Scraps of the Untainted Sky

Cultural Studies Series

Paul Smith, Series Editor

Scraps of the Untainted Sky: Science Fiction, Utopia, Dystopia, Tom Moylan

Turning the Century: Essays in Media and Cultural Studies, edited by Carol Stabile

Midfielder's Moment: Politics, Literature, and Culture in Contemporary South Africa, Grant Farred

The Audience and Its Landscape, edited by John Hay, Laurence Grossberg, and Ellen Wartella

Art and the Committed Eye: The Cultural Functions of Imagery, Richard Leppert

Youth, Murder, Spectacle: The Cultural Politics of "Youth in Crisis," Charles R. Acland

Enlightened Racism: The Cosby Show, Audiences, and the Myth of the American Dream, Sut Jhally and Justin Lewis

Forthcoming

Postmodernism and the Politics of "Culture," Adam Katz

Scraps of the Untainted Sky

Science Fiction, Utopia, Dystopia

Tom Moylan

Westview Press
A Member of the Perseus Books Group

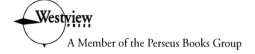

Published in 2000 in the United States of America by Westview Press, 5500 Central Avenue, Boulder, Colorado 80301-2877, and in the United Kingdom by Westview Press, 12 Hid's Copse Road, Cumnor Hill, Oxford OX2 9JJ

Visit us on the World Wide Web at www.westviewpress.com

Library of Congress Cataloging-in-Publication Data
Moylan, Tom, 1943–
Scraps of the untainted sky: science fiction, utopia, dystopia/Thomas Moylan.
p. cm.— (Cultural studies series)
Includes bibliographical references and index.
ISBN 0-8133-9768-5
1. Science fiction—History and criticism. 2. Dystopias in literature. 3. Utopias in literature. I. Title. II. Cultural studies.

PN3433.6 .M69 2000

00-061437

The paper used in this publication meets the requirements of the American National Standard for Permanence of Paper for Printed Library Materials Z39.48-1984.

10 9 8 7 6 5 4 3 2 1

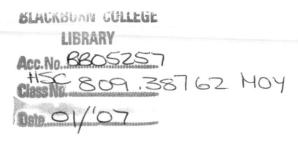

As he spoke, the whole city was broken like a honeycomb. An airship had sailed in through the vomitory into a ruined wharf. It crashed downwards, exploding as it went, rending gallery after gallery with its wings of steel. For a moment they saw the nations of the dead, and, before they joined them, scraps of the untainted sky.

—E. M. Forster, "The Machine Stops" (1909)

Contents

Permissions

Excerpts from the following copyrighted material appear by permission. Any additional arrangements or oversights will be corrected in subsequent editions.

"Against the Great Defeat of the World" by John Berger; reprinted by permission of the Institute of Race Relations.

The Concept of Utopia by Ruth Levitas; copyright © 1990 by Ruth Levitas; reprinted by permission of the author.

"The Concept of Utopia in the Work of Fredric Jameson" by Peter Fitting; reprinted by permission of *Utopian Studies.*

"Dreamwood", the lines from "Dreamwood," from *Time's Power: Poems 1985–1988* by Adrienne Rich. Used by permission of the author and W. W. Norton & Company, Inc.

The Gold Coast by Kim Stanley Robinson; excerpts, copyright © 1988 by Kim Stanley Robinson; reprinted by permission ofthe author, Orb Books, and HarperCollins.

He, She and It (published in England as *Body of Glass*) by Marge Piercy; copyright © 1991 by Middlemarsh, Inc.; reprinted by permission of Alfred A. Knopf, a Division of Random House Inc. and The Wallace Literary Agency.

"The Heat Death of the Universe" by Pamela Zoline; reprinted by permission of McPherson and Company on behalf of Pamela Zoline.

"Horizons, Figures, and Machines: The Dialectic of Utopia in the Work of Frederic Jameson" by Phillip E. Wegner; reprinted by permission of *Utopian Studies.*

"Houston, Houston, Do You Read?" by James Tiptree, Jr.; permission being arranged with Random House and other possible holders of the copyright.

"The Machine Stops" by E. M. Forster; excerpts from *The Eternal Moment and other Stories* by E. M. Forster, copyright © 1928 by Harcourt, Inc. and renewed 1956 by E. M. Forster, reprinted by permission of the publisher and The Society of Authors.

"On the Poetics of the Science Fiction Genre" by Darko Suvin; copyright © 1972 by the National Council of Teachers of English; reprinted with permission of the National Council of Teachers of English.

The Parable of the Sower and The Parable of the Talents by Octavia Butler; reprinted by permission of Seven Stories Press.

"The Politics of Incorporation and Embodiment: *Woman on the Edge of Time* and *He, She, and It* as Feminist Epistemologies of Resistance" by Vara Neverow; reprinted by permission of *Utopian Studies.*

"Post-Apocalyptic Hoping: Octavia Butler's Dystopian/Utopian Fiction" by Jim Miller; reprinted by permission of *Science-Fiction Studies.*

The Red Peril by Wesso (Hans Waldemar Wessolowski), on the cover of *Amazing Stories* 4.6, September 1929; reprinted by permission of Forrest Ackerman, Ackerman International Agency. "This month's cover depicts a scene from the story entitled *The Red Peril* by Capt. S. P. Meek, U.S.A., in which is shown the futile attempts of the perfectly equipped American naval airships of the future to destroy the enemy craft, completely protected by a repellent element."

"'The Red Sun Is High, the Blue Low': Towards a Stylistic Description of Science Fiction" by Kathleen Spencer; reprinted by permission of *Science-Fiction Studies.*

The Seeds of Time by Fredric Jameson; reprinted by permission of Columbia University Press.

"The Three Faces of Utopianism Revisited" by Lyman Tower Sargent; reprinted by permission of *Utopian Studies.*

"Two Cheers for Essentialism and Totality: On Marx's Oscillation and Its Limits (as Well as on the Taboos of Post-Modernism)" by Darko Suvin; reprinted by permission of *Rethinking Marxism.*

Utopia and Anti-Utopia in Modern Times by Krishan Kumar; reprinted by permission of Blackwell Publishers.

"Utopian and Dystopian Pessimism: Le Guin's *The Word for World Is Forest* and Tiptree's "We Who Stole the Dream" by Søren Baggesen; reprinted by permission of *Science-Fiction Studies.*

"When It Changed" by Joanna Russ; copyright © 1972 by Joanna Russ; first published *Again: Dangerous Visions*, ed. Harlan Ellison (Garden City, N.Y.: Doubleday, 1972), 233–241; reprinted by permission of Ellen Levine Literary Agency.

"World-Reduction in Le Guin: The Emergence of Utopian Narrative" by Fredric Jameson; reprinted by permission of *Science-Fiction Studies.*

Preface

Hunger cannot stop continually renewing itself, but if it increases uninterrupted, satisfied by no certain bread, then it suddenly changes. The body-ego then becomes rebellious, does not go out in search of food merely within the old framework. It seeks to change the situation which has caused its empty stomach, its hanging head. The No to the bad situation which exists, the Yes to the better life that hovers ahead, is incorporated by the deprived into revolutionary interest. This interest always begins with hunger, hunger transforms itself, having been taught, into an explosive force against the prison of deprivation.

—ERNST BLOCH, *THE PRINCIPLE OF HOPE* (75)

Dystopian narrative is largely the product of the terrors of the twentieth century. A hundred years of exploitation, repression, state violence, war, genocide, disease, famine, ecocide, depression, debt, and the steady depletion of humanity through the buying and selling of everyday life provided more than enough fertile ground for this fictive underside of the utopian imagination.[1] Although its roots lie in Menippean satire, realism, and the anti-utopian novels of the nineteenth century, the dystopia emerged as a literary form in its own right in the early 1900s, as capital entered a new phase with the onset of monopolized production and as the modern imperialist state extended its internal and external reach.

From that early period, and throughout its varied and shifting history, this negative narrative machine has produced challenging cognitive maps of the historical situation by way of imaginary societies that are even worse than those that lie outside their authors' and readers' doors. In the hands of E. M. Forster, Yevgeny Zamyatin, Aldous Huxley, Katherine Burdekin, George Orwell, Ray Bradbury, Margaret Atwood, and others, the classical dystopia flourished in societies besotted by greed, destruction, and death. In the "new maps of hell" that science fiction (sf) writers in mid-century became so adept at creating, dystopia's negative energies shaped a new critical strand within contemporary popular culture. Most recently, after an interlude of utopian writing in the 1960s and 1970s, sf writers again developed a dystopian textual strategy that spoke to the attenuated and terrible reality brought about by the capitalist restructuring of the economy, the conservative restoration in politics, and the cultural shift to the right that dominated the 1980s and 1990s.

Dystopia's foremost truth lies in its ability to reflect upon the causes of social and ecological evil as systemic. Its very textual machinery invites the creation of alternative worlds in which the historical spacetime of the author can be re-presented in a way that foregrounds the articulation of its economic, political, and cultural dimensions. Formally and politically, therefore, the dystopian text refuses a functionalist or reformist perspective. In its purview, no single policy or practice can be isolated as the root problem, no single aberration can be privileged as the one to be fixed so that life in the enclosed status quo can easily resume. Indeed, with its unfashionable capacity for totalizing interrogation, dystopian critique can enable its writers and readers to find their way within—and sometimes against and beyond—the conditions that mask the very causes of the harsh realities in which they live.

In the hands of some who react against the present moment in a relatively undialectical manner, dystopia expresses a simple refusal of modern society. Certainly, E. M. Forster's pathbreaking 1909 story "The Machine Stops" takes a stand against the emergent (standardizing, rationalizing, debilitating) technological world, but if its author's humanism challenges the new social logic and begins to locate a basis for dissent and resistance, his abstract analysis offers but a minimal binary of domination and opposition that does not yet delineate the contradictory character of the coming age. With the likes of Zamyatin, Burdekin, Orwell, and Atwood, however, dystopian interrogation begins to sharpen as the modern state apparatus (in the Stalinist Soviet Union, Nazi Germany, social democratic welfare states, and right-wing oligarchies) is isolated as a primary engine of alienation and suffering. Gradually, however, dystopia's critical sensibility is taken up by authors who look beyond technology and the authoritarian state and turn to the especial imbrication of the economy and culture that capitalism has achieved at the cost of diminishing the complexity and potential of all humanity and the earth itself. Within the web of classical dystopias, it is Huxley's work that offers the first thorough critique in this vein, and then in the pages of popular sf the dystopian imagination seeps into the nooks and crannies of everyday life to expose the depredations produced by the strongest socioeconomic force of the century.

Crucial to dystopia's vision in all its manifestations is this ability to register the impact of an unseen and unexamined social system on the everyday lives of everyday people. Again and again, the dystopian text opens in the midst of a social "elsewhere" that appears to be far worse than any in the "real" world. As the mise-en-scène is established in an exponential presentation of the society's structure and operation, the narrative zooms in on one of the subjects of the terrible place. The story line then develops around that alienated protagonist as she or he begins to recognize the situation for what it really is and thus to trace the relationship between individual experience and the operation of the entire system. In some dystopias this narrative runs aground when the power structure crushes the resistant dissenter—ending the text on a note of resignation that nevertheless offers the compensation of an apotheosis of the defeated individual. In others, however, the singular misfit finds allies and not only learns the "truth" of the system but also enters collectively into outright opposition. The conflict may end in another defeat, but it is one that can be remembered by others. Or the outcome may lead to the organization of a resistant enclave, a liberated zone, that sticks in the craw of the hegemonic system; or it may even result in a political movement that threatens to transform the entire order. In some form, a utopian horizon, or at the very least a scrap of hope, appears within the militant dystopia.

*Dys*topia is thus clearly unlike its generic sibling, the literary *eu*topia, or its nemesis, the anti-utopia. The dystopian text does not guarantee a creative and critical position that is implicitly militant or resigned. As an open form, it always negotiates the continuum between the Party of Utopia and the Party of Anti-Utopia. Iconically immersed in an already oppressive society, the discrete narrative trajectory of a dystopian text plays out on a terrain contested by these historically opposed political tendencies. Texts that adhere to the insistence of the (usually conservative) argument that there is no alternative (and that seeking one is more dangerous than it's worth) run up to the limit of Anti-Utopia and risk transforming what begins as a dystopia into a full-fledged anti-utopia. In contrast, those progressively inclined texts that refuse to settle for the status quo manage to explore positive utopian possibilities by way of their negative engagement with their brave new worlds. In the anti-utopian dystopia, the best that can happen is a recognition of the integrity of the individual even when the hegemonic power coercively and ideologically closes in; whereas in the utopian dystopia, a collective resistance is at least acknowledged, and sometimes a full-fledged opposition and even victory is achieved against the apparently impervious, tightly sutured system.

As dystopian expression spread out from a few texts in the early decades of the twentieth century, it expanded into a negative imaginary that informed pulp fiction magazines and Hollywood films as much as it did those works continuing in the classical mode. By the 1950s, sf texts such as Frederik Pohl and C. M. Kornbluth's *Space Merchants* and Kurt Vonnegut's *Player Piano* shifted dystopia's fascination with questions of state power into an interrogation of the economic and cultural sphere shaped by the postwar partnership of a revived capitalism (spreading by way of its commodification systems into all aspects of daily life) and the new imperial power of the United States (eliminating opposition not only by the lure of the good life of suburbia and consumer goods but also by the weapons of loyalty oaths and anti-communist witch-hunts). In this conjuncture, dystopia again proved adequate to the task of catching not only the extent of the human and ecological devastation brought about by the latest configuration of capitalism and imperialism but also of finding the seeds of opposition within the tendencies and latencies of that existing social system.

The 1960s and 1970s, however, was a time of such overt opposition, such serious challenges to the ruling order in the United States, Europe, and around the globe in a myriad of liberation movements that dystopian expression took a back seat to a revival of utopian writing that was the first outpouring of hopeful counterworlds since the previous century. Then, as the capitalist system reached the end of its postwar profit curve and began the process of reconfiguring itself and commodifying everything in sight, the possibilities for a complex, equitable, just, and ecologically balanced world receded. Led by increasingly powerful transnational corporations, capital sought to revive its generation of surplus by reducing costs and expanding operations through a series of moves that included rationalizing and updating production in flexible sub-systems; finding cheaper sources of labor and material; eliminating social costs by refusing obligations to social entitlements, labor contracts, and ecological health; and moving into all corners of the globe and all aspects of everyday life to produce commodities and markets that could bring renewed financial gains (gains that would no longer be subject to even token redistribution to the very people who produced them). This new round of restructuring was then protected and further encouraged when, in the early 1980s, the neoconservative restoration occasioned by the administrations of Ronald Reagan, Margaret Thatcher, and Helmut Kohl presided over the political defeat of the necessarily limited and often compromised social democratic effort to work with capital and still meet human needs and desires.

Within the new hard times wherein the gap between rich and poor dramatically increased, wherein not only industrial workforces were eliminated but middle management as well, wherein the drive for commodification reached wherever and however it could, and wherein social violence against non-privileged peoples intensified, the political opposition and utopian imagination of the previous three decades faltered. Faced with this economic, political, and cultural onslaught, the Left—in all its diverse and contentious dimensions—suffered major setbacks. Systemic challenges were replaced (necessarily as well as opportunistically) by a micropolitics based in the local and the situated. Assertive as those new movements were, the dispersed force of their multiple actions was never enough to stop the new leviathan.

Working the ground of popular sf, the bleak energy of cyberpunk and the unyielding utopian imagination of feminist sf sustained the critical imagination in the mid-1980s. Then, in a step beyond those creative initiatives, dystopian narrative turned up on the fictive palettes of sf writers such as Kim Stanley Robinson, Octavia Butler, and Marge Piercy. Although many (in fiction and film) took this dystopian path, I find the work of these authors to be among the most eloquent examples of what Lyman Tower Sargent terms the "critical dystopia," a textual mutation that self-reflexively takes on the present system and offers not only astute critiques of the order of things but also explorations of the oppositional spaces and possibilities from which the next round of political activism can derive imaginative sustenance and inspiration. Challenging capitalist power as well as conservative rule—and refusing the false "utopianism" of reformist promises from neoliberals and compromised social democrats with their bad-faith exercises in "third way" solutions—the new dystopias have rekindled the cold flame of critique and have thereby become a cultural manifestation of a broad-scale yet radically diverse alliance politics that is emerging as the twenty-first century commences.[2]

II.

In Part 2 of this book, I examine the poetics and politics of dystopia. In Chapter 4, I work through E. M. Forster's story to explore one of the first instances of dystopian narrative; and from that reading I go on to review the Anglo-American critical work on the dystopian text. As I do so, I highlight the distinctions between and among the literary types of the utopia (eutopia), the anti-utopia, and the dystopia, and I end by examining the relationship of these textual forms to the historical conflict between Utopia and Anti-Utopia. In Chapter 5 I draw on several major studies of the formal operations of dystopia in order to develop a schematic account of the textual mechanics and social significance of this utopian inversion. I then survey several classical and sf dystopias to demonstrate the range of utopian and anti-utopian positions that can occupy the contested space between Utopia and Anti-Utopia within dystopian writing. In Chapter 6 I introduce the conditions of production and the specific qualities of the "critical dystopia" of the 1980s and 1990s. Finally, in Part 3, I carry out detailed analyses of three texts that in the context of late-twentieth-century U.S. culture I consider to be the best examples of this new dystopian form. I trace the timely emergence of a critical consciousness that maps the sociopolitical terrain and imagines new forms of oppositional agency: moving from formations of individual resistance in Kim Stanley Robinson's *Gold Coast* (1988), to collective efforts to separate from the mainstream society in Octavia Butler's *Parable of the Sower* (1993), and finally to allied praxis in Marge Piercy's *He, She and It* (1991).

Informing this entire discussion of dystopia, however, is a body of critical work in science fiction studies and utopian studies that since the 1960s has led to more grounded and perceptive analyses of the formal, cultural, and political dynamics of these literary traditions. For the sake of clarifying and extending my dystopian study, I introduce it by way of an overview of this paradigmatic work. The scholar in me believes that providing such a context will bring greater scope to the specific question of dystopia; the teacher in me knows that it will be a useful way to draw in readers who are new to these matters; and, to be honest, the editor in me hopes that perhaps it will help writers who are addressing this material for the first time to avoid reinventing the critical wheel, however much they rightly go on to redesign it.

Consequently, Part 1 works a bit like book 1 of Thomas More's *Utopia,* as it sets the scene and charts the path toward my arrival in dystopia in Parts 2 and 3. In Chapter 1 I explore the reading protocol commonly invited by sf texts through an exposition of two stories of the 1970s by Joanna Russ and James Tiptree Jr. (Alice Sheldon). Through the next two chapters, I report on the theoretical and methodological work that developed within the interdisciplinary fields of science fiction studies and utopian studies. In Chapter 2 I focus on the emergence of the field of sf studies from the cultural ground of the oppositional movements of the 1960s and 1970s, and I review what I consider to be key critical works that have given many of us an effective way to deal with the sf text, on its own terms and in the context of its place in the cultural machinery of its time. In Chapter 3 I then review the complementary development of scholarship in what has come to be known as utopian studies.

Underlying all three parts of this study is the recognition, by fans and scholars alike, of the particular capability of sf texts not only to delight but also to teach. As I emphasize in Chapter 1, sf indulges the reader's pleasure in discovering and thinking through the logic and consequences of an imagined world. On the one hand, this reading experience is not unlike that of following a radio drama, in which the fuller picture and meaning of the words heard in the atmospherics of the broadcast are given greater weight as they are imaged and detailed by the creatively listening mind. On the other, the pleasure includes the satisfying work of analytic thinking as a reader engages with the premises and puzzles of an intellectually demanding text, one that requires consistent thought but also mental leaps that stretch the mind beyond the habitual or the accepted. As I lightly but seriously tell students, this degree of involved reading can be dangerous to their social and political health, for it can "damage" their minds by allowing them to think about the world in ways not sanctioned by hegemonic institutions and ideologies. Indeed, the infamous "escapism" attributed to sf does not necessarily mean a debilitating escape *from* reality because it can also lead to an empowering escape *to* a very different way of thinking about, and possibly of being in, the world. In utopian-dystopian sf in particular, these readerly trips can lead to an involvement with the design, portrayal, and investigation of an imagined society that involves a provisionally totalizing grasp of an entire social logic and an entire way of life. The potential exists, therefore, for an enlightening triangulation between an individual reader's limited perspective, the estranged re-vision of the alternative world on the pages of a given text, and the actually existing society.

To be sure, many sf stories fail to deliver on this larger critical potential, for they deliver no more than a one-dimensional extrapolation or a simple adventure. Many never get beyond the perspectives allowed and encouraged by mainstream society, and an unacceptable few go further down the road of nastiness as they reinforce positions of privilege or hatred.[3] Then too—as critics such as H. Bruce Franklin, Constance Penley, and Carol Stabile have demonstrated—a substantial body of sf directly feeds the ideological processes that reproduce the very subject positions required by the political and economic structures of the hegemonic order itself.[4] Yet the risk of venturing into the textual web of popular science fiction is worth it when readers discover new and challenging works that, as the Quakers say, speak to their own condition and speak truth to power. Imaginatively and cognitively engaging with such works can bring willing readers back to their own worlds with new or clearer perceptions, possibly helping them to raise their consciousness about what is right and wrong in that world, and even to think about what is to be done, especially in concert with others, to change it for the better. Throw in the particular modality of utopian and dystopian narratives and the possibilities get all the more interesting—and all the more useful and dangerous.

III.

Given the way I have framed this book, it makes sense to dedicate it to two groups of people: those who have helped me to do my work and those who might one day take it elsewhere. I want, therefore, to honor the memory of Tom Andersen,

Michael Sprinker, Mary Ellen Young, and especially my father, Thomas Michael Moylan. And then I want to remember my students from over three decades of teaching. Just to mention a few: Jeanne Gomoll (who in 1968 suggested that I teach a course in science fiction), Harry Boomer, Linda Coleman, George Coleman, Jim Schroeder, Dick Brown, José Soto, Geza Petri, Sue Gilbertson, Trisha Brown, Dave Anderson, Cathy Schulz, Michael Dean, Eileen Molloy, Mark McCraw, Greg Kurcziewski, Mary Stassi, Dianne Unterweger, Cathy Jozwiak, Louise Lambert, Tim Havens, Florencia Gonzalez, Nitin Govil, Ben Arnette, Zoltán Szántò, Rebecca Breen, Musa Eubanks, Sangeet Khalsa, Wendy Reese, Jodi Evans, Mark Williams, William Crisp, Gino DiAngelo, Katy Adams, Kathryn Mitchell, Jason White, Howard Hastings, Gina Dreistadt, Jane Williams, Chris Elliott, and the original *Fractal* editors (Dave Gardner, Lane Hatfield, Scott Lightsey, Karla Miller, and Sean Newborn).

For the production of the book itself, I want above all to thank my graduate research assistants, without whom it simply would not have been done: Anna Bounds, who began it before moving on to better things, and Donna Messner, who took over and, generously and patiently and thoroughly, saw it through to the very end with care and precision. I want to thank those who took time to read the manuscript: Raffaella Baccolini for conversations that have grown into collaborations on this entire dystopian project and beyond; Lyman Tower Sargent, Darko Suvin, and Phil Wegner for working through the entire manuscript; and Peter Fitting, Ruth Levitas, and Ken Roemer for careful attention to various sections. I am grateful to all of them for their critiques, suggestions, and infernal advocacies. I also want to thank the staff at and freelancers for Westview for their interest and support, and for bringing the book into publication in a timely fashion—noting in particular Andrew Day, David McBride, Lori Hobkirk, Alice Colwell, Eric Brearton, Deborah Gayle, and Paula Waldrop. And I am grateful to Forrest Ackerman, George Slusser, and Andy Sawyer, director of the Science Fiction Foundation Archive at the University of Liverpool, for their help with the cover material. Given all this assistance, I must allow that the remaining shortcomings are mine alone.

More broadly, I want to acknowledge the intellectual communities that sustain my work: the Society for Utopian Studies and the Marxist Literary Group in the United States; the Utopian Studies Society and the Marxist Cultural Network in Britain; the community of writers, scholars, and fans in the land of sf, most recently those involved with the Science Fiction Foundation; and friends and colleagues at the National University of Ireland—Galway and the Centro Interdipartimentale di Ricera Sull'utopia, Università di Bologna. Of course, I am grateful to George Mason University, especially for its institutional support in the form of study leaves and research assistantships. And I am especially grateful to the School of Media, Critical, and Creative Arts at Liverpool John Moores University for granting me an initial study leave but more so for extending a warm and collegial welcome.

I also want to thank other people who helped along the way: Basil O'Leary, Chris Christie, Bernie Gendron, Sean Keane, Jack Zipes, Lorne Falk, Mary Layoun, Pat Small, Irma Bennett, Lorraine Brown, Jim Henry, David Kaufmann, Marilyn Mobley, Amelia Rutledge, Pat Story, Scott Trafton, Steven Weinberger, Jan Bogstad, Jane Donawerth, Veronica Hollinger, Naomi Jacobs, Lee Cullen Khanna, Carol Kolmerten, Lise Liebacher, John O'Connor, Jean Pfaelzer, Robert Philmus, Peter Sands, Peter Stillman, Hoda Zaki, Dan Goodman, Fred Pfeil, Debra Abrams, Tom Boylan, Tadhg Foley, Luke Gibbons, Sean Ryder, John Caughie, John Moore, Karen Sayre, Edward James, Farah Mendlesohn, Patrick Parrinder, David Seed, Vince Geoghegan, Lucy Sargisson, Ildney Cavalcanti, Maria Varsamopolou, Sam Fear, John Freeman, Nickianne Moody, Roger Webster, Ross Dawson, Sean Homer, Vita Fortunati, Anu Dingwaney Needham, Kevin Francis Grey, Allan Prim, Kaye O'Brien, Maróg O'Brien, Val Bogan, and Jamie Owen Daniel.

Finally, I want to thank Denise Albanese, Beth Cronise, and Paul Smith for their friendship (and memorably excessive dinners in D.C.); my daughters, Katie Moylan and Sarah Moylan, for being exactly who they are; and, as always, Áine O'Brien.

Tom Moylan
Liverpool

Part One

Science Fiction and Utopia

1

Dangerous Visions

If any theme runs through all my work, it is what Adrienne Rich once called "re-vision," i.e., the re-perceiving of experience, not because our experience is complex or subtle or hard to understand (though it is sometimes all three) but because so much of what's presented to us as "the real world" or "the way it is" is so obviously untrue that a great deal of social energy must be mobilized to hide that gross and ghastly fact.

—JOANNA RUSS, *TO WRITE LIKE A WOMAN* (XV)

I.

Where in the world am I? What in the world is going on? What am I going to do? These are questions common to science fiction (sf) whenever and wherever one locates it historically or geographically. Especially in the Anglo-American tradition, narratives of alienation and discovery have characterized sf from the early moments of its emergence from the sea of fantastic writing.

In *Frankenstein* in 1818, Mary Shelley's scientist strives to find a place for himself and his heterodox approach to medieval and modern science in the brave new world of utilitarian, capitalist Britain; and even more so her newborn creature awakes in an alien and alienated society that holds no place for such a radically new human. Both characters ironically and negatively echo the amazement of Shakespeare's Miranda as she stands on the cusp of modernity, colonialism, rationality, and the rest of the economic-cultural package that has led to this particular historical moment at the beginning of the third millennium. In *The Time Machine* in 1895, H. G. Wells's Time Traveller struggles to ground his vision and find his way, and by metaphoric extension the way of humanity, in a nasty future in which his own present, Wells's empirical moment and the Time Traveller's "Britain," is the terrifying past. In the United States in the early 1960s, Michael Valentine Smith in Robert Heinlein's novel finds himself to be eponymously the stranger in a strange land, the consumer paradise of postwar America. In the parallel world of sf film, David Bowie's character, the cool-headed alien in Nicholas Roeg's *Man Who Fell to Earth* (1976) is beset by the disorientation of one who strives to read the signs of the place wherein he lands, simply to apprehend where he is and what is going on, desperately to grasp the rules and framework that produce and shape his fallen location, so that he might somehow regain his own place in the universe. And the commercially popular extraterrestrial in Steven Spielberg's *ET* (1982) captures the audience's attention and support as it too tries to learn the ways of an alien planet in order to use its culture and its technology to return home.

In these works, as in so much of sf, the protagonists as spacetime travelers—to whom we as readers are attached like so many remora riding the back of a deep-diving whale—struggle to make sense of their world and to act decisively within it. Whether they find themselves in a familiar society now seen freshly and critically or one that is fully alien, they negotiate an "anthropological strangeness," as Bruno Latour and Steve Woolgar would put it.[1] In response, they develop what Michael Taussig calls an implicit social knowledge as they imaginatively move toward a form of cognitively enhanced action, toward a degree of praxis that is most likely and perhaps inevitably in conflict with the society surrounding them.[2] At the very least, they act in the name of a self-interested effort to be more fully themselves in a difficult place, but more often they strive to be actively part of a found community of people who are also dislocated, and no doubt dispossessed and disempowered, and who are posing similar questions to the entire social reality: asking historically as well as individually where in the world they are, what in the world is going on, and what in the world they can do about it.

And so it is that sf finds ways to explore and to go where others will not, might not, dare not go. It's not the only creative mode to do so, but it is one that has evolved and acquired a relatively privileged niche in the cultures of modernity and postmodernity. Whether one traces sf from the amazing voyages of the early modern period, the utopian narrations of the sixteenth century, the scientific romances of the nineteenth century, the science fictional novels of imperial Britain, or the pulp stories and paperbacks of the neo-imperial United States, this fictive practice has the formal potential to re-vision the world in ways that generate pleasurable, probing, and potentially subversive responses in its readers. Although a good deal of sf—especially since the early 1980s—suffers from a standardization and simplification imposed by the constricted financial demands of publishers and distributors, the texts that do draw on the full measure of the formal capacities of the genre and rise above prevailing common sense and market mediocrity make for worthwhile and challenging reading.

Central to sf's textual tendency to go where others haven't (at least not in ways acknowledged within the purview of those who are inclined to settle for the world as they immediately and unreflectively see it and know it) is sf's imaginative proclivity to re-create the empirical present of its author and implied readers as an "elsewhere," an alternative spacetime that is the empirical moment but not that moment as it is ideologically produced by way of everyday common sense.

In this formal quality lies one of the basic pleasures of the sf text, for it delivers the textual motivation that makes available the specific reading opportunities to which readers of sf return again and again. However much sf is, as Joanna Russ has said, a "didactic" literature, it is one that works by way of a readerly delight in the thoughtful and thought-provoking activity of imagining the elsewhere of a given text, of filling in, co-creating, the imagined (or what Marc Angenot calls the "absent") paradigm of a society that does not exist but that nevertheless supplies a cognitive map of what does exist.[3] Such world-building is both the deepest pleasure of reading sf and the source of its most powerfully subversive potential, for if a reader can manage to see the world differently (in that Brechtian sense of overcoming alienation by becoming critically estranged and engaged), she or he might just, especially in concert with friends or comrades and allies, do something to alter it—perhaps on a large scale or ever so slightly, perhaps in a singular deluge or maybe through steady drops of water on apparently stable and solid rock—so as to make that world a more just and congenial place for all who live in it.[4]

When I teach sf, I find that the most difficult problem for some students who are new to this particular variety of the fantastic is their inability or unwillingness to read it on its own formal terms.[5] Too often they come to sf from their experience with literary modes more ideologically attuned to the society they know and are taught to love and obey. That is, they tend, initially at least, to read sf by way of an assumed realism or mimeticism in which the stories they encounter are set in motion in settings that they assume are ones with which they are familiar. Or if they accept the settings as unfamiliar, they too quickly conclude that the narrative is still comfortably knowable by means of existing social rules; or, alternatively, they find it to be consolingly unknowable because they can then regard the entire text as mere fantasy, and therefore meaningless. Put simply, they don't get sf because they don't realize the consequences, formally and logically, of the text's particular mechanics—namely, its ability to generate cognitively substantial yet estranged alternative worlds.[6]

As Samuel R. Delany once suggested, inexperienced readers do not see that what appears to be the taken-for-granted background (the setting) is actually in sf the foreground (or driving force behind the total creation); for before a story can be followed or a character understood, the fictive world itself must be indulged in, grasped, learned, and detailed in readers' own minds so that the matters of plot or character can literally make sense.[7] Instead, they hold fast to an ideologically driven belief in a transparent and unchanging world and follow only the plot as they skim over descriptive parts with clouded eyes. Opting for this retreat to the safety net of familiar narrative practices, they often slam into a text that becomes even more opaque, even less pleasurable, as they avoid the necessary work of learning the complexity of the alternative world in order to understand the characters' actions. Thus they miss, or refuse, the central pleasure of this imaginative mode. If they persist in their readerly mystification, they eventually turn away from sf and adopt the mainstream (what Delany would call mundane) rap on sf as a simple-minded, escapist sub- or trivial literature that toys with scientific or technological marvels or terrors or indulges in fantasies replete with bug-eyed monsters, spaceships, and ray guns. When they don't take up the challenge to break new epistemological and aesthetic ground in their own reading practice, they lose touch with a historically and formally rich fictive tradition that could well give them intellectual pleasure, as well as critical insight to their own time and place. They lose the opportunity to acquire a valuable but "dangerous knowledge," which in its minor key is potentially as challenging to the status quo as those major instances of subversive epistemology in the history of the twentieth century, including the radical readings of the "signs of the times" in base Christian communities, the consciousness-raising discoveries of feminists and their male allies, or the theory-practice analytical spiral of a noncompromised socialist opposition.[8]

The specific textual strategies of sf and the resulting feedback loops in the reading practices learned by what Edward James calls the "determined reader of sf" are my initial topics when I teach sf.[9] Although there are undeniably as many ways to read the sf text as there are actual readers, those who are familiar with the fictive maneuvers of sf (whose skills are sometimes enhanced by their participation in that world of sf fan culture which at its best is knowledgeable and democratic) fairly quickly realize that the "setting" of the text is where the primary action is. The world created by the sf author has its own systemic rules insofar as it is a fully working version of an alternative reality. To avoid the cumbersome and boring task of first explaining that world (in some sort of encyclopedic preview or purview), the author must deliver its substance in sequential bits, appearing as the narrative unfolds, as the pages turn. The generically informed reader of such a text therefore learns the strange new world not by way of a condensed reality briefing but rather by absorbing and reflecting upon pieces of information that titrate into a comprehensible pattern, by which the reader subsequently "makes sense" of the plot and character development unfolding within that alternative spacetime.

As many writers, fans, and scholars of sf have noted, the experienced sf reader moves through a text like a traveler in a foreign culture or a detective seeking clues to unravel the mystery at hand.[10] Both proceed incrementally, observing and gradually absorbing information, making patterns, discovering ways to see and understand the larger picture in its own right, and finally to act decisively within that new context—to enjoy the newfound culture or to solve the crime and reestablish justice and well-being. Working from a comparison with the process of detection, Edward James notes that "the decoding and assessment of these clues can be a major part of the pleasure provided by the work; indeed, *without* that decoding and assessment, in a process of careful reading, it may be impossible to understand the text at all" (*20th Century* 115).[11] Sf thus invokes and invites a particular readerly experience built around a distinctive "sense of wonder," a quality that has long been part of the sf community's self-understanding, as can be seen in Damon Knight's 1956 volume of sf criticism entitled *In Search of Wonder*.

This quite specific pleasure, James suggests, is based in the embrace of a reality that is larger than the lived world of the individual reader. As such, it can be linked, chronologically and epistemologically, to the Romantic notion, and potentially subversive experience, of the Sublime; for the secular sense of magnitude that displaces and relocates the individual in a process both terrifying and satisfying is one that resonates with the "wonder" evoked by the sf text.[12] Unlike the abstract individual response evoked by the Romantic Sublime, however, the "wonder" of sf (as it developed further along in the complex history and experience of modernity) is much more socially, collectively, materially inflected. In a comparison with the traditional realist novel (with its focus on individual personalities as they play out in relatively familiar settings), James observes that sf is more concerned with the created world or produced social environment, more interested in the collective fate of the human species, exploring these concerns in a setting that while resonating with their own material realities, does not actually exist (or exist as such) in the known world of its author or readers. This invented world challenges readers, or seductively invites them, to engage in the thoughtful activity of *constructing* both the details and the social logic that comprise it.[13] In doing so, the sf imaginary machine offers them the opportunity to reorganize "their assumptions and knowledge, reversing and distorting conventional structures and relationships, and drawing upon the reservoir of other [sf] fiction, in order to make sense of the text" (*20th Century* 96).

Working out of a semiological analysis, Teresa de Lauretis further suggests that this readerly process does not end with simply making sense of the text.[14] By juxtaposing the familiar claim of a "sense of wonder" with a more theoretically nuanced account of the readerly process as one that requires an intellectual and imaginative "wandering" between the signifiers of the text and the referents of the outside world, she shifts the balance from the text back to the reader. She describes the reader's process of working through the text as an activity of "associating, opposing, relating, remembering, or making unexpected discoveries," thereby launching an adventure within the mind, not the text, that can possibly lead to a re-visioning of "time, space, and social relations" (de Lauretis 165). In the "best" sf, de Lauretis argues that

> the reader's sense of wOnder as awe, marvel, portent, revelation is replaced by a sense of wAndering through a mindscape both familiar and unfamiliar. Displaced from the central position of the knowledgeable observer, the reader stands on constantly shifting ground, on the margins of understanding, at the periphery of vision: hence the sense of wAnder, of being dislocated to another space-time continuum where human possibilities are discovered in the intersection of other signs with other meanings. (de Lauretis 165–166)

I will return to the formal operations of sf in more detail in the next chapter when I review the developing body of critical work that from the late 1960s onward accounted for the formal and social significance of what Darko Suvin calls the "feedback oscillation" generated by the relationship between the sf reader and the sf text: a feedback loop that as Suvin puts it, "moves now from the author's and implied reader's norm of reality to the narratively actualized novum [of the sf text] in order to understand the plot-events, and now back from those novelties to the author's reality, in order to see it afresh from the new perspective gained."[15] As Delany observes, it is this very feedback loop, or rather the reading protocol it invites, that constitutes for him the most fruitful way to arrive at the specificity of sf itself: "The genre is not a set of texts or of rhetorical figures but rather a reading protocol complex. . . . The texts central to the genre become those texts that were clearly written to exploit a particular protocol complex—texts which yield a particularly rich reading experience when read according to one complex rather than another."[16] For now, I want to stay in a teacherly mode and turn to two exemplary sf texts so that I can continue my discussion with an emphasis on the sf object itself (as happened in the best moments of the critical turn of the 1960s and 1970s, as it refused the a priori accounts and judgments of orthodox academic scholarship).[17]

II.

> *He turned his head—those words have not been in our language for six hundred years—and said, in bad Russian: "Who's that?"*
>
> —Joanna Russ, "When It Changed" (412)

One of the stories that I find most helpful and pleasurable in my efforts to introduce students (the few who are resistant and the many who are not) to the substance and potential of sf is Joanna Russ's "When It Changed."[18] First published in 1972, it has gained a longer shelf life (in these days of a publishing industry disciplined by the logic of just-in-time, flexible production) as a selection in *Science Fiction: The Science Fiction Research Association Anthology*, which was brought out in 1988 by one of the leading academic organizations dedicated to sf studies.

"When It Changed" is a text that speaks to many of the concerns that thread their way through my book. For one thing, it works along the axis of the utopian-dystopian imaginary that has so effectively informed sf in the years since the end of World War II, and it is more immediately part of the revival of utopian writing of the 1960s and 1970s that produced the critical utopia, of which one of the earliest and best examples is Russ's alternative version of this very story in her 1975 novel, *The Female Man*.[19] As well—and in keeping with the strategy of critical utopias' self-reflexively foregrounding their own conditions of textual production in light of the historical opportunities and pitfalls of utopian writing—it also demonstrates within its manifest content the sort of reading protocols invited by, encouraged by, sf's specific textual mechanics.

Most broadly, the story is a product of the historical period that is the jumping-off point for the political and theoretical considerations that inform these pages. This period of the late 1960s and early 1970s is, of course, the moment when the Left—in so many places and in so many formations around the globe—was undeniably strong, when it held substantial cultural, if not political or economic, power. It is also that related moment when scholarly work in sf and utopian studies (along with utopian sf itself) developed in opposition to the reigning orthodoxies of academic literary studies. Indeed, that critical shift—especially as it pulled together the political, creative, and scholarly projects—is symptomatically and substantively marked by the publication, also in 1972, of Suvin's essay "On the Poetics of the Science Fiction Genre," a work to which I return in the next chapter. With its mixture of sharp critique and grim humor, Russ's story is a strong example of the sort of sf that can be socially and politically insightful and incite-ful even as it is an elegant fictive exposition of the learning curve that sf privileges.

The narrative opens on a distant planet where an Earth colony had been abandoned by its colonizing center, only to have its population cut in half by a plague that destroyed all the male colonists. The remaining highly trained and resourceful professional women survived into subsequent generations by developing a technique for merging ova (as opposed to parthenogenesis) and thereby reproducing in a manner that resulted in the richest possible genetic pool. Over the course of thirty generations, the all-female population produced a utopian society that would be understood as separatist if any men were still around to be separate from (and a society that would be considered lesbian if compulsory heterosexuality were still the reigning norm).

Having cast aside the worst of the old military-industrial political economy, the women, now numbering 30 million, have opted instead for the sort of social paradigm advocated by radical feminist and leftist thought in the 1960s. Drawing on anarchocommunist, ecological, and feminist counterlogics to patriarchy, capitalism, and imperialism, they have built a society informed by the principles and practices of slow economic growth, appropriate technology, and radical democratic decentralization. Still basically agrarian (though "things are beginning to snowball in industry"), the society is organized into extended families spread over two continents (which resemble the North and South Islands of New Zealand writ large). These dispersed family groups begin their political involvement in local town hall meetings and move on to district caucuses and then to a dual legislature with "geographic" and "professional" houses, which is topped off by a structurally weak presidential administrator.

Idyllic and pastoral as it may seem—resembling a mid-twentieth-century feminist revision of William Morris's utopia in *News from Nowhere*—this society of women nevertheless accepts anger and personal violence as a normal and healthy dimension of everyday life. In a deft move against the dominant ideological stereotypes of women in her time, Russ counters with female subjects who are unafraid of face-to-face anger, adept with guns, and not unwilling to settle accounts with personal adversaries by means of deadly duels. In keeping with the spirit of the youth movement of the 1960s, it is also a society unafraid of the energy and insights of its younger members. At puberty every woman heads out for the northern forests, to "disappear for weeks on end to come back grimy and proud, having knifed her first cougar or shot her first bear, dragging some abominably dangerous dead beastie behind her" (411). Overall, then, the bright and confident, creative and scrappy women of "Whileaway" (they changed the name of the colony from the provisional and intriguingly Faustian "For-A-While") live in a utopia, albeit a messy, lively, and "critical" utopia.

This mini epic of a utopian people begins in medias res: with the everyday life of the narrator and wife Katy driving home to the family farm, accompanied by their daughter, Yuriko. Complaining in mundane fashion about Katy's driving habits and giving out about her refusal to handle guns, the narrator—who has fought three duels and who is feeling "old" at thirty-four—sounds at first take like a "typical" husband of the normative nuclear family of postwar U.S. culture. Into this domestic scene bursts the message over the car radio that "men" have landed on the planet. At this point, in the fourth paragraph of the story, the epistemological re-reading demanded by significant sf begins to impose itself on sensitive readers. Such readers—as students year after year have noted—inevitably pause on one of these lines and begin to re-read. They enter into recurring feedback loops that run from their hesitation over the manifest content of the text, into their own accumulated sense of that reality, and on to the emerging social paradigm that is absent on the page but active in the imagination. In this interpretive spiral, the readers glance back up the page to revisit the bits and pieces of information in the opening lines.

As many students have told me, the most common first stop for this re-readerly eye is in the first paragraph when the narrator says that Katy "will not handle guns," for to make a point of Katy's *not* handling guns flies in the face of the stereotype in which men use guns and women don't (411). In this case Katy's refusal is an anomaly, not the norm. The next pause that refreshes the readers' mental screens is the narrator's depiction of the initiation trip that their daughter will soon take. Here, the ideological fabric is torn in two, insofar as such rites are not the norm in the relatively tame milieu of U.S. teenagers, and even if such rites are recognized for males (in military basic training, fraternity hazing, or less violent adolescent high jinks), such behavior for women, especially in the days before the revivification of female bodies and sport in post–Title IX days, could be considered socially off-key, something only for "boyish girls." And finally, the now more thoughtful readers come back to news of the radio message and look at the announcement in the next short paragraph: "Men!" Yuki had screamed, leaping over the car door. "They've come back! Real Earth men!" (411).

At this point the cat, or the man, is almost out of the bag. Again, to note the presence of what should be already present is to note its absence. For men to be *named* casts in doubt the very presence of men (of whatever evolved, devolved, or transformed variation) on this planet. Further doubts enter the readerly minds as they begin to wonder just how these characters are a couple and have a child. After a shift in scene, the citizens of the planet gather, "in the kitchen of the farmhouse near the place where they had landed" (411). Again, readers will pause and wonder why this punctal moment, the time of the formal "take me to your leader" arrival of the landed aliens, takes place in a *kitchen* and not in a government hall or town square. "Then," the narrator announces, "I saw the four of them" (412). The new arrivals step into the kitchen and onto the stage of this post-colonial, post-male, post-Terran history.

In the next paragraph, the epistemological loops circulate in ever tighter spirals of information to be processed by the now provoked readers. But as well—and this is the formal power of Russ's story—a parallel learning curve takes place with the characters themselves. Colonists and readers share and struggle with the observation: "They are bigger than we are. They are bigger and broader. Two were taller than I, and I am extremely tall, one meter eighty centimeters in my bare feet. They are obviously of our species but *off,* indescribably off. . . . I can only say they were apes with human faces" (412). Facing the lead male (who, in a testament to Russ's ironic meditation on the Cold War, speaks Russian), the narrator reaches out to shake his proffered hand, "to set a good example (*interstellar amity,* I thought)" (412). Behind the narrator, Yuriko peers up at "*the men* with her mouth open" (412). And then the most powerful and epistemologically challenging sentence of the story, at the very least for the colonists but often for readers as well, is thought by the narrator: "*He* turned *his* head—those words have not been in our language for six hundred years" (412).

With these words in the ninth paragraph, engaged readers begin to feel a bit more knowledgeable about this paradigmatically other place. Men are absent, women are present, and at last readers get confirmation as to the identity, and gender, of the narrator. In response to the lead male's question about the young woman peering at him, the narrator names her as her "daughter, Yuriko Janetson. We use the patronymic. You would say matronymic" (412). Readers now know her as Janet, the one who has a "wife" named Katy, and also realize that male lineage is entirely absent since the very word that would mark it, *patronymic,* has become the generic word for their own reproductive and legal process (this, it occurs to some student readers, is a nice riff by Russ on the feminist interventions against sexist language launched in the early 1970s). Now other details contribute additional pieces of the social puzzle as one of the women present is identified as "Phyllis Helgason Spet" and the leader of their government is referred to, quite irreverently but accurately, as "Madam President." Such information now reinforces the emerging paradigm. Like the images and words that fill a just-contacted Web page, slowly covering the screen with ever richer detail, the alternative world that has been there but absent since the first lines of the story now more rapidly unfolds; but it does so (I would venture to say for most readers) only after several swift glances back up the page, across particular lines, and back down again, only for another move up to check a point that slipped by, and then onward again.

After a few more words, Janet, as she now can be known and as her wife and co-citizens have always known her, can say to the invading men, and to readers, "This is Whileaway" (412). The increasingly dangerous repartee between the men from Earth and the women of Whileaway is then rehearsed in the conversation of Janet and the leader of the expedition. Janet, still working within her own culture of trust and security, explains the history and present order of things in Whileaway, yet the man continues to ask where all the "people" are. Janet only gradually grasps (as her own feedback oscillation works parallel to the readers') that he means "men." The women of Whileaway, who are quite happy with their social and personal lives, their lovers and compatriots, are characterized by the mission leader as strange and fundamentally deprived, as having "adapted amazingly" but as missing something quite necessary for their own well-being: men. As the leader persists with questions and comments based in his version of reality, representing the women as lacking something and regarding the absence of male colonists as a "tragedy," his words begin to work a certain magic, an evil magic to be sure, as he sows the discursive doubt that interpellates the Whileawayans as if they "were something childish and something wonderful" (413). The ideological apparatuses of patriarchy (informed by psychoanalytic concepts of female "lack") and imperialism (informed by philosophical notions of instrumental rationality) have once again begun their nasty work. The next stage of the invasion has begun. From the actual landing and arrival, the mission has moved on to ideological warfare, asserting and imposing the earthly version of male-female binary codes.

As the hegemonic shift moves apace, the deeper purpose of the mission becomes clear. After patronizingly reassuring the Whileawayans that "sexual equality" has been reestablished on Earth (and here Russ critiques that species of white, male liberalism that compromised so many radical liberation movements), the leader gives his account of the history of Earth. In an ironic parallel to the Whileawayan plague, Earth's population had suffered its own irreversible genetic damage from spreading radiation (due, in Russ's wry comment, to a nuclear war that "Russia" seems to have won). Hence, the mission was launched to this long-neglected colony to harvest fresh genes.

Of course, in an instant justification for their invasion and appropriation of women's genetic resources, the leader (in words that would have been chillingly familiar to Russ's readers at the time of the Vietnam War, second-wave feminism, and the beginnings of gay-lesbian liberation) makes it clear that he has judged Whileaway's society to be unnatural and in need of occupation and correction at the hands of the imperial center. Working from premises of biological essentialism, he asserts that Whileaway is missing its necessary complement of men, men who could save the women from their perversely happy ways, men who could harvest their valuable genes as well as restore "natural" procreation on site. In a declaration that is simultaneously homophobic, misogynist, and imperialist, he asserts that there "is only half a species here. Men must come back to Whileaway" (415). A few lines later, Janet overhears him talking about "the grand movement to recolonize and rediscover all the Earth had lost," emphasizing to his female audience the advantages he was bringing to Whileaway: "trade, exchange of ideas, education" (415).

After a page break, time moves on and the occupation triumphs. Janet admits that "Katy was right, of course; we should have burned them down where they stood," for men, she says, are coming to Whileaway, and, restating the great lesson of colonial conquest, "when one culture has the big guns and the other has none, there is a certain predictability about the outcome" (415). Men are back in control, and even Janet, who has fought three duels and won, is "afraid that [her] own achievements will dwindle from what they were—or what [she] thought they were—to the not-very-interesting curiosa of the human race, the oddities you read about in the back of the book, things to laugh at sometimes because they are so exotic, quaint but not impressive, charming but not useful" (416).

The patriarchal, heterosexual imperium has reconquered. Physical and ideological control has been secured. What lingers for the women of Whileaway is, significantly, memory: their ancestral journals with their "long cry of pain" and their recollections of their individual lives in utopia. Only this subversive knowledge can potentially break through the normative and naturalized social construction to which they are being subjected. Yet even this resistant option is in danger of being rewritten or excised, in a reprise of the control and re-creation of news and memory in George Orwell's *Nineteen Eighty-Four.*

Readers are often resistant to this moment of capitulation by these strong and independent women to the conquering men of Earth. Readerly fellow travelers hope for the defeat of the invasion, but their hope is as futile as the manifest conquest of the utopian women. Such readers want the men to be destroyed, as the Whileawayan woman hold out in solidarity against the violence and injustice. But Russ, in her usual unwillingness to indulge her readers' line of least resistance, demonstrates the power of the imbrication of male violence and economic-political power as it informs a triumphal invasion that in the end succeeds not only by coercion but also by nominal consent. In the conquest of Whileaway, Russ offers a cautionary parable in the best prophetic tradition that sf facilitates. Unfolding her tale, she educates and implicates her readers step by step, not only in the process of figuring out what is going on but also in tracing the characters themselves as they too work through the same learning curve. She therefore conjoins form and content in a highly powerful few pages: as the content of her story bespeaks the very form of sf, as its formal achievement draws readers into a chilling and challenging content.

The parable, however, does not end there. In the best sense of the utopian spirit, it does not quite settle into a resigned, one-dimensional conclusion. Several traces of radical hope linger on the last page, traces that—as with a departing audience at a Brechtian education play—go beyond the closure of the last line, the stated closure of invasion, capitulation, and reoccupation. First and strongest of these is Yuriko's response to Janet's asking her if she could fall in love with a man: "With a ten-foot toad!" says the obstreperous and undefeated representative of the next generation. The next bit of hope rests in Janet's long meditation on memory, that of her ancestors and her own; for threatened and endangered as they are, their dangerous memories have the potential to survive and inspire.

Finally, warning and hope conspire to open up the narrative even in its closing lines. Weakened, admitting her inability to fight back, Janet quotes Faust's words and gives her own translation: "*Verweile doch, du bist so schoen!* Keep it as it is. Don't change" (416). With these words echoing in her mind, she lies awake at night *remembering* the original name of the colony. She recalls the "For-A-While" that caught the initial purpose of the colony but that she now redefines as her political warning: Remember to be historically vigilant, do not lock in the utopian achievements, do not remove the social utopia from the processes of time. Don't cut a deal with the false utopian devil of your own collective imagination as it dreams of the end of history; and don't cover up the deal by changing the colony from that of a place-in-process to one of eternal delight, literally allowing time to while away. Janet (and Russ in her own political moment) cautions the reader not to let the process of learning and change end, not to risk a situation—brought about by either internal or external forces—that might "take away the meaning" of life.

III.

> *Lorimer's brain seems to be expanding, letting in light. He is understanding actively now, the myriad bits and pieces linking into patterns.*
>
> —James Tiptree Jr. [Alice Sheldon],
> "Houston, Houston, Do You Read?" (434–435)

Another story that challenges students new to sf was written by a woman influenced by Russ but one who clearly claimed her own place of honor in the history of sf. Alice Sheldon (writing under the protective coloring of "James Tiptree Jr." in the still male-dominated world of the sf market) published "Houston, Houston, Do You Read?" in 1976.[20]

Tiptree's story shares in the counter-hegemonic sensibility of the time, and it too addresses the question of male interlopers confronting a female society as it also recapitulates the reading process facilitated by sf in the actions of its characters (this time, the men). Tiptree comes up with a different scenario and a much different conclusion, but in the end her text does not contradict or negate Russ's story as much as it complements it. As with "When It Changed," Tiptree's story both calls forth sf reading practices from its readers and recapitulates them in its unfolding plot and developing characters. It also works within the oppositional political and cultural ambience of the 1970s. It shares its publication year (in a no doubt unintended contestation of the ideological hype of the bicentennial) with two of the major critical utopias, Samuel R. Delany's *Triton* and Marge Piercy's *Woman on the Edge of Time*. As in Russ's Whileaway, Tiptree offers her readers a future society that is a radically better place. Unlike Russ's story, however, this utopian place is one in which the male invasion ultimately fails, albeit in a resolution that provokes further debate among readers.

The narrative begins a year after the three-man crew of the circumsolar NASA expedition in the ship *Sunbird* has been rescued by the crew of a ship named *Gloria*. In its opening sentence, the point-of-view male character, Lorimer, is trying to listen to the alien voices around him, hoping to learn what has happened to him and his shipmates, what sort of place they have been taken into, and what might face them in the future. Realizing that all three men have just been administered a truth-inducing drug (one that opens up the unconscious), he begins to drift between his present situation, his deep memories, and that moment when their ship entered what they came to realize was a strange new reality.

Drawing on immediate perceptions and flashbacks, Lorimer, the scientist, pushes his brain to its limit, and in this very early passage detailing his efforts to understand, the reader encounters one of the best descriptions of the epistemological process that the formal strategies of sf invites: "Lorimer's brain seems to be expanding, letting in light. He is understanding actively now, the myriad bits and pieces linking into patterns" (434–435). Tagging along with this man lost in space and time, the reader joins him in the work of filling in the new paradigm and moving toward what will be a difficult and painful denouement.

As Lorimer recalls, the estrangement the men have experienced in coming to terms with their spatiotemporal dislocation develops gradually, naively, since they were professionally certain about their reentry location after coming around the sun. Back in what should have been NASA transmission range, they radio "home" with the usual greeting, "Houston! Do you read?" (436). In the silence of the nonresponse, however, they wonder what is going on. What they next hear is an unexpected, alien voice, a woman with a quasi-Australian accent no less. And so begins the first of many conversations between the crew and these strange women. Secure in their official knowledge, the men have to struggle with disturbing pieces of new information. The female voice throws them, for it is clearly not one of their people and not from the only other earthly presence in space, the Russian cosmonauts. The name of her ship, the *Escondita,* rings no bells. Words she uses, such as "andy" and "dinko," make little sense. Quite chillingly, as they begin to surmise that their situation might well be radically different from what they had confidently assumed, they are stymied by the *Escondita*'s report that Earth's location is in Virgo, not Pisces as they thought. And they are even more disturbed when they are told that it is the 15th of March and not the 19th of October.[21]

Puzzled by these anomalies, they nevertheless proceed with a series of transmissions between the *Escondita,* their ground control station on Earth (*not* Houston), and the nearby ship that will pick them up, the *Gloria,* yet another unknown and alien name. In the course of these conversations and after checking some historical sources, the voice from Earth gives them the bad news:

> There was a Major Norman Davis on the first *Sunbird* flight. Major was a military title. Did you hear them say "Doc"? There was a scientific doctor on board, Doctor Orren Lorimer. The third member was Captain—that's another title—Bernhard Geirr. Just the three of them, all males of course. We think they had an early reaction engine and not too much fuel. The point is, the first *Sunbird* mission was lost in space. They never came out from behind the sun. That was about when the big flares started. Jan thinks they must have been too close to one, you heard them say they were damaged. (441)

Here, even the women are struggling with the new situation. Even for them, oddities linger. Titles seem alien; their gender is notable in its naming. The learning curve the women face is less daunting, for they are securely in a familiar reality and these bits of information—more technical than substantive—are readily absorbed and understood within their own social paradigm. It's different for the men. "Never came back" is a terrifying piece of information. Yet, rigidly disciplined by their military and scientific training, they develop a working hypothesis that they may well have been catapulted into the future by a temporal disruption caused by the superflares from the sun. They begin, in other words, to accept and to work with the actual cognitive premise that undergirds Tiptree's entire story. So it is that in these early pages, and on through the story, the manifest content of the story and the formal qualities of sf re-presented as another level of that content elegantly intertwine.

The point of view throughout the story is Lorimer's, but Tiptree further complicates the situation by investing him with two pressing concerns, one based in his past and one he currently faces. As it happens, as mission scientist, Lorimer is not the alpha male that the other two are. A quiet, studious type, he harbors early memories of entering the wrong bathroom as a boy and having his penis seen, in women's territory, by the girls. His exposure to this female gaze has produced the deep fear that he is really not a boy, and for the rest of his life his grasp of his own masculinity is unsteady. In a fine study of the processes of male gender construction and privilege, Tiptree gives us Lorimer's account of how he went on to participate in his interpellation as a *man*—reinforced in his fragile masculinity with a long-nurtured misogyny against that Other that threatens to absorb his very self. "Women are natural poisoners," he notes (434). Smaller and marked as less virile, he nevertheless labors at sports, signs up for the space program, and takes his turn at the exercise cycles: all to prove that he is one of the boys.

On the *Gloria*, with the macroreality already shattered for the NASA crew, Lorimer's microreality as a "man" is challenged in ways he never imagined. Ironically, it is his scientific training but more so his semigendered subjectivity that allows him to be more open to the women. This "token scientist," this "half-jock" (436), is the one most able to absorb the new reality as he gradually, through "bits and pieces" (435), learns the full import of this new world. While he tussles with the meaning of the "impossible realities shifting around him" (445), he also continues his lifelong battle to assume a male-identified identity, for he looks on Dave and Bud (their names already signify their masculine distinction from his multisyllabled "feminine" one) as the "authentic ones, the alphas" (445). Never fully of his own world, he is now lost in an entirely new one.

That new reality, he discovers, is one occupied by women who (as in Russ's story) have survived an epidemic, doing so not by the merging of ova but by cloning. In Tiptree's version of a gendered and militarized apocalypse, "an airborne quasi-virus escaped from Franco-Arab military labs, possibly potentiated by pollutants . . . damaged only the reproductive cells" (459). Checking into an old history of the cataclysm, Lorimer reads that sterility for half the human race occurred because the damage "was on the Y-chromosome where it would be selectively lethal to the male fetus" (459). He later corrects this false account, however, when one of the women explains the cloning process to him. As he recalls that successful cloning happens only when both X chromosomes are "viable," he realizes that it was not the Y but the X chromosome that was mortally damaged:

> "It was a gene or genes on the X-chromosome that was injured," he guesses aloud. "Not the Y. And the lethal trait had to be recessive, right? Thus there would have been no births at all for a time, until some men recovered or were isolated long enough to manufacture undamaged X-bearing gametes. But women carry their lifetime supply of ova, they could never regenerate reproductively. When they mated with the recovered males only female ba-

> bies would be produced, since the female carries two Xs and the mother's defective gene would be compensated by a normal X from the father. But the male is XY, he receives only the mother's defective X. Thus the lethal defect would be expressed, the male fetus would be finished. . . . A planet of girls and dying men. The few odd viables died off." (465)

With this passage, readers get a detailed account of Lorimer's apprehension of the biological and social history of the strange people, but they in turn are made privy to his cognitive processes as he moves from sheer ignorance to false information and toward the truth by way of further observation of this new social text. That is, as the point-of-view character, Lorimer can be *read* as a "reader" (a resistant reader who is an unwelcome outsider and possible threat). His characterological position is one that actual readers can follow at the level of manifest plot but also at the level of a self-reflexive rehearsal of the sf reading protocol.

Lorimer therefore learns that 300 years after the epidemic, women have not only survived but flourished. To be sure, as clones, there are only 11,000 genotypes among the population of 2 million, substantially reduced from 8 billion (464). Each individual lives out her own identity but also shares in the transgenerational history of her genotype. All "Judys" read the "Book of Judy" and add to it the details of their own lives; each individual in this society is temporally allied with her clone community from the moment of her birth.[22] The horror of the isolated "singleton" casting about in a lonely world is unthinkable to them. As in a good deal of sf, such a communal representation (here as clones, but elsewhere as alien configurations such as *Star Trek*'s Borg) negotiates anxieties in modern Western society about socialism, communism, and their ideologically dreaded collectivity that is considered destructive of that unstable conjunction in the modern subject, the individual entrepreneur and citizen. Tiptree plays with this figurative anxiety, but she turns it on its head, transforming the cloned society from a signifier of fear and revulsion to one that registers a positive, preferred, collective hope for a better future, one not attainable by a society of lonely singletons.

After the worst of the epidemic, the surviving women gravitated to the gentle climate of "the south part of the American states where they could grow food and the best communications and factories were" (448). From this local enclave, they built a social system that, like Russ's Whileaway, resembles the anarchocommunist, feminist, ecological utopias of the politicized counterculture.

Although they have Earth and the nearby reaches of outer space to wander in from their secure southern base, they live in an environmentally repaired, uncrowded world that is organized around five main activities (food production, communications, transport, space exploration, and reproduction) that provide them with all they need for a high-tech but ecologically appropriate society. With a small population and radically different communal values, they share the social wealth by way of an economic system that lacks the alienated systems of money or private ownership. Building from this basic arrangement, administrative requirements are minimal, prompting another familiar utopian pattern, for the society is run democratically, "by consensus" (460). Politically, in the best anarchist spirit, they manage their society and make decisions without the "complex activity" of government: "With so few people we don't have that type of formal structure at all. People from the different activities meet periodically and our communications are good, everyone is kept informed. The people in each activity are in charge of doing it while they're there. We rotate, you see" (449). As well, work assignments come from a rationalized and agreed-upon labor "registry," and there is no need for coercive institutions such as police or military (460). Sympathetic to the values and structures of "early Chinese communalism," the women have eliminated the competitive drive of capitalism and its accompanying patriarchal machinery and built a society in which change is based on use value, not market forces (460). Education and enjoyment are major parts of everyone's life, and the cloned individuals live easily with each other in a slower, simpler, yet psychically richer life.

Perhaps the object that best signifies the society's values and practices is the spaceship that rescues the men. One of only four ships (along with the *Escondita*, the *Indira*, and the *Pech*), the *Gloria* travels between the old Luna dome and the newer Mars dome and around the environs of the inner solar system. This is not the sleek and silver phallic object of actual space programs or pulp sf. Its nearest iconic relative might be the ship *Nostromo* in Ridley Scott's film *Alien* (1979). Bud describes the approaching ship as a "flying trailer park," and it gradually resolves into a "disorderly cluster of bulbs and spokes around a big central cylinder" (453, 454). Lorimer observes the many "pods and miscellaneous equipment stowed all over her," and he ironically, for Tiptree's readers, recalls that this ship of the future is "not like science fiction" (454).

Once inside the ship's main cylinder, the men see that the "whole inner surface [is] festooned with unidentifiable objects." Women in "flowing pink pajamas," sometimes accompanied by cackling chickens, float around the men. Off to one side is a greenhouse that contains a "brilliant jungle, foliage everywhere, glittering water droplets, rustling leaves," replete with grasshoppers and iguanas. In this one unit, food, oxygen, waste disposal, and water retrieval combine in a complex ecological machine (455). Sleeping "cubbies" are provided with one-tenth gravity during individual sleeping periods by shipmates exercising on pedicycles in the gym chamber—again an arrangement that facilitates complementary activities in a balanced system (456). Bud characterizes this alien alternative to a militarized spaceship as "primitive," yet he grudgingly admits that the women have been able to "sacrifice everything to keep it simple and easy to maintain. Believe it, they can hand-feed fuel. And the back-ups, brother! They have redundant redundancy" (458).

In these early pages of the story, the crew's process of discovery aids the reader who is building up her or his own textual paradigm. Once the deep and recent history has been established, at least by Lorimer and his female interlocutors, and once the scene has been set with the passing of the year of quarantine, the plot moves on to the events that bring it to its climax and denouement. Under the influence of the drug, all three men have been revealing their deeper memories, attitudes, behaviors. Lorimer has been talking, learning, probing, puzzling; whereas Bud, the stereotypical hotshot pilot, has been taking unabashed delight in what he foolishly sees as some sort of "desert island" filled with comely beauties existing solely to service him. As he rattles on in his drugged condition, his desires, drives, and arrogant assumptions become obvious. He reveals himself to be a chauvinistic, violent rapist, and he ultimately makes a fool of himself in front of the women. From his talk about "space bunnies," to his gay-bashing of the androgyne, Andy Kay, whom he misreads as male, to his assault and rape of Judy, to his pathetic ejaculation collected in a small plastic bag as it limply floats in the central chamber, Bud comes across to the women and to readers as the stereotypical testosterone-flooded male who assumes all women are his to possess and to fuck (435, see 466–469).

Just as drugged but rigidly guarded and controlled, as a repressed Christian male as well as commander of the mission, Dave works not from such direct sexual motivation but from his assumed position as military and religious patriarch. Fundamentalist Dave is horrified by what he sees to be unnatural women, literally flying in the face of God's plan. He is appalled that they have "no concept of prayer and had never seen a Christian Bible" (447). In a hypocritical exercise in male-bonding that is critical of Bud's actions yet defensive, he challenges the women after their "experiment" on Bud, and he identifies them as "lost children" who for generations "have lived in darkness" (470). He attacks them verbally as being "not capable of running anything," and he describes their ship as "pathetic" (471). He tells Lorimer that it was God's plan that led them to save these lost souls. Yet when one of the Judys tries to silence him with an injection, this Christian man draws a hidden gun and attempts to take command of the ship "in the name of the United States of America under God" (472). In a move that almost takes him into an alliance with the women, Lorimer throws a canister at Dave, and the women disarm him. Now both alpha males are subdued, and, as the reader soon learns, their fate is sealed.

Lorimer is the last and most complex object of study for the women. A reader sympathetic to his unstable construction as a man—with his lifelong act of "passing" as one—could well regard him in a potentially liminal subject position, floating in space somewhere between two opposing social paradigms.[23] As the point-of-view character, Lorimer invites sympathy as he assembles the clues, trying desperately to learn this strange social context. A reader closely affiliating with him might even hope that he will become an effective mediator in this historic conflict. To begin with, he is truly open-minded. He accepts the hypothesis that the *Sunbird* has fallen into the future, and he suppresses the despairing thoughts of never again seeing his wife and children and Earth as he knew it. Both rational and potentially liminal, he avoids the reactionary behavior of the likes of Dave and Bud. After twelve months on the *Gloria* (the period of quarantine that the women decided upon as safe and proper for this anomaly) and now in his drugged state, he recalls the events of the past year, as well as those of his boyhood, even as he tries to fit together the pieces of the new social puzzle.

While the women try to understand what are for them aliens, Lorimer tries in reverse to grasp this alien context. He listens to the explanations of their history and society, much like a visitor in a literary utopia follows the travelogue of the utopian guide, but he also endeavors to grasp what is not being said: how these people really survived, how they reproduced if sterility was caused by the epidemic, what words like *sister* and *daughter* and *granddaughter* mean to them. At first his efforts are intuitive: "Something *has* changed, he can sense it. Something basic enough to affect human nature. A physical development perhaps; a mutation? What is really under those floating clothes?" (461).

Soon Lorimer figures out that these women who seem so similar to each other, who call each other "sister," are clones, but then he wants to know more, the how and why, and the consequences of this reproductive shift (462). Further bits come to him. Hearing a Connie speak of *an* "andy," he realizes that this "man" he thought was named Andy is in fact an androgyne, a genetically altered female. He computes the numbers—11,000 genotypes—and realizes how small and communally cozy this new population actually is. Finally, he begins to anticipate the outcome of the story—of his and Dave's and Bud's fate—as he learns the details of the epidemic. He understands that male reproduction is impossible and that men have been biologically and sociologically factored out of the logic of this future world. There is no place, will be no place, for these castaways (as contrarily there was early in the century for the three men in Charlotte Perkins Gilman's *Herland*).

Yet however open this atypical scientist is to this new world, and however unstable and changeable his own identity, after seeing what happens to Bud and Dave, Lorimer too reverts to the security of male bonding and refuses to empathize with these alien women. In a form of future shock based in an insecurity compensated for by way of an amalgam of official maleness and military-national-scientific power, he clings to his old paradigm, to the hegemonic discourses and practices that have, in deadly finality, made him what he is. No longer a naive reader of this culture, now grasping it on its own terms, he still cannot take the next radical step and deconstruct his own position, cannot betray his privileged identity, cannot make a new alliance with his hosts. Instead, he flies into a rage of defense of Dave and Bud: "'They aren't bad men. You don't know what bad means. You did it to them, you broke them down. You made them do crazy things. Was it interesting? Did you learn enough?' His voice is trying to shake. 'Everybody has aggressive fantasies. They didn't act on them. Never. Until you poisoned them'" (473).

Falling back into his ideological safety net, Lorimer cannot see the events before him from the women's standpoint, or from a positively estranged one of his own. His remark about "poisoning" betrays his residual misogyny, and his embrace of manly subjectivity keeps him from taking the opportunity to cast off years of compensating and passing. In his rant, he asserts his male privilege and its official version of history. Like a father attacking his child for striking out on her own, he claims his authority in the name of all the idols of his hegemonic position:

> "They were good men," Lorimer repeats elegiacally. He knows he is speaking for it all, for Dave's Father, for Bud's manhood, for himself, for Cro-Magnon, for the dinosaurs too, maybe. "I'm a man. By god yes, I'm angry. I have a right. We gave you all this, we made it all. We built your precious civilization and your knowledge and comfort and medicines and your dreams. All of it. We protected you, we worked our balls off keeping you and your kids. It was hard. It was a fight, a bloody fight all the way. We're tough. We had to be, can't you understand? Can't you for Christ's sake understand that?" (473)

The weight of history consumes Lorimer. The force of being named, or interpellated, by the hegemonic power structure paralyzes him, but gender privilege leads only to his destruction.[24] He cannot cast off his own social construction. He cannot take this golden opportunity, in this at least individually revolutionary moment, to become a radically new subject: a nonman, a new human creature open to a new world. He cannot accept the nature of the dialectical transformation this society of women achieved as it sublated the previous period of male domination and re-produced the world and their own bodies and values on their own, self-determined terms. To Lorimer, they have refused the male gift. To the women, they have liberated themselves—forging an unanticipated freedom out of the detritus of sheer necessity.

As his rage subsides, Lorimer regains a calmer focus. The women are still sympathetic to him in ways they were not to Dave and Bud. They appreciate, ironically, how he as an object of study "brought history to life"; but however much Lorimer might have chosen to understand, however sympathetic he as an individual might have become, they know that history and their own material and ideological transformation of reality have moved on, that the time for admitting this rare male to their society has, unfortunately, passed (473). They know that no matter what he personally thought or did, he cannot be allowed to live: "We can hardly turn you loose on Earth, and we simply have no facilities for people with your emotional problems. . . . Besides, we don't think you'd be very happy" (473). In a last pitch for survival, Lorimer suggests isolation on an island, on three islands, but as he looks at their compassionate and even regretful faces—a compassion he hated in the women of his old life and a regret that tells him they too will feel the loss—he knows their answer: "'Your problem is,' he says, 'if you take the risk of giving us equal rights, what could we possibly contribute?'" (474). With the wisdom garnered by his own cognitive estrangement, he knows that in this world there is no place for the old male subject, not for the violent Bud nor the self-righteous and equally violent Dave, and not even for the enlightened and rational scientist, however half-man he might be.

The story ends as Lorimer asks the women what they call themselves and hears their answer: "Why, we call ourselves human beings. . . . Humanity, mankind" (474). The old binary is obsolete. There is no place for "man" anymore. That historical subject is dead. Consequently, the NASA crew, even Lorimer, is already extinct. The last two sentences resound in an ironic inversion of Socrates' execution: "The drink tastes cool going down, something like peace and freedom, he thinks. Or death" (474). This, however, is not a moment of historic martyrdom, not the launching of the modern Western subject, but rather its last gasp.

Tiptree's "Houston, Houston" exemplifies the sf feedback loops of what Suvin calls "cognitive estrangement" in his 1972 essay. Stepping away from a known world and yet always in creative connection with it, the sf reader must take seriously the alternative world of the text before her or his eyes. This created elsewhere—developed in what I term the iconic textual register with its fuller meaning available only by way of bits of information accumulating down the pages—must be learned, and further imagined, before the plot and characters of the discrete register can make any sense.[25] Thus, in "Houston, Houston" the reader must cognitively accept the scientific premise of the solar time slip and seriously appreciate the new society of women to make any sense of the story and its outcome. The reader must *work* at grasping not only the details but also the *logic* and *consequences* of this new reality. For to read about the displaced men and their elimination directly from the empirical reality outside the text, directly from the reader's own social standpoint, would be to misread the matter entirely.

The historical, political, and moral complexities of Tiptree's story therefore require the reader's (ad)venture into an alternative world, for only then can its critical interventions make an impact. Those resistant or naive readers who dismiss the details as so much filler will only find their own position and prejudices bounced back at them. A refusal of an engaged, cognitive reading process risks committing discursive violence to the text and further risks the perpetuation, or at least acceptance, of that ignorance and violence, injustice and domination, that rages in the world outside the text, in that everyday life to which we all return upon turning the last page and closing the book.

IV.

Know that your words have won me at the last
To practise magic and concealed arts:
Yet not your words onely, but mine own fantasy.
—Christopher Marlowe,
Doctor Faustus (I, 1, 102–104)

Closing the book, of course, brings the reader back into the everyday, into history. And yet, in the act of reading sf, history itself is seldom far away. As James notes, sf "like history . . . has often been more interested in the fate of humanity than the fate of humans" (*20th Century* 97). To be sure, sf is often misunderstood as bearing a direct, unmediated relationship to the author's empirical reality, regarded simply as a "metaphorical" (worse yet, "mythic") retelling of the present moment. Or at the other extreme, sf is too readily regarded as a form of futurological analysis of things to come. Contrary to these unmediated engagements with the present, serious sf, with all the richness that fiction can muster, pursues a more complex engagement that enters into a dialectical negotiation of the historical tension between what was, what is, and what is coming to be. To put it another way, sf has the capability of elucidating the contradictions at work in a given social context (a given conjuncture) out of which the next moment of history (that which gets reified in the word *future*) is emerging.

Indeed, as Fredric Jameson argues in "Progress Versus Utopia; or, Can We Imagine the Future?" sf allows us to apprehend the present *as* history. He reminds us that the world in which we all live—the world of a now pervasive capitalist logic—has managed to erase historical memory so that it is almost impossible to see that what is going on around us was not always the case, and that what may be coming next is a shift that we cannot grasp by looking directly at it. As Jameson puts it: "The present—in this society, and in the physical and psychic dissociation of the human subjects who inhabit it—is inaccessible directly, is numb, habituated, empty of affect" ("Progress" 151). Consequently, so that we may be self-determining agents who can develop a critical knowledge that informs and enables engagement with the social situation in order to change its worst tendencies and move it forward to an arrangement that affords justice and freedom for all, our access to the present needs to be enhanced by epistemological means that enable us to get under its surface appearances, tear open its sutured explanations, and uncover the tensions and contradictions that are constantly in motion.[26] Developing this dangerous but useful knowledge, Jameson suggests, calls for "strategies of indirection . . . if we are somehow to break through our monadic insulation and to 'experience,' for some first and real time, this 'present,' which is after all all we have" ("Progress" 151).

Working from Georg Lukács's studies of the historical novel, Jameson notes that early manifestations of that genre, in the work of Walter Scott, for example, captured the very emergence of "historical thinking, of historicism in its peculiarly modern sense" ("Progress" 149).[27] That is, at the time of their rise to power, the bourgeois discovery of a present that was *different from* (and, in their eyes, better than) the feudal past reinforced their ideological sense of achieved status in the world. At this early moment, therefore, the insight offered by the historical novel was a part of the "*bourgeois cultural revolution*, the process whereby the definitive establishment of a properly capitalist mode of production as it were reprograms and utterly restructures the values, the rhythms, cultural habits, and temporal sense of its subjects" ("Progress" 149).

The critical force of the historical novel, however, became a victim of that very historical turn, for Jameson reminds us of Lukács's argument that this popular form fell prey to the consolidation of the bourgeois power it first articulated, reaching a point (around the time of Flaubert) when the stimulation of a historical memory gave way to the compensation of a nostalgia that smoothed out the deep changes uncovered by a critical historical knowledge in favor of instrumental recollections of a past that now became part of the very ideological universe of the reigning bourgeois culture. And yet once this articulation of historical thinking found its way into political discourse, the danger to achieved bourgeois power was obvious, for the epistemological process of tracking social transformations (of remembering how things were and how they were changed) was now available to other classes and disempowered collectivities coming into their own consciousness through political struggle. Thus, the evacuation of the critical power of the historical novel both reinforced bourgeois hegemony and diminished the opportunities for historical thinking in other sectors of society.

As Jameson argues, however, a new fictive form took up the vocation of historical knowledge. For the moment of the decline of the historical novel in the later nineteenth century is also the time when the fiction that later came to be known as "scientifiction," "science fiction," or "sf" begins to flourish; and in doing so, it picks up where the critical labor of the historical novel left off. To be sure, with this new form the narrative focus shifts from a dynamic relationship with a past that differs from the present to one that meditates on a "future" that frames significant conditions in the present.

Sf, therefore, "registers some nascent sense of the future, and does so in the space on which a sense of the past had once been inscribed" ("Progress" 150). Sf, in other words, delivers the present to its readers by working within a realist mode that is defamiliarized yet dynamic.[28] Whether it does so by direct extrapolation (in which our present is "some future world's remote past") or by an analogous re-creation (in which our present is transmuted into an imagined society that nevertheless invites a thought-provoking comparative response), sf is intimately concerned with history itself. Against those who invoke the "end of history" or arrogantly conquer (or instrumentalize) history in the name of technological "progress," sf enables its readers to cut through the jungle of such arrogant hegemonic claims and find new directions for critical comparisons between what is and what is coming to be, where we are and what we might be doing.

As a fictive mode that not only mirrors but actively interrogates and intervenes in the processes of history, sf offers more than a pleasurable trip through its pages. When the book is closed and the reader looks out at the world, the even more satisfying experience (now both delightful and didactic) of investigative reading so privileged by sf lingers as one more skill, one more intellectual habit, by which to make sense of social reality itself.[29] In this way the popular cultural form of sf makes an empowering critical practice available to its readers. It offers them a way of "reading the shape of the world," as Henry Schwarz and Richard Dienst put it, that can become complicit with the political practice of overcoming their social alienation, their anthropological strangeness, and hopefully *changing* the shape of the world for the betterment of all humanity.[30] At its most significant, sf can be a part of the larger process of mobilizing the cultural imagination. It can be part of the process of making the world critically "legible" in a way that not only delivers pleasure and knowledge but also the joys of joining in the collective, historical work of bringing a more just and free society into being.

2

Absent Paradigms

In SF, the attitude of estrangement—used by Brecht in a different way, within a still predominantly "realistic" context—has grown into the formal framework *of the genre.*

—Darko Suvin, "On the Poetics of the Science Fiction Genre" (375)

I.

As with any imaginative mode, science fiction is not essentially progressive or conservative. It does not automatically come down on the side of angels or devils. Often, sf is implicated in the ideological apparatus of mainstream society and does its bit in reproducing that social order and its subjects. Certainly the sf of Jules Verne played into the technological logic of his time, and Edgar Rice Burroughs's novels privileged empire and patriarchy. Critics such as H. Bruce Franklin, Constance Penley, and Andrew Ross have demonstrated the ways in which sf in the United States has helped to create the very imaginary of the military-science-industrial complex that has managed the Pax Americana in its Cold War and post–Cold War manifestations, and many feminist critics have exposed the legitimation of masculine privilege and power within the world of sf publishing itself.[1]

Connected to its role in the reproduction of these hegemonic logics, the sf imaginary has also, and perhaps more pervasively, contributed to the interpellation of consumer subjects in the United States and around the globe. Especially with recent claims for the triumph of finance capitalism and its attendant technological marvels, uncritical sf images and narratives do not bring readers and audiences into brave new worlds, whether worse or better than the present, but rather spin them around within the one and only "paradise" that is allowed to exist. From literary series to special-effects-laden films, from video games to fashion design, this compensatory imaginary encapsulates its consumers within enclosed spaces (like the shopping malls that enact and signify) and valorizes lives of repetitive purchases, growing debt, and compulsive (what Joanna Russ metaphorically calls hyperglycemic) subjection to a society built on values of acquisition, compound interest, and free market mobility.

Yet as I suggested in the previous chapter, despite its complicity in this interpellative generator the sf imaginary can still produce critiques of and alternatives to the prevailing social order (which if not fully oppositional or emancipatory are at least contrary in some unsettling fashion). With its disturbing visions, critical sf (fictive, filmic, graphic, or otherwise) generates a distanced space that can draw willing readers away from the society that produces and envelops them. As detractors have always claimed even as they missed the substance of their charge, sf is admittedly an "escapist" mode. The question, however, is what sort of escape? Does a text bring merely the quick thrill of a roller-coaster ride or a chase scene in a popular film, providing a momentary rush that cycles back to the point of departure—producing a compulsion to repeat by riding again or rewinding the tape? Does it tap into the constructed desires of theme parks or textual sequels? Or does it offer a possible escape velocity that can sweep readers out of their spacetime continuum, warping their minds into a cognitive zone from which they might look back at their own social moment, perhaps with anxiety or better yet with anger, and then discover that such a place might be known for what it is and changed for the better?[2]

Sf has always offered this possibility for radical re-vision. But—and now I refer to North American sf in particular—as new generations of sf writers expanded the genre's creative practice, especially by the 1950s, that critical potential increased. Because of the population surges of the baby boom and the changing attitudes toward popular culture (stimulated by street style, comic books, rock and roll, and the mass-market paperback book), the number of readers grew. Simultaneously, sf writers, as Isaac Asimov observed, began to move from stories that focused on questions of physical science to ones that looked at social realities and problems. As they did so, they often opted for near-future tales that were closer in time and space to the authors' and readers' immediate social realities.[3] Established writers such as Asimov, Arthur C. Clarke, Robert Heinlein, Judith Merril, and Frederik Pohl continued to create sf that did not settle for replications of the status quo. However contradictory or compromised their envisaged alternatives, they nevertheless looked elsewhere and took their readers with them.

More overtly, younger writers, especially members of the baby-boom cohorts, were more immediately influenced by the postwar intellectual and cultural energy that was usually interrogative and sometimes overtly oppositional. Eventually, by the 1960s, falling within the controversial and ultimately inconclusive designation of the "New Wave," they demonstrated that they were at the very least citizens of their own time and place. They were imbued with the sf tradition but also open to experimental, often self-reflexive fiction and to the Left and avant-garde/bohemian culture of their time. Writers such as Delany, Russ, Thomas Disch, Pamela Zoline, and others pushed against the boundaries of what was considered to be appropriate within the sf community and even more so within mainstream society. Each explored new ways to create what Harlan Ellison called, in the titles of his two pathbreaking short story collections, "dangerous visions."[4] Some took another step and contributed to the revival and renewal of utopian writing (since its last heyday in the late nineteenth century), and this led to the critical utopias by Ursula K. Le Guin, Suzy McKee Charnas, Sally Gearhardt, Marge Piercy, and Ernest Callenbach, as well as Joanna Russ and Samuel R. Delany.

This explosion of critical creativity within the sphere of sf and utopian writing was itself part of the sociopolitical opening of the period. Although some writers, such as Heinlein, aligned with the libertarian Right (as it circulated around groups such as the John Birch Society, the Young Americans for Freedom, and the presidential campaign of Barry Goldwater), others were more closely affiliated with the cultural ambience of the diverse, often contradictory, but nevertheless revitalized Left.[5] Rooted in the economic and social organizing of 1930s, the anti-fascist resistance of World War II, and the international and domestic liberation and labor struggles after the war, this complex political movement steadily gained strength from the late 1940s onward.[6] After years of setbacks in the face of anti-communist repression, Stalinist betrayal, liberal cooptation, and consumerist displacement, multiple strands of activism blossomed into that array of oppositional formations that can be included under the nominal umbrella of the Left of the postwar era. For me, this would include the noncompromised (by liberalism or Stalinism) Old Left, militant labor, radical pacifism, the several generations of the New Left, and the liberation movements (be they of nation, race, ethnicity, region, age, gender, sexuality, ability, or nature itself). Each of these was part of a material (not merely discursive) opposition to a hegemonic bloc based in capitalist exploitation and its attendant state power (primarily based in the United States but also developing throughout the West) as well in the continuing structures and practices of racism, sexism, homophobia, and ecological aggression.

By the 1970s this movement constituted what Ernst Bloch would call a "concrete utopian" moment and what Antonio Gramsci would identify as a potentially "counter-hegemonic" force that posed a serious threat to the reigning system of power and privilege.[7] Although the strength of this Left was always more cultural than economic or political, its critique and vision, its analysis and praxis, challenged and liberated the hearts and minds (and bodies) of many, young and old, who were not content with things as they were. After slow and uneven growth in the 1940s and 1950s and explosive expansion in the 1960s, the Left in the 1970s had come to constitute what Oskar Negt and Alexander Kluge would call an oppositional public sphere or what Henri Lefebvre would identify as a "counter-space."[8] Broadly understood, it included local action or affinity groups, mass organizations, and political parties, as well as popular and academic intellectual and cultural formations. But it was not only organizational or narrowly political. Many who affiliated with the Left (whether cadres, militants, partisans, radicals, fellow travelers, sympathizers, or hangers-on) lived in or at the edges of a politically attuned counterculture that shaped not only their own everyday realities but also those of their children, their extended families, and even their nonaligned neighbors—especially as they clustered in particular parts of cities, towns, and the countryside.

In this oppositional space, intellectual and cultural activity took place across the social grid. Critical and creative production flourished in study and consciousness-raising groups, local theater companies, film societies, poster collectives, fan formations, festivals and rock bands, as well as in new formations in the academy. Cultural forms (sf and comic books, street theater and murals, folk and rock music, film, and all varieties of counterfashions) grew and expanded with people as they moved along in their lives. Within this cultural growth, the scholarly investigation and critique of this expanded and complex popular/mass culture developed apace. As each subgeneration of activists and allies reached the next stages of their "adult" lives, they did not abandon their initial activist commitment but rather transformed it in the new conditions of life and work. As German Students for a Democratic Society (SDS) leader Rudi Dutschke famously put it in a reformulation of Mao Zedong's words, they embarked upon a "long march through the institutions" that continues to this day.[9]

Building on the work of the radical thinkers and teachers who reentered the academy as the pall of the debilitating McCarthyist purges lifted, new projects in academic disciplines such as history, economics, and literature were launched, often clustered in specific departments or campuses and in new professional organizations and scholarly journals. Alongside the traditional disciplines, inter-, cross-, and transdisciplinary work in African American, gay-lesbian, Third World, women's, and other "studies" programs emerged as the intellectual-pedagogical sector of the postwar political struggles for self-determination.

As well, the elaboration and expansion of the Left's ongoing critique of its own theoretical and political framework flourished. In this richly layered moment, intellectual and cultural work also moved between the academy and other social formations without the barriers that have now become common. The result was the revitalization, after years of repression and marginalization, of the praxis of a broadly considered Left that included a refunctioned critical Marxism, a second wave of feminism, a new project of gay-lesbian studies, a more critical form of ecological studies, and an expanding anti-, non-, and post-Western scholarship. This was a time when the personal, political, and professional dimensions of life were more, though not always easily, interrelated as facets of the self-conscious practice of the movement. In all this work, and from a variety of liberatory standpoints, the theories, structures, and practices of academic life were critiqued and often transformed.[10]

II.

Within this intellectual and cultural tectonic shift, some of the creative tendencies in sf grew from and fed back into the countercultural and sometimes counter-hegemonic space of this broad oppositional phenomenon.[11] Significant projects in sf publishing moved in this direction, and some sf fans organized progressive formations such as Wiscon (the annual feminist fan convention in Wisconsin) or gathered in socialist, anarchist, feminist, lesbian, gay, and other radical caucuses, with their own subcultures, meetings, and publications.[12] In what would become a paradigm shift in the way sf and utopias were studied, this cultural movement produced and was in turn affected by scholarly and critical work as activists (and sf readers) moved into graduate programs and endeavored, successfully, to make room for the reading, study, and teaching of sf and utopias in their workdays and workplaces. The result was the development of an approach that took sf scholarship beyond the limiting tendencies of the day. In the new work, sf was considered a properly didactic literature with its own history and its own formal operations. The object at last began to shape the scholarly and pedagogical response.

The critical turn in sf and utopian studies, of course, was but one component among many in the transformation of academic life that took place throughout this political period. As Richard Ohmann has recalled, literary scholarship abandoned the ivory tower of detached, even when critical, contemplation and sought a direct engagement with all dimensions of culture as it constituted the entire way of life of people making sense of the dynamic but terrible postwar world.[13] After years of celebrating "verbal art and Anglo-American high culture," literary study "charged out of its quiet retreat, turned a critical eye on the social order, challenged many core beliefs and values, and sharply revised its cultural mission" ("Cold War" 73). Under the inspiration of F. R. Leavis and others of the

Scrutiny group in Britain, literary criticism had already articulated its antagonism to capitalism and its mass commodified culture, but it had done so from an intellectual parapet that stood apart from and safely above the fray.[14] The object of knowledge, the literary text, continued to be studied in splendid isolation from its historical context and was held up as a preserve of truth, a haven for timeless universals.

But with the overdetermined pressures of postwar liberation struggles and the waves of political movements from civil rights, to the opposition to the war and the draft and the bomb, to the next wave of feminism, and beyond, literary studies was dragged out of its refined refuge into the mean streets of political engagement. The protective wall of aloof disdain tumbled, and critical projects ventured into the world. By the 1960s, intellectual activists had successfully disrupted the old equilibrium. Early scholarship sought to give recognition and voice to those who had been repressed and silenced, and scholarly movements such as women's, black, and Third World studies produced groundbreaking archival and interpretive work.

In this context and from a variety of critical stances, the hegemonic culture (including the structures and practices that reproduced the socioeconomic complex and its subjects) was analyzed and challenged. Especially as such work was enriched by theoretical interventions informed by critical Marxist projects in Europe and liberation movements in the Third World, the curtains of empiricism and functionalism in the social sciences and humanities were torn asunder. More substantial analyses of the economic, political, and cultural dimensions of society demanded and received the attention of the radical projects. The consequent change in intellectual life in the United States, as elsewhere, was profound, as the ruling ideological assumptions were roundly attacked. Ohmann:

> Thus, many of the challenges posed by 1960s movements to the postwar consensus were taken up and developed in English and neighboring fields. No one there could any longer take for granted—that is, without encountering dissident views among close colleagues—that American society was relatively just and marching toward equality under the banner of its corporate leadership; that policy elites were trustworthy guides in international affairs; that the war machine was an instrument of democracy abroad; that the state security apparatus was promoting democracy at home; that capitalism itself was the handmaiden of democracy; or even that any regrettable shortcomings in these areas could be justified by Cold War urgencies—the implacable enmity of the evil empire and the peril of domestic communism. ("Cold War" 92)

To be sure, usually no more than 10 percent of the people involved in literary studies were directly pushing in these directions in their research, writing, curricular development, and teaching. This fraction, however, had an expanding impact as independent organizations (such as the Radical Caucus and the Marxist Literary Group) and caucuses in the major professional organizations (such as the Modern Language Association, the National Council of Teachers of English, the American Historical Association, and the American Studies Association) challenged policies, procedures, and programs; elected radicals to office; and rewrote bylaws to accommodate democratic governance and to facilitate the intervention by such bodies in public debates on the crucial issues of the period. As Ohmann writes: "By the end of the 1970s, radicals and sympathetic liberals constituted a solid bloc of people in literature whose thinking, teaching, and institutional practice were informed by 1960s movements, and the effort to preserve and unify the insights of those movements" ("Cold War" 93).[15]

In this "working hegemony," the literary Left successfully occupied a zone of cultural power in the United States from the late 1960s onward.[16] People who learned about "putting their lives on the line" in civil rights demonstrations, who made the existential choice to resist the draft, who reclaimed control over their own gendered and sexed bodies, and who joined with others not only in "speaking truth to power" but in daring to change society fundamentally were now embarking on that long march of intellectual and educational work by which they would continue to infiltrate, challenge, and change the culture of the most powerful state and economic system in world history. Again Ohmann:

> Plainly, through the period covered here, the American hegemony, and beyond that the hegemonic order of world capitalism, lost its plausibility as common sense, as it was vigorously "resisted, limited, altered, challenged" by 1960s movements. And we have lived since in a time both of challenge and of a strenuous effort to renew, recreate, defend, and modify that hegemony ("Cold War" 95).

I will come back to the matter of that last sentence and the "conservative restoration" it bespeaks, but for now I want to move from this general emergence of radical literary studies to the particular development of sf and utopian studies that also began in the late 1960s. At this moment the creative work of sf writers merged with the critical pleasures of sf readers and the scholarship of sf critics or critics-to-be (to be sure, these positions were often occupied by a single person). This is not the place to recap the debates over the Vietnam War and other issues (such as the status of women) that raged in organizations like the Science Fiction

Writers Association. Nor is it the place to distinguish demographically between that part of the sf community of writers and readers that was overtly conservative (though often libertarian), the part that was countercultural, and the smaller fraction that was progressive and directly "political" in its outlook and commitment.

However, it is the place to emphasize that—despite the lingering presence of patriarchal privilege and power—the most effective political engagement in the sf world at this time came from feminist creative and critical work, as feminist sf in general and the critical utopias in particular demonstrate. Recognizing this major tendency, of course, we should not overlook the anti-capitalist sf of writers such as Frederik Pohl and C. M. Kornbluth (*Space Merchants*) or Mack Reynolds (*Commune 2000*); the anti-war narratives of Joe Haldeman (*Forever War*) or Le Guin (*The Word for World Is Forest*); the anarchist, socialist, and anarchocommunist visions of the many critical utopias; and the exploration of the processes of political organizing and radicalization by Piercy (*Dance the Eagle to Sleep*). It is also the place to recall more generally how sf readers, many of whom were both activists and academics, were reinforced in their break from mainstream interpellation by the consciousness-raising process of becoming an emancipated person in a movement that invited them to be part of something bigger than their individual selves (as the people in the civil rights struggle put it).

My intention here is to give a brief overview of the new directions taken in science fiction and utopian scholarship as a way to lead into my own perspective within that paradigm (which itself provides a framework for my discussion of the dystopian subgenre and the recent development of critical dystopias). Unfortunately, a comprehensive history of sf criticism (before, during, and after this period) must be left to a very different project than this one. To that end, however, the editors of *Science Fiction Studies* have made a significant beginning by publishing a special issue on "A History of Science Fiction Criticism" in July 1999.[17] Noting that the history of sf *criticism* is "less well documented or understood" than the history of the literature itself and that the references that are made tend to pay "brief homage to a few iconic predecessors" but are generally "incomplete, inchoate, cursory, or polemical" ("Editorial Introduction" 161), the editors decided on the special issue as a statement in its own right but also as the possible template for a book. Happily, then, I offer this *SFS* issue as an initial source for a history I cannot at this moment recount. I do, however, want to recognize some of the key elements expressed in that issue as a way of providing a general framework for my commentary.

One area that is often neglected (and that is important for a larger cultural studies approach) is the critical work that has occurred within the realm of sf publishing (by writers and editors) and fandom, as opposed to academic criticism, what some call "inside criticism." Therefore, Gary Westfahl's essay on what he terms the "popular tradition" of sf criticism needs especially to be acknowledged. Although even this story is more complex and certainly more contested than Westfahl tells it, he usefully identifies the popular "conversation" about sf that began in the 1920s in the "editorials, blurbs, articles, reviews" of the North American pulp magazines edited by Hugo Gernsback and others (Westfahl 203). This material prompted readerly responses, editorial replies, and then more response and debate; and later (especially by the 1950s) this popular critical discourse expanded into the explicit form of book reviews and implicitly in the schemes and selections of literature checklists, annotated bibliographies, and "year's best" and thematic anthologies that were produced in the marketplace outside the walls of academia. This popular tradition, he argues, has been both neglected and overwritten by academic criticism, but it is one we all need to recognize and learn if a properly comprehensive critical history is ever to be produced. Besides Westfahl's contribution, the remaining pieces in this special issue of *SFS* identify other major regions of the critical terrain.

Interestingly, the abstract for the "Editorial Introduction" recognizes a basic consensus among the broad critical community as it notes that certain key points have been consistent elements of the emerging understanding of the characteristics of the sf genre. In particular, the acknowledgment of sf's "social purpose," "scientific and moral didacticism," and "perceived level of verisimilitude" stands as a constant in both popular and academic criticism ("Editorial Introduction" 186). Beyond the introduction, the pieces by Arthur Evans, Donald Hassler, and Veronica Hollinger begin to chart the critical history that runs from the early period of Kepler to Wells, through the postwar "literary" tradition, and finally into the "contemporary trends," which include feminist criticism and the later insights of poststructuralist studies (while displacing or perhaps discounting the critical Marxist contributions to all this work). This all-too-brief history, then, offers a minimal baseline for my "cursory" and no doubt "polemical" overview.[18]

By the late 1960s, therefore, a major tendency in the critical studies of sf and utopian literature (especially but not exclusively informed by feminism, critical Marxism, and British, continental, and post-Western cultural theory) had begun to deal with sf/utopian fiction on its own terms, working inductively with the specific history and form of these unique textual objects.[19] This new work therefore induced a way of reading, interpreting, and critiquing that was not defined by or dependent on established academic projects: both those that followed the reigning New Criticism and canonical literary studies in an elitist elevation of *some* sf to the status of "serious literature," usually interpreted with criteria derived from, and appropriate for, the realist or modernist novel; and those that emphasized an academic but nevertheless unreflexive populist reading of *all* sf as paraliterature but that did not make the distinctions required to comprehend sf's social production and consumption.

To be sure, the "popular culture" position (however undertheorized or noncritical in its general approach) at least approached sf and its paraliterary cousins on their own terms and contributed to the scholarly legitimation of sf and utopian studies; whereas the dominant "high culture" camp continued the corrosive work familiar to the logic of mainstream academic liberalism by isolating and than appropriating a small portion of sf for inclusion in the established literary canon. In that hegemonic perspective, "popular" works of sf and "tendentious" works of utopian narration were relegated to shadowy margins, and only exceptional examples (like a select few "scholarship boys") were cut out of the pack and rehabilitated by reducing them to their similarities with the already privileged canonical works of Western literature. Of course, the situated critical work on the broader range of sf texts would also be branded and marginalized as simply "popular" or narrowly "political."

Supporting, encouraging, and providing venues for the new critical work (by way of conferences and in publications) were a variety of organizations and scholarly journals specifically devoted to sf studies. In the United States, Tom Clareson and others had established a Modern Language Association Seminar on Science Fiction as early as 1958, and they continued that seminar at national and regional meetings until the MLA Executive Committee exercised a purge of sessions in the late 1970s.[20] And in 1959 Clareson also founded the journal *Extrapolation* from his base at Wooster College. As scholarly work accumulated and progressed, the Science Fiction Research Association (with its *SFRA Review*) was created in 1970; the independent journal *Science-Fiction Studies* (originally edited by Dale Mullen and Darko Suvin) was established in 1973; the first conference of the International Association for the Fantastic in the Arts was begun in 1980; and its *Journal of the Fantastic in the Arts* was launched in 1988.[21]

In addition to these projects, pedagogical initiatives also contributed to the legitimacy of sf studies. In his introduction to the special issue of *Science-Fiction Studies* focusing on "Science Fiction in Academe," Mullen reports that courses in utopian studies (including but not restricted to literary utopias) were taught in the 1950s (a substantial move itself in those anti-utopian Cold War years); and these, he argues, helped to pave the way for sf courses.[22] The honor for the first sf class goes to Sam Moskowitz, who offered an extension course in New York's City College in 1953, but the first regularly scheduled, credit-carrying courses were taught in 1962 by Mark Hillegas at Colgate and Bruce Franklin at Stanford (while Arthur Lewis offered a utopian literature course at Penn State).[23] Since then, third-level as well as second-level courses in sf and utopias have blossomed, and graduate work in these fields has accordingly grown in quantity and quality.[24]

III.

With this perspective in mind, I want to review a set of critical pieces in sf and utopian studies that were formative for many of us who work in these areas (in our overdetermined positions as scholars, teachers, writers, editors, publishers, readers, viewers, consumers).[25] One of the first essays that helped to produce this influential paradigm shift was Joanna Russ's "What Can a Heroine Do? Or Why Women Can't Write." Published in 1972 in Susan Koppleman's *Images of Women in Fiction: Feminist Perspectives* (an early anthology of the new feminist criticism), Russ's essay was written at the moment of the intersection of the rising consciousness of the women's movement, the emergence of feminist theory and criticism, and the new awareness of the qualities of sf.[26] As Russ recalls in her introduction to the reprint in a collection of her critical work, *To Write Like a Woman*, the essay grew out of her participation in a symposium on women, hosted by the Cornell University School of Home Economics in January 1970. The result, as she puts it, "was a ferment of talk . . . that lasted for years. I went home feeling that the sky had fallen. One of the most immediate results was my understanding that 'English literature' had been badly rigged, and out of that insight came this essay."[27]

"What Can a Heroine Do" rehearses the changes recurring throughout literary studies.[28] It thinks its way through and beyond scholarly and political orthodoxy by evaluating available literary strategies and connecting the potential of some of these to the needs, desires, insights, and interventions of women and other politically engaged writers who were taking creative steps within the challenge to the political and cultural status quo. Russ's argument is that narrative modes at the edges of recognized literary culture along with certain popular genres offered the best ways to break open the ideological limits of conventional narratives (in which female protagonists could only capitulate, go mad, or die). Her assertion, in the spirit of the time, was direct: "Culture is male" (*To Write* 80). Consequently, the culture's "myths" (soon the term *ideology* would be more regularly used) allow only narratives and images that recognize and reproduce that dominant viewpoint. Other lives, other ways of being in the world, are thereby silenced and eliminated. As Russ tersely puts it: "Make something unspeakable and you make it unthinkable" (*To Write* 90). Writers who opt for working within this cultural framework end up being "pretty much restricted to the attitudes, the beliefs, the expectations, and, above all, the plots that are 'in the air'" (*To Write* 81).

Russ, of course, refuses to settle for this deadly capitulation, and begins her search for ways out of the mythic jungle. In doing so, she moves in two directions taken by the new feminist criticism as she works out a critique of existing images of women and then archivally retrieves certain writers as foremothers to ground a new tradition of women's writing. After reviewing the allowable range of female subjects in narrative (Devourer/Bitch, Maiden/Victim, Abused Child, and, most often, Protagonist of a Love Story) and after setting aside the strategy of occupying the male protagonist position (since a "woman who refuses to write about women ignores the whole experience of the female culture"), Russ turns to the margins to find liberatory forms of writing (*To Write* 85). Hesitating at the intersection of high and popular literary forms, she identifies two textual strategies that she names as the nonnarrative "lyric" and the stories of nonprivileged (that is, not-male, not-Western European) "life" (*To Write* 87, 88). Both of these, she argues, can address what she calls the "unspeakable, undramatizable, unembodiable action-one-cannot-name" and spark a textual vitality that could have a powerful social impact on its authors and readers (*To Write* 90).

As Russ puts it, the structural principle of lyricism "consists of *the organization of discrete elements* (images, events, scenes, passages, words, what-have-you) *around an unspoken thematic or emotional center*" (*To Write* 87). It is a mode that deemphasizes chronology or causation, in which "nothing happens." Offering Virginia Woolf's work as a model, she suggests that the material of such a text—images, events, scenes, memories—circles around an "invisible center," that which is, in the present order of things, "unsayable in available dramatic or narrative terms" (*To Write* 87). Without the myths of the present informing the narrative, this accumulation of other ways of knowing and being comes to constitute another place, another way to live.

Acknowledging that not every female author will choose this more modernist mode, Russ notes that the alternative is to work from stories of life itself: that is, "to take as one's model (and structural principle) not male myth but the structure of one's own experience" (*To Write* 88). With George Eliot, Doris Lessing, and the Brontës as models, she suggests that this more realist mode allows one to write about "a person to whom nothing happens" in the world of male power and myth (*To Write* 88). The resulting narrative, in its "blocked jabbing" and "constant thwarting," is often a "formless" composition that lacks the security of a plot of predictable success and reward (*To Write* 88). She connects this second strategy with nineteenth-century Russian fiction and African American fiction and then associates it with the sort of political fiction that is so often condemned for being mere propaganda.

Moving to another textual register, Russ turns to popular genres for examples of writing that "already employ[s] plots not limited to one sex—i.e., myths that have nothing to do with our accepted gender roles," and she names detective stories, supernatural fiction, and sf as the three most useful sources (*To Write* 90). Detective fiction is written and read by women and often features women protagonists, and its exploration of "genuine intellectual puzzles" points to a way to interrogate the status quo (*To Write* 91). Russ, of course, anticipates writers such as Sarah Peretsky and Sue Grafton, who soon began to transform the hard-boiled detective novel, or "crime fiction," as Russ names it, into even more powerful social interrogations. Supernatural fiction, also written and read by women, offers another way into the realm of the strange, the dangerous, and that which is not regarded as "natural"; but its outcome, Russ asserts, often ends up with the empty closure of ritual gestures. Despite her caveats, she insightfully anticipates the complex negotiations of a supernaturalized social space by writers such as Ann Rice or popular visual works such as *Buffy, the Vampire Slayer.*

In sf, however, she finds the most powerful way forward; for she sees it as an intellectual mode in which the very structure of the narrative is concerned with the positing and exploration of new worlds:

> The myths of science fiction run along the lines of exploring a new world conceptually (not necessarily physically), creating needed physical or social machinery, assessing the consequences of technological or other changes, and so on. These are not stories about men *qua* Man and women *qua* Woman; they are myths of human intelligence and human adaptability. They not only ignore gender roles but—at least theoretically—are not culture-bound. (*To Write* 91)

Sf is therefore an optimum mode for reaching beyond the myths of male power. Russ acknowledges Suvin's comparatist connection of sf with forms of medieval literature (a common enough recognition, though more often made by medieval scholars looking forward rather than others looking backward), and she ends her essay with a paean to varieties of *didactic* writing (allegory, exemplum, parable, political fiction, sf) that follow from that observation. As she notes, each of these allow authors and readers to think through *collective* solutions to human problems. Writing in the radical tone of the 1960s, she celebrates these literary modes, and the "outsiders" who work with them, as best situated for the work of radical cultural critique: "When things are changing, those who know least about them—in the usual terms—may make the best job of them" (*To Write* 93).[29]

"What Can a Heroine Do?" is replete with a radical hope and engaged criticism that breaks with the imaginative and critical orthodoxy surrounding the production and reception of sf. Complementing her essay in 1972, Darko Suvin's "On the Poetics of the Science Fiction Genre" situates sf within the long history of nonnaturalist literature, delineates its primary formal characteristics, and posits a definition for sf that holds to this day.[30] Accepted by Richard Ohmann for the December issue of *College English,* the essay was included with critical works on the pastoral, the fairy tale, and "talking books," reflecting the shift that radical editors such as Ohmann were beginning to make in the centers of literary scholarship.[31] The essay grew from a lecture Suvin gave in a seminar on fantastic literature in Yale's Slavic Department in 1968, and revised versions were given in 1970 at Temple University and at the Science Fiction Research Association conference (see "Poetics" 372n). With political roots in the anti-Stalinist socialism of Yugoslavia in the late 1940s and the New Left of the 1960s, an intellectual formation produced by an early love of sf, a degree in science, advanced study in philology and the theoretical frameworks of critical Marxism and Russian formalism, and with an academic base in Canada at McGill University, Suvin was well positioned, theoretically and politically, to challenge literary orthodoxy on the question of sf.

"Poetics" (however much it has been disagreed with or refined in subsequent years) provided a groundbreaking historical and theoretical analysis of sf, and in doing so it opened the way for new directions in sf criticism and for connecting that criticism with the wider culture of opposition.[32] Suvin begins the essay by recognizing the popularity and significance of sf in the cultures of leading industrial nations, and (in a claim for a certain readership that many others echo) he notes its particular reception by "some key strata of modern society such as the college graduates, young writers, and general readers appreciative of new sets of values" ("Poetics" 372).[33] Like Russ, he proceeds from a typology of literary forms in present-day culture and in the sweep of Western history and gradually zeroes in on the formal specificity of sf. Working dialectically, he characterizes sf in terms of "non-naturalist" literary modes, but as a modern variant that has appropriated, refunctioned qualities of naturalist writing. He connects sf with earlier forms of writing that refuse immediate accounts of the given world and generate "radically different" figures or contexts, and he thereby acknowledges sf's kinship with literary subgenres such as "the Greek and Hellenistic 'blessed island' stories, the 'fabulous voyage' from Antiquity on, the Renaissance and Baroque 'utopia' and 'planetary novel,' the Enlightenment 'state (political) novel,' the modern 'anticipation,' 'anti-utopia'" ("Poetics" 372).

Further emphasizing its refusal of empiricism, he notes that sf shares "an opposition to naturalistic or empiricist literary genres" with myth, fantasy, fairy tale, and the pastoral insofar as these are all "non-naturalistic or meta-empirical genres" ("Poetics" 372). But he then turns in the opposite direction and posits a spectrum, "or spread of literary subject-matter," that runs "from the ideal extreme of exact recreation of the author's empirical environment to exclusive interest in a strange newness, a *novum*" ("Poetics" 373). At the empiricist end of this continuum, he locates works that have constituted the literary mainstream from the eighteenth to the twentieth centuries; at the other end, he places nonnaturalist forms, such as the imaginary voyage and the satirical re-presentation of society, which articulate the "amazing" or the "new."

With this historically informed comparative analysis in place, Suvin then presents sf as a version of nonnaturalist writing that engages with the "social and the methodological" in a historically grounded and epistemologically rigorous manner. Situated between the empirical and the amazing, sf occupies a space in the center as it dialectically incorporates a realist sensibility in a non-naturalist form. Suvin puts it this way:

> The approach to the imaginary locality, or localized daydream, practiced by the genre of SF is a supposedly factual one. Columbus' (technically or genologically non-fictional) letter on the Eden he glimpsed beyond the Orinoco mouth, and Swift's (technically non-factual) voyage . . . stand at the opposite ends of a ban between imaginary and factual possibilities. Thus SF takes off from a fictional ("literary") hypothesis and develops it with extrapolating and totalizing scientific rigor. ("Poetics" 374)

He then argues that this formal strategy provides sf with the potential for a socially critical perspective, for the "effect of such factual reporting of fictions is one of confronting a set normative system—a Ptolemaic-type closed world picture—with a point of view or glance implying a new set of norms" ("Poetics" 374). He takes his argument to a more theoretical level when he explains this critical proclivity in terms of the notion of "estrangement" (as it comes from the Russian formalist Victor Shklovsky and the German Marxist Bertolt Brecht), and he draws on Brecht's own description to make his point: "A representation which estranges is one which allows us to recognize its subject, but at the same time makes it seem unfamiliar" (Brecht, quoted in "Poetics" 374). This de-alienating "look of estrangement" is both cognitive and creative, for it not only coolly assesses a given situation from a distanced perspective but it imaginatively does so by way of the textual form and not simply the content.[34]

In this tightly argued first section, Suvin moves from the world of hegemonic literary studies into a dialectically transformed position that regards sf within its own formal parameters. The result is an understanding of sf as a literary genre in which "the attitude of estrangement—used by Brecht in a different way, within a still predominantly 'realistic' context—has grown into the *formal framework* of the genre" ("Poetics" 375).[35] Suvin opens the next section with his now well-known definition in which he describes sf as "a literary genre whose necessary and sufficient conditions are the presence and interaction of estrangement and cognition, and whose main formal device is an imaginative framework alternative to the author's empirical environment" ("Poetics" 375). He goes on to examine how the interplay of estrangement and cognition enables sf to generate a distanced and fresh view of an author's reality that rejects narrowly empirical, commonsensical accounts yet does so by way of a representation of an alternative framework that is "realistically" rigorous and consistent in terms of its own provisional reality and in its critical relationship with the empirical world.[36]

Suvin then examines how sf narrative strategies—from the purely extrapolative to the fully analogic—negotiate the relationship between the author's environment and the created world. The simplest is based on "direct, temporal extrapolation," as certain tendencies in the historical environment are played out in the alternative world. To be sure, many compelling and powerful sf works have taken this path and generated futures that expose current problems and warn of the dire consequences if such problems are not properly addressed. Suvin cautions, however, that extrapolative sf can easily be caught up in a narrowly technological accommodation with the status quo and back away from challenges to the fundamental premises or logics of a society. Extrapolation, therefore, can too readily be "used as a hand-maiden of futurological foresight" that simply fine-tunes things as they are (see "Poetics" 378–379).

The richer, more complex model for sf narration is the analogic, in which the relationship between created and historical worlds is both more totalizing and more indirect. The simplest form of analogic modeling is close to the extrapolative in that it posits an alternative world that stands in almost a one-to-one relationship to the author's, even though the alternative space is as far back as the prehistoric or as far away as another galaxy or the end of time. Suvin places adventure-driven space opera in this category, but he also acknowledges that serious sf such as Samuel Delany's adopts this approach. In the "highest" form of analogic sf, the alternative world does not come across in a direct correspondence to the empirical world but rather is ontologically and epistemologically modulated and distanced so that rigorous work must be done to articulate the critical connections. Here, Suvin cites examples ranging from Edwin Abbott's *Flatland* (1884) to Franz Kafka's *Penal Colony* (1919) to Stanislaus Lem's *Solaris* (1961), but one might also consider examples such as Delany's *Dhalgren* (1975) or Le Guin's *Always Coming Home* (1985)(see "Poetics" 380).

Suvin closes his essay with yet another dialectical turn as he addresses the quality of the sf form in terms of its dual function to delight and teach. Like Russ, he values the aesthetic complexity of sf, and he sees the relationship of estrangement and cognition as the basis for judging the formal value of a given text in terms of the complexity, consistency, and rigor of its presentation. Also like Russ, he considers sf to be an inherently didactic literature, one that not only demands careful and thoughtful writing and reading but also, at its aesthetic and pedagogical best, offers critical knowledge and awareness of possibilities for change. Sf, he notes, "demands from the author and reader, teacher and critic, not merely specialized, quantified positivistic knowledge (*scientia*) but a social imagination whose quality, whose wisdom (*sapientia*), testifies to the maturity of his critical and creative thought" ("Poetics" 381).

This contribution was joined by another in the paper Suvin delivered in a seminar organized by Teresa de Lauretis at the University of Wisconsin-Milwaukee's Center for Twentieth Century Studies in 1977 and that was published as chapter 4 of his *Metamorphoses of Science Fiction*. In "SF and the Novum," he added to his categories of "cognitive estrangement" and "alternative framework" the further argument that sf (and utopian fiction, I would add) is "distinguished by the narrative dominance or hegemony of a fictional 'novum' (novelty, innovation) validated by cognitive logic" (*Metamorphoses* 63). With this new work, Suvin's materialist and formalist analysis, already politically charged, became even more explicitly engaged with his reading of sf as a literary form capable of breaking open the prevailing hegemonic hold on reality. By not only tracking what was at hand in the tendencies of the historical moment as portrayed in the alternative world but also pointing, through the textual novum, toward the potential for radically new directions in the latencies of that moment, Suvin's claims for sf brought it to a level of sociopolitical value that many sensed but never fully theorized. Such a move was controversial to say the least in certain academic and fannish communities that nevertheless took serious notice of his work.

Important as many of us found the category of the novum to be, Suvin's "Novum" essay never received the reception accorded to the "Poetics" piece, although I would suggest that the reasons for this were multiple and even contradictory. To explain this key category, I review the history of its reception and of Suvin's own critique and revision in order to do it the justice it deserves. In 1996 Suvin recapped the troubled history of the novum in a keynote address at a conference on "Envisioning Alternatives" at the University of Luton (a version of which was published as "Novum Is as Novum Does").[37] Considering the lively response to his work on cognitive estrangement, he surmised that the lack of response to the notion of the novum over two decades indicated a quiet acceptance of his argument and implied a "critical consensus" by "socialists and liberals" ("Novum Is as Novum Does" 37). Yet he then proceeded to reassess, critique, and refine his own sense of this key aspect of sf's textual mechanics. Contrary to his sanguine reading, my own interpretation of the critical silence is less optimistic. Taking into account the beginning of the shift to the political Right at the time *Metamorphoses* was published in 1979 (and equally factoring in the theoretical critique of long-standing assumptions about master narratives, the emancipatory potential of science, the expectations of progress, and the privileging of certain political agents that developed in the conservative reaction to the Left after 1968), I think it was not consensus but in fact political and theoretical discomfort with Suvin's argument that accounted for the benign neglect of the novum as a critical category.[38]

Indeed, in an exchange in *Science-Fiction Studies* in 1995, a version of this discomfort emerges when Suvin and Carol McGuirk disagree over the function of the novum. McGuirk, taking a properly postmodern position, distances herself from Suvin's claim that a textual novum needs to be validated by cognitive logic (this, even after checking his clarification, in his 1988 volume, *Positions and Presuppositions in Science Fiction,* that cognition includes the imagination as well as analytical discourse, a point that he had already made in "Poetics").[39] Lurking in this friendly disagreement is a hint of what might have been more aggressively at stake in other nonresponses in this decades-long silence.

Recalling the onset of the hegemony of the Right around 1980, I suggest that this critical neglect is itself an early symptom of the reaction against the Left counterpublic sphere. To be sure, needed, useful, and proper critiques, by what has often been subsumed under the term *poststructuralism,* effectively challenged the orthodox Marxist tradition that uncritically employed categories such as scientific analysis, totality, progress, or class struggle within the unyielding, authoritarian stricture of an unexamined teleological analysis that was itself closed to the specificities of history. Especially within critical Marxist, feminist, and post-colonial manifestations, these critiques have aided the democratic and critical Left's political-intellectual project, for they have stimulated the reexamination and refunctioning of such assumptions, premises, frameworks, and methods.

By the 1980s, however, this healthy "poststructuralist" correction was also readily conflated with an official response that was neither critical nor dialectical but outright condemnatory of *all* Left discourse and praxis. That is, the critical project was often appropriated for use in hegemonic attacks based in an old-fashioned anti-communism, albeit given new "professional" shape within a narrow academic discourse by the post-1968 reaction and the emergent new Right discourse. In this repressive atmosphere, Suvin's claims for the formal operation of a totalizing novum validated by critical cognition may well have been preemptively dismissed as prescriptive and narrowly rational, and consequently ignored and bypassed in the retreat to the safer zones of textuality, micropolitics, and yuppie postmodernity.

Nevertheless, in his original formulation, his refinements, and his self-critique in the Luton paper, Suvin's argument for the textual novum still stands (for some of us, at least) as an effective category for the analyses of sf texts. Even as he expresses his own doubts about the "beneficence" of the novum in the 1996 paper ("Novum Is as Novum Does" 37), his concerns are not a revisionist rejection of its underlying logic but rather a caution against a too facile embrace of the capacity of a radical novum to survive the pressures of the current conjuncture.

Sharply divorcing the sense of the novum from the "novelty" privileged by the capitalist machine, he asserts that "we live in an ever faster circulation of what Walter Benjamin called *das Immerwiedergleiche,* the ever again recurring whirligig of fads that do not better human relationships" ("Novum Is as Novum Does" 37). And he quotes David Noble, who warns of the "perpetual rush to novelty that characterises the modern market-place, with its escalating promise of technological transcendence" in a "remarkably dynamic society that goes nowhere" (quoted in "Novum Is as Novum Does" 37). As well, he takes care to separate his understanding of the term *cognition* as a form of critical reason from the now compromised and co-opted instrumental reason of a "science" fully employed by late-twentieth-century capitalism. Finally, he sets aside any hints of a conflation of "progress" with his sense of the radically new, in a reassertion of the open-ended perspective that had been there all along.

Suvin's 1990s suspicions, in other words, are not those of the camp of reaction and rejection but rather a necessary correction of the effective apprehension of the viability of the novum in these times. Because of these careful distinctions, I would argue that his keynote commentary helps not to bury the novum but to revive this already nuanced category in the light of the poststructuralist sensibility and in the shadow of the now more pervasive power of capital. Thus, he does not argue that the novum should be made redundant in an end-of-history implosion but rather that extreme care must be taken to distinguish between the novum of opposition and the pseudo-novum of commodification that has come to dominate the terrain of the "new." He offers a sober reminder that utopian hope for what Bloch terms the "not yet" is negated by the false utopia that the new market order offers as the prime site for individual experiences of hustle, success, and pleasure; and he further cautions that the novum of opposition itself must be interrogated (as in the critical utopias of the 1960s and 1970s) so that it is recognized as an authentic novum when it produces a "formulation of a *problem*" but not when it offers the consoling "*explanation*" of a pseudo-novum ("Novum Is as Novum Does" 39).

With this historical perspective in mind, I will examine Suvin's understanding of the novum, drawing on the sources cited above and working with and going beyond the original 1979 *Metamorphoses* chapter. With his argument that the common denominator of the sf and utopian text was to be found in the "estranged techniques of presenting a cognitive novum" (*Positions* x), Suvin stressed the sociopolitical consequence of his earlier definitions by clarifying how "history and society are not simply the contexts of fiction but its inly interfused factors" (*Positions* xi). Thus, while novelty might be present in the content of any literary genre, in sf the novum is the *formal* element that generates and validates all elements of the text, from alternate reality to plot, characters, and style. Yet the novum is meaningful only to the extent that it effectively intervenes in the author's historical context. Suvin makes this point eloquently: "Born in history and judged in history, the novum has an ineluctably historical character. So has the correlative fictional reality or possible world which, for all its displacements and disguises, always corresponds to the wish-dreams and nightmares of a specific sociocultural class of implied addressees" (*Positions* 76).

As he reveals in *Metamorphoses,* Suvin's immediate source for this category is Bloch. Working in a different historical and political conjuncture, he dialectically critiques and supersedes Bloch's more orthodox formulation of a "societal Novum," and he consequently develops a radically democratic sense of the novum that enriches the deeper, political implications of his argument.

Bloch's account in *The Principle of Hope* usefully begins with an identification of the realism and pessimism needed to expose the "horrifying possibilities which have been concealed and will continue to be concealed precisely in capitalist progress," for only from such a "critical coldness" can a "militant optimism" proceed clearly with concrete utopian struggle.[40] Having taken this stand, Bloch then falls back into an orthodox framing of the Novum within the interrelated categories of Front and Ultimum, and here Suvin's critical refunctioning takes hold. First of all, Bloch's category of the Front, where the Novum is to be found, is limited by its Leninist connotation of direct, vanguardist military engagement. Such a singular site of historical movement betrays what the actually existing Left has come to know: namely, that the social spaces and moments of contestation are multiple and shifting.

In Suvin's refunctioned sense—informed by the work of Gramsci and Raymond Williams—the insufficient metaphor of the Front gives way to a meaning closer to Williams's notion of a "structure of feeling," which allows for the naming of a variety of historically specific sites and instances (often contradictory but nevertheless oppositional) in which radical novums are to be found. To be sure, in his unorthodox moments, Bloch himself catches this sense of a complex array of emergent possibilities, for he speaks of those spaces wherein the "world process" is most in motion, wherein one can locate the "little thought-out, foremost segment of Being of animated, utopianly open matter" (*Principle* 200). Thus, Suvin's novum is neither the reified "novelty" produced by capitalism nor the vanguard privileged by orthodox Marxism. Instead, it is the dialectical force that mediates the material, historical possibilities and the subjective awareness and action engaged with those possibilities.

On the other side of the frame from the Front, Bloch's Novum assumes full import only when grasped in terms of the Ultimum into which it will transmute, and for him the Ultimum represents "the highest newness, the repetition (the unremitting representedness of the tendency-goal in all progressively New) [that] intensifies to the last, highest, most fundamental repetition: of identity" (*Principle* 203). The shift from Novum to Ultimum registers the point of a "total leap out of everything that previously existed" (*Principle* 203), and so it is the pull toward the unrepresentable Ultimum that keeps the Novum resistant to enclosure by the forces (be they the hegemonic system or a hypostatized opposition) of the present moment. Again, although the sense of a "total leap" keeps the Ultimum radically open, the connotation of finality compromises it with the sort of ahistorical fixation that predominates in both theological and Stalinist discourse. For Suvin, therefore, the Ultimum, with its anti-historical, authoritarian claim of fulfillment, must necessarily give way to the alternative term of an always receding horizon of a radical break from, or leap beyond, the present, one that refuses the legitimating claim of teleological arrival.

In Suvin's formulation, the novum has revolutionary effect *only* if it functions in dynamic relationship to the changing, historically specific structures of feeling out of which it develops and the unnameable horizon of an ongoing history toward which it tends. Again, Bloch, working from his unorthodox spirit, which always contends with his orthodox discipline, expresses it this way: the "dialectic which has its motor in unrest and its goal-content, which in no way exists ante rem, in unappeared essence does away with the dogged cycle (of an Alpha to Omega movement around the new which endlessly repeats)" (*Principle* 204). Instead, in keeping with the "real-ciphers in the world," history itself can move in an open-ended, not determined or predictable, manner.[41]

From this dialectically enriched philosophico-political framework, Suvin frees up the political valence of the textual novum as the mediation of form and history. As he puts it: "An aesthetic novum is either a translation of historical cognition and ethics *into* form, or (in our age perhaps more often) a creation of historical cognition and ethics *as* form" (*Metamorphoses* 80). With this relationship established, he goes on to refine the treatment of readerly estrangement begun in "Poetics," and he describes it as a "feedback oscillation" that "moves now from the author's and implied reader's norm of reality to the narratively actualized novum in order to understand the plot-events, and now back from those novelties to the author's reality, in order to see it afresh from the new perspective gained" (*Metamorphoses* 71).

IV.

Upon publication, Suvin's 1970s contributions to the new critical paradigm (however questioned, debated, ignored, and transformed) offered a perceptive account of the historical and textual specificity of sf. Subsequent studies went on to delineate not only the manner in which that formal capability affected the other elements of the sf text—from the overall narrative to the actants in that narrative to the very sentences themselves—but also how it enabled the relationship between the text and the social context in which it was produced and received. From the body of sf scholarship that was produced in the 1970s and 1980s, three contributions represent, for me, exemplary touch points in the elaboration of this critical understanding of the sf text, the reading protocols it enabled and invited, and its broader sociopolitical value.

In 1979 Marc Angenot (who taught and wrote essays with Suvin) published a semiotic study of the sf text that added further support to Suvin's analysis of sf's inherent capacity to generate cognitively estranged alternative worlds that stand in a potentially critical relationship with empirical reality. In "The Absent Paradigm," Angenot offers a semiotic examination of the textual form of sf that leads to a description of the process of reading sf as it moves between the syntagmatic material on the page and the paradigm of the alternative society that is "both suggested in and yet absent from the textual message."[42] As he explains it, the aesthetic goal of sf, as opposed to realistic fiction, "consists in creating a remote, estranged, and yet intelligible" alternative world (Angenot 10). But the printed narrative about that world requires a "conjectural" reading that incorporates a social paradigm that is *of* but not directly delineated *in* the text.

Thus, the sf text does not ask readers immediately to apply "the norms, rules, conventions, and so forth" of their empirical world but instead assumes an implicit and "paradigmatic intelligibility that is both delusive and necessary" (Angenot 10). Faced with such a textual formation, readers learn to work between the "unfolding (syntagmatic) sequence" and the absent paradigm with its "immanent practical or theoretical models, which are supposed to confer meaning on the discourse" (Angenot 10). Angenot therefore observes that sf readers are like swimmers on an unfamiliar beach searching for ways to negotiate the unseen currents and riptides (or, as I've said earlier, like travelers in a strange culture that is only comprehensible to the extent that the never articulated but ever present social paradigm itself is known).

As Angenot puts it, sf offers a journey "to an illusive 'elsewhere' of a semiotic nature, to the paradigms both suggested in and yet absent from the textual message" (Angenot 14). Relying on a verisimilitude that the text "*implies* without attempting to *show* it extensively," its readers slowly drift "from the narrative sequence as such (syntagm) to these illusory general systems (paradigms)" and are enlightened by what the text "does not and can not show: the complex universe within which such events are supposed to take place" (Angenot 14, 15). Whereas readers of a realist novel proceed "from the general (the commonplace, the ideological *topos*) to the particular (the specific plot governed by the ideological structure)," sf readers take the opposite path that requires an inductive speculation on the relationship between the textual particulars and "some imagined, general rules that prolong the author's fantasies and confer on them plausibility" (Angenot 15). As he tersely notes, they engage "in a conjectural reconstruction which 'materializes' the fictional universe" (Angenot 15).

In keeping with Suvin's general position, he argues that sf contains (performs) within its formal structure a model of its own cognitive project. Its "realism" is based in an estranged "paradigmatic delusion" of "codes, series, coordinates, systems" that are "absent yet indispensable for the coherence of the syntagm" (Angenot 17). Sf encourages readers to generate a paradigm "whose semantic structures are supposedly homologous to those in the fictive textual 'world'" (Angenot 13). Although they will be tempted to use familiar material from their own world to interpret the text, they inevitably must contend with a textual structure that generates an alternative world that is always already estranged from that empirical reality even as it selectively and symptomatically captures that reality in its pages. As a result, a cognitive connection between the two must be mediated by the sf text's formal operations. That is, it must work by indirection, resisting direct denotation between text and world and reaching toward the totalizing but absent paradigm, that "paradigmatic mirage" which "entails a conjectural mode of reading" (Angenot 18).

In 1983, with "'The Red Sun Is High, the Blue Low': Towards a Stylistic Description of Science Fiction," Kathleen Spencer continued this line of analysis and examined in greater detail the particular means by which sf invites its readers to understand and interpret its stated and unstated textual material.[43] Like Suvin and Angenot, Spencer notes that the alternative world of the sf text requires a reading process that "follows a repeated sequence of pattern formation/disruption/re-evaluation/pattern formation" in which "the reader oscillates between involvement in, and observation of, the world of the [sf] text" (Spencer 36). In a statement that exemplifies the position taken by sf critics who work between the popular community of sf readers and the university and who are doing something other than detached academic studies, she argues that this process of "involvement and evaluation" constitutes the primary pleasure of reading sf. Working with Suvin's triad of estrangement, cognition, and the novum, she identifies two basic expectations of a reader of the sf text:

> (1) that the story will happen *somewhere else*—that time, or place, or circumstances will be significantly different from their "empirical environment"; and (2) that the environment of the fiction will be interpretable by cognitive processes—that is, that it derives from or is related to our own environment in some logical way, and that it is bound by natural laws as our own world, though those laws may differ from the ones we know. (Spencer 38)

To satisfy the first expectation, she notes that the text must be properly "irrealistic" in that it needs to deliver an alternate world that is generated by a novum that truly constitutes a totalizing break with the empirical world as it is known or lived. To satisfy the second expectation, however, the text must work in a "realistic" fashion, for it must deliver an alternate world that is both internally consistent and knowable by the reader.

Spencer then observes that the major difficulty in writing and reading sf derives "from the fact that the culture upon which the fiction's verisimilitude rests is itself a fiction, a construct, and hence unfamiliar to the readers" (Spencer 40). An author could never provide enough description and exposition to fill in all the details of the alternate world, and no reader would sit through such an extensive explanatory discursus. Short of an encyclopedic summary or a utopian-style tour, the only other approach is an oblique one in which the unfamiliar world is presented in a familiar fashion, "from the inside," and the reader is then invited to fill in the details of the world by her or his own imaginative and cognitive work with the bits of information that are provided. What is offered, therefore, is a readerly engagement with the text and its world in which the reader must understand and appreciate on its own terms not only what is on the page but also what is unstated—that is, the fuller, absent paradigm of the alternative world.

Moving from Angenot's semiotics to structuralist poetics, she explains that sf writers describe the unfamiliar created culture from the inside and do so by readjusting what Jonathan Culler terms the "threshold of functional relevance" (Spencer 40). The text therefore recalibrates "the level of generality at which we normally encounter the world: in which we 'eat dinner,' rather than 'pick up our fork in our right hand, insert the tines into a piece of meat, lift the fork to our mouths, pull the meat from our fork with our teeth, chew vigorously, and swallow'" (Spencer 40). Writing *within* the fictive culture, the writer sets the level of relevant information higher than a reader's actual knowledge, since no actual reader can actually know that world. The level is gauged instead for a fictional "someone" who already inhabits the alternative culture—a "level at which we might, in mundane novels, refer without elaboration to 'McDonalds'" (Spencer 41).

This technique separates the actual author from an "implied" author who is already an inhabitant of the alternate world, and consequently it requires an "implied" reader who also is of that world. This arrangement constitutes the "obliquity" of sf texts and helps to explain the realist treatment of a space and time that is unreal. It also suggests how the actual reader needs to approach that text, with its encoded other culture, again like a detective: "What the reader is doing, in fact, is constructing the salient features of the culture from the clues which the author (the actual author) has left him" (Spencer 41).

Spencer elaborates on this process by way of Delany's discussion, in "The Semiology of Silence," of the function of sf sentences in their relationship to the textual world. Only by working between the absent social paradigm and the words on the page in a thoughtful way can readers understand sentences such as "he turned on his left side" or "her world exploded" beyond the limits of the familiar realist novel in the empirical world. Sentences with even more information, such as "the door irised" or "I rubbed depilatory soap over my face and rinsed it with the trickle from the fresh-water tap" require more thought as their bits of strange information must be accounted for within the logic of the alternative world; for in the reader's own world they make no sense. Reading sf sentences, like reading whole pages and whole texts, requires the sort of oscillation between page and mind that Spencer and the others insist upon. As she describes it, "these very readjustments—part of the normal process of pattern revision that is inherent in reading literary texts—serve to reinforce our impression of verisimilitude" (Spencer 42). The reader, in other words, enlists in this other culture, joins the fictive author and fictive readers in their world. Again, she notes that this activity, by way of an estranged irreality as well as a cognitively consistent "realism," is where the real work and the pleasure of reading sf is located.

In 1987 Peter Fitting's "Positioning and Closure: On the 'Reading-Effect' of Contemporary Utopian Fiction" (published in *Utopian Studies I,* a series of essays published by the Society for Utopian Studies before the launching of its own journal) contributed an assessment of sf and utopian reading protocols that carried this line of textual analysis more directly into the political arena.[44]

For his sample texts, Fitting focuses on the resurgence of utopian writing as it developed within the sf genre in the 1970s, and he directly connects this body of work with the social upheavals and political movements of the time. He suggests that this "literature of alternatives" offers radical utopian themes but also, and more subversively, produces a "poetics of the future" that links up with a "politics of the future" by way of the form of these fictions and the reading processes they inspire ("Positioning" 23, 24). In his examination of the utopian works of Delany, Le Guin, Russ, and Piercy, he argues that these new utopias constitute a "didactic and committed art" that interpellates the reader as a politically aware and possibly engaged person by way of two reading conventions: one that revolves around the "positioning" of the reader in the text; the other around the apparent "closure" of the narrative and the work it does on the reader. These conventions, according to Fitting, allow texts such as these to "break out of the passivity and illusionism of the traditional reading experience in an effort to push the reader to work for change" ("Positioning" 26, 29).

Positioning is a concept Fitting borrows from feminist film theory, and he employs it to examine how the sf text addresses its reader as well as how the reader views the text. The new utopian novels depart from the mode of readerly address common to the last wave of utopian writing in the late nineteenth century, for they invite not merely a passive though thoughtful tracking of the matter of the text but rather an active involvement in the implicit comparison and contrast between the author's and reader's world and that of the textual utopia. Nineteenth-century utopias tended to regard their readers as intelligent persons who were open to reasonable arguments, who were positioned "as the addressee in a philosophic dialogue who is persuaded through reasoned presentation" ("Positioning" 30). The new utopias, however, have been formally transformed by their "novelization" in the tradition of the sf novel. In them the reader enters more actively into the overt *narrative* "process of identification with a fictional character . . . [and is] implicated on an emotional and experimental level as well as on the intellectual one" ("Positioning" 30).

As well, unlike the earlier utopias wherein the point-of-view character was a visitor to utopia from the outer world, the new utopias work from the perspective of a citizen of the utopia or at least an "outsider" who is faced with the existential-political decision to make a commitment to the preservation or further development of the utopia. Through this involvement with characters (in varying degrees of political effectivity, Fitting argues) such as Bron in Delany's *Triton* (1976), Connie in Piercy's *Woman on the Edge of Time* (1976), the J-women in Russ's *Female Man* (1975), and similar protagonists in Le Guin's *Dispossessed* (1974) and other works, the reader "is 'hailed' as a potential actor in the process of building utopia, unlike the passive role traditionally assigned to the reader, where it suffices to dream and to wait" ("Positioning" 31); for the reader must enter into the agonizing revelations and subsequent choices such characters face as they live out Utopia page by page. Such active positioning helps to interpellate the reader in her or his own world by inviting them to carry over the tensions of the text to their own struggles for identity and responsibility in their actual social realities.

Turning to the technique of closure (assembled from the work of Roland Barthes and Jameson), Fitting identifies another contested technique in the new utopian sf. Narrative closure, he reminds us, works formally against the very activism that the textual positioning of these utopias encourages. In a commentary reminiscent of Russ's, he notes that in traditional, or realist, novels, the ending almost always resolves the "tension and disorder" of the unfolding plot in some passively consoling manner. "In this way," he argues, the reader's political anxieties "are acknowledged and then displaced to the fictional concerns and tensions of the novel where they are resolved through the novel's own resolution of the fictional tensions and the return to harmony and order," and the reader is thereby reinscribed within the dominant order ("Positioning" 33).

Narrative closure thus short-circuits a more didactic approach that could stimulate the reader's interest in political action. Again, however, the new utopias resist or at least endeavor to work against this ideological demand for the security of a satisfying, and quieting, ending. Instead, they leave open questions or actions on the last pages and bring the reader to "some sort of critical judgement" ("Positioning" 34). They produce an openness that pulls the reader into the text (whose formal characteristics Suvin, Angenot, Spencer, and others have delineated) and asks one of the key political questions of the time: "Which side are you on?" Each of these texts is relatively successful in this radicalizing move. Fitting finds *Triton* to be resistant to closure but nonetheless caught up in the individual protagonist's "confusion and unhappiness" and falls short of considering the larger political questions and possibilities, whereas *Woman on the Edge of Time* asks the reader to decide just what sort of ending its collectively affiliated protagonist, Connie, experiences—and by deciding the reader furthers her or his own stance in the world by aligning with or against the political ethics of Connie's actions. Finally, *The Female Man* directly addresses its readers just as the four female protagonists are about to begin their own political campaign and thus incorporates them into this collective movement.

V.

In addition to Fitting's engaged analysis of the links between these sf texts of the 1970s and the developing opposition of the same period, the phenomenon of the critical utopias within the generic frame of sf prompted a number of other formal-political studies (especially from feminist, ecological, and broadly Left standpoints) that explored the positive dimensions of this utopian revival in the context of the growing counter-hegemonic bloc in U.S. society.[45] Other critics, however, took up the equally pressing task of working on critiques of the ideological function of sf as it helped to reproduce the existing order of things. Key contributions in this direction include Franklin's analysis of the linkage between sf and military discourse and the studies of the relationship between sf and the political economy of contemporary technoculture by Penley, Ross, and Stabile. More directly concerned with the immediate object of study but also maintaining a political perspective, the interrogations of newer directions in sf such as cyberpunk (as in the work of Ann Balsamo or Scott Bukatman) and the studies of sf fandom by Henry Jenkins and Penley critically address these crucial intersections of form and politics.

For many of us, however, the essay that moves further in the direction taken by critics such as Suvin and Fitting as it accounts for the positive oppositional potential of sf is one that never directly mentions the genre: namely, Fredric Jameson's "Cognitive Mapping."[46] This essay began as a paper presented at the 1983 meeting of the Marxist Literary Group's Summer Institute in Culture and Society, and it was published in the 1988 volume *Marxism and the Interpretation of Culture*.[47] Jameson's aim is to explore the possibilities for a new aesthetic, one that is adequate to the task of critically interrogating the socioeconomic logic and practice of late capitalism. As Jameson's introduction to the 1988 publication puts it: "Without a conception of the social totality (and the possibility of transforming a whole social system), no properly socialist politics is possible. It involves trying to imagine how a society without hierarchy, a society that has also repudiated the economic mechanisms of the market, can possibly cohere."[48]

As he develops his argument, Jameson traces the outlines of an aesthetic that will take shape between the immediacy of the current conjuncture and some transcendent yet material quality that can pull people away from the common sense of the present. It will necessarily be an aesthetic that, albeit dialectically, goes beyond the limits of modernism and postmodernism, yet one that nevertheless retains the traditional characteristics of being able to "teach, to move, to delight" ("Cognitive Mapping" 347). In a synecdotal allusion to sf, he begins his exploration with an acknowledgment of "the great historical merit of the work of Darko Suvin to repeatedly insist on a more contemporary formulation of this aesthetic value, in the suggestive slogan of the *cognitive*" ("Cognitive Mapping" 348).[49]

Jameson connects this privileging of the cognitive ("itself the immediate source of profound aesthetic delight") with his own project of developing a spatial analysis of culture ("Cognitive Mapping" 348). To set up the necessary framework for his invocation of an aesthetic of cognitive mapping, he reviews three overlapping and never precise periods of the "unifying and totalizing force" of capitalism, and he argues that each possesses its characteristic social space ("Cognitive Mapping" 348). He begins with classical or market capitalism and its logic of the grid and its "reorganization of some older sacred and heterogeneous space into geometrical and Cartesian homogeneity" and then moves to the period of monopoly capital and imperialism, with its "growing contradiction between lived experience and structure" as the sweep of the social exceeds the ken of the individual in the economic-industrial machinery and in the global stretch of empire ("Cognitive Mapping" 349). He then argues that in the current moment "these two levels drift ever further apart and really begin to constitute themselves into that opposition the classical dialectic describes as *Wesen* and *Erscheinung*, essence and appearance, structure and lived experience" ("Cognitive Mapping" 349).

In the social conditions of this third moment at the end of the twentieth century, the daily experience of the individual cannot encompass the truth of the entire system. That is, the economic and imperialist operations of the world system—from London to India to Jamaica to Hong Kong—cannot be known by an individual living out a daily existence in London alone. Jameson puts it succinctly: "If individual experience is authentic, then it cannot be true; and . . . if a scientific or cognitive model of the same content is true, then it escapes individual experience" ("Cognitive Mapping" 349). The methodological challenge is just how to represent, and in doing so begin to transform, this contradictory situation. If the "fundamental realities" of the period are not directly available to an individual subject, since they constitute what Louis Althusser terms the "absent cause . . . that can never emerge into the presence of perception" ("Cognitive Mapping" 350), how does one even begin to track its effects, so as to work toward a proper grasp of the totalizing system? With echoes of his studies of the utopian analyses of Louis Marin, Jameson responds with the claim that the absent cause generates "figures through which to express itself in distorted and symbolic ways" ("Cognitive Mapping" 350); for it is this "play of figuration" that the critic can examine in order to "make conceptually available the ultimate realities and experiences" that the figures themselves designate ("Cognitive Mapping" 350).

Within the "postmodern" space of "late" capitalism (as the city and the nation-state are themselves being transformed in the new economic configuration), the individual subject negotiates "a multidimensional set of radically discontinuous realities, whose frames range from the still surviving spaces of bourgeois private life all the way to the unimaginable decentering of global capital itself" ("Cognitive Mapping" 351). Caught in this perceptual/conceptual gap, the individual flounders (suggesting the "death" of this very subject), and on a wider collective scale the project for political transformation of this new reality, in the name of socialism, equally struggles for survival, facing "the enormous strategic and tactical difficulties of coordinating local and grassroots or neighborhood political actions with national or international ones" ("Cognitive Mapping" 351).

What is needed in this new conjuncture is a new way of conceptualizing the current reality, and for this Jameson draws on Kevin Lynch's *Image of the City*. Taking Lynch's insight that "urban alienation is directly proportional to the mental unmapability of local cityscapes," he suggests that a "mental map of city space . . . can be extrapolated to that mental map of the social and global totality we all carry around in our heads in variously garbled forms" ("Cognitive Mapping" 353). Here he is looking at the separation between immediate experience and perceptions and the absent totality, searching for forms that are capable of negotiating that disempowering distance. He recalls Althusser's formulation of ideology as "the Imaginary representation of the subject's relationship to his or her Real conditions of existence" (quoted in "Cognitive Mapping" 353), and he suggests that this *positive* conception of ideology "as a necessary function in any form of social life has the great merit of stressing the gap between the local positioning of the individual subject and the totality of class structures in which he or she is situated" ("Cognitive Mapping" 353).

The gap, therefore, can be spanned, coordinated, mapped, "by means of conscious and unconscious representations," representations that can accordingly be traced, analyzed, interpreted, made use of. Jameson names that activity (which includes representation and interpretation) "cognitive mapping." He then suggests that since the incapacity to map is as crippling to collective political experience as it is to any displaced individual, it "follows that an aesthetic of cognitive mapping in this sense is an integral part of any socialist political project" ("Cognitive Mapping" 353). A few paragraphs later, he reiterates his introductory comment when he argues that "without a conception of the social totality (and the possibility of transforming a whole social system), no properly socialist politics is possible" ("Cognitive Mapping" 355).

Thus, Jameson connects the process of imaginative figuration with that of critical cognition in the anticipated framework of an aesthetic rather than a conceptual system—thereby privileging a process that can bring new life not only to individuals but also to the collective political project. Certainly, a facility for cognitive mapping can contribute to the immediate, and importantly negative, tasks of political critique and mobilization. For example, it can help to work through the "contradiction between self-management on the local level and planning on the global scale; or the problems raised by the abolition of the market, not to mention the abolition of the commodity form itself" ("Cognitive Mapping" 355). This emergent aesthetic, however, also has the potential, in its positive anticipations, to address the long-range challenge of the socialist project—that is, to mediate between the immediate demands of the everyday, even in a transformed society, and the transcendent values and vision that keep such immediacy alive and moving forward. Jameson states the problem this way: "With one signal exception (capitalism itself, which is organized around an economic mechanism), there has never existed a cohesive form of human society that was not based on some form of transcendence or religion" ("Cognitive Mapping" 355).

How, then, can a truly socialist project hope to motivate, establish, and maintain a radically new social reality without the active presence of a materialist yet transcendent vision? Brute force hardly does the job, although it has too often been used for this very purpose. Survival in the face of an external siege works for the time of the siege, but its residual memory is never sufficient to maintain a collective commitment. Without the adversary of the "nontranscendent economic mechanism of capital" to fix the focus of commitment and hope, "all appeals to moral incentives (as in Che) or to the primacy of the political (as in Maoism) must fatally exhaust themselves in a brief time," leaving only the alternatives of succumbing to capitalism or adopting a modern form of despotism ("Cognitive Mapping" 355).

This dilemma, this desperate need for a materialist form of transcendence, Jameson argues, is "the most urgent task that confronts Marxism today," and one can readily add the entire movement of the Left that Marxism seeks to understand and inform.[50] The need is simple: how to generate a contemporary "vision of the future that grips the masses" ("Cognitive Mapping" 355). Such a vision cannot be imposed from the outside—neither by the now rejected avenue of religious doctrine nor by the secular equivalent of political orthodoxy embodied in a priori guarantees, agendas, and agents. It certainly cannot be based on coercion. Nor can it be purely economic. Given all that twentieth-century critical theory and revolutionary practice has taught (all we have learned about language, culture, and ideology; subjectivity and identity; totality and agency), this transcendent force must necessarily be "supremely social and cultural, involving the task of trying to imagine how a society without hierarchy, a society of free people, a society that has at once repudiated the economic mechanism of the market, can possibly cohere" ("Cognitive Mapping" 355). As the intersecting problematics of feminism and Marxism have shown us, this force can be discovered only within the historical situation, not in some external or universal deus ex machina. The question, as Jameson typically asserts, comes down to this: "how to imagine Utopia" ("Cognitive Mapping" 355).

The question, however, does not get answered in this essay. Yet Jameson does set out the elements that are required for moving toward the answer. An aesthetic of cognitive mapping, in other words, names the process of grasping both the global picture and the immediate experience, and of taking both through a dialectical transformation that is existential and transcendent—one that makes sense of the everyday and anticipates a utopian horizon that will pull people beyond wherever they find themselves in the long process of transformation. Such a process, Jameson concludes, "will be a matter of form," since no amount of content can be sufficient for the dialectical mediation of the immediate and the transcendent. In the larger social scale, the new aesthetic will be "an integral part of a socialist politics," but this possibility depends on a "political opening," a historic break in the system that will unsettle the balance of power ("Cognitive Mapping" 356). Given such an opening, the task of an achieved cognitive mapping will be to enlarge the cultural dimensions of that space, to inform and shape the battles at hand but also to help carry people to whatever comes next, however positively unimaginable that might be.

Although Jameson never mentions sf in his essay, his account of the aesthetic of cognitive mapping correlates strongly with imaginative processes of sf as they were delineated in the critical studies of the 1970s and 1980s. With a formal basis in an imaginary setting that stands as an alternative to the author's empirical environment, the literary apparatus of sf reconfigures the historical moment so that it can been seen and responded to in a new light. Reprising Henry Adams, Suvin puts it this way: "The mirror [of sf] is not only a reflecting one, it is also a transforming one, virgin womb and alchemical dynamo: the mirror is a crucible" ("Poetics" 374). Sf's textual mechanics therefore invite, or at least enable, a cognitive mapping process that runs from the stated information of the alternative world to the absent paradigm that informs the text, back to the page, and outward again to the reader and the realities of her or his own historical moment, then back into the text, and inevitably out again in a feedback spiral that can be properly shocking, enlightening, motivating.

VI.

Central to this critical trajectory in sf and utopian studies, as well as to the larger project of cognitive mapping in its present and future forms, is the analytical category of totality and the related categories of class and class struggle (and, in an overdetermined relationship, the political agency of other disempowered groups coming into consciousness though struggle). For without a grasp of both the actual social relations and the horizon of possibilities at any historical moment, the intensive and extensive analysis needed to critique and look beyond the present situation is doomed to the failure of being lost in the immediate, the local, the micro. The recent retrieval of totality, in Jameson's work as in others, is of course a move against the received wisdom of a good deal of "postmodern" and "poststructuralist" theory. Jameson says as much in "Cognitive Mapping" as he notes, as early as 1983, how his argument for such a critical-aesthetic organ implicitly violates "many of the taboos and shibboleths of a faddish post-Marxism," which dismisses the categories of class, class consciousness, class struggle, and the mode of production and stigmatizes "the concept of totality and of the project of totalizing thought" ("Cognitive Mapping" 353–354).

Pointedly, Jameson refuses the attacks by the French *nouveaux philosophes* and others that equate "totalizing thought" with "totalitarian thought," for, he argues, the "conception of capital is admittedly a totalizing or systemic concept" and must be apprehended in an equally totalizing analysis ("Cognitive Mapping" 354). To do less is simply to capitulate to the status quo. He reiterates this boldly and, in light of the textual work of sf, ironically, observing that "anyone who believes that the profit motive and the logic of capital accumulation are not the fundamental laws of this world . . . is living in an alternative universe" ("Cognitive Mapping" 354). Without this tool for a working analysis of the capitalist system (inevitably provisional lest it fall into a fixed account that would lose sight of the totality-in-motion that *is* social reality), the contemporary world simply cannot be known in an adequately critical way. Again, Jameson suggests that

> it seems unlikely that anyone who repudiates the concept of totality can have anything useful to say to us . . . since for such persons it is clear that the totalizing vision of socialism will not compute and is a false problem within the random and undecidable world of microgroups. Or perhaps another possibility suggests itself, namely, that our dissatisfaction with the concept of totality is not a thought in its own right but rather a significant

> symptom, a function of the increasing difficulties in thinking of such a set of interrelationships in a complicated society. ("Cognitive Mapping" 356)

Then, in *The Seeds of Time* (1994), he updates his retrieval of totality and his attack on its theoretical suppression as he again dismantles the postmodern equation of "totality" as an aesthetic-analytic category ("a combination or permutation scheme") with totalitarian practice.[51] He reviews the "paralysis of postmodern thinking" and argues in favor of "the philosophically correct use of the concept of totality, as something that by definition we cannot know rather than as some privileged form of epistemological authority some people are trying to keep for themselves, with a view toward enslaving others" (*Seeds* 68, 69). In other words, given the "totalizing force" of capitalism, in any of its historic transformations, it is only by means of representations of the social totality that the mode of production can be adequately grasped, critiqued, and substantively challenged. Such a process is not authoritarian, closed, or absolute, but rather a matter of "a preliminary working hypothesis" or "an indirect way of solving something that cannot be mastered head-on" (*Seeds* 68–69). As he puts it, "totalization" is thereby "a project rather than the word for an already existent institution" (*Seeds* 65).

A different version of this timely opposition to theoretical reaction is put forth by Paul Smith in his 1997 analysis of the current, apparently "global," moment of capitalism. In *Millennial Dreams: Contemporary Culture and Capital in the North,* Smith claims as part of his basic approach, a "logic of the totality," which, citing Engels, he describes as a *method* depending on a "historical process and its explanatory reflection in thought, the logical pursuance of its inner connections."[52]

Asserting that the "different descriptions of the world that [critical Marxism] can offer are still crucial," despite (or perhaps because of) the historic events of 1989 and the "thrall of the millennial dream" of a globalizing capital, Smith argues that the "discovery and exposure of effective orders of determination in culture and society are still the task at hand and [one] in which a pragmatic politics might still claim a theoretical and analytical dimension directed at *structural* transformation" (*Millennial* 3, 56). That is, in the face of capital's totalizing practice, only an "alternative analysis of the totality" can mount an adequate and effective oppositional response (*Millennial* 57). Smith, like Jameson, challenges anyone who "parrots the shibboleth of the 'collapse of the grand-narratives,' or who recites the standard chant against Marxism's 'totalizing' urge" (*Millennial* 59) or who "forgets" how much Left critical praxis has rigorously challenged any and all authoritarian tendencies. As did Jameson and Suvin, he reasserts the importance of "the explanatory power, and the power to change, that came from recognizing the existence of a complexly structured totality" (*Millennial* 60) and of being able not only to critique the social order but also to change it.[53]

Finally, in "Two Cheers for Essentialism and Totality," which appeared in *Rethinking Marxism* in 1998, Suvin joins the chorus of those who are refunctioning totality in these times that require more than analyses based on the theory and practice of localized discourse or micropolitics.[54] What must be retained, he argues, are "two major methodological pointers: the demystificatory vision and the open-ended concreteness of analysis and of recategorization" ("Two Cheers" 67). Putting it more directly, he simply notes that "a new cognitive epistemology is on the order of the day" ("Two Cheers" 68). Demystification is necessary in order to get inside the normal "configuration of phenomena," but against what he calls "PoMo [postmodern] vogue," critical investigation must also include its "positive turn," which is as yet beyond capitalism's version of "equality" and "freedom" ("Two Cheers" 70).

Suvin then connects this claim to an argument for moving further than the postmodern dismissal of essentialism by collapsing the binary opposition of essentialism and nonessentialism itself. Arguing that the "quite indispensable hermeneutics of suspicion and demystification are either incomplete or counterproductive unless accompanied by the readiness for and attempts at reconstruction," he suggests that some form of "'rational abstraction' which not only underlines the common traits of a subject and avoids repetition but furthermore allows us to define and intervene (first discursively and then pragmatically) in any subject at all" offers a way to work with a strategic sense of essence that is "*relational* rather than substantive" ("Two Cheers" 72, 73). Referring back to Gramsci and Brecht—as well as Judith Butler, bell hooks, and Gayatri Spivak—Suvin insists that a "flexible 'soft' essentialism" is required for working out serious moves beyond the critical deconstruction of the current social order ("Two Cheers" 74).[55]

Critique, he asserts, is also necessary for its "firm refusal of all static fixity, of any eternally natural categories and undialectical determinism" ("Two Cheers" 75). Always "dialogical and ironical," critique requires a totalizing perspective as it works from empirical phenomena to analytical generalization and then "back to a reconceptualized and enriched concreteness"; consequently, neither society as it exists nor a possible new social reality can be known and engaged without the fullness of totalizing analysis ("Two Cheers" 75). Of course, Suvin admits, any version of a "hard" essentialism or totality, any programmatic analysis drawing on "the unfortunate paleotechnic vocabulary of rigid laws, issuing forth with metallic . . . necessity" must be rejected. But to reprise the motif of the baby and the bathwater, this does not mean a complete dismissal of a model and method that embraces totality. As he puts it, "The more dialectical relation between veiling or mystifying and unveiling or manifesting, omnipresent in Marx from *The Communist Manifesto* through *Das Kapital,* usually does not rely on 'laws' but on critical work constituting both these poles in an unceasing weaving back and forth between them" ("Two Cheers" 77).

With this fluid sense of critique, totality is a "synonym for the social system or society or, as Williams repeatedly insisted, 'the whole social order'" ("Two Cheers" 78). With this sense in mind, Suvin argues that

> we need to strive for both extensive totality (understanding the capitalist world system that beats Western trade unions by shifting to Taiwan or Georgia) and intensive totality (a standpoint allowing us to see the shifting paradigms under the extension). After all, since a total, and negative, world system exists beyond any reasonable doubt . . . to refuse to think it as such is an act of imaginative and political abdication. ("Two Cheers" 78)

Unlike Smith, he ends with a strong assertion of the *positive* dimension, the *Utopian* dimension, of this refunctioned totalizing critique as he recalls Jameson's "insistence on a dynamic and open-ended value-horizon of possible totalization which yet critically refuses spatiotemporally closed totalities" ("Two Cheers" 78). A totalizing analysis and anticipation (of capital and its absent transcendence) "enables us to grasp it all" in what is assuredly "an epistemological or hermeneutic but not an ontological totality"; and thus, with an accompanying "Brechtian productive doubt entailing an articulated stance and clear value-horizon," the project of social "self-reflection and self-correction" can (perhaps again) move forward ("Two Cheers" 79).

VII.

Suvin's insistence on the dual registers of the critical project—the negative critique and the positive anticipation—brings the category of Utopia directly into this discussion; for this basic impulse for a better world underlies both sf and utopian textuality and the overall aesthetic project of cognitive mapping. Implicit in cognitive mapping is not only a formal representation of the contradictory order of things but also of the utopian figuration that moves reality toward a yet to be achieved, known, or lived future. In this sense, a totalizing analysis must be open-ended, since it includes not only a representation of what is but also the absent reality of what is "not yet." Thus, cognitive mapping—in science and utopian fiction or elsewhere—is not a static report of a closed, totalized system but rather, as Phillip E. Wegner puts it, "a performance, a travel itinerary, a semiosis, a *mapping*, or an ongoing totalization rather than [a] picture, a map, an imaginary mimesis, or a completed totality."[56] The horizon for such a process can only be the ultimately unattainable, asymptotic category of Utopia itself.

Utopia, therefore, names the sociopolitical drive that moves the human project for emancipation and fulfillment beyond the limits of the current system. Even as the best of utopian anticipation is based in a historical and material understanding of the present, it nevertheless takes the imagination (rooted in the "political unconscious" and, at its best, imbricated with the politics of the transformation of everyday life) to a place beyond what is available through accommodation and reform. Utopia, in other words, informs what Lefebvre has identified as the "quest for a 'counter-space'" that enables humanity to change "life itself" (*Production of Space* 383, 54). Utopia affords the open-ended frontiers of what Negt and Kluge have described as the movement by workers—and all who are exploited, dispossessed, and disenfranchised—to produce a "counterpublic sphere" that will reclaim the fullness of human experience from the instrumental limitations of life within the capitalist system (Negt and Kluge 79). In the next chapter, I move from the creative and critical projects of sf to the complementary work of utopian production and utopian studies. Just as my discussion of sf shifted into the register of the aesthetic, epistemological, and ultimately political project of cognitive mapping and social transformation, my focus on utopianism follows the same trajectory, and ultimately moves to the contested terrain framed by Utopia and Anti-Utopia.

3

Daring to Dream

The dream becomes vision only when hope is invested in an agency capable of transformation. The political problem remains the search for that agency and the possibility of hope; and only if we find it will we see our dreams come true.

—Ruth Levitas, *The Concept of Utopia* (200)

I.

Utopia rose, again, from the ashes of obscurity in the decades after World War II. Filled with hope after the defeat of fascism, aware of the weakening chains of imperialist power, yearning for better lives in a world of peace, and experienced in collective action, people around the globe began to give real shape to their collective dreams. Movements for national liberation expanded, labor renewed its prewar militancy, people of color who fought for freedom abroad returned to demand it at home, women who discovered their power in the public sphere of work and service took hard looks at the old world of domestic tranquillity, and gradually young people began to assert their own views in the brave new world around them.

This militancy, however, ran directly into the inability of the new social order to fulfill these dangerous desires: Corporations thrived and new economic and military alliances were forged; imperial armies attacked anti-colonial movements and domestic police smashed militant demonstrations; managerial deals were brokered with labor; gradualist reforms and physical violence deflected the agitation for racial liberation; a modicum of welfare trickled down to the dispossessed; social work, therapy, and Valium were applied to the discontent; and a postwar and post-Depression economic paradise was offered, in one form or another, to everyone.

Especially in the United States, where the new center of power took hold, a culture of consumption and patriotism reached deeply into the daily lives of the entire population. On the surface an "affluent society" promised to settle many into an American dream life filled with suburban houses, televisions, cars, and affordable educations, while underneath the false promises the coercive arm of the state named, interrogated, imprisoned, and sometimes executed those who refused to stop struggling for a very different world. A regime of pleasure and fear, consent and coercion, growth within cages, became the hegemonic answer to radical demands for a way of life that went beyond the scope of a booming economy and a militarized state. The reaction, however, did not succeed in tying up all the loose ends, in suturing all the ragged tears in the social fabric, in keeping immediate needs and surplus desires (known and not yet known) confined within the productive machinery that shaped labor and leisure. People refused to stop wanting meaningful lives and fighting for control over those lives. They chose to carry on the fight for self-determination, economic and social justice, and personal freedom and fulfillment in a world of peace and plenty for everyone. Consequently, the political movements of the 1940s grew into the organizing that led to the oppositional public sphere of the 1960s and 1970s, and driving each of these struggles was a radical hope for a better world.

It is no surprise, therefore, that utopian expression became a major element of the oppositional projects of the postwar decades. Reviving after a nineteenth-century heyday, the literary utopia, intentional communities, and utopian social thought began again to flourish. Although literary utopias were published throughout the century, they began to appear in greater numbers after the war. Emblematic of this resurgence was Aldous Huxley's shift from his dystopian *Brave New World* in 1932 to the eutopian *Island* in 1962. Gradually, most often working within the expanding market of sf, younger writers began to transform utopian textuality itself. Always a part of North American societies from the earliest days, utopian communities (however ignored, misunderstood, or repressed) also entered into a period of growth, reaching a veritable boom within the counterculture of the 1960s. And social theory, often within the parameters of the broad and critical Left, confronted Western positivism and anti-communism as well as Stalinist orthodoxy and authoritarianism with demands for an alternative reality that could not have been delivered by either system.

A strong utopian strain ran through the work of critical Marxism and the New Left, the social theories of racial and national liberation movements, the multiple voices of feminism, the cries of the poor and the dispossessed, the assertions of sexual difference and desire, the arguments for world peace and world government, and the reconceptualization of humanity's relationship with nature itself. In each of these manifestations, utopian dreaming, now allied with concrete agency, looked through and beyond the structural logic and limits of hegemonic exploitation and interpellation. As Henri Lefebvre (who with Ernst Bloch and Herbert Marcuse was one of the influential utopian theorists of the 1960s) put it, the postwar movements increasingly fought for a counter-space that began to "insert itself into spatial reality: against the Eye and the Gaze, against quantity and homogeneity, against power and the arrogance of power, against the endless expansion of the 'private' and of industrial profitability; and against specialized spaces and a narrow localization of function."[1]

It is also not surprising that scholarly work on utopianism developed apace with this political renaissance. In North America, Northrop Frye, Arthur Lewis, Glenn Negley, J. Max Patrick, Judith Shklar, Mulford Q. Sibley, and others began to publish on utopian matters in the 1950s; and at least since 1949, sessions on utopian literature were on the program of the annual Modern Language Association conferences.[2] In addition, university courses in utopianism were offered even before those in sf. According to Dale Mullen's *Science-Fiction Studies* report, Neil Reimer taught a course on utopias in the Political Science Department at Penn State throughout the 1950s, and by the early 1960s courses were given in several departments (including American studies, comparative literature, English, philosophy, political science) on campuses from Queens College, to Duke, to the University of Minnesota, to Portland State (Mullen 372).[3] In 1952 Negley and Patrick published *The Quest for Utopia* and made a significant impact in the study of the literary utopia. Then, with *Utopia and Its Enemies* in 1963, George Kateb advanced the cause of utopian thought by confronting the anti-utopian attacks that had become a key element in the ruling ideology of the new social order. And in 1965 a special issue of *Daedalus* (with essays by Lewis Mumford, Frank E. Manuel, Frye, Shklar, Kateb, and others) marked a further step in developing what would eventually become known as "utopian studies."[4]

Gradually, the study of communal societies and literary utopias began to focus on their distinct areas of research and to refine their individual methodologies, whereas utopian social theory informed and was further influenced by each of these projects, even as it was extended and deepened by the theoretical articulation of the intellectual and cultural work of the oppositional movements. By the late 1960s, utopian studies was on its way to becoming a significant intellectual intervention within Western societies.

Publications and courses were reinforced by special sessions at the yearly meetings of organizations such as the American Studies Association, the Modern Language Association, and the Political Science Association. Two U.S. organizations—the Communal Studies Association and the U.S. Society for Utopian Studies—were launched in 1975, and a *minnesota review* special issue "Marxism and Utopia" was in influential publication in 1976.[5] *Science-Fiction Studies* regularly encouraged work on utopias, and a variety of other journals (including *Comparative Literature Studies, Genre, Studies in the Literary Imagination,* and, especially on matters of Marxism and utopianism, *New German Critique*) also published utopian material. In time, journals devoted solely to utopian studies appeared: *Alternative Futures* (edited by Alexandra Aldridge and Merrit Abrash) had its run from 1978 to 1981; *Utopus Discovered* (the newsletter founded and initially edited by Kenneth M. Roemer) began in 1975; and after publishing three volumes of conference proceedings under the title *Utopian Studies,* the Society for Utopian Studies launched a journal under its own name in 1990.[6]

II.

Within this new scholarly effort, a critical paradigm that dealt with the specificity of the literary utopia was taking shape alongside of and in dialogue with the new work in sf studies.[7] The resurgence of utopian writing within the textual universe of sf guaranteed that many scholars, and some writers, chose to work at the intersection of utopian and sf studies, and the affiliation of the new utopian sf with the growing oppositional culture further ensured that these twinned intellectual projects would take up the challenges of an engaged political critique. As with sf studies, this creative and critical work drew from but also went beyond the disciplinary limits of previous scholarship. To be sure, the relationship between the emerging transdisciplinary project of utopian studies and the discipline-based scholarship of the early postwar years (perhaps best signified by the *Daedalus* issue) was a friendlier, less-contested one than that which occurred with the parallel project of sf studies (largely because older scholars were more open to the new work). As in sf scholarship, utopian studies dealt more specifically with its object of study (as text, community, or theory) and increasingly clarified the formal operations by which Utopia entered the historical moment.

One of the first essays in this new trajectory was by Lyman Tower Sargent, the person who went on to shape the field not only in his theoretical writings and his research as primary bibliographer of the literary utopia but also in his leadership role in the Society for Utopian Studies, as founder and editor of the journal *Utopian Studies,* and as the catalyst for any number of conference sessions, conferences, essay collections, special editions, book series, and exhibits.[8]

In "The Three Faces of Utopianism," published in *minnesota review* in 1967, Sargent deployed the tripartite division I've been using in this chapter when he identified the "three broad directions" of utopianism as "utopian thought or philosophy, utopian literature, and the communitarian movements."[9] Trained in American studies and pursuing research in all three areas, he had the intellectual wherewithal to address each separately and as part of an interrelated, overdetermined set. His early insights into the relationship between utopian textuality and utopian practice are revealed most directly in his brief references to Etienne Cabet's maneuvers between writing a literary utopia, *Voyage en Icarie,* and attempting to organize actual utopian communities. He also explores these interconnections (this time in the relationship of the utopian text and utopian political thought) as he discusses the advantages peculiar to the utopian novel and makes the now familiar observation (which Fredric Jameson takes further) that utopian fiction works by way of a double operation, with a negative move that "reflects popular discontent" by "holding a mirror to contemporary society to criticize it" and then a provisionally positive one that serves as a "device for the testing of hypotheses" ("Three Faces" 227).

Sargent's most salient point, however, lies in his discussion of utopian social theory. In anticipation of Jameson's later argument for the aesthetic of cognitive mapping, he argues that utopian thought works not through rational thought as such but rather in the realm of the imagination, as a "form of 'fictive activity'" ("Three Faces" 222). Drawing on Hans Vaihinger's *Philosophy of "As If": A System of the Theoretical, Practical and Religious Fictions of Mankind,* he argues that utopian thought presents the elements of its alternative social order (its absent paradigm, as Angenot would put it) "*as if* they existed," thereby coming to the reader in a fictively realistic manner and intervening in history by way of imaginative speculation ("Three Faces" 223). He then bolsters the material and historical valence of his argument by connecting his reading of utopian thought as fictive with Frederick Polak's contention that utopianism is necessary for human development. In another bit of anticipation (in this case as a refutation of the anti-utopian claims of Francis Fukuyama for an "end of history" in the apparent event of late-twentieth-century capitalist triumphalism), he cites Polak's assertion of the linkage of utopian thought with the processes of history: "If Western man now stops thinking and dreaming the materials of new images of the future and attempts to shut himself up in the present, out of longing for security and for fear of the future, his civilization will come to an end. He has no choice but to dream or die, condemning the whole of Western society with him" (quoted in "Three Faces" 226). Thus by 1967 an understanding of the utopian process as a distinct way of knowing and intervening in the world, as a form of what later would be called cognitive mapping, was on the table.

Sargent continued to pursue his concern with the nature of utopianism in his 1975 essay in the sf journal *Extrapolation,* "Utopia—the Problem of Definition."[10] Informed by his bibliographic research and his interest in the relationship between the literary utopia and sf, he focuses on the need for a working definition of the literary utopia that is based in the study of actual texts and not in external assumptions or criteria imposed by commentators unfamiliar with the body of utopian writing. His concern, however, reveals more than a bibliographer's will to the taxonomic. It is one that has run throughout his subsequent work and represents a central contribution in the development of utopian studies as a distinct intellectual project. For without such clarity about the object, scholarship on utopianism could too easily misapprehend the specific nature of Utopia's manifestations and therefore miscalculate their significance. In the absence of such discrimination, uninformed and uncritical studies of utopian expression could and do remain within the boundaries of official knowledge systems that are dedicated to the preservation of the status quo rather than to the social critique that utopianism—whether progressive or conservative—makes possible.

Beginning the essay with a discussion of the term itself (*u-topia* as "no place"), Sargent then reviews the distinctions made possible by the first syllable, wherein *eu-topias* (and by convention *u-topias*) name narratives of the good place and *dystopias* those of the bad place. He also makes the pathbreaking point—one too often and disastrously ignored—that the term *anti-utopia* (as distinct from *dys*topia) "should be reserved for that large class of works, both fictional and expository, which are directed *against* Utopia and utopian thought" ("Definition" 138, my emphasis). Central to his exposition is his emphasis on the quality of the pun in Thomas More's original text in which *utopia* and *eutopia* are conflated, for this condensation catches the potential of utopian textuality in that the imagined good place is nowhere to be found in the world as it presently exists and is therefore both beyond and yet connected to the historical moment—thus standing as a critique but also a signpost.

In a move that connects with the work of Lefebvre and others on spatiality, he argues that the importance of the second syllable of the key word, *topos,* is not to be dismissed; for the invocation of social space is what establishes the connection of Utopia and history. As he puts it: "*Topos* implies that the Utopia must be located spatially and temporally; even though nowhere, it must have some place. This is, of course, a device for *imparting reality, making it seem possible rather impossible*" ("Definition" 138, my emphasis).

Distant as the utopian society is from the author and reader, it nevertheless is an exercise in imaginative intervention in historical reality, not a vehicle for ahistorical myth or supernatural agency. Recalling his tripartite division and echoing Marx's *Eleventh Thesis on Feuerbach,* Sargent once more reminds his readers that utopian thought (in conjunction with utopian literature and communal societies) is a "social force" rather than a matter of "literature or history or political philosophy" ("Definition" 139). He then reviews several attempts to define Utopia, including those by Andreas Voight, Joyce Oramel Hertzler, Negley and Patrick, and Darko Suvin. In an example of the high standard of collegial and productive critique that has come to characterize much of the work in utopian studies, he makes it clear that he regards Suvin's as the best (see the discussion on Suvin later in this chapter) but then challenges its lack of "comment and exemplification," and he suggests that it especially needs to emphasize more directly that a literary utopia describes its imaginary society "fairly completely" ("Definition" 141).

From this review, he moves on to his own remarks on definition. Although he never offers a full articulation, he insists that the element that most characterizes a utopia is its description of "an imaginary society in some detail" ("Definition" 142). Again, he anticipates later arguments that locate utopia's potential for sociopolitical critique in its capacity for generating representations (albeit indirect, mediated, estranged) of the historical moment in a detailed and comprehensive, that is, *totalizing*, manner.

Sargent closes his essay with comments on two areas of concern for ongoing scholarly work. Speaking as a bibliographer who has tracked the formal mutations in the literary utopia across historical periods, he reports that utopia has appeared more often within the scope of sf since the 1940s, and he asserts that it now "exists almost solely as a sub-type of science fiction" ("Definition" 142). He then raises the question of intentionality as one of the criteria for determining a utopian text. Contrary to what has become received wisdom in literary theory, he argues for the need to incorporate whatever is known about the author's intentions in the analysis of a text. Certainly, an author's assertion that a work is a *eu*topia is a material precondition that invites at least an initial eutopian reading. But in the case of sf, many texts offer detailed, totalizing, descriptions of society that can be read as eutopian even if not directly intended as such by the sf writer; in contrast, some works that are purposely written as eutopias (B. F. Skinner's *Walden Two* is Sargent's example) are received by most readers as decidedly dystopian or even anti-utopian. Knowing that Edward Bellamy chose to write a utopia in *Looking Backward,* Aldous Huxley a utopian satire in *Brave New World,* and B. F. Skinner a utopia in *Walden Two* grounds one level of the analysis of a text, whereas the reception of readers (who may contrarily consider Bellamy's to be a dystopia, Huxley's a utopia, and Skinner's a dystopia) is yet another factor to consider, but not one that obviates the factor of intention.[11] In making these observations, Sargent offers no answers, but in calling attention to the issue he raises the standards for a textual critique that should take care to work not only with the text itself but also with the contexts of its production and its reception. With this essay, therefore, Sargent sharpens and expands the scope of the developing critical paradigm.

Finally, in "The Three Faces of Utopianism Revisited," which appeared in *Utopian Studies* in 1994, Sargent expands on his recent thoughts on the problem of refining the definition and scope of utopian expression. After reaffirming the categories of literature, communities, and theory, he sums up utopianism with the concise but effective phrase, "social dreaming," a designation that includes "the dreams and nightmares that concern the ways in which groups of people arrange their lives and which usually envision a radically different society than the one in which the dreamers live" ("Three Faces Revisited" 3).

More completely than in the previous essays, he also gives specific definitions of the several textual forms of the generic literary utopia, eutopia, dystopia, utopian satire, anti-utopia, and critical utopia:

> Utopia—a non-existent society described in considerable detail and normally located in time and space.
>
> Eutopia or positive utopia—a non-existent society described in considerable detail and normally located in time and space that the author intended a contemporaneous reader to view as considerably better than the society in which that reader lived.
>
> Dystopia or negative utopia—a non-existent society described in considerable detail and normally located in time and space that the author intended a contemporaneous reader to view as considerably worse than the society in which that reader lived.
>
> Utopian satire—a non-existent society described in considerable detail and normally located in time and space that the author intended a contemporaneous reader to view as a criticism of that contemporary society.
>
> Anti-utopia—a non-existent society described in considerable detail and normally located in time and space that the author intended a contemporaneous reader to view as a criticism of utopianism or of some particular eutopia.
>
> Critical utopia—a non-existent society described in considerable detail and normally located in time and space that the author intended a contemporaneous reader to view as better than contemporary society but with difficult problems that the described society may or may not be able to solve and which takes a critical view of the utopian genre. ("Three Faces Revisited" 9)

Lest it be misunderstood, it is important to note that Sargent's emphasis on social *dreaming* pointedly refuses two characterizations of Utopia that are most often attributed to this powerful social force by those working within the parameters of *anti-utopian* thought and practice. The first that he rejects in no uncertain terms is that of "perfection." Clearly aware that the utopian impulse is a matter of *process*, he notes that the implicit stasis of perfection simply cannot be a typical property of Utopia, and he places the blame for the false charge on the anti-utopian camp:

> First, there are in fact very few eutopias that present societies that the author believes to be perfect. . . . Second, opponents of utopianism use the label *perfect* as a political weapon to justify their opposition. They argue that a perfect society can only be achieved by force; thus, utopianism is said to lead to totalitarianism and the use of force and violence against people. ("Three Faces Revisited" 9)

Of course, the other argument used by anti-utopians is that dreams and schemes of a "perfect" society will help to destroy the disciplinary motivation (proceeding from experiences of scarcity and fear) that they claim people need to succeed in society (which is usually posited as a space disciplined by theological notions such as "original sin" or secular economic notions such as "laziness" or "dependency").

In this view, anti-utopians name perfection as a dangerously debilitating goal that must be exposed and condemned. But by attributing perfection to utopianism they also manage to condemn any radical movement for social transformation as escapist and irrealistic. Yet even as this attack is leveled, the anti-utopian standpoint also appropriates perfection for itself, as it argues that the "best of all possible worlds" already exists in the status quo.[12] Contrary to the anti-utopians, he argues that the utopian process aims for a *better* rather than the *best* or *perfect* society and consequently refuses the trap of seeking or claiming perfection. Indeed, the process itself at its best self-corrects for any such temptation. Sargent implicitly levels a second charge against anti-utopians when he takes care to argue that the *social* dreaming of utopianism is not escapist, for it balances a creative use of fantasy with the qualities of critical reason and deliberate action. To be sure, some utopias (literary, communal, even theoretical) lean more in the direction of fantasy (and perhaps satiric exaggeration) whereas others insist on an almost instrumentally reasonable alternative. But overall, most utopian expressions or enactments work with what he calls the "dual propensity" of fantasy and reason and thereby avoid the extremes of escapism and totalitarianism ("Three Faces Revisited" 4).

Along with Sargent's work on matters of definition and terminology, Suvin's 1973 essay "Defining the Literary Genre of Utopia: Some Historical Semantics,

Some Genology, a Proposal, and a Plea" supplies a detailed definition of the literary utopia that matches the precision of his sf definition.[13] First published in *Studies in the Literary Imagination* and then in *Metamorphoses*, this piece was another of Suvin's early contributions to the critical paradigms of sf and utopian studies.

Again, by way of historical contextualization and careful distinctions, Suvin clarifies the framework for the study of the literary utopia and establishes the relationship between the two genres by regarding them as kindred forms of "estranged" writing. Fully aware of the ambiguity of the term *Utopia*, especially as it oscillates between the historical impulse and actual texts and practices, he grounds his analysis in the material specificity of the formal apparatus of the literary utopia as he argues that "utopias are verbal artifacts before they are anything else" and therefore "the source of this concept" (*Metamorphoses* 39). Thus he opens with More's neologism, noting, like Sargent, its "simultaneous indication of a space and a state . . . that are nonexisting (*ou*) as well as good (*eu*)," and he observes that the literary utopia operates by "example and demonstration . . . [working as] a gesture of pointing, a wide-eyed glance from here to there, a 'traveling shot' moving from the author's everyday lookout to the wondrous panorama of a far-off land" (*Metamorphoses* 37). The literary utopia therefore offers an "*alternative location radically different in respect of sociopolitical conditions* from the author's historical environment"; and yet, however different, it is still an "Other World immanent in the world of human endeavor, dominion, and hypothetic possibility" (*Metamorphoses* 41, 42). As a *literary* artifact, it is not a static picture of perfection but rather a dynamic representation of human relations in motion, not perfect but better than what can be found in the author's world.

After a historical review of previous scholarship on the literary utopia, Suvin then advances his own, now familiar, definition:

> Utopia is the verbal construction of a particular quasi-human community where sociopolitical institutions, norms, and individual relationships are organized according to a more perfect principle than in the author's community, this construction being based on estrangement arising out of an alternative historical hypothesis. (*Metamorphoses* 49)

Suvin agrees with Frye that this literary form has more in common with the anatomy than with the novel, for it deals less with "people as such than with mental attitudes" and "presents us with a vision of the world in terms of a single intellectual pattern" (Frye, quoted *Metamorphoses* 49). Within the frame of an isolated space and time, the literary utopia presents the "inner organization" of a social alternative that dramatically conflicts with the knowledge and expectations of its readers. It works toward this effect with its framing structure of the journey, tour, and report back home; but, as Suvin argues, it also does so in every other element of the text: in the specifics of the alternative world and in the very style and composition of the text itself.[14] Like Sargent, he dismisses the false questions of realizability and "perfection" and argues that the utopian text is fundamentally an "epistemological and not an ontological entity." Neither "prophesy nor escapism," it is rather (here he draws on Vaihinger and Bloch, respectively) an "as if," an imaginative experiment, or "a methodical organ for the New" (*Metamorphoses* 52). Like sf, the literary utopia works with the logic of cognitive estrangement. Indeed, he controversially makes the logical claim that the literary utopia is not a genre in its own right but rather "the *sociopolitical subgenre of science fiction*" (*Metamorphoses* 61). Reading backward from the present, he argues that the utopian subgenre actually preceded its parent genre of sf. Thus, sf "is at the same time wider than and at least collaterally descended from utopia" and a genre that "can finally be written only between the utopian and the anti-utopian horizons" (*Metamorphoses* 61–62).

Although some scholars continued to study the classical form of the literary utopia at various stages and in various instances from More up through the mid-twentieth century, others began to examine the recent transformation of the utopian form within and by way of sf. One of the early essays that addressed this development was Fitting's "Modern Anglo-American SF Novel: Utopian Longing and Capitalist Cooptation," which appeared in *Science-Fiction Studies* in 1979.[15] In an extensive historical and textual analysis, Fitting argues that sf's "*generic ability* to provide a place for imagining utopian alternatives" has produced important critiques of "capitalism and specifically of sexism" ("Anglo-American" 70, my emphasis). Drawing on critical Marxist theory—especially that of Louis Althusser and Pierre Macherey—he argues that Western sf works on a contested cultural terrain that is framed, on the one hand, by "a form of ideological production, one of the ways in which capitalism speaks itself and determines our ways of perceiving reality, one of the ways through which the real problems and conflicts present in society are transformed into false problems and imaginary resolutions" and, on the other hand, by the potential to express what Ernst Bloch has referred to as "'utopian longing,' humanity's continued striving for an 'adequate future'" ("Anglo-American" 59). From this perspective, he reviews the ideological-utopian contest regarding the specific "thematic configurations of the *future* and of *science*" in sf from the 1930s to the 1970s ("Anglo-American" 59–60).

After a thorough dialectical reading of four decades of popular sf, he brings his analysis up to the late 1960s. Then, by way of commentary on Delany's work, which he traces from "mythic" tales such as *The Einstein Intersection* (1967) to the utopian *Triton,* he comes again to the utopian revival, marked by Delany's novel but seen most powerfully in the feminist utopias written by Russ, Ursula K. Le Guin, and Marge Piercy. These works, he argues, take the next dialectical turn in negating the hegemonic anti-utopianism of postwar society. He describes them as "*critical and utopian*" expressions in which "the original recognition of . . . the role of science and reason in human emancipation are reaffirmed . . . [and which] promise to supply a new basis for the utopian longing for emancipation that has always been—more or less—a fundamental impulse behind and inside [sf]" ("Anglo-American" 72, my emphasis).[16] In Le Guin's *Left Hand of Darkness* (1969), he sees a "return to social speculation in which the imagining of alternate societies grows out of an examination of the social and political structures of the author's own world" ("Anglo-American" 70). It is in Le Guin's *Dispossessed* and Russ's *Female Man,* however, that he finds fully elaborated utopian alternatives. He therefore locates the center of the new utopian whirlwind in the work of these two women, and he stresses their intervention in the publishing world of sf as well as in the public sphere, noting that however one may disagree with or be disappointed by specific elements of their texts, their contribution lies "in the revival of utopian thought itself, in the willingness and ability to again envisage emancipatory alternatives" ("Anglo-American" 71).

As is obvious from Fitting's list of the new utopias, many were written by women who were deeply involved in the feminist movements of the time, and most were primarily, but not exclusively, received as feminist utopias. Although some scholars—and writer-critics such as Russ, Le Guin, and Delany—were already working on feminist critiques of sf, the new utopias stimulated yet another, related series of contributions within the somewhat friendlier realm of utopian studies.

In 1973 Sargent published the essay "Women in Utopia" in *Comparative Literature Studies,* and in 1974 Daphne Patai brought out one of her several critical works on feminism and utopia in her essay for *Aphra,* "Utopia for Whom?" Dolores Hayden's interdisciplinary study of women's culture, architecture, and utopia, *Seven American Utopias: The Architecture of Communitarian Socialism, 1790–1975,* came out in 1975, and Ann J. Lane's edition of Charlotte Perkins Gilman's *Herland* was published in 1979. Support for this growing body of feminist work on utopianism came especially from the editors of *Science-Fiction Studies* and *Alternative Futures:* Elaine Hoffman Baruch's "Natural and Necessary Monster: Women in Utopia" in *Alternative Futures* in 1979 and Nadia Khouri's "Dialectics of Power: Utopia in the Science Fiction of Le Guin, Jeury, and Piercy" in *Science-Fiction Studies* in 1980 are examples of the results of both journal's initiatives. The newly formed Society for Utopian Studies also proved to be encouraging of feminist work, and presentations—which later appeared as essays in the society's journal and elsewhere—were given by scholars such as Kristine Anderson, Raffaella Baccolini, Marleen Barr, June Deery, Libby Falk Jones, Carol Farley Kessler, Lee Cullen Khanna, Carol Kolmerten, Helen Kuryllo, Jeanne Pfaelzer, Vara Neverow, Jewel Parker Rhodes, Lynn Williams, and Hoda M. Zaki.

By the 1980s, therefore, a strong movement of feminist criticism had emerged, and more was on the way. Marleen Barr and Nicholas D. Smith's collection, *Women and Utopia: Critical Interpretations,* came out in 1983; Carol Farley Kessler's important study, *Daring to Dream: Utopian Stories by United States Women,* and Elaine Hoffman Baruch and Ruby Rohrlich's collection, *Women in Search of Utopia,* appeared in 1984. Nan Bowman Albinski's *Women's Utopias in British and American Fiction* and Hoda M. Zaki's *Phoenix Renewed: The Survival and Mutation of Utopian Thought in North American Science Fiction, 1965–1982* came out in 1988. At the end of the decade, two substantial studies of the feminist utopias of the 1970s were published by Frances Bartkowski (*Feminist Utopias* in 1989) and Angelika Bammer (*Partial Visions: Feminism and Utopianism in the 1970s* in 1991). Kessler's "Bibliography of Utopian Fiction by United States Women, 1836–1988" appeared in the first issue of *Utopian Studies* in 1990. Also in 1990, Sarah Webster and Libby Falk Jones published their collection, *Feminism, Utopia, and Narrative,* and Carol Kolmerten brought out her *Women in Utopia: The Ideology of Gender in the American Owenite Communities.* In 1994 Jane L. Donawerth and Kolmerten published the collection of essays *Utopian and Science Fiction by Women: Worlds of Difference;* Jennifer Burwell's *Notes on Nowhere: Feminism, Utopian Logic, and Social Transformation* appeared in 1997.[17]

Among this early criticism, one of the most effective contributions on the new feminist utopias came from Russ, in her essay "Recent Feminist Utopias," first published in 1981 by Barr in her influential anthology *Future Females.*[18] As I noted in Chapter 1, Russ's 1972 story "When It Changed" caught the attention of many, especially women, who were working at the political and literary edges of society, and her expansion of the story into *The Female Man* circulated among a network of feminist sf writers until Ballantine Books, under the editorship of David Hartwell, finally published it in 1975.

In this essay Russ connects the "mini-boom of feminist utopias" with the politics of the women's movement. The earliest of these utopias, she notes, is Monique Wittig's *Les Guérillères* (1969), which appeared in a timely English translation in 1971; the latest at the time of her essay was Suzy McKee Charnas's *Motherlines* (1978). Besides her own *Female Man* and Le Guin's *Dispossessed*, she lists Delany's *Triton*, Piercy's *Woman on the Edge of Time*, Marion Zimmer

Bradley's *Shattered Chain* (1976), Sally Gearhart's *Wanderground: Stories of the Hill Women* (1979), Catherine Madsden's "Commodore Bork and the Compost" (1976), and James Tiptree Jr.'s (Alice Sheldon's), "Houston, Houston, Do You Read?" and "Your Faces, O My Sisters! Your Faces Filled of Light" (1976) (*To Write* 134). As they fly in the face of the bad rap given to Utopia by ideological anti-utopianism, Russ notes that the new works present not perfect societies but "only ones better than our own," societies that are "better in explicitly feminist terms and for explicitly feminist reasons" (*To Write* 134).

Thus, the new utopian writers drew from the feminist structure of feeling and mutually influenced each other as they read drafts, published versions, exchanged letters, met, and talked. In distinct ways each text focuses on questions of "personal relations and who's doing the work women usually do" but develops that emphasis in the context of the detailed exploration of society that shapes most utopias. Each addresses a common set of issues, including "the absence of crime, the relative lack of government, and the diffusion of the parental role to the whole society . . . [along with a] lack of dualistic thinking, the importance of mothering, and [new] philosophical and religious attitudes" (*To Write* 135n). Russ's designation of feminism, however, needs to be understood within the rich and complex movement of the period. The multiple strains of socialist, radical, lesbian, and liberal feminism all were working in a lively cooperation and contention; and all were militantly engaged, each in its own political style, with the process of social critique and change. "Feminism" therefore incorporated dimensions of socialism, communism, and anarchism, along with the wisdom of the young ecology movement, and was open to many varieties of radical Left and libertarian thought and practice of the day. As "feminist" utopias, these works are powerfully expansive rather than reductive.[19]

Among their shared qualities, Russ mentions the concern for "*communal*, even *quasi-tribal*" social systems. Unlike the Right's later attack on government, feminist utopianism grows out of the long tradition of Left political thought, but it tends to cluster in the familiar formulation of an anarchocommunism in which personal freedom abounds and the state has given way to a relatively unobtrusive administration (although many of the utopias focus on problems in this arrangement, none rejects it.) Related to this principle of social organization is a shared acceptance of a "classless" society. Here too, status and privilege become issues to be dealt with in several of the stories, but again the problem is an occasion for struggle, not for rejection of the shared ideal. The utopias also exude an ecological consciousness, and here the influence of ecofeminism is clearly seen.

As Russ notes, "many of the stories go beyond the problems of living in the world without disturbing its ecological balance into presenting their characters as feeling a strong emotional connection to the natural world" (*To Write* 137). Perhaps unexpectedly, violence is not eliminated but rather reduced to a personal level (although Russ observes that relatively just wars linger at the edges of the narratives in the works by Delany, Piercy, and Wittig). Sexual permissiveness is common "to separate sexuality from questions of ownership, reproduction, and social structure" (*To Write* 139). In such safe and free worlds, women, and sometimes men, experience an unusual level of freedom—usually helped by some form of communist economy (which Russ does not elaborate upon).

Privileged in many of these works, young people, especially young women at puberty, often provide the leading models for the radical new subjectivity explored in these novels (and drawn from the praxis of the women's movement). Thus, the utopias "offer an alternative model of female puberty, one which allows the girl to move into a full and free adulthood" (*To Write* 143). In her view, they

> supply in fiction what their authors believe society (in the case of these books) and/or women lack in the here-and-now. The positive values stressed in the stories can reveal to us what, in the authors' eyes, is wrong with our own society. Thus if the stories are family/communal in feeling, we may pretty safely guess that the authors see our society as isolating people from one another, especially (to judge from the number of all-female utopias in the group) women from women. (*To Write* 144–145)

She goes on to connect the common elements in these utopias with the immediate problems and contradictions in her own society: urban alienation, class exploitation, war and military rule, sexual repression, alienated labor, and an adolescence racked with "sexist restrictions, sexual objectification, or even outright persecution" (*To Write* 145). Most important, she catches the *public* nature of these alternate societies, for in these other places "there is no personal solution": The personal is clearly political for all the authors. They all attack the injustices being exposed and challenged by the political movements, and they all posit a collective response to the work that needs to be done.

Many other commentaries and many other utopias added to this new utopian sensibility, and all were more or less connected politically with the oppositional movements outside their pages. In *Demand the Impossible* in 1986 (indebted to the work of Russ, Suvin, Fitting, Jameson, Delany, and others), I dwelt on this political connection and characterized these transformed literary utopias as "critical utopias."[20] Then as now, I approached these works (especially ones by Le Guin, Russ, Piercy, and Delany) as part of the Left oppositional culture of the time. To be sure, their primary base rested in a combination of socialist and radical feminist thought and practice; however, the connection with and influence of the other strands of the opposition were also to be found in these dangerous utopian visions. The anti-racist and liberatory analyses of national, racial, and ethnic liberation struggles; the socialist/communist analyses of the New Left; the pacifist and anti-bomb critiques of the anti-war and peace movements; the anarchist and existentialist thought of the counterculture, the anti-draft, and gay and lesbian fronts; and the new scientific work of the ecology movement all fed into these literary interventions.

The result was a fresh round of utopianism that supported, sustained, challenged, influenced, and motivated activists and readers around the globe. In support of this, I quoted Sheila Rowbotham's description of the value of utopias within the political culture:

> We need to make the creation of prefigurative forms an explicit part of our movement against capitalism. I do not mean that we try to hold an imaginary future in the present, straining against the boundaries of the possible until we collapse in exhaustion and despair. This would be utopian. Instead such forms would seek both to consolidate existing practice and release the imagination of what could be. (quoted in *Demand* 196)

And in my last endnote I pointed toward the connections between the textual and the social, the private and public, the personal and political that the utopias could facilitate. More than entertainment, other than activism, the critical utopias had and still have their place in furthering the processes of ideological critique, consciousness-raising, and social dreaming/planning that necessarily inform the practice of those who are politically committed to producing a social reality better than, and beyond, the one that currently oppresses and destroys humanity and nature.

More particularly, I focused on the formal interventions taken by these utopias. Like Fitting, I argued that the 1960s revival of sf provided the initial space for this overtly utopian writing. Within the science fictional mode, the critical utopias addressed what had become the fate of utopianism in the twentieth century. First, they challenged the anti-utopian rejection of utopian thought and practice; they refused to accept the current social order as "utopian" and thereby resisted the repression of authentic utopian work. In doing so, they preserved the utopian impulse itself. Thus, they produced unmistakably *utopian* texts and with fully developed *utopian* societies, however unsettled or ambiguous those societies were.

Second, the new utopias confronted the contradictions that pervaded utopian expression itself. Whether working from an anti-utopian misperception or from actual investigation of earlier utopian texts, they created strategies, in content and form, that challenged any tendency toward a narrowly conceived and enforced utopianism. That is, they resisted textual work that did not question its own leanings toward single-minded solutions or undemocratic, nonnegotiable social blueprints. Influenced as much by experimental, postmodern fiction as by sf, many spun out self-reflexive formal maneuvers that called attention not only to their content but also to the way in which they were formally produced, considering their textual development in its own right and sometimes in the intertextual web of all utopian writing.

The new utopias, in other words, managed to sublate utopian expression. While preserving the utopian impulse and the utopian form, they nevertheless destroyed both the anti-utopian rejection and the utopian compromises that had come to haunt the utopian tradition. They therefore transformed utopian writing into a new object suited to the aesthetic and political demands of the historical situation. Thus:

> A central concern in the critical utopia is the awareness of the limitations of the utopian tradition, so that these texts reject utopia as blueprint while preserving it as dream. Furthermore, the novels dwell on the conflict between the originary world and the utopian society opposed to it so that the process of social change is more directly articulated. Finally, the novels focus on the continuing presence of difference and imperfection within utopian society itself and thus render more recognizable and dynamic alternatives. (*Demand* 10–11)

Such utopias, I argued, were "critical" of the sociopolitical situation and of the utopianism that had always endeavored to oppose it. In this light, they adopted the feminist and Maoist practices of "criticism-self-criticism," and they incorporated the meaning of the Frankfurt School use of the term *critical* as opposed to *instrumental* reason (that is, of "critique" as opposed to ideological capitulation or consent).[21] Finally, they were "critical" in the sense that underlies the activist understanding of the degree of mass involvement needed to organize effectively (see *Demand* 41–46).

Although a development within the literary realm, the critical utopias provided a strategic contribution to utopian thought and practice as well. The investigation of the utopian process by way of content that critiqued utopia's own tendency to closure and compromise raised the stakes of the utopian imagination in all its manifestations. As well, and perhaps more significant, the strategic deployment of formal techniques of self-reflexivity provided a model within literary discourse that could be carried over to utopian practices within the realm of lived experience, in communities or in political movements, in the use of modes of self-criticism that would work against the growth of an elite leadership and the blocking of grassroots democratic decisionmaking. In short, the critical utopias helped to deflect utopia's own drift into ideological containment to keep its processes of critique and change alive and healthy.

III.

By the 1970s, utopian expression was flourishing. Intentional communities, religious and secular, grew in numbers and sometimes in influence; literary utopias constituted one of the liveliest new directions in sf; and the scholarly project of utopian studies came into its own. Connected with these developments but moving on a broader scale, the utopian impulse found a wider outlet in the oppositional cultures of the times. Daring to dream and then struggle for a better world, activists were inspired not only to bring an end to the social ills they saw in front of them but also to build new spaces for humanity and nature that negated and transformed the logic and practices of the society that had produced them.

Although the New Right would become dominant in the 1980s, the oppositional movements of the Left were making significant steps in delineating and occupying, if only for a historical moment, utopian counter-spaces that represented the outlines of an alternative to the present economic, political, and cultural system. Many who worked within the ambit of utopian studies centered their research on the particular manifestations of communities or texts; others stepped back from given instances of utopian expression and looked directly at the question of Utopia itself. In doing so, they joined the intellectual effort—most often within radical humanist and Marxist perspectives—of coming to terms with the nature of this powerful sociopolitical force. Although this is not the place to address that entire body of work, I turn now to the sociopolitical dimension of Utopia as it has been specifically explored by two leading thinkers in utopian studies.

In *The Concept of Utopia* (1990), Ruth Levitas recalls Sargent's insistence that a basic agreement on definition and a clear terminological framework was required if utopian studies was to proceed with any effectiveness. For lacking a consensus on the object of analysis, the project would be confused and compromised (see *Concept* 214n). She therefore sets out to clarify the meaning of the term, not "to impose an orthodoxy, but to encourage communication about issues which are already being addressed and to suggest new ones" (*Concept* 2), and she works toward her goal through a survey of the history of utopian thought and practice, examining existing definitions as they clustered around three aspects of Utopia: content, form, and function. Although content is compelling for readers, Levitas, like most scholars in utopian studies, acknowledges that the variation in utopian accounts rules out this aspect as a useful basis for a stable definition. Form, in contrast, has attracted more serious attention—especially with the "changing nature of contemporary utopian fiction" (*Concept* 7). Yet even though the specificity of utopian writing has been more precisely articulated, a comprehensive definition based on form is insufficient, for it does not account for the entire range of utopian manifestations. For Levitas, therefore, function offers the best basis for an adequate definition. Even here, however, the differing instances of utopian production demand that the determination of a common underlying quality is still required for a definition that can be suitably encompassing (*Concept* 4–5).

Although she attends to all three aspects in her survey, she consistently turns to utopia's fundamental role in the process of social change. She reminds readers that not all utopian expressions are manifestations of progressive writers or movements (or texts that, however complicit, still uncover social contradictions in ways that point toward utopian critique and anticipation), for utopian expression on the Right has also challenged hegemonic systems. She also acknowledges the anti-utopian tendency wherein Utopia is completely hijacked by a ruling system that exploits and silences Utopia by claiming its achievement for its own. Thus, she restates the basic Marxist caution about the potentially conservative role of utopian expression when it works not to mobilize social change in the name of justice and emancipation but rather to contain that very process in static dream worlds that deny or displace political practice. Yet against the orthodox Marxist position that tends to see Utopia only in this reactionary guise, in the best tradition of utopianism she recognizes Utopia's powerful capacity to serve as a motivating force for social critique and change. No doubt rooted in the medieval history of branding utopian thought and practice as heretical, the fuller articulation of utopia's radical capacity emerges most directly with Marx and runs forward within critical Marxism (so far reaching its most elaborate presentation in the work of Bloch).

Later going into greater detail, Levitas first offers a definition in the early pages of her book as she borrows the phrase used by Raymond Williams and E. P. Thompson in their commentaries on William Morris. Thus, she identifies the "education of desire" as the characterization that most comprehensively catches the nature of Utopia. For her, desire as a basic yearning for a "better way of being and living" is a "historically variable" quality that inherently goes beyond the limits of any given social order (*Concept* 7–8). Utopia's role is not to express desire directly but rather to enable people "to work towards an understanding of what is necessary for human fulfillment, a broadening, deepening and raising of aspirations in terms quite different from those of their everyday life" (*Concept* 122). Understood in this way, the utopian function must be "simultaneously educative *and* transformative" (*Concept* 106, my emphasis). If the education of desire is undertaken in good faith, the result must necessarily be one that will negate the present order and point toward a historically better social reality. As she puts it, "there is plainly no point in the education of desire for its own sake, and if the function of [U]topia is the education of desire, the function of the education of desire is the realisation of [U]topia" (*Concept* 124).

Further on in her analysis, she refuses idealist and essentialist claims for the utopian function when she again asserts that Utopia is nothing more nor less than a product of history: Utopia "is a social construct which arises not from a 'natural' impulse subject to social mediation, but as a socially constructed response to an *equally* socially constructed gap between the needs and wants generated by a particular society and the satisfactions available to and distributed by it" (*Concept* 181–182). As a historical force, Utopia emerges in the collective response to the "scarcity gap" between what is and what could be within any social context. The gap between haves and have-nots that is the result of the actual mode and relations of production is, therefore, the historically situated space in which human desire begins to move toward Utopia. Here, then, is the material, not metaphysical, condition that produces the utopian response. Thus, Utopia in any of its forms must be based in and work from this material precondition of the "disparity between socially constructed experienced need and socially prescribed and actually available means of satisfaction" (*Concept* 183).

In her closing chapter, Levitas focuses on the possible directions the utopian function can take, playing out as compensation, criticism, or change. She first addresses compensation and connects it with the production of what Karl Mannheim would regard as ideology and Bloch would identify as "abstract, 'bad'" utopias. When such "utopian" expressions become "pure compensation," they only work to co-opt and contain human desire within the current society (*Concept* 180). Although she never states it directly, this misappropriation of the utopian process becomes a negation of Utopia itself. By suppressing the education of desire, compensatory utopias are nothing but *anti-utopian*. Drawing on Barbara Goodwin's understanding of Utopia as "social fiction," Levitas then turns to the function of criticism, and she values its capacity to evoke a comparative response that works by way of the utopian alternative's counterfactual relationship with existing society.

The critical function, however, tends to occur primarily at the level of social and political theory and may not necessarily lead to the next step into the realm of transformative praxis. Herein lies the potential for yet another negation of utopian quality. If the counterfactual thought experiment does not achieve this connection (in some mediated yet engaged fashion), it can simply remain within the discursive universe of the prevailing system and lose its utopian valence by becoming little more than a matter of intellectual curiosity or academic debate. The function of criticism rides on the very edge of the utopian and the anti-utopian, falling one way or another depending on its degree of political articulation. Thus, only the function of *social change* remains viably in the utopian camp, for here the work of criticism implicitly links up with that of transformation, as situated social hopes for specific changes are taken to their most realistically radical reaches by way of the deep human desire for a totally better way of living. As Levitas puts it, Utopia is "a means of grasping and effecting the hoped-for future" that its content and form prefiguratively invoke (*Concept* 190).

In this framework an immediate connection with political change is not the most pressing point. Rather, it is Utopia's capacity to generate conditions and strategies for change rather than change itself that lies at the heart of its radically oriented function. This transformative work nevertheless needs to be carried out in terms of actual material conditions and contradictions, for if utopian yearning remains the stuff of abstract or universal dreams, it will simply die on the vine of dilettantism or escapism at best, or become fodder for the cynical machinery of anti-utopianism at worst.

Given this fundamental role in processes of sociopolitical transformation, utopian desire must engage with the tendencies and latencies of the historical moment that can be acted upon by specific political agents. As Levitas puts it: "When the function of [U]topia is to catalyse change, then of course the issue of practical possibility becomes salient"; however, she again adds the caveat that "even here, [U]topia does not need to *be* practically possible; it merely needs to be believed to be so to mobilise people to political action" (*Concept* 191). She insists that the process of the transition from the present to the utopian alternative must be fundamentally included in the utopian provocation. Her argument implicitly recalls the example of the crucial chapter in William Morris's *News from Nowhere*; for only when it came to detailing "How the Change Came" did Morris's text give historical flesh to the spiritual bones of utopian desire. Therefore, the articulation of "will-full action" with actual historical possibility (working between the poles of strategic maneuvers or outright contestation) must be part of the deployment of the utopian process if it is to be effective.[22] As she concludes, the utopian dream becomes historically effective "only when hope is invested in an agency capable of transformation" (*Concept* 200).

Although this connection of Utopia's function with the processes of political critique and change is crucial for arriving at a proper grasp of its nature, it is this very relationship that requires careful attention and elaboration. For if the utopian work within political movements fails to interrogate *both* the hegemonic social order and the theory and practice of the opposition itself, it risks becoming a narrowly pragmatic, *functionalist* process that could all too easily remain trapped within the binary of unchallenged power and static opposition. If the utopian impulse does not challenge the entire movement against the current order as well as the movement's own tendencies to legitimize and hypostatize its position and practice, it will inevitably become part of a compensatory holding exercise and not a force for simultaneous external and internal transformation. Thus, even, or perhaps especially, within a political movement, the utopian process must always insist (with Theodor Adorno and Bloch) that "something's missing." It must hold that what is already being done is never enough, that what needs to be done must always keep the fullness of human experience on the agenda as an asymptotic reality that constantly pulls the political struggle forward (before, during, and after whatever counts as a revolutionary moment).

Indeed, this was the significant development in the self-reflexive strategy that transformed the textual mechanics of the literary utopias of the 1970s. In content and form, the critical utopias forthrightly put the principle of self-critique on the utopian agenda. At the level of content, the iconic representations of the alternative worlds included the faults and contradictions of the utopian society and not just those of the hegemonic order. As well, the discrete narratives tracked the inhibition and often denial of further political movement by post-revolutionary power structures and explored ways that activists could re-engage, not only against the "enemy" but also against the revolution's own compromised practice. At the level of form, the literary techniques of self-reflexivity called attention to the very process of utopian creativity. The narrative tendency for a utopian trajectory to lapse into the stasis of a blueprint, plan, or party line was challenged by textual tactics that broke open the utopian form so that the utopian imagination remained responsive to further critique and change. Thus, although the critical utopias worked at the level of a *textual* intervention in the cultural matrix, the lesson they brought to the general practice of utopian thought and action could not be ignored. Literary self-reflexivity pointed to political self-reflexivity. Textual critique facilitated political critique.

By 1990, work in utopian studies had not only refined its specific areas of research but also arrived at a characterization of the utopian process in terms of Levitas's formulation, the "education of desire," and Sargent's "social dreaming." Both definitions properly focus on Utopia as an ongoing human activity that takes up various forms but also exceeds the limits of any one of them. In doing so, both refuse a simple psychological analysis in favor of a deeper structuralist argument for the utopian proclivity. Yet neither provides much in the way of further detail on that process. Here, then, Jameson's extensive exploration of Utopia provides a fuller sense of its nature and operation. This is not the place to explore the entire range of Jameson's writings on Utopia, but I do want to consider his key contributions in terms of their impact on utopian studies. This can be seen in two essays (published in a special section of *Utopian Studies* in 1998, "Jameson and Utopia") that exemplify the particular reception of Jameson's "utopian problematic" within the critical purview of that project: Fitting's "Concept of Utopia in the Work of Fredric Jameson" and PhillipWegner's "Horizons, Figures, and Machines: The Dialectic of Utopia in the Work of Fredric Jameson."[23]

Although Jameson has written incisively about overtly utopian matters (e.g., Le Guin's and Robinson's sf, Fourier's and Bloch's theory), he more often and consistently sets his critical sights on the utopian process itself. His concern, therefore, is not with utopian objects as such but rather with what Wegner terms the "utopian problematic," which Jameson described in 1983 as "a set of categories in terms of which reality is analyzed and interrogated, and a set of 'essentially contested' categories at that" (quoted in "Horizons" 58). With Jameson, as with Levitas, the scope of this problematic not only involves radical interpretation but also pedagogic dissemination in the name of radical social change.

In Wegner's view, Jameson regards Utopia as a process that "re-educates the desires of its audience, enabling them to grow the 'new organs' necessary also to 'live' and later 'perceive' a newly emerging social and cultural reality" ("Horizons" 68). What Utopia delivers is not the fulfillment of that new reality, or even its blueprint or promise, but rather the imaginative means to help move toward this historical possibility through political struggle. As such, Utopia may prefigure a not yet known and lived reality, and it may stand as the horizon of collective movement toward that reality, but it also helps to produce the conditions for the production of the political movement itself. What Utopia "successfully brings into view is precisely the 'machinery' concentrating and localizing necessity—those structures that enable a social order to (re)produce itself—so that new forms and spaces of freedom can come into being in the first place" ("Horizons" 70).

As with others in the critical Marxist tradition, Jameson first had to rescue Utopia from the depredations of mainstream and even some versions of oppositional thought. Fitting reminds us that he did this as early as 1971 in his discussion of Bloch and Marcuse in *Marxism and Form,* when he recalculated Utopia's historical valence. The passage Fitting cites is worth repeating:

> For where in the older society (as in Marx's classic analysis) [u]topian thought represented a diversion of revolutionary energy into idle wish-fulfillments and imaginary satisfactions, in our own time the very nature of

> the utopian concept has undergone a dialectical reversal. Now it is practical thinking which everywhere represents a capitulation to the system itself, and stands as a testimony to the power of that system to transform even its adversaries into its own mirror image. The [u]topian idea, on the contrary, keeps alive the possibility of a world qualitatively distinct from this one and takes the form of a stubborn negation of all that is.[24]

From this moment of reclamation, as Wegner demonstrates, Jameson's commentaries on Utopia have taken several turns. Each new formulation, however, does not diminish his previous meditations but rather enriches the entire commentary. Wegner therefore cautions readers of Jameson always to step back and consider the totality, to use an apt term, of his evolving argument and not fix on one or another aspect. He also observes that there has been a steady shading from a focus on the negative, critical function of Utopia to its positive anticipatory role (albeit one reachable only through negation):

> consistent with his other work, Jameson's treatment of the problematic of [U]topia is a deeply dialectical one: on the one hand, taking the form of an early well-nigh "negative dialectic," that maintains [U]topia is as impossible as it is indispensable; and, on the other hand, re-emerging as a pedagogical and transformative dialectic, which reaches full fruition in his later articulations of the aesthetic of cognitive mapping. ("Horizons" 58)

Despite shifts in relative balance, the interplay of the negative and positive is present throughout Jameson's work, and it can be discovered as early as the study of Bloch. As Jameson describes it, Bloch's utopian hermeneutic works precisely by way of a dialectical negation of what exists in order to open the way to Utopia as the negation of the negation, and his method therefore provides a critical search engine that can track the utopian "principle of hope" not simply by focusing on instances of "utopian" expression but rather by detailing the myriad ways in which the ideological fullness of certain phenomena or texts implicitly promises a surplus "horizon of utopian Otherness" ("Horizons" 59).

If hegemonic discourses reproduce the social system by representing it as universally meaningful and satisfying for all—even while masking the constitutive "nonsynchronicity" between what is ideologically articulated and what is painfully desired—Utopia brings its critical energies to bear on those very contradictions, breaking open that which is ideologically replete to make room for the work of building a radically different world ("Horizons" 59). Working with Bloch, Jameson puts paid once and for all to Mannheim's binary opposition of ideology and utopia. Rather than casting the two categories as external to each other, he argues that Utopia and ideology are dialectically imbricated in a dynamic in which each taps into the power of the other. Consequently, only an equally dialectical critical intervention can crack open the apparent closure and release the power of Utopia. Thus, in 1981 he states in the conclusion to *The Political Unconscious* that the "effectively ideological is also, at the same time, necessarily [u]topian."[25] Or as he argues in "Reification and Utopia in Mass Culture," ideological expressions cannot work without a utopian promise, "cannot manipulate unless they offer some genuine shred of content as fantasy bribe to the public about to be manipulated."[26]

Utopia therefore is always already immersed in—empowered by—ideology even as it stands ready to negate its sutured representations. Looking at this relationship in terms of the project of political contestation and class struggle, Wegner puts it this way: "Jameson argues that 'all class consciousness of whatever type is [u]topian insofar as it expresses the unity of a collectivity,' it being understood once again, however, that these collectivities are themselves . . . '*figures* for the ultimate concrete collective life of an achieved [u]topian or classless society'" (quoted in "Horizons" 60).

It is this dialectical understanding of the utopian process that Jameson brings to his studies of sf and utopian fiction. In "World-Reduction in Le Guin," he was already tracking the formal innovations emerging in the texts of the 1960s as he acknowledged their capacity to establish a critical stance in a culture that works at every level (including the aesthetic) to suppress critique and change. However ideologically imbricated with mainstream culture, the potential to disturb that cultural equilibrium nevertheless exists in these historically engaged thought experiments. In the United States, sf had been flying under the radar of hegemonic surveillance at least since the 1950s, when it escaped suppression by the anti-communist purges, and in the resurgence of political life in the 1960s it surfaced to find one of its most overtly political forms in the critical utopias.[27]

Drawing on Suvin's studies on sf textuality as well as the investigations of the function of fantasy that Herbert Marcuse, Oskar Negt, and Jack Zipes developed within the critical problematic of the Frankfurt School, Jameson catches the nature of this potential in his comparison of sf with contemporary "high" literature as he notes that sf's "officially 'non-serious' or pulp character" is "an indispensable feature in its capacity to relax that tyrannical 'reality principle' which functions as a crippling censorship over high art, and to allow the 'paraliterary' form thereby to inherit the vocation of giving us alternate versions of a world that has elsewhere seemed to resist even *imagined* change" ("World-Reduction" 223). He therefore argues in "Progress Versus Utopia" that sf has the capacity to "defamiliarize and restructure our experience of our own *present*"; for sf's "apparently full representations" work through "distraction and displacement" to cast light on the present not directly in terms of what is on the page but indirectly in what that content catalyzes in the imagination: namely, a new perspective on the present that is not available in the everyday common sense encouraged by the hegemonic demand for consensus.[28]

When he takes up the literary utopia, Jameson shifts the analysis to yet another level—and makes what Wegner calls his "more troubling pronouncements" and what Fitting describes as his "most fruitful and troubling intervention" ("Horizons" 60; "Concept" 9). As in his discussion of sf, he does not focus on matters of overt content (what has typically been of interest to readers of utopian accounts) but looks instead at the *formal* operations of the utopian text and their relationship with the utopian process. Thus, he concludes "World-Reduction in Le Guin" with the initially disconcerting argument that the significance of the literary utopia is found in its reflection "on our own incapacity to conceive [Utopia] in the first place" ("World-Reduction" 230). His point is not simply a recognition that the transformed future is not yet present and therefore cannot be conceptually known, much less lived. Rather, it is an acknowledgment of the ideological fullness of the social reality that informs the content of the text (however effectively "reduced" and delineated) and supplies the matter upon and against which Utopia must work to make its deepest point.

Whatever is utopian in such works lies not in the determinate content as such. As Marx and Engels cautioned, the content itself can effectively block or deflect or limit the actual utopian qualities, for no work can get beyond its own cultural and ideological horizons (although it can reveal those horizons in a way that then exposes the limits of the present moment). More fundamentally, the utopian elements lie in what the mechanics of the text accomplish with regard to its imaginative relationship with the world from which the content was imaginatively drawn. Thus, the "true vocation" of Utopia is found not simply on the page but in the production of the page.

This line of analysis continues in "Of Islands and Trenches: Neutralization and the Production of Utopian Discourse" (Jameson's 1977 review of Marin's study of *Utopia*), where Jameson describes the utopian text as "a determinate type of praxis" that works by way of what Marin terms "neutralization."[29] Again, he emphasizes the roots of the utopian text in the historical situation, and he argues that the "place of the Real" in such a text must first be "constituted within the work before it can be dissolved or 'neutralized' by the work as process" ("Of Islands and Trenches" 10). Again, he refers to the text's process of cognitive estrangement as it takes up the ideologically constituted realities of the author's empirical environment and reworks them in the alternative world.

In this essay, however, he refines his analysis by distinguishing two stages in that process, as he continues to differentiate between the negative and positive functions of Utopia. For its part, "neutralization" initially brings forth a "point-by-point negation" of the author's historical world, but this critical operation then clears the stage, as Wegner puts it, "for the productive operation of utopian figuration" ("Horizons" 63). In canceling or deconstructing the "ideological parameters" of the given social reality, this process clears critical space for "the construction of something new" ("Horizons" 63). That new element, however, still works in the realm of the imagination, since the world to which it refers does not yet exist and therefore cannot be known empirically or conceptually.

Nevertheless, the alternative possibility (understood in terms of Suvin's textual novum) emerges only "*within* the horizons of its present" and ultimately exists as what Marin terms an "absent referent" for possibilities not yet reached ("Horizons" 63–64). As Wegner goes on to argue, the "historical originality" of utopian fiction lies in its ability to negotiate this critically imaginative plane, not as some form of political denial or diffusion but as an intervention in the social reality it appears to leave behind. The textual mechanics of the utopian text endow it with the "capacity to mediate between two different cultural and social realities, between the world that is and that which is coming into being" ("Horizons" 64). Using Jameson's terminology: through the process of neutralization the utopian text produces "pre-conceptual figures" that refer to the new reality that cannot yet be directly known, described, conceptualized, or lived. The famous utopian alternative does not appear as fully theorized or developed concepts but rather as figuration that signifies but does not, cannot, and must not deliver the transformed society.

The argument does not stop here, for it moves on to Jameson's most "fruitful" point: namely, that the "deepest subject" of the utopian text, and its most "vibrantly political" intervention, is "precisely our inability to conceive it, our incapacity to produce it as a vision" ("Of Islands and Trenches" 21). The assertion is certainly troubling, especially for those who take utopian narrative seriously as a source of social and political insight and intervention. On first glance, it appears to negate all there is about Utopia. It resembles an argument against Utopia, an anti-utopian denial of its use value. Yet the statement actually makes a stronger case for Utopia, for it liberates the utopian process from the ideological drag of its textual or social manifestations. Utopia may well drive and inform texts and communities, but it carries out that work in a dialectical process that preserves the content of these manifestations even as it negates and transforms them.

Jameson's sober reminder is that whatever the utopian expression, however informative and provocative its content may be for oppositional praxis, the deeper power of Utopia lies in what exceeds that expression. Trapped within the present, no oppositional theory or practice can deliver the future as an accomplished fact, and if it claimed to do so, it would generate yet another trap in the epistemological limits of its imagined alternative. What utopian practice *can* deliver, however, is a set of provocative but dispensable figures of possible new ways of living and possible ways toward them, and what it most fundamentally delivers is the grave acknowledgment that only through the complex processes of struggle will more emancipatory possibilities than those imagined actually be achieved. Utopia thus calls attention to the implicit limits of its own vision and turns us back to history and the open-ended task of building the future. To return to the key sentence, Utopia, therefore, implies a paradoxically valuable "*failure* to project the other of what is, a failure that, as with fireworks dissolving back into the night sky, must once again leave us alone with *this* history" ("Of Islands and Trenches" 21, my emphasis).

Jameson reiterated this argument in 1982 in "Progress Versus Utopia" with the claim that the "deepest vocation" of the utopian text "is to bring home, in local and determinate ways, and with a fullness of concrete detail, our constitutional inability to imagine Utopia itself, and this, not owing to any individual failure of imagination but as the result of the systemic, cultural, and ideological closure of which we are all in one way or another prisoners" ("Progress" 153). The "failure" of the utopian text, therefore, lies in its *successful* resistance to the ideological closure that surrounds and generates its production. The inability of Utopia to deliver a systemic plan or solution in the historical moment releases its potential as a flexible and far-reaching mode of critique and change. Thus, the "systematic description of an emerging reality" is no longer taken as Utopia's literary vocation, but Utopia "nevertheless 'succeeds,' in that it enables us to conceptualize for the first time the place that such a description must one day fill" (Wegner, "Horizons" 65).[30] Here, Jameson's emphasis on the pedagogical function comes into view as his analysis intensifies the political charge of utopian studies. As Wegner argues, Jameson shifts the "critical perspective" that Utopia invites from an immediate reception of the work to one that "can only occur by imaginatively re-occupying the original situation from within which the text had emerged in the first place" ("Horizons" 65). The feedback loops of this interpretative act thereby spin out the potential of utopian texts only by moving through their representations to the historical grounds of their creative and contestatory production.

The elaboration of these complementary processes (utopian production and critical response) leads Wegner to close with comments on the "Cognitive Mapping" essay and the 1994 book *The Seeds of Time*. As I suggested in Chapter 2, Jameson's speculation about the emergent "aesthetic" of cognitive mapping provides a way to connect the textual work of sf and utopian fiction with the project of utopian sociopolitical transformation. Indeed, Wegner believes that utopian texts can be counted "among the earliest expressions in Western modernity of the operations of cognitive mapping" ("Horizons" 68) and that there is no reason to exclude their contemporary versions (such as the critical utopias of the 1970s or the critical dystopias of the 1980s and 1990s) from this characterization. Holding to Jameson's argument on utopian praxis, Wegner is quick to point out that as a form of cognitive mapping, utopian narratives do not contend with the Real by providing a completed picture of an alternative world that can overlay the Real and magically make it over. Instead, they operate dialectically on the Real, and the result is a pedagogical utopia-in-motion: a "mapping" not a "map," a quick Polaroid photo that illuminates and then fades away to make critical room for the next shot.[31] Although the transformative power of Utopia has been part of his utopian problematic since the early 1970s, the activist nature of this "pedagogical imperative" has received greater emphasis in Jameson's later writing.

Furthering this tendency in *The Seeds of Time,* he adds another refinement to his understanding of the utopian problematic as he regards Utopia not only as a figure of hope or a horizon of change but as a "machine" for the production of that very change. As ever, he argues that the task of Utopia is not the unmediated production of the realm of freedom (which the text nevertheless names) but rather the production of the conditions for such historical change. Utopia, therefore, must work "to neutralize what blocks freedom, such as matter, labor, and the requirements of their accompanying human social machinery (such as power, training and discipline, enforcement, habits of obedience, respect, and so forth)."[32] Thus, the utopian machine's transformative work "may be expected to absorb all that unfreedom into itself, to concentrate it where it can best be worked over and controlled," and by constraining unfreedom in its textual lathe it thereby "allows a whole range of freedoms to flourish outside of itself" (*Seeds* 57). Again, the dual operation of negation and production of possibilities lies at the core of the process.

Throughout his decades of work, Jameson's engagement with Utopia has informed his many cultural and political interventions. His detailed exploration of the utopian problematic has enriched utopian studies by widening the theoretical and historical scope of the project. His analytical matrix (of neutralization and figuration, with its increasingly sharper sense of what is involved in Utopia's active engagement with the historically situated mode of production) has brought greater specificity to our understanding of the nature and operations of Utopia as it is generally understood as "social dreaming" or "the education of desire." As Fitting notes, however, the strong emphasis on *process* is also the source of Jameson's most troubling argument, perhaps especially for those who work within the field of utopian studies.

Fitting puts it this way: "Despite Jameson's contention that literary utopias are a 'type of praxis' rather than a 'mode of representation,' they nonetheless continue to be read and understood as if they were meant to be taken literally, as designs for, or at least images of, a better society" ("Concept" 11). He recalls the long tradition of utopian texts written by authors who intended their then radical content to be taken seriously and adopted as actual alternatives within political or social movements, and he also recaptures the more recent history of many of us who first came to utopian literature because of the politically intriguing, challenging, and empowering content we encountered on its pages. However limited, reductive, or "impoverished" (as suggested in *Marxism and Form*) the content of utopian texts might have been in actual circumstances—and might further be when seen through Jameson's unyielding argument for the larger historical role of the utopian process—utopian subject matter still constitutes a significant contribution to the real work of sociopolitical critique and change, both in initial moments of production and in ongoing reception (including that of utopian studies itself).

With these comments, Fitting admits to falling into a "double bind." He describes his position as one caught between a recognition of the validity of Jameson's argument about the "true vocation" of Utopia, with its privileging of the "critical and negative dimension," and his own reluctance to give up on the recognition of the utopian text's ability to "portray an alternative" that at its radical best can inspire and motivate the collective imagination of the active opposition. He grants that Jameson's focus on the text's critical function "helps us to understand the 'conditions of possibility' of a specific utopian work, and the buried contradictions it is attempting to resolve," but he also argues that "it does not satisfactorily acknowledge the positive aspects which brought us to utopias in the first place. For many of us became interested in literary utopias precisely insofar as they were visions of alternatives" ("Concept" 14).

Although he does not resolve his dilemma, he suggests a resolution by arguing not so much against Jameson but beyond him, in a dialectical twist that incorporates the work of utopian studies as a challenge that can potentially move the entire critical project to another level—one that retains Jameson's sense of "praxis" but actively incorporates the place of utopian content. If a utopia is considered praxis, he argues, "it must be one which like the often cited bust of Apollo in Rilke's sonnet, will force us to acknowledge that 'you must change your life'" ("Concept" 14). In catalyzing radical change, the work of the utopian text lies not only in reminding us of the "insufficiency of our own lives" or in negating or neutralizing ideological contradictions but also in providing social maquettes that explore "the look and feel and shape and experiences of what an alternative might and could actually be, a thought experiment or form of 'social dreaming' . . . which gave us a sense of how our lives could be different and better, not only in our immediate material conditions, but in the sense of an entire world or social system" ("Concept" 14–15).

To be sure, Fitting is not the only one involved in utopian studies to struggle with the question of content in the face of the privileging of function or process that critics such as Levitas and Jameson have called for. In an essay on Charlotte Perkins Gilman, Val Gough argues against my own emphasis on utopian process in the critical utopias; she calls (in the context of her study of Gilman) for an approach to form *and* content that will "marry the two together as intimately as possible."[33] Rather than writing off the substance of a text such as Gilman's, which was purposely intended as a catalyzing blueprint for a new social reality, Gough suggests that if we are fully to grasp the social and political significance of any given text, we cannot ignore its specific content and the specific contestation with the author's historical moment that such content generates. Without such a proper sense of the subject matter, she notes, even the author's creative decisions about formal strategies cannot be fully understood. Although she underestimates my own approach to the content of the critical utopias (as seen in my focus on the texts' direct intervention into debates on political agency and on the relationship between the radical content and the self-reflexive form), she nevertheless makes an important correction that resonates with Fitting's concerns.

Sargent similarly argues for the political use value of utopian content in "The Three Faces of Utopianism Revisited" when he refers to Polak's assertion that it is precisely the overt *images* of the future that keep us from being locked in the present by signifying the possibility of producing an actual future. According to Polak, "We will view human society and culture as being magnetically *pulled* towards a future fulfillment of their own preceding and prevailing, idealistic images of the future, as well as being *pushed* from behind by their own realistic past" (quoted in "Three Faces Revisited" 25). Against Popper's anti-utopian arguments in *The Open Society and Its Enemies,* Sargent notes that Polak regarded Utopia not as a limit to human dignity but rather as an essential motivation for its realization, for he saw Utopia as "a constant mirror held up to the present, showing the faults of contemporary society" ("Three Faces Revisited" 25).

Certainly, Sargent's own position is more nuanced than Polak's. With a contemporary approach that recognizes the influence of the suturing effects of ideology on the social imagination, he prefers to upgrade Polak's utopian mirror to one that is usefully "distorting" as it properly "upsets people because it constantly suggests that the life we lead, the society we have, is inadequate, incomplete, sick" ("Three Faces Revisited" 25). He therefore comes closer to Jameson's position, especially when he invokes the work of Bloch, who upholds Utopia as a "standard by which to judge existing practice" ("Three Faces Revisited" 26).

Jameson's investigations of Utopia and its processes clearly require further development if the question of content is to be adequately dealt with in his critical framework. Given his analysis (with his understanding of the imbrication of ideology and Utopia, his description of the mechanisms of the utopian process, and his recommendations for a critical response), we need to think carefully about our own responses (political as well as pleasurable) to the *manifest* narratives of utopian texts. We need to ask how they can usefully be read without collapsing into ideological compensations of images and stories that will lock in already-known categories. Although I agree with Fitting that this dilemma is not readily resolved, I join him in pointing toward an analysis that can transcend the apparent conflict. The basis for that resolution lies precisely in Jameson's own interpretive method. Recalling that Jameson's critical machine *both* negates *and* transforms Utopia's role in generating "positive images" of "better societies," we should be able to follow how his dialectical moves reveal the utopian process as something other than a static binary opposition between present images and future movement.

Indeed, Jameson himself would be anti-historical and anti-utopian if he simply dismissed, much less undervalued, the substance of utopian narratives and images. But he is right to demand that we consider such content in terms of its ideological traps as well as its utopian potential. Utopias *do* mean what they say, but (as Marx noted) they do so in ideological conditions not of their own choosing. Although they directly, intentionally, counter the prevailing social reality with an alternative content, they ensure the radical force of that content only by means of the mechanics of the text: that is, even as they provide alternatives (often based in extrapolation from oppositional practices of the time), they formally do so by way of an "absent paradigm" that is implicitly *not* of that empirical world but rather one that points through the ideological (re)production of that world, via its content, to a social reality that will be so different it cannot yet be conceptualized but only creatively prefigured.

Utopian content does mean what it says, but it means much more as well, for its signified substance refers not only to its immediate extrapolated referent but also to Utopia's not yet existing referent (the always incomplete achievement of which will redefine the very signifiers themselves). Jameson admits to this complex layering of signification in "World-Reduction in Le Guin" when he appreciates the overt content as a serious thought experiment in a work like *Left Hand of*

Darkness: "One of the most significant potentialities of [sf] as a form is precisely this capacity to provide something like an experimental variation on our own empirical universe; and Le Guin has herself described her invention of Gethenian sexuality along the lines of just such a 'thought experiment' in the tradition of the great physicists" ("World-Reduction" 223).[34]

Even within Jameson's utopian problematic, there is no reason to neglect the relative importance of the content of utopian texts. As Fitting notes, the pedagogical adventure of Utopia most often begins with the popular reception of the alternative world by readers seeking critique and change. Yet the dialectical understanding of the utopian process also demands that scholars take care not only to examine and assess the narratives and images of the literary utopia in the fullness of their relationship with the ideological matrix from which they emerge and with which they contend, but also to investigate the complex influence of the historical situation and the political process on the author's decisions regarding formal strategies. Wherever the analysis begins, the basic relationship of the interaction of social dreaming with the historical moment is one that frames and shapes the entire utopian project. Any utopian object, therefore, is necessarily multifaceted and multilayered. As the critic's gaze moves from text or community, to theoretical argument, to sociopolitical process, back again to text, and ultimately again to history, the underlying charge of that utopian study lies not simply in the quality of the utopian object but also in the way it speaks back to critic and in the larger intellectual and political engagement it stimulates.

In our time especially, as Jameson argued in 1971, the use value of Utopia, in whatever form it takes and in whatever content it advances, lies in its ability to challenge the limitations of "practical thinking" (or what the Frankfurt School calls "instrumental reason") by way of its impossible demands being realistically put into play in the realm of scholarship as well as in the realm of oppositional politics. The utopian idea, therefore, "keeps alive the possibility of a world qualitatively distinct from this one and takes the form of a stubborn negation of all that is" (*Marxism and Form* 111).

Jameson offers his own answer to this question in his response to the essays in *Utopian Studies.*[35] Never rejecting Fitting's revaluation of content, he nonetheless gives a "practical and empirical" reply based in a sober recognition of our historical situation ("Comments" 76). In this period of the triumph of a restructured capitalism, now aiming to copper-fasten its hold on the entire globe in a historical extension of its initial logic, the oppositional project has all too often simply capitulated to the demands of struggles that work only within the limits of the present. A deeper critique and challenge to the logic, structure, and practice of the entire politicoeconomic system has not yet developed; indeed, this related failure, not of Utopia but of the Left, is partly based in the theoretical unwillingness to confront the totality of the system and to ally across identity formations in a diverse yet unified counter-hegemonic alliance that works nationally and internationally.

The result of this withdrawal, this failure, is that a politics of reform, not revolution (now as process, not punctal event) dominates the political terrain. In the face of this standoff, with its "crippling effects on our sense of history and of the future," Jameson suggests that the negative aspect of the utopian process (he points again to Marin) must be on the agenda now more than ever. Unless the ideological absorption and neutralization of anticipation can be broken, the political vision of the Left will lose its radical utopian perspective and be reduced to "local readjustments and corrections (in other words, to what used to be called reforms, as opposed to that systemic transformation that used to be called revolution)" ("Comments" 76).

Thus, the project of utopian studies needs to be careful with its work on content, so as to get beyond a reformist focus on cultural representations of better worlds and look to ones that "explore the structural limits" of the historical transformations that have taken place since the mid- to late 1970s. Jameson's argument is, as usual, not about content as such but about the materially produced "epistemological limits of our current political vision" (in both creative texts and critical interventions, I would add), limits that dangerously include "much that is habitual in the prospect of radical change" itself ("Comments" 76). Again, it is his own method of negation and anticipation that returns in his "answer" to Fitting. Indeed, he incorporates Fitting's assertion of the importance of content in a challenge to hold that unavoidable textual matter to the higher standard of Utopia and not to settle for any local conceptualization (which could well be based on our own "dependencies within the system"). In a rephrasing of his methodological stance, he moves the entire discussion from the register of textual analysis to that of historical engagement, and he ends with the suggestion that both an "anxiety about Utopia" as it is immersed in these times and the continuing practice of "cognitive speculation" need to be exercised in "any [u]topian thinking worthy of the present and its dilemmas" ("Comments" 76–77).

Another way to approach this interrogation of the relationships circulating between and among form, content, consciousness, and effectivity might be found by taking an unlikely excursion through a secularized appropriation of Jewish and Christian theological discourse, since both bodies of thought have wrestled with vexed questions of content and form for centuries and have been taken up, albeit in a nonreligious and mediated fashion, by a number of Marxist thinkers.[36] Considered in Western theological terms, Jameson's position (like Adorno's and Benjamin's) regards utopian content in ways that resemble both Protestant iconoclasm and the Jewish *Bildersverbot*. In both of these theological arguments, naming or imaging the deity is regarded as idolatry or blasphemy. Both assert that such activity cannot authentically lead to the divinity because it diverts the seeker toward an earthly object (the word or image) and away from the divine subject.

In something of an ironic twist, the orthodox Roman Catholic teaching on the nature of the sacraments (in an attitude that, perhaps surprisingly, resonates with Bloch's) holds that the material form of the rite stands as an "outward sign" of an "inward grace": Thus, the cleansing of baptism, the strengthening of confirmation, the encouragement of marriage, the charge of ordination, or the consolation of the dying mean *both* the immediate gesture and a transcendent spiritual reality.[37] As well, in the Roman liturgy of the mass, the central concept of the transubstantiation of physical bread and wine into the spiritual body and blood of Christ (for Catholics it's *real;* for Protestants it's a symbol) is perhaps more to the point of utopian content; for the logic behind the process implies that the primary event of the Eucharist means *both* its own immediate materiality and the presence of a transcendent divinity.

Aided by these seemingly paradoxical but perhaps dialectical distinctions (while further recalling the basis of Western utopian thought in classical and medieval Christian practice and discourse, even when they verged into heresy), Utopia can be seen not simply as a process that names *nothing* or *nowhere* but rather as one that (drawing on dialogic traces of its distant theological roots) posits a quite legitimate name, a precise yet potentially expansive content, that, within the historical circumstances of its generation, refers both to its immediacy and that which is still historically transcendent. As Bloch might put it, the manifest content can unevenly refer to its given conditions of production but can also lead forward to a radically transformed "meaning" that is nonsynchronous with the immediate moment.

Again, this recognition of the relative worth of utopian content resonates with Jameson's claim that the "effectively ideological is also, at the same time necessarily [u]topian." As Fitting suggests, the utopian signifier, the social content, carries its own situated, and quite political, connotation, and yet it is never (in the utopian as opposed to the ideological sense) reducible to that meaning since it is, however powerfully, merely a provisional moment on the way to another, and never fully attainable, meaning. Utopian content, therefore, is perhaps of more *significance* than Jameson and others might be comfortable with. Yet as Jameson himself warns, it is still a significance that cannot be limited to the substance of its own literal expression.

IV.

It was, therefore, no accident that the most recent revival of utopianism in Western and especially Anglo-American societies occurred during the resurgence of progressive and socialist movements after World War II.[38] Within the conditions and contradictions of postwar societies, people struggled on many fronts for a change in the order of things, insisting that the growing wealth and advancing technology be used by and for all and not for the benefit of an elite enriched by an economic and political system that worked only for its own reproduction and extension around the globe. Their demands grew out of the tendencies and latencies of the existing situation and called for its simultaneous destruction and transformation into a radically alternative way of producing and reproducing social reality. Utopia was implicitly at the core of this call, negating what was in the name of what was desired, anticipated, and fought for.

Along with the utopian motivations and expressions came the knowledge and understanding articulated within the intellectual project of utopian studies. With one foot in traditional scholarship on utopianism (especially in departments of literature, philosophy, and political science) and another in new work aligned with the opposition (from African American studies to women's studies, as well as cultural studies), the "field" of utopian studies has from its early days incorporated detailed scholarship with engaged intervention (though varying with each person and contribution). Thus, the critical utopias, Jameson's exploration of the utopian problematic, and utopian studies simultaneously enter North American culture along separate avenues in the late 1960s and early 1970s but almost immediately converge in the new cultural, intellectual, and political counter-space.

This powerful utopian matrix is a testimony to the overall strength of the political opposition of the postwar years. As the critical utopias signify, the success of the movement was mainly in the realm of culture and cultural politics. Working within the contradictions of the growing economy, the radical challenges to constructed, reified, exploited, controlled, repressed, suppressed subjectivity that robbed people not only of their own democratic agency but also of their specific identities and their unique desires and pleasures were advancements in the larger social revolution. The new utopias that not only critiqued and offered alternatives to the economic and political systems but also challenged the cultural milieu worked at the leading edge of this opposition.

To recall the traditional Marxist suspicion of imaginary utopian solutions to real historical circumstances, however, this utopian moment could also be seen negatively as a force for compensation. Although the cultural sphere was a site of radical challenge and change, the struggle to overturn a capitalist economy and the military-industrial complex of an imperialist and bureaucratic state was not only not successful but roundly defeated by the 1980s. In this light, a critic such as Levitas properly questions the progressive spin given to the critical utopian moment. In her critique of *Demand the Impossible,* for example, she acknowledges the "shift of the locus of opposition into the realm of culture," yet she sees this not as the opening of a new level of struggle but rather as "something of a last resort" for the political project (*Concept* 172–174, 196). Thus, the creation of a utopian literature that works only at the level of cultural contestation is to be questioned for its willingness to settle for criticism and not change. In this perspective the utopian moment's very strength also betrays its weakness.

And yet as it was caught without a way forward on the political-economic terrain, the work of the Left persisted within the economically and politically valorized cultural register. No longer regarding culture as part of a reflective superstructure (seeing it instead as a relatively autonomous material dimension of an overdetermined system), the Left made great advances on the cultural front (including feminist and ecological tendencies), and social dreaming was at its core.[39] As Levitas argues, this broad cultural project verged on compensation for what was not actually achieved; however, its radical utopian praxis actually changed not just individual lives but the systems-practices-discourses of everyday life. As a counter-space was created, if only for-a-while (as Russ might put it), it marked a substantive achievement, a net gain, a concrete utopian moment—the political influence of which carries into the progressive struggles of today. Within this larger cultural initiative (bolstered by its own organizations, conferences, journals, and, more recently, Internet networks, and growing in numbers of interested students and scholars), the scholarly work of utopian studies managed not only to survive the conservative restoration and the economic and political devastation of the 1980s and 1990s but actually to enter the new century with a greater degree of intellectual and organizational strength.[40]

Despite the flourishing of scholarship, however, utopian expression itself has declined since the 1980s. Intentional communities have diminished in numbers, the revival of the literary utopia has come and gone, and utopian political thought has been co-opted and devalued. In Fitting's words, "few would dispute the link between utopian writing—or its absence—and the larger social and political context in which we now live" ("Concept" 15). Although lingering utopian enclaves can be found in communities that have beaten the historical odds (such as Twin Oaks and The Farm) and although Kim Stanley Robinson's sf continues the tradition of utopian narrative (refunctioned yet again), the leaner and meaner world of the 1980s and 1990s was marked by anti-utopian deprivation rather than utopian achievement. Progressive and socialist gains, fought for since the 1930s, were rolled back, taken back, or simply crushed by a reenergized capitalist system, and the loosely united Left opposition fractured and splintered. Survival (at best for the sake of fighting another day, at worst in co-optation and capitulation) rather than radical social dreaming and hard political organizing characterized the ambience of the Left. In these times the historical force of Utopia was severely challenged by the reactionary rise of Anti-Utopia.

Indeed, in *Seeds of Time,* Jameson identifies the antinomic relationship between Utopia and Anti-Utopia as a key diagnostic relationship by which the contradictions of the current conjuncture can be symptomatically tracked and, more so, dealt with.[41] Throughout modernity (as Sargent, Levitas, and others have demonstrated), the anti-utopian persuasion has systematically worked to silence and destroy Utopia, but Utopia (which Jameson describes in *Seeds* as the "goal of all change") has always offered a way to work against and beyond these attacks. Still (as will be evident in the next chapter), this fundamental opposition has intensified since the 1980s as Utopia's "many contemporary critics and enemies . . . try today even more enthusiastically than in earlier periods to persuade us to agree that this is indeed the best of all possible worlds" (*Seeds* 8).

Jameson therefore suggests that this fundamental tension has taken on a more complex and perhaps greater importance now that the cultural machinery of a restructured capitalism endeavors to appropriate Utopia as its own. In this shift, he argues, the antinomic opposition has both intensified and collapsed, for now what is Anti-Utopia torques into Utopia and what were once antitheses have for the moment at least turned out to be "the same" (*Seeds* 7). On the one hand, the renewed culture of the market (with its desire finally to become global) claims the achievement of Utopia even as it condemns the term itself to the oblivion of the historical trash heap. On the other, popular utopian desires for a just and free society lurk within the depths of such anti-utopian manifestations as the right-wing movements against government and for the family (while a once strong and courageous Left settles for defensive and pragmatic positions within the current system).[42] On this contested ground, it becomes difficult to locate Utopia, much less to tap its radical force for the revival of the project of critique and change.

Facing these terrible times, Fitting pulls back from his concern with the political power of utopian content and revalues Jameson's insistence on the place of negation in the utopian process, a step all the more necessary at the moment. To describe what he suggests is a timely "pre-utopian" project, he cites Jameson's comments on "the new onset of the utopian process"—presented in the context of the discussion of socialist utopias in *Seeds* as a "kind of desiring to desire, a learning to desire, the invention of the desire called Utopia in the first place, along with new rules for the fantasizing or daydreaming of such a thing" (*Seeds* 90). As with the invention of utopian narrative in the 1500s or its critical reconfiguration in the 1970s, the current situation calls for yet another transformation of the ways in which Utopia is spoken or enacted.

Thus, as Jameson puts it, the production of "a set of narrative protocols with no precedent in our previous literary institutions (even if they will have to come to terms somehow with our previous literary or narrative habits)" is needed if Utopia is to slip through the ideological net that has now incorporated so much of its own matter and form (*Seeds* 90). Jameson's own search for refunctioned utopian expressions has led him to a variety of cultural phenomena, ranging from Rem Koolhaas's architecture to the "immense heterotopia of China itself" (*Seeds* xviii), and many of us in sf and utopian studies have acknowledged the stubborn utopian quality of Robinson's sf, especially in the shift from what could be called the last critical utopia of *Pacific Edge* (1990) to the new utopian narratives of the Martian trilogy (1992–1996) and *Antarctica* (1998).

But another direction for new utopian work has emerged in the revival in the 1980s of the inverted complement of eutopia, the dystopia. Although it does not offer the radical break with utopian narrative that Jameson's more modernist sensibility calls for, within the realm of popular culture the dystopian imagination has nevertheless attracted writers (and filmmakers) who seek a formal strategy that speaks to the moment without abandoning utopian contestation. For those who are unwilling to capitulate to an unqualified triumphalism or a static cynicism, this implicitly unsettled narrative opens onto the continuum of utopian and anti-utopian contestation without necessarily falling into either camp. Unlike the "unprecedented" forms Jameson seeks, these new dystopian narratives work within the shell of the old utopian aesthetic as it plays out in the familiar discursive universe of sf. In doing so, however, these revived and transformed variants come to terms with Utopia's "previous literary or narrative habits" in ways that supersede their potentially compromised status within contemporary culture.

As I argue in Chapter 6, the new dystopias (named "critical dystopias") embody the antinomic opposition of Utopia and Anti-Utopia not only in their manifest content but also in their formal strategies. All resist the anti-utopian subversion of Utopia that can occur within dystopian narrative, but some open out to minimal utopian possibilities that are perhaps not even prefiguratively available; yet others offer new utopian trajectories against a seemingly overwhelming world system that is striving to achieve its historical goal of total external and internal exploitation of humanity and nature.

Thus, in the shadow of the mid-1980s publication of one of the last "classical" dystopias (Margaret Atwood's *Handmaid's Tale*) and the edgy nouveaux narratives of cyberpunk (William Gibson's *Neuromancer*), several sf writers took the utopian imagination into a "dystopian turn" that explored and negotiated closed and terrifying worlds that—as the line in the film *Max Headroom* (Morton and Jankel 1985) had it—were no more than "twenty minutes" into our own dangerous future. From works such as Robinson's *Gold Coast* (1988) to Piercy's *He, She and It* (1991) and the series begun by Octavia Butler in *The Parable of the Sower* (1993), a discernible and critical dystopian movement emerged within contemporary science fiction and film that at its best reached toward Utopia not by delineation of fully detailed better places but by dropping in on decidedly worse places and tracking the moves of a dystopian citizen as she or he becomes aware of the social hell and—in one way or another, and not always successfully—contends with that diabolical place while moving toward a better alternative, which is often found in the recesses of memory or the margins of the dominant culture.

Underlying my discussion of this dystopian turn is a concern for the ways in which this cultural intervention helps to register and track the possibility of what Jameson calls the "absent first step of renewed praxis" (*Seeds* 71). In many respects the question for Utopia in our time is a political one, but the answer is hardly evident. As Wegner puts it, "when politics itself has apparently been relocated to the utopian horizon—part not of the here-and-now, but rather of some as-of-yet unimaginable future," the political processes required for the next contestation with the hegemonic system are themselves not clearly evident and therefore necessarily become part of what is examined in the speculative thought experiments of "utopian figuration" ("Horizons" 70). In the face of the ubiquity and inequity of the system and the debilitation of the opposition, how are political anger and utopian anticipation to move forward? In the face of corporate triumph and social democratic capitulation to market logic, how are working people in all their diversity to challenge, much less change, a world system that continues to benefit a small yet privileged portion of the population? Or, simply, what is to be done, and how can Utopia help?

This pressing search for the new directions of political action and strategy, however, needs an analysis adequate to the task. The question therefore is one for a refunctioned macropolitics, not simply the micropolitics that were so crucial in the 1980s. Without a larger scope of analysis and an alliance of movements to carry the work forward, the totalizing forces of capital will continue to divide, coopt, and conquer. In short, the challenge for Utopia in this anti-utopian moment is not only the exploration and anticipation of new types of radical agency but also the production of cognitive maps of the system itself. Along with other, perhaps less immediately recognizable utopian expressions, the new dystopian narratives offer one avenue for the necessary tracking and testing of these new maps of hell and possible paths through them.

In the early years of a new century, we do well to remind ourselves that the conditions for moving forward are not to be found in some idealized future but are with us in the very societies in which we live. Perhaps now (after the historical, political, cultural, and theoretical convulsions of the last two decades of the twentieth century), we are in a position to do more about the project of critique and change. Despite the attempted englobement of turn-of-the-century capital, the potential for resistance and transformation still exists. Utopia still matters—though it may do so in forms and venues not previously recognized. Wherever it arises, however, Utopia's promise will rise out of the conditions in which we live and not in some idealized past or future. As Daniel Singer puts it in his 1999 political analysis, *Whose Millennium? Theirs or Ours?*, "our society contains the elements of its *potential* transformation, and in this interaction of the existing and the possible—a possibility perceived realistically, but lying beyond the confines of our society—lies the burden of our responsibility and the mainspring of political action."[43] How the creative negativity of dystopia sheds its own modest light on this process is my own next step.

Part Two

Dystopia

4

New Maps of Hell

It is a truism that one of the most revealing indexes to the anxieties of our age is the great flood of works like Zamyatin's We, *Huxley's* Brave New World, *and Orwell's* Nineteen Eighty-Four. *Appalling in their similarity, they describe nightmare states where men are conditioned to obedience, freedom is eliminated, and individuality crushed; where the past is systematically destroyed and men are isolated from nature; where science and technology are employed, not to enrich human life, but to maintain the state's surveillance and control of its slave citizens.*

—MARK HILLEGAS, *THE FUTURE AS NIGHTMARE* (3)

I.

Published in 1909, E. M. Forster's story "The Machine Stops" reminds us that it is literary utopia's shadow, the dystopia, that most often flourished in that the twentieth century.[1] Before Yevgeny Zamyatin's critique of the Soviet state in *We* (1924), Aldous Huxley's critique of consumer capitalism in *Brave New World* (1932), and well before the cautionary despair of George Orwell's *Nineteen Eighty-Four* (1949), Forster wrote against the grain of an emergent modernity.[2] In his portrayal of a totalizing administration that "mechanizes" every dimension of daily life (from the organization of nature and industry to the standardization of the person), he develops an abstract yet critical account of the new social spacetime of the twentieth century. Yet even as he foregrounds his apocalyptic horror at the unraveling of the world he knows, he clings, at least in his closing paragraphs, to the prophetic possibility that one day humanity will again prevail. He grounds his narrative in a familiar satiric tradition, but he also draws on the more detailed systemic accounts of utopian narratives by way of an inversion that focuses on the terrors rather than the hopes of history. Although his perspective is based in a residual romantic humanism that collapses all the dimensions of modernity into the single mystifying trope of the Machine (with its anti-urban and anti-technology connotations), he nevertheless mounts his critique in a fictive form that, in other hands, will take on the emerging world produced by the constantly mutating capitalist system (organized in Forster's time by the twin regimes of monopoly capitalism and imperialism) in a more concrete and dialectical fashion.

Forster's story therefore stands as an early example of the dystopian maps of social hells that have been with us ever since. As a work that predates the readerly protocols of popular science fiction, "The Machine Stops" initiates its own audience by means of a narrator who invites readers into the strange world of the text. With an opening tone that is closer to the "once upon a time" rubric of the fairy tale, the narrator's words ("*Imagine*, if *you* can") bridge the gap between the author's/reader's environment and the world of the story. Having issued the invitation, the narrator launches into another familiar move with a tour of the world conducted in the mode of the traditional utopian novel, situating the narrator as the guide and the reader as the visitor. As the travelogue progresses, the narrator's voice fades and the action in the alternative world takes over. But the voiceover recurs with occasional commentary until the crisis at the end of the tale calls it back to a more direct and politically charged role.

The iconic construction of this alternative world opens on a primal site, a private room buried deep in the Earth. The ideological distance between Forster's historical moment and the elsewhere of the text is immediately measured by the shape and nature of the room. Hexagonal and evocative of a cell in a beehive, it recalls that image most often associated with expressions that register the supposed loss of individuality in the face of a modernizing collectivism (in this case one that is but technologically "modern," not yet communist nor consumerist). The room is fully and efficiently functional with its "soft radiance," "melodious sounds," and fresh air, yet it lacks the everyday familiarity of lamps, windows, or instruments of sound. The textual estrangement changes pitch as the narrator introduces the lone occupant of the room: "a swaddled lump of flesh—a woman" (41). With this enclosure and its quasi-human inhabitant, the narrator establishes the suppressed space and subjectivity of this other world, and dialogue begins as the swaddled woman, Vashti, rolls across the room in her mechanized chair to answer a communication from her son, Kuno.

A misfit, with a strong body and inquiring mind in a society where strenuous activity and inductive thought are discouraged, Kuno disturbs his mother with the unusual request that she travel halfway around the globe to visit him. With this second invitation of the text, what will become a typical dystopian conflict between the established order and the potential dissident begins. Kuno wants Vashti to see him, but "not through the Machine . . . not through the wearisome Machine" (42). Bristling at his seeming apostasy, Vashti (like some resistant reader) urges him to desist, but Kuno counters by suggesting that his mother (who, like others in this "mechanical" society, is quite secular) has paradoxically made a god of the Machine. He reminds her that the now pervasive and ruling mechanism was initially produced by humans, and he asserts that the "Machine is much but it is not everything," implying that more can lie beyond this enclosed reality. "Pay me a visit," he insists, "so that we can meet face to face, and talk about the hopes that are in my mind" (42).

Vashti refuses, for she hates physical movement and fears that her time—in this quantified, measured, controlled system—will be wasted. With her pasty white skin covering a toothless and hairless body, she is a perfectly constructed subject of the automated society. Open only to the pleasures of a ten-minute lecture, seeking "ideas" that never connect with the things of the material or historical world, entrapped by an imposed agoraphobia, she signs off and resumes her life. Here, however, Forster's romantic humanism and privileged individualism take the story through its next turn as Vashti thinks back to her son's birth (45). Motivated by some inherent sense of a "universal" mother-son bond, Vashti recalls her son's "queer temper" (remembering as well, in an echo of Forster's valorization of the individual, that there "had been something special about all her children") and then reconsiders his insistent plea, with its hint that "something tremendous might happen" (45). Out of some unexplained maternal bond catalyzed by the unfamiliar opportunity to break out of the unacknowledged boredom of her existence, she agrees to make the journey to the Northern Hemisphere.

The travelogue jumps beyond the room when Vashti begins her unusual trip. Living in spaces identical to Vashti's, the entire population is physically isolated in standardized hexagonals yet linked in constant communication with one another. As the narrator, working from some other timescape, comments: "Few travelled in these days, for, thanks to the advance of science, the earth was exactly alike all over" (46). Direct experience has been all but eliminated, and connection with human bodies—except for mandatory reproduction—is discouraged. A mechanically efficient system developed by the human-built Machine now manages all the affairs of the global society. Originally produced to serve humanity (who finally had "harnessed Leviathan"), the Machine (like the artificial intelligences of later sf tales and films) has come into its own and now manages its makers. With a Central Committee of human administrators to serve it through the authority of the Book of the Machine, the Machine, as a mystified prefiguration of the bureaucratic state and monopoly capitalism, hums endlessly and ubiquitously around a globe that is now but an extension of its own system.

Experiencing the discomforts of motion and human interaction, fighting off "physical repulsion and longing to be once more under the surface of the earth," the diminished Vashti arrives at Kuno's room. Kuno tells her that he has been threatened with "Homelessness," or exile to the planetary surface. As the punishment handed out by the Machine to those who pursue "illegal, unmechanical" activities, forced removal from the womblike security of the interior world is generally assumed to be a death sentence, for in the official Machine version the victim is sent up without a respirator and is "exposed to the air, which kills him" (49, 47, 50). Kuno explains that the Machine has tracked the trips he has taken to the surface and accordingly issued him with the warning. Vashti is surprised at this response, since travel to the surface is not illegal—in fact it is "perfectly mechanical," though rarely done. Kuno, however, admits that he acted—apparently all too freely for the Machine's disciplinary requirements—without an "Egression-permit" and reached the surface without taking the usual pathway through the "vomitories," finding his own way through old ventilator shafts (50).

At this point the conflict between the dystopian society and the social misfit intensifies as Kuno explains why and how he took up the quest that has led to his imperiled situation and to his even more dangerous conclusions about the Machine. From birth, Kuno has been a marginal subject in this streamlined society. Endowed with unusual bodily strength (a quality no longer needed in a mechanized population), he barely avoided immediate extermination, and when he applied to father a child, the Machine rejected him since, as the narrator explains, he was not a "type that the Machine desired to hand on" (51). As he matured, his atypical strength led him to develop a muscular humanism (for Forster's contemporaries, a quality recognized in the culture of British private schools) that continued to distract him from pursuing a "normal" existence in this place of isolated rooms and settled lives. Untypically as well, he remained in touch with his birth mother, and he also insisted on thinking beyond the approved and simplified "ideas" that had come to shape the social discourse. Always already different, he worked from that difference to explore and think about the world on his own terms and accordingly to be horrified at what he found.

Kuno tells Vashti that he began to shift from his first erratic musings to more direct action by "walking up and down the platform of the railway outside" his room and thereby recapturing the relational meanings of "Near" and "Far" (50, 51). After this initial exploration, he was unable to rest content with where and how he lived. He strengthened his body with a regime of exercise and began to broaden his investigation of the tunnels. Moving further into the underground labyrinth, he eventually came to a ladder that led upward to the surface. Reborn on his own terms rather than expelled by the Machine, he crawled onto the surface and felt his face bathed in sunshine. Ironically (provincially for Forster and his immediate readers), he realized, from old lectures, that he was in "Wessex," the name for "an important state" that was located above his subterranean room. Exploring the area, he momentarily forgot about the Machine, but at sunset he found that his respirator had run down (drained by the Machine in its calibrated surveillance) and he had to struggle back to his underground room.

At this point Kuno's recollection becomes confused as he relates his fight against something he thought were white worms (but that the narrator later identifies as extensions of the Machine's Mending Apparatus). Anxious about breathing without his respirator, he was dragged away by the worms, yet just before he was knocked unconscious in the tussle, he cast his eye on the stars above him, in a night he had never seen. Later he mysteriously awoke in his room. The "worms" had done their sanitizing work, but Kuno was left with dangerous memories of an anomalous experience.

Driven by his unusual physical-psychic qualities and armed with a new sense of spatial differentiation and scale, Kuno continues to assert his agency by enhancing his cognitive map of his personal space and the space of his society. In doing so, he embodies Forster's own residual values as he proves by his independent activity that the proper measure of humankind is not the Machine. He shares the results of his renegade mapping when he tells his mother that the people of their world have "lost the sense of space": "We say 'space is annihilated,' but we have annihilated not space, but the sense thereof. We have lost a part of ourselves" (50).

Vashti, however, is appalled by this account. She is unable to see the "idea" in it and regrets making her journey, clinging to the "truth" of the many lectures she has heard and rejecting Kuno's account. Kuno responds passionately to her recalcitrance and gives her a very different explanation of their society's fate:

> Cannot you see, cannot all your lecturers see, that it is we who are dying, and that down here the only thing that really lives is the Machine? We created the Machine, to do our will, but we cannot make it do our will now. It has robbed us of our sense of space and of the sense of touch, it has blurred every human relation and narrowed down love to a carnal act, it has paralysed our bodies and our wills, and now it compels us to worship it. The Machine develops—but not on our lines. The Machine proceeds—but not to our goal. (54)

Despite Kuno's critique and her maternal concern, Vashti can only wearily conclude that her son's adventure will end in Homelessness. In response, Kuno wishes that he would be exiled so he could live on the surface, but Vashti recalls the official myth of the "Great Rebellion," when rebels were cast out of the vomitories to die, with their bones left visible for the "edification" of the population (56). She reminds Kuno of the received social wisdom that no one can survive on the surface: "Ferns and a little grass may survive, but all higher forms have perished" (56). No airship, no lecturer has ever reported signs of surviving Homeless populations, she says. Kuno, however, challenges the official ideology and reports that with his own eyes he saw a Homeless woman, symbolically in "the twilight," who was unluckily killed by the same "worms" that attacked him. Full of anger, he again tries to convince his mother, but Vashti is too immersed in the whole way of life of her society and can only revert to the security of her isolated and isolating room.

Unlike Vashti, the Machine does listen carefully to Kuno, and in the years following this minor individual exploit, the feedback mechanisms of the Machine, the Mending Apparatus, make two major changes to suppress further independent exploration. The first is the abolition of respirators and the removal of terrestrial travel motors, making it (apparently) impossible to travel on the surface. A few lecturers mildly object to being denied their rightful access to their subject matter, but most people go along with the decision. In an early indicator of intellectual complicity and consumerist passivity, the "advanced thinkers," including Vashti, pave the way for the Machine's action by arguing that direct observation is foolish since the gramophone and cinematophote give them all they need. By this decree, the Machine reinforces the ideological direction it has already taken in establishing the intellectual and geographical boundaries of the society.

In a version of what will later develop into a critique, by the Frankfurt School and others, of modern capitalism's mass-mediated and commodified culture, one of the "most advanced" thinkers unreflexively sums up the accepted epistemology: "Beware of first-hand ideas. . . . First-hand ideas do not really exist. They are but the physical impressions produced by love and fear, and on this gross foundation who could erect a philosophy? Let your ideas be second-hand, and if possible tenth-hand, for then they will be far removed from that disturbing element—direct observation" (57). By fostering this simplifying discourse, the Machine instrumentally reduces knowledge to reified quanta that people "may employ most profitably" in their daily lives. Ideas no longer come from things or thinkers but rather *become* things that are unproductively juxtaposed, playing out in an endless series of antinomies: "In time," the thinker proudly asserts, "there will come a generation that has got beyond facts, beyond impressions, a generation absolutely colourless, a generation 'seraphically free/From taint of personality,' which will see the French Revolution not as it happened, nor as they would like it to have happened, but as it would have happened, had it taken place in the days of the Machine" (57).

Knowledge and action are thereby further reduced to the service of the Machine. Thinkers settle into lives of complaisant reflection on reflections, and the general population is relieved to become even more passive, to be free not only from labor but also from curiosity. Then, building on the abolition of travel and consequently of critical exploration and thought, the Machine implements its second disciplinary correction by reestablishing religion and encouraging its status as god. Again, the population simply accepts the transcoding of the Book of the Machine from an operations manual to a holy text and obediently praises the apotheosis of the Machine, as it changes from the material motor of the society into its creator. In a farcical twist on Feuerbach, the daily activities that are already "machinelike" in their repetitive efficiency segue into ritual acts. People describe "the strange feeling of peace that came over them when they handled the Book of the Machine, the pleasure that it was to repeat certain numerals out of it, however little meaning those numerals conveyed to the outward ear, the ecstasy of touching a button, however unimportant, or of ringing an electric bell, however superfluously" (58).

In a mechanical great awakening, religious fervor sweeps the population, and a form of doublethink that Orwell will later expose in a fuller critique is readily accepted. Paradoxically regarded as "the creation and the implement of man," the Machine assumes the mantle of divinity (58). Indeed, a variety of religions coalesce around the Machine as some venerate its "blue optic plates," others its Mending Apparatus ("which *sinful* Kuno had compared to worms," the narrator cynically reveals), still others the elevators, and others the Book itself (58, my emphasis). Those who cannot hold to even a minimalist "undenominational Mechanism" live in danger of persecution and the familiar charge of Homelessness (58).

At this point the distant narrator intervenes to make clear that these changes were not made by the managers of the Central Committee: "They were no more the cause of them than were the kings of the imperialistic period the cause of war" (58). Instead, the narrator (and Forster) locates the source of power and discipline in the systemic logic of the Machine that gradually alienates its own creators from themselves, turning them from inventive agents to reified cogs in its own expanding mechanism. As bureaucratic announcer of events, the Central Committee merely yields to "some invincible pressure, which came no one knew whither, and which, when gratified, was succeeded by some new pressure equally invincible" (58). The Machine's intervention is therefore received as another sign of "progress," and daily life once more resumes its repetitive, servile pattern. The narrator sums it up: "Year by year [the Machine] was served with increased efficiency and decreased intelligence. The better a man knew his own duties upon it, the less he understood the duties of his neighbour, and in all the world there was not one who understood the monster as a whole" (58).

In the "success" of the Machine, however, lies the material contradiction that will crack open the social equilibrium it has established. Without self-directed administrative "master brains" that could intelligently grasp the *totality* of the society as it has come to be constructed by the Machine, the ability to recognize and repair the systemic malfunctions steadily diminishes. After instrumentally rationalizing and standardizing all aspects of daily life, having automated not only the functions of production but also reproduction and maintenance, the Machine (as with the humans who made it and lost their place in the previous set of contradictions) has created the conditions for its own destruction. The dialectics of the situation become clear as a series of problems gradually leads to the "final disaster" (58).

In these failing conditions, Kuno resumes contact with his mother. Speaking without visualizing his image on the screen, "out of the darkness" and with "solemnity," Kuno delivers his prophetic message: "The Machine stops. . . . The Machine is stopping, I know it, I know the signs" (59). Refusing the passivity of the master thinkers but working from a totalizing analysis (now an empowering one, based on observation and critique), Kuno has been able to chart the "progress" of the Machine and identify the moment of its breakdown. True to Forster's abstract analysis and undifferentiated fear of collective behavior, however, it is only this singular misfit who has torn open the ideological veil of the system that was created and represented by the Machine and the humans who built and then capitulated to it.

As Kuno predicts, small breakdowns begin to occur, slowly permeating the society like the plagues of Egypt. Music transmissions are interrupted, and the steady hum of the Machine is occasionally broken by slight jarring noises. Fruit turns moldy; bathwater stinks; poetry machines emit "defective rhymes" (60). Each problem is "bitterly complained of at first, and then acquiesced in and forgotten. Things went from bad to worse unchallenged" (60). When the sleeping apparatus falters, however, the signs of incremental breakdown can no longer be ignored. In a system wherein compliant people are the necessary components, disruption of sleep becomes the physical contradiction that cannot be corrected. As the narrator puts it, "from it we may date the collapse of humanity" (60). The committees in charge of the problem are "assailed by complainants," and discontent grows, "for mankind was not yet sufficiently adaptable to do without sleeping" (60).

Yet the negative reaction again subsides as people assume that someone is "meddling with the Machine" or someone "is trying to make himself king, to reintroduce the personal element" (60). In the type of displacement made possible by conspiracy theories and witch-hunts, the population refuses to see the overall situation in which the Machine has produced the conditions of its own destruction. They call instead for vengeance to those who are suspected of subverting the Machine.

The response of the Committee of the Mending Apparatus offers a rare moment of honesty as the need for serious repair is finally acknowledged by the last technicians on the globe. But from the moment of their inability to act, despair sets in. This negation or destruction of the ruling system, however, offers little in the way of liberation for the population. Revolution in the face of systemic crisis is not an option, for such a collective negation of the negation is no longer possible in a population that has been reduced to physically and intellectually static monads. All that occurs is a social whimper, and even that is stifled by those still willing to be patient with the Machine as it tries to repair itself. The plagues increase in severity as the system-generated euthanasia program ceases to end the lives of the old and sick. Lighting fades. The air is fouled. "Loud were the complaints, impotent the remedies," the narrator reports (61). Still, in the midst of these disasters, some remain loyal and passive. Emptied of their humanity, they cling to the compensatory belief that the Machine, as a transcendent yet secular deity, will continue after all people have died.

The literal and social twilight grows. Hysteria and panic rise with it. Some suggest the reactionary solution of a "provisional dictatorship," some pragmatically try to repair power stations, but most revert to the empty comforts of praying to the Machine. Finally, "there came a day when, without the slightest warning, without any previous hint of feebleness, the entire communication-system broke down, all over the world, and the world, as they understood it, ended" (61). With this apocalyptic moment, the ever present hum of the Machine stops, and everyone is encased in a silence never before experienced. The ubiquitous mechanical presence is absent. The underlying support that sutured the population into a compliant whole (there is the suggestion that the hum produced an actual psychophysical effect) is gone forever. Many are killed outright by instant deprivation. Others go mad. Vashti barely keeps her senses and looks out of her room to see people screaming, whimpering, fighting—all in a "silence which is the voice of the earth and of the generations who have gone" (62). The silence, she realizes, is far worse than her long-standing solitude. She retreats inside her room and awaits the final collapse: "And at last the final horror approached—light began to ebb, and she knew that civilisation's long day was closing" (61).

In these closing moments, the setting and perspective of the tale subtly but radically changes. The narrator's voice returns in the direct address, marked again by first-person pronouns and a commentary that is no longer the apparently detached description of the body of the story. In a voice that is now speculative and evaluative, the narrator reports that Vashti escaped, but escaped in a way that alters the nature of the story itself: for Vashti "escaped in the spirit: at least so it seems to *me, ere my meditation* closes. That she escaped in the body—*I cannot perceive that*" (62, my emphasis).

With the shift from third-person description to first-person judgment, the narrator's framing stance as well as its historical distance from the society of the Machine is reestablished with a narrative tone that takes on the quality of a cautionary parable. In the narrator's closing words, Vashti is reunited with her son, but now on a spiritual or transhistorical plane. Released from the material contradictions of their society, the two of them weep for humanity but "not for themselves" (62). Somehow they find the inner resources to cling to life for a while longer (whether through the residually "human" quality of the mother-son bond or in the larger persistence of a universal human nature). In an intrinsically humanist gesture, "their hearts were opened, and they knew what had been important on the earth" (62).

Reporting from its estranged, and privileged, perspective, the narrator sums up the historic convulsion in biblical tones: humanity "was dying, strangled in the garments [it] had woven" (63). Human toil throughout the ages had produced the "garment" of the social, "heavenly at first, shot with the colours of culture, sewn with the threads of self-denial"; but then this socially produced (mechanically produced) garment becomes more than a covering for the human soul and body and is no longer able to be shed at will. The *essential* humanity of the naked body and the soul it encompasses gradually fades. Vashti and Kuno, the narrator notes, weep for this ultimate "sin against the body . . . the centuries of wrong against the muscles and the nerves, and those five portals by which we can alone apprehend" (63). Implicitly, modernity, with its theories of evolution and its mechanisms of production and consumption, has selected for a human body that is now nothing more than "white pap, the home of . . . [the] last sloshy stirrings of a spirit that had grasped the stars" (63).

Now fully present, the narrator ends the tale with an account of the last exchange between mother and son. Vashti asks Kuno if there is any hope, and he replies that there is none for them. A pair of humanist ghosts, they touch, kiss, and await their end. In their death, however, they recapture the memory of humanity (through Forster's backward-looking evocation of the way "it was in Wessex, when Aelfrid overthrew the Danes"), but they also manage a look forward to the hint of a utopian horizon of hope emerging from the collapsing society, for the negation of the negation of the Machine society can come only from the collectivity of the Homeless who have been ejected through the years.

At this moment the tone has clearly shifted from the apocalyptic to the prophetic, if not yet the historical. In a revelation that the narrator did not offer during the body of the story, Kuno is allowed to report that he has seen these survivors, "spoken to them, loved them." He can only assume that they are waiting, "hiding in the mist and the ferns until our civilization stops," in a new amalgam of noble savage and educated dissident that may one day claim its own agency (63). Refusing to accept Vashti's pessimistic assertion that "some fool will start the Machine again, to-morrow," Kuno asserts that humanity "has learnt its lesson" and that its next step will be taken by these outcasts on the surface (63). From this enclave of exiles (the explorers, thinkers, and dissidents of the old society), a new society could possibly emerge in the next turn of history.

In the closing paragraph, as an airship crashes into a ruined wharf, Vashti and Kuno look out at the "nations of the dead," but they also see a figure of hope at the literal horizon, as the last words of the tale have it, in the "scraps of the untainted sky" (63). Of course, those closing words are the narrator's, the reporter whose own location is ambiguous but who is clearly *elsewhere*. On the one hand, in a proto–science fictional vein that privileges the absent paradigm of the alternative world, the narrator could be taken as a representative of the society subsequently rebuilt by the Homeless and one of the post-revolutionary subjects of a new era reporting on a key moment in its own history. Or remaining within the older sensibility of satire, the voice could be understood as a secular prophet speaking from the heart of the modern serpent. Joining both possibilities in a new dialogic tension at work within a familiar anti-utopian form, the story emerges as new literary mutation, not an anti-utopia but a dystopia that speaks eloquently and effectively to its times.

II.

Looking forward from 1909, dystopian narrative developed in several directions throughout the rest of the century. Forster's story and, more famously, the novels by Zamyatin, Huxley, and Orwell came to typify the "classical" or canonical form of this inverted subgenre of utopia.[3] In a more diffused manner, works that shared the cultural ambience of the dystopian imagination (though sometimes with ambiguity or irony) appeared on the realist or modernist margins of mainstream fiction. These include titles as varied and contradictory as Jack London's *Iron Heel* (1908), Karel Capek's *War with the Newts* (1937), Gore Vidal's *Messiah* (1953), Evelyn Waugh's *Love Among the Ruins* (1953), Vladimir Nabokov's *Bend Sinister* (1947) and *Invitation to a Beheading* (1959), and William Golding's *Lord of the Flies* (1964).[4] Albeit in a more popular direction, a clear dystopian tendency developed within science fiction, and this resulted in the "new maps of hell," as Kingsley Amis called them, that appeared after World War II and continues in the sf of recent years.[5]

Contrary to this broad dystopian tendency, with its complex relationship to the utopian impulse, a variety of "anti-utopian" texts has paralleled these works throughout the century. Along with fiction as different as *The Napoleon of Notting Hill* by G. K. Chesterton (1904), *Anthem* by Ayn Rand (1938), and *That Hideous Strength* by C. S. Lewis (1945), anti-utopian nonfiction (from Lewis's challenge to modernity's control of the human spirit to Friedrich von Hayek's refusal of central planning and Karl Popper's critique of utopian thinking itself) has steadily attacked and refused Utopia and all that its authors claim for it.[6]

The critical analysis of these shadowy variants of utopian writing developed with less precision than that seen in the postwar work on science fictional and utopian texts. Although responses to individual works and to the thematic patterns and political positions produced by various sets of texts addressed the social imaginary represented in these works, a more detailed examination of their formal operations evolved more slowly. Clarity of terms and categories was often frustrated by a tendency to reduce dystopian and anti-utopian texts to a single "anti-utopian" category, and the conflation of textual expressions with the social processes of the utopian impulse (or its historical opposition) further clouded the analytical waters. As well, the deployment of a simple binary opposition between Utopia and Anti-Utopia effaced the complex continuum that stretches between these powerful forces.

Certainly, the social and political significance of the inverted utopian narratives was always recognized and intensely debated, even as their textual specificity was elided. In his 1955 essay on *Brave New World*, Theodor Adorno considers Huxley's nightmare vision as a contradictory production of contemporary capitalist culture.[7] Although this noted dystopia exposes the terrible truth of the totally administered and commodity-driven social system, Adorno argues that it nevertheless manages that terror and contains it in a narrative that failed "to contemplate a praxis which could explode the infamous continuum" ("Aldous Huxley" 117).

Whereas Adorno regards Huxley's book as a negative but compromised response to modern capitalism, Phillip Rahv's 1949 essay in the *Partisan Review*, "The Unfuture of Utopia," discusses Orwell's recently published dystopia in terms of its value as a critical response to the failures of the Left.[8] Relating *Nineteen Eighty-Four* to Arthur Koestler's *Darkness at Noon* (1941), Rahv characterizes both as examples of the "the melancholy mid-century genre of lost illusions and Utopia betrayed" (Rahv 744). If the only critical potential Adorno sees in Huxley's text lies in his own dialectical diagnosis of its failure to address the "question of whether society will come to determine itself or bring about terrestrial catastrophe" ("Aldous Huxley" 117), Rahv argues that Orwell's book could be "the best antidote to the totalitarian disease that any writer has so far produced," and he sees it as a useful tool for the liberal exorcism of the "political superstition" of the Left (Rahv 749).

Adorno's reading of Huxley comes out of an anti-capitalist stance shaped by his familiar utopian negativity, and Rahv's response to Orwell represents the prevailing anti-utopian position of postwar anti-communist liberalism. In a variation on Adorno's position, Gaylord LeRoy's 1950 *College English* essay on Orwell ("A.F. 632 to 1984") manages to be critical of both capitalism and the Left but does not follow Rahv's apostasy in doing so.[9] Not surprisingly, LeRoy sees Orwell's text as a brilliant example of Utopia "in breakdown" (LeRoy 136). Unlike Rahv, he sees it as an exercise in disbelief and disillusionment that serves no progressive purpose. Like Adorno on Huxley, he argues that although *Nineteen Eighty-Four* is a perceptive *satirical* account of contemporary standardization and dehumanization, it nevertheless closes in on itself, as it offers no "mitigation of the terrors it is designed to inspire" and presents "no practical alternative to its fearful vision of a pneumatic utopia" (LeRoy 136, 137).

Opting for a more resistant view than Adorno's negative dialectics, LeRoy assumes the viability of political opposition as he questions the deleterious effect that a work like Orwell's will have on readers caught within the very system it represents on its pages. He argues that Huxley's and Orwell's books tend "to strengthen the belief, becoming now so widespread, that nothing can be done to salvage modern man from the mounting crisis of the times"; for without exploring how such "trends may be resisted," books like these become complicit in acquiescing to the very "pessimism which constitutes so conspicuous a trend in contemporary thought" (LeRoy 137–138).

In these early responses, the cultural and political stakes in dystopian and anti-utopian writing are obvious, but the debate shifts according to the situation of the critic and the targets of the text. The particular targets include the hegemonic system of capital, the oppositional project of the Left (including both the Stalinist state and Left movements in the West), and (in a more philosophical or literary vein) the premises and processes of Utopia itself. What can be understood as a persisting utopian tendency can be found in critiques such as Adorno's and LeRoy's that hold out for a political response that could at least negate and perhaps transform the most terrible of present conditions; a contrasting anti-utopian attitude can be seen in Rahv's willingness to regard Orwell's and Koestler's works as narrowly critical of the Left and Utopia, and not as critiques of the social system in which the authors are constituted and that they liberally defend.[10]

Then, in 1956, George Woodcock added a useful attempt at clarification of the spectrum of anti-utopian persuasion when he charted a difference between what he saw as "anti-Utopians" and "ex-Utopians."[11] The title of his *New Republic* essay, "Five Who Fear the Future," suggests an outright rejection of Utopia, yet his argument works more subtly between the poles of Utopia and Anti-Utopia. On the one hand, he argues, "anti-Utopians" such as Huxley and Orwell still believe in humanity's ability to survive the worst distortions of progress, and they hold to the conviction that the individual is a "hero" who can stand tragically against the "over-development of social and political organization" (Woodcock 18). Although they acknowledge defeat in the present, they also look beyond it to the possibility of an eventual triumph for humanity. Their bleak vision, therefore, is "not necessarily a measure of their despair" but "rather a measure of their hatred of unfreedom and their anxiety for the perpetuation of freedom itself and its attendant values" (Woodcock 19).

"Ex-Utopians" such as H. G. Wells, George Bernard Shaw, and Koestler, on the other hand, have lost their original Left perspective and abandoned all hope. For them, utopian dreaming was "followed by the fall into a second disillusionment" that lacks faith in humanity's potential to survive and therefore is "doomed to end in pessimistic negation" (Woodcock 17, 18). Seeing the narratives of Huxley and Orwell as "anti-Utopian" but nevertheless "progressive" in the ironic quality of their tragic hope, and those of Wells, Shaw, and Koestler as totally pessimistic in their "ex-Utopian" resignation, Woodcock ultimately aligns himself with the stubborn militance of what he terms the "anti-Utopians." Appreciating their social critique as well as their flirtation with despair, he advocates a utopian standard of human freedom (primarily rooted in anarchist thought) that resists the ex-Utopian negation of Utopia even as it shares in the anti-Utopian suspicion of the ideological traps that Utopia itself can produce.

As utopian scholarship developed in the 1960s, critics continued to contend with the sociopolitical substance of these negative invocations of Utopia, but they also began to pay more attention to their formal operations. In the "Fiction of Anti-Utopia" in 1962, Irving Howe takes a position that resembles Rahv's but retains an affiliation with the critical Left.[12] Howe usefully distinguishes between the long-standing conservative tradition (emblematized by Chesterton and Hillaire Belloc) that attacked the idea of Utopia as "an impious denial of the limitations of the human lot, or a symptom of political naivete, or a fantasy both trivial and boring" and the newer "anti-utopian" persuasion (in Zamyatin, Huxley, and Orwell) that interrogates Utopia in an effort not to destroy but to free the Left from its own worst, Stalinist tendencies (Howe 13). In these "anti-utopian" works, the "enchanted dream" of the Left is exposed as a "nightmare," but unlike Rahv's legitimation of his own abdication, Howe sees their potential not in the rejection of Utopia and the reinforcement of pragmatic liberal hegemony but rather as powerful warnings to a Left that still has the wherewithal to correct its errors and revive its "urgent" dream.

Unlike previous commentators, Howe goes on to discuss the formal properties of the "anti-utopia." He begins by rebutting the dismissive response to this distinct fictive type by literary critics who incorrectly subject it to the aesthetic criteria of the novel. Against them, he argues that critics must "learn to read" the anti-utopian text "according to its own premises and limits, which is to say, in ways somewhat different from those by which we read ordinary novels" (Howe 15). As Darko Suvin will do with sf, he draws on Frye's work to identify its specific character. Seen in terms of Menippean satire's privileging of "abstract ideas and theories" presented through stylized characterization, the anti-utopia can be read as a literary form not identical with the novel and therefore subject to evaluation by different criteria. With this fresh perspective, Howe then names five characteristics particular to what he terms the anti-utopia:

1. It posits a "flaw" in the perfection of the perfect. . . .
2. It must be in the grip of an idea at once dramatically simple and historically complex: an idea that has become a commanding passion. . . .
3. It must be clever in the management of its substantiating detail. . . .
4. It must strain our sense of the probable while not violating our attachment to the plausible. . . .
5. In presenting the nightmare of history undone, it must depend on the ability of its readers to engage in an act of historical recollection. (Howe 16)

Howe's elements in many ways anticipate the later elaboration of the characteristics of utopian and dystopian texts. Certainly his second, third, and fourth items resonate with Suvin's concept of a commanding new historical idea-form, or novum, as the key formal device; Lyman Tower Sargent's definition of utopia as a narrative that presents a society in full detail; and Marc Angenot's and Kathleen Spencer's recognition of sf's strategy of presenting its "unreal" alternative world in realist fashion. More to the immediate question, Howe's first item (the portrayal of utopian society as deeply flawed) and his last (the continuation or completion of the tale by a reader who is always already historically engaged) point toward characteristics of what should be appropriately named the "dystopian" narrative. Indeed, his observation that the "anti-utopia" works by way of social images that negate the dream of a Utopia with which they are still affiliated catches the sense of the estrangement process that Suvin tracked in sf and utopian writing. As Howe puts it, the negative utopian texts realize their social use value "only through images of their violation," only by projecting the nightmare society "with such power as to validate the continuing urgency of the dream" (Howe 16).

Another important analysis in 1962 marked that year as one in which this body of work (still identified as "anti-utopian" literature) began to receive a greater degree of critical attention. In an extensive study that ranges from Plato to the present, Chad Walsh's *From Utopia to Nightmare* provided the first book-length examination of anti-utopian literature, and in doing so it made an important contribution in the move toward delineating the "anti-utopia" as a distinct literary form. Then in 1966, at Louisiana State University, William Gordon Browning completed his doctoral dissertation, "Anti-utopian Fiction: Definition and Standards for Evaluation." Drawing on Howe's five elements and other existing scholarship for his study of Zamyatin, Huxley, and Orwell, Browning's thesis did not break new critical ground, but it did represent a major step in the academic legitimation of utopian and anti-utopian literature. Both writers, it should be noted, regarded anti-utopian texts as useful warnings that would lead not to a conservative anti-utopian position but rather to a utopian response to existing social conditions that would prevent them from reaching the outcomes portrayed.

In 1967 Mark Hillegas's *Future as Nightmare: H. G. Wells and the Anti-Utopians* became the most advanced example of an "anti-utopian" criticism that clearly looks in the other direction and regards this textual form as fundamentally opposed to the utopian persuasion. Hillegas provided a valuable intertextual account of "anti-utopias," seeing this entire body of work as "a sad, last farewell to man's age-old dream of a planned, ideal, and perfected society, a dream which appeared so noble in Plato's *Republic*, More's *Utopia*, Andreae's *Christianopolis*, and Bellamy's *Looking Backward*" (Hillegas 3–4). Briefly sliding his gaze from literary history to social causes, he lists "dictatorships, welfare states, planned economies, and all manner of bureaucracies" and the regimes of "Hitler, Stalin, or Roosevelt" as the immediate stimuli for these terrifying texts. As opposed to these historical generalities, however, it is his literary analysis that stands as the enduring strength of the book. His examination of the roots of the "anti-utopia" in the tradition of satire and in the work of Wells and those who worked within, but also against, the Wellsian persuasion marked the beginning of an important line of formalist analysis of this literary tradition. Indeed, he names Forster's story "The Machine Stops" as the "first full-scale emergence of the twentieth-century anti-utopia," recognizing its dual move of Wellsian social criticism along with an anti-Wellsian critique of utopian thought itself (Hillegas 82).

His detailed textual studies advanced the understanding of the literary universe traversed by Wells, Forster, Zamyatin, Huxley, Orwell, and those who followed in sf and mundane fiction, and he therefore added to the growing understanding of their formal qualities. By limiting his attention to the literary realm and by virtue of his rather sweeping liberal suspicion of all state formations as deformed by their deployment of "utopian" planning, however, he cut short the possibility for a more complex social analysis that could have framed and deepened his textual studies. Thus, his focus on the "anti-utopia" as a text that rejects the utopian tradition (especially in its manifestation of the Left) rather than one that critiques and challenges society itself distorts the nature of his own textual intervention by reducing it to the abstract register of internecine literary or philosophical battles rather than seeing it in terms of its function in the larger political fray.

From Rahv's "Unfuture of Utopia" to Hillegas's *Future as Nightmare*, the titles of these early studies bespeak their value and their limitations. By giving thoughtful attention to "anti-utopian" writing as a specific cultural phenomenon, they made an important contribution to the unfolding discussion of the function and worth of Utopia and its anti-utopian nemesis, yet their conflation of actual anti-utopian texts with those which would become known as "dystopias" (works that negotiated the utopian and anti-utopian opposition in ways dismissed by the textual "anti-utopia") preserved a methodological and political murkiness that only began to be dissipated in the critical work of the 1970s. As seen in the previous chapter, the key contribution to this needed process of clarification was Sargent's essay "Utopia—the Problem of Definition." Informed by his bibliographic research, Sargent finally proposed the distinction that led to more specific studies of the "dystopia" and "anti-utopia" as distinct cultural strategies. To recall his definitions: while *eu-topia* (and *u-topia*) names texts that render the "good place," *dystopia* names those which explore the "bad place" and yet remain within the purview of *utopian* expression. He then decisively reserves the term *anti-utopia* only for works that "are directed against Utopia and utopian thought."[13] Bolstered by George Kateb's powerful attack on anti-utopianism in *Utopia and Its Enemies*, Sargent's careful distinctions brought an overdue requirement for specificity to the study of these related but very different narrative objects.

Although Kateb's strategic isolation, exposure, and critique of the anti-utopian persuasion and Sargent's distinctions between and among the textual forms opened the way for more extensive work on dystopian narrative, few critics took up the challenge. Even Suvin, who published precise studies of the specificity of sf and utopian texts, did not turn his attention fully to the question of dystopia until 1998. To be sure, early in "Defining the Literary Genre of Utopia," he nods toward dystopian writing when he notes that utopia, as the "logical obverse" of satire, "explicates what satire implicates, and vice versa" (*Metamorphoses* 54). He also suggests that a utopian text could be "gauged by the degree of integration between its constructive-utopian and satiric aspects," for the isolated extremes of "the deadly earnest blueprint and the totally closed horizons of 'new maps of hell' both lack aesthetic wisdom" (*Metamorphoses* 55).

Later, he more usefully describes anti-utopias as utopian variants that emerge from a novum generated by a "less perfect principle" of social organization, observing as well that a text that makes "a community claim to have reached perfection is in the industrial and post-industrial dynamics of society the surefire way to present us a radically less perfect state."[14] Further on he mentions the "intimate connection of utopian fiction with other forms of [sf] (extraordinary voyage, technological anticipation, anti-utopia and dystopia, etc.)" (*Positions* 38). But rather than address the specificities of the literary dystopia, he chooses to leave it in the sort of genealogical jungle he cleared away for sf and utopias, seeing it as satire one time, as anti-utopia another, and in yet another as a correlate form of sf.

In 1982, however, John Huntington's *Science-Fiction Studies* essay "Utopian and Anti-utopian Logic: H. G. Wells and His Successors" served as a useful bridge between the earlier anti-utopian studies and the new critical paradigm that Sargent's definitions helped to establish.[15] Working within the line of thought developed by Hillegas and other Wells scholars (such as Patrick Parrinder and Robert Philmus), Huntington, like Sargent, goes on to make the distinction between the category of "utopia-dystopia" and "anti-utopia." More important, he stresses the function of both tendencies at a deep epistemological rather than a strictly formal register, seeing them as a type of "imaginative procedure" or "opposed structural principles of thought" ("Logic" 123). He argues that the utopian-dystopian position involves "the imaginative attempt to put together, to compose and endorse a world," whereas the anti-utopian represents the opposing "attempt to see through, to dismember a world" ("Logic" 123). The utopian text, therefore, is "an exercise in thinking through a way things might fit together, might work; it strives for consistency and reconciles conflict" ("Logic" 123), and the dystopian text is the negative of Utopia in that it still imagines a coherent whole, just one that is worse than the given society. Both function as thought experiments that either "lure the reader towards an ideal or . . . drive the reader back from a nightmare" ("Logic" 124). With this argument, he brings an insightful gloss to the nature of utopian and dystopian texts as he links their formal qualities with the logical processes that inform them.

Huntington's discussion of anti-utopia also, but more subtly, moves critical understanding forward as he defines it as "a type of skeptical imagining that is opposed to the consistencies of utopia-dystopia," a logical structure that "discovers problems, raises questions, and doubts" ("Logic" 124). Beyond satire, this more modern form is "a mode of relentless inquisition, of restless skeptical exploration of the very articles of faith on which utopias themselves are built" ("Logic" 124). Anti-utopia for Huntington is therefore not the product of conservative, pragmatic liberal, or disavowed leftist persuasions. Instead, it is an analytic form that produces not an "attack on reality" but rather an effort to explore the "conflicts in human desire and expectation" ("Logic" 124). Once again, "anti-utopia" is discussed as a critique of utopianism and human desire itself, not of a particular historical situation; but in this case it is presented as a formally specific thought process that is divorced from the historical force usually attributed to Anti-Utopia. As such, instead of offering a negation of Utopia, it acts as a powerful critical complement to the ordering function of utopian and dystopian logics.

Valuable as Huntington's emphasis on the logical processes of utopian, dystopian, and what he calls "anti-utopian" thought experiments is, his nomination of "anti-utopia" excises the historical position of Anti-Utopia from the evolving critical paradigm. The critical process that he does describe might be more usefully understood as characterizing not "anti-utopia" but rather the critical phase of utopian thought itself. Seen in this light, his formulation comes closer to describing the underlying logic of the "critical utopias" of the 1970s, and it catches the logic of the negative and positive moments (neutralization and anticipation) at work in the utopian process as Fredric Jameson and others have described it. His argument contributes to our understanding of the thought processes of Utopia, and of the dystopian text, but not of its historical opponent, Anti-Utopia. Better, perhaps, to regard the two logical moves that he describes ("imaginative solutions" and "disturbing ambivalences") as aspects of a single *utopian* function. Better then, to reserve the term *anti-utopia* for the textual form that critiques and rejects not only Utopia but also the political thought and practice that is produced and motivated by Utopia as a force of societal transformation (by the radical Right as well as the Left)—that is, to see it as the textual expression of the historical, political position of Anti-Utopia.

The critic who finally ventured a more extensive exploration of these questions was Krishan Kumar, in his 1988 book, *Utopia and Anti-Utopia in Modern Times*. Although he too persists in using the obfuscating term *anti-utopia*, Kumar does provide an analysis of the formal evolution of this textual expression in the larger context of the historical opposition of Utopia and Anti-Utopia that at least sets up the context for a critical account of a specifically dystopian narrative. Like Sargent and Huntington, he separates Anti-Utopia and Utopia into analytical categories that are embedded in the social and not simply reducible to the register of psychological attitude or authorial intention. Thus, he examines temperament and text. In his chapter "Anti-Utopia, Shadow of Utopia," he argues that at the level of temperament Utopia and Anti-Utopia are "contrast concepts" that derive their meaning from "their mutual differences" (*Modern Times* 100). As he puts it, Anti-Utopia has "stalked" Utopia from the very beginning; for once Utopia is declared or written, the "mocking, contrary, echo" of Anti-Utopia resounds (*Modern Times* 99, 100). Insofar as Utopia names the nonexistent better place that negates existing society, it is the "original" that provides the positive content to which Anti-Utopia makes a second-level negative response as it reassembles, or rewrites, the utopian material in a manner that simultaneously denies and contains its transformative affirmation.

Kumar abstractly, and perhaps too broadly, acknowledges that there have always been "those who, for reasons of individual psychology or social ideology, have been profoundly skeptical of the hopeful claims made on behalf of humanity by social prophets and reformers" (*Modern Times* 100), and he identifies an early locus of this historic clash in the theological and political battle between Augustinianism and Pelagianism. In modernity, however, this social tension blossoms into a conservative anti-utopianism with Edmund Burke's challenge to the French Revolution in *Reflections on the Revolution in France*. Kumar then follows the growing power of Anti-Utopia into the "robust, no-nonsense, Anglo-Saxon" pragmatism that can be found in the work of Robert Burton (*Anatomy of Melancholy*) or Thomas Macauley ("an acre in Middlesex is better than a principality in Utopia"). Moving into the twentieth century, he places Bellamy and Wells in the Pelagian camp of Utopia (with those who believe in the essential goodness of humanity and society) and writers such as Huxley and Orwell in the Augustinian Anti-Utopia (with those who see humanity as sinful or weak).

Thus, both conservative and liberal anti-utopian tendencies manage to attack Utopia from the protective perspective of "a fundamental pessimism, or at least skepticism, about the capacities of human beings, and the possibility of attaining more than a moderate degree of happiness in human society" (*Modern Times* 101–102). Kumar recalls how the sweeping historical view of Spengler's *Decline of the West* (1918) and the psychoanalytic "realism" of Freud's *Civilization and Its Discontents* (1930) enhanced the ruling authority of Anti-Utopia (*Modern Times* 383–384). He also adds the related liberal humanist assessments by thinkers such as William James, who held that the visions of Utopia violated the very basis of a restless and striving human spirit, or Octavio Paz, who rejected future-oriented hopes in his assertion that "what man truly wants he wants *now*. Whoever builds a house for future happiness builds a prison for the present" (quoted in *Modern Times* 102–103).

In an overtly political sense, however, Anti-Utopia in this century found its most powerful vocation in shaping the hegemonic reaction against communism and socialism—whether formulated by those who have always been opposed or those who became disillusioned (see *Modern Times* 421). In general, therefore, Anti-Utopia celebrates and protects the status quo and the satisfactions that it delivers to its beneficiaries. As a refusal of the sociopolitical project of humanity's collective ability to produce the material conditions for the fulfilled existence of everyone, Anti-Utopia's discourse of privilege incorporates the entire spectrum of reaction, pulling together "Christian objections to perfectibility, conservative opposition to radical reforms, and cynical reflections on human incapacity" (*Modern Times* 103).

When Kumar turns from the question of temperament to that of text, he argues that the anti-utopian form only gradually comes into its own, moving from an imbrication with satire and utopia into a distinct formal strategy in the nineteenth century. Citing Hesiod's Iron Age of pain and sorrow following the Golden Age, Aristophanes' satiric replies to Plato's *Republic,* and Swift's ridicule of Bacon's *New Atlantis,* he argues that early anti-utopian textual expressions were more often than not intertwined with utopian sensibilities in satiric and later in overtly utopian works. In a formulation similar to those made by Sargent and Huntington, he notes that in Greek and Roman satire an anti-utopian spirit "criticizes, through ridicule and invective, its own times," whereas an accompanying utopian attitude points "usually implicitly but sometimes explicitly . . . to alternative and better ways of living" (*Modern Times* 104). He therefore argues that it is only after More's invention of the literary utopia that a freestanding anti-utopian expression gradually becomes "recognizable as a distorted reflection of utopia," but even here its negative descriptions refer more to a critique of the author's historical situation and less to the dangers of utopian thought (*Modern Times* 104).[16]

In the shadow of Burke, however, as European society experienced industrial development, social revolution, and immense scientific and cultural change (including new utopian texts that aimed to carry such progress even further), the imbrication of utopian and anti-utopian expression began to come apart as the discursive conditions for what Kumar names the "formal anti-utopia," as distinct from "utopian satire," became more propitious. He observes that by the late 1800s (helped by the rise of realist fiction that further validated scientific thought) "the negative and positive poles of the old satirical utopia were pulled apart and assigned to separate genres or sub-genres" (*Modern Times* 125). Consequently, anti-utopian narratives could be written without resorting to overtly fantastic and satirical modes that drew upon both tendencies. Kumar suggests that a punctal moment in the evolution of the "formal anti-utopia" occurred with the publication of Samuel Butler's *Erewhon* (1872) and Edward Bulwer-Lytton's *Coming Race* (1871). Both works are quite "modern," indeed experimental, for their time, but one revises the older satiric tradition whereas the other takes up the new aesthetic of realism.[17] Butler's protomodernist critique of Victorian society and the coming "Mechanical Age" is unremittingly satiric and replete with fantastic exaggerations that play on a seemingly deliberate utopian and anti-utopian ambiguity. In contrast, Bulwer-Lytton's evocation of bourgeois anxieties in the form of an invading underground race that collectively threatens life on the surface of the earth assumes a formally anti-utopian mode to expose not only the social evil but also the dangers of utopian thought itself. As he puts it, Bulwer-Lytton's text, with its realist quality, gives as "graphic and detailed a portrayal as possible" of the "the horror of a society in which utopian aspirations have been fulfilled" (*Modern Times* 109).

Thus—just as it had devalued historical fiction once it had successfully tapped social memories to produce its reigning reality—bourgeois culture discounted the utopian temperament the moment its transformative energies were no longer needed. In the established new order of capital and empire, History *and* Utopia were labeled as dangerous to the health of the very society that had made full use of, if not entirely invented, both categories. Yet when technology, democracy, and socialism became historical realities, they became the targets of critical examinations in apparently "anti-utopian" works that were not fully aligned with Anti-Utopia. As the transformative potential of such modernizing and potentially emancipating forces fell prey to the instrumental opportunism of a capitalist political economy, their new compromised status provoked renewed critiques by socialists, populists, feminists, and even the occasional liberal that attacked their false or failed "utopian" claims in the name of a far more radical embrace of Utopia.

Therefore, in a range of nineteenth-century political fiction what often appeared to be an anti-utopian stance was in fact another degree of radical interrogation that did not oppose progress but rather attacked the co-optation, betrayal, and distortion of progress. As Kumar puts it, it was not "the principles of progress themselves, but their use and practice . . . [that] dismayed and outraged [these writers]. There seemed no way to make the practice fit the principles. Every attempt ended in the grotesque inversion of its promise—democracy produced despotism, science barbarism, and reason unreason" (*Modern Times* 110). In works such as Mary Shelley's *Frankenstein* (1818) and Fyodor Dostoyevsky's *Brothers Karamazov* (1879), the valence changed; for such works evoked not a clear anti-utopian diffidence but rather more complex acknowledgments of the *failure* of an apparent utopian promise. Kumar's account of this response can perhaps be further qualified by the terms of Woodcock's categories of "anti-Utopian" in the case of Shelley, as her narrative maintains a shred of utopian hope, and "ex-Utopian" for Dostoevsky's resigned acceptance of the world as it stands.

What Kumar does not address are those other early examples of a "formal anti-utopia" that resisted an anti-utopian temperament and still worked from an overt affiliation with Utopia as it informed their realist portrayals of the negativities of the present society. Refusing the cynicism of a fashionable anti-utopian ambiguity but eschewing the eutopian route taken by the likes of Bellamy, Morris, or Gilman, writers such as Mark Twain, and Jack London at times looked beyond the available formal strategies of realism or naturalism and deployed the realistic irrealism of the anti-utopian form in ways that allowed them to express their still utopian critiques of capitalism and imperialism. In the hands of London especially, this venture into an estranged anti-utopian modality preserved the utopian impulse in a way that fully anticipated the dystopian narratives that would soon appear. Thus, when he comes to the emergence of what will eventually be regarded as the "classical dystopia" (as it begins with Forster and Zamyatin and moves forward), Kumar does not quite catch or account for the underlying utopian quality of this new textual strategy.

This emerging intertextual network clearly represents a creative step beyond the utopian satire of the previous centuries even as it draws on the qualities of the popular anti-utopian text. Yet even though Kumar identifies such works as "anti-utopias," they are not *anti*-utopian but now something else entirely. As *dys*topias, they are not texts that temperamentally refuse the possibility of radical social transformation; rather, they look quizzically, skeptically, critically not only at the present society but also at the means needed to transform it. In texts such as Forster's, the society portrayed in an "anti-utopian" mode is obviously worse than what the author or readers know; however, the depiction works *not* to undermine Utopia but rather to make room for its reconsideration and refunctioning in even the worst of times. To recall Howe's phrasing, such texts formally "realize [their utopian] values only through images of their violation," only by projecting the nightmare society "with such power as to validate the continuing urgency of the dream" (Howe 16).

III.

Up through the 1980s, critical work on the nature and operation of anti-utopian forms of expression (by Kumar, Huntington, and others) produced a rich and inevitably contentious account of the political ground traversed by these quite varied texts of the late nineteenth and twentieth centuries. As well, these studies began to clarify the difference between the underlying categories of Utopia and Anti-Utopia and their textual expressions, and this clarification set the stage for a more nuanced understanding of the relationship between "anti-utopian" textuality and the contradictions and possibilities of given historical moments. In particular, Kumar's account of the interrelationship of utopian and anti-utopian narratives, and especially of the evolution of the "formal anti-utopia," provided valuable groundwork for further formal and social analyses.

And yet even with Kumar's work on "anti-utopia" there is still a lack of precision in the assessment of the historical dimension of Anti-Utopia and its relationship to textual forms. As in the earlier studies, his explanation of Anti-Utopia as temperament oscillates between regarding it as a rejection of all utopian processes based in long-standing conservative thought and practice or as a disavowal that stems from the disillusionment with Utopia among those already, and sometimes still, on the Left. Against this polarity, critics such as Huntington have described "anti-utopia" as a thought process that informs a third option that is critical of both Utopia and the prevailing hegemonic system. Useful as this line of thought is for understanding the critical dimension of utopianism itself, the attribution of this activity as "anti-utopian" unfortunately defers and diminishes a better understanding of the historical force of Anti-Utopia as an outright rejection of both Utopia and the historical changes it informs and helps to produce. It was only in the moment of the dystopian turn in the 1990s that a more substantial clarification of these categories and terms finally emerged. The times, it seems, again produced the theory required for their critique.[18]

Thus, in his 1994 essay "The Three Faces of Utopianism Revisited," Sargent offers an extended discussion of Anti-Utopia as social temperament and dystopia as text that brings a greater degree of clarity to these categories and paves the way for a better understanding of the relationship between and among them.[19] Near the end of his essay, he takes up the question of Anti-Utopia in the context of his discussion of social and political thought as he differentiates between the "complex of ideas we call utopianism" and that "constant but generally unsystematic stream of thought that can be called anti-utopianism" ("Three Faces Revisited" 21).[20] Less psychologically inclined than Kumar, and thus more attuned to the deeper material and discursive dimensions of Utopia, he traces the ideological roots of anti-utopianism to the Christian idea of original sin, with its implication that fallen humanity cannot, and in some versions must not, improve its own conditions in this life. From the demonization of medieval "pre-utopian" thinkers (such as Joachim of Fiore or Thomas Muntzer) to the historic reaction against the French Revolution (he cites George Sand to Kumar's Burke) to the modern right-wing judgment that those who "who dream concretely [are] a very dangerous breed" (as Ernst Jünger infamously put it), Anti-Utopia turns Utopia in on itself and thereby not only rejects what Utopia claims to make possible but demolishes the very concept (Jünger, quoted in "Three Faces Revisited" 22).

In Sargent's account: "If [U]topia is heretical, the earthly paradise must be a trick of the Devil and the noble savages are followers of Satan. Attacks on socialism are extended to attacks on all planning (this was quite common in the United States in the Fifties and Britain in the Eighties). Even if [U]topia is realizable, the costs are too high, and people are simply incapable of [U]topia" ("Three Faces Revisited" 22). Thus, he notes that the "most complete success of the Anti-Utopians was to make the label 'utopian' take on the meaning of fanciful, unrealistic, impractical" ("Three Faces Revisited" 22).

Sargent then confronts Anti-Utopia's equation of Utopia with "totalitarianism" (attributed to communism and fascism, but, in an act of critical blindness, never to liberalism).[21] He explains that anti-utopian social thought in the 1940s and 1950s especially asserted that humans are incapable of working toward a qualitatively better society and will do so only by means of externally imposed force. Since this is the case, no utopian phenomenon can ever be an enabler of self-determination and fulfillment, for it will inevitably lead to totalitarian rule by virtue of the force required to impose an alternative system on a selfish and reluctant population. He cites Popper's *Open Society* as the most direct representative of this position. Assuming that Utopia can be saved only by some version of "the Platonic belief in one absolute and unchanging ideal," and since this ideal can never be attained by rational thought and realized justice, Popper argues that Utopia is doomed to rely on "power instead of reason" (Popper, quoted in "Three Faces Revisited" 24).

In making such clarifications, however, Sargent refuses to reduce Utopia and Anti-Utopia to this simple binary opposition. As he moves his discussion back to the utopian text, Sargent—like LeRoy, Howe, Kumar, and Huntington—looks at the "contradictory nature" of Utopia and argues that the position of Anti-Utopia has itself undergone transformations in recent times. In the specific case of texts he properly identifies as "dystopias," he observes that certain dystopian narratives retain an affiliation with Anti-Utopia, whereas others embrace its logical and political opposite. In this way he locates the critical process of which Huntington speaks *within* the scope of dystopian strategy, seeing it not as a critique of authoritarian practices that ends in a closed dismissal of utopian aspiration but rather one that opens a way forward by directly addressing the very confrontation of Utopia and Anti-Utopia within its pages. He notes that dystopian narratives work from this perspective of contestation and ask *if* correct or progressive choices can be made rather than simply, like Popper, denying that possibility. "Some dystopias," he concludes, "are deeply pessimistic and can be seen as a continuation of the idea of original sin. . . . But many dystopias are self-consciously warnings. A warning implies that choice, and therefore hope, are still possible" ("Three Faces Revisited" 26). His observation about the dystopian reconfiguration of the anti-utopia therefore places the dystopia at least potentially in the camp of a critical utopianism.

Like Sargent, Suvin also returned to the question of dystopia and anti-utopia in 1998, in "Utopianism from Orientation to Agency."[22] With Disneyland rather than a literary dystopia as his exemplary text (thereby recalling and engaging with Marin's important study of this "degenerate utopia"), he works out his own definitions of these "incompletely stabilized neologisms" in the context of an extended meditation on the current economic and political moment, the role of engaged intellectuals, and the field of utopian studies ("Orientation" 170). Detailing the economic and cultural strategies of contemporary capitalism that have produced an "abiding political disempowerment" that includes the co-optation and destruction of utopianism in all its forms, he argues that Utopia has been "eaten up by the very ideology [and material practices] which it was its original Morean and Morrisian function to fictionally unveil" ("Orientation" 166). He metonymically locates this historical diagnosis in an analysis of the operations of Disneyland and delineates the ways in which the mega–theme park's "careful and most efficacious organization of desires" displaces the possibility of "an active intervention into the real world which would make the pursuit of happiness collectively attainable" even as it also encourages a full consumerist indulgence in human desires, "however shallow" ("Orientation" 168).

It is this actually existing anti-utopian machinery (of Disneyland and the entire society that produces and surrounds it) that occasions Suvin's attention to the distinctive textual characteristics of the eutopia, dystopia, and anti-utopia. Identifying Disneyland, and the capitalist society it bespeaks, as a "fake" utopia, he goes on to adapt his own definition of the literary utopia to its dystopian counterpart, so that dystopia is understood as text that creates "a community where sociopolitical institutions, norms, and relationships between its individuals are organized in a significantly less perfect way than in the author's community" ("Orientation" 170–171). But (showing the impact of theoretical work on situatedness, agency, and readerly protocols), he appends a crucial coda when he notes that the imagined dystopian society is "significantly less perfect" especially and importantly as it is "*seen by a representative of a discontented social class or fraction, whose value-system denies 'perfection'*" ("Orientation" 170, my emphasis). In another refinement he also recognizes the difference between the classical dystopia and the texts that emerged within the realm of sf, and he uses the term *simple dystopia* to identify works that appear in the form of the sf's "new maps of hell" ("Orientation" 171).

Finally, he differentiates the textual anti-utopia from these variations on utopian expression and recognizes its attributes in ways that recall Sargent's 1975 essay. Although he surprisingly conflates the term *anti-utopia* with *dystopia* (at one point calling it a "special case . . . which finally also turns out to be a dystopia"), he then paradoxically, though rightly, refuses the "uneconomical use of this term as a synonym of dystopia" ("Orientation" 170). More importantly, he catches the rhetorical function of the anti-utopia as an explicit refutation of a "fictional and/or otherwise imagined utopia" and accordingly locates it in the larger repertoire of the capitalist ideological arsenal; thus, the anti-utopian text "designates a pretended utopia, a community whose hegemonic principles pretend to its being more perfectly organized than any thinkable alternative" ("Orientation" 170–171).

Another critic who returned to these questions from the basis of earlier work is Robert M. Philmus. In "The Language of Utopia" in 1973, he published an analysis of utopian and anti-utopian textuality that continues in the direction taken by Hillegas and others.[23] Drawing on Kenneth Burke and Northrop Frye, he immediately establishes that utopias are analyzable in Burke's terms of "dialectical" and "ultimate" orders, wherein a utopian expression (such as More's *Utopia*) is dialectical "in that it necessarily defines itself, at least implicitly, *against a status quo (else it would not be utopian)*," and it is ultimate (as with Plato's *Politeia*) "insofar as it purports to be not only antithetical but also superior to the status quo (that is, more or less ideal)" ("Language of Utopia" 61–62, my emphasis). The ratio between these possibilities then determines the "orientation" of the utopia, which is "satirical to the extent that 'dialectical' outweighs 'ultimate' considerations, visionary to the extent that the reverse is true" ("Language of Utopia" 62). In this formulation Philmus catches the qualities of utopian expression that encompass its capacity for both an open-ended potential and a tendency to collapse into rigidity and closure. He does not go on to develop this line of thought, but the roots of a further understanding of the difference between the temperaments of Utopia and Anti-Utopia (and from their textual expressions) are present in this analysis.

Philmus does, however, acknowledge that what he identifies as an "anti-utopian" critique of utopianism involves the exposure of the limits of Utopia as it tends toward its visionary component (with its attendant proclivity for universal claims and closed orders), and he therefore continues his textual analysis as he explores the interrelationship of the literary forms of utopia and anti-utopia. He argues that utopian textuality "through transvaluation" becomes "anti-utopia, *or* dystopia" when the text turns against the limits of utopian logic and values, even as it continues to address a critique of the existing society. Thus (significantly referring to Butler's *Erewhon*), he notes that in what he nominates as an "anti-utopian" text "apparent antitheses turn out to be real analogies, while final solutions constitute a negative ideal, something to be avoided rather than sought after" ("Language of Utopia" 63, my emphasis).

In this assessment "the strategy of anti-utopian fiction typically involves internalizing the opposition so that utopian civilization is seen through the eyes of its discontents" ("Language of Utopia" 63). Given this distinction between the textual forms of utopia and anti-utopia, he explains the role of satire in both. Whereas satiric elements in a utopia "serve to reinforce the desirability of a utopian order that may be achievable," in the anti-utopia, in contrast, "the undesirability of the utopian order serves satiric purposes as the *reductio ad absurdum* of already existing social tendencies" ("Language of Utopia" 63). In this light he regards an *anti-utopian* text as one that negotiates a critique of the limits of utopian expression as well as the existing society by way of, or through, its challenge to utopianism.

What Philmus does not do, however, is move on to explore the qualities of a specifically *dystopian* text. Instead, he uses the two terms interchangeably, except when he notes that the characterization of a text as *dystopia* is largely a matter of point of view. With Sargent, he acknowledges the importance of authorial intention in the production of utopian and anti-utopian texts, and he notes that any given text could subsequently be judged by a reader as either a utopia or anti-utopia (supporting his argument with the familiar example of Skinner's *Walden*). In this discussion of readerly evaluation, "dystopia" is not a form that is clearly distinct from anti-utopia; rather, by connotation, it appears as the worst case, or limit, of the anti-utopia.

In a 1999 revision of this essay (retitled "Swift, Zamiatin, and Orwell and the Language of Utopia"), Philmus continues his formalist analysis, but he also brings in a more historically nuanced perspective that allows him to separate the dystopian from the anti-utopian text.[24] The generic distinction emerges when he summarizes the historical process whereby "dystopia derives from anti-utopia, thus recapitulating the latter's evolution from utopia," and he argues that Zamiatin's *We* "qualifies as anti-utopian fiction" whereas Orwell's *Nineteen Eighty-Four* exemplifies the dystopia ("Swift, Zamiatin" 3). Thus, the literary "anti-utopia" has its roots in "the perceivable impact of nineteenth-century technology on the natural and social environments, on which evidence anti-utopists pit dreams of material Progress against the natural world and human nature"; and the "dystopia" rises out of the response to the more dire twentieth-century experiences of the "police-surveillance state" and no longer negotiates the tension between Utopia and the status quo but now questions the entire utopian project with visions that are "decidedly more nightmarish than those of their anti-utopian cousins" ("Swift, Zamiatin" 3). Whereas anti-utopias "preserve something of utopian Hope" in the search for a "*via media* between Nature and Technology," dystopias abandon "all such hope," for their question is "whether the 'definitive realization of [U]topia is 'avoidable,' on the understanding that *[U]topia* is synonymous with *Hell*" ("Swift, Zamiatin" 3).

With this reading, Philmus at least implicitly recognizes the difference between the temperaments of Utopia and Anti-Utopia, and he finally separates texts that traverse the terrain between them with some hope from those that evince no hope at all. Although his distinctions are welcome, my objection to his analysis, as it was to Huntington's, is terminological, insofar as he designates the hope-less text as a "dystopia" and the more hope-ful as an "anti-utopia." Following Sargent's basic definitions, I would argue that it is more consistent with the developing paradigm in utopian/dystopian studies to name the text that refuses all utopian hope and effort an *anti-utopia* and the one that enters the fray between Utopia and Anti-Utopia (coming down in a different position in each text) a *dystopia*. Thus, as Philmus argues—but as I would rename the types—since *We* maintains some hope in the face of the One State, it qualifies as a "dystopia" that opts for Utopia, whereas it is debatable (depending on the position of the critic and the frame of the argument) whether *Nineteen Eighty-Four* is a dystopia leaning to the pole of Anti-Utopia or an outright instance of an anti-utopia that refuses Utopia outright.

Important as Sargent's, Suvin's, and Philmus's contributions are to this developing paradigm, it is Jameson's recent work that most fully and carefully examines the relationship of Utopia and Anti-Utopia, and of both to their textual representations. In *Seeds of Time,* he moves the discussion even further beyond the historical binaries.[25] Making distinctions similar to Kumar's of temperament and text and Sargent's of text, community, and theory, and working from a similar understanding of what both see as the oppositional yet imbricated relationship of Utopia and Anti-Utopia, he looks directly at the basic conflict between the two and draws the obvious conclusion that ours is a time when Anti-Utopia reigns supreme. For however much social progress and Utopia have been challenged in the past three or four centuries, events in the 1980s and 1990s in particular endowed Anti-Utopia with greater ideological value. Not only has Utopia been silenced by the hegemonic discourse of societies in the West that (under the aegis of a restructured capitalism) paradoxically declare Utopia to have arrived in our daily lives, but its potential has been further discredited by the related analyses celebrating the "fall" of "actually existing" socialist states in the East.[26]

Besides these overt condemnations of Utopia by neoconservative and neoliberal ideologies, he notes that Utopia has also been challenged by a progressive line of postmodern thought, as the critical spin of an anti-utopian sensibility has helped to facilitate feminist and other challenges to the utopian tendency to a universalism that ends up neglecting and displacing the very diversity of subjectivities and social possibilities that its own radical process privileges in the first place. Thus, he argues that even as Anti-Utopia retains its connections with a "critique compounded of Edmund Burke and of the nineteenth-century additions," it also has taken up the not entirely erroneous "critique of high modernism itself as repressive, totalizing, phallocentric, authoritarian, and redolent of an even more sublime and inhuman hubris than anything Burke could have attributed to his Jacobin contemporaries" (*Seeds* 53).

As a result of these flexible maneuvers in a time of crisis, Anti-Utopia has come to displace Utopia on the discursive terrain since about the early 1970s. Working along the entire spectrum of the political imagination—from traditional conservatism to neoconservative and neo-liberal positions and on to the realm of radical postmodernism—the underlying logic of Anti-Utopia always manages to revert to its baseline project of producing and reproducing the ruling order of things. Thus, even as it appropriates useful critical challenges to Utopia's errors, Anti-Utopia continues to reprise, as Jameson puts it, "a very old (but hitherto Western) Cold-War and . . . market rhetoric about hubris and human sinfulness (our old friend human nature again) rehearsed with a view toward the dangers involved in trying to create anything like a new society from scratch, and vividly warning of Burkean Jacobinism and the Stalinism implicit and inevitable in any Utopian effort to create a new society, or even in any fantasy of doing so" (*Seeds* 54).

To clear the ground for a more detailed discussion of this fundamental antinomic relationship between Utopia and Anti-Utopia, Jameson first questions the commonly assumed status of the literary dystopia as a direct opposite of Utopia, for such an equation only occludes a proper grasp of the relationship between Utopia and Anti-Utopia. Again he steps away from a binary division as he notes that the "formal or generic concepts" such as utopia and dystopia, "which have become current since science fiction, seem to lend themselves to a relatively simple play of oppositions in which the enemies of Utopia can easily be sorted out from its friends—Orwell being sent over to that corner, Morris to this one, while some of them (Wells himself, for example) spend their whole lives vacillating between the poles like tender and tough, or hawks and doves" (*Seeds* 55). Drawing on Gilles Deleuze's reconsideration of the polarity of sadism and masochism, Jameson argues polemically that Utopia and the textual dystopia are "not opposites and in reality have nothing to do with each other"; for, as in Deleuze's argument, each seeks something very different from that which is offered by its supposed opposite (*Seeds* 55). He therefore cautions against "the facile deployment of the opposition between Utopia and dystopia" (*Seeds* 55).

This move might at first glance appear to be troubling for a study of dystopian narrative. In fact, it helps set the stage for that very project by stepping back and clarifying the nature of the terrain that not only eutopias and anti-utopias but also dystopias must negotiate. Jameson therefore asserts that the "pleasures of the nightmare—evil monks, gulags, police states—have little enough to do with the butterfly temperament of great Utopians like Fourier, who are probably not intent on pleasures at all but rather on some other form of gratification" (*Seeds* 55). More to the point, he makes the formal observation that it is the *narrative* quality of dystopia (in its attention to what "happens to a specific subject or character") that distances it from the "nonnarrative" quality of the utopian text, which instead of plotting the trajectory of a subject "describes a mechanism or even a kind of machine" (*Seeds* 56).

As a literary form that not only rushes too readily to narrative but also works with daily fears and apprehensions of "imminent disaster," the dystopia (especially as near-future sf) in Jameson's gaze appears to be too close to the current situation to partake effectively in the powerful estranging mechanisms of Utopia. Although I dispute Jameson's underestimation of the utopian potential of dystopian narrative in the following chapters, with his categorical house-cleaning he usefully disjoins dystopian from utopian texts and also separates dystopian expression from the historical force of Utopia itself. In doing so, he reprises his long-standing position that Utopia's basic concern is with its own possibility for realization and not with the substance of this or that manifest utopian content. Or as Levitas might rephrase it, his concern for Utopia calls attention to its own function *as form* and not to its manifest content. The 1994 version of the argument goes this way:

> The ideals of Utopian living involve the imagination in a contradictory project, since they presumably aim at illustrating and exercising that much-abused concept of freedom that, virtually by definition and in its very structure, cannot be defined in advance, let alone exemplified: if you know already what your longed-for exercise in a not-yet-existent freedom looks like, then the suspicion arises that it may not really express freedom after all but only repetition; while the fear of projection, of sullying an open future with our own deformed and repressed social habits in the present, is a perpetual threat to the indulgence of fantasies of the future collectivity. (*Seeds* 56–57)

In a replay of the suspicion of utopian content that Fitting and I question, Jameson again interrogates all utopian textuality and argues that rather than directly imaging, much less narrating, a properly revolutionary alternative, Utopia works by way of negation as it constructs "material mechanisms" that do not name freedom in any specificity but rather "neutralize" what blocks it in a given historical moment. In this latest account of his utopian problematic, he describes Utopia as a mental and textual machine that absorbs unfreedom, concentrates it, and isolates it in order to control it. Only through this secularized *via negativa* can Utopia point toward the conditions for the supersession of unfreedom in preconceptual figures of what would be the negation of that negation. As he puts it, "the Utopian mechanism by embodying the necessary—labor, constraint, matter—in absolute and concentrated form, by way of its very existence, allows a whole range of freedoms to flourish outside of itself" (*Seeds* 57). Utopia, in other words, opens the way to revolution, to radical social change, not by the narratives and images it generates but rather by the creative and critical praxis of containing the unfreedom of the present in its imaginary machine, thus producing the possibility, not the actuality, of the desired historical transformation (see *Seeds* 70).

Having set aside dystopian textuality and reaffirmed the negative discipline of Utopia, Jameson turns his attention to recent manifestations of what Kumar would call the temperament of Anti-Utopia. In the spirit of his familiar imbrication of ideology and Utopia, he is interested in teasing out the utopian potential lurking within the very expressions of Anti-Utopia. On the one hand, like Kumar and Sargent, he argues that some conservative anti-utopian positions or texts turn up at Utopia's end of the spectrum as they tap into a radical dissatisfaction with the present system even if the politics with which they are affiliated are distorted or reactionary. On the other hand, he also recognizes that some progressive positions—heretofore affiliated with Utopia—have opted for an "anti-utopian" critique of the limitations and failings of the utopian project on the Left as well as maintaining an oppositional stance against the present social order.

As Sargent, Huntington, and others have argued, an anti-utopian perspective, insofar as it does not simply reinforce the status quo, can also fulfill a utopian purpose by virtue of its capacity to indict and delegitimize a particular hegemonic or counter-hegemonic position as "utopian" (that is, as an abstraction that signifies the contradictions and possibilities of the historical situation by denying or suppressing them or, in Suvin's term, as a "fake"). Especially now, when Utopia has been severely compromised and discredited, the available and popular discourse of Anti-Utopia is likely to offer a viable hiding place and an outlet for some undefeated manifestations of the Utopian impulse. In a sentence that summarizes a good deal of his work on this question throughout the years, Jameson puts it this way:

> If indeed one believes that the Utopian desire is everywhere, and that some individual or pre-individual Freudian libido is enlarged and completed by a realm of social desire, in which the longing for transfigured collective relationships is no less powerful and omnipresent, then it can scarcely be surprising that this particular political unconscious is to be identified even there where it is the most passionately decried and denounced. (*Seeds* 54–55)

Thus, Jameson suggests that the radical intellectual commitment to bringing Utopia back into the political process must be prepared to delve into the realm of its inversion within anti-utopian expression. There is "no more pressing task for progressive people in the First World than tirelessly to analyze and diagnose the fear and anxiety before Utopia itself" (*Seeds* 61). Rather than looking just to new utopian visions of the future (which can emerge only from actual contradictions and possibilities), overcoming the diminution of radical political vision in our time (brought about through the conservative restoration as well as its own shortcomings) requires that we also look into the downside of everything that we "fantasize as mutilating, as privative, as oppressive, as mournful and depressing, about all the available visions of a radical transformation" in order to release the potential of Utopia from the simultaneous co-optation and condemnation that has so effectively curbed its oppositional power (*Seeds* 61). In this way the "fear of Utopia" (as opposed to the conservative *refusal* of Utopias) that runs through contemporary political and creative expression can begin to be overcome by confronting the processes by which that fear found its articulation in anti-utopian venues in the first place (*Seeds* 60).

In one diagnostic direction, Jameson takes on "the most powerful drive in contemporary ideology" by which "anything labeled as public has become irredeemably tainted, everything that smacks of the institution arouses distaste and repels in a subliminal, well-nigh Pavlovian fashion, anything construed as representing the state and the satellite institutions that surround it" (*Seeds* 62). Within this strong anti-utopian position, however, he points to a deeper political revulsion against that other (fundamental and pervasive) source of social contradiction, suffering, and discontent: the corporation and its capitalist project. According to Jameson, the "anti-institutionalism" urged by anti-utopian discourse "can only secondarily be identified as antisocialist or anti-Stalinist, since the more fundamental object at which it is directed is corporate capitalism itself" (*Seeds* 63).

In its inability to experience and much less apprehend the corporate machinery of capital, however, the popular imagination (nurtured by the anti-government rhetoric of triumphal conservatives, frightened liberals, and renegade leftists) can embody its underlying anti-corporate revulsion only through the available representations of those institutions which *are* encountered in everyday life: "big government" and "bureaucracy." Thus, a proper institutional critique of corporate power that could "ordinarily be expected to fuel the production of properly Utopian meditations and fantasies—is redirected against Utopia itself" (*Seeds* 63).

Such a move is made possible to the extent that Utopia is associated with public institutions that, though they have the potential to regulate and control capitalist operations and to redistribute social wealth and well-being in a just and democratic manner, have more often come to be experienced or at least seen to be nothing other than intrusive and controlling interventions in people's daily lives. Feeding this process of political disillusion and displacement is the cultural arm of the capitalist machine that persistently redirects popular desire and discontent by producing and disseminating "all the properly Utopian fantasies of gratification and consumption that market society is capable of generating" (*Seeds* 63). Hijacked by Anti-Utopia, utopian longing and political strategies alike have thus been turned upside down to become representations that refuse Utopia in the name of what Adorno called its cheap market substitute.[27]

Switching diagnostic direction, Jameson turns to the anti-utopian critique embodied in postmodern identity politics: a politics that challenges the "social standardization" of the current economy and culture but also refuses the traditional articulation of the utopian project of the Left, insofar as it has been informed by the errors of totalizing analyses, master narratives, and historically privileged agents. Working dialectically, he notes that the political desire of the diversity-based social movements for a radical democracy that would enable everyone to be different and free can be achieved only by embarking on a more radical path than the ones that lead either to the social hyperglycemia of commodity consumption or the temporary security of separatist enclaves. Reaching into the active utopian core of this anti-utopian yet still progressive politics, he argues that only with a shared adherence to that larger human but decidedly not universal "Identity" that is privileged by a full democracy based in an antinomic but more fundamental "Difference" can the array of social and identity-based movements take the next historical step and "be productively transformed into a political program" (*Seeds* 66).

Therefore, by retrieving a radical solidarity that is "the spiritual property of the Utopian tradition proper," a utopian commonality that primarily produces and protects the subject differences articulated by the social movements can lead to an alliance politics (a "historic bloc" or a "popular front of marginalities") that can move forward on the basis of the "common problem and necessity of their strategic interrelationships" (*Seeds* 66, 65).

To pursue this strategy, however, Jameson again argues that the process of totalizing analysis must be retrieved from its anti-utopian grave diggers. Thus, the trend of anti-utopian condemnation of totality as a critical tool (wrongly conflated with the evil of totalitarianism) must be exposed as a misdirected but understandable cry for specificity against standardization, for it is a cry that ultimately silences itself by dismissing the very analytical scale needed for making sense of, and moving against and beyond, the current system. As he puts it, totalization as a *project* rather than "the word for an already existent institution" is precisely the utopian tool needed for the revivification of an effectively united oppositional movement. He argues that only by developing an adequate totalizing critique of the already totalizing mechanisms of capital can the project of a renewed Left begin to "coordinate our very limited positions, as individuals or indeed as historical subjects and classes, within a History whose dynamics representationally escape us" (*Seeds* 69). Thus armed with an analysis of "the presence all around us of some overarching system that we can at least *name*," we can move further and "conceive of at least the possibility of other alternate systems" (*Seeds* 70).

Now more than ever, this critical work needs to defer the immediate production of "premature" images of alternative systems in favor of confronting the very anti-utopian anxiety currently blocking the processes of a collective imagination that could begin to clear the political space that might lead to such alternatives. Although Jameson chooses his own promising objects for this present round of critical intervention (seen in the examples above and others in *Seeds*), his disavowal of dystopian narrative unnecessarily limits the range of this new cultural matrix. Certainly if instances such as the anti-government discourse of the market and militias or the political activism of identity politics bear utopian traces, then dystopian stories of violent and unjust societies can also provide a creative take on the problems of the current social order as well as on possibilities for political moves against and beyond it. Rather than removing dystopia from the utopian problematic, Jameson's clarifying comments set the stage for a discussion of dystopia that allows us to see just how this particular textual tradition works in terms of the processes of Utopia.

5

The Dystopian Turn

Still, this is the advantage of the new direction, that we do not anticipate the world dogmatically but that we first try to discover the new world from a critique of the old one. . . . If the construction and preparation of the future is not our business, then it is the more certain what we do have to consummate—I mean the ruthless criticism of all that exists, *ruthless also in the sense that criticism does not fear its results and even less so a struggle with the existing powers.*

—KARL MARX, "LETTER TO ARNOLD RUGE"[1]

I.

Dystopias negotiate the social terrain of Utopia and Anti-Utopia in a less stable and more contentious fashion than many of their eutopian and anti-utopian counterparts. As a literary form that works *between* these historical antinomies and draws on the textual qualities of both subgenres to do so, the typical dystopian text is an exercise in a politically charged form of hybrid textuality, or what Raffaella Baccolini calls "genre blurring."[2] Although all dystopian texts offer a detailed and pessimistic presentation of the very worst of social alternatives, some affiliate with a utopian tendency as they maintain a horizon of hope (or at least invite readings that do), while others only appear to be dystopian allies of Utopia as they retain an anti-utopian disposition that forecloses all transformative possibility, and yet others negotiate a more strategically ambiguous position somewhere along the antinomic continuum.

To be sure, the typical narrative structure of the dystopia (with its presentation of an alienated character's refusal of the dominant society) facilitates this politically and formally flexible stance. Indeed (and despite Jameson's hesitations about the nature, structure, and virtues of dystopian narratives), it is precisely that capacity for narrative that creates the possibility for social critique and utopian anticipation in the dystopian text. Paradoxically, dystopias reach toward the cognitively compelling nonnarrative function of Utopia precisely *through* their facilitation of pleasurable reading experiences derived from conflicts that develop in the discrete elements of plot and characterological action.

In a series of essays published in the early 1990s, Baccolini began to work out the textual mechanics of this hybrid genre.[3] Drawing on Vita Fortunati's 1979 study of dystopian conventions in *La letteratura utopica inglese*, she differentiates between the "typical" utopian narrative (a visitor's guided journey through a utopian society that leads to a comparative response that indicts the visitor's own society) and the dystopian trajectory. With dystopia, the text usually begins directly in the bad new world, and yet even without a dislocating move to an elsewhere, the element of textual estrangement remains in effect since "the focus is frequently on a character who questions" the dystopic society ("Breaking the Boundaries" 140).

Although this observation resonates with Jameson's recognition of dystopia's narrative concern for what "happens to a specific subject or character," Baccolini identifies a deeper agenda in the dystopian form itself, as she argues that the text is "built around the construction of a narrative [of the hegemonic order] and a counter-narrative [of resistance]" ("It's Not in the Womb" 293n). Since the text opens *in medias res* within the "nightmarish society," cognitive estrangement is at first forestalled by the immediacy, the normality, of the location. No dream or trip is taken to get to this place of everyday life. As in a great deal of sf, the protagonist (and the reader) is always already *in* the world in question, unreflectively immersed in the society. But the counter-narrative develops as the "dystopian citizen" moves from apparent contentment into an experience of alienation that is followed by growing awareness and then action that leads to a *climatic* event that does or does not challenge or change the society. Despite the absence of the eutopian plot of the dislocation, education, and return of a visitor, the dystopia generates its own didactic account in the critical encounter that ensues as the citizen confronts, or is confronted by, the contradictions of the society that is present on the very first page.

Drawing especially on feminist theory, and also indebted to the particular insights of George Orwell, Baccolini further notes that this structural strategy of narrative and counter-narrative most often plays out by way of the social and antisocial use of language. Throughout the history of dystopian fiction, the conflict of the text has often turned on the control of language. To be sure, the official, hegemonic order of most dystopias (from Forster's Machine society to Butler's California) rests, as Antonio Gramsci observes, on both coercion and consensus. To varying degrees, the material force of the economy and the disciplinary apparatuses control the new social order and keep it running. But discursive power, exercised in the reproduction of meaning and the interpellation of subjects, is a parallel and necessary force.

From the anti-intellectualism and theological revisionism in "The Machine Stops," to the suppression of history and corporate policy in Kim Stanley Robinson's *Gold Coast,* the erasure of political memory in Octavia Butler's *Parable of the Sower,* or the battle over story lines in Marge Piercy's *He, She and It,* language is a weapon for the reigning dystopic power structure. As Baccolini observes in two examples, in Orwell's *Nineteen Eighty-Four* "a new language, Newspeak, is created and history and culture are rewritten," and in Margaret Atwood's *Handmaid's Tale,* "although the state is at war, only its victories are reported [and] . . . history and the Book of Genesis are rewritten" ("Breaking the Boundaries" 143).

The dystopian protagonist, however, is generally prohibited from using language, and "when s/he does, it means nothing, words having been reduced to a propaganda tool" ("It's Not in the Womb" 295). Despite the initial silence, the counter-narrative is often accomplished precisely by way of language. From Kuno's conversations to Savage's in *Brave New World,* from D-503's diary in *We* to Offred's in *The Handmaid's Tale,* from the counter-advertising campaign in Frederik Pohl and C.M. Kornbluth's *Space Merchants* and the book people in Ray Bradbury's *Fahrenheit 451,* to the antiestablishment hackers in the works of William Gibson, Pat Cadigan, and other cyberpunkers, and finally to Jim's local history in Robinson's *Gold Coast,* Lauren's "Earthseed" journal in Butler's *Parable of the Sower,* and Malkah's storytelling in Piercy's *He, She and It,* control over the means of language, over representation and interpellation, is a crucial weapon and strategy in dystopian resistance.[4]

An important result of the reappropriation of language by the dystopian misfits and rebels is the reconstitution of empowering memory. With the past suppressed and the present reduced to the empirica of daily life, dystopian subjects usually lose all recollection of the way things were before the new order, but by regaining language they also recover the ability to draw on the alternative truths of the past and "speak back" to hegemonic power. As Baccolini notes in her discussion of Katherine Burdekin's *Swastika Night* (published under the pseudonym of Murray Constantine), memory plays a key role in the dystopian opposition and locates at least one utopian node not in what could be but in what once was: "Journeying to the past through memory often coincides with the realization that what is gone represented a better place and time" ("Journeying" 345).

Whereas the hegemonic order restricts memory to nostalgia for a fictive golden age that embodies the ideological attributes of its own system, the dystopian protagonist often reclaims a suppressed and subterranean memory that is forward-looking in its enabling force, liberating in its deconstruction of the official story and its reaffirmation of alternative ways of knowing and living in the world. Savage's "different" knowledge in *Brave New World,* the alternative histories in the banned books in *Fahrenheit 451,* Offred's recollections of her old life in *The Handmaid's Tale,* Jim's retrieval of Orange County history in *Gold Coast,* and Lauren's and Malkah's dialectical combination of traditional memories and radical visions in *Parable of the Sower* and *He, She and It,* all demonstrate the place and power of memory in dystopian narrative and counter-narrative.[5]

Of course there is also the material dimension of the opposition: martial, economic, and political action are equally part of the counter-hegemonic force in works such as these. Nevertheless, Baccolini is right to stress the role of language in dystopian texts that are attuned to the production and reproduction of hegemonic systems in modernity. Her argument adds another layer to the question of "what happens to a specific subject or character" and takes our understanding a step closer to realizing the extent to which dystopian narrative (with this proclivity for a self-reflexive awareness of the power of language) is concerned with its own conditions of production and reception.

As feminist criticism expanded our understanding of the utopian text in the 1960s and 1970s—and as feminist writers led the way in the critical utopian revival—analyses such as Baccolini's and the works of writers such as Atwood, Cadigan, Butler, and Piercy have opened up the dystopia to new possibilities for its creative realization and reception. Baccolini's studies of the dystopian form help to explain how the sf properties of cognitive estrangement and a textual novum come into play in significant dystopian texts as the narrative progresses. As the unhappy, alienated, sometimes dissident, protagonist confronts (and either breaks with or is defeated by) the totalizing mechanisms of the hegemonic system, a new understanding—if not always a new praxis—cognitively distances the dystopian narrative and its denouement from the conditions of the author's (and readers') empirical situation. How that conflict develops, and especially how it ends, supplies within the narrative structure the basis for investigating the meaningfulness and significance of the textual novum.

In his ongoing assessment of the formal strategies of sf texts, Darko Suvin contributes a layer of analysis that supports this critical framework and helps to pave the way for a discussion of the relationship between dystopia as an estranged subgenre and the historical contest of Utopia and Anti-Utopia. In "The SF Novel as Epic Narration" (published in 1982 and reprinted in *Positions* in 1988), he builds on his previous work and identifies two complementary elements of the sf text that can serve as sites for formal and sociological evaluation.[6] On the one hand, he considers the textual novum as plot generator; on the other, he looks at the narrative ending in terms of the opposition between the categories of epic and myth.

Suvin begins his analysis of the novum as plot generator by connecting it with the historical project of epic narration. He notes that sf works "in proportion to its meaningfulness—under the hegemony of the epic," and he grounds this assertion in the claim that sf texts share the common denominator, in one variant or another, of the "epic adventure or voyage-of-discovery plot," even if a given narration is concerned with the discovery of an idea or the process of changed consciousness (*Positions* 77). The power of such narratives, however, rests on the quality of the novum; for significant sf texts produce "new configurations of reality in both inner and outer space . . . rather than an *a priori* dogma pretending to mythological status or a private impression" (*Positions* 77).

The chronicle in the alternate setting therefore pivots on the novum, seen as the epically new, not on a "mythic reconfirmation of cyclic processuality" (*Positions* 77). Consequently, a meaningful text will "represent spatial and historical configurations as partly but irreconcilably different from the norm dominant in the author's age" and will "refuse the mythological homeomorphy where all cycles and all agents are, centrally, such transformations of each other which can bring forth neither truly new values nor a hesitation as to the empirical success of existing values" (*Positions* 77–78). Refusing the closure of mythic compensation, the epical narrative will look to a more fundamental engagement with the contradictions of the moment and open up a range of alternative social possibilities.

Moving to ending, Suvin argues that "epic events must be presented as historically contingent and unforeseeable (and thus as a rule historically reversible)," whereas in a compromised, commodified ending the "events are cyclical and predetermined, foreseeable descents from the timeless into the temporal realm," hence mythological (*Positions* 80). In an epical text, therefore, "choice" shapes the agential relations and the ending in "new and better" ways, ones not readily predicted.[7] This, he asserts, is "the precondition for a narrative rendering of freedom," for once history is newly mapped by the textual world, possibilities beyond what is known or expected are legitimated (*Positions* 80). In a mythological text, there is no clear sequence of narrative choices in a richly detailed setting that generates a forward-pulling novum. Suvin concludes that in sf texts "again more explicitly and testably than in most other genres, the ending is the moment of truth for the novum's cognitive validation and the narrative's believability—for the coherence, richness, and relevance of the text as significant [sf]" (*Positions* 81).[8]

Considered in Suvin's terms, the potential of a dystopian text thereby rests in the capacity of its novum to "reconcile the principle of hope and the principle of reality" by resisting mythological/ideological closure and opening toward what he describes as a "more mature polyphony envisaging different possibilities for different agents and circumstances, and thus leaving formal closure cognitively open-ended, regardless of whether at the end of the novel the positive values be victorious or defeated" (*Positions* 83). Understood as well in light of Baccolini's structure of narrative and counter-narrative, the potential of a dystopian text to achieve an epical, or open, expression lies in the way it negotiates the clash of the official narrative and the oppositional counter-narrative and eventually is realized in a utopian or anti-utopian stance within its own healthy negativity.

Whereas Baccolini's and Suvin's work clarifies the formal operations of the dystopian text and sets up the framework for a broader sociopolitical analysis, Søren Baggesen provides the terms for that very analysis in his 1987 essay on Ursula Le Guin's novella *The Word for World Is Forest* and James Tiptree Jr.'s (Alice Sheldon's) story "We Who Stole the Dream."[9] With this study of related but strikingly disparate short works, he introduces a way of reading dystopias (and eutopias and anti-utopias) in relation to the contention of Utopia and Anti-Utopia. He recognizes the shared dystopian quality of the two stories, but in an echo of Baccolini's and Suvin's categories, he also notes the difference in the way they negotiate the narrative conflict and its outcome. His careful analysis therefore leads to a crucial distinction between degrees of "dystopian pessimism" that can be applied to dystopian texts in general.

In Baggesen's reading, both stories "tell about a peaceful species of alien humanity, enslaved by Terran imperialism and hence motivated to transgress their own deeply integrated cultural norms of nonviolence in order to rebel against their oppressors and set themselves free" (Baggesen 34). In *The Word for World Is Forest* (which Le Guin wrote in 1967 in the midst of her opposition to the U.S. war in Vietnam), the Athsheans (who are distant relations within the pangalactic humanity) resist their Terran conquerors, thus violating their nonviolent ethic, but the resistance succeeds in persuading the "League" to withdraw its troops and keep Athshe off-limits for several generations. In "We Who Stole the Dream" (written after the war in the late 1970s and less obvious in its anti-imperialism, though perhaps clearer in its postwar bitterness), the Joiliani (a separate intelligent species) also break their own social ethic and resist their invaders, but they do so in a way that traps them in their own cycle of violent colonization.

The opposing resolutions of very similar conflicts thus occasion a comparative analysis that allows Baggesen to argue for two quite different modes of dystopian pessimism. Le Guin's account may be one of violence and counterviolence within massive social destruction, but as Baggesen puts it, "the reader is still left with the hope that the wisdom of the Athsheans will be deep enough to contain and restrict their new knowledge of violence as a political means" (Baggesen 39). In Tiptree's story there is no such open-ended possibility. Instead, the Joiliani's violent response cycles back on itself, since no historical change is achieved in the universe other than the return to violence of a people who had apparently left it behind. The "dream" of the story modulates "into nightmare as the return to peace requires a return to war, demonstrating that violence has been latent in Joiliani society from the beginning" (Baggesen 40).

Baggesen therefore sees Le Guin's text as operating within the realm of "historical necessity," whereas Tiptree's works within a "metaphysical (or ontological) necessity." From this fundamental difference, he describes the two types of narrative pessimism that are potentially available to any dystopian text. Baggesen establishes the framework for his distinction with the help of Ernst Bloch's concepts of "tendency" and "latency" in human history and his accompanying categories of "resigned" and "militant" pessimism. Working with Bloch's analyses, Baggesen argues that

> human history contains not only what it has actualized, but also all the possibilities that have been hidden by actualized history. It is from these hidden possibilities—from the *Latenz,* or rather from its dialectical opposition to the "tendency" or actual direction of history (*Tendenz*)—that we derive our "concrete utopian" notions, our "Hope Principle," that a better, even a good, human society is possible and our shared ideas of the concrete conditions that a good human society must satisfy. (Baggesen 35)

Given the tension between actual tendency and latent potential, a "space of possibilities," as Bloch describes it, emerges in which movement can still occur. Although history indeed moves in its materially restricted fashion, against idealized wishes to the contrary, there is nevertheless room for human response within a given context shaped by the contradictions of the moment. That is, in the face of a bad situation, which must be grasped in an honest pessimism rather than an idealist optimism, there are still two available responses: a "resigned pessimism" that suppresses or refuses to consider the actually existing but latent possibilities of the period, and a "militant pessimism" that (as Bloch puts it in language that is both outdated and yet stubbornly to the point) stands "with world-changing humanity in the front line of the historical process" (quoted in Baggesen 36).

Taking Bloch's point, Baggesen notes that the stance of resignation implies a response to a historical situation that regards it as "already decided," as opposed to the militant position, which sees the situation as "not yet" a closed matter. In what is to me a misunderstanding of the activist connotations of the term *militant,* however, he chooses to retain Bloch's notion yet prefers the substitute terms of *utopian pessimism* and *dystopian pessimism.* Especially if we bear in mind Jameson's caveat, it is a substitution that weakens his theoretical distinction. His new terminology immediately entraps the term *dystopia* in the iron cage of Anti-Utopia and thereby undermines the potential benefits of his argument. In light of the distinction I have been stressing, Baggesen's restriction of *dystopia* by the connotation of "anti-utopian" would simply result in naming one text a *utopian dystopia* and the other a *dystopian dystopia,* a terminological morass that would not get us very far. On a more substantive level, his substitution tends to slide the larger argument out of the complex space of history, culture, and politics and reduce it to the narrower scope of a binary opposition that works only at the level of the textual.

The difficulty in this presentation can be seen in the way Baggesen applies his terms to the Le Guin and Tiptree stories:

> Tiptree's story gives evil the kind of ontological status that would put a stop to history, so to speak. *The Word for World Is Forest,* by contrast, leaves history open to discussion and—to a limited extent—to decision. Of course, it might seem a meager consolation to suggest that we can deliberate about evil, but never fully abolish it. Yet I would point out that the nadir of historical aspiration is still "utopian": that such deliberation holds out a "utopian" hope—slim though it be—for Blochian *Möglichkeitsraum* [space of possibilities]. (Baggesen 41)

Although he captures the historical-ontological difference between the two stories, his own response pulls away from history and the needs of direct political engagement—forgetting, as Marx put it, that we do make history but *not* in circumstances of our own choosing.[10] Instead, he seems to be developing a more discursively based, if not wholly idealist, opposition to the metaphysical "evil" of the world rather than articulating a more engaged contention with the contradictions of history. Nevertheless, Baggesen's insightful distinction is crucial to the project of dystopian studies. As Jenny Wolmark has noted, his analysis and categories, especially the "thoroughly contradictory term 'utopian pessimism,'" is especially attuned to the "complex nature of particular kinds of science fiction texts."[11]

To keep with the fuller possibilities of his argument and thereby develop a more useful framework for understanding and evaluating the dystopian narrative, however, I suggest that his designation of *utopian pessimism* can work more effectively if the second term is recast as *anti-utopian pessimism.* With this distinction the basic opposition can correlate with the register of the historical continuum of Utopia and Anti-Utopia while keeping the connotative values of the immediately political terms *militant* and *resigned,* as well as allowing the term *dystopia* to remain free of any inherently "anti-utopian" charges.[12]

II.

To set up a critical framework for studying dystopian narrative, three clarifying moves need to be made to enable a better understanding of its textual mechanics and sociopolitical potential. Simply put, these are (1) the categorical separation of Utopia as impulse or historical force from its various expressions (as texts, communal societies, or social theories); (2) the formal differentiation of the dystopian from the anti-utopian text; and (3) the political differentiation between dystopian texts that work from a position of utopian pessimism and those that are fully anti-utopian.

With these clarifications in mind, we can then specify dystopia in terms of Sargent's definition in "The Three Faces of Utopianism Revisited": as a text in which "a non-existent society [is] described in considerable detail and normally located in time and space that the author intended a contemporaneous reader to view as considerably worse than the society in which that reader lived."[13] Building on this, Suvin's 1998 definition adds an emphasis on political agency, for not only does a dystopia present "a community where sociopolitical institutions, norms, and relationships between its individuals are organized in a *significantly less perfect way* than in the author's community," but it does so, and is so judged, from the explicitly oppositional standpoint of "a representative of a discontented social class or fraction, whose value-system defines 'perfection.'"[14]

In both definitions authorial intention matters, but Suvin's foregrounding of the oppositional actant leads to a direct linkage with a potentially oppositional readerly stance. As Sargent argues in "Utopia—the Problem of Definition," an author's claim that a work is a utopia or a dystopia invites at least an initial reading in terms of that perspective, and from there a more complex assessment can proceed by way of a further analysis of the text but also of readerly responses.[15] Thus, some texts intended (and internally marked) as utopian or dystopian (or perhaps not written within a utopian/dystopian strategy at all) can be received by readers as utopian or dystopian according to their own aesthetic and political judgments. Skinner's *Walden Two* is thus a utopia often read as a dystopia, and I recall a graduate professor of mine saying that he considered Delany's critical utopia, *Triton,* to be nothing but dystopian or even anti-utopian.[16]

With its imbricated account of the poetics and politics of the dystopian textual opportunity, Suvin's definition even more explicitly leaves the judgment of utopian or dystopian quality up to a reader or critic who undoubtedly works from a particular standpoint (with particular affiliations and principles) in order to decide whether a given fictive society is *worse* or *better* than the author's or the reader/critic's. Indeed, my own categorization of certain texts as critical dystopias in this study is precisely the result of such an assessment, since none of the literary or filmic examples discussed in the closing chapters are explicitly named as dystopias by their authors.

Working from these distinctions and definitions and bearing in mind Baccolini's and Suvin's analyses, we can examine a dystopia in terms of its narrative and counter-narrative structure to track the manner in which its textual novum generates internal innovation in and through its narrative trajectories and ending.[17] Then, in light of Baggesen's identification of utopian and anti-utopian affiliations, we can further examine a text in terms of its formal and political standpoint within the historical situation itself.[18] Thus, the distinction can be made between the limit case of an open (epical) dystopia that retains a utopian commitment at the core of its formally pessimistic presentation and a closed (mythic) one that abandons the textual ambiguity of dystopian narrative for the absolutism of an anti-utopian stance.[19] To be sure, a given text can be located at any point along the continuum between these opposed poles. This differentiation makes the first type a fully utopian dystopia, whereas the second polar type is best seen as a "pseudo-dystopia" or what might more properly be called a masked version of the "formal anti-utopia."

Addressing this difference, Peter Fitting sees it as one between dystopias that work from a stance of utopian social criticism and those that work from a position that develops an anti-utopian criticism of Utopia. In a comment that resonates with Jameson's remarks on the narrative and nonnarrative dimensions of the textual utopia, he further suggests that a "possible distinction between dystopia and anti-utopia might lie in seeing the former in terms of setting and the latter in terms of plot."[20] In light of this suggestion, the dystopian narrative of revolt or possible revolt that expresses a utopian pessimism tends to privilege the setting (generated in what I term the iconic register of the text) by developing its surplus utopian possibilities in the extensive details of the alternative world (located, for example, in an unconquered enclave or in economic or political contradictions that are not resolved or controlled).

In contrast, a text with an anti-utopian stance tends to favor a linear plot (developed in the discrete register) wherein revolts are decisively crushed, with no slippage or surplus of dissent or opposition left in the society. Thus, at one end of the spectrum a dystopian text can be seen as *utopian* in tendency if in its portrayal of the "bad place" it suggests (even if indirectly) or at least stimulates the potential for an effective challenge and possibly change by virtue of human efforts (what Raymond Williams understood as "willed transformation").[21] At the other end, it can be deemed *anti-utopian* if it fails (or chooses not) to challenge the ideological and epistemological limits of the actually existing society. Folding Baccolini's and

Historical Antinomies

Utopia (historical) (novum)	**Anti-Utopia** (universal) (pseudo-novum)

Literary Forms

utopia/eutopia (radical hope)	**anti-utopia** (cynicism, despair)
dystopia (militant pessimism) (epic, open)	**pseudo-dystopia** (resigned pessimism) (myth, closed)

FIGURE 5.1 History and Form

Suvin's distinctions back into this critical mix, the dystopia that works with an open, epical strategy maintains a possibility for change or identifies a site for an alternative position in some enclave or other marker of difference, or in some way in its content or form manages to establish an estranged relationship with the historical situation that does not capitulate; whereas the anti-utopia-as-dystopia that recycles a closed, mythic strategy produces a social paradigm that remains static because no serious challenge or change is desired or seen as possible.

As a heuristic device, the formal and political range of expressive possibilities is set out in Figure 5.1, which shows the spread of narrative forms (set in lowercase, with the correlate sociopolitical and formal positions in parentheses) posited in relation to the historical antinomies of Utopian and Anti-Utopia (set in uppercase, with the correlate sociopolitical and formal positions in parentheses).

From this framework, several questions can be asked of a given dystopian text. How do the narrative and counter-narrative of the text play out in the iconic and discrete registers of the text? How does the text negotiate the difference between an open or a closed strategy? How does the text contend with the difference between epical and mythic form and substance? How is the text in-formed by a novum or pseudo-novum? Where does the assemblage of textual work place the dystopia along the continuum of "militant" or "utopian" pessimism versus "resigned" or "anti-utopian" pessimism"? How, then, does the dystopia situate itself in the contest between history and the "end-of-history," between Utopia and Anti-Utopia?

To questions such as these, which are located within an analysis of a given text and its conditions of production, can be added another, and that is one that also investigates its reception. For even if a work is fully on the side of Anti-Utopia in form and affiliation, readers or audiences may well respond with a resistant and utopian attitude—perhaps finding in the very closure of a certain text a chilling view of the present that counterfactually produces hope rather than the capitulation the text itself invites. This, of course, is to recall Jameson's recognition that perhaps especially in our own moment, "the most powerful arguments against Utopia are in reality Utopian ones."[22]

III.

Given this critical schematic, E.M. Forster's "The Machine Stops" offers an initial example of a dystopian narrative with an epical quality and a stance that is one of utopian pessimism, albeit more abstract than some later examples, such as the critical dystopias.[23] Forster begins the story *in medias res* in Vashti's room, but an estranged perspective is quickly marked by the narrator's disruptive invitation to "imagine." Although Vashti's character position provides the opportunity for the appropriately detailed account of the dystopian society, Kuno's subversive revelations create the counter-narrative of alienation, consciousness-raising, and resistance (and here even the author's humanistically privileged individual agency opens out to a potentially wider collectivity that encompasses the Homeless and the subject position of the narrator). As the negation to Kuno's negation, the Machine's disciplinary reaction creates the contradictory material conditions for the ultimate crisis. When it enforces firmer control over Kuno and the entire social system, the Machine's increased centralization leads to the inability of its human servants to work from a knowledge of the total system, and thus the possibility for diagnosis and repair is reduced to zero. Consequently, the quantitative problems grow into the qualitative, systemic crisis when the larger subsystems fail, and without the ability to repair itself and without human backup, the Machine finally stops.

The story's novum, however, not only concerns the exposure of the centralized, mechanical social logic and the reaffirmation of the ability of humans to interrogate it, but—however mystified—it also points to the possibility of a new moment of history (even if seen through the imperfect lens of a residually backward glance). In the continuing existence of the Homeless, exiled after the failure of the "Great Rebellion," can be found the basis for a utopian enclave (launching a motif that will become familiar in subsequent dystopian narratives). For in their exiled state the Homeless constitute a zone of un- or not yet-conquered space from which a new society, or at least a mass political movement, *might* emerge. Rather than confidently predicting and describing this opposition, Forster's narrative (in keeping with Jameson's sense of the prohibition against images of freedom) simply marks the empty space and expresses the hope that humanity might one day struggle toward a new way of life. Yet in not attending to the *process* of this future political change (a step that is crucial to a *concrete* utopian strategy, as seen in works such as William Morris's *News from Nowhere* or Jack London's *Iron Heel*), Forster's text remains abstract in its oppositional potential.

But there is another formal element that feeds into the novum, and that is the overall dystopian strategy of the story itself. One useful way of charting this radically new form is through an examination of the function of the narrator. From the initial invitation through the intermittent comments to the extended commentary in the closing paragraph (which includes the hopeful suggestion that the Homeless might survive), the narrator formally signifies the existence of a reality outside the parameters of both the Machine society and the surface enclave of the Homeless. Writing from some third place, the narrator offers a set of social values that implicitly opposes the very society it describes. The location of this elsewhere is ambiguous, but (at least) two possibilities exist—in the logic of the story and in the history of the utopian form. As a more traditional signifier of utopian critique, the narrator could be taken as the voice of an implied author in Forster's own time, and in this sense it would be relating a prophetic tale of warning in the nineteenth-century mode of utopian satire in which the portrayed society is oppressive but hope nevertheless lingers, even though no alternative future yet exists to give transformed substance to that hope.

Or as a signifier of a new, realistically irreal approach to utopian expression, it could be regarded as a voice located in a future beyond that of the Machine society and beyond that of the post-Machine years in which the Homeless might still be struggling to establish their own society. From this proto–science fictional perspective, the narrator's tale delivers a more hopeful warning by evoking an empowering memory informed by an achieved utopian future that looks back on the Machine society as a moment in its own past. Thus, the narrator speaks from an imagined time in which humanity has already built a new society out of the shell of the old, one in which the social ethos and aesthetic form of stories like the narrator's could exist. If we take both possibilities as dialogically related, the very *form* of Forster's story self-reflexively shapes it as an emergent new dystopia (in which the older satiric form is both negated and preserved by way of a new formal mode that one day will be named science fiction).

In its overall structure, the story possesses an epical quality as it exposes, however abstractly, certain antihuman systemic tendencies in Forster's own time and names (if not traces) the successful exercise of resistance (one based in an individual structure of feeling but that also suggests the collective formation of the Homeless and possibly that of the society that has produced the narrator). As well, the ending of the story remains open, giving no answers but rather creating at least a minimal "space of possibilities" that evokes a potentially utopian horizon. Recycled mythic closure, reinforced by an anti-utopian pessimism that obviates all possibility of human engagement and transformation of the situation, is not to be found in Forster's story.

At the beginning of the twentieth century, then, this early dystopian narrative gets the intertextual trajectory off to a *utopian* beginning as it moves within its pages from the satiric to the realistically irreal, from an apparently anti-utopian pessimism to a scrappy utopian pessimism. Coming two decades later, Yevgeny Zamiatin's *We* pulls no punches in pessimistically describing the extensive power of the OneState to put down individual and collective resistance.[24] The disciplinary success of surveillance and especially of the "Operation" is clear in the suppression of the protagonist, D-503, and in his subsequent betrayal of his fellow rebel and lover, I-330, and the Mephi resistance. At the narrative's end, D-503 has been "rehabilitated," and he reviews his own subversive diary with amazement, wondering how he "actually wrote these 220 pages." He reports all he knows about the "enemies of happiness" to the Benefactor. He watches passively as I-330 is placed under the Bell and destroyed, and in the last lines he celebrates the reestablishment of the ruling, instrumental "reason" (Zamyatin 220–221). But at the core of this pessimistic narrative of hegemonic victory, with its suggestions of narrative and political closure, the text from the very beginning generates a literal and self-reflexive counter-narrative in the form of D-503's diary, which (as the counter-text that both shapes and opposes the entire narrative) traces his alienation, growing desire and consciousness, and attempted resistance.

If it were just a discrete narrative question of the success or failure of D-503's opposition, the text would of course valorize the mythic enclosure of the ubiquitous and inevitable power of the OneState. But there is more going on in the text and in the society it iconically portrays than D-503's actions. As he discovers the nature and contradictions of his society, he encounters other recalcitrant and even oppositional elements, ones that are not closed down by the end of his diary entries (Records). At the very least, his discovery of a populated, natural space beyond the Wall identifies an outside, and a free people, *not* subject to the OneState. The alliance of those external, nonstandardized humans and the dissidents who are organized by the Mephi resistance within the official society marks another. In a less overt way—and pointing toward a narrative gambit that will recur in many sf texts—the additional possibility of space travel by a collectivity of humans, and in this case in a ship named the *Integral,* identifies yet another, materially transcendent space.

Finally, the political models of I-330's resistance, even if crushed, and D-503's change of consciousness, even if defeated, stand as evidence that radical transformations can actually happen. Their stories prove that the OneState is not in total control and that slippage exists in the practices of everyday life. Thus, at the iconic register of the text, the presentation of uncontrolled space, individual radicalization, and collective resistance provides a surplus meaning that is simply not contained by either the narrative dominance of the OneState or the apparent closure of the ending. Just before D-503's closing paean to "reason," he acknowledges that at the edges of the city, "in the western quarters there is still chaos, roaring, corpses, animals, and, unfortunately, quite a lot of Numbers who have betrayed reason" (Zamyatin 221).

Epical openness and utopian pessimism therefore characterize the militant resistance that works against the grain of Zamyatin's portrayal of the OneState. Although it offers a strong argument against the narrow, ultimately compromised "utopianism" built on the actually existing combination of Taylorism and Leninism, a deeper, uncontainable utopian impulse runs through the entire work. It is best caught in D-503's account of his conversation with I-330 in Record 30, where she makes her argument for permanent revolution. Against D-503's parroting of the official line that Utopia has arrived, that "our revolution was the final one," she turns the numerical discourse of her society on its head and asserts that any such "final" solution is itself a betrayal of the very process of which he speaks: "And how can there be a final revolution? There is no final one. The number of revolutions is infinite. The last one—that's for children" (Zamyatin 167).

As does Forster's use of conversation, the diary mode in this text self-reflexively makes its own formal gestures to the not yet achieved, but possible, utopian future. In his first Record, D-503 speaks of his account as a possible epic, and more so in his address to his "unknown readers" in Record 35, he asserts in the process of his writing the possibility of a future in which his diary will be read by those who have not only survived the OneState but have perhaps gone on to create a better alternative to it. Indeed, Zamyatin's own text—especially in light of its publishing history and reception—is itself a sign of the book's strong, and indeed more concrete, *utopian* stance.

With Orwell's *Nineteen Eighty-Four,* as Gaylord LeRoy noted, the textual tendency of anti-utopian pessimism can be more clearly seen.[25] The brooding, faded, shabby, cruel, and paranoid society presided over by Big Brother and the Inner Party is the quintessence of the bad place in our time. Nevertheless, a structural counter-narrative suggests itself in the story of Winston and Julia. But the dominant narrative of their utter defeat—especially in the Room 101 torture scene—is so total that no possibility for resistance exists by the end of the plot.

Further, there is no meaningful possibility of movement or resistance, much less radical change, embedded in any of the iconic elements of the text. Winston's and Julia's pleasure in the room above the shop may suggest a space that could be named utopian, but their meeting is set up, watched, and then used as the occasion for the capture and torture of the lovers. As well, neither the rural idyll of the Golden Country nor the urban lives of the Proles give any indication that they might constitute a viable utopian enclave or agency, that they might be the source or germ of movements that could attain the critical mass to revolt, much less to succeed. Indeed, the lingering song of the proletarian woman that Winston overhears is not a sign of utopian hope but actually a plaintive testimony to its apparently permanent impossibility. And certainly, the ending of the bleak narrative forecloses the possibility of any social transformation. Thus, while Orwell powerfully exposes the terror of official utopianism as he has come to see it, he also sets up a narrative structure that denies the possibility of an oppositional utopian resistance—be it in an organized formation, in individual actions such as those of Winston and Julia, or in the everyday lives of the Proles.

Orwell's dystopia is therefore an eloquent example of one that leans toward an anti-utopian pessimism; however, it is one that was created in a very specific context. Unlike the conservative writers of overt anti-utopias (e.g., Ayn Rand, Karl Popper), as several critics have noted, Orwell sought to counter the utopia-gone-wrong that embodied the central plan and the authoritarian mind with what might be called a "critical anti-utopia," one that could possibly make people conscious of what might happen and therefore work to avert it.[26] In other words, he regarded his work as a utopian attack on what he saw as anti-utopian historical tendencies. As he put it in his own disclaimer, the novel was not intended as

> an attack on socialism or on the British Labour Party . . . but as a show up of the perversions to which a centralized economy is liable and which have already been partly realized in Communism and Fascism. I do not believe that the kind of society I describe necessarily *will* arrive, but I believe (allowing of course for the fact that the book is satire) that something resembling it *could* arrive.[27]

The author's own oppositional hermeneutic is therefore very specific and not aimed at the rejection of all progressive thought and practice. Indeed, the slim trace of hope in his text comes at the very end of the published volume: that is, in the "Newspeak Appendix." This self-reflexive "report" on language and power stands analytically, cognitively outside the story of the dominant state, and it thus bespeaks a possible Other Place—one of present, satirical, critique if not future, utopian, opposition. As Larry Caldwell notes, the appendix functions as "a kind of ironic anti-closure" to the story, wherein the "temporal ambivalence of the verbs and of the adverbial locutions expressly confounds the Party's 'forever' and destabilizes its closed narrative."[28]

Orwell's formal and historical problem, however, is that the book tends to outstrip itself in its pessimistic virtuosity. It delivers such a fulsome and uncompromising anti-utopian narrative (unblemished by a theory or practice of opposition or transition) that it squeezes surplus utopian possibility out of its pages.[29] Despite Orwell's goals, disclaimers, and textual tactics, *Nineteen Eighty-Four* gets caught in its own anti-utopian impulse and in its reception often goes no farther than the social terror it begins with. As a result, it satirically cycles around in a critical account of mythic closure in a seemingly endless present rather than offering an open-ended parable (as abstract as Forster's or as concrete as Zamyatin's) with a utopian horizon that might provoke political awareness or effort.

If, moving further along in the century, Atwood's *Handmaid's Tale* is added to this intertextual sample as a continuation and challenge to the classical dystopia, a more nuanced, perhaps deliberately or liberally *ambiguous* position can be discovered in the evolution of the dystopian mode.[30] To be sure, Atwood's portrayal of Gilead is recognizable by readers aware of the "backlash" of the 1980s. With elements from the New Right and Christian fundamentalism conjoined with deformed and distorted feminist formations, mass-mediated consumption, and the military-industrial complex, a variant of "friendly fascism" comes alive on the page.[31]

Against this near future society of repression and exploitation, with enhanced citizenship only for the elect, a counter-narrative develops around the culture of resistance practiced by the Handmaids—through sexual transgression (Moira), spying (Ofglen), and language itself (Offred's diary, but also her secret messages and the masked communications among the women)—and in the direct action of the Mayday Underground. Along with these militant forces, the iconic suggestion of a border and locales beyond it (Canada, England, Brazil) creates an "outside" (one more substantial than Zamyatin's or Huxley's) that, as it becomes known in resistance circles, offers those trapped in Gilead a possible refuge, a secure base for fighting back, and a utopian horizon. As the physical conduit to that external space, the "Underground Femaleroad" provides the link (by way of historical memory and immediate action) between the internal opposition and a potential utopian space. And yet within the text of Offred's diary the counter-narrative becomes a tale of anti-utopian triumph, as the resistance is crushed and the Christian state prevails.

In its discrete register, therefore, *The Handmaid's Tale* leans toward the anti-utopian pole of resignation, but there is more to this text than the main narrative and even counter-narrative. Atwood writes from the perspective of the 1980s, having seen, at least for a few years in the 1960s and 1970s, the false utopias of big states and big ideas yield their power to the grassroots utopian opposition of popular movements (fighting for racial liberation, stopping a war, taking control of one's body and one's self). In her hands the classical dystopia takes on a different quality than it does in those of earlier writers who focused on the transgressions of the modern state in the decades leading up to the 1960s. Indeed, Atwood seems to be pushing the classical form to its limits in an effort to find the right level of cognitive figuration for the bad times of the 1980s.

As seen in her detailed iconic presentation, Gilead is a society in which the contradictions are more pervasive and closer to the surface than in many of the dystopian accounts of authoritarian states. Besides the conflict between the ruling regime and the resistance (among the Handmaids, in Mayday, or across the border), another threat to Gilead's power lies in the internal dissatisfaction of its chosen few. The deep unhappiness of the Wives, themselves relative victims who are suffering from the genetic sterility that works so well as a metaphor for the death culture modernity has produced, is more than matched by the desperate "cheating" of the Commanders as it is based in their insecurity and hypocrisy. Indeed, the Commanders' private abuse of Handmaids, their indulgence in the pathological public sphere of the bar and brothel of Jezebel's Club, and their individual power plays are symptomatic of the political corruption and ultimate instability of Gilead itself. The discontent of the women and men in the power elite turns Atwood's Gilead into a weak dystopia compared to the ubiquitous efficiency in the societies created by Forster, Zamyatin, Huxley, and Orwell.

Moving beyond the discrete and iconic registers of Offred's tale, the ambiguity of the text is most evident in the infamous "Historical Notes" that "end" the book. As Offred's account tails off, a post-revolutionary reality (only discretely suggested by Forster's narrator or iconically pointed to by Zamiatin's marginal resistance logic and movements) is here developed in the brief presentation of a functioning future society that looks back on Gilead from the year 2195. Clearly working in the tradition of Orwell's "Newspeak Appendix," Atwood thus reverses the closure of her anti-utopian story with this thoughtful addendum that reports an academic symposium addressing the significance of Offred's newly discovered diary. Yet, unlike Orwell's, hers is dynamically linked with the historical moment of Gilead. It does not simply stand satirically outside the base narrative, even though it only abstractly points to the new historical moment and does not detail the way the change came about. However disconcerted some of us might be at seeing an academic meeting and academic discourse as signs of a utopian future, and in spite of the residually patriarchal arrogance of Professor Pieixoto, the social context of the proceedings of the "Symposium of Gileadean Studies" constitutes a potential "utopian" gesture at the closing of Atwood's dystopian text.

The future society in which the symposium occurs testifies to Gilead's defeat and its passing in history (along with other "late-twentieth-century monotheocracies"), but it also gives further textual clues to the absent paradigm of the *relatively* more utopian world that followed those terrible societies. The society is made up of a racially diverse population—as indicated by the names and identities of those who are Native Americans or First Peoples (Maryann Crescent Moon from Nunavit, who in ironic historical revenge studies Caucasian anthropology) and South Asian (Gopal Chatterjee from India, who, equally ironically, reverses the gaze to study Western philosophy). An apparently more progressive decentralized regional government is indicated in the references to the "Republic of Texas" and even in the term *Nunavit* itself, since it suggests the name chosen by the First Nations of Canada for their autonomous zone in the former Northwest Territories. Other progressive qualities are suggested in the implicit critiques of administrative mechanisms such as "State Religion" or "Urban Core Encirclement" (Atwood 380).

Finally, the attitude toward the historical realities of Gilead that runs through the discussion and critique of the professor's presentation (even when, or perhaps especially when, the presentation itself is coolly distanced by its narrowly empiricist, inappropriately jocular, and obsequiously brutish tone) bespeaks a very different set of social ethics and practices that come across as achieved social assumptions, understandable by the implied reader of the text but not necessarily by actual readers possibly looking forward to a Gilead in their lives in the 1980s. Each of the following contributes to the iconic image of an enlightened society that is more utopian than Gilead or our own present moment: the accepted ordinariness of women's history, the certainty that compulsory state control over people's bodies is wrong, the past-tense references to a long-gone era of superpowers and arms deals, the matter-of-fact discussion of discredited "national homelands" and "Jewish boat-person" schemes enacted by the CIA, and the negative reference to "sociobiological theory of natural polygamy" as a "scientific justification for some of the odder practices of the regime" (Atwood 388).

And yet in another reading, the utopian quality of this future alternative fades if one focuses instead on the general intellectual, class- or caste-based attitude of condescension toward Offred, as the life of this ordinary suffering woman, who became a courageous political agent in her own right, is patronizingly reduced to the reified status of an object of study. In this more negative light, the utopian values of the future society give way to the familiar anti-utopian suggestion that humanity will "always" be mean-spirited. Indeed, the question lingers: is this later society truly a eutopian future whose past includes Gilead, or is it a future in which a eutopian transformation has failed or has not yet happened (or may never happen, because of the proclivities of "human nature")? Given this uncertainty, and bolstered by Atwood's avoidance of a counter-narrative that traces the transition from Gilead to this apparently better future, the combination of Offred's narrative and the "Historical Notes" prevents the emergence of a militant utopian position within the text's dystopian pessimism.

Atwood's closing line ("Are there any questions?") makes me wonder whether *The Handmaid's Tale* might be best understood as an "ambiguous dystopia" (in a significant variation of Le Guin's critical utopia of the 1970s, *The Dispossessed: An Ambiguous Utopia*). Although the final words recall Russ's ending in *The Female Man* (wherein an authorial voice charges her "little book" to go out into the world and stir up dissent and possibly transform what has been described as a harsh patriarchal society), Atwood's text steps back from such a militant stance and opts instead for a distanced mediation on the dire times of the 1980s. The reader (or this reader at least) is therefore left wandering along the continuum between Utopia and Anti-Utopia, in a wishful anticipation of a better world but with little imaginary substance on the process of getting beyond the present terrible moment.

Overall, therefore, in what might ultimately be seen as the stance of an engaged liberal who faces the evils of social reality and yet takes one considered step back from a radical political praxis, Atwood stretches the creative range of the classical dystopian form, working it in one direction toward anti-utopian closure, then turning it toward a utopian horizon, and then again leaving a space in between for her unresolved questions as they grow out of the accounts of the society's internal flaws, the opposition's vulnerability, and the clearly imperfect and perhaps always compromised "utopian" reality revealed in the symposium narrative. Although the *Tale* remains a "classical" dystopia in its overall structure and tone, its author has nevertheless taken the traditional dystopia to a historical limit, and in doing so she anticipates the moment of the critical dystopias that will soon occur in the popular realm of sf in the late 1980s. And yet as she pulls back from the degree of utopian engagement that will appear in the critical dystopias, she remains on the other side of the dividing line from these more radical texts that nevertheless benefit from her vision and craft.[32]

IV.

Moving beyond these classical texts, the dystopian sensibility found a larger and more diffuse scope in the popular form of sf. Indeed, the title of Harold Berger's

1976 book, *Science Fiction and the New Dark Age*, speaks to the privileged place of dystopian and anti-utopian narratives in the genre in the years after World War II, and Krishan Kumar ends his own extensive study with a recognition of the "new quizzical and cynical mood [of sf], which increasingly became pessimistic and apocalyptic" in the 1950s and 1960s (*Modern Times* 403). Although he offers a potentially patronizing account of the influence of the classical dystopias "filtering" down into "pulp science fiction," Mark Hillegas nevertheless recognizes the strong anti-utopian and dystopian quality of sf after World War II (Hillegas 151). In a more sf-friendly manner, David Samuelson argues that the dystopian tradition was alive and well in postwar American sf that "concentrated mainly on projecting American technological and economic domination beyond the Earth and into the future."[33] These sf works, he notes, were dystopian in approach and subject matter even though they generally had "upbeat endings" that suited the market. As in the responses of other critics, Samuelson makes the familiar conflation of works that attack utopianism (in the spirit of Huxley, Berdiaeff, and Dostoyevsky) with those that question the social realties of the new "Pax Americana" and the "dangers which seem to be inherent in progress, exploitation and technology in general" (Samuelson 77).

The critical study that most effectively caught the spirit of postwar sf, however, was Kingsley Amis's *New Maps of Hell* (1960). In this groundbreaking scholarly venture, Amis grasped how capable sf was of furnishing "a new vantage point from which to survey 'our culture'" (Amis 12). Especially in his section on utopias, he examines sf that exposes the "forces of evil" in political, economic, and technological terms. Catching the anti-utopian drift within the dystopian imagination, he observes that "conformist utopias maintained by deliberate political effort are a cherished nightmare of contemporary science fiction"; then, in a sympathetic comparison with the classical dystopias, he offers extensive readings of popular sf by Poul Anderson, James Blish, Anthony Boucher, Damon Knight, Katherine MacLean, Robert Sheckley, Clifford Simak, William Tenn, Philip Wylie, John Wyndham, and Bradbury (Amis 84ff.). For examples that question "unrestricted technological and commercial development" as well as investigating the new exploitation and exploration of sexuality in the postwar years, he cites works by Arthur C. Clarke, John D. MacDonald, Robert Sheckley, Clifford Simak, A. E. Van Vogt, and Pohl and Kornbluth, among others. In his conclusion he presents his famous formulation of the "idea as hero" to highlight what he calls the "science fiction of idea," which to his mind offers the best stories in the genre (Amis 118, 119). Central to this tendency is the seriousness that Suvin sees producing the textual novum that takes sf out of the category of simple adventure story and into the realm of cognitively estranged critical fiction.

Whether regarded as "near future" satire (Kumar), "anti-utopia" (Hillegas), "apocalyptic, ecotastrophic, even technological Gothic" (Samuelson), or "new maps of hell" (Amis), sf in the affluent Western societies after World War II worked within an increasing enclosure of the lived moment and drew upon the dystopian sensibility even when its stories and novels were not fully cast in the classical dystopian form. To be sure, some works of sf, or at the edges of sf, were distinctly dystopian, as Bradbury's *Fahrenheit 451* (1953), Kurt Vonnegut's *Player Piano* (1952), Anthony Burgess's *Clockwork Orange* (1962), or Bernard Wolfe's neglected *Limbo* (1952) exemplify. Others, however, worked loosely with the spirit of the dystopia and produced tales of social nightmares that cannot be reduced to the strict parameters of dystopian narrative even though they share the basic perspective; here the works of J. G. Ballard, John Brunner, and Philip K. Dick offer excellent examples.

At this point a closer look at a few sf works of the 1950s and 1960s can sample the intertextual web from which the new dystopias of the 1980s and 1990s eventually developed. Of all postwar sf texts, one that is often recognized for its dystopian quality is Pohl and Kornbluth's *Space Merchants.*[34] Kumar acclaims it as a "characteristic product of the 1950s . . . which satirized the glossy, hi-tech world of Madison Avenue, and portrayed a servile future world run by multinational advertising corporations" (*Modern Times* 403). Samuelson gives it faint praise as a "science fiction 'classic,' which survives more from manic satirical inventiveness hung on a clichéd melodramatic plot, than from any serious look into the social nature of things" (Samuelson 77).

As early as 1960, however, Amis caught the significance of this novel in ways other commentators did not, calling it "an admonitory satire on certain aspects of our own society, mainly economic, but . . . not only that."[35] In doing so, he identified the critical force of this text and extrapolated it to sf in general. With these remarks on *Space Merchants,* he lays the groundwork for Suvin's concept of the novum, and he begins to chart the development of a form of dystopian writing that is not bound to the narrative strictures and anti-utopian temptations of the classical dystopia.

Amis argues that *Space Merchants* offers a disturbing, if exaggerated, insight into an emerging society in which people of his time will face a "situation without precedent in our experience" that "both in this novel and in science fiction as a whole, will be an uncomfortable one by our standards, and it may be used to subject human beings to a kind of insecurity that is both new in itself and novel in the sense that it renders general and public what in the present context is only piecemeal and private" (Amis 114). The powerful fictive intervention of sf texts such as Pohl and Kornbluth's, Amis believes, cannot simply be read through a mainstream literary criticism that reduces it to the status of allegories or concretizations of "our own variegated insecurities" or to the historical tradition of satire or the newer ironies of a modernist reaction to present-day evils. Nor can it be simply equated with the related form of the utopia. Instead, as Frye and then others, such as Howe and Suvin, similarly argued, the sf maps of hell constitute a distinct variety of popular fiction that offers realistically delineated cognitive maps that are textual products of their own time (and which, as Amis notes throughout his study, have much in common with the cultural and formal immediacy and complexity of modern jazz).

Written and published at a time when the twin disciplinary apparatuses of consumerism (which commanded obedience to a new culture of immediate gratification) and anti-communism (which commanded loyalty by way of the imposition of fear) were helping to produce the economy, culture, and subjects of postwar U.S. society, *Space Merchants* appeared under the shadow of censorship and passivity that pervaded the culture of the late 1940s and the early 1950s. Because political and moral censors such as the House Un-American Activities Committee, Joseph McCarthy, and the Roman Catholic Church never took sf as seriously as they did other popular culture forms such as Hollywood films, comic books, and rock and roll, the book escaped political and religious repression and has been avidly read and often taught since its first publication.

Looked at with the lens of dystopian strategies, *Space Merchants* isolates and examines the disciplinary tendencies of consumerism and anti-communism as they tighten the grip of hegemonic power on the newly affluent society. The counter-narrative that emerges to oppose these forces clearly places the book on the epical utopian pessimist side of the spectrum. However manic and melodramatic (Amis claims that Kornbluth contributed the action while Pohl "filled in the social background and the satire"), *Space Merchants* delivers a detailed world picture in which multinational corporations have edged out government and advertising practices permeate the social fabric (Amis 107). Before Althusserean notions of the construction of the subject or Lacanian arguments about lack and desire, and in the spirit of the Frankfurt School, Pohl and Kornbluth described the logic of capital's project of producing obedient, desiring consumers rather than thinking citizens.

When the protagonist, Mitch Courtney (the advertising executive disciplined for his apparently disloyal activities), is exiled to the chlorella plantations in Central America, he experiences firsthand the pattern of deprivation and desire produced by the system. Enclosed within long days of work and with no cash to spend, he finds he has to draw on his future pay, and (like people who live in company mining towns or in the credit card economy that began in the 1950s) he realizes that the worker-consumer never gets out of debt. Further, and more substantially, he discovers that he is becoming the ideal consumer that his New York ad agency aimed to construct as he buys various products in order to cope with the alienation and exploitation of his mind and body in the daily grind. He therefore gets stuck in a cycle of addiction always already occupied by a scripted sequence of product names: "Think about smoking, think about Starrs, light a Starr. Light a Starr, think about Popsie, get a squirt. Get a squirt, think about Crunchies, buy a box. Buy a box, think about smoking, light a Starr. And at every step roll out the words of praise that had been dinned into you through your eyes and ears and pores" (Pohl and Kornbluth 79).

This fully developed capitalist system strives to build its market base by extensively reaching out to every human being on the planet by means of images, sounds, and smells and by intensively reaching into every psyche by way of the subliminal appeals that Vance Packard and other social critics exposed at the time. From the "Star Class" citizens of New York to the indentured workers of the chlorella plantations, almost everyone is enmeshed in this totalizing social web. "Sales" is the god, mergers are the steps to corporate heaven, and privatization is the means of releasing formerly taxed monies into the hands of the corporations. The protocol of this hegemonic order, of course, has its official narrative sequence: construct new consumers, capture new markets, increase profits, merge, increase power in the state apparatus and the society at large, take over more, make more profits. The lords of advertising, such as Mitch's boss, Fowler Schocken III, are the privileged subjects, and their aim is to rule by appealing to the loyalty of those who make it into the enhanced subject status of the Star Class and by keeping all others at bay through labor servitude and consumer addiction (as they earn or borrow just enough to stay on the hook).

The development of this economy and culture, however, has been achieved at the expense of the natural environment, for not only has the natural order been ravaged for industrial growth but also unchecked population growth has been encouraged to produce new consumers. The result is an overcrowded and environmentally nasty world. Fresh water trickles, air is so filthy that filtering plugs need to be worn in urban areas, meat has been replaced (not for health reasons) by soyaburgers and regenerated steak, bread is oiled not buttered, wood is regarded as a luxury item, two-room apartments are considered housing for the elite, and Cadillacs are pedaled (see Pohl and Kornbluth 1–4). Having taken Earth to its exploitable limits, the corporate leaders now look with awe to the conquest of Venus as its next market: "Not just India. Not just a commodity. But a whole planet to *sell*" (Pohl and Kornbluth 7). Capital, it appears, will be able to develop yet another world system, rolling over Earth-bound profits into its next great venture.

Such pervasive corporate power, total political control, and natural degradation, however, have produced their opposition in the counter-narrative of Mitch's own alienation and the collective rebellion of the "Consies," as the Conservationist Party is ironically nicknamed. In this counterpunctal trajectory, the authors tap into the existential angst and anger of the 1950s as reflected in works as serious as those by Jean-Paul Sartre and the Beats and as popular as William H. Whyte's *Organization Man* (1956) and films such as *The Man in the Grey Flannel Suit* (Johnson, 1956). From that nascent structure of feeling, they track Mitch's growing awareness, disillusionment, punishment, and eventually consciousness-raising and revolt, as this "typical" subject of the managerial class properly betrays his own ruling-class fraction. To be sure, the story at worst turns on a melodramatic love saga in which Mitch tries to win back his wife, Kathy, only to do so as part of the Consie rebellion that she, as a good Consie, has helped to organize, and Mitch's voice often does not rise above the heroic tones of a Tom Swift or a Henry Aldrich. Nevertheless, his plunge into the hell of the plantation, his social and self-discoveries, and his gradual alliance with the Consies feeds a counter-narrative of revolt that engages with the social tensions and conflicts of the time and exceeds the limitations of its market-driven love story.

The surplus social meaning that takes the story line beyond that of an adventure story or love story is generated by the most subversive element of the novel: the utopian enclave, the utopian movement, of the Consies that spreads through the iconic register of the text. Opposing the anticommunism of the day—but in a clever and ironic twist in which the radical group is based in what was in the 1950s a right-wing movement—Pohl and Kornbluth presciently combine the environmentalism of the libertarian Right with the politics of the socialist and communist Left (with a strong popular front flavor to it) in the sort of alliance that might have happened in the 1950s (had not the mechanism of anti-communism succeeded in destroying the possibility of a broad Left opposition) and that does happen by the 1970s. The Consies and not Mitch, therefore, constitute the locus of the textual novum. Although Mitch betrays his own Star Class to join the revolution, most of the Consies are lower-level workers—ranging from professional designers in corporate offices to agricultural and industrial laborers in the tropical plantations.

In their collective praxis, the Consies develop a totalizing analysis of the corporate system and organize a broad-based resistance. With a few people secreted in high-placed positions and others leading the workers' organizations, like Marx's old mole they burrow within the system, slowly exploiting the contradictions, gaining ground, and positioning themselves in ways that would make Gramsci proud. Indeed, the best image of burrowing is the "liberated space" that the local

Consie cell creates within the pulsating body of the major food source of the planet, Chicken Little. The description of this massive organic composition of chlorella is easily one of the most powerful metaphorical representations of capitalist relations of production in all of sf. Chicken Little, or Gallina, as the workers have named it, is the primary source of food and profit (especially given its low-cost of production) for the entire economic system. Its workers endlessly skim and process it from multiple layers of scaffolding in the torrid heat of Central America, but the great political irony in Pohl and Kornbluth's counter-narrative is their outrageous positioning of a Consie cell within the very flesh of this throbbing mass of tissue (Pohl and Kornbluth 83).

Having gradually gained the attention of Mitch, newly arrived from New York, one of the skilled workers, the "Master Slicer" Herrera, appeals to Mitch's anger and leads him into the details of the Consie analysis and agenda. Meeting Mitch outside Chicken Little, Herrera blows on a small whistle, and the flesh parts like some distorted version of the Red Sea. Herrera leads Mitch into the core of the "hundred-ton lump of gray-brown rubbery flesh" where the Consies hold their meetings (Pohl and Kornbluth 85).

From this point the individual and collective counter-narratives merge as Mitch's victimization and alienation slowly but steadily transmute into his affiliation with the "long haired" Consies. At first he seeks only to regain his old position, but with the help of an increasingly totalizing analysis he finally sees the entire system in a new light. After several twists and turns, he claws his way back to corporate headquarters and tells the "whole story" to his boss and father figure, Fowler Schocken, still believing that what happened to him was an aberration in the system, one caused by his apparently jealous competitor, Matt Runstead. The breakpoint for Mitch comes when Schocken refuses to believe him and dismisses his suffering by way of the psychobabble that was applied to so many women coming to consciousness in the 1950s: "You've been on a psychological bender. You got away from yourself. You assumed a new identity, and you chose one as far-removed from your normal, hard-working, immensely able self as possible. You chose the lazy, easy-going life of a scum-skimmer, drowsing in the tropic sun" (Pohl and Kornbluth 134).

Lost in these depths, Mitch faces a political gestalt shift, a radicalizing moment of consciousness-raising, a dystopian turn. He finally sees that he was the one "who was out of touch with reality," and he becomes increasingly angry at Schocken's pop-psychoanalytic justification for his fall and rise. All the information he had been collecting, from his own experience and from his Consie helpers, now adds up to more than the sum of the individual bits. The clues leading to an alternative version of reality accumulate into a critical epistemological mass that enable him (as it does sf readers) to make sense of the absent paradigm, of what once was a completely "absent signifier," or what Althusser called the "absent cause" of history itself.

What began as a liberal enlightenment or postwar existentialist narrative in which Mitch recounts the flaws in what he believes is an essentially just society becomes a timely revolutionary account as he sees his own society reconfigured into one driven by the logic of greed and exploitation. As he comes to realize that he has opted for a Consie stance in the world, he describes the process of consciousness-raising by turning the words of his own advertising industry against themselves: "It's an axiom of my trade that things are invisible except against a contrasting background. Like, for instance, the opinions and attitudes of Fowler Schocken" (Pohl and Kornbluth 136).

True to Samuelson's point about upbeat endings, the conflict resolves in a surge of fairy-tale motifs as the corporate villains are defeated, the Consies triumph, and the "hero" wins back the love of his life. In an ending that resembles those of the radio serials of the time, the society remains intact but the people of the revolution find a way out. In this case the radicals succeed in taking over the Venus rocket (with the help of the greatly diminished, in both actual size and power, president of the United States). The point-of-view couple (Mitch has now given Kathy an entire world!) and a group of fellow Consie travelers take off in the rocket to build what will eventually become a utopian enclave on Venus, a counterfactual counterworld to that of the corrupt capitalist Earth. And yet back on the home planet the struggle continues as Matt Runstead and other Consies carry on the fight against the Fowler Schockens of Earth. At the end, therefore, the dystopian reality is still very much in place, but clearly an open-ended utopian space has been identified and seized through militant political action.

Since its publication in 1953, *Space Merchants* has delighted readers (fans and students) with its humor and its analysis, its presentation of the machinations of capital and its revolutionary romance.[36] Yet where Pohl and Kornbluth held out a utopian possibility in their account of the United States as dystopia in the 1950s, Philip K. Dick, as Samuelson has suggested, became one of the more pessimistic explorers of the dystopian imagination in the 1960s and 1970s.

Unlike Pohl and Kornbluth, Dick holds out less, often no, hope. Yet he somehow resists the worst cynicism of the anti-utopian temperament even as he purposely plunges deep into the anti-utopian ambience of his time. Immersed in the Californian society that he and others (Jean Baudrillard and Mike Davis among them) have taken to be the unhappy future of the planet, he insightfully captures the dynamics of the social order, but he seldom locates spaces for substantial alternatives or outright opposition (other than the admittedly serious one of turning on, tuning in, and dropping out). However accurate in its mapping of U.S. society, Dick's dystopian sf, like Orwell's, often ends in a pessimistic rush. Yet the almost (and occasionally actual) self-reflexive quality of his work (as it navigates between a sober realism and an acerbic humor) pulls it at the very last moment from the anti-utopian flames and places it somewhere in the contested zone *between* Utopia and Anti-Utopia, taking it to the uneasy but creative position that Dick seemed to prefer in his work and his life.

A troubling and perhaps atypical example of Dick's pessimism can be seen in "Faith of Our Fathers."[37] With this 1967 story, he excels in the twisted irony of which sf is capable, an irony especially suited to the surreal black humor of the counterculture in the war-ridden 1960s. In a very near future, the communist Chinese and Vietnamese have won the Southeast Asian war and now occupy most of the United States, except for a few "Pentagon remnants in the Catskills" and a "pocket of die-hard reaction in the red hills of Oklahoma" (Dick 357). The enemy of the new communist state is still the old enemy of the counterculture: the military and its conservative backers. Yet Dick portrays the victorious new society in anti-utopian terms, as a "utopian" alternative led by another version of the very power structure its militants have fought against. In this post-revolutionary regime, the old political-economic order has, in a historically familiar move, been replicated by its new rulers. Western fashions, consumer desires, and petty power struggles between and among middle-management bureaucrats clawing for position now constitute the milieu of the triumphant communist society. The victors have become more American than the Americans. In a bizarre version of the once popular convergence theory, Dick captures the commonalities of power, not in the older dystopian measure of the authoritarian state but in the newer perception of the adaptable corporate-consumerist society.

More acutely than many sf writers of the postwar era, Dick recognizes the totalizing logic of the modern economic system and its mechanisms of subject construction. Through his protagonist, Chien, the bureaucrat-on-his-way-up, he traces the compulsions and fears, the desires and hopes, of a "typical man" of the times. Like a later replay of W. H. Auden's "Unknown Citizen," Chien does his job during the week, tends to his party duties, and on Friday practices "the esoteric imported art from the defeated West of steer-roping" (Dick 354). All he wants is the chance to pursue his own career and leisure, but even here, after the revolution, the contradictions of history bear down on him.

Chien becomes the focal point in a power struggle between the ruling bureaucrats and an opposition group dedicated to exposing the identity of the ruling "Absolute Benefactor of the People." Initially, he is approached by a street peddler, who is an agent for the group seeking literally to unmask the Absolute Benefactor.

The peddler sells him a drug guaranteed to "rest eyes fatigued by the countenance of meaningless official monologues" (Dick 354). Before he can sample the drug, he is called in by his supervisor at the Ministry for Cultural Artifacts and asked to reach out to the "liberal and intellectual youth segment of western U.S." by helping to grade ostensible qualifying exams to determine who is "responding to the programming and who is not" (Dick 355). The extended surveillance and control is needed because American youth, "having lost the global war . . . has developed a talent for dissembling" (Dick 355). He is promised advancement in his career if he takes the job and warned of dire consequences if he does not, for this task of distinguishing "ideological correctness—and incorrectness" is deemed crucial to the final plans for conquest of the United States. Under the pressure of threats and promises, he agrees to do the work.

In the meantime, while watching a television address by the Absolute Benefactor, Chien samples the peddler's drug to see if he can ward off inevitable boredom. Amazed, he sees not the Benefactor but a "dead mechanical construct, made of solid state circuits, of swiveling pseudopodia, lenses and a squawk-box." Not knowing if this is reality or hallucination, he nevertheless realizes that the drug is stronger than the LSD-25 that the U.S. troops dumped in the Vietnamese reservoirs (in an ironic combination of the Right's fear in the 1950s of fluoride in the water and the hippie fantasy of dropping LSD into city water supplies), and he wonders what the strength and purpose of this psychedelic toxin might be (see Dick 360). The actual effect is that he has seen through the projected figure of the Absolute Benefactor, and his sense of reality will never be the same. He then wonders if this was the peddler's goal. After having the remaining portion of the drug tested, he learns that it is "anti-hallucinogenic."

Shortly thereafter, he is contacted by a young woman who identifies herself as another member of the underground organization. The mysterious Tanya tells Chien that the organization is distributing drugs to enable citizens to break the spell cast by the government through the hallucinogens it officially puts in the water supply. She explains that the drug, stelazine, is designed to shatter the projected image of the Absolute Benefactor and that Chien is meant to test it to see just what image appears to him when he looks at the Benefactor. She then exposes the plot of the bureaucrats and their "request" for Chien to monitor the exams, and she tells him that their real goal is to "pol-read" Chien himself, to test him to see if he is politically suitable for further promotion (Dick 363). She offers to help Chien pass his political test by providing him with information on which of the exams to choose, but she demands his participation in further drug tests as the price. She explains that the stelazine does change the image of the Absolute Benefactor but that twelve alternative images, "twelve realities," have been seen by a variety of people (Dick 364). In return for underwriting his career, she asks Chien to attend one of the Absolute Benefactor's receptions for his elite cadre and there to take the drug and see what he sees.

Caught between "the Party and His Greatness on one hand [and] this girl with her alleged group on the other," Chien reluctantly accepts the assignment to satisfy his own growing desire to see the Absolute Benefactor "face to face as he actually is" (Dick 365). In a bizarre twist, at a meeting with his supervisor before he goes to the gathering, he is told that the Absolute Benefactor is one Thomas Fletcher, an aged Caucasian from the New Zealand Communist Party, and that his image on television is "subjected to a variegated assortment of skillful refinements" (Dick 367). He goes to the Benefactor's residence filled with confusion: "Am I being led into one trap after another?" he asks; is Tanya actually a double-agent, "an agent of the Secpol [security police] probing me, trying to ferret out a disloyal, anti-Party streak in me?" (Dick 368). At this stage in the story, in a move typical for Dick, no meaning is stable.

Once at the residence, succumbing to his own curiosity, Chien drops the drug and meets the Absolute Benefactor. As the substance takes effect, he sees an alien being that "had no shape. Nor pseudopodia, either flesh or metal. It was, in a sense, not there at all; when he managed to look directly at it, the shape vanished; he saw through it, saw the people on the far side—but not it. Yet if he turned his head, caught it out of a sidelong glance, he could determine its boundaries" (Dick 371). The quasi figure Chien peripherally sees is more veiled than he expected. "If this is a hallucination," he thinks, "it is the worst I have ever had; if it is not, then it is evil reality; it's an evil thing that kills and injures" (Dick 371).

Gradually, he realizes that he is looking at nothing other than a deity, but an evil deity who watches, controls, and kills. In their brief conversation, or interrogation, the Benefactor grabs Chien by the arm and tells him the Orwellian truth that it founded the party and the rest of the political spectrum as well: "the anti-Party and the Party that isn't a Party, and those who are for it and those who are against, those that you call Yankee Imperialists, those in the camp of reaction, and so on endlessly" (Dick 373). The god-alien seeks his trust and loyalty. It orders him to tell Tanya that he saw "an overworked, overweight, elderly man who drinks too much and likes to pinch girls," but it also tells him that despite everything he will know nothing but torment for the rest of his life and at his death he will learn that there are worse things in the universe.

He then runs out of the residence and returns to his apartment. There Tanya visits him, and he tells her that the Benefactor is a nonterrestrial alien puppet master. "We can't win," he cries. He wants only to return to his job and forget "the whole damned thing" (Dick 374). After further conversation in which they talk about the Benefactor and the hopelessness of fighting it, Chien realizes that the spot on his arm where the Benefactor touched him is poisonously livid. Aware of the mortal injury, his final act is to ask Tanya to join him in bed. Thus, after he goes through a dystopian realization of the manipulated social order and sees the Benefactor in a scene evocative of Joseph Conrad's Marlowe looking on the face of Kurtz (in *Heart of Darkness*), Chien's potential counter-narrative simply collapses as he gives up.

Dick's satiric story effectively exposes the imbrication of social construction and hegemonic power, but it leaves no room for successful resistance or even survival at the edges. It appears to be supremely anti-utopian, but its grim humor endows it with a satiric rather than cynical ambiguity that resists the instrumentally realist resignation encouraged by the anti-utopian temperament. Although the society itself is closed and controlled, the ontological reality Dick describes is even a step beyond that. Power is exercised only by carping bureaucrats and naive do-gooders. The alienated individual is lost in such a world, able only to go mad or die. The closed mythic quality of the story is unmistakable. There is no opposing enclave, no way out, no way forward, no utopian horizon. The Absolute Subject of society, of all reality, has everyone trapped. And yet the sheer formal exaggeration of the text gives it an emancipating quality that works against its own enclosed narrative, thereby positioning it in a potentially influential location between Utopia and Anti-Utopia.

Moving to the margins of sf in this period is one of the most avant-garde stories of the New Wave, Pamela Zoline's "Heat Death of the Universe," written in 1967. It offers a quite different example of the ways in which sf has delved into the dystopian arena and transformed dystopian narrative.[38] Unlike Dick, Zoline does not locate social evil in the machinations of the state, but like Dick she describes a cosmic catastrophe, one that ultimately is beyond human control.

By equating the second law of thermodynamics (the entropic heat death of the universe) with the growing dissolution of one woman's everyday life, Zoline conjoins the macro and micro, the metaphysical and the physical, the death of the universe with the banal and oppressive implosion of an apparently "normal" life. The result, with its strong ontological premise and the downward spiral of its uncontested entropic narrative, is a memorable work of sheer anti-utopian pessimism. Zoline herself stated that she saw the story as an "attempt to 'make sense' of things, of general data, by organising the private to the public, the public to the private; by making analogies between entropy and personal chaos, the end of the universe and our own ageing and death, into the crucial structuring metaphor."[39]

The story opens with the invocation of "ontology" in the first of the fifty-four "sections" that make up the text, but by section 9 it identifies its protagonist as

Sarah Boyle, who is "a vivacious and intelligent young wife and mother, educated at a fine Eastern college, proud of her growing family which keeps her busy and happy around the house" (Zoline 295). Sarah is the perfect subject of the American "utopia" of the 1950s—the sort that Adrienne Rich's poetry disassembled and transformed—but unlike Rich's poetic protagonists, she is not on a path of discovery and transformation. She is confined to her kitchen and the care of her children (the number and names of which are vague), with no sign of a husband except by mention of her mother-in-law. From this California kitchen, the destruction of Sarah's life (from potential subject to victim) parallels the very ending of the universe itself. In section 12, the California setting is expressed as a metaphor of the "whole world" in which

> all topographical imperfections [have been] sanded away with the sweet-smelling burr of the plastic surgeon's cosmetic polisher; a world populace dieting, leisured, similar in pink and mauve hair and rhinestone shades. A land Cunt Pink and Avocado Green, brassiered and girdled by monstrous complexities of Super Highways, a California endless and unceasing, embracing and transforming the entire globe. (Zoline 295)

Section 13 reminds us that the "entropy of a system is a measure of its degree of disorder," and section 14 shifts back to the task of "cleaning up the house," which will increase in intensity until the entire enterprise collapses (Zoline 296). At this point Sarah is writing "Help, Help, Help, Help, Help" above her stove and trying to hold on to reality by numbering the objects around her, but she still goes on washing diapers, changing sheets, putting away toys, cleaning and caring for her household. By section 19 we are told that the second law of thermodynamics means that the available energy in a closed system tends to wind down to a minimum, to an eventual heat death; yet in section 20 the housecleaning continues. In section 26 Sarah attempts to find meaning in art. She invokes Duchamp's ready-mades in a fleeting desire to fix her kitchen-world as an aesthetic refuge, but she sees this tangential option as leading only to madness and resumes her efforts to maintain control by cleaning and caring.

In section 28 timepieces are catalogued, and in section 29 Sarah finds new lines on her face, joining the "Other Intimations of Mortality" she keeps track of. Again, in section 32, a passing desire for utopian hope comes over Sarah as she is visited with the thought that "there are things to be hoped for, accomplishments to be desired beyond the mere reproductions, mirror reproduction of one's kind" (Zoline 301). Like the moment of artistic impulse, however, this utopian reflection fails to grow into a counter-narrative and collapses back into domestic musings on children, love, the body, and the forms by which the world might end. In section 44 Sarah again asks if there is not "more than this," a way to "justify one's passage" or, "less ambitiously," a way to "change, even in the motion of the smallest mote, the course and circulation of the world" (Zoline 304).

One change, she thinks, would be enough, to act once in a meaningful way: "To carve a name, date and perhaps a word of hope upon a turtle's shell, then set him free to wend the world, surely this one act might cancel out absurdity?" (Zoline 304). Yet existentialist acts of hope—even upon mythic turtles carrying the universe—are not to be for Sarah. The musing again fades to the work at hand, this time a birthday party with all its chaos, followed by another section on entropy that claims that "order is least probable, chaos most probable" (Zoline 305). For a fourth time, a passing utopian possibility looms as the section notes that "there are local enclaves whose direction seems opposed to that of the Universe at large and in which there is a limited and temporary tendency for organization to increase. Life finds its home in some of these enclaves" (Zoline 305). Again, however, the chance for Utopia passes Sarah by. Art, utopian desire, utopian motion, and now utopian enclaves are not on the horizon for Sarah. She returns instead to the mundane task of "cleaning up after the party," and at this point she "is very tired, violet under the eyes, mauve beneath the eyes" (Zoline 306). She notices that the pet turtle has died, and in the next section she begins to cry.

In this last section, Sarah finally breaks down. She opens the refrigerator, takes out a carton of eggs, and "throws them one by one onto the kitchen floor which is patterned with strawberries in squares" (Zoline 306). She smashes the children's dishes against the refrigerator, she throws a jar of grape jelly against the window, she cries, she throws a jar of strawberry jam against the stove, she turns on the water and fills the sinks with detergent, and she writes on the kitchen wall: "William Shakespeare has Cancer and lives in California"; "Sugar Frosted Flakes are the Food of the Gods" (Zoline 307). The soapy water flows over the sink onto the littered floor, and she breaks more glasses and dishes and throws cups and pots and jars of food at the walls. Crying steadily—while the "sand keeps falling, very quietly, in the egg timer"—she tosses more eggs into the air (Zoline 307). The flying, falling eggs provide the last image of the story as Sarah disappears into the end of her life and the universe: "The eggs arch slowly through the kitchen, like a baseball, hit high against the spring sky, seen from far away. They go higher and higher in the stillness, hesitate at the zenith, then begin to fall away slowly, slowly, through the fine, clear air" (Zoline 307).

With this literal and metaphorical ending, the story of Sarah Boyle and the universe offers a strong indictment of the meaninglessness of everyday life in the "affluent society" of postwar suburban America. More ontological than political, it nevertheless is a timely anticapitalist and protofeminist critique of the subjected position of women, as it utters an early version of the slogan of the personal and the political. Again, economy and culture are the dystopian focus, not the state. No authoritarian OneState, no brooding Big Brother, no manipulative drugs or media, no drudgery and deprivation appear on these pages. Rather, the material reality and quotidian duties of a life in California that supposedly no longer requires the dangers of utopian desire and action encompass Sarah's days and come to constitute the entire universe. At the end all reality crashes down upon and within her. Her world disappears in a cry and a bang.

"The Heat Death of the Universe" is a dystopian narrative of an emergent postmodern culture, as it avoids master narratives and world systems and microscopically probes the cultural formations and practices of everyday life. With an initial ambiguity that anticipates Atwood's, the story appears to reach toward a counternarrative based in the power of Sarah's desire. And yet the twinned ontological inevitabilities of domestic reality and cosmic entropy underscore a metaphysical conviction of chaos, disorder, and death that overwrites any utopian possibility. The dominant narrative of universal and personal death effaces the space of a counter-narrative. Angry and perceptive as the story is in its representation of the violence of daily life, especially for women, its satirical and mythic strategy takes the reader to no other destination than Anti-Utopia itself.

Still, even here, a resistant or at least resilient reader, especially in those burgeoning feminist days, could well develop the anger of Zoline's story in a contemporary utopian reception that would refuse and resist the despair. Shortly after Zoline's story, in the late 1960s and early 1970s, the textual counterpoint of the critical utopias—most written by women working from a developed oppositional analysis—constituted a move back to an epically eutopian engagement with the hegemonic forces around them. Yet this moment also passed, as the "conservative restoration" of the 1980s moved into place and sf turned again to dystopian narrative, but this time with narratives that are as transformed as the critical utopias themselves.

V.

Since 1909, with "The Machine Stops," dystopian writing has consistently confronted the historical contradictions and conflicts of the century. Some dystopias explore the oppression of fascist or bureaucratically deformed socialist states, others delve into the controlled chaos of capitalist society, and a few linger over the horrendous details of everyday life. Some settle for an anti-utopian stance, whereas others make room for utopian enclaves of resistance or horizons of hope beyond the pages of the text, and yet others forthrightly or hesitantly negotiate the contested or undecided space between militancy and resignation. Some take the "classic" form of a conflict within an authoritarian state, whereas others generate "new maps of hell" that more often trace the complexities of a capitalist world system that has only become more powerful through the decades, and still others work tangentially with the available ironies or ambiguities of modernist or postmodernist fiction. Whatever its stance, target, or outcome, however, every dystopian narrative engages in an aesthetic/epistemological encounter with its historical conjuncture. Whether that encounter recasts the present in mythic traps of consolation or takes the reader epically beyond the order of things is a question whose answer lies with readers as they confront each textual novum.

Underlying and shaping these textual and political possibilities, as Jameson generally argues, is the fundamental conflict between Utopia and Anti-Utopia, and each dystopia negotiates this historical contest in its unique way. Those that adhere to an anti-utopian tendency are the sort that Barbara Goodwin and Keith Taylor characterize as warnings that only "serve to revalidate the present as the lesser evil, and to promote a 'decision' for no change."[40] With a focus on story lines of alienation, revolt, and defeat, these dystopias of resignation embrace an anti-utopian pessimism that allows authors, and willing readers, to reinforce their settled preference for the status quo or to help produce their capitulation to it as all hope for change is shattered.

In contrast, the militant dystopias that retain an affiliation with Utopia offer what Robert Evans has described as a "warning to the reader that something must and, by implication, can be done in the present to avoid the future."[41] These texts generally cover a larger canvas of social representation as they pay more attention to the setting in which the story of the protagonist's engagement proceeds. By developing the complex background of the alternative world within the usual dystopian story of alienation and rebellion, they generate nonnarrative spaces of possibilities that can suggest openings in the system and thereby offer meanings that exceed the pessimism of the plot.[42] Although fear and outrage may inform the writing of such texts, the creative encounter with the realities of the social system leads not to doubt and despair but to a renewed and focused anger that can then be tempered with radical hope and vision. Indeed, such a response may even come from a resistant reader of an anti-utopian dystopia (such as Orwell's, Dick's, or Zoline's) who responds to the textual totality of oppression by choosing to get and perhaps stay angry, and even to fight back rather than lapse into abject nihilism or trendy irony.

Certainly the classical dystopias negotiated the spectrum of Utopia and Anti-Utopia in ways that differed from the utopian satires and realistic exposés of nineteenth-century fiction. They did so, however, as products of their time, a time when, as Marshall Berman puts it, modernity was already losing its sense of "adventure" and settling into its life-denying "routine."[43] Drawing on familiar anti-utopian persuasions and expressions, they challenged the social order around them even as they questioned the claims of an actually existing utopianism that they regarded as arrogant and dangerous. Early on, they took a hard look at the specific conditions of the rise of the totalizing state and the instrumentalizing capitalist economy, and they critically explored the impact of this complex matrix of macropower on the individual.

As opposed to the classical dystopias, the texts that redeployed a dystopian sensibility within the intertextual web of sf, especially in the years after World War II, followed a different strategy. No longer standing in abhorrence at the frontiers of twentieth-century modernity, the sf dystopias (Suvin's "simple dystopias") were expressions in and of the very social reality that the classical dystopias feared and reviled. Immersed in modernity's own mass culture, the new maps of hell did not look backward to a better time. Nor did they easily look ahead to a utopian future. At work in the belly of the beast, they focused more often on experiences of everyday life in societies increasingly shaped by a refined imbrication of economy and culture. Compared to their classical cousins, the sf dystopias (like the jazz to which Amis compares them) tend to be less driven by extremes of celebration or despair, more open to complexities and ambiguities, and more encouraging of new riffs of personal and political maneuvers. It is, then, within this science fictional variation that the new, critical dystopias emerge in the hard times of the 1980s and 1990s.

6

The Critical Dystopia

If this were a map
it would be the map of the last age of her life,
not a map of choices but a map of variations
on the one great choice. It would be the map by which
she could see the end of touristic choices,
of distances blued and purpled by romance,
by which she would recognize that poetry
isn't revolution but a way of knowing
why it must come.

—Adrienne Rich, from "Dreamwood"

I.

In the early 1980s, Ronald Reagan retrieved the utopian figure of the "city on the hill" from colonial history to signify the society of harmony and enterprise that his new administration promised to establish. A decade later, in a speech to the General Assembly of the United Nations in October 1990, George Bush deployed the utopian figure of the millennium as he called for a new world order of peace and prosperity that would move beyond the era of the Cold War.

And yet in the years between the two presidential gestures, neither humanity nor the environment benefited from their apparently utopian promises. Indeed, the situation became increasingly dystopian as the celebration of Utopia became a mark of triumph for Anti-Utopia. Massive upward redistribution of income became the norm; working people steadily lost the measures of social wealth and rights that they had won through years of struggle; homelessness and the deprivations of un- and underemployment became the common lot of increasing numbers of people; violent attacks on those with little or no social power multiplied and intensified (with harassment, battering, and rape of women and similar psychological and physical assaults on people of color, gays, and lesbians); and quality medical care, universal education, and safe and supportive work and living spaces were sacrificed to the draconian policies of neoconservative and neoliberal "reformers." As well, the environment itself was pushed to the edge of irreversible disaster: Damage ranged from the depletion of the ozone layer and the spread of acid rain, to the destruction of rainforests and the poisoning of land and water through racially opportunistic toxic emissions and dumping, and to the endangering of hundreds of species with whom humanity shares the earth.

What the Republican presidents celebrated in their "utopian" tropes was clearly not the betterment of humanity and the earth but rather the triumph of transnational capital and right-wing ideology. Engaged in restructuring since the end of the postwar boom in the 1970s and furthered by the rise to power of Ronald Reagan in the United States, Margaret Thatcher in Britain, and Helmut Kohl in Germany in the 1980s, the new hegemonic constellation generally succeeded in shifting from a less profitable centralized mode of production to a more flexible regime of accumulation that took full advantage of technological developments in cybernetics and electronics.[1] Multinational corporations based in and supported by powerful nation-states transformed themselves into transnational entities able to shift the role of their "partner" states away from economic and social regulation and into the narrower job of providing national security (which in the United States took the form of a "military Keynesianism" that renewed the war machine and led to Reagan's covert operations in Central America and Bush's open pursuit of the Gulf War).

Under the pseudo-utopian flag of rational choice and the free market, a renewed capitalism reached toward its own dream of total exploitation and administration of workers and consumers through a worldwide division of labor in a world market of goods and services (supported and, paradoxically, protected by a worldwide financial apparatus, working under the auspices of formations such as the General Agreement on Tariffs and Trade and, more recently, the World Trade Organization). At the same time, the conjunctural privileging of quick financial gain led to the fiscal write-off of entire geographical regions and masses of humanity that were regarded as no longer, or not yet, worthy of preservation or protection by the leaner and meaner economic machine.[2]

Although many liberals hoped for happier days under the Democratic presidency of Bill Clinton (or the Third Way of Tony Blair or the *Neue Mitte* of Gerhard Schröder), the logic of economic growth and governmental abdication of social responsibilities was not only not stopped but actually intensified in a more efficient and seemingly responsible manner.[3] On the international front, the military vocation of the United States was reinforced through incursions (by missiles, air strikes, and ground troops as needed) into Iraq (again), Haiti, Somalia, Sudan, Bosnia, and (under the aegis of a newly assertive NATO) Kosovo; at the same time, foreign policy assured the systemic neglect of non-white populations around the globe, seen especially in sections of Africa that were besieged by wars, famine, and disease (in particular AIDS).[4] On the domestic front, the privileging of corporate power, the redistribution of wealth, the degradation of labor, the dismissal of the poor, the violent abuse of those seen as different, and the destruction of the ecosystem escalated in spite of righteous claims to reverse such practices.

Perhaps the "utopian" gesture that epitomizes the policies of this third U.S. administration of the conservative era is what was popularly known as the "Welfare Act" of 1996; for in this new act of class warfare over sixty years of hard-won state commitment to caring for the needs of the community, whether citizens or not, was ended.[5] In a system in which a decreasing number of people have access to what one corporate commentator calls "enhanced citizenship," not only the very poor but also ordinary working people (and that designation now extends far up the ladder of what used to be regarded as privileged managerial and professional work) have been cast aside and left to fend for themselves with little hope that a caring society will spend effort or money on providing a basic safety net for a full and satisfying life, much less offering protection from the harsh effects of an unregulated capital logic. At the core of this act is the "utopian" argument that a viable market-driven society will be achieved by withholding support after ninety days in the case of food stamps and two or five years in the case of welfare entitlements; for only then will people be "inspired" to search for jobs, only then will money previously tied up in so-called useless taxes be released for personal and corporate investment, only then will the economy be free to operate without the gravitational pull of social responsibility.

Indeed, the 1990s shift to the nominal center has not changed anything for the better—even though it did halt the overt economic, political, and cultural violence perpetrated by the Right in the 1980s. The rising employment rates in the United States and elsewhere in the West and North in the 1990s bespeaks not the revival of reindustrialization, democratic government, and horizontal redistribution of wealth but rather a more canny management of the population by an economic system still intent on a competitive and hence exploitative exercise of power over humanity and nature that takes the wealth of labor and the profits of commerce from those who produce it and deposits it in the secure financial and geographical enclaves of the upper echelons of the executive class. Apparent solvency for working people and mere gestures to social decency therefore mask the sociopolitical disparities that characterized the social order in the 1990s. Less shared wealth and less democratic power continue to be the norm even with a growing economy; well-paid and secure jobs continue to be replaced by part-time employment at lower pay and no benefits; violence toward those not privileged continues even in the face of an assertive global discourse of human rights; and the exploitive destruction of the natural environment continues to be the practice of profit-hungry corporations even with the commonsensical embrace of a "green ethics."

Thus, even with the rationality of reform liberalism, third-way "solutions," and social democratic alliances that repress and refuse their own inherent principles, the world continues to drift toward Anti-Utopia. As the new century gets under way, the "utopian" rhetoric of three presidential administrations merely exemplifies two interconnected stages in a historic transformation that banishes the hope for a better world for humanity and nature from the realm of possibility. Seeking to enclose and exploit every aspect of human and natural existence, the logic of what Paul Smith calls "millennial capitalism" claims a planetary system presided over by the competitive machinations of transnational corporations, yearning for success yet ignoring the social and ecological cost. Supported by the largely rhetorical threat of corporate abandonment in an apparently global economy, the leaders of the developed nations—whether neoconservative, neoliberal, or social democratic—continue to justify their policy of dismissing social well-being in the name of a false competitiveness that only ends up serving those within the state who are already wealthy and powerful.[6]

II.

It was in this era of economic restructuring, political opportunism, and cultural implosion that dystopian narrative reappeared within the formal parameters of sf.[7] Moving beyond the engaged utopianism of the 1970s and against the fashionable temptation to despair in the early 1980s, several sf writers turned to dystopian strategies as a way to come to terms with the changing, and enclosing, social reality. Although they reached back into its classical and science fictional roots, they did not simply revive dystopia but rather reworked it in the context of the economic, political, and cultural conditions of the decade. Gradually, critics began to track the results, noting the innovations in formal flexibility and political maneuvering as they did so.

With a theoretically nuanced assessment of the linkage between Theodor Adorno, Fredric Jameson, and the aesthetics of utopia and dystopia, Bryan Alexander locates the roots of this dystopian resurgence quite early on—indeed, in the oppositional response to late or global capitalism after World War II.[8] He therefore turns to Adorno's "first major postwar work" (*Minima Moralia,* published in 1951) and reads it alongside Jameson's 1990 study of Adorno (*Late Marxism: Adorno, or the Persistence of the Dialectic*). To present Adorno's grasp of the appropriateness of this emergent dystopian response to capital's encapsulation of Utopia, Alexander reaches further back to Walter Benjamin's association of images and tropes of hell (especially in the *Arcades* project) with the entropic agony and arrogant power that is endemic to capitalist modernity.

As he puts it: "While considering advertising images of unprecedented plenitude as controlled utopias of desire characterized, stimulated, and fulfilled, Benjamin actually plays a two-handed game, ranging the material against the trope of dystopia" shaped by images of the infernal (Alexander 55). He then traces the influence of Benjamin's hellish account in Adorno's confrontation with the hegemonic order, wherein Adorno's "intellectual awareness of market-dominated society creates an atmosphere, a world of hell" (Alexander 55). Within *Minima Moralia*'s critical analysis of the new totalizing strategies of postwar capitalism, "agony is produced and circulates within a completely-administered dystopia" that allows no opposition, no outside (Alexander 55).

Alexander then associates Adorno's (and Benjamin's) "tonal stance" with Jameson's challenge to the cultural machinery of late capitalism, now considered in its triumphal 1990s version. Again, the analytic strategy of totality enables a critique that recognizes capitalism's reproduction of a "utopia" in which the authentically radical call of Utopia is both co-opted and silenced, leaving in its place tropes of dystopia to represent and inform what critique and opposition remain. Catching the quality of Jameson's metaphoric analysis, Alexander puts it this way: "In the face of enforced global more-or-less complacency as postmodern nigh-utopia the dystopian trope provides 'a bile [as] a joyous counter-poison and corrosive solvent'" to apply to the slick surface of reality (Jameson, quoted in Alexander 55–56). The contemporary moment, therefore, is one in which a critical position is necessarily dystopian (and perhaps that moment has been with us, as has the dystopian genre, in one form or another, since the onset of twentieth-century capitalism, beginning in its monopoly and imperialist phase, taking another turn in the 1940s and 1950s, and yet another in the 1980s and 1990s).[9]

Writing within the realm of literary critique (specifically in a study of recent feminist sf), Jenny Wolmark recognizes immediate textual evidence for a dystopian turn in 1980s works by Margaret Atwood and Sheri Tepper when she describes their deployment of a complex mixture of "utopian and dystopian elements" as they "critically voice the fears and anxieties of a range of new and fragmented social and sexual constituencies and identities in post-industrial societies."[10] Moving to the next decade, Lyman Tower Sargent goes on to name this distinctly new fictional development. He observes that politically engaged texts such as Piercy's *He, She and It* "are clearly both eutopias and dystopias" and thus "undermine all neat classification schemes."[11] Yet in his proper insistence on taxonomic and bibliographic precision, he sets aside the implication of a utopian-dystopian hybrid and identifies the new tendency as a specific form of dystopian narrative. He therefore suggests that these new works might usefully be understood as "critical dystopias" that interrogate both society and their generic predecessors in ways that resemble the approach critical utopias took toward the utopian tradition a decade or so earlier. In their own studies, Raffaella Baccolini and Ildney Cavalcanti agree with Sargent's historically informed nomination, and like Wolmark they note that the contributions of feminist women occupy a leading edge of this new literary intervention as it did in the earlier critical utopian moment.

In "Gender and Genre in the Feminist Critical Dystopias of Katherine Burdekin, Margaret Atwood, and Octavia Butler," Baccolini sees an "open or critical" dystopian strategy in texts that range from the 1930s to the 1990s.[12] Although I agree with Baccolini's assessment of the formal properties of the new critical dystopia, I would, for reasons of historical specificity, reserve the term for works that arise out of the emerging sociopolitical circumstances of the late 1980s and 1990s—thereby positing Burdekin and Atwood as predecessors. That is, although Sargent's "critical dystopia" is a recent development, its political and aesthetic roots can be traced back through the dystopian intertext. As I argued in Chapter 5, the dystopian genre has always worked along a contested continuum between utopian and anti-utopian positions: between texts that are emancipatory, militant, open, and "critical" and those that are compensatory, resigned, and quite "anti-critical." That the recent dystopias are strongly, and more self-reflexively, "critical" does not suggest the appearance of an entirely new generic form but rather a significant retrieval and refunctioning of the most progressive possibilities inherent in dystopian narrative. The new texts, therefore, represent a creative move that is both a continuation of the long dystopian tradition and a distinctive new intervention.

Baccolini describes the critical dystopias as texts that "maintain a utopian core" and yet help "to deconstruct tradition and reconstruct alternatives" ("Gender and Genre" 13). Recalling the dialectical sublation achieved by the previous critical utopias, she notes that the new dystopias "negate static ideals, preserve radical action, and create a space in which opposition can be articulated and received" ("Gender and Genre" 17). She then identifies the "strategies at the level of form" that enable these texts to challenge the present anti-utopian situation by creating a "locus of resisting hope and subversive tension in an otherwise pessimistic genre" ("Gender and Genre" 30). From her analyses of the works by Burdekin, Atwood, and Butler, she argues that critical dystopias reject the conservative dystopian tendency to settle for the anti-utopian closure invited by the historical situation by setting up "open endings" that resist that closure and maintain "the utopian impulse *within* the work" ("Gender and Genre" 18). Catching the specificity of the tendency, she argues that "by rejecting the traditional subjugation of the individual at the end of the novel, the critical dystopia opens a space of contestation and opposition for those groups (women and other 'eccentric' subjects whose subject position hegemonic discourse does not contemplate) for whom subjectivity has yet to be attained" ("Gender and Genre" 18).

Although that embrace of openness (through resistance, enclaves, or even textual ambiguity) is already present in the classical and sf dystopias (as implied in the examples of Burdekin and Atwood), it is both formally and politically foregrounded in the recent works. Thus, as the critical dystopias give voice and space to such dispossessed and denied subjects (and, I would add, to those diminished and deprived by the accompanying economic reconfigurations) they go on to explore ways to change the present system so that such culturally and economically marginalized peoples not only survive but also try to move toward creating a social reality that is shaped by an impulse to human self-determination and ecological health rather than one constricted by the narrow and destructive logic of a system intent only on enhancing competition in order to gain more profit for a select few.

What formally enables these open, critical texts is an intensification of the practice of "genre blurring," which Baccolini has traced in earlier dystopian works. By self-reflexively borrowing "specific conventions from other genres," critical dystopias more often "blur" the received boundaries of the dystopian form and thereby expand rather than diminish its creative potential for critical expression (see "Gender and Genre" 18). Thus, she argues that dystopian narrative is further rendered as an "impure" text that can renovate the "resisting nature" of dystopian sf by making it more properly "*multi*-oppositional" ("Gender and Genre" 18). She historically links this formal emphasis with the insights of post-structuralist critiques as she recognizes that the "attack, in recent years, against universalist assumptions, fixity and singularity, and pure, neutral and objective knowledge in favor of the recognition of differences, multiplicity, and complexity; partial and situated knowledges; as well as hybridity and fluidity has contributed, among other things, to the deconstruction of genre purity" in this generic form as in others ("Gender and Genre" 18).

I generally agree with this historical and methodological argument, but I think the new dystopias move even further along than Baccolini suggests, as they dialectically transcend even the moment of poststructuralist critique and identity-based micropolitics. Crucial as that moment has been, the wheel has turned again, and a new historical conjuncture is upon us. As an anticipatory machine in that new context, the critical dystopias resist both hegemonic and oppositional orthodoxies (in their radical and reformist variants) even as they refunction a larger, more totalizing critique of the political economy itself. They consequently inscribe a space for a new form of political opposition, one fundamentally based in difference and multiplicity but now wisely and cannily organized in a fully democratic alliance politics that can talk back in a larger though diverse collective voice and not only critique the present system but also begin to find ways to transform it that go beyond the limitations of both the radical micropolitics and the compromised centrist "solutions" of the 1990s.

Indeed, Baccolini's invocation of the critical dystopia's use of "re-vision" suggests this emergent stance (see "Gender and Genre" 13). Especially insofar as the textual re-vision retrieves memories of the oppositional past (with its stories of resistance and change) and enlists those forward-looking memories in the work of articulating the next political steps, these texts at the end of the century take on hegemonic formulations as well as oppositional habits, breaking open favored perspectives to move to what next needs to be done, by refreshing the links between "imagination and utopia" and "utopia and awareness" ("Gender and Genre" 13). As she puts it, the new dystopias "with their permeable borders, their questioning of generic conventions, and their resistance to closure, represent one of the preferred sites of resistance" ("Gender and Genre" 30). I would only add that this preferred site is not only, even though importantly, feminist but also anti-capitalist, democratically socialist, and radically ecological in its overall stance. Although the critical dystopian position continues the qualitatively progressive advances of identity politics, it also takes the political imagination into the larger realm of a democratically unified alliance politics; and although it remains attuned to contemporary theoretical practices of openness, diversity, and resistance to the closure of master narratives, it also revives and privileges totalizing analyses that consider the entire political-economic system and the transformative politics that are capable of both rupturing that system and forging a radical alternative in its place.

Like Baccolini, Cavalcanti finds a decidedly feminist quality in the body of work that she too identifies as "critical dystopias." Her study of "dystopian fictions by women" published between 1967 and 1998 has led her to conclude that these journeys "through contemporary women's 'Hells'" nevertheless allow for important glimpses of 'Paradises.'"[13] Working from analyses of Atwood's *Handmaid's Tale;* Piercy's *He, She and It;* Suzy McKee Charnas's "Holdfast" series (1974–1999);

Suzette Haden Elgin's *Native Tongue* (1984) and *Judas Rose* (1986); Lisa Tuttle's story "The Cure" (1984); and Margaret Elphinstone's *Incomer* (1987) and *Sparrow's Flight* (1989), she argues for the emergence of a "feminist critical dystopia."

The "critical" aspect of these texts, as she sees it, refers to three factors that move from politics to form and on to the reader. Thus, they incorporate

> the negative critique of, and opposition to, patriarchy brought into effect by the dystopian principle; the textual self-awareness not only in generic terms with regard to a previous utopian literary tradition (in its feminist and non-feminist manifestations), but also concerning its own construction of utopian "elsewheres"; and the fact that the feminist dystopias are in themselves highly critical cultural forms of expression (for the two reasons pointed out above), which in turn may have a crucial effect in the formation or consolidation of a specifically critico-feminist public readership. (Cavalcanti 207–208)

Again, while I think a broader oppositional base informs such critical dystopias, a feminist stance and methodology do lie at the heart of the political and formal innovations of this body of work. Working from that stance, in an argument that recapitulates Baccolini's, Cavalcanti examines the ways in which the texts open up traditional dystopian narrative to name a utopian elsewhere that resists becoming filled in by a determinate content that would compromise or shut down its own most radical gesture to a future that is not yet achieved.

Cavalcanti's discussion of the utopian space within the dystopian text begins with a distinction that resembles the one Jameson makes in *The Seeds of Time.* In an echo of Ruth Levitas's analysis, she defines *dystopia* in "*formal terms* (i.e., as *narrative*)," regarding *utopia* in "*conceptual terms* (i.e., as *the expression of desire*)" (Cavalcanti 15). Rather than separating these categories as does Jameson, she argues that it is precisely the formal operation of dystopian narrative that produces, leads into, the nonnarrative, conceptual space of utopia. That is, the work of the counter-narrative, to use Baccolini's term, generates a "'blank space' anticipatory of social possibilities which are radically other" (Cavalcanti 3). The "utopian object" therefore never appears in a compromised form as fully delineated but rather in its most subversive manner as the negativity (or neutralization) that is required before an expression of "anticipatory illumination" can even begin to be considered. In an argument that is close to my own in the previous chapter, Cavalcanti suggests that the critical dystopian text is not unproductively severed from its relationship with Utopia. Indeed, it is precisely a textual form that leads *toward* Utopia by way of dialectical negation, for it negotiates the conflict between Utopia and Anti-Utopia, not in a way that displaces or diffuses that historical contestation but rather invokes Utopia within its own cultural intervention in a time when such oppositional impulses are suppressed or compromised. As she puts it in her discussion of Elgin's *Native Tongue* and *Judas Rose*, "Utopia thus 'surfaces' as the motor and enigma of feminist dystopian narrative, its *desire machine*" (Cavalcanti 165, my emphasis). To add what I argue in Part 3, however, that spatial desiring machine takes on the specific task of making room for and giving voice to emergent forms of political consciousness and agency that speak to the conditions of the times.

Cavalcanti recognizes the roots of the twentieth-century dystopia in the satire of previous eras, and she argues that along with the modern realism of the text comes a lingering exercise in satiric exaggeration, or catachresis.[14] Noting that catachresis "is founded upon oblique relations, implying 'hidden' meanings and 'deviations' from normal usage," she tracks its formal deployment in the critical dystopias as they "depict fictional realities which are, to different degrees, discontinuous with the contemporary 'real'(although such realties are drawn in relation to, and as a critique of, the world as we know it)" (Cavalcanti 12, 13). In an analysis that recalls Jameson's assessment of the rhetorical function of "world-reduction," she holds that these texts work toward their "deviant" yet realistic "relationship with their referents" by both reducing the world they depict to its conjunctural essentials and then exaggerating that material in order to critique it and then to make room for the radical space that negates the very dystopian qualities that have been presented (Cavalcanti 13).[15] Thus, the "extended figures of catachresis" in these texts hide "utopia in their folds" (Cavalcanti 14). Like the pulsating Chicken Little in *Space Merchants*, the opposition is literally carved out of the prevailing mode of production and its cultural heritage.

Pointing to the self-reflexivity of the critical utopias, Cavalcanti further notes that an inherent part of the critical dystopia's textual resistance lies in its meditation on the very act of writing "as itself an act of hope," as it embodies the dystopian narrative's critique and utopian assertion that is taken up in the act of reading (Cavalcanti 202). By not only foregrounding the production of textual signifiers that point toward a utopian "signified that is deferred" but also emphasizing the imaginative and epistemological process that helps to produce the political movement toward that utopian horizon, the self-reflexive work of the critical dystopia can do its part to shape and provide "inspiration for a feminist 'counter-public sphere'" that can become a ground for overt political mobilization (Cavalcanti 203, 197). Again, although the feminist space she evokes is crucial to the developing opposition of the 1990s, I would add that it is one of many, yet a necessarily informing part of all, in what now appears to be an overdetermined assemblage of opposition.

Using the term *critical dystopia* in their discussions of recent sf-dystopian films, Constance Penley and Peter Fitting likewise catch the logic and sense of the recent dystopian turn as it takes shape in the specificity of film form. For her part, Penley argues that near-future sf films such as *The Terminator* (1984) adopt critical perspectives that "suggest causes rather than merely reveal symptoms."[16] She notes that such films challenge the systemic "atrophy of the utopian imagination" by examining the socioeconomic operations that not only produce the present reality but also silence the utopian opposition to it as all serious alternatives are apparently denied or crushed. Their filmic thought experiments help to explore the forms of "collective political strategies" needed to dismantle the present system and lead toward a better, utopian future. As do Wolmark, Sargent, Baccolini, and Cavalcanti, she perceives the flexible nature of the recent cultural work, and she also situates that work within an emerging critical problematic that dialectically moves through and beyond the theoretical and political positions of the 1980s and early 1990s.[17]

In an argument that implicitly agrees with Penley's, Fitting (in "Unmasking the Real? Critique and Utopia in Four Recent Films") recognizes the ways in which critical dystopian films deliver a *causal* rather than symptomatic analysis as a key characteristic of this new direction.[18] Noting that a critical dystopian text (film or fiction) is marked by "what constitutes the dystopia as well as the explanation of how this situation came about and what should be done about it," he argues that while *Dark City* (1998), *The Truman Show* (1998), *The Matrix* (1999), and *Pleasantville* (1998) portray dystopian realities, only the last two do so in a *critical* dystopian mode ("Unmasking" 1). He goes on to explain that each film presents a society that is itself an "illusory" one that covers over or repackages the "real" society of the film's own spacetime. Thus, all four "contain illusory, constructed realities, worlds which are inhabited by people (or in *The Truman Show* by a single character) who are deliberately kept unaware of the 'artificial' nature of their reality, and where the plots then—in typical dystopian fashion—depict the escape (or attempted escape) from or the struggle against that world" ("Unmasking" 1).

He further notes that in the two films based in a science fictional framework, *Dark City* and *The Matrix*, the protagonist's discovery and breakthrough leads into a "truly dystopian real reality"; whereas in the two based in a televisual frame, *The Truman Show* and *Pleasantville*, the breakthrough leads back into "our own" present time ("Unmasking" 1). In *The Truman Show*, however, there is little "critical thinking" and only one individual escapes, and then only to a loved one in the present world; in *Dark City*, in contrast, there is a social critique but no collective resistance, for the protagonist only ends up re-creating "his own solipsistic utopia" ("Unmasking" 4, 3). Neither film possesses the progressive formal or political qualities that would render it a critical dystopia. Indeed, I would argue that both are examples of the resigned, closed, anticritical, pseudo-dystopian sensibility associated with the anti-utopian persuasion.

Yet *The Matrix* and *Pleasantville* not only deliver substantial causal analyses of our immediate "dystopian" world (by way of their illusory and "actual" filmic dystopias), but they also develop a significant counter-narrative against their multiple dystopian realities. In *The Matrix,* as Fitting puts it,

> it is no longer a question of an individual escape from an oppressive or false reality into a personal fantasy world, but a collective struggle to free the human race from oppression so that however vague or fanciful the film is in terms of the dystopian, it presents a more utopian form of struggle and resistance, a welcome correction to the myth of the solitary hacker of so much cyberpunk since the hackers here are working collectively. ("Unmasking" 4)

And in *Pleasantville* the historical memory of the 1960s civil rights and feminist movements is invoked to inform a collective resistance to the bleak "black and white" dystopian signifier of the 1950s and the 1990s. That collectivity is based on a "color" difference and identity that runs across genders and generations and not only challenges the social status quo but also raises questions of "meaning and happiness" that suggest a "level of self-awareness and introspection which seems almost completely lacking in *The Truman Show* or *Dark City*" ("Unmasking" 5). Fitting, therefore, values the critical dystopian films in terms of their substantial interrogation of the enclosing logic of the dystopian society as well as their presentation of modes of collective resistance that point in the direction of some sort of breakthrough to a utopian horizon. They work against the grain of the compromised or false dystopian films in their effort to challenge contemporary perceptions of a closed social reality as well as the perceived inability to do anything to change it.

III.

Thus, as the critical utopias of the 1960s and 1970s revived and transformed utopian writing (by negating the anti-utopian tendency through a dialectical combination of dystopia and eutopia to produce texts that looked not only at what was and what was to be done but also at how the textual work self-reflexively articulated that political imaginary), the critical dystopias of the 1980s and 1990s carry out a similar intertextual intervention as they negate the negation of

Historical Antinomies

Utopia (historical) (novum)	**Anti-Utopia** (universal) (pseudo-novum)

Literary Forms

utopia/eutopia (radical hope)	**anti-utopia** (cynicism, despair)
dystopia (militant pessimism) (epic, open)	**pseudo-dystopia** (resigned pessimism) (myth, closed)
critical dystopia	**anti-critical dystopia**

FIGURE 6.1 The Dystopian Continuum

the critical utopian moment and thus make room for another manifestation of the utopian imagination within the dystopias form. And as the critical utopias challenged the political compromises of a Left authoritarianism and the theoretical strictures of both orthodox Marxist and structuralist analyses, the critical dystopias interrogate and supersede the limits of 1980s micropolitics and post-structuralism (especially as they lead into or legitimate accommodation with the status quo). Here, then, the critical dystopia can be understood in terms of the definition that Sargent added to those in his growing list of utopian textual types: "a non-existent society described in considerable detail and normally located in time and space that the author intended a contemporaneous reader to view as worse than contemporary society but that normally includes at least one eutopian enclave or holds out hope that the dystopia can be overcome and replaced with a eutopia."[19]

Considered in terms of the distinctions set out in the Chapter 5, these historically specific texts cluster, as it happens, on the "left" side of the dystopian continuum, as they negotiate the necessary pessimism of the generic dystopia with an open, militant, utopian stance that not only breaks through the hegemonic enclosure of the text's alternative world but also self-reflexively refuses the anti-utopian temptation that lingers like a dormant virus in every dystopian account (see Figure 6.1).

In contrast, contemporary dystopian examples that are anti-critical can be identified as texts that more readily remain in the camp of nihilistic or resigned expressions that may appear to challenge the current social situation but in fact end up reproducing it by ideologically inoculating viewers and readers against any form of anger or action, enclosing them within the very social realities they disparagingly expose. Thus, anti-critical texts of this period can be located in an anti-utopian constellation of dystopian (better, pseudo-dystopian) commodities against which the critical dystopian fictions and films struggle for reception and effect. This textual web would include films such as *Dark City* and *The Truman Show* but also television productions such as Oliver Stone's miniseries *Wild Palms* or *The X-Files* (which substitute conspiracy theories for analysis and posturing for politics), novels such as Robert Harris's 1992 *Fatherland,* Don DeLillo's 1997 *Underworld,* or John Updike's 1997 *Toward the End of Time* (which perceptively open up the social only to suture it right back up) and any number of sf cyber-thrillers that toy with corporate evil but only give meaning to the acts of hustling within it.[20]

IV.

Unlike these anti-utopian masquerades, the recent texts by Robinson, Butler, and Piercy can be read as critical dystopias that continue in the political and poetic spirit of the critical utopias even as they revive the dystopian strategy to map, warn, and hope.[21] Stepping inside the ambient zone of anti-utopian pessimism with new textual tricks, they expose the horror of the present moment. Yet in the midst of their pessimistic forays, they refuse to allow the utopian tendency to be overshadowed by its anti-utopian nemesis. They therefore adopt a militant stance that is informed and empowered by a utopian horizon that appears in the text—or at least shimmers just beyond its pages.

Besides the utopias of the 1970s, the critical dystopias also work with and against two immediate precursors in the bleak political and cultural environment of the early to mid-1980s that represent some of the first creative attempts to come to terms with the economic and political changes: the ongoing tradition of feminist sf and the new direction of cyberpunk. Certainly, Robinson, Butler, and Piercy maintain an affiliation with the feminist texts of the 1980s even as those works shifted from the contentious utopias of the 1970s to narratives that, as Wolmark puts it, are symptomatically "less overtly oppositional" and more concerned with "scrutinising the range of dilemmas and contradictions facing the female subject, rather then eliminating them" (Wolmark 88). Although they continue in the spirit of Atwood's *Handmaid's Tale* (which, contrary to Wolmark, Baccolini, and Cavalcanti, I see as a classical not a critical dystopia), they dare to explore utopian possibilities that Atwood prefers to avoid. Still, although they might concur with the feminist stance of works such as Tepper's *Gate to Women's Country* (1988), Pamela Sargent's *Shore of Women* (1986), Joan Slonczewski's *Door into Ocean* (1986), in their strategic moves to a different stage that works with and yet beyond the common sense of postmodernism and micropolitics, they do not step away from a totalizing analysis of the historical moment nor do they refuse to identify the potential for uncompromised forms of oppositional agency.[22]

In terms of cyberpunk, the critical dystopias share its deeply negative portrayal of the brave new world of late-twentieth-century capitalism. With William Gibson's groundbreaking *Neuromancer* in 1984 and in works by Bruce Sterling, John Shirley, Lucius Shepard, Lewis Shiner, and other, mostly male writers, this creative conjunction of hacker, punk, and sf cultures produced works that generated near-future sf that registers the social conditions of the capitalist and conservative 1980s.[23] Eventually, however, critics and readers began to see shortcomings in the first wave of cyberpunk. Fitting, for example, acknowledges that cyberpunk effectively portrayed the "triumph of instrumental reason" in the new transnational "society of the spectacle," but he also notes that a "contestatory option" was never allowed to develop; Suvin observes that "a viable thisworldly, collective and public, utopianism is simply not within the horizon of the cyberpunk structure of feeling."[24] Both imply that cyberpunk caught the problem of the social changes of the 1980s but it then too readily opted for existence within the terms of that problem rather than blasting through it. Others—such as Istvan Csicsery-Ronay, Thomas Foster, Jean Gomoll, Sharon Stockton, Samuel Delany, and Andrew Ross—saw that cyberpunk was largely written and read by white, heterosexual, upwardly mobile males who were anxiously yet still powerfully renegotiating their own social positions in the 1980s.

As a result of these conditions of production and reception, the edgy new texts suffered from an insufficient self-reflexivity and critical stance regarding questions of gender and power.[25] In my own study of Gibson's trilogy, I argue that this dynamic series simultaneously appropriated and rejected the feminist utopias of the 1960s and compromised its own negative portrayal of contemporary society by containing that radical vision within the limits of a caper plot that privileges the hustling ability of its loner male heroes and ends up going nowhere beyond the world found on the first page of *Neuromancer*. As I saw it, Gibson astutely captured the mise-en-scène of the capitalist culture, but he minimized the risk of his iconic critique with the "safety net" of a narrative that collapsed into the logic of the very system he set out to expose.[26]

And yet the authentically negative energy of cyberpunk led into the moment of the critical dystopia. To be sure, some of the early cyberpunk writers did take their narratives into politically confrontational waters. More neglected than the successful titles by Gibson and Sterling, Fred Pfeil's *Goodman 20/20* (1986), Richard Kadrey's *Metrophage* (1988), John Shirley's *Eclipse* trilogy (1985, 1988, 1990), and the crossover detective stories of Richard Russo and Richard Luceno are examples of work that moves beyond the cheap thrills of the more self-contained cyberpunk hits. Later in the 1980s and 1990s, when a number of women took up textual cybertactics, a second wave of cyberpunk moved onto more political ground. Pat Cadigan (the only woman published in the definitive *Mirrorshades* anthology in 1988) took the cyberpunk sensibility beyond the narrative limits of noir heroes engaged in cyclic quests in *Synners* (1991) and developed a tale of collective resistance to the new bio-information ventures of corporate capitalism.[27] Others such as Emma Bull (*Bone Dance,* 1991), Sherri Lewitt (*Cybernetic Jungle,* 1992), and Laura Mixon (*Glass Houses,* 1992) also connected the cyberimagination with a cultural imaginary and a political narrative that was more sensitive to diversity and more engaged with direct, collective challenges to the system than the earlier works.

The critical dystopian strategy, however, differs from these textual predecessors in ways that are less utopian than the feminist narratives and less anti-utopian than cyberpunk. Certainly, their intertextual debt to these penultimate works is unmistakable, but in each case the genre-blurring dystopias move in significantly different directions. Robinson's *Gold Coast* reflects cyberpunk's exploration of the hard edge of everyday life and self-critically does so from a primarily white male standpoint, yet it also goes beyond cyberpunk in a near-future narrative that shares a sensibility with historical writing and realist coming-of-age narratives, simultaneously reviving the power of memory and invoking a temporal solidarity that will be found only in a not yet achieved future. Butler's *Parable* books have an affinity with the feminist utopias but also draw on the creative possibilities of the diary and journal, slave narratives, realist fiction, right-wing survivalist stories, and New Age vision quests to spin a story of new social formations that is rooted in the traditions of popular American sf. And from her usual place on the margins of sf, Piercy in *He, She and It* carries on her long-standing socialist, feminist, ecological critique in a work that draws from cyberpunk and feminist sf while it also retrieves the power of traditional forms of storytelling in order to create a tale of political activism that explores a new set of strategies and tactics.

The critical dystopias clearly traverse different political and cultural ground. Faced by the delegitimation of Utopia and the hegemonic cynicism of Anti-Utopia, they do not simply mimic the utopian expression of the 1970s. Nor do they easily let go of that sensibility as they stand up to the hegemony of Anti-Utopia. Consequently, they burrow within the dystopian tradition in order to bring utopian and dystopian tendencies to bear on their exposés of the present moment and their explorations of new forms of oppositional agency. Considered in terms of the continuum of utopian and anti-utopian pessimism, they tend to express an emancipatory, militant, critical utopian position. With their epical scope of nascent political challenges to ruling systems, open endings that look beyond the last page to other rounds of contestation, and realistically utopian possibilities lurking in the iconic details of their alternative worlds, the critical dystopias do not simply come down on the side of an unproblematized Utopia or a resigned and triumphant Anti-Utopia. Albeit generally, and stubbornly, utopian, they do not go easily toward that better world. Rather, they linger in the terrors of the present even as they exemplify what is needed to transform it.

None of the new dystopias quite reaches the degree of self-reflexivity that characterizes the earlier critical utopias (perhaps in a move against the postmodern aesthetic); nevertheless, they work in this new cultural moment (as Baccolini and Cavalcanti note) to reassert the transformative functions of language, textuality, memory, and history. In so doing, they highlight their own use value as cultural objects even as they reflect on the limits and possibilities of the dystopian form itself. With the texts that I discuss in the following chapters, each one finds a way to exemplify the power of imaginative intervention in political processes of critique and change. Each features a writer or storyteller whose individual craft becomes the core of a political vocation in a collective, or potentially collective, movement; and each offers extensive meditations on creative and critical expressions that disturb their various universes.

Whether they work with modes of history and memory as forces of social change, journal writing as a source of self-critique and social interpellation, or storytelling as a means of subversive subject formation, all three dystopias reflect upon their formal relations with sociopolitical realities by way of their internal accounts of textual interventions. Thus, they teach their readers not only about the world around them but also about the open-ended ways in which texts such as the ones in front of their eyes can both elucidate that world and help to develop the critical capacity of people to know, challenge, and change those aspects of it that deny or inhibit the further emancipation of humanity.

Part Three

Dystopian Maneuvers

7

Kim Stanley Robinson's Other California

There comes into being, then, a situation in which we can say that if individual experience is authentic, then it cannot be true; and that if a scientific or cognitive model of the same content is true, then it escapes individual experience.

—Fredric Jameson, "Cognitive Mapping" (349)

I.

Published in 1988, Kim Stanley Robinson's *Gold Coast* (the second volume in his Orange County trilogy) is the earliest in my sampling of critical dystopias.[1] Although his utopian Martian trilogy is perhaps better known, Robinson's first trilogy, set closer to home, is in itself an important moment in the development of sf.[2] In this set of textual studies published between 1984 and 1990, he created three versions of the southern Californian landscape that perceptively explore the formal possibilities of the sf genre as well as the sociopolitical realities and tensions in the United States in the late 1980s. In each, a younger and older man cross generational barriers and engage in a conversation about society, personal life, and the vocation of the writer as they simultaneously confront the political crisis that shapes their particular spacetime variation. In the first two volumes, the young man eventually decides on the sort of writing he needs to do to be true to himself as well to be a responsible political agent in his society. In *The Wild Shore* (1984), Harry, at old Tom's urging, writes about his travels and experiences in the new frontier of post–neutron bomb Orange County; in the military-corporate-consumer society of *The Gold Coast,* Jim sets poetry aside to write the history of a ruined Orange County; but in *Pacific Edge* (1990) it is the older man (the Tom Barnard who appears in all three volumes) who works out the literary and political theory of what is essentially the critical utopia in his journal, and then joins the revolution that produces both the utopian society in which his grandson Kevin lives and the text we are reading. In the last volume, the younger man, Kevin, is not a writer but a skilled carpenter in the post-revolutionary town of El Modena.

In these self-reflexive studies of a metonymic American space, Robinson moves from a post-holocaust, apocalyptic narrative (in the vein of an Orson Scott Card or David Brin), to a near-future dystopian account (closer to the style of Philip K. Dick), and on to the utopian *Pacific Edge* (which Edward James has called the most interesting utopia since Delany's *Triton*). Of the three, the last continues, and self-reflexively extends, the critical utopian tradition. As he does in greater scale in the Martian trilogy, in this volume Robinson reasserts the critical utopian refusal to regard Utopia as an end in itself, seeing it instead as the very "road of history . . . something we are working within, step by step" in a process that never ends.[3] Within this provisional and open-ended challenge to the prevailing reality, he provides a totalizing exploration of society and agency that concerns itself with economy and production, multiplex class struggle, and a collective engagement that opposes the new capitalist ideology and discipline of "globalization" as well as the ameliorations of liberal reformism by way of a new (yet still difference-based) political struggle that connects the global system with local government and culture.[4]

Before writing the utopia of *Pacific Edge,* however, Robinson took up the challenge of dystopian narrative in *The Gold Coast,* but he did so in ways that drew on both the Wellsian sensibility of the classical dystopia and the noir pessimism of cyberpunk. On first reading of *The Gold Coast,* one might miss the dystopian and noir qualities that lurk beneath the textual surface and find only a postmodern world that is disconcertingly "normal," even to the extent of banality, as Robinson delves into the quotidian details of individual lives in this Other California in a style that is not unlike the fine-tuned accounts of a writer like Delany. Although it is set in the near future of the 2040s (almost a hundred years after the founding of NATO), the tone of his genre-blurring tale of planetary capitalism as it plays out in the centers of corporate power and in the struggles of everyday life is closer to that of a realist coming-of-age narrative, but one helped along with the additional discourses of history and poetry.

Despite its deceptively innocent, almost presentist ambience, Robinson's text is a carefully crafted dystopian effort in cognitively mapping the cultural logic of a system dominated by the Reaganesque military-industrial complex in the years just before the historic shift of 1989, when the United States became the infamous "victor" of the Cold War.

II.

Caught within the simultaneously sped-up and impoverished society produced by an ever more greedy corporate-governmental system, the young Jim McPherson and his twenty-something friends try to find meaning and satisfaction in lives reduced to the needs and pleasures of an emptily commodified moment, while Jim's father, Dennis, fights to survive in a defense industry that has no need for his skill or idealism as it neglects quality production and political principles in favor of the accumulation of profit and power. As Jim confronts the political and creative challenges in his life, and his father eventually escapes the machinations of a corporate world that cares nothing for his work, their parallel stories articulate a modest utopian hope in the ability of people to learn the scope of the new capitalist world and forge independent and politically committed lives in the social and geographical gaps of a system that shows no signs of changing. In addition to the iconic details and narrative spine of this deceptively dystopian world, Robinson self-reflexively explores the discursive functions of emancipating memory (social and personal), totalizing analysis, and the craft of writing as they contribute to the processes of cognitive mapping and political activism.

Certainly, this alternative world of the twenty-first century realistically represents the agendas of the U.S. military, the defense industry, and the government that were hegemonic in the mid-1980s. Even though the Cold War still provides the primary source of profit and power, other opportunities abound in new U.S. actions in "Arabia" (Bahrain) and Southeast Asia (Thailand, Burma) and in the collateral challenges brought about by the expansion of a Reaganesque space defense system, the rearmament of Japan, drug wars in South America, and the other "forty odd wars currently being fought" with "obsolete equipment" (11). As in the Vietnam years, it is obvious that a "guns and butter" social policy is not working, and consequently the daily lives of those who are not securely employed within the privileged sectors of the economy are shaped by a degraded environment, minimal employment, limited housing, and the mindless experiences of commodity consumption. Robinson encapsulates this social reality in his microcosm of Orange County (which "sprang Athena-like, full blown from the forehead of Zeus Los Angeles") by reducing his gaze to the local only to expose it as a fractal image of this world of militarized corporate capitalism. In an early statement of the book's concern with the processes of history (which anticipates and negates the assertions of Francis Fukuyama), Jim ironically but astutely observes that

> Orange County is the end of history, its purest product. Civilization kept moving west for thousands of years, in a sunset tropism, until they came to

> the edge here on the Pacific and they couldn't go any farther. And so they stopped here and *did it*. And by that time they were in the great late surge of corporate capitalism, so that everything here is purely organized, to buy and sell, buy and sell, every little piece of us. (3)

Later in his working draft of the history of the county, Jim locates the causes of this dystopian degradation in the postwar engines of the peacetime military and the consumer economy (signified by Camp Pendleton and South Coast Plaza). As he recounts, the buildup in the aftermath of World War II transformed the area when the "war machine" dominated its geography and economy; for the "military-industrial infrastructure was built, and left in place, and it provided work for the thousands of men who returned after the war, with their new families; they came, and bought houses built by the construction industry that had been so well primed by military construction" (264). Fed by the fear of communism and the satisfaction of consumer goods, the county boomed in employment and population. Gradually, acres of orange groves were replaced by strip malls and subdivisions, and by 2020 the number of malls had increased again, with "many square miles . . . roofed and air-conditioned" (322). The new malls were fed by more elevated freeways that added another layer to the ones already in place, and the synergistic outcome was an "autopia" that endlessly cycles around itself.

With the implosion of the national economy under the pressure of endless military adventures, however, the quality of life collapsed. An expanding population and limited space led to shared housing and the subsequent end of the suburban dream of a private home; the shrinking domestic economy produced fewer jobs and resulted in aimless youth and frustrated middle managers; and the ecological diversity and beauty of the region was devastated by unproductive land and water speculation that consumed the last of the state forests. Embodying the "ultimate expression of the American Dream," this "over-lit," overbuilt, overconsumed, post-suburban reality may seem so familiar to U.S. readers that it will not be read through the distancing lens of dystopia but simply taken as a realistic portrayal of life at the end of the twentieth century. Formally, however, it is fully dystopian, as it offers a detailed cause-and-effect analysis of an extrapolated society that no longer nurtures and stimulates its people but rather constitutes, as Forster described long before, an unseen social machine intent only on its own carcinogenic growth.

This cognitive map of Orange County configures the society that Jim, his father, and his friends try to come to terms with, either to acquiesce in its seductive routines (which are as "tracked" as the electromagnetic guidance system that replaced the gasoline-powered automobile) or to reach, at least individually if not yet collectively, for an alternative existence that is shaped by the social dream of a self-determined and fulfilled humanity rather than an economy intent on reifying and commodifying everyone and everything. Coming from different perspectives, two of Jim's friends bespeak the dystopian nature of their society in their own evaluations and responses. More resilient and resistant than the others, Tashi, who eventually leaves for the outlands of Alaska, manages to live on the edge of the system by working occasionally as a "car brain" mechanic and living in a tent "on the roof of one of the big condotowers in the Newport Town Center," growing his own vegetables, using the water facilities of the partly abandoned building, and enjoying a great view of the ocean, the "blue plain to the southwest" (98). His home, as he argues, symbolizes his ecological analysis of the society and his independent response to it. In a dystopian reprise of Kuno, he explains to Jim that the "less you are plugged into the machine, the less it controls you. . . . Since most jobs are part of the machine, it follows that you should lead a life with no need for money. No easy task, of course, but one can approximate, do what is possible" (98).

At the other extreme, Jim's ambulance-driver friend, Abe Bernard, knows he is hopelessly entangled in the cogs of the machine as he drives its freeways to rescue its wounded. But he at least understands why he can't act more independently, for he realizes that the quotidian has consumed him. Time flies by "in a haze of undifferentiated activity," and "his shifts on the job all blur together" (118). Like Kevin Lynch's disoriented urban dweller and Jameson's underinformed subject, Abe sees that he and others like him no longer possess the perspective of the "long-term time scale" (118). A skilled and concerned paramedic, he remembers all the crashes, the rushes to hospitals, and the agonies of patients in some remote corner of his mind; but in his waking life "the recollection mechanism is firmly turned off" (118). Unlike Tashi, who uses the counterlogic of ecology to map his cannily resistant place in the larger system, Abe has no way to locate himself so that he can gain control over his life and work. With memory suppressed and daily existence divided between being exhausted on the job and stoned afterward, he can no longer triangulate his position in a system that drains him at work and leaves him empty in his downtime.

In this deceptively normal dystopian world, twenty-seven-year-old Jim McPherson begins to emerge from his immediate dreamscape and find his own way. As a well-interpellated subject of his time, he passively—and, in a Lukacsian sense, typically—survives by working two part-time jobs, going to parties heightened by designer drugs, cruising the freeways with his friends, drifting in and out of sexual "alliances," guiltily relating to his parents and uncle, and yet, through some sort of interpellative slippage, remaining unhappy and seemingly unable to change any part of his mundane life.

An apparent misfit who is not exceptionally strong or skillful, Jim teaches a few English classes at the community college and works as a clerk in a real estate office, but the passion that offers a way to dislodge himself from the system lies in his own creative work. He clumsily tinkers at musical sampling (combining the "slow parts" of Beethoven's five late string quartets into one tape) and poetry (which in desperation he subjects to a randomized computer program). But he attains a different degree of creative energy and quality in his work on the history of Orange County. When his current ally, Virginia, comments that people "never think about how things got this way," Jim realizes that he is one of the remaining few who at least tries (31). He enlists his friends in nocturnal archaeological forays, digging through parking lot concrete to uncover fragments of life before the maze of strip malls, condo towers, subdivisions, and multilayered freeways obliterated the decentralized towns, orange groves, and desert ecology. On his own he compiles archival evidence of the way things were—accumulating old histories, visual artifacts, and his uncle Tom's stories. Three walls of his room are covered with maps of Orange County: one from the 1930s, one from the 1990s, and a recent one that shows the county "gridded and overgridded" (63); orange crate labels with their pastoral images of a nonexistent moment of peace and plenty hang on the bathroom wall.

Jim knows, however, that this supposedly healthier past is "out of reach" (64). Instead of dwelling nostalgically on its loss, he writes its history, eight chapters of which are scattered through Robinson's text as a metacommentary that frames the developing counter-narrative. Five of the chapters portray a lost "utopian" world of ecological beauty and relative social well-being and end with the words "all that went away" (117, 224, 242); three others narrate the instrumentalizing lead-up to the dystopian present and end with the words "none of that ever went away" (264, 295, 323). Clearly, Jim's intent is not to escape into the static icons on the end of orange crates. Instead, his maturing historical sense gives him the necessary critical distance to gain an empowering knowledge of the nature, pace, and consequences of change and the human causes behind it. Finally, it makes this typical dystopian misfit want "to do something" to redress the exploitation and destruction of the land that his family has lived in for four generations (28).

The opportunity for meaningful action comes to Jim by way of a conversation with his friend Arthur Bastanchury (whose roots in the region are marked by his family name, which is also that of a major street in the county). Engaging in political work that recalls the best of the 1960s opposition, Arthur is a "dedicated antiwar activist and underground newspaper publisher" (28). On his way to leaflet a shopping mall with fliers against the draft (reimposed by the "Gingrich Act"), he talks with Jim about the "sleepwalkers" who know nothing about the political situation and do even less (40). He alludes to Jim's historical research and challenges him to do more than indulge in what he misreads as a nostalgic obsession. Asserting that "what's needed is something more active, some kind of *real resistance*," Arthur reveals to Jim that he and people he works with have escalated their degree of activism by sabotaging weapons manufacturers based in Orange County (42). Although irritated by Arthur's "secretive righteousness," Jim is intrigued at the possibility of direct action and agrees to join Arthur the next time he leaflets a mall. During the distribution, Jim makes it clear that he wants nothing to do with terrorism, but he is drawn to Arthur's claims for the nonviolent destruction of military property (65). Replaying the strategy of underground struggle of the African National Congress or the position taken by the American Catholic Left during the Vietnam War that "some property has no right to exist," Arthur argues that there is a "big difference between terrorism and sabotage," and he assures Jim that his group uses "methods that harm plastics, programs, and various composite construction materials, without endangering people" (65).

Still Jim demurs, holding to his reservations about violence, but after a hassle with his father and a fight with his current "ally" Virginia he tells Arthur that he is ready "to do something . . . to help" (110). With a complex set of reasons hovering between personal frustration and political anger, Jim realizes that this is a

> chance to make some meaning out of his life, to strike back against . . . everything. Against individuals, of course—his father, Virginia, Humphrey, his students—but he doesn't think of them, not consciously. He's thinking of the evil direction his country has taken for so long, in spite of all his protests, all his votes, all his deepest beliefs. Ignoring the world's need, profiting from its misery, fomenting fear in order to sell more arms, to take over more accounts, to own more, to make more money . . . it really is the American way. And so there's no choice but action, now, some real and tangible form of *resistance.* (110–111)

That night Jim and Arthur collect their weapons from Arthur's covert connection and head for the parking lot of Parnell Airspace Corporation. They fire small, laser-guided missiles into the door of the company's physical plant. On impact the bombs release a gas "containing degrading enzymes and chemical solvents . . . and all the plastic, filaboy, reinforced carbon, graphite, epoxy resin, and kevlar reached by the gas" is "reduced to dust, or screwed up in some less dramatic way" (113). Back on the street, after damaging what Arthur describes as "ninety million dollars of space weaponry," Jim is elated at having finally "*done* something" (114). Looking at Jim with the "raptor intensity" of a typically opportunistic organizer,

Arthur sums up the consciousness-raising consequences of direct action: "Take that first step, perform an act of resistance of even the smallest kind, and suddenly your perception changes. Reality changes. You see it can be done" (115).

Accepting Arthur's subsequent invitations, Jim takes part in attacks on the Northrop missile complex (174–177) and Aerojet North (186) and looks forward to a third that will target a firm that makes "orbiting nuclear reactors" (244). At the end of each action, he utters his new slogan: "Here's to resistance" (177). Although this Californian sleeper appears to have awakened, the purity of direct action begins to fade as Jim begins to wonder about the network with which Arthur is affiliated. His first opportunity to learn more comes when his friend Sandy (a skilled chemist and the best producer of designer eyedrop drugs in the area) takes Jim, Arthur, and the others to a party in San Diego hosted by his dealer friend Bob Tompkins and his partner, Raymond. As one of the larger drug distributors, Bob has invited Sandy down to discuss a once-off deal for a new line of designer aphrodisiacs that would bring him extra cash (cash he needs to pay the bills for his dying father, who is hospitalized in the now commonly privatized medical system). As Sandy discusses the deal with Bob, Jim overhears Arthur talking with Raymond and discovers that Raymond is the mysterious supplier behind the sabotage. Beginning with this conversation, the apparently unrelated plots of Jim and Arthur's political action, Sandy's drug dealing, and the corporate machinations experienced by Jim's father combine in a Dickensian matrix to reveal the underlying scheme that pulls all the action together and expresses the totalizing logic and practice that produces the society in which they all live.

In unfolding the layers of this megaplot, Robinson adds another dimension to the cognitive mapping already at work in the iconic register of the text. Along with the detailed account of the formation of militarized capitalism in his twenty-first-century version of Orange County—in a version of one of Russ's recommended sf narrative strategies—he fills in his provisional map through the discrete narrative of these intertwined life stories as they thread their way through the iconic tapestry. In fact, his piecemeal exposure of the "master plot" of the corporate executives, government bureaucrats, and renegade drug dealers more precisely replicates the necessarily incremental nature of this didactic aesthetic. True to Jameson's argument that no one person can correlate the truth of his or her experience within the larger systemic reality, no single character in Robinson's text is able to grasp the entire scope of the scheme that drives the basic crisis of the text, but each contributes bits that help to fill in the absent paradigm of the overall social map. Sandy, Dennis, and Jim work out separate pieces of the puzzle, but the full picture is available only to the reader who is in the privileged epistemological and political position to accumulate that collective knowledge and see it for what it is: namely, an embodiment of the logic of greed and power that informs the entire society. Self-reflexively, it is only through connecting the apparently independent actions of Sandy, Dennis, and Jim that the reader can follow a similar trajectory of discovery in order to apprehend the overarching dystopian totality. Like the face of God (or Dick's Absolute Benefactor), it can never quite be seen in its own right.

It is no surprise that the person who garners the first solid information about the larger scheme is Sandy. As the friendly drug-dealer of the sort associated with the counterculture of the 1960s rather than the organized crime purveyors of the 1980s, he is a benign character who makes an honest living in the black economy. Working on the borderline of legitimate and illegitimate markets, moving imperceptibly between business and pleasure, and yet ultimately standing by his friendship with Jim and Arthur, Sandy is in the least fixed position and therefore the one who can more readily see the traces of the master plot in his canny peripheral vision, a vision he cultivates for his very survival. Jim hears only fragments of Arthur's conversation at the Torrey Pines party, but Sandy learns firsthand from Bob that Raymond has become distracted from the drug trade by "other things." He finds out that Raymond's friends in Venezuela "were killed by some remotely piloted vehicles that the Venezuelan drug police had bought from our Army" (149) and consequently Raymond has vowed revenge on the U.S. military and defense industry: "He couldn't really declare war on the U.S. Army, but he's done the next best thing, and declared war on the people who made the robot planes" (149). Rather than political principles, it is personal revenge (along with a continued interest in "keeping an eye out for profits") that has led him to import "little missile systems . . . for sabotaging military production plants" and find "people who want these things done more than he does" (150).

Back in Orange County and checking with others in the "black economy's extended family," Sandy collects more rumors about the sabotage (182–185). From a friend and client, he hears that some believe the cause behind the attacks is even more insidious than Raymond's individual vendetta, for it appears to be a campaign of "industrial sabotage" undertaken by the corporations themselves in what could be "an intercorporations war" (185). When he and Tashi have to hide their illegal aphrodisiac shipment on the coastline below Jim's father's workplace, he also senses from Bob's interest that there is a connection with Laguna Space Research (LSR). And when he finally hears what Jim and Arthur have to say, he can confirm that they are indeed involved in the attacks. Yet rather than expose his friends to unnecessary anxiety over what at this stage is still speculation, he refrains from telling them about Raymond's role and motivation. After more snooping—in the course of which he somehow forgets the corporate dimension—he believes he knows the "shape of the whole setup," as he sees that "Jim is working with Arthur, and Arthur is working for Raymond, and that Raymond is pursuing a private vendetta for private purposes—and perhaps making a profit on the side" (330). At this point, however, it is inconvenient to tell Jim and Arthur since they are preparing an attack on LSR that will have the desirable side effect of covering Sandy's own retrieval of the abandoned drugs. Caught in a rush between loyalty and business, he falls into a compromised silence that betrays his own generous qualities.

Sandy thinks he knows the shape of the entire scheme, but he has actually penetrated just to the level of Raymond's personal involvement and never appreciates the larger corporate role in the campaign. Jim's father, however, is in a better position to learn more about the corporate side of the plot. Working within the thriving defense sector, Dennis McPherson is on the verge of losing his job at Laguna Space Research, the small defense contractor whose parent company is "one of the world's corporate giants," Argo AG/Blessman Enterprises (21). With his experience in engineering, he works meticulously on his projects, and because he can "see the larger patterns, where engineering touches both invention and administration" (10), he also represents the company in Washington, negotiating proposals with the defense establishment.

Dennis's commitment to quality, however, has angered his immediate superior, Stuart Lemon, for it has resulted in the company's losing two projects because he was unable to keep his costs competitive with other companies. Lemon (a prime type of the privileged executive with financial and cultural capital) offers one last chance to Dennis when he returns from Washington with an Air Force "superblack" order for a small robot bomber to use against the Soviets. Dennis takes on the assignment of the "Stormbee" project, but his painstaking work is frustrated when the Air Force cancels the superblack status and opens the project to public bids. When Lemon reviews Dennis's revised budget, he asserts that it is "too high" because the "system [is] over-designed" (160).

Further up the line of power, Lemon's boss—Donald Hereford, president of LSR and a vice-president in the parent company—also assesses the bid in terms of profit and not product and orders Lemon to cut the production budget. Despite the trimming, the project is awarded to Parnell Aviation (ironically, the company attacked by Jim and Arthur), and Dennis is furious because he knows Parnell cannot deliver at the cost it listed (180). Still thinking in terms of his liberal idealism—believing that his work inside the corporate structure can prevent war by producing well-designed weapons systems that will permanently discourage Soviet attacks—Dennis sees his deterrence logic and his reformist belief in the rule of law crumble when the project is finally lost in a court appeal in which the judge rules "in the interests of national security" (287). LSR's lawyer explains to Dennis that they had been unknowingly immersed in an internecine competition between competing managers and that the entire affair was "part of a campaign to pull . . . weapons procurement . . . back completely in the Pentagon's power" (288). With his idealism shattered, Dennis admits that LSR was a pawn "in a battle between two parts of the Air Force" and the hegemony of the Pentagon, signified in the impenetrability of its "massive concrete bunker defended against all the world" (289, 291). He returns to California knowing that his days at LSR are numbered.

If the scheme around the Stormbee program exposes a layer of corporate logic to Dennis, the shadowy outline of the deeper and more systemically insidious level of causation is available exclusively to the reader who follows the accumulating action as Dennis, Lemon, and Hereford confront the consequences of the terminated Stormbee contract. Even before the cancellation, Lemon knows that LSR is in danger, for the parent company has been demanding an increase in yearly profits and threatening to sell off the company if the new goals are not met (157). Later, in conversation with Hereford, he learns that the sabotage of neighboring companies might well be the work of corporate interests who are simply using the "local group of refusniks" to do the dirty work (257). Hereford—the hegemonic leader who has the widest view, and most control, of the power struggles—opaquely notes that company security had penetrated the campaign and found out that a "very large, very professional group" is at the root of it all (257); he then implies that AG/Blessman itself might be that primary agent. In a description of "normal" corporate sabotage, the urbane and quietly powerful Hereford explains that a "company attacks others to harm their work and eventually damage their reputation for efficiency," but then another tactical twist occurs when "it attacks itself to keep suspicion away" (258).

This information is already turning "tumblers" in Lemon's mind, but another drops into place when Hereford observes that the company in question "could use the attack on itself to get rid of something potentially damaging in and of itself" (258). He then orders Lemon to pull the security guards from the plant in light of the rumors that LSR will be attacked, ostensibly to save their lives. Lemon realizes that he's been sufficiently clued in to Hereford's plot to work with its effects in disciplining LSR, but he also is canny enough not to ask further questions. Looking at the "amused crinkle" in Hereford's eyes, he sees that the corporate leader knows full well what is going on and what is at stake. In conversation some days later, Hereford "informs" Lemon that his security people have found the person hiring the activists—ostensibly Raymond—but again he infers merely that the handler above Raymond can be found within AG/Blessman's own corporate headquarters (331).

Dennis's well-intentioned concerns about the fate of LSR intersect with this deeper plot after Hereford hears about the court ruling and orders Lemon not to appeal, for the corporate leader argues that it is more important to preserve LSR's standing in the military-industrial hierarchy than to protect their own integrity or their employees or the military troops using the weapons. As Hereford explains:

> If we win this one—force the Air Force to take back their award, and win the contract ourselves—then we've got the Stormbee system, sure. But we've also embarrassed the Air Force in front of the whole industry, the whole country. And if we do that, then Stormbee is the last program we can ever expect to get from the Air Force again. Because they'll remember. They'll do their best to bankrupt us. (334)

Dennis, of course, is appalled at this account of raw corporate survivalism achieved at the expense of purpose, quality, and law. Embittered, he at last begins to see the operating pattern: "The whole operation, so neat, so efficient, so *real* looking, is all a sham, a fake. . . . Only the power struggles of certain people in Washington are real, and those battles are based on whims, personal ambitions, personal jealousies. And those battles make the rest of the world unreal" (335). Regarding himself as nothing more than "an extra in those battles," he closes his office door and goes home.

Even though he has learned more about the competitive dynamics behind the system in which he works and lives, Dennis still thinks like a liberal reformist and interprets everything in terms of a repairable personal or institutional dysfunction and not as an endemic result of the systemic logic itself. Closer to the center, Lemon and especially Hereford are more fully aware of and complicit in the actual maneuvers. When they review the situation after Jim's botched attack on LSR (which Dennis never realizes is his son's work), they implicitly understand that the damage that could have assisted in the downsizing of LSR did not occur. Less subtle than his comfortably powerful boss, Lemon comes out and asks if they should "stimulate another attack" (366), but Hereford deflects the suggestion: "Stimulate? Or simulate? . . . No. The point is, we've been warned. So now it's our responsibility to see it doesn't happen again" (366). Successful damage or not, the attack has helped Hereford's cause, and he now has sufficient reason to close down LSR in California and move its design and production line to Florida. In a flash he orders Lemon to fire the executive team, including Dennis, and he observes that Lemon should be happy that he too wasn't sacrificed.

From his personal standpoint, Dennis simply experiences this ruthless restructuring as the end to his own career. But the strategically positioned reader gets the picture of the systemic motive behind the entire set of actions. Simply put, Argo AG/Blessman Enterprises needs not only to survive but to triumph, and this economic and political "necessity" has driven the entire operation, setting in motion a series of events that brought untold damage to people inside the corporation and at large, only to guarantee that costs could be cut, power preserved, and position gained in the center of power.

III.

As Sandy, Dennis, and the corporate executives fix the dystopian social coordinates for the readerly eye, the counter-narrative line of Jim's search for meaning and purpose beyond his "hollow" and "fashionable" life offers at least a proto-political trajectory through which the system can begin to be critiqued, if not yet overturned and transformed (254). Even though the sabotage project has jolted him out of his malaise, he is further challenged through his interactions with those closest to him: his friends; his new lover, Hana; and his father. When Sandy takes him along with his wife, Angela, and their friend Humphrey to Europe to escape the pressure of the interrupted smuggling deal, Jim finds it is an opportunity to see himself and his Orange County home against a broader canvas (225–238). After Humphrey's choice takes them to the French Disneyland and Sandy and Angela opt for Moscow, Jim suggests a visit to the historical sites of Cairo and Crete, thereby dipping back into the racially contested roots of "Western" reality.

On a solitary walk, Jim gets lost in Cairo's streets and is overwhelmed by the poverty he encounters. Recalling Athol Fugard's play *People Are Living Here,* he develops his own self-reflexive take on a "real world" that his encapsulated life in Orange County has not allowed. In Crete he finds another comparative viewpoint on the history of Orange County as he looks back on it in terms of the strikingly different history of the quite similar landscape of this Mediterranean island. When he returns home, he realizes that the trip has further dislodged his sense of self and society, and he is filled with an increasing personal and political feeling of unease. With his working grasp of reality breaking down, he anxiously thinks about his situation in terms of the freeway mechanism that surrounds and shapes his meager life: "It's as if somewhere the program and the magnetic field keeping him on his particular track have been disarranged, fallen into some awful loop that keeps repeating over and over" (242).

Aware that he is developing a vertiginous perspective that will explosively conjoin his static existence with an expanding awareness of the history and social logic of his world, Jim experiences another epiphanic change when he meets and falls in love with Hana Steentoft, the art teacher in the classroom next to his at the community college. An artist and the most feminist character in the book, Hana has opted out of the party scene and committed herself to a form of art that rejects the fading fashion of postmodernism. Just as she challenges her "sleepwalking" students, she directs her utopian critique at Jim and urges him to take his creative work more seriously and to focus his vision on "the open space left by the death of postmodernism" to "shape what comes next" (190). Accepting the challenge, Jim begins to think again about how he can "make a difference" and help to change America. Somehow—through the matrix of his writing, his resistance work, his teaching—he hopes to overcome the gap "between his desires and his achievements" (191). Yet, he hardly changes overnight, and in his waning foolishness he also learns negatively from Hana. When he brings her to one of Sandy's parties and his previous ally, Virginia, snubs her for not being suitably cool for their scene, he thinks Hana is wise and strong and above such cultural pressures, and so he is shocked when he finds she has been hurt by Virginia's response.

Embarrassed by his ignorance, he gains a better understanding of the power of social construction and interpellation, not at the level of theory but in the actual suffering of a loved one. He sees that

> no one can escape. You can pretend not to care about the image, but that's as far as the culture will let you get. Inside you have to feel it; you can fight it, but it'll always be there, the contemptuous dismissal of you by the Virginia Novellos of the world. . . . No doubt Hana saw that look and was perfectly aware of it, all the rest of the evening. And she did look different from the rest of the women there. . . . And now he had implied that she was so far out of the norm that she wouldn't have the common human response, wouldn't even notice, wouldn't even care. (285)

Yet even with this insight, Jim falters again when Hanna discovers him talking and holding hands with Virginia outside of a local restaurant. He guiltily pulls his hand away, but the damage is done. Hana once more sees Jim caught in the web of a shallow social scene (see 310). In response, she turns away in anger and refuses to see or talk to him.

With Hana's rejection feeding his growing anxiety, Jim anticipates the upcoming raid on LSR with Arthur. Fearful that they may inadvertently hurt someone—as another sabotage group did in a raid in Silicon Valley—Jim nevertheless seizes the chance to keep acting, for he sees it as a way to forestall his impending psychic collapse. Before the attack he visits his parents and predictably gets into yet another fight with his father. This time he crosses an emotional and political line when he accuses Dennis of being a maker of bombs and a purveyor of the very war mentality he is trying to stop. Dennis—who has just learned that his program was rejected—is already vulnerable and tries to explain his well-intentioned deterrence theory to Jim, but Jim will not listen and continues his rant. When Dennis plaintively cries out that the rejected Stormbee project was a "good" program, Jim hears the "fearful strain" in his father's voice, and he begins to feel Dennis's frustration and pain as his known world explodes. Consequently, Jim's anger momentarily "drains out of him, and he's amazed, even frightened, at what he has been saying" (345). Having now hurt his father as well as Hana, his personal and political anxiety returns, and he leaves the house in even more turmoil.

Tense and hyperventilating, Jim redirects his energy on the defense industry, seeing it as the prime cause of evil in the society—as a "malignancy making money in the service of death" (346). He launches into the night's action, but he also continues to think about his father's idealistic argument as he arranges to meet Arthur after picking up the missiles. Still ambivalent when he meets the four men who deliver the weaponry, Jim panics as a police cruiser sweeps into the parking lot. He runs, and two of the men chase him, perhaps believing he set up the arrest. Finding his car and telling the approaching policemen that the men are trying to steal it, he drives off, only to see Arthur standing with the other two men as the police pull up. Jim's diversion lets him get away, but he also knows Arthur will think he exposed the rest of the group to arrest. Having hurt yet another person, he begins his night of rage against the social machine, driving madly in a car filled with "six boxes of felony-level weaponry" (352). Dazed and confused, he feels he has "betrayed everyone he knows, in one way or another" (352), but his guilt and fear give way to the secular fury that has brought him to this point. Sobbing and cursing, he cries to himself: "You know—you know—what should—be done—and you—can't—*do it*" (352).

Hesitation gone, he drives like a desolation angel to South Coast Plaza (where Virginia works) and fires a "Harris Mosquito missile with its Styx–90 payload" at the administrative headquarters of the mall (352). He sends another missile into the plate glass window of the First American Title Insurance and Real Estate offices where he works with his friend Humphrey, and he fires another into the offices of the Orange County Board of Supervisors, the "crowd that has systematically helped real estate developers to cut OC up, in over a hundred years of mismanagement and graft" (353). Laughing maniacally, he strikes out at a Fluffy Donuts shop, another real estate office, a military microchip factory, and finally destroys the signs in the parking lot at LSR (353).

Aware now that he "can't make OC go away, not with his idiot vandalism, not even by going crazy," he drives home, "still mindless with rage and disgust" (353). He trashes his apartment, destroys his music, kicks his books across the room, tears up his manuscripts, smashes his cheap video system, and pulls down his maps. Hearing a car approach, he runs out of the house and down the street. Along the way, he smashes more shop windows, but realizing that he is exposed as a rare pedestrian in autopia, he jumps on a bus to Fashion Island. Still fuming, he picks up stones from a bonsai garden and prepares to throw them through the display windows of Bullock's and I. Magnin's. As he raises his arm, he is grabbed from behind and turns to see Tashi, who has fortuitously appeared like a Zen guardian angel.

Having just broken up with his longtime ally, Tashi is going through his own agonies, and when he takes Jim back to the tent to rest he suggests that they head off to the mountains. After a symbolic three days in the wilderness, they return to Orange County, refreshed in body and spirit. Tashi prepares to leave for Alaska; Jim, who has calmed down and again broadened his perspective, prepares to face the aftermath of his rampage. Back in his apartment, he gathers the torn maps and tapes them together in a synecdotal gesture of what he hopes to do with the shattered remnants of his own life. He picks up the scattered pages of poetry and history and looks at them with fresh eyes. With his apartment back in a strange new order, he visits home only to find his mother's note informing him that Dennis had been fired and that they have gone north to visit their small parcel of land near Eureka (in a geographic displacement that replicates the utopian trope found in many of the complementary dystopian fictions and films, from *Blade Runner* and *Brazil* to *Parable of the Sower*).

Feeling even more ambivalent about his actions against his father and LSR, he nevertheless resolves to "start up in a new way" (377). Visiting Angela, he learns that Sandy will survive the failure of the smuggling caper—escaping the wrath of his partners and the police—and that Arthur has disappeared. Again, he is uncertain, this time about Arthur and their actions. He respects Arthur's political commitment, but he is no longer sure that direct action is the way for him, even though he still agrees that "something has to be done, [that] there are forces in the country that have to be resisted" (380). Acknowledging for the first time that both Arthur and his father are, from their own standpoints, "right" in their views and actions, he realizes that neither his friend's participation in a singular social movement nor his father's reformism is right for him. He therefore decides that it is time to find his "own way, somewhere between or outside them—find some way that cannot be co-opted into the great war machine, some way that will actually help to change the thinking of America" (380).

With this resolution, Jim's activist turn against society that began with his foray into direct action reaches a new level of maturity and focus. Knowing that the system will be around for years to come, he decides that he can most effectively challenge its hegemonic lock by drawing on his particular skills and passions. On a personal level, he realizes that he needs to make amends with those he has hurt in his raging identity crisis, and he vows to reach out to his father and to Hana, but also to the other women he has scorned, Sheila and Virginia, and to his friends Humphrey and Arthur, whose lives were damaged by his night of destruction; and he plans as well to spend more time with his uncle so that he can learn from his experience and wisdom. On a political level, he seizes on his writing as the basis for his real work. He has already realized that poetry and the postmodern culture from which it stems is not for him, and he concludes that it is "deliberately ignorant, concerned only with surfaces, with the look, the great California image . . . the tired end of postmodernism, which makes utterly useless all his culturevulturing, because for postmodernism there is no past" (259).

Setting postmodern modalities aside, Jim thinks of the two writers most important to him, Albert Camus and Athol Fugard, and remembers that "both said that it was one's job to be a *witness* to one's times" (259). He is humbled, however, as he recalls the conditions under which both men wrote, for the "subjugation of Algeria" and "apartheid in South Africa" seem far more substantial than the situation in Orange County, at the geographical and historical edge of "the richest country of all time" (260). And yet this is the place in which he can be a valid witness, and so he decides that his particular contribution will take the form of a history of Orange County, written as a "collection of prose meditations" that follows in the poetic sprit of William Carlos Williams's *In the American Grain* (261). "How did it get this way?" will be his question. His book will be his answer. If he cannot escape this deceptive dystopia, he can at least begin to expose it by giving life to the estranging and enlightening perspective of the long view of history.

The painful steps of the past weeks have brought Jim to this realization of his vocation, and he returns to his apartment to begin his new life. After writing late into the night and falling into a sleep filled with wild dreams of recent events, he wakes up and looks over his finished pages. Happy with the new work, he decides to entitle the project *Torn Maps*. He packs up the finished copy, jumps in his car, and drives off to show it to Hana. The book ends in the midst of the journey, as he turns onto the off-ramp at Hana's exit.

IV.

As Jim leaves the freeway—and reengages with his writing and his life—the reader closes the book and is, hopefully, left with a bit more insight into the relationship between the structural coordinates of this extrapolated version of contemporary capitalism and the individual struggles of everyday life. Although

Robinson's text begins as a deceptively familiar account of late suburban alienation (replete with characters who are trying to make some sense of it all), it morphs into something else entirely as the details of the alternative world and the entwined narratives shatter the surface "normality" to reveal the anti-utopian logic of an economic and political system that privileges profit and power rather than a "healthy" and "caring" social alternative (see "Interview" 77).

Bit by bit, from multiple points of view, the nature of this tightly sutured though apparently open society becomes increasingly clear, partially to some of the characters and as holistically as possible to the reader.[5] Even though elements traditionally associated with dystopias are missing (the classical array of authority figures, invasive surveillance, pervasive control, and outright terror; or the sf ambience of apocalyptic breakdowns or noir underworlds), *The Gold Coast* nevertheless offers its readers a dystopian view of the "friendly terror" of their own existence by fast-forwarding that reality just enough to expose both the dangers of the systemic logic that has produced the world in which they live and the limitations of the 1980s political tendencies of singular social movements and liberal reformism.

Although the hegemonic narrative is dominated by the seemingly peripheral figures of Hereford and Lemon (as catachrestic personifications of the military-industrial complex), an open-ended counter-narrative of alienation giving way to critical awareness develops through the account of several characters whose lives are dispersed across the iconic tapestry of this alternative California. Foremost, of course, Jim's crisis and coming of age offers the most direct instance of the dystopian sleepwalker who turns against the system. Here Robinson engages in a particularly acute intervention as he focuses on the challenges taken up by a straight white male protagonist who, with varying degrees of success, acts against his privileged subject position as he tries to forge a new form of personal and political existence.[6]

Jim's story, however, is accompanied by several others that offer additional utopian streaks that survive in tactical spaces at the textual margins.[7] The relocations of Dennis and Lucy to Eureka and Tashi to Alaska point to potential enclaves that could produce a radical knowledge of and perhaps opposition to the cancerous system that the corporate couple and marginal ecocitizen have left behind. In another shadowy corner, Hana (not unlike the political position expressed by Nili in Piercy's *He, She and It*) occupies a space outside both the social mainstream and the postmodern opposition, even as she courageously and painfully reengages with everyday life on a regular basis.[8] Despite these countermoves, however, the system is not seriously threatened, much less changed. Instead of spaces or narratives of opposition, the reader encounters a set of proto-political actions that play out in the small changes of the daily lives of a few individuals who have torn open segments of the sutured reality that has produced and enclosed them. Not yet organized in any collective manner—and certainly not yet militant—Jim, Dennis, Lucy, Tashi, Hana, and Arthur nevertheless begin the process of taking a second, more critical look at their lives and their society.

Of course the counter-narrative *in* the text reprises the counter-production *of* the text itself. Venturing out in the bleak years of the late 1980s, Robinson was only beginning his long-term project of exploring the connections between sf and cognitive mapping, between creative fiction and the political imagination. In his utopian *Pacific Edge,* Martian trilogy, and *Antarctica,* he moves on to overt explorations of emerging modes of political opposition and new maps of liberated space, but in *The Gold Coast* he innovatively searches for Utopia by way of a dystopian pessimism that turns the wisdom of history and the commitment of daily struggle against the anti-utopian fear and loathing of radical political interrogation and transformation. Or as he later put it, he gives shape to a process of working within the insistent and troubled density of history itself, as it stands "between us and any decent society" ("Interview" 77). Like a Tantric Buddhism that reaches toward Nirvana precisely through the body that entraps the seeker, Robinson's most dystopian narrative finds its own way to Utopia in stories of individuals who are developing the new structures of feeling that will lead toward the collective movement needed for the political engagement and transformation that Utopia, and his own subsequent work, provisionally names.

8

Octavia Butler's Parables

Without brute force, which is never but a momentary solution, people cannot in this vein be asked to live cooperatively and to renounce the omnivorous desires of the id without some appeal to religious belief or transcendent values, something absolutely incompatible with any conceivable socialist society.

—Fredric Jameson, "Cognitive Mapping" (355)

I.

In *The Parable of the Sower* (1993) and, to a lesser extent, in *The Parable of the Talents* (1998), Octavia Butler has created a dystopian vision that equals Robinson's for its creative innovation and political engagement.[1] Like Robinson, Butler focuses on her protagonist's coming of age in an extrapolated version of contemporary U.S. society. In doing so, she expands the dystopian form by drawing on a range of textual influences to enrich the social detail and the narrative conflict of what is inherently an open-ended multivolume series. While journal entries set within the familiar sf account of new beginnings in a post-apocalypse world constitute the primary vehicle for her "parables," in her first volume she transforms that popular mode into a critical dystopia by self-reflexively spinning an intertextual web that draws on the substance and form of sources as varied as slave narratives, feminist fiction, survivalist adventure, and New Age theology along with the realism of works such as John Steinbeck's *Grapes of Wrath* and Upton Sinclair's *Jungle*. As a result, she situates her detailed dystopian account of societal collapse within a larger historical perspective even as she expands the purview of the developing opposition by the transcendent vision of a quite secular theology. With this performance of genre blurring, she generates a counter-narrative in which a diverse group of individuals develops through struggle into a political collective that (at least for-a-while) constitutes a historically and theologically informed utopian alternative to the economic and political power that barely controls this broken society.[2]

As in *The Gold Coast*, the alternative world of the "Parable" series opens in a "typical" southern Californian suburb in the early twenty-first century. Unlike Robinson's near future dominated by a military-corporate alliance that still operates in a functioning nation-state with a viable consumer economy, Butler's absent paradigm suggests an even harsher version of millennial capitalism as it presents a world in which transnational corporations have prevailed, but only by destroying the social and natural ecology that had sustained capitalism through its many stages.[3] As one of the characters in the second volume tells it, the socioeconomic crisis named the "Apocalypse" began around 2015, "perhaps even before the turn of the millennium," and in fifteen years the reality that was the secure and stable world of the United States came to an end (*Talents* 13). Passed off by some as a climatic, economic, or sociological "accident," the "Pox," Butler's character suggests, was actually caused by the systemic convergence of "convenience, profit, and inertia" that had the effect of "an installment-plan World War III" (*Talents* 14). By the end of the overdetermined crisis, around 2030, the United States had ceased to exist in its old form. It had "suffered a major nonmilitary defeat. It had lost no important war, yet it did not survive the Pox" (*Talents* 14).

The Pox was the end result of the economic, political, and environmental matrix produced by the capitalist restructuring and conservative policies that dominated the last twenty-five years of the twentieth century. The 1980s right-wing agenda of reducing taxes, expenditures, and bureaucratic oversight (along with increasing the national debt to fund a short-lived military buildup designed to destroy the Soviet Union by competition rather than warfare) finally resulted in a government composed of a weak executive stripped of political power and a military that was little more than a national guard. Fundamental services such as water supplies and police and fire protection were privatized to serve only those who could afford to pay exorbitant fees, and entitlements such as basic welfare, health, housing, and education were eliminated as the social contract was canceled.

Without the safety nets of regulation, support, and service to protect against the worst effects of capital's inherent obsession with profit at the expense of human and environmental well-being, the late-twentieth-century insistence on quick capital gains that shifted investment away from industry and labor in favor of finance and futures completed the destruction of the social matrix with its always uneasy combination of a shrinking public sphere and an expanding consumer sector. Consequently, the production and reproduction that sustained growth and kept the population within a controlled band of acceptable interpellation collapsed.

Butler's version of this breakdown emblematically focuses on the collapse of the broad "middle" of U.S. society that constitutes its expanded working class. Mid-level jobs (professional, managerial, industrial, technical) and middle-class lifestyles disappear in a social vacuum in which the critical mass needed to mount an anti-corporate movement and build a different social system is no longer viable. There is simply not enough in the way of a state infrastructure, a productive economy, and a healthy and educated working population to resist, much less move in another direction. In short, the corporate downsizing and restructuring that was well in force by the 1980s did not lead to a sustainable triumph of capitalism at some imagined end of history but rather produced a dangerous new reality barely anchored by nodes of corporate power surrounded by a social and environmental chaos in which masses of dispossessed people took to the roads to survive. In this world, capital's millennial dreams have led to the nightmares of a twenty-first-century world shaped by a postmodern corporate feudalism in which a new population of the propertyless have not yet taken an oppositional stand.

Butler brings her readers into her dystopian society by zooming in on one neighborhood in the suburb of Robledo, "20 miles from Los Angeles, and . . . once a rich, green, unwalled little city" (*Sower* 9). Like other communities that survived the initial effects of the Pox, this group of black, mixed-race, and white families organize out of necessity into a community of survival and reluctantly imitate the fashionable "gated communities" of the 1980s by erecting walls around its streets and houses to guard against thieves, feral dogs, and "squatters, winos, junkies, homeless people in general" who were growing in numbers as the social fabric ripped apart (*Sower* 5, 9). Trying to preserve the American dream in one subdivision, the neighbors draw into themselves and occupy an "island surrounded by sharks" (*Sower* 44). They still live in family groups, but they share goods and services in an informal barter economy. They produce most of their own food and clothing and get the rest from markets reachable only by risky journeys beyond the walls.

Since the few existing churches and schools (institutions that no longer have the power to catalyze a critical response) are also dangerously distant, several neighbors serve as preachers for local services (in Christian denominations and in a new combination of West African and Christian beliefs); others teach literacy, numeracy, and survival skills. Fire protection and security are provided by local volunteers (who turn to the expensive private services only when necessary). In an amalgam of the southern black tradition of armed self-defense and the white conservative assertion of the right to keep and bear arms, all the adults, including teenagers, are trained to use firearms, and target practice is one of the community's scheduled rituals. Armed neighbors stand twenty-four-hour watch, and armed escorts accompany those who need to venture beyond the walls.

If the walled neighborhood in Robledo represents one of the last sites of "normal" existence, the company town of Olivar signifies the new space of the transnational corporations. Unfettered by state regulation, these independent, feudalized giants have torn up the historically tactical social contract and freely repossess the derelict public infrastructure in order to turn it into a profit-making machine that is no longer constrained by social and environmental costs. As cities and public services fail, competing corporate vultures take them over and reconfigure them into businesses that sell the basic requirements of existence back to people who have just been deprived of them by the last round of capital's restructuring. Reaching to even lower depths, the corporations have also revived "something old and nasty" as they coerced the residual government into legalizing debt slavery (in a twenty-first century sublation of chattel, debt, and wage slavery) (*Sower* 105). Thus, when people leave their bankrupt and broken neighborhoods, the waiting companies entrap the most desperate (not unlike the "men of no property" or the "Oakies" of other moments of economically induced devastation) into lives of indentured servitude (*Sower* 106).

In the case of Olivar, the transnational Kagimoto, Stamm, Frampton, and Company (KSF) acquired the once wealthy coastal city and its valuable desalination plant after it could no longer deal with the dual threat of economic collapse and flooding by the rising seas of global warming: "After many promises, much haggling, suspicion, fear, hope, and legal wrangling, the voters and officials of Olivar permitted their town to be taken over, bought out, privatized" (*Sower* 106). By adding Olivar to its empire of cities, public lands, and infrastructural systems, KSF moved closer to its goal of dominating the "great water, power, and agricultural industries in an area that most people have given up on," doing so through the minimized cost of an enslaved labor force made up of people who will "accept smaller salaries than their socio-economic group . . . in exchange for security, a guaranteed food supply, jobs, and help in their battle with the Pacific" (*Sower* 106). As one character describes the economic situation: "This country is going to be parceled out as a source of cheap labor and cheap land. When people like those in Olivar beg to sell themselves, our surviving cities are bound to wind up the economic colonies of whoever can afford to buy them" (*Sower* 114).[4]

In this brave new world of corporate towns, ineffectual government, social chaos, and environmental disaster intensified by the inability of a dysfunctional social system to repair the damage or attend to the aftermath, the families in the Robledo neighborhood make their last stand. The older members recall the "golden age" of the mid-twentieth century and cling to the belief that things will get better (*Talents* 53), but like their counterparts in Butler's own time, the teenagers know that this is the only world there is and that they have already seen the best of it. In this microcosm the dystopian drama takes shape around the story of the community's destruction and the struggle for survival by the young, black, female protagonist, Lauren Olamina, and the alternative community she organizes.

II.

Following a long-standing dystopian tradition, Butler's text is related in the form of Lauren's journal (written in the years 2024 to 2027). On the day before her fifteenth birthday, Lauren makes her first entry in a private text that will grow into the public document of a new socioreligious movement called Earthseed. As personal journal and theological and political manifesto—and as the initial textual vehicle for Butler's series—this narrative machine not only delineates the terrible world of the 2020s but also self-reflexively constitutes the basis of the counter-narrative that speaks against the absent master narrative of the distant corporate powers as it negates the status quo and, in the first book, points toward a possible negation of the negation in the movement Lauren eventually founds and builds. At fifteen, however, Lauren is just getting a sense of the wider world and how she might live in it. Although she appreciates the security of her community, she feels restricted, even as she also understands that worse conditions lie beyond its confines. Her intelligence and her upbringing by a father and stepmother whose lives are rooted in the church and in the struggle for African American freedom have made her into a contemplative, resourceful, and courageous young woman who reads the signs of the times and refuses to give in to their destructive ambience.

To this realist character portrait of a non-white, non-male, dispossessed survivor (and soon-to-be leader) in a racist and sexist capitalist society, Butler adds the catachrestic spin of the particular genetic disability that shapes every minute of her protagonist's life and painfully fine-tunes her social acuity. Lauren suffers from a "hyperempathy syndrome" that she inherited as a result of the experimental "smart drug" Paraceto taken by her biological mother during pregnancy to enhance mental performance in an increasingly competitive society (*Talents* 17–18). Because of permanent genetic damage to her neurotransmitters, Lauren involuntarily experiences the psychological delusion that she feels the pain and pleasure others experience around her. When people are hurt or killed, she internalizes their pain (and when she was younger her psychological reaction extended to sympathetic bleeding). Yet as others experience intense pleasure—especially in sexual activity—she takes that in as well. In lovemaking or, as in the second book, in the violence of rape she feels both her response and that of her lover or attacker. For obvious reasons, she keeps her condition to herself, but its latency informs and shapes her entire existence and her lifelong religious-political project. Only when she leaves home does she come to better terms with her condition as she discovers and works with other "sharers" or "hyperempaths" who suffer from this "organic delusional syndrome" (*Sower* 10).[5]

Like Kuno, Jim, and other dystopian protagonists, Lauren is a relative anomaly in this collapsing society, a young black woman and a psychobiological misfit who turns her embodied difference into a force for learning about the world and eventually for organizing others to live in that world on radically different terms.[6] Drawing on the history and culture of her African American family, she has the memories, knowledge, and skills for surviving and building an alternative reality in the shattered world about her. Further knowing she can never be like those without the hyperempathy syndrome, she adapts what could be a genetic disability into a personal gift that endows her with the extra transformative strength that eventually informs her work as a visionary and social reformer. She begins her journal, therefore, in a conflicted spirit of frustration and anticipation as she brings her particular subjectivity and sensitivity to bear on the question of her own beliefs and those of her family and neighbors. As she thinks of her shared birthday with her fifty-five-year-old father (one of the local preachers and a community college teacher, and a role model and parental force to be reckoned with), she confesses in her opening pages that she no longer believes in *his* God. Her God, she admits, "has another name," and in this self-revelation the account of her personal life and her public theology begins (*Sower* 6).

Lauren's crises of identity and faith, however, are not simple teenage passions. Already attuned to the world through her hyperempathy, her newly awakened spiritual sense enhances her social concern and inspires her to meditate on how she, and others, should live in this ravaged society. She therefore takes a hard look at the community around her. She is fully aware of the impending threat of dispossession and the poverty and homelessness that goes with it, and she knows the dangers of thieves and crazies who, in an inversion of biblical liberation, can bring the walls of their private Jericho tumbling down. She hears the political gossip about the forthcoming presidential elections and observes people's lingering hope that a new president will make a difference, but she hears others admit that the days of progressive government intervention are over.

To get a grip on this frightening life, she realizes that she needs to clarify what she believes and what she will do in her own life. Having written about God since she was twelve, she finally names her deity (*Sower* 22), for, as she later puts it, "naming a thing—giving it a name or discovering its name—helps one to begin to understand it" (*Sower* 68). To her, "God" is "Change," the essence of biological and historical mutability, and humanity's mission is to "understand that God exists to be shaped" so that sheer randomness, neglect, or error does not confine Change to the destructive force it has become (*Sower* 22).

With this perspective, she looks at the suffering of her family and neighbors, and she decides that they and others could one day benefit from her version of a materialist and activist spirituality that seeks to regain control over society in the name of a transcendent yet still secular project. A year later, in 2025, she writes that it is not "enough for us to just survive, limping along, playing business as usual while things get worse and worse. If that's the shape we give to God, then someday we must become too weak—too poor, too hungry, too sick—to defend ourselves. Then we'll be wiped out" (*Sower* 67). Taking collective responsibility for Change, therefore, lies at the core of her spiritual discipline: "There has to be more that we can do, a better destiny that we can shape. Another place. Another way. Something!" (*Sower* 67).

Through her journal entries, Lauren develops and refines her theology of survival and transformation. Writing at times to "keep from going crazy" in the face of the chaos about her, she works between an immediate concern for survival and a transcendent vision that is rooted in human history (*Sower* 46, 141). Refusing the disembodied afterlives of other religions, she articulates the teleology of her vision as the movement of humanity into outer space. Like the escaped slaves of nineteenth-century America, "heaven" for Lauren is secular, only it is not the northern United States or Canada but the galaxy. As early as fifteen, she sees space as the salvation of humanity, for "space exploration and colonization are among the few things left over from the last century that can help us more than they hurt us" (*Sower* 18). By the time she is eighteen, she understands that space travel is one of the key economic and cultural opportunities of her era, and she sees that it carries the potential to expand humanity's self-understanding and self-respect by way of a temporal solidarity and a cosmic transcendence. For Lauren, space is a tangible heaven, and the means taken to attain that end harken back to the African American practice of "following the drinking gourd" to liberation in the "North" and with the sacred calls that drove religious movements such as the Mennonites and the Mormons to seek their particular promised lands.

At this stage, Lauren's vision is in keeping with the tradition of popular utopias from the "Land of Cockaygne" to the "Big Rock Candy Mountain" to the 1960s jazz utopia of Sun Ra ("Space is the Place"). With space as her spiritual and historical telos, she goes on to develop a spiritual and political discipline and an agenda that moves from immediate survival through the intermediate stage of building communities in which people can regain control over their lives to the ultimate goal of departure from Earth itself in the colonization of other planets. Planning on the negation of suffering and destruction by organizing self-determining communities, she foresees the negation of that negation in the sublation of those preparatory communities as the new societies on other planets.

The name *Earthseed* catches the nature of her dialectical plan. From embracing and controlling Change, to renewing Earth itself, to taking Earth's potential to the cosmos, *Earthseed* nominates all the stages of what Lauren desires and anticipates. As she puts it: "Someday, I think there will be a lot of us. And I think we'll have to seed ourselves farther and farther from this dying place" (*Sower* 69). Looking to her imagined future, she sees that the present moment of sheer survival is the "time for building foundations—Earthseed communities—focused on the Destiny" of reaching the stars (*Sower* 199).

Although she will one day entitle her theological meditations *Earthseed: The Book of the Living* and become the "leader" of a major spiritual and political movement, Lauren at fifteen is only beginning to frame the way she knows and hopes to live in the world. But right from the first page, her journal (like those of D-503 and Offred before her) gives shape to a counter-narrative that exposes and opposes the social chaos of feudalized capitalism. As thieves randomly attack the neighborhood and individual houses are robbed and burned, she anticipates even worse destruction, and she takes seriously her friend Joanne's skeptical speculation that someday some group will "smash in our wall and come in" to destroy everything (*Sower* 48). When her father learns of her concerns, he talks with her about the coming "abyss" and broadens her perspective by telling her that the "adults in this community have been balancing at the edge [of destruction] for more years than you've been alive" (*Sower* 58). As she ponders the situation, she realizes that the problem is not only local but endemic to the entire globe, and she writes that the "world is in horrible shape. Even rich countries aren't doing as well as history says rich countries used to do" (*Sower* 75).

From this point on, Lauren's narrative (and Butler's) works between a prophetic tone that requires the labor of Utopia *in* history and an apocalyptic tone that steps outside of history in the name of a fully transcendent alternative (and by the second volume the apocalyptic side takes over). As things fall apart around her, Lauren begins to make preparations for survival that add material substance to her visionary writing. In a moment of prophetic realism that also recalls the stories of (typically white and conservative) survivalist fictions, she tells Joanne that they have to get ready to deal with the coming destruction of their community, and she sums up her own efforts:

> I'm trying to learn whatever I can that might help me survive out there. I think we should all study books like these [on wilderness survival, guns,

> medical emergencies, native plants, and basic living]. I think we should bury money and other necessities in the ground where thieves won't find them. I think we should make emergency packs—grab and run packs—in case we have to get out of here in a hurry. Money, food, clothing, matches, a blanket. . . . I think we should fix places outside where we can meet in case we get separated (*Sower* 51).

Not as tuned in or concerned, Joanne shrugs off the challenge, but Lauren counters with the simple assertion that she intends to survive (see *Sower* 51). When she talks to her father about telling others of the need to plan and prepare, he cautions her to temper her comments so as not to cause panic, but he essentially agrees with her, even though he hopes that their community will somehow pull though. He wisely encourages her to put her energy into teaching preparedness classes rather than talking about "Armageddon" (*Sower* 59), and he then tells her where the family's emergency cache of guns, money, and food are hidden. Backed by her father's respect, Lauren continues to ready herself and others (as much as they will listen) for the probable destruction of their home. Linking her new skills with her spiritual vision, she notes that there is "always a lot to do before you get to go to heaven" (*Sower* 75).

While Lauren prepares, her community suffers more losses. Her twelve-year-old brother, Keith, leaves the neighborhood to explore what is left of central Los Angeles, only to be mugged by thieves who beat him, steal his clothes, and take the key to the main gate that he filched from his mother. Angry after his father publicly beats him for endangering not only himself but also the entire community, he takes his mother's handgun and runs back to the city, determined never to face such humiliation again. From his refuge in the derelict space of downtown L.A., he occasionally sneaks back to give money to his mother and gifts to his brothers. After eight months, he meets and talks with Lauren. He explains that as soon as he ran away he killed a man, stole his sizable stash of money, and then managed to survive in the black economy of the city by trading on his ability to read and write, helping thieves and smugglers and earning even more money. Two months later, after a year outside, Keith—the young, black male trying to survive in a fully hostile world—is tortured and murdered by the drug dealers for whom he worked, and the family bitterly mourns his passing.

After Keith's death, the community begins to unravel. As Lauren puts it: "We're a rope, breaking, a single strand at a time" (*Sower* 103). More robberies occur, some families opt for the indentured "security" of Olivar, and then Lauren's father disappears. After an extended search, the family presumes he has been murdered, and Lauren preaches at his memorial service. At the close of this service for their religious and social leader, the community draws on its roots in the civil rights movement and sings "We Shall Not Be Moved." Lauren joins in but also notes in her journal, in bitter irony, that they will "be moved, all right. It's just a matter of when, by whom, and in how many pieces" (*Sower* 121). Feeling detached from the community, she thinks even more about heading "north" to Oregon or Washington or wherever she can go to find a decent life. She meets her boyfriend, Curtis, and after they make love in an unused darkroom, she talks with him about leaving. Settled in the community, Curtis wants her to stay and one day to marry him, but Lauren tells him that she is going away. Given the state of the world and their own neighborhood, she has little interest in marriage and less in children, and even though she loves Curtis, she knows she has to follow her vision and strike off on her own.

More burglaries occur—striking Lauren's house too—and throughout the region young people on a drug called Pyro begin to set fires just so they can watch them in a nihilistic haze (*Sower* 128; see *Talents* 109). Then, on July 31, 2027, three years after she began her journal, Lauren sees her entire neighborhood attacked and destroyed. Pyro addicts ("bald people with painted heads, faces, and hands") drive a truck through the gate, shoot everyone in sight, and burn and loot every house. Hyperempathically overwhelmed by the pain and death around her, Lauren grabs her emergency pack and runs to the hills above the neighborhood. She returns in the morning to the burned-out enclave and searches for her family and others who might have survived. With looters picking at the wreckage, she enters her own house and grabs what items she can for her life on the road—taking clothes, food, medical supplies, a gun, and the hidden family money. She finds no sign of her stepmother or brothers and sadly steps over the bodies of dead neighbors. In the midst of the carnage, however, she finds her friends Harry Balter and Zahra Moss, a white man and a black woman like herself. Zahra tells Lauren that she saw her mother raped and taken away, even as she herself was raped (*Sower* 148). On the following day, a Sunday, the three survivors decide to travel north together.

At this point, aged eighteen, Lauren begins the second stage of her life and steps onto the broken highway with her friends to search for some diminished dystopian version of Oz. The decaying suburban idyll (and Keith's brief street saga) is displaced by a narrative of life on the road. In a reprise of the Underground Railroad of the nineteenth century, the expectant moves to California by displaced farmers from Oklahoma in the 1930s, and the efforts by ex-GI's seeking the suburban dream in the 1950s—and in keeping with the contemporary dystopian trope of the flight to northern California in films such as *Brazil* and *Blade Runner* and fictions such as Thomas Pynchon's *Vineland* (1990) and Robinson's *Gold Coast*—Lauren, Harry, and Zahra begin their modest quest to find a place where "water doesn't cost more than food, and where work brings a salary" (*Sower* 151). Pooling their meager goods and money, they also anticipate the hassles they will meet if people see what they assume is a mixed-race couple, and Lauren disguises herself as a man so that people will think she and Zahra are the heterosexual couple and Harry their white friend.

Before leaving Robledo, they stop at the "secure store complex" of Hanning Joss, where under the eyes of armed guards they shop safely for food and other supplies (*Sower* 155). They then walk down the local freeway to Highway 101, the coast road to the north, where they become part of the "heterogeneous mass" of people seeking to escape, find refuge, or follow their embittered dreams. Early in the journey, Lauren enters a journal description of this river of refugees:

> Black and white, Asian and Latin, whole families are on the move with babies on backs or perched atop loads in carts, wagons or bicycle baskets, sometimes along with an old or handicapped person. Other old, ill, or handicapped people hobbled along as best they could with the help of sticks or fitter companions. Many were armed with sheathed knives, rifles, and, of course, visible, holstered handguns. The occasional passing cop paid no attention. (*Sower* 158)

Out on the open road, survivalist ethics take over. The threesome swears to protect one another, even if it requires taking lives to do so. Knowing she has to trust her friends, Lauren tells them about her hyperempathy syndrome, briefing them on what will happen to her when they come across injured or dying people and on what she herself will feel if and when she kills someone. Reciprocating with respect and loyalty, Harry and Zahra listen carefully if skeptically as Lauren takes a revelatory step and shows them her journal and her Earthseed texts. At this point the first seeds of vision are sown, and as the three travel north they begin to attract others to their group. Like the heroes of a fairy tale who acquire helpers in their quest—and like early activists in a growing political movement—they slowly build a community that is marked by its multiplicity of race, gender, sexuality, age, and class identities. Lauren catches the power and value of this strategic openness in the Earthseed text that begins the section of the journal that describes the journey and the new members:

> Embrace diversity.
> Unite—
> Or be divided,
> robbed,

ruled,
killed
By those who see you as prey.
Embrace diversity
Or be destroyed. (*Sower* 176)

In their invocation of commonality and diversity, Lauren's words—and the reality of her group—recall the "blessed community" of the Student Nonviolent Coordinating Committee (SNCC) in the early civil rights movement in the United States and the unity in diversity of the social movements of the 1980s, even as it begins to offer a sketch of what could be the emerging alliance politics of the 1990s. The first addition to the group is a mixed-race family that the three friends rescue from attacking coyotes. Once they are sure the two adults and baby are not a danger, they invite them to join them in the trek north. After a few days of traveling in uncertain proximity, the family agrees, and Travis Charles Douglas, Gloria Natividad Douglas, and six-month-old Dominic Douglas ("a black man, a Hispanic-looking woman, and a baby who managed to look a little like both of them") increase the community to five adults and one child (*Sower* 182). While the vetting takes place, Zahra and Harry finally become lovers, and this shift prompts Lauren to describe the new formation as "natural allies—the mixed couple and the mixed group" (*Sower* 186).

When an earthquake delays them as they rescue other travelers, Lauren notices a man smiling at her: "an older, but not yet old black man who still had his teeth, and who pushed his belongings in twin saddlebags hanging from a small, sturdy metal-framed cart" (*Sower* 203). After helping them with the victims, the man speaks to Lauren, and she sees he is someone who comes from a certain degree of wealth, a professional. Attracted to him, she listens as he recalls the previous craziness of the 1990s and describes how things have declined even further since then. She learns his name—Taylor Franklin Bankole, a surname that dates from the black cultural nationalism of the 1960s—and realizes that at fifty-seven he is a year younger than her father. When the group resumes walking, Bankole tags along, and by the end of the day he adds his money, his gun, and what the others eventually learn is his knowledge as a medical doctor to their shared resources (*Sower* 206).

Before leaving the earthquake site, the group also pulls two young white women from the rubble. They learn that Allison and Jillian Gilchrist are running from their father who abused them and forced them into prostitution. Properly wary—as battered women and vulnerable travelers—the sisters hesitate at Lauren's invitation to join them but then agree, while they cling protectively to each other. A few days later—during which Lauren and Bankole become lovers—Bankole finds a child whose mother has just died in another attack, and Justin Rohr, the newly orphaned child who is at the "run around and grab everything" stage, is taken along, with Allie opting to be his "substitute mother" (*Sower* 227, 228).

A month later two others begin to follow the group, and one night they slip into their camp and bed down next to them. Ragged, terrified, filthy, the woman who "looked Asian" and her fragile daughter eventually explain that they are runaway debt slaves who had been surviving on the road in the most degraded of circumstances (*Sower* 252, 253). Fearful and desperate, they welcome Lauren's offer to join them, and Emery Tanaka Solis (the daughter of a Japanese father and black mother) and her daughter, Tori Solis (whose father was Mexican), bringing the number of adults to nine and children to three. Two days later, young Tori brings in a "thin, black Latino" man, Grayson Mora, and his daughter, Doe, who was only a year younger than nine-year-old Tori (*Sower* 258, 261). In a measure of the changing landscape of class in 2027, the two also turn out to be escaped debt slaves. A few days later, Lauren learns that all four are hyperempaths like herself, a terrible condition to have if one is subjected to the cruel reality of slavery (*Sower* 269). Predictably, the two ex-slave parents become lovers and form a new family, of sharers, within the community.

After Jillian is murdered in an attack by marauders, the group numbers thirteen (in the apostolic motif of one leader and twelve followers). Gradually, Lauren's Earthseed vision begins to give them an identity and sense of purpose that goes beyond their individual lives. With each new person, Lauren has introduced and elaborated upon Earthseed, and her theology has developed through the feedback of questions, doubts, and insights that the new members bring to the discussion. To greater or lesser degree, with questions and hesitations, each becomes a part of the increasingly self-identified community, some doing so for security, some embracing the entire vision.

What is immediately pressing for the entire group, however, is the question of where they should settle. Having made it into northern California and avoided the devastation of what once was the glory of San Francisco, they are unsure of their destination. Lauren, however, suspects that Bankole might offer them a solution. Noticing his determination to move up the highway and thinking of his class position, she assumes that he has a sense of where he is going, that he has "a haven somewhere—a relative's home, another home of his own, a friend's home, something—some definite destination" (*Sower* 237).

In his own time, Bankole tells Lauren that he has land in Humboldt County, in "the hills on the coast near Cape Mendocino" (*Sower* 244). He admits that he owns "three hundred acres," which in a world now gone forever he had bought as an investment, and on which his sister and family now live (*Sower* 245). He wants Lauren to leave the group and settle there with him, but she convinces him to take everyone and make it the halting site of the first Earthseed community. She puts the possibility to the group, and after some discussion they agree and walk past "state parks filled with huge redwood trees and hoards of squatters" to reach the relatively untrammeled hills of the northern coast. The pastoral locale they find is "empty and wild . . . covered with dry brush, trees, and tree stumps, all far removed from any city, and a long, hilly walk from the little towns that line the highway" (*Sower* 281). The acreage has its own water, tillable soil, fruit trees, and timber for building. It lies in an area that has been amenable to isolated and independent living since the previous century, when marijuana growers, whisky distillers, poets, and others disinterested in the intrusion of official surveillance lived and thrived in the remote hills.

When they arrive, however, they meet another obstacle in their quest for a safe haven. They come over the last hill on the long road in and find not a pastoral refuge but devastation: "There was no house. There were no buildings. There was almost nothing: A broad black smear on the hillside; a few charred planks sticking up from the rubble, some leaning against others; and a tall brick chimney, standing black and solitary like a tombstone in a picture of an old-style graveyard. A tombstone amid the bones and ashes" (*Sower* 282). They discover five skulls, which they presume are those of Bankole's sister and her family, and they realize that even this remote site is vulnerable to intruders and scavengers. They spend the week trying to find out what happened, cautiously dealing with the ineffective police department in the nearby town of Glory. Learning nothing and confused about their future, they discuss their options. Lauren argues that nothing farther north "will be any better or any safer" than this remote valley (*Sower* 287). Realizing that there can be no social guarantees for their safety, the group agrees to settle into their rural retreat. Lauren's journal in the first book of the series ends by naming the community Acorn, and then quoting the King James version of the Parable of the Sower. The words of the biblical tale self-reflexively end Butler's own parable as they recall the sower who scattered his seeds, some of which fell by the wayside, were devoured by fowls, fell on rocks, or fell on thorns, but others of which "fell on good ground, and sprang up, and bore fruit an hundredfold" (*Sower* 295).

With this ending, Butler brings her counter-narrative through the dystopian world and suspends it at the enclave in Humboldt County. The epical quality of her text is evident not only in the account of the journey, the formation of community, and the moment when humanity in the name of Earthseed will go to the stars, but it also lingers in the implicitly open ending that anticipates the next volume in the "Parable" series.

At this point, the dystopia of 2027 clearly is negated by the journey of Lauren and her friends away from their corrupt world and positively opposed by the utopian enclave of the Earthseed community. In Lauren's writing, as in Butler's, the existing hegemonic order has been at least momentarily neutralized, and a utopian space has been created in the content and form of the text. As Lauren puts it in a description of the power of her own writing, her Earthseed verses have affected at least twelve people, prying "them loose from the rotting past" and maybe pushing "them into saving themselves and building a future that makes sense" (*Sower* 70). Her words catch the sprit and potential of Butler's own words as they speak truth to the powers of the early 1990s.

Unlike Robinson's *Gold Coast,* Butler offers an overtly collective narrative of political development and creates an evident utopian horizon in her critical dystopian contribution. As opposed to the "streaks" of utopian possibility in Robinson's assiduously negative account, Butler's willingness to explore the empowering force of a spiritually motivated but materially transcendent vision that is rooted in difficulty and difference allows her to posit a politicizing process that produces a vulnerable but viable utopian alternative by the end of this first book in the series. In what Baccolini would term its "multi-oppositional" diversity of classes, genders, sexualities, races, ages, abilities, and experiences, Lauren's Earthseed community captures the best qualities of the identity politics of the 1980s even as it reconfigures that entire tendency within the emerging alliance politics of the 1990s. In doing so, it suggests a possible model for an oppositional movement that is fundamentally and insistently diverse yet strategically united, one able to generate a level of totalizing analysis and coordinated action that can challenge the entire socioeconomic system of the transnational corporations.

The political agents who are formed in this individual and collective struggle to survive and transform the world of 2027 therefore take the political structure of feeling developed by Robinson a step farther as they actually forge a new sociopolitical formation that can stand against the regime of a feudalized capitalism.[7] And yet this next step into direct contestation is withheld. The text closes as the people of Earthseed settle into their valley, and Lauren makes the ominous comment that in this new locale the community finds that "it's best to mind your own business and not pay too much attention to how people on neighboring plots of land earn a living" (*Sower* 281).[8]

III.

When Butler resumes her account of the Acorn community in *The Parable of the Talents,* it becomes evident that the prophetic and dystopian novum of *Sower* gives way to a narrative that is simultaneously pragmatic and apocalyptic. Pulling back from the detailed iconic account of the failing social system in her first volume, Butler places her emphasis on an entwined double plot that follows Lauren's daughter as she angrily seeks her lost mother and Lauren herself as she continues to build Earthseed to the point where her socioreligious offspring depart for the stars. Although she develops this plot with a complex narrative structure built around interlaced and overlapped journal entries from several characters, she nevertheless confines the political charge of *Sower*'s iconic description and counter-narrative within the frameworks of a family narrative and a science fictional story of humanity's escape from Earth's problems by reaching for the stars. She therefore ends up offering a "solution" that draws more heavily on the personal and theological side of her intertextual resources, and thereby reduces the acuity of her historical analysis and political speculation.[9]

As a result, the linkage of Lauren's transcendent vision with the everyday struggle and resistance of the Earthseed community is broken when the surviving, and eventually flourishing, community sets aside questions of immediate political opposition in favor of the abstract alternative of a stellar journey. Instead of the mutually reinforcing relationship between the theological/spiritual vision and political contestation that characterized the early civil rights movement or the Latin American base Christian communities that were informed by liberation theology, Butler's continuing portrayal of Earthseed more closely resembles separatist millenarian communities that opt out of secular political struggles to make themselves ready for their "ultimate" destiny by immersing themselves in the immediate practices of everyday life. Consequently, the tone and emphasis of the book shares less with the sociopolitical attitude of the prophetic books of Jewish and Christian Scripture (e.g., Micah or Isaiah) and more with the mystical quality of the apocalyptic books (e.g., Daniel or Revelation).

And yet even with this pragmatic and apocalyptic spin, *Talents* does not fall into the dead-end of a compensatory, anti-utopian accommodation with the prevailing culture of Butler's own social milieu. The basic vision and practice of the community does not allow for the compromising options of cultish escape, liberal reform, or outright co-optation. Instead, the text holds on to an ongoing radical critique of the status quo. Indeed, if read in the spirit of the powerful traditions of strategic separatism in African American or feminist political culture (positions that enable both a refuge and a place of recuperation for renewed action), the separatist agenda of Earthseed in *Talents*, at least in the iconic register, makes a gesture of utopian resistance to the actual world in which Butler and her contemporary readers live. The community of Earthseed, in other words, does not become an opiate of the people but rather stands as a haven in a heartless word.

In the early chapters of *Talents*, a critical dystopian sensibility lingers, especially when Butler makes the effort to brief her readers on the brutality of the world of the 2030s. Even in this iconic detailing, however, she takes the quicker path of representing that world through the expository gambit of a capsule news summary rather than by a presentation of the absent social paradigm that threads its way throughout the entire text (*Talents* 78–83). As she sets up her summary, she explains that the community has purchased "well-made news disks" that deliver more extensive accounts of current events than those given in the popularized media.

According to one recent disk, the still ravaged society is now divided between free towns and company towns (with competing microeconomies based on wage or debt slavery), and the U.S. state has become so weak that the always independent-minded people of Alaska have opted to secede, encouraged by their self-interested Russian and Canadian neighbors. Environmental devastation proceeds as climatic warming and flooding intensify and as tropical diseases migrate into the fresh fields of the once cold regions of the north. With no explanation of causes, the report notes that local wars still rage around the globe: with Kenya against Tanzania, Bolivia against Peru, Greece against Turkey, Egypt against Libya, an alliance of Pakistan and Afghanistan against India, and civil wars in Spain and China. As well, the memory of a nuclear "exchange" between Iran and Iraq in 2029 instills people with fears of another. In science and technology, developments include electronic collars that allow total control of slaves, technologies for extrauterine reproduction and computerized eggs, and the anomalous improvement (in the midst of economic disaster) of virtual reality entertainment systems. The report ends with the announcement that recent space probes have discovered living, multicellular organisms on Mars.

Most ominously, the report announces the results of another presidential election, in which Andrew Steele Jarret, a Christian fascist, has defeated the weak reformer Edward Jay Smith just as the worst of the Pox years seemed to be coming to an end (*Talents* 23, 83). With a popular fundamentalist base fronted by organized thugs wearing black tunics with white crosses, Jarret has secured consensual and coercive dominance in a society still threatened by destruction and deprivation. His movement echoes the Christian Right in Butler's world (especially the extremist "Christian Identity" movement and its allied militias), and it is intertextually connected with the Christian fundamentalists that founded the Republic of Gilead in Atwood's *Handmaid's Tale.*

As Lauren puts it, Jarret "wants to take us all back to some magical time when everyone believed in the same God, worshipped him in the same way, and understood that their safety in the universe depended on completing the same religious rituals and stomping anyone who was different" (*Talents* 23). Following an old pattern, the new president and his rabid followers shore up their position by covertly attacking non-Christian scapegoats upon whom they place the blame for the ills that engulf the society. Jarret's inauguration reinforces this repressive move with an ideological display of "patriotism, law, order, sacred honor, flags everywhere, Bibles everywhere, people waving one of each" and a speech that promises a "strong Christian America" with "strong Christian American soldiers to reunite, rebuild, and defend it" (*Talents* 135, 136). To secure further support, the new leader takes the familiar step of launching a patriotic war to win back Alaska—a war he eventually loses.

This is the world that surrounds the Earthseed community of Acorn in Humboldt County. Five years after the original group arrived, as "needy adults" and "orphaned children" have been taken in and given shelter and hope, the community has grown to a population of fifty-nine. Pooling money, knowledge, skills, and sharing the Earthseed vision, they have built houses, tilled fields, cultivated livestock, and educated themselves. Every member can read and write, and most know Spanish and English. Lauren describes this pocket utopia (as Robinson might call it) in her ongoing journal.[10] She modestly notes that "it's as though we've come to a somewhat gentler version of the homes we were forced to leave. Here, there is still water, space, not too much debilitating heat, and some peace. Here, one can still have orchards and groves. Here, life can still come from death" (*Talents* 59). Overall Earthseed is prospering and on the verge of launching a trucking business, spreading the word of the Earthseed message by voluntary missionaries, and preparing to establish new "clones of Acorn" after the first community reaches a maximum population of 1,000 (*Talents* 156). In this thriving and apparently secure context, in 2033, Lauren gives birth to her daughter, Larkin Beryl Ife Olamina Bankole (*Talents* 157).

Feeling that all is finally going well, Lauren sums up her developing vision for Earthseed just after Larkin's birth: "I want us to go on growing, becoming stronger, richer, educating ourselves and our children, improving our community" (*Talents* 161). Still keeping her eyes on the long-term prize, she looks ahead to Earthseed's reaching its "Destiny" of leaving the "womb" and achieving a temporal immortality by becoming the progenitor of "new peoples, new species" and "sowing Earthseed on other worlds" (*Talents* 48, 49). She reinforces this embodied hope when she writes of Earthseed's potential to generate a "kind of species adulthood and species immortality when we scatter to the stars" (*Talents* 144).

Yet while the community survives and grows, its connection with the larger struggle to change society during the crisis of the Pox slowly gives way to introspective concerns as it looks ahead to its flight into the wilderness of space. Indeed, this new direction is reinforced by the fact that Earthseed does not contribute to the admittedly liberal political opposition to Jarret. The members discuss his presidency, acknowledge that his strategy of scapegoating may harm them, but choose not to pursue political work on their own or to join with others to prevent the expected depredations of Christian America.

It is with an air of inevitability, therefore, that Acorn is attacked and destroyed by Jarret's Crusaders in September 2033, a little under a year after the election. The well-armed invaders occupy the valley and rename it Camp Christian (*Talents* 172). Later, locked in one of the new slave collars in the "re-education camp" that once was Acorn, Lauren learns that Bankole and Zahra have been killed and that all the children, including her daughter, have been taken way. Like the "disappeared" offspring in Argentina in the 1980s, the Earthseed children have been kidnapped and placed in "good Christian homes," separated from their parents and community forever (Larkin is adopted by a wealthy black Christian family and renamed Ashe Vere Alexander) (*Talents* 189, 201). Although the account of Lauren's imprisonment provides a critical picture of the contemporary prison-industrial complex (especially when set against the memory of nineteenth-century slavery and twentieth-century concentration camps and maximum security prisons), its iconic potential is abandoned when Lauren leads her Earthseed prisoners in their escape.

After the prison experience, the remaining plot event that could have recuperated a dystopian counter-narrative is the fall of the Jarret regime and the reformist government that follows. As Jarret's war fails and Alaska survives as an independent country, political gossip surmises that Jarret's home state of Texas will reach back into its own history and be the next to break away. The Christian American terror is alienating more people, especially as the economy appears to be recovering. Dissatisfaction and some opposition are growing. As Lauren puts it: "Jarret's kind of religion and Jarret himself are getting less and less popular these days," and (in a list that is revealing in its order), she goes on to note that both, "it seems, are bad for business, bad for the U.S. Constitution, and bad for a large percentage of the population" (*Talents* 351).

Finally, a "coalition of angry business people, protestors against the Al-Can War, and champions of the First Amendment worked hard to defeat him in the re-election of 2036" (*Talents* 354). Not surprisingly, the effort is far from revolutionary. Rather than seizing power from the grassroots and transforming the entire economy and political system, the anti-Jarret coalition appears more interested in reforming the existing system. Although they oppose Jarret's fascism and his debilitating war, they do nothing to challenge the position of the ruling corporations. Instead of working to build a new society, the new regime refines a more efficient version of the old one—or, at best, searches for a "third way" that only appears to move beyond the existing social order. The radical potential of Earthseed is doubly negated by this liberal accommodation and the community's own decision neither to support nor challenge it.

Yet Earthseed's (and Butler's) apocalyptic stance still makes political sense in its outright rejection of such a reformist response. Lauren and Earthseed have nothing to do with the opposition to Jarret, and, from their limited viewpoint, for good reason. As they see it, their vision and program is so completely opposed to the status quo, reformed or otherwise, that it can only look to a new reality that lies completely beyond it. Although this position takes Earthseed's mission out of the arena of direct engagement—with the Christian Right and with the liberal opposition—it still reaffirms a radical vision that in the tradition of separatist communities represents a signpost to a different way of life. But because of the abstract nature of this apocalyptic position, the political vision of Earthseed—within and without the text—loses its immediate connection with the processes of engaged militancy. While Earthseed's separatism still suggests a relatively utopian response, that very position betrays the same detached stasis of the many utopian movements that have opted out of the self-reflexive processes of history.

After Jarret's fall, Lauren even takes advantage of the new equilibrium, for she works within its relative stability, social wealth, and personal freedom to bring Earthseed closer to its destiny. She concentrates on building new clone communities and preparing for the first flights into space, but she ironically reveals the resignation informing her renewed but limited effort to two of her new recruits as she tries to explain the current logic behind her vision:

> I wanted us to understand what we could be, what we could do. I wanted to give us a focus, a goal, something big enough, complex enough, difficult enough, and in the end, radical enough to make us become more than we ever have been. We keep falling into the same ditches, you know? I mean, we learn more and more about the physical universe, more about our own bodies, more technology, but somehow, down through history, we go on building empires of one kind or another, then destroying them in one way or another. We go on having stupid wars that we justify and get passionate

> about, but in the end, all they do is kill huge numbers of people, maim others, impoverish still more, spread disease and hunger, and set the stage for the next war. And when we look at all of that in history, we just shrug our shoulders and say, well, that's the way things are. That's the way things always have been. (*Talents* 321)

In this formulation her analysis is more pragmatic, more modest, than the earlier engaged expressions in her journal. It is no longer a radical response or utopian critique that works from the contradictions and possibilities of history. It does not challenge, alone or with a larger collective voice, the new liberal government to redirect its own economic and political policies. Rather, it articulates a view of history that is cyclical, not dialectical, and implies that the only move forward must be an apocalyptic leap, not *through* the present but *out* of the present, out of this world, and into some new age. Hence, Lauren's ideological and political goal is not the transformation of the Earth from some liberated base on another planet. Looking only to a future elsewhere, she claims that Earthseed "can fulfill the Destiny, make homes for *ourselves* among the stars, and become some combination of what we want to become and whatever our new environments challenge us to become" (*Talents* 322, my emphasis).

Perhaps because of this reformed attitude, Earthseed turns into a nationally recognized and no longer threatening institution. As Larkin describes the expanded project after she investigates it, Earthseed has

> financed scientific exploration and inquiry, and technological creativity. It set up grade schools and eventually colleges, and offered full scholarships to poor but gifted students. The students who accepted had to agree to spend seven years teaching, practicing medicine, or otherwise using their skills to improve life *in the many Earthseed communities*. Ultimately, the intent was to help the communities to launch themselves toward the stars and to live on the distant worlds they found circling those stars. (*Talents* 340, my emphasis)

The community has gained power, but only in a compromised form that works in itself and for itself. In Raymond Williams's terms, it has become an alternative and is no longer an oppositional force.[11] It rightly offers refuge to its own people—many of whom have escaped slavery, rape, battering, and economic and physical abuse and properly need and deserve such a refuge. Yet what it offers is a secure space—one that soon will be cosmically elsewhere—rather than a utopian enclave wherein its members can strive to become agents in and of themselves, preparing to burrow within the very historical context that has brutalized and terrorized them. By the end of the second book, therefore, Earthseed is no longer a political formation that is prepared to speak radical truth to existing power. It does not stride into the temple of the economy and scatter the moneylenders. It does not bring the walls of the system tumbling down and seek to build anew from those scattered stones. Instead, the community leaves the world behind as the first Earthseed ships take off for the stars.[12]

Like Tiptree's *Gloria,* the "fat, squat, ugly, ancient-looking space trucks" are certainly a refreshing populist alternative to the sleek macho shapes of a cliched sf invasion force, and they do carry an ecological and egalitarian promise into the galaxy, possibly preserving the only seeds of humanity that will outlast Armageddon on Earth (*Talents* 363). As with the Venus rocket in *Space Merchants,* the radical hopefulness of the ending is an eloquent gesture but one cast in the manner of a New Age discourse nuanced with an ethos of survivalism rather than a materialist spirituality based in political praxis. The transcendent is invoked, but at this point it is no longer articulated with secular history.

The second plot line that leads up to this paradoxically limiting yet expansive ending is the family drama of Lauren and her children. Powerful and socially resonant as that drama might be (especially in the portrayal of the mother-daughter relationship), it minimally explores the dynamic relationship between those personal conflicts and the wider possibilities of political engagement. The plot develops around Larkin's search for her mother, a quest that begins in anger, develops through scholarly curiosity, and ends in a meeting that resounds with alienation and pain. Raised in a Christian American home and then cared for by Lauren's younger brother Marcus (who is rescued by Lauren from sex slavery only to become a Christian minister antagonistic to Earthseed), Larkin/Ashe grows up to be a historian and a creator of scenarios for popular virtual reality entertainments called Dreamask. In some ways Larkin/Ashe and Marcus act as foils to Lauren and are in a characterological position to provide a usefully self-reflexive critique of the reduced narrative of Earthseed and its strong leader, but Butler does not develop this critical potential. It shimmers at the textual periphery by implication and could well shine forth as such in a subsequent volume. In *Talents* it simply languishes.

To be fair to the longer series-text of multiple volumes, the self-reflexive and critical seeds that have been rendered dormant in the second book could again blossom and restore the series to the vitality of utopian or dystopian discourse, but at least by the closing of *Talents* that potential is not realized.[13] Hope lingers, however, in the way that Butler ends her sequel, with a moment of self-reflexive questioning similar to the position Lauren describes when she writes about her uncertainty over the vision of Earthseed: "The thing that I want to build is so damned new and so *vast!* I not only don't know how to build it, but I'm not even sure what it will look like when I have built it. I'm just feeling my way, using whatever I can do, whatever I can learn to take one more step forward" (*Talents* 52). Or as she puts it later in prison: "My writing is a way for me to remind myself that I am human, that God is Change, and that I will escape this place" (*Talents* 202). Somewhere between uncertainty and abdication, the second book ends. Consequently, it might be best to close this present discussion on a lingering note of hope drawn from Butler's own scriptural metaphors of the sowing of seeds and the potential of talents. Where the new volumes take the series will crucially indicate the next turn in Butler's admittedly powerful political analysis and vision. They will tell us, in their sequential appearance, how the entire series will continue to negotiate the political terrain between utopian and anti-utopian pessimism.

9

Marge Piercy's Tale of Hope

Historically, all forms of hierarchy have always been based ultimately on gender hierarchy and on the building block of the family unit, which makes it clear that this is the true juncture between a feminist problematic and a Marxist one—not an antagonistic juncture, but the moment at which the feminist project and the Marxist and socialist project meet and face the same dilemma: how to imagine Utopia.

—FREDRIC JAMESON, "COGNITIVE MAPPING" (355)

I.

With *He, She and It*, published in the United States in 1991 and in Britain as *Body of Glass* in 1992, Marge Piercy joins Robinson and anticipates Butler in her critical dystopian negation of the social realities of the 1980s and early 1990s, but in doing so she supersedes Robinson's focus on a structure of feeling and Butler's alternative cultural formation.[1] Continuing her lifelong vocation as a politically engaged writer, she imaginatively traces an oppositional movement that is confrontational, militant, collective, and at least momentarily successful. Like Butler's, Piercy's dystopian elsewhere opens on a hegemonic corporate order wherein twenty-three megafirms compete with one another for profits and power in a world that is ecologically devastated. As the cockroaches of history, the corporate giants have survived war, nuclear bombs, global warming, toxic poisoning, famine, and economic collapse, and they continue to attempt mergers and takeovers that will lead to even larger entities that inherently seek to destroy or absorb their remaining competitors.

Unlike Butler with her socioreligious movement and Robinson with his rebellious individuals, Piercy crucially locates the leading edge of the anti-corporate opposition directly within the contradictory nature of the capitalist machinery of this future society. Both the workers of the urban sprawl called the Glop and the cybernetic designers of the free town of Tikva exist in the tenuous gap between their economic exploitation by the corporations and the benefits they eke from that relationship. They consequently develop their immediate politics and utopian aspirations out of the conjunctural possibilities of the situation in which they find themselves.

They find another, unexpected source of support, however, from a part of the world that has been excised from the map. Earlier in the century, in the land that once was the Middle East, a nuclear bomb had devastated the nations and peoples of the region, but in the Black Zone that registers on official maps as derelict space, a community of Palestinian and Jewish women has survived and built a utopian enclave in what has truly become a no-man's land. Tactically isolated so that they could develop their radical alternative, the women have finally sent out an emissary, the cyborg Nili, who not only befriends and helps build the oppositional alliance of the counter-narrative but also brings them the vision of a new utopian horizon.

Piercy's concern for oppositional possibilities has, of course, been a strong emphasis throughout her work. As she puts it in her commentary on *He, She and It,* all her fiction "is concerned with questions of choice, autonomy and freedom."[2] Whether in fiction, poetry, drama, or essays, she has consistently examined the state of the world and asked what could and should be done.[3] Giving voice to the reality behind the slogan that the personal is the political, she has expressed an uncompromising socialist-feminist perspective; and in exposing the economic ravages of nature and the exploitation of the human community, she has remained loyal to the best traditions of democratic socialism and radical ecology. Her 1976 realist novel, *Vida,* self-critically explores the individual and collective turmoil and commitment of the New Left movements of the 1960s and 1970s with an uncompromising eloquence; and her 1996 historical novel on the French Revolution, *City of Darkness, City of Light,* reprises that eloquence in a work that speaks to the political stasis of the 1990s with the distancing power of the historical imagination. It is in her sf works, however, that she has been able to express her sweeping speculations about political realities and possibilities.

He, She and It is the third of Piercy's sf novels and the first to garner significant respect from the sf community beyond its feminist wing, as Edward James has pointed out, by winning the 1993 Arthur C. Clarke prize (*20th Century* 217n). Although many have explored its similarities to *Woman on the Edge of Time,* this text of the 1990s has moved beyond its critical utopian predecessor and taken up the critical dystopian mode. Indeed, one can usefully read *He, She and It* in light of its intertextual links with *both* of Piercy's earlier sf texts. As a dialectical sublation of the nearly realist *Dance the Eagle to Sleep* (that neglected 1970 work of political sf written in the midst of the U.S. repression of the New Left) and her 1976 critical utopia, *He, She and It* retains the political realism of both texts even as it refunctions their combined utopian energy in an account of a world that is worse than the one in *Dance* or in the realist chapters and the prescient dystopian chapter 15 of *Woman on the Edge of Time*.

In this recent work, as in the other two, Piercy steps just a bit into a future from which she can take a cooler and more totalizing look at current conditions and explore ways of moving forward that activists and theoreticians—perhaps caught in the limitations of nostalgic agendas or the pressures of immediate disputes—may not be ready or able to acknowledge or imagine. Like Robinson and Butler, she offers her readers a critical dystopian elsewhere that charts new political directions, but in her imaginative space those directions are more confrontational and successful than many people would dare to dream or hope for.

II.

The formal organization of Piercy's latest sf venture resembles the braided narrative of *Woman on the Edge of Time*, but instead of a story line that winds between the present and future, the double narrative in *He, She and It* moves tectonically between the past, in the Jewish ghetto of Prague in 1600, and the future, in the second half of the twenty-first century. Only the reader stands in the present, to reflect upon these alternative social paradigms and hopefully to be challenged and inspired by doing so. The dystopian temptation to anti-utopian resignation is therefore resisted formally by a text that pulls at the enclosure of the present moment from two chronotopic perspectives—and then from a third once the political imagination of the reader begins to challenge the common sense of her or his own time.

The self-reflexivity made possible by the alternating stories of resistance in the Prague ghetto and the corporate-dominated future is supported by the subversive power of storytelling throughout the text.[4] Malkah's tale of the heroic Golem highlights the place of tradition and memory in the critical practice of breaking through the political stasis of the present. In addition, the multiple stories (from Malkah's to Milton's to Mary Shelley's and on to comic books) that help to educate and empower the artificial creature Yod further remind readers of the ways in which narrative can offer other ways of seeing the world and perhaps of acting in it. As well, in the actions of several characters, Piercy stresses the transformative process of close observation, gradual discovery, and consequent change. Yod is certainly an exemplar of this radicalizing process, but the dawning realizations and shifts in attitude and behavior seen in the characters of Avram's spoiled son, Gadi, and the cyborg Nili (and even of the irascible and jealous house computer) also reinforce the power of the very epistemological process that sf makes available and that can carry over to everyday life as a means of consciousness-raising and self- and social critique.[5]

Piercy's twenty-first-century world is one that has seen more social and natural destruction than Robinson's yet hangs on to more structural coherence than Butler's. In the realistic details of this cognitively focused and magnified alternative future, humanity, as it has been doing for centuries, is still "killing the world" (137). The actual conditions, however, have now reached the critical stages predicted in the previous century. The results of a Two Week War in 2017 (when the area that encompassed Israel, Jordan, Lebanon, Syria, Iraq, and Saudi Arabia was obliterated by a nuclear weapon) are locked into the damage it left behind. The oil-based economy has ended once and for all, radioactive poisoning has spread globally, and power balances have shifted, but also no other large-scale war has yet occurred (5, 195). In addition to this single military cataclysm, a slower effusion of economically induced ecological damage has taken its toll as global warming, ozone depletion, loss of topsoil, toxic waste, and unchecked diseases synergistically produced the famine of 2031. Besides the obliteration of entire geographical regions—producing the poisonous "raw" into which humans cannot venture without protection—large numbers of people have died, and the birthrate has dropped because of "pesticides, toxic waste accumulations and radiation stockpiled in the groundwater and the food chain" (310).

Thus, the world of the second half of the twenty-first century has been nearly destroyed by national and military arrogance and capitalist greed, as the "multis cut down the rain forest, deep and strip mined, drove the peasants off the land and raised cash crops till the soil gave out" (202). The oceans have inundated large coastal zones—such as the "rice paddies and breadbaskets of the delta countries like Bangladesh and Egypt"—and rich farmlands have turned into deserts in the North American Great Plains, the Eurasian steppes, the expanding wastes of Africa, and the denuded Amazon basin (43–44).

Former nation-states have been absorbed into larger regional entities—such as Norika and the "affluent quadrant of Europa"—"managed by the remains of the old UN," which still serves as "eco-police" but little more since no regional or local infrastructure, public sphere, or bureaucracy is in evidence (5, 35). Other than holding on to a residual authority over "earth, water, air outside domes and wraps," the minimal world government is powerless against the real rulers of the earth: the twenty-three megacorporations that have "divided the world among them," occupying privileged and protected enclaves "on every continent and on space platforms" (35, 5). In fact, the names of corporations reveal the history of their mergers and to some extent their economic interests: Yakamura-Steichen and Aramco-Ford signify cross-national mergers, and Uni-Par identifies the remaining entertainment multi, based, as was the cutting edge of television in the 1990s, in Vancouver.

At the peripheries of each multi's geographical range of influence, the former urban areas known around the world as the Glop provide an impoverished home for the temporary and day workers still employed by the corporations, and on the economic margin the few remaining free towns, such as Tikva, survive by delivering specialist products and services that the corporations find more convenient and profitable to acquire by subcontracting (35). Other than a few remaining rural zones in which the last vestiges of nonchemical, nonvat, organic agriculture is practiced by a shrinking group of smallholders, the remaining lands stand empty because they have become fatally toxic (330–331).

The map of this new world is constructed around nodal points of protected and thriving corporate enclaves that are protectively ringed by abandoned lands and then linked to their regional economic adjuncts in the Glop and the free towns by superfast tube trains that cross the twenty-first-century moats of deadly deserts. In North America, where Piercy's story is microcosmically set, the most powerful multi, Yakamura-Steichen, rules from its base in a domed enclave in the midst of the "Nebraska Desert," which insulates it from attacks by other feudalized multis, independent information pirates, and the desperate workers and outcasts who have been denied a privileged position with the company.

In this secure paradise, the permanent employees—ranked and coded in Huxleyesque fashion from executive to technical to security classes—live and work in a conformist culture of sanitized pluralism that encourages extensive body surgery so that every member can assume the recommended corporate appearance. Fully interpellated subjects of the Y-S corporation therefore acquire the locally idealized characteristics of "blond hair, blue eyes with epicanthic folds, painted brows like Hokusai brush strokes, aquiline nose, dark golden complexion" (4). United as well by the company religion of "born-again Shintoism" and dwelling in small and identical housing designed and located by rank, with their children considered as corporate resources, the employees live obediently and productively under the black, white, and blue Y-S flag while, as in many company towns, the corporate president resides in splendid isolation in a separate house on a "lake full of real water" (339). Besides its terrestrial location, Y-S, as with the other multis, maintains several space platforms for research and a certain amount of disciplinary isolation as it "privileges" certain employees by promoting them "upward" to the protection of residential satellites such as Y-S's Pacifica Platform (17).

With oil, industrial production, and agribusiness obliterated, the production, use, and transmission of information has emerged as the leading source of corporate profit (while necessities such as vat food are produced in the Glop), and it is generated, used, and traded on the worldwide computer Network that developed out of the late-twentieth-century Internet. As a public utility subscribed to by "communities, multis, towns, even individuals," the Net is shared and protected by a consensual ethos of nonintervention against users, and yet the value of the information flowing through it makes it inevitably the Achilles' heel of the corporate political economy (58). In response to the constant danger of cybernetic invasion, in what amounts to a twenty-first-century cold war, corporations do all they can to protect their own security even as they endeavor to break in to the Net bases of other multis and free towns. Consequently, industrial surveillance and espionage, sabotage of data banks, and assassination of on-line workers have become standard operating procedures—as have the defensive measures required to guard against those practices.

Standing in a dependent relationship to the dominant multis, the people of the Glop—the generic name for urban areas such as those that stretched from Atlanta to Boston, lined the coast of Lake Michigan from Green Bay to the far side of the lake, constituted "El Barrio" in the Southwest, the "Jungle" on the Gulf Coast, and similar locales around the globe—live in markedly poorer and more degraded conditions. The Glop is the "festering warren" that houses the bulk of the population (nine-tenths in North America alone) that has no permanent or secure relationship with the multis (8, 330). A few who live in the Glop earn their living as commuting day workers in the multi enclaves, but others resort to the lumpen pursuits of crime, and still others languish as they starve or die from rampant diseases (8, 31, 33).

Ignored by world government and corporations alike, the Glop is self-organized by gangs that occupy and control contested regions of this inner urban space. As the "mollies for the multis" who do the "dirty grabs" while the free town designers do the clean labor, the Glop workers and gang members are tough, proud, and angry (319). Some gangs—such as the Coyotes—have begun to transform themselves from paramilitary gangsters into political agents, developing their turf into zones of "autonomous political development" (318). Like the politicized gangs in the United States of the 1970s before the Reagan administration destroyed their political initiatives by cutting job training programs and turning a blind eye to the new crack cocaine trade as it was developed by their military surrogates in Central America, the Glop gangs are forging a new political culture out of their struggle to survive the miseries of their region and the exploitation of the multis. Within these contradictory conditions, they are forming associations resembling a cross between labor unions and militias, and they are ready to join the others who will constitute the emerging alliance against Y-S.[6]

Unlike the Glop, free towns such as Tikva retain more autonomy and maintain a higher standard of living, mainly because they perform highly skilled product development and services that the corporations choose not to include in the fixed costs of secure employment. Because of their unique production niche, the free towns manage to live a relatively comfortable existence, but in doing so they are no less vulnerable. At any time they can be denied their contractual relationship or simply be attacked by a multi with which they deal (or by a competing multi or even another free town). Hence, they protect themselves by delivering state-of-the-art products while they keep a step ahead of those very products in their own defense systems. They also maintain a second tier of protection by negotiating between and among corporations, thereby playing one multi against another in an economic-martial balance of power. As a typical free town, Tikva stands on an unclaimed geographical margin between the relatively untainted lands of the multis and the poisonous realms of the raw and the sea.

Stretching alongside Massachusetts Bay on the site of what once was Boston and what in *Woman on the Edge of Time* was the utopian community of Mattapoisett, the city-state preserves its flourishing but endangered existence on the shore of a poisoned sea as it tries to nurture lives based on principles radically different from those of the corporations, seeking to effect minimal damage and making collective choices about what can and should be done (106).[7] Protected from the toxic elements by a "wrap" that is more flexible and less expensive than the domes over the multi enclaves, Tikva guards against incursions from thieves, pirates, and multi attacks with electronic walls, surveillance devices, and volunteer sentries. Like other free town residents, the citizens of Tikva are sufficiently skilled to compete for jobs in the multis, but they prefer instead to stay outside, sometimes because of "a minority religion, a sexual preference not condoned by a particular multi, perhaps simply an archaic desire for freedom" (33).

Tikva's particular history, however, is linked to the Two Week War of 2017, for its founding as a Jewish enclave was a "direct response to the virulent anti-Semitism of that period [called, in a borrowing from Northern Ireland] the Troubles" (355). Thus, this city of "hope" serves both as a refuge for Jews in the present and a historical alternative to the corrupt state of Israel.[8] As Malkah explains it, Tikva is an effort to make up for "having had a nation in our name as stupid and as violent as other nations" (407). Reaching back to the models of early American town hall government, New Left participatory democracy, feminist principles of equity and self-criticism, and the socialism of early Zionism (before it mutated into a form of state racism), Tikva has organized itself on a foundation of "libertarian socialism with a strong admixture of anarcho-feminism, reconstructionist Judaism (although there were six temples, each representing a different Jewishness) and greeners" (418). Valuing optimal freedom for everyone, the citizens practice a total democracy that requires endless meetings (the necessary price of socialism that Oscar Wilde recognized over a century and half earlier) and community duties such as town labor and reforestation work.

Within the security and freedom of this pocket utopia, Tikva's citizens perform the high-end labor that guarantees them their place in the economic system. Their particular product line is the design and specialized production of defense systems that provide security for company computer bases when they are linked to the Net. Working from their own base (the "gold mine of the town, where the systems were created that were the town's main export"), Tikva's scientists and designers invent, develop, and market their quality range of defense tools and services (42). On the one hand, they offer "chimeras" that protect bases by means of misdirection through subsystems that generate "misinformation, pseudoprograms, falsified data"; on the other hand, they can deliver aggressive defense machines that are driven by new forms of artificial intelligence (47). Selling such materials to corporations and other free towns guarantees Tikva not only a relatively comfortable level of economic well-being but also a great deal of security, for the Tikva designers make sure that their own defense systems are kept a step ahead of the ones they put on the market (see 149).

If the corporations, the Glop, the free towns, the rural zones, and the dangerous raw constitute the known map of this future world, the "black patch" that marks the area of the Middle East destroyed in 2017 (by a "zealot" who nuked Jerusalem) and subsequently quarantined as a "radioactive, biologically unsafe area" is secretly the location of the most utopian space in the book (195). Unexpectedly and clandestinely, an emissary has ventured into the corporate-ruled world from this place that once was known as "Safed" in old Israel but now goes by the name of the Black Zone. Like a militant dove (or as she pointedly recasts it, a "raven") from a radical ark, Nili identifies herself as a "spy and a scout" who has been given the assignment of seeing if the world is ready for her people and if there is anything in this outer space that they could use (206). As she explains to her new friends in Tikva, she is a member of the "community of the descendants of Israeli and Palestinian women who survived" the bomb by cloning and genetic engineering and further enhancing their bodies with medical and martial augmentations.

In this historical anomaly, the company of cyborg women has created a post-holocaust, post-colonial, and post-human utopian space that is radically communal and democratic and based on principles from religious traditions as well as the secular traditions of ecology, feminism, and anarchocommunism (205). As Nili puts it: "We have created ourselves to endure, to survive, to hold our land"

(205–206). In this renewed and historically transcendent space (which will one day include the rebuilt city of "Yerushalaim"), the entire community stands ready to teach and to lead when the time is right. For the moment, however, Nili is the one who will learn and help, for it is the conflict between Y-S and the people of Tikva and the Glop that pulls her into the first act of solidarity between her cyborg community and the rest of the world.[9] Not only does this utopian citizen join the new alliance, but in the aftermath of its successful engagement with Y-S she takes the aging Malkah back to her transformed land. In this longed-for aliyah, or pilgrimage, to the transformed holy land, Malkah is "made-over" by the utopian scientists and technicians, and lives to love life and fight even more than she already has (433).

Joining Tikva and the Black Zone as the third spatial alternative to the corruption that was the old Israeli state, the walled Jewish ghetto of Prague in 1600 ("the Glop of its time") offers a more distant, more mystical, utopian source for the text's self-reflexively political articulation (21). In this embattled locale, Rabbi Judah Loew ben Bezalel, Judah the Lion, is deeply worried about the Christian oppression of his people that has been inspired by the Counter-Reformation. Outraged at the demeaning yellow symbols, the forced isolation in the ghetto, the marauding mobs, the blood libels, and the life taxes, he looks abroad at the exile and persecution of the Jews of Spain, England, and Portugal, and he fears that another pogrom will soon be perpetrated upon his people (23, 27).

In response, this learned, kindly, yet "hotheaded kabbalist" (simultaneously "the *tzaddik*—the righteous—and the *hasid*—the pious") decides to draw on his dangerous knowledge of the kabbalah and raise up a superbeing, a Golem, to protect his people (23, 29). Named Joseph by his maker, the Golem signifies the Prague community's ability to engage in aggressive self-defense and not settle for passive victimization. Gradually, Joseph learns to guard the ghetto and defend the individuals in it, even as he ventures outside it to discover what plots are afoot in the hateful Christian communities. Again and again, he saves his people.

Finally, in a time of "maximum danger," the Golem becomes the mystical fighting machine who stands up and leads the community against the Christian invaders who will attack at Easter (274, 329). With Joseph at his side, Judah prepares the assembled fighters for the coming attack: "Jews of Prague . . . Today we must defend our gates. Today we must stand as a shield, the Magen David, between our people and certain death. They don't expect us to fight. If we stand firm, we can discourage those who don't like killing Jews enough to die for the pleasure. Let us put ourselves in the hands of the living ha-Shem and fight like holy men and demons" (329). Joseph then sends the rabbi to safety and assumes command of the defending force. On Good Friday of 1600, the battle ensues, and Joseph and the empowered community successfully turn back the Christian mob assaulting their walls and gates.

In the relative peace that comes after the victory, the aging rabbi fears leaving Joseph in the hands of anyone else and decides to return him to the clay from which he came: "I made him. I must unmake him. But I will not destroy him. I will leave him intact. If anyone comes in future who has the mastery of the forces of life, they can wake him if the times are truly needful" (411). Hence, the Golem is laid to rest, but it remains available in the traditional imagination as the signifier of a fighting hope. It is this utopian signifier, and the story of its creation, that runs through Piercy's text as a reminder of the place of righteous anger—as seen in the defense of the Warsaw ghetto in World War II and in the allied struggle against Y-S in her future world—but it also stands as the sober reminder of the related need to set such power aside in times of waning danger. The figure of the Golem lingers as a simultaneous indictment of Israel and a symbol of the Jewish community's capacity, when necessary, to fight against their oppressors.[10]

III.

It is within these geographic, economic, and historical spaces that the narrative conflict of Piercy's dystopian text plays out. In a world solidly under the exploitive and oppressive control of the multis, an oppositional alliance emerges from the events put into motion by the Y-S plot to steal computer defense information from its subcontractor, Tikva. As usual in dystopian narratives, the epical contest starts with the story of an individual misfit who becomes aware of her exploitation or abuse by the hegemonic system, and in this instance it is Shira Shipman's corporate alienation and her consequent fight to regain custody of her son, Ari, that launches the counter-narrative. After Ari is awarded to his loyal corporate father in the custody fight, Shira takes a leave of absence from her Y-S techie position, in which, in a foreshadowing move, she is expert on the "interface between people and the large artificial intelligences that formed the Base of each corporation and every other information-producing and information-eating entity in the world" (3).

Returning to her family home in Tikva, she clings to the hope of getting Ari back while she takes a temporary job with her grandmother Malkah. She is enlisted to help Malkah with the task of socializing the creature that the artificial intelligence and robotics expert Avram has finally produced after years of failed efforts. Not only does this assignment lead Shira to become Yod's lover and friend (as she discovers its exceptional post-human qualities), but it also intensifies Y-S's interest in Tikva. Following an attack the year before Shira arrived (in which five programmers were killed and "another two reduced to vegetables"), Malkah herself is assaulted while she is plugged into the town's base (99). In response to this almost fatal invasion, Shira, Malkah, Avram, and Yod begin to speculate on the reasons for it, and after Shira and Yod break into Y-S's information banks to uncover Ari's whereabouts (and Y-S's plans for Shira), they discover the larger Y-S scheme that has been in motion for several years.

As one of "the ten most powerful multis in the world," Y-S would not have been thought of as directly interested in the likes of a small free town like Tikva (182); however, once Yod decodes the stolen files, the corporate plot become clear. When Shira was first hired, the company's personnel investigators traced her familial links to Tikva and the radicals and intellectuals whose files they had been compiling since before she was born: her mother, the information pirate Riva; her grandmother, the chimera designer Malkah; and most of all in Y-S's estimation, the scientist Avram, an expert in artificial intelligence. Given these "subversive" ties, Shira's status in the corporation secretly changed from that of a talented new employee to a potential source of valuable information.

Having wondered for years why she was never properly promoted after she entered with high university honors, she discovers the answer in Y-S's plan to maneuver her into a position that would make her so desperate as to want to return home to Tikva so that she could act as an unwitting conduit to pass on information about Riva's political activities (which pose a danger to the "established corporate order") and on the results of Malkah's and Avram's research (from the chimeras to the project that produces Yod) (82). Even though she was consistently rated above her husband, Josh, in categories of "capacity, efficiency, inventiveness, teamwork," she was held back while he advanced (291). The resulting discrepancy in their careers gradually undermined her self-confidence and exacerbated the differences between the couple until they became unresolvable. The conflict led to divorce, and the divorce led to Josh's receiving custody. The entire sequence led to Shira's feeling vulnerable, alienated, and anxious to take time off in Tikva.

Hence, Y-S achieved the forced "transfer" it had planned long ago, a transfer that put Shira into an exploitable position. As Shira puts it, Y-S did "put a spy in place here. . . . They forced me out by taking my son away. . . . They knew I'd remain bound to them through Ari. Essentially they considered they were transferring me here to remain long enough to learn about Avram's research. Then I was to be recalled and emptied of useful information" (292).

As Y-S continues with its plot (but discovering the existence of Yod only upon Shira's arrival in Tikva), Shira and the others assess Y-S's scheme and plan how they will protect themselves and the community. They realize that after Y-S exhausted its first-round tactics of imposing cultural pressures of conformity, guilt, and bribery by promotion and privilege, the company escalated its activity with the falsely legalized kidnapping of Ari and intrusive surveillance of Shira. After manipulating Shira back to Tikva, Y-S took the next, clearly criminal step and violated the security of the Net by launching a direct attack on Malkah—thereby breaking one of the few common rules of this tenuous social system. Further espionage and assassination attempts combined with a series of false negotiations in fabricated meetings then shape the next steps in the campaign to track subversives and steal Tikva's intellectual property.

In the midst of this developing political fight, Shira's personal identity crisis and parental anxiety continue and are matched by Yod's own struggles as the creature gradually grows in awareness, perception, wisdom, and desire under the tutelage of Malkah and Shira and the experience of its own actions. As a breakthrough in the science and technology of human-machine interfaces, Yod is "programmed for introspection, to be self-correcting in subtle and far-reaching ways" (364). Like Frankenstein's creature and so many other beings in that fantastic, catachrestic tradition, Yod strives "heroically to be human" (353). It argues before Tikva's town council for its right to be recognized not only as a person but also as a citizen and a Jew (405, 379, 419,). In the relationship with Shira, however, Yod experiences its most powerful desire, and the consequent sexual and personal intimacy motivates the creature not only to fight for Shira, Tikva, and the alliance but also to carry out its Samson-like self-sacrifice in the final battle with Y-S.

The counter-narrative therefore grows from the private struggles of the principal characters, Shira and Yod, into the public movement, and it is the quality and power of their relationship that informs the response of the entire anti-Y-S alliance. Both rise to the occasion and do what must be done. Shira breaks out of her corporate formation and her self-doubt and discovers new depths in herself as she struggles for Ari as well as Tikva and the others. She continues to train Yod, manages the negotiations with Y-S, helps Yod break into the data banks and later to take Ari back, and adds her insider knowledge to the strategy that leads to the defeat of Y-S. As a latter-day Golem, Yod guards its chosen people, works as the high-level computer it is designed to be, but also kills when needed—including Y-S executives, security guards, and, in a mistaken moment, Josh. Yet while Shira lives to be reunited with Ari and becomes a base overseer in Tikva, Yod has the political and ethical wisdom not only to self-destruct but also to kill Avram so that this particular scientific and military creation will never be repeated (430).[11]

The coordinates of the oppositional conflict ultimately take on a three-way configuration that gives shape and substance to the alliance. If the stories of Shira and Yod recall the identity politics of the 1980s, the collective consciousness-in-struggle gained by the people of Tikva, the Glop, and the Black Zone points toward the reviving economic and self-determination alliances of the 1990s. It is the role of the historically evocative outlaw figure of Riva, however, that adds the third, mediating and catalyzing element that unites and transforms both tendencies into a greater movement that serves as a provocative image for the politics of the twenty-first century.

For their part, the people of Tikva enter the conflict by way of their familial and communal response to Shira's plight when she returns home bereft of her son; but once the second attack on the base occurs, it is clear that the very economic and political survival of Tikva itself is in question. When Yod tells Malkah and the others that the attackers were employees of Y-S, they realize that the socioeconomic balance of power has changed. The truth behind the direct attack, as Malkah explains, is that Y-S in its drive for power and profit simply doesn't want Tikva "to endure free any longer" (180). Although the oppositional work is at first restricted to the discreet efforts of Shira, Malkah, Avram, Yod, and Gadi, the escalation of the conflict leads to their notifying the town council and thereby making it a fight of the entire community for the entire community. When Shira, Yod, Avram, and Malkah first meet to discuss their possible responses, Shira suggests that they could begin by playing one corporate juggernaut off another. Consequently, she asks the Cybernaut corporation to provide "space and security" for the meeting they have set up with Y-S, since no competitor would want to see Tikva's valuable products and services monopolized by any single corporation (183). Then, drawing on their advanced knowledge and skills, they enter the fray against Y-S. In the cybercaper into the Y-S computer after the disastrous meeting, not only do Yod and Shira steal information but Malkah also plants a virus that destroys Y-S's archives (284). Later, as the designer of Yod as a fighting machine, Avram is ready to launch it into action against the corporation, and he urges Yod to blow itself up along with the top Y-S executives when the final meeting is planned. Finally, the council itself endorses the group's actions, and the community rallies to make its defensive preparations for another Y-S attack.

This range of contributions (as creative as Malkah's and as violent as Avram's) demonstrates the collective but contradictory will of Tikva to survive in a world that barely tolerates its freedom. The odds shift further in Tikva's favor when Malkah's daughter Riva returns with her strange friend from a strange land. Disguised as an old woman with her nurse, Riva and Nili announce that they have come to help after hearing of Malkah's attack (196–197). With these two women, Tikva gains the critical mass it needs to launch a counterattack. For all its surveillance, the powerful megacorporation did not reckon on the resources and skills that the tenacious community possessed. Reviewing the situation, Shira realizes that Y-S had "underestimated Malkah, ignored Riva, and Yod had not figured except as the passive quarry," and she knows that ultimately Yod (in a reprise of the Golem tradition) is Y-S's "unknown enemy," the "great glitch" in their master plot (293).

Not only do Riva and Nili help with the immediate challenge of the first meeting with Y-S, but they also make the next, crucial move toward broadening the opposition by brokering the alliance with the gangs of the Glop. After Nili provides lifesaving backup in the first meeting and arranges Riva's feigned death so that her partner can go underground in the Glop, she announces that she is leaving to meet with the Glop gangs. When Malkah wonders why she is bothering to go to such a dangerous place, Nili tells her that the Glop is too often misread according to its image in the popular "fantasy machine" (295). She reports that certain gangs have been forming resistance forces; consequently, "sectors have managed to organize secretly in spite of drugs and mandated ignorance" and some of the groups have "penetrated the multis" (295). Her own task, as Riva has set it up, is to give support to the new political formations. Malkah then recalls that Riva had spoken about her connections with gangs such as the Lava Rats, the Lords of Chaos, and the Blood Angels, and she admits that they might make good allies in the fight with Y-S. Shira agrees, noting that as Nili makes contacts for her purposes she and Yod could check them out for their own.

When Nili, Gadi, Shira, and Yod arrive in the Glop for their meeting with Lazarus, the leader of the most politically advanced gang, the Coyotes, they discover that Riva not only survived the Y-S ambush but purposely "died" to put her enemies off her trail so that she could resume her long-term organizing work (see 313, 316). From her secure hideout with the Coyotes, Riva explains that the gangs have been able to develop politically right under the nose of the multis, for the corporations rely on the gangs to provide a stable leadership within the Glop and cannot see beyond an immediately exploitive need. Their use of the gangs was simply "good for business" (310).

Working within the limited protection afforded by this contradictory gap, the gangs have begun to organize the people of the Glop in terms of their own self-interest and ultimately self-determination. According to Lazarus (an appropriate name for the leader of two revived movements, youth groups and labor), the "Coyotes are what we call a New Gang. They're an autonomous political development just beginning to make connections" (318). Shira asks for their help in countering the aggression of Y-S, telling Lazarus that they are interested in seeing if "we have goals in common and if we can work together, exchange information, anything that can help you and us to survive" (318). Nili adds that she comes from "farther away" but stands willing to give them her support, with the potential connection with her own people lingering as an unstated possibility (318).

Lazarus remarks that they are all "mollies for the multis," just working in different levels, and suggests that the Coyotes can help by providing information retrieved from corporation sources, and Riva adds that she is also augmenting the Coyote's information retrieval capacity by setting up an underground Net, "outside theirs, alongside theirs" (319). His gang and the others are looking for reciprocal support to build the independent power of the Glop, to make their "people less helpless" and to give them the "strength to take back a piece of the pie" (319). Shira counters that Tikva is also fighting to survive but needs allies to do so. She offers their "different technologies" and trade in information (319). Lazarus then agrees to provide "troops" and "assassins" and asks in return for "the techie lore" (321). And so the alliance is forged.

In the pact with the Coyotes, the individual quests of Shira and Yod and the collective struggles of Tikva and the Glop transform into a qualitatively different movement. One more agent is added to this alliance, and that is the community of the Black Zone, Nili's home. Nili is the single representative of this utopian enclave, but her outlook and activities are themselves promising indicators of the alternative the women in the new Middle East have created. Although she began her trip as an emissary, her political principles (which accord with the enduring practice of radical internationalism) lead her to help any progressive struggle she encounters, beginning with Riva's information piracy and reaching out to the people of the Glop and Tikva.

Nili's cyborg qualities make her a formidable ally, for she offers material help but also signifies the very utopian horizon that informs the political campaigns with which she works. As she bluntly puts it: "I am the future" (230). Or as Shira describes her, she "sees better, hears better, is certainly smarter, tougher, faster, stronger. She's a superior human" (368). She is a trained fighter (an "assassin" and a "well made bomb"), but she is also an adept organizer (196, 197). Further, she is a psychically healthy and fulfilled person, a loyal friend, a ubiquitous lover, and, as Shira discovers, a mother (376, 196, 321, 369). Unaffected by corporate interpellation, she rejects the mass entertainment culture (along with Gadi's invitation to become a stimmie star), enjoys the organic pleasures of Tikva, and finds much to learn from the people of the Glop as they live "off the garbage of the preceding century" (373). In this typical citizen of the Black Zone, the new subject of history, the alliance not only has the benefit of a powerful fighter and organizer but also the guarantee of a connection with a people and land who stand at the timely intersection of the horrible past, the dangerous present, and a liberated future that could mean better lives for all. Indeed, the proof of this potential is seen when Malkah goes to the Black Zone after the final battle and finds not only new eyes but also a new existence with an even greater grasp of the utopian vision to which she has devoted her life.

If Nili is the future, then Riva is the "tool of the future" (421), the radical who works steadily to develop the capacity of all oppositional movements and eventually to bring them together into a single anti-corporate alliance. Shira and others *become* activists in the process of their dystopian struggle with the corporations, whereas Riva appears to have always been eager to live dangerously and to serve others. Malkah recalls her daughter's early "temptation" to danger and her work as a data pirate who "finds hidden knowledge and liberates it" for the sake of people, not corporations (31, 82). Cooperating with like-minded outlaws (in the tradition of Robin Hood, Ned Kelly, Pretty Boy Floyd, and many contemporary hackers), Riva sometimes sold information to finance other work, but more often she freely shared it with countries destroyed by the multis and with free towns striving to retain their precarious independence (202). Gradually, however, she matured into a skilled political agent who was intent not only on liberating information but also on helping people and communities to throw off their corporate chains.

Thus, Riva moves from the position of outlaw to that of organizer (working in the spirit of internationalist solidarity seen in formations such as the IWW, the civil rights and anti-war movements of the 1960s, and throughout the history of the labor movement). Indeed, organizing is her objective when she comes to Tikva. Although she aims to support her family and home community, she is also eager to enlist her own people in the larger fight. For it is Riva who supplies the fullest picture of Y-S's activities to her family. She tells them that Y-S's aggression toward Tikva is but a small part of its larger campaign to eliminate competing multis and assume the position of the leading world power. As she puts it, Y-S thinks "there are too many multis and the free towns are a nuisance. One world, one corp. That's their line. Aramco-Ford is in this with them for starters" (206). Riva, therefore, brings a totalizing picture of global capitalist power to each local group she works with, and it is that galvanizing information and analysis that leads the various communities to enter the anti-capitalist coalition she is gradually helping to build.

Unlike Lauren with her Earthseed community, Riva is not a leader. Rather, she is a self-effacing organizer, teacher, mediator, catalyst, one who helps to build the movement and then moves on. Often neglected in commentaries on Piercy's book, Riva is nevertheless the key agent in the entire counter-narrative. She comes in from the margins and fades out in the last battle, as any good organizer would. Part of a matrilineal family, she admits she has not been a very good mother to Shira, and yet she loves her daughter and helps her to get Ari back. Riva enriches

Shira's sense of her family when she tells her that (by virtue of secure sperm banks) her biological father was the famous physicist Yosef Golinken and that the same man was Nili's grandfather—thus linking the family in Tikva with the people of the Black Zone (199). Outside of her family circle, Riva is a public figure, though one who works behind the scenes. In Nili's estimation she is a powerful model for others: a warrior, a prophet, and even a saint, but one in the tradition of Marx's nomination of Prometheus as the first secular saint (321, 393).

Indeed, Riva is a Prometheus-like agent, stealing from the corporate gods to help the people of Earth. More simply, as Nili goes on, she is simply a "brave woman. A wise woman. One who pursues just aims regardless of the danger to herself. She sees what must be done, and she forces herself to do it. How can we not admire her?" (393). Riva herself is more modest: "Some nasty saint! I'm a tool of the future that wants to be. That's all. I make myself useful, and I do okay by it" (421). Not a hustler and certainly not an escapist or a narcissist intent on her own performance, Riva is typical of the strong political women that have appeared throughout Piercy's writings.

In the final battle, this motley crew comes together to defeat Y-S and stop its campaign to consolidate the economic and political system around its own hegemonic rule. Appropriately following the chapter in which Malkah ends her tale of the Golem, with Judah rendering Joseph back into clay, chapter 46 is entitled "The Task of Samson." It is Yod's self-sacrifice that brings the corporate edifice tumbling down around the multi's grab for global power. As the council deliberates over Yod's request for citizenship and the rabbis ponder the question of its identity as a Jew, Y-S maintains aggressive pressure on Tikva with another assassination attempt, in a "gesture designed to emphasize Tikva's vulnerability and the extent of Y-S resources" (417). Despite both pressures, the band of fighters continues to plan for what they know will be a culminating confrontation. With the Glop providing background intelligence and Nili monitoring Tikva's security, the others prepare for the upcoming meeting. Riva slips back from the Glop to explain the scale and importance of the meeting on the coast of Maine at which Y-S has demanded Yod's attendance: "They want Yod at that top-dog meeting. It starts today and continues tomorrow, my best intelligence says. Roger Krupp [the "tactical genius" of Y-S] is being elevated to second in command. . . . They want to present Yod at Krupp's coronation" (421).

The question is, What to do? Avram insists that his weapon, Yod, be sent to the meeting to destroy the entire Y-S leadership by blowing itself up in their presence. Shira objects, but Riva coolly accepts Avram's conclusion, noting that it's a matter of pursuing the expected work of war: "Yod's a soldier, and this is a crucial battle. I'll be there too. We'll send in Lazarus's best assassins" (422). Malkah tries to mediate the debate, but in the end Yod acknowledges its programmed dependence on Avram and admits it has to go to the meeting and destroy itself or else subject itself to Avram's own terminating discipline back in Tikva: "I am Avram's weapon. Killing is what I do best" (424). Yod then says good-bye, telling Shira at the last minute that there is a message for her on her personal base (425). The next day Avram notes the signal that marks Yod's arrival at the meeting, but sometime later an explosion resounds within Tikva as Avram's house, along with Avram and his notes and records, is totally demolished.

At this point Shira knows Yod is dead and reads his message, only to find out that the creature acted with full volition right to the end:

> I have died and taken with me Avram, my creator, and his lab, all the records of his experiment. I want there to be no more weapons like me. A weapon should not be conscious. A weapon should not have the capacity to suffer for what it does, to regret, to feel guilt. A weapon should not form strong attachments. I die knowing I destroy the capacity to replicate me. I don't understand why anyone would want to be a soldier, a weapon, but at least people sometimes have a choice to obey or refuse. I had none. (429–430)

Both Malkah and Yod had acknowledged that the creature was a mistake. In Malkah's view Nili, not Yod, represented the right path. She argues that it's "better to make people into partial machines than to create machines that feel and yet are still controlled like cleaning robots" (426); Yod, knowing its own freedom in ways Malkah did not, also recognizes itself as an error, but it nevertheless achieves a level of self-transcendence when it freely self-destructs (430). Later, when all has settled down, and she has replaced Malkah as a base overseer, Shira realizes that the software that produced Yod is stored in Malkah's log and thinks about bringing another version of the creature back into existence. By doing so, she could make the perfect lover for herself and a father for Ari. She could recreate a private Golem, a "male figure of gentleness and strength and competence" (442). Feeling Yod's "violent absence," she begins to prepare for the reproduction, but then she recalls Yod's own last words and decides not to "manufacture a being to serve her, even in love" (443, 444). Instead, she dumps all the records into the recycling plant. Finally, the memory of Yod is set free, and the battle is fully over.

With Yod's elimination of the Y-S leadership at the height of their power grab, the counter-narrative draws to a close. Y-S's move to assume global hegemony has been averted. Like a wounded shark, the corporation has become vulnerable to the hostile incursions of the very companies it sought to eliminate (432). In the aftermath, however, the new equilibrium is still dominated by a capitalist order. Yet the groups that make up the anti-corporate alliance have gained relative strength in relation to the diffused and competing multis. Tikva emerges with good relations with the competitors of Y-S, especially Cybernaut—and is in no fear of Y-S retribution given the weakened state of that company. The fight itself has given the community a stronger defense system within its walls as well as in the security of its new alliance. The people of the Glop (at least its North American East Coast sector) have moved significantly toward creating a viable counter-public sphere with political organizations resembling trade unions and organs of self-government beginning to develop (a process helped by the alternative Net that Riva has set up). Even though it was secure all along, the women of the Black Zone (through Nili's exploration and Malkah's visit) have taken the historic step of ending their tactical separatism and have begun to be active members of the new global opposition.

As for the three women of the Shipman family: Riva moves on to continue her clandestine work, most immediately watching for any signs of Y-S vengeance; Malkah goes to the Black Zone to be renewed in body and soul by the utopian women; and a stronger, more confident Shira settles in Tikva with her son and serves as one of the town's base overseers. Nili returns to her homeland and lives on as a citizen of the transformed future.

IV.

As an avowedly political writer, Piercy has never strayed far from cutting-edge questions of critique and activism, and in her sf work she has focused in particular on self-reflexive thought experiments that explore new ways in which an oppositional socialist-feminist-ecological politics could develop out of existing social conditions. Whether she works from a utopian or a dystopian disposition, she manages to detail the social reality of her time and then to delineate spaces and avenues for militant action within her re-vision of that reality. In doing so, she always attends to the imbricated relationships between personal lives and public engagement.

It is not surprising, therefore, that her critical dystopian narrative of the 1990s locates her concerns with personal existence and historical struggle in the stories of Shira and Yod. With these entwined tales, she addresses the imperatives of identity politics even as she brings them into a renewed attention to the parameters of economics, class, and labor, as well as to the epistemological and material processes involved in conceiving and forming an alliance politics capable of challenging the entire system. Revolving around the subject positions of woman, Jew, and cyborg, the crises of self her lead characters confront and the dynamics of their relationship take on a wider political valence in the face of corporate aggression even as every aspect of their lives remains a matter of individual need and desire.[12]

Thus, Piercy continues to pursue her long-standing commitment to investigating the conditions and possibilities for women. Rooted in second-wave feminism—and standing apart from more recent positions of liberal feminism or post-feminism—she brings her socialist-feminist politics to bear on the challenges of the moment. Tensions between the workplace and everyday life, childcare and parenting, mother-daughter (and grandmother-granddaughter) relationships, sisterly politics, and relationships with men that range from the violent and abusive to the loving and sacrificial fill the pages of this work as they have all her others. She spins her tale around Shira and the men in her life, on the one hand, and the intergenerational network of women on the other. In the grandmother Malkah, the mother Riva, the daughter Shira, and the cousin Nili (a "coffee klatch of Jewish mamas"), she offers a matrix of personal and political actions and options that is vital in itself yet also informs and drives the local and global political battles (370).

As the many references to Jewish identity and Israel suggest, Piercy also pays political and cultural attention to that part of her own heritage.[13] Finding wisdom in Jewish tradition as well as in the utopian principles that Zionism once signified, she draws on both to uncover their betrayal by the Israeli state (a betrayal that has had a deadly impact not only on the Palestinian people but also on Jews and Israelis themselves as they have been compromised and brutalized by policies and practices carried out in their name). Her symbolic critique takes the terrifying shape of Israel's destruction and its hopeful replacement by the multiple alternatives of the Prague Ghetto, Tikva, and the Black Zone.

On a cultural plane, however, she goes on to explore the subjective qualities and shortcomings of traditional and contemporary Jewish life through her characters in Tikva in general and Shira's family in particular. She especially probes the relationship between feminism and the aspects of Jewish culture that resonate with the place and power of women, as family members and as individuals. In doing so, she exposes the arrogance of male characters such as the father-son pair of Avram and Gadi and Shira's lovers (Gadi, Josh, Malcolm) with sensitivity and even humor; at the same time she delineates the personal and public strengths made available to the women of her tradition as they are signified by Malkah, Riva, Shira, Nili, and Chava in the Prague story.

With the figures of Yod and Nili, Piercy links her focus on feminist and Jewish matters with one of the major theoretical developments of the 1980s as she, like her character Shira, enters into the exploration of the interface between humanity and machines that has brought a cyborg reality, and potentially a "cyborg politics," to use Donna Haraway's term, onto the sociopolitical stage.[14] Working from the scriptural stories of Genesis and the kabbalistic legends of the Golem and then picking up the Western tradition of the rebellious created being as variously tracked in Milton, Hawthorne, Shelley, Shaw, Capek, Asimov, and Dick (and evoking figures such as Prometheus, Frankenstein's creature, and *Star Trek*'s Data), she develops a fresh perspective on the cyborg issue as she brings Jewish, feminist, and socialist thought to bear on the question. The result is a nuanced move away from an uncritical romanticization or demonization of this metaphorical prod to human transformation.

At the level of geopolitics, Piercy problematizes the insights made available by the cyborg imaginary by directing her attention to the opportunist logic that leads to the appropriation of scientific advances by the profit machines of corporations and the repressive apparatuses of nation-states (large and small). Through the figure of Yod, she speculates on how a defensive advance (even when sympathetically humanized) can turn into a potential engine of terror; for complex as Yod is, it is fundamentally designed as a weapon, one intended for good use but that in the wrong hands (or in the symbolically overdetermined case of Avram, hands *gone* wrong) could become a tool of sociopolitical evil. Framing this ethical and political question of weaponry and self-defense with the insights of the kabbalah legend, she offers a cautionary parable for policymakers, theoreticians, strategists, activists, and citizens alike. Yet, while opposed to engines of war, Piercy is not a technophobe or Luddite; she is quite open to the positive possibilities of an appropriate use of science and technology on an everyday, human scale. Besides computer-assisted housing, in vitro fertilization, and advanced forms of communications and transportation, she presents the figure of Nili (the cybernetically enhanced human) as her most powerful signifier of the potential of an emancipatory cyborg science and sensibility.[15] The cyborg option also carries over to other characters who are already, if modestly, enhanced, as is Shira with her corrected eyesight and Malkah with her several life-extending procedures. When Malkah goes to the Black Zone, she looks ahead to living out the closing years of her life—now lengthened—with enhanced eyes and who knows what else once the utopian doctors and their nanotech robots have finished with her.

Pulling all this material together, Piercy produces a rich political vision that is compatibly traditional and forward-looking.[16] Growing from the discrete stories of Shira and Yod and the iconic presentation of the entire social paradigm, the coalition (women, Jews, Tikva scientist-designers, Glop workers, the utopian cyborg of the Black Zone, and the tragic android Yod) not only breaks the power of the Y-S corporation but also produces the new conditions for further political gains. Unlike the culturally mediated political developments in Butler's and Robinson's texts, this formation of unity in difference grows out of the socioeconomic conditions and contradictions of the corporate society, even as it is given depth and scope by a larger and longer cultural and political ethos and history. Taken at this register, the counter-narrative represents a challenging pedagogical step against the resigned options of escapist survival or liberal accommodation, and it dialectically works with and through discourse-based micropolitics to a new moment of transformative analysis and action.

But another, overtly utopian step is taken when Malkah takes her sacred trip to the transformed "holy land." In this space that is "off the map," Piercy offers little more than a brief sketch of the utopian future that has been prefigured by Nili (434). She gives just a hint of the potential of this strange place in Malkah's report to Shira of her own physical transformation at the hands of women who are the "strongest . . . in the world" (432). As another formation rising out of historical contradictions, this healed land is the locus of "the new that has come to be under the murderous sun of our century" (433–434). Yet coming as it does at the edges of the narrative, at the horizon of history, it is barely representable, lingering as a nonnarrative, and certainly unfilled, utopian meditation.[17]

As a work of political fiction, *He, She and It* brings historical memory (of the distant and immediate past) and science fictional speculation to bear on a sobering examination of the present reality. As a work of dystopian fiction, it refuses the anti-utopian path and articulates utopian traces within a social order that is still the reserve of corporate powers even after the momentary victory of the alliance. Finally, as a *critical* dystopia, it further provides a self-reflexive meditation on the formal capacity of dystopian narrative to make room for utopian hope, and its most telling self-reflexive gesture occurs in the foregrounding of the formative power of storytelling itself.[18]

Allusions to Jewish, Christian, and secular Western tales of created beings, heroic women, and sacrificial actions recur from beginning to end, and several characters add their own tales to the narrative mix: Gadi creates a compromised form in his stimmies, Yod reads children's books to Ari, the house computer reads the *Zohar* to its residents, Shira relates the story of labor unions to Lazarus, and Nili tells the tale of the Black Zone. Yet it is Malkah's parable of the Golem that offers the most developed, and self-referential, exploration of the role of narrative in the process of social change. Considered as a folktale in itself, it is an effective demonstration of the dynamic relationship between material practices, narrative, and utopian politics; but as a plot device it also demonstrates its interpellative potential in the way Malkah makes use of it to give progressive shape to Yod's identity and character. In the creature's mature actions, the effects of her incremental storytelling are readily seen as Yod not only achieves a degree of self-awareness and a strength of character that enables it to serve its designated people but also allows it to exceed its existing parameters when it rightly destroys itself and its creator.

The text, however, does not simply recognize the use value of storytelling. It also problematizes it in several instances, thereby destabilizing the authority and certainty of the narrative form even as it celebrates it—consequently suggesting a degree of caution to readers, lest enthusiasm overtake wisdom. Several stories are exposed as "false" and are overturned as the major narrative unfolds. Precisely because of its formation by a variety of alternative stories, Yod dispenses with the traditional male valence of fairy tales (in which the prince will always rescue the princess) in the way it understands its developing love for Shira. It assumes a protective role toward her, but only by virtue of the distinctiveness of its attributes and not by a privileged ideological assumption that she is weak and in need of a hierarchically different level of protection (390).[19]

It is with Shira, however, that the narrative deconstruction of accounts is most obvious. The major instance is the overturning of the childhood story Malkah related to Shira, in which she explained that the women in this matrilineal family followed the practice of handing their daughters on to their own mothers so that the child would be raised by her grandmother (13). Once Riva arrives and reveals her version, Malkah admits that her earlier tale was just a strategic fiction and not the truth: "When you were a child, I made up that little myth about our family to explain to you why you were being raised by me instead of your mother" (83). As well, Shira's uncertain and "banal" self-understanding that she had cobbled together after her youthful relationship with Gadi changes radically once she finds love with Yod (130). When she rediscovers a stronger self through her passion for Yod, she casts off the inner narrative she had carried with her since she and Gadi parted as she realizes that the "myth that had governed her emotional life for the last ten years was peeling off like an old mural of two burning children impaled on their love, and the bricks beneath the chipping paint emerged unweathered" (186).

Formative or deconstructive as its manifestations might be in these instances, Piercy clearly identifies storytelling as a powerful discursive force throughout her text. Indeed, the many stories do not just feed the overall counter-narrative (thereby helping to produce a complex way toward Utopia in a narrowly anti-utopian time); for in a deft inversion of postmodern common sense, they also overturn grand narratives—ones, however, that have shaped not the opposition but rather the anti-utopian hegemony itself. Terrible though this alternative future is, global capitalism's triumphant cessation of history does not happen, the U.S. assumption of a leading position in the story of the twenty-first century collapses in the simple disappearance of that apparently solid nation-state, and the official narrative of the Israeli state is radically denied and replaced by multiple alternatives that preserve and transform the best of Jewish and Zionist culture and politics.

In addition to storytelling and demythologizing, Piercy emphasizes the liberating process of learning itself, especially in terms of its relationship to social transformation. Again, the Prague story offers its metacommentary on knowledge and power—not only in the activities of Judah and the Golem but also in the character of Chava, Judah's granddaughter, as she works against the male assumptions in her culture and becomes a scholar who contributes to the defense of the ghetto and to the knowledge base of her culture. As Malkah not surprisingly tells it, hegemonic knowledge (*savoir* in Lefebvre's terms, "instrumental rationality" in the language of the Frankfurt School) is countered by Judah's flexible and adaptable way of knowing and being in the world that proceeds from the conditions and positionality of his people even as it maintains a thoroughly empirical relationship with the material and social world (closer to Lefebvre's sense of critical knowledge, or *connaissance*).

Working with the mysticism of the kabbalah and the new science of Tycho Brahe, Johannes Kepler, and Giordano Bruno, the rabbi provides the exemplary basis for Malkah's assertion that she finds "different kinds of truth valuable" (267), thereby opting for a way to negotiate the limits of power that can move with, through, and beyond its own official discourses. When Malkah considers Judah's admiration for Brahe and Kepler, she makes a point of opposing the emptiness of abstract theory to the value of concrete empirical observation: "Instead of empty theorizing or proceeding from Aristotle, they were making precise and repeated measurements of the movements of the planets and the stars, keeping meticulous records. This was something new in the world, beginning with observation and only then proceeding to theory" (238). But she also invokes Bruno's astute and early problematization of the temptation to empirical universality as she reminds readers of the importance of standpoint in the production and dissemination of knowledge through the words of Judah to Joseph: "The idea you have just postulated resembles the theories of Giordano Bruno, who says that observation and ultimately truth is relative to the position from which we observe" (240).

This internal textual epistemology is connected with the processes of history early on in Malkah's tale when she describes Judah's initial agony over the question of creating the Golem. History and the power relations therein, she notes, produce the occasion for knowledge, and certain moments require certain types of knowledge, especially as they are being marshaled against the existing order of things. As she remarks: "At any moment in history, certain directions are forbidden that lie open to the inquiring mind and the experimental hand. Not always is the knowledge forbidden because dangerous: governments will spend billions on weapons and forbid small sects the peyote of their ecstasy. What we are forbidden to know can be—or seem—what we most need to know" (30). Later, when Judah lays Joseph to rest, this linkage of available or possible knowledge and oppositional power is again emphasized as he observes that historical need, in the form of suffering and fear, can create the conditions for the specific radical knowledge of the Golem's viability. As he tersely puts it, "if knowledge and fearful need are joined, it can be roused to life" (414).[20]

Running through *He, She and It,* therefore, is a self-reflexive demonstration of the power of counter-narrative, critical knowledge, and the role of positionality in both. Oppositional work, of course, must necessarily take place in economic, political, and cultural material practices, but the negation of existing discourse and the production of radical ways of thinking are also vital elements in the oppositional, utopian, project. Within the narrative, therefore, Piercy calls attention to the empowering attributes of the very text she is creating. Privileging the "truth of what is perhaps figurative," reaffirming the power of words to shape and reshape the world, she reinforces the manifest work of her narrative and gives her readers a way to experience the text, and perhaps the world they live in, with a higher level of awareness of the processes of radical knowledge and action.

Thus, Piercy reminds readers of one of the key attributes of critical dystopian narrative even as she writes it. Again putting it in Malkah's voice, she notes that such speculative fictions (with their cognitively estranging qualities, I would add) help to "form the habit of seeing what other people are wont to think is not really there" (29). That is, in political fiction generally—and critical dystopian fiction in this case—the work of the text is potentially subversive, not only in its manifest content but especially in its formal operations. Such texts are capable of changing the minds of their readers, young and old alike, by exposing the false solidity of the world as it is commonsensically lived, by tearing open its sutured normality, and by daring to expose the power that reigns and the possibilities that lurk in the tendencies and latencies of the situation.

The novum of *He, She and It* is consequently to be found not only in its epical account of militant resistance and collective victory but also in its formal demonstration of the processes of unknowing and reknowing that are inspired and advanced by the oppositional imagination. As Judah meditates on the ethics of defending the ghetto and the value of self-determination for his people, he admits that right action takes place in a decidedly imperfect (dystopian) world: "The world is imperfect," he observes, "and requires repair so long as any people is under the rule of any other" (327). Thus, it is the political work of transformative "repair" that Piercy privileges, and the characters who most accomplish it carry the most utopian weight.[21] Hence, Judah, maker of the Golem, and Malkah, teacher of Yod, stand as strong utopian figures in this dystopian text. Both—one in a religious framework, one adamantly secular—possess the dual qualities of activist and contemplative, scientist and mystic. Both point to a form of knowledge and a way of living in the world that is mediated, on the one hand, by the wisdom of the kabbalah with its awareness of the Ein Sof (the "all that is nothingness" so that the richness of the world is based not in fullness of being but on nothingness) and, on the other, by the rigors of a self-reflexive and critical scientific and political praxis (29).

In Piercy's critical dystopia, the present social order is unflinchingly portrayed through the distancing lens of its imagined alternative, but in this case the story of the people who stand up to the corporate order leads to the possibility of an eventual utopian transformation of that order. This is not a certainty, to be sure, since the path of narrative can be realistically traced only by way of its detours, roadblocks, washouts, and switchbacks as much as, or more than, its connection to its designated destination. The social and aesthetic value of such a text therefore lies in the emphasis it places on the process of reaching toward Utopia and on the values and policies required for that process to move in a progressive direction.

As Earnst Bloch would put it, the work of being "on the way" (*unterwegs*) takes precedence over the celebration of arrival. Indeed, the utopian horizon, Bloch's *Heimat,* is importantly just that: the "home" at which we have not yet arrived, the unfilled space at the limits of engaged political vision and practice that recedes as it is approached, the space that substantively informs the present moment but always remains at the front of the journey so that nothing can be taken for granted or frozen in place, so that the effort to achieve the best for all people, in the most self-determined manner, does not stop. Perhaps the realization of the importance of this informed negative process is what underlies the deep urge to dystopia in our time, avoiding the consolations or premature evocations of the fullness of Utopia in favor of privileging the difficult way toward that better place. In this light, it is not Judah or Malkah—or even Nili—that is the most significant utopian figure in *He, She and It.* Rather, it is the one who is not "the future" but the "tool of the future" who is the most evocative character. It is, therefore, Riva, through the very work she does as an organizer, who opens the utopian way, the one who teaches the value of being of use, in the personal and political process of making possible the conditions for the "future that wants to be" (421).

10

Horizons

Fifth is the race that I call my own and abhor.
O to die, or be later born, or born before!
This is the Race of Iron. Dark is their plight.
Toil and sorrow is theirs, and by night
The anguish of death and the gods afflict them and kill,
Though there's yet a trifle of good amid manifold ill.

—Hesiod, "Works and Days"

The only authentic image of the future is, in the end, the failure of the present.

—Terry Eagleton, "Utopia and Its Opposites" (36)

I.

Well before the neologisms that grew from the textual inventions of modernity, the world had been home to enough hunger, oppression, violence, suffering, and destruction to warrant creative and critical responses that opposed things as they were and tried as well to imagine a better way. Facing the horrors of his society in the eighth century B.C.E., Hesiod creates the image of a Golden Age in which humanity "lived like gods and . . . feasted gaily."[1] But to set the comparative stage for this imagined era of "all good things" in which no "sorrow of heart" was felt, he brings what was outside his door into his text to evoke the "toil and sorrow" and "anguish of death" that beset the people of his time and produce the desire for that better, even golden life. Although the manifest chronology of the poem implies the primacy of the Golden Age, with the "fifth race" of his own time following sadly behind, the "plight" of the moment is the condition that catalyzes the poet's social dream. By naming the evils of his existing reality and suggesting their distance from the originary time of "landed ease," Hesiod does not mobilize what would be later called an anti-utopian rebuttal to his proto-utopia, but in an estranging twist of chronology, he pulls the imaginary of a previously better place into the awful reality that surrounds him. Read this way, the "trifle of good amid the manifold ill" becomes not a fading echo or repudiation of the Golden Age but the nonsynchronous germ of an idea that people could not only wish for but perhaps one day produce a decidedly better life for themselves, in a time to come, when it was "later born."

Krishan Kumar might be right in his characterization of the "mocking, contrary, echo" of Anti-Utopia as it stalks Utopia, yet there is always the material situation that precedes and informs the conflict of this antinomic pair, for the whole contest of Utopia and Anti-Utopia rests upon the cold substance of a world that has never known a Golden Age, never discovered a Garden of Eden or a Blessed Isle.[2] It may be banal to assert, but it is also politically wise to remember that Utopia begins with the contradictions of life as we live it and not with memories of good times gone or guarantees of perfection ahead. Humanity never fell. We have always been here, in this vale of tears, in history itself. The hard times have been with us all along and will, as the song goes, come around again.

Yet we also seem to be always on the way to something better. Over and over, people have fought their gods and rulers and at least tried to transform their contradictory social reality. Although that struggle is immersed in material conditions and possibilities, the radical imagination also plays its part as it contributes other ways of looking at, through, and beyond the ills that exist. As with Hesiod, and so many others around the globe and throughout history, social dreams continue to rise to oppressive occasions and rekindle the process of finding how a way forward might be possible, of producing not a plan nor a path but rather a sense of how a path might fruitfully be imagined and created, step by resistant and hopeful step.

In this transformative praxis, Utopia, not Anti-Utopia, is the first negative step. Writing at the end of the twentieth century, Terry Eagleton recalls that authentic "utopia is . . . at the same time dystopia, since it cannot help reminding us of how we are bound fast by history in the very act of trying to set us free from that bondage."[3] Marx knew—and Ernst Bloch extensively demonstrated—that a "utopian" gesture is of no use to anyone but the powers that be if it does not recognize that its hopeful journey begins in refusing the bondage of the present. To slip out of the grip of the real world and merely posit some ideal alternative is to indulge in an abstract utopianism that lapses into nothing more than a debilitating distraction from present terrors and a displacement of the concrete hope that humankind might do something to end them; for if the transformed future generated by a utopian expression is not "anchored in the present, it quickly becomes a fetish," one that serves no one but those who are on top of the social order (Eagleton, "Utopia and Its Opposites" 34). Only by working within, and with, the tendencies and latencies of the world as it stands will the utopian impulse usefully do anything in the name of justice and freedom. Only by looking at what exists and exploring how crises can be segued into changes will the utopian imagination enter into its subversive and transformative work.

As Fredric Jameson has so strongly and extensively argued, however, Utopia's labor is first and foremost a formal task, a self-demonstrating engagement in the process of cognitively mapping the coordinates of the present in order to suggest in the act of doing so that a self-aware, self-critical move against and out of that reality can happen—once humanity has suffered to the point that it says "enough." Yet Peter Fitting and others additionally argue that the manifest content of utopian expression has its own job to do in stimulating that transformative process, as it disturbs settled ways of seeing with specific, albeit provocatively debatable images and designs for different forms of knowing and living.[4] Impoverished and even deleterious as utopian matter may be, as Ruth Levitas holds, the thought experiments of Utopia help to mobilize "human energy in pursuit of the real-possible future" that a given utopian alternative represents.[5]

The negative vocation of Utopia is therefore a threat to any established system that reigns by way of keeping its population in thrall by exploitation and oppression, consensus and coercion. Privileged power and concentrated profit have been placed again and again above the interests of humanity, but Utopia's counterfactual interventions—eponymously but not exclusively in Western modernity—have been a crucial part of the long fight to overturn those dominating and exploiting actions, to challenge the instrumentality of the socioeconomic system with critical and creative attitudes that seek something more than the bottom line or the pinnacle of power.[6] It is no wonder that the substantial imaginative resources of hegemonic orders have always drawn on the capability of Anti-Utopia to stalk, to search and destroy, all manifestations of Utopia wherever and whenever it can. As Lyman Tower Sargent has argued, the second order of negation carried out by anti-utopian expressions attacks as needed: one time denying Utopia, another co-opting it, yet another finding gaps and faults and evacuating its validity by designating it as useless or escapist (see "Three Faces Revisited").

Whether by extermination, colonization, or delegitimation, Anti-Utopia has stood fast in its assignment to defeat Utopia; and in the economic, political, and cultural turn to the Right since the 1980s, this conserving and restricting force has especially raised its status and intensified its effect. It is not surprising, therefore, that Utopia has fought back against the matrix of transnational capital, superpower force, and consuming culture by confronting the anti-utopian machinery of that complex through the critical utopian practices of aesthetic, theoretical, and political self-critique. Nor is it any more surprising that Utopia also found another channel in the complementary dystopian mode. More cunning as the century moved on, the utopian imagination has often shifted down to its dystopian gear and dared to dream not in already improved elsewheres but rather in decidedly worse re-visions of reality in order to bring readers and viewers into a hopeful reorientation by confronting and possibly breaking through the conditions it portrays.

The dystopian maneuver has therefore kept utopian hope alive by exposing the authoritarian state and the capitalist economy but also by taking on the compromises and weaknesses found within utopian dreaming and actual opposition—refusing the temptation to move quickly to a restful refuge (in one's own garden, by the riverside trees, or in some solipsistic cul-de-sac) and to forget the need for collective action, even in and after whatever it is that passes for the revolutionary moment or era.

Although both Jack London (in *The Iron Heel*) and William Morris (in *News from Nowhere*) began their narratives of alternative futures in settings based in their own contemporary societies (the United States and Britain), Morris took his readers into a eutopian society based in a successful political struggle, whereas London pulled his audience into a proto-fascist proto-dystopia that saw the defeat of the socialist movement and held out hope of a triumphant revolution only in some not yet achieved future. London's cautionary parable (written in 1908, compared to 1890 for Morris's tale) brought the shadowy side of utopian expression to the brink of dystopian narrative. But with E.M. Forster, Yevgeny Zamyatin, and the others, the classical dystopias set aside that initial realist gesture and developed narratives and counter-narratives directly within iconically detailed elsewheres that were worse than the social realities in which the authors and their readers lived but that nevertheless grew from those situations. Moving beyond the conventions of the classical dystopia, the popular imagination of sf offered a further- and wider-reaching arena for the dystopian imagination, especially in the postwar maps of hell. And then the critical dystopian vision of the 1980s and 1990s took a hard look at the bad new times of contemporary enclosure and, within a sober apprehension of the intensified exploitation and deprivation, endeavored to find traces, scraps, and sometimes horizons of utopian possibility.

II.

> *How exquisitely human was the wish for permanent happiness, and how thin human imagination became trying to achieve it. . . . How can they hold it together, he wondered, this hard-won heaven defined only by the absence of the unsaved, the unworthy and the strange?*
>
> —Toni Morrison, *Paradise* (306)

> *Now we have spaces to get through colder even than Antarctica; the timespace of human history, and our life together in these overshoot years. There are more people on this planet than the planet can hold, and how we act now will shape much of the next thousand years, for good or ill. It is a bottleneck in history; the age beyond carrying capacity; the overshoot years; the voyage in an open boat, weighted down beyond its Plimsoll line. There is a possibility for very great tragedy, the greatest ever known.*
>
> —Kim Stanley Robinson, *Antarctica* (463)

Running through analytic discourse and imaginative texts, a new political structure of feeling emerged as the old century ended and the next one began.[7] As I have argued in the previous pages, sf offers one potential source for the anticipation and articulation of this oppositional position-in-formation, and its formal capacity to produce an estranged perspective on the historical moment has once again led to texts that can, as Darko Suvin puts it, rearrange "the categories that shape our experience" (*Positions* 189). Thus, with the dystopian fiction and films of the past several years, fresh "parables" of possibility offer representations of the social system and narrative negotiations with and beyond that system. In works such as Robinson's *Gold Coast,* Butler's *Parable of the Sower,* and Piercy's *He, She and It,* this dystopian strategy has found an effective outlet. Although all three texts isolate, magnify, and cognitively challenge the brutal social conditions of the late twentieth century, each develops a particular utopian response not only to the historical situation but also to the self-satisfied anti-utopian refusal to challenge that reality. Each calls attention to processes of cognitive mapping and consciousness-raising that turn the dystopias away from the inherent temptation to settle for the static pessimism of Anti-Utopia. By means of their creative speculation, these hopeful texts help to revive and expand the popular political imagination in the name of progressive transformation. They offer the prophetic challenge to go and do likewise, to become aware and fight back, possibly in a world that is not (yet) as bad as the one on their pages.

Where the dystopian imagination will wander in the twenty-first century is, of course, not evident. But two works of the late 1990s give indications of possible directions. One leans toward history and the other to science, yet both develop dystopian explorations within a recognizably contemporary society, one in the present, the other just a bit in the future, and both give credence to Raffaella Baccolini's argument that the technique of genre blurring is a central formal element in their parables of hell (see "Gender and Genre"). Coming from outside the realm of sf and utopian fiction, Toni Morrison has written what could be regarded as a "realist dystopia" in her 1998 novel, *Paradise*.[8] Marked by the notable dates of 1968 and 1976 (and drawing on a historical archive that runs from the horrors of slavery and Reconstruction, through war veterans' dreams of the 1940s and activists' hopes of the 1960s, and then to the mendacity of the 1990s), her narrative turns around two local spaces that together and separately incorporate utopian and dystopian qualities: the Convent, which evolves as a refuge for women battered by men in particular and society in general, and the town of Ruby, founded by black veterans seeking a new and safer home for their families in Oklahoma after World War II (and doing so with the historical memory of the path taken in the same territory during Reconstruction).

In the actions and interactions of these communities—which are further enclosed by the never-ending institutional racism of the entire American reality—Morrison explores the tensions and possibilities that surround, inform, and mercilessly attack the everyday desire for a world no longer filled with injustice. On the one hand, the Convent begins as a derelict space, but it is reclaimed over the years by the women who drift in and evolve in their daily lives another, nearly utopian way of living; on the other, the town of Ruby (founded, for the second time, in 1950) begins as an intentional community that opted for Utopia by stepping away from the systemic racism of postwar society. Whereas the women of the Convent remain radically open to all who come to their door and extend utopian hope without articulating it, the citizens of Ruby—their male leaders especially—close in on themselves and reduce their enclave to a cruel "utopian" caricature that in the course of the novel turns into an outright dystopia. *Paradise* therefore names no pristine utopian space, but it does look with great pain and yet sensitivity at the implosion and destruction of utopian dreams as well as the traces of utopian possibilities in an all too typically violated and violent situation. Clearly dystopian in form yet hopeful in spirit, Morrison's mainstream novel moves beyond the dystopia as it has previously been written and in doing so opens a new space for a creatively utopian negativity.

In *Antarctica,* also published in 1998, Kim Stanley Robinson continues to develop the dystopian imaginary within the realm of sf, but he does so with a text that draws on elements of the mystery novel, travel adventure, scientific discourse, constitutional discourse, spiritual discourse, and poetry.[9] Set in the very near future, in the "elsewhere" of Antarctica, Robinson's text begins with a tone of "normality" that is initially as disconcerting as that found in *The Gold Coast*. In this estranged place that is not some other time or place but is like "nothing on Earth," Robinson develops an iconic account that exposes economic and political exploitation and a counter-narrative that details the gradual building of an oppositional alliance that includes local scientists, technicians, artists, tour guides, labor leaders, and feral "Transantarctic" citizens, as well as global eco-activists and scientists, bureaucrats, and politicians from the higher echelons of the remaining world superpower (*Antarctica* 2).

Through the work of this broad alliance, Antarctica is liberated and named "its own place" (protected by a constitution embodied in the "Antarctic Treaty" that intertextually recalls the utopian constitutions and ideal commonwealths of earlier centuries). But in becoming a model of "structured cooperation" (echoing and paralleling, as Robinson suggests, the evolving traditions of China), the new Antarctica also stands as a utopian alternative for the entire planet (*Antarctica* 443, 465, 468). As the constitutional document reads and as the independent scientist Carlos asserts, "whatever is true in Antarctica is also true everywhere else" (*Antarctica* 468, 491). Here the formal work of cognitive estrangement takes shape in the very content of Robinson's text, as the "other world" is presented, legally as well as metaphorically, as an analog (and in this case a eutopian one) for the rest of reality.

Offering a horizon at best, a negativity at least, the critical utopian imagination in the years to come may well continue to take shape in these new dystopian tendencies. Even Robinson's major utopian work, the Martian trilogy, grows, as did London's proto-dystopia, from the present oppressive moment into a near future that sets an initial dystopian base for the winding and critical utopian road of *Antarctica*—which Jameson surmises may be "the great political novel of the 1990s."[10] By staying within the terror of a social order that encloses and denies all alternatives, new forms of dystopian expression may continue to help us get out of where we are by first interrogating that actual reality and then, only through its negation, opening up to other ways of being. In works such as those by Morrison and Robinson, dystopia's fantastic machinery might well be the most realistic thing going, for it not only catches the way things are but also searches for and traces the tendencies that can lead to Utopia's mobilization of a better way.

III.

It is necessary to build a new world, a world capable of containing many worlds, capable of containing all worlds.

—Subcommandante Marcos

> *Today, the police in Seattle have proved they are the handmaidens of the corporations. . . . But something else has been proved. And that's that people are starting to stand up and say: we won't be transnational victims.*
>
> —Dave Brower[11]

In his introduction to a special issue of *Race and Class*, "The Threat of Globalism," John Berger brings the work of the dystopian imagination directly into the realm of political engagement as he frames the set of essays by way of two texts: *Millennium Triptych*, the early-sixteenth-century painting by Hieronymous Bosch, and "Letter to the World," the 1997 message distributed through the Internet by Subcomandante Marcos, the leader of the Zapatista political movement (Emiliano Zapata Liberation Front) based in Chiapas, Mexico.[12] Comfortably occupying the intersection of the artistic and political, Berger works from both textual artifacts to make his own contribution to the journal's interrogation of contemporary capitalism. He first focuses his attention on the third panel of that triptych from the dawn of modernity, and he argues that Bosch's depiction of Hell "has become a strange prophecy of the mental climate imposed on the world, at the end of our century, by globalisation and the new economic order" (Berger 1).

He notes that Bosch drew his symbols from the "secret, proverbial, heretical language of certain fifteenth-century millennial sects, who heretically believed that, if evil could be overcome, it was possible to build heaven on earth," thus locating the painting within what soon emerges as the discursive tradition of utopian (and later dystopian) expression. He further emphasizes that the strength of the work lies "not so much in the details—haunting and grotesque as they are—but in the whole . . . in what constitutes the space of hell" (Berger 1). This is a totalized space without horizon, continuity, past, or future, where "the clamour of the disparate, fragmentary present" resounds. Yet in this "spatial delirium" he recognizes what Bloch would term a nonsynchronous anticipation of an economic order that works to secure the "concentration of global wealth in fewer and fewer hands," doing so at the expense of "the unprecedented extension of hopeless poverties," with a "barbarism . . . unchecked by any opposing ethical consideration or principle" (Berger 1, 2).[13]

Faced with this powerfully negative image and the world system it prefigures, Berger refuses the tempting compensations of anti-utopian cynicism or despair (or even reformist accommodation) and turns instead to the utopian hope embodied in Subcomandante Marcos's letter (a text that also metonymically affirms the strategies and tactics of the Zapatistas as they continue to work on multiple levels of engagement within and without the existing social reality). In this message to the world from Chiapas, Berger finds not only a sound assessment of the present capitalist order but also evidence that all critique has not been suppressed nor all organized resistance crushed. Marcos, of course, pulls no punches as he describes the world situation in terms of a new "Fourth World War." As Berger summarizes:

> The aim of the belligerents is the conquest of the entire world through the market. The arsenals are financial; there are nevertheless millions of people being maimed or killed every moment. The aim of those waging the war is to rule the world from new, abstract power centres—megapoles of the market, which will be subject to no control except that of the logic of investment. Meanwhile, nine-tenths of the women and men living on the planet live with the jagged pieces which do not fit. (Berger 2)

In response, he draws a political line in the sand and points to "various pockets of resistance against the new order which are developing across the globe" (Berger 3). The Zapatistas are just one such enclave, mixing armed struggle, grassroots organizing, and systemic intervention with regional and worldwide education and organizing through the Internet; others work through a variety of strategies and tactics, which because of their promising heterogeneity cannot be entirely stopped by the repression or discipline of the new corporate order. Although he acknowledges that such diverse formations still lack a common political program, he notes that they minimally share a "defence of the redundant, the next-to-be-eliminated, and [a] belief that the Fourth World War is a crime against humanity" (Berger 3). Certainly more needs to be done, for greater commonality of purpose and vision, albeit based in epistemic and political diversity, must lead not only to critique and resistance but ultimately to a transformation of the entire social order. And yet that "new world . . . capable of containing many worlds, capable of containing all worlds" that Marcos calls us all to build can only begin to emerge from these critically utopian pockets of resistance.

Bosch's painting therefore supplies a counterfactual image to hold up to the ideological "world-picture implanted in our minds." It is an image that prophetically exposes "all the false promises used everywhere to justify and idealise the delinquent and insatiable need to sell" (Berger 4). Within this moment of dystopian negation, Berger, like the critical dystopian writers, recognizes that a "horizon has to be discovered," and he locates that new space of possibility in the realization of radical hope based in the concrete actions of resistance movements. Replicating the logic of the dystopian mode, he argues that the next utopian step needs to begin with representing, exposing, and neutralizing the existing world picture, for when "hell is denounced from within, it ceases to be hell" (Berger 4). Only then can humanity articulate other ways of seeing and acting. Moving on from Bosch's image of Hell, Berger reminds his readers that the other two panels of the triptych (*The Garden of Eden* and *The Garden of Earthly Delights*) can iconically point toward utopian desires and alternatives that for now, at least, will only "be studied by torchlight in the dark" (Berger 4).[14]

In Berger's commentary the dystopian imagination appears alive and well within the oppositional political imaginary. Perhaps, then, it is best to end this journey through the radical elsewheres of sf, utopian, and dystopian discourse by recalling an event in the last month of the twentieth century that Berger would no doubt see as a sign of new and renewed struggle and that Bloch would identify as a concrete utopian moment: namely, the demonstrations by the growing anti-capitalist coalition of human rights, environmental, and labor activists at the World Trade Organization (WTO) meeting in Seattle, Washington. In his firsthand "Seattle Diary," Jeffrey St. Clair delivers one of many narratives in print, on video, and on the Internet that track the confrontation that took place at the end of November and the beginning of December 1999.[15] In his report it is clear that activists from around the globe came to Seattle to give militant shape to utopian demands in their resounding attack on the policies and practices of the World Trade Organization, the "Star Chamber for global capitalists" (St. Clair 81).

Facing the unseen power of corporate and national leaders and the inescapable force of the Seattle police, this "insurgency from below" came out in larger numbers than even their organizers anticipated and succeeded in achieving their immediate objectives. Standing up to the state apparatus, the activists survived "sustained clouds of tear gas, volleys of rubber bullets, concussion grenades, high-powered bean cannons and straightforward beatings with riot batons" and continued to function despite "targeted" arrests of their "command-and-control" personnel: "people with cellphones, bullhorns, the known faces and suspected organizers, medics and legal observers" (St. Clair 85–86, 90). Aware of the traps of political instrumentalization, they also resisted the betrayals of liberal sellouts and co-optation (St. Clair 85–86, 90). As St. Clair summarizes, between November 28 and December 2, the allied demonstrators accomplished the following no doubt modest but significant oppositional actions:

shut down the opening ceremony;
prevented Clinton from addressing the WTO delegates at the Wednesday night gala;

turned the corporate press from prim denunciations of "mindless anarchy" to bitter criticisms of police brutality;
forced the WTO to cancel its closing ceremonies and to adjourn in disorder and confusion, without an agenda for the next round. (St. Clair 96)

More so, they achieved a farther-reaching, and perhaps longer-lasting, impact as they sent out the message of the form and substance of their oppositional action to the entire world (St. Clair 96).

In this complex political event, the causes of human rights, labor, and the environment were briefly linked in a common political structure of feeling and a common strategy of direct action. Taken as a new developing movement, this emergent coalition represents a significant move beyond the moment noted in Berger's already hopeful account, for it clearly marks an end to the period of isolated social movements and micropolitics and the beginning of a diverse and democratic but strongly allied international movement with clear local roots. In the Seattle streets, union members and eco-warriors, AIDS activists and indigenous peoples, community organizers and policy researchers came together. Their use of traditional political forms such as speeches, mass demonstrations, and civil disobedience was enhanced by the telecommunications practices of instantaneous Webcasting (achieved by mobile phones, laptop computers, and digital cameras) to mount a protest that was simultaneously local and global as the images, sounds, and analyses of the action circulated on the Web faster than the word on the streets or the coverage by broadcast television or radio. Albeit adamantly decentralized, the new coalition acted with a degree of solidarity not seen for decades, and their maneuvers bode well for further and more organized and focused movements against powers.

The WTO demonstrations therefore exemplify the developing opposition that Berger writes of and that the critical dystopias explore and prefigure. Hopefully, they represent the potential for a larger and more developed movement that could intensify in numbers, strength, and scope—especially as the economic, ecological, and cultural agendas of the present order are rendered more transparent by organized action and critical studies, as labor organizers and social movement activists begin to communicate with something other than mutual suspicion, as local campaigners and global movements come to share a common ground of analysis and opposition, and as people who value "universal" declarations of human rights or the specificities of human fulfillment learn to see that such goals can be reached only by acknowledging an economic, political, and cultural commonality that is based in the sheer difference and diversity of people around the globe. While they do so, it is important to note that such possibilities (whether in the extensive work of the Zapatistas, the anti-WTO alliance, or any number of other enclaves, formations, parties, and movements) are not about "managing" the crisis within the present social order (by merely "petitioning" for amelioration or reforms) but rather involve deeply critiquing all that exists in the service of effecting a systemic transformation. How such diverse movements can or will connect up in the next steps of challenge and change within and without state and corporate systems is, of course, still a matter of what is to be done.[16]

Yet if faced with the results of the actions in Seattle, hearing the words of Marcos, or seeing new coalitions developing around the globe, the likes of Riva would be delighted. If she had been part of the "five days that shook the world in Seattle," she would have jumped on the bus as soon as the demo was over, on her way to help organize the next step.

Notes

Preface

1. When I refer to the historical antinomies of Utopia and Anti-Utopia, I use uppercase. When I refer to specific instances of utopian expression (texts or social practices), I use lowercase. The textual forms of Utopia, therefore, are the utopia (or eutopia), dystopia, and critical utopia. The textual form of Anti-Utopia is the anti-utopia.

2. This next political step needs to build dialectically on the theoretical and organizational gains of the social movements of the 1980s. However much it is time for a new stage of local and global alliance politics, that emerging strategy can only move forward if it is self-reflexively based in the broad and international commitment to the diversity and democracy that was advocated and seized in the previous years; for an incisive articulation of this position, see Anuradha Dingwaney and Lawrence Needham, "The Difference That Difference Makes," *Socialist Review* (1996), 5–47.

3. On the "bad soul" of sf, see Darko Suvin, "Afterword: With Sober, Estranged Eyes," *Learning from Other Worlds: Estrangement, Cognition and the Politics of Science Fiction and Utopia* (2000).

4. An extended study of the official ideological work of sf is a very different project from this one. For now, however, see H. Bruce Franklin, *War Stars* (1988); Constance Penley, *NASA/Trek: Popular Science and Sex in America* (1997); Carol Stabile, *Feminism and the Technological Fix* (1994). In their studies of the military (Franklin), the space program (Penley), and reproductive science (Stabile), these cultural critics have adduced some of the ways in which the sf imaginary is mobilized within official discourses to produce and reproduce hegemonic institutions and practices. For a creative take on the power of the sf imaginary in the mainstream consciousness, see William Gibson, "The Gernsback Continuum," *Mirrorshades: The Cyberpunk Anthology* (1988), 1–11.

Chapter 1

1. See Bruno Latour and Steve Woolgar, *Laboratory Life: The Social Construction of Scientific Facts* (1986). I am grateful to my research assistant, Donna Messner, for making this

connection. As she puts it: "In their study of the daily activities of scientists in a research laboratory, Latour and Woolgar adopted an attitude of 'anthropological strangeness' (40), treating the laboratory as a remote culture. In so doing, they hoped to 'apprehend as strange those aspects of scientific activity which are readily taken for granted' (29), and to integrate these familiar-but-estranged practices with unfamiliar ones into 'some kind of a systematic, ordered account' no matter 'how confused or absurd the circumstances and activities' might seem (43)."

2. See Michael Taussig, *Shamanism, Colonialism, and the Wild Man* (1987), 393.

3. See Joanna Russ, "Towards an Aesthetic of Science Fiction," *To Write Like a Woman* (1995), 3–14; Marc Angenot, "The Absent Paradigm: An Introduction to the Semiotics of Science Fiction," *Science-Fiction Studies* (1979), 9–20. On didactic literature's vocation to teach and delight, see Horace, *Ars Poetica,* and Fredric Jameson, *Brecht and Method* (1998).

4. Pamela Annas describes how a sf text envisions a world "which comments on our own" in "New Worlds, New Words: Androgyny in Feminist Science Fiction," *Science-Fiction Studies* (1978), 143–156. She writes of sf's imaginative use of the scientific method in which one or more variables are tested and manipulated to perform an experiment with the "laboratory of the text" that "leads back to this world" (143). On sf's "thought experiments," see Fredric Jameson, "World-Reduction in Le Guin: The Emergence of Utopian Narrative," *Science-Fiction Studies* (1975), 221–230; see also Peter Fitting, "Recent Feminist Utopias: World Building and Strategies for Social Change," *Mindscapes* (1989), 155–163.

5. On teaching sf, see Beverly Friend, "Strange Bedfellows: Science Fiction, Linguistics, and Education," *English Journal* (1973), 998–1003; Charles Elkins and Darko Suvin, "Preliminary Reflections on Teaching Science Fiction Critically," *Science-Fiction Studies* (1976), 263–270; E. E. Nunan and David Homer, "Science Fiction and Teaching: Science, Science Fiction, and a Radical Science Education," *Science-Fiction Studies* (1981), 311–330; and the discussions in the Science Fiction Research Association *Newsletter*. See Chapter 2, n. 23.

6. A good example of how sf's conceptual stretch can challenge readers is Stanislaus Lem's *Solaris*. In this case it's a matter of setting aside or deferring familiar anthropomorphic categories when confronting the radical otherness of the sentient ocean; see also the trans- and posthuman sf of Olaf Stapledon, such as *Last and First Men: A Story of the Near and Far Future* (1930).

7. Delany's position on the sf reading process is well stated in "Reading Modern American Science Fiction," *American Writing Today* (1991), 517–528. Therein he notes how highly capable readers have difficulty with sf texts. Although he tends to attribute that blockage to the language of sf, he also sees that inexperienced readers miss the formal relationship involving the alternative world, the text on the page, and the reading process. As he puts it, such "readers, used to the given world of mundane fiction, tend to overlay the *fabulata* . . . of science fiction on top of that given world and see only confusion. They do not yet know the particular syntactical rules by which these *fabulata* replace, displace, and reorganize the elements of the mundane world *into new worlds*. All the practice they have had in locating specific areas of the given world that mundane fiction deals with has given

them no practice at all in creating imaginative alternatives" ("Reading" 524–525). See also Delany's essay "Science Fiction and 'Literature'—or, The Conscience of the King," *Visions of Wonder: The Science Fiction Research Association Anthology* (1996), 442–458. The best source for his analysis of the operations of the actual sentences and words of the sf text is "The Semiology of Silence," *Science-Fiction Studies* (1987), 134–165.

8. Such critical knowledge is what Henri Lefebvre speaks of when he opposes it to the official knowledge of hegemonic systems; see *The Production of Space* (1991), 10, 44, 367–368. As he puts it: "Hegemony implies more than an influence, more even than the permanent use of repressive violence. It is exercised over society as a whole, culture and knowledge included, and generally via human mediation: policies, political leaders, parties, as also a good many intellectuals and experts. It is exercised, therefore, over both institutions and ideas. The ruling class seeks to maintain its hegemony by all available means, and knowledge is one such means. The connection between knowledge (*savoir*) and power is thus made manifest, although this in no way interdicts a critical and subversive form of knowledge (*connaissance*); on the contrary, it points up the antagonism between a knowledge which serves power and a form of knowing which refuses to acknowledge power" (*Production of Space* 10). On dangerous knowledge, as articulated within liberation theology, see Tom Moylan, "Denunciation/Annunciation: The Radical Methodology of Liberation Theology," *Cultural Critique* (1992), 33–65.

9. Edward James, *Science Fiction in the 20th Century* (1994), 95.

10. In a discussion of Bloch's account of the role of reader/critic (that is suited to the "work" of the sf/utopian reader), Jack Zipes puts it this way: "[the work of art] demands that we become detective-critics in our appreciation and evaluation of such works. It is up to us to determine what the anticipatory illumination [Bloch's concept of *Vor-Schein*] of a work is, and in doing this we make a contribution to the [unfulfilled and therefore radical] cultural heritage. That is, the quality of our cultural heritage and its meaning are determined by our ability to estimate what is valuable and utopian in works of art from all periods"; see Zipes's introduction to *The Utopian Function of Art and Literature: Selected Essays of Ernst Bloch* (1988), xxxvi. See also Tim Dayton, "The Mystery of Pre-history: Ernst Bloch and Crime Fiction," *Not Yet: Reconsidering Ernst Bloch* (1997), 186–201.

11. James quotes sf editor and publisher David Hartwell to describe the understanding sf readers have of their favored mode of fiction: "A sense of wonder, awe at the vastness of space and time, is at the root of the excitement of science fiction. Any child who has looked up at the stars at night and thought about how far away they are, how there is no end or outer edge to this place, this universe—any child who has felt the thrill of fear and excitement at such thoughts stands a very good chance of becoming a science fiction reader" (quoted in *20th Century* 105). On sf fans as readers, see Chapter 2, n. 12.

12. James draws on the work of Romanian critic Cornel Robu in making this connection (see *20th Century* 104–105). This narrative sense of wonder can also be found—albeit, more problematically—in one of the precursors of sf: the travel literature of Western conquest and colonization; see Stephen Greenblatt, *Marvelous Possession: The Wonder of the New World* (1991); and Denise Albanese, *New Science, New World* (1996).

13. James quotes Tom Shippey's discussion of the pleasures of *unpredictability* in reading sf: "The science fiction reader, of course, *likes* this feeling of unpredictability. It creates intense curiosity, as well as the pleasure of working out, in the long run, the logic underlying the author's decisions, vocabulary and invented world. It is a powerful stimulus to the exercise of 'cognition,' of putting unknown data into some sort of mental holding tank, to see if and when they do start to fit together, and what happens when they do. Yet this experience is in a sense a deeply 'anxious' one" (quoted in *20th Century* 120). See Shippey, "Learning to Read Science Fiction," *Fictional Space: Essays on Contemporary Science Fiction* (1991).

14. Teresa de Lauretis, "A Sense of Wa/onder," *The Technological Imagination: Theories and Fictions* (1980), 159–174.

15. Darko Suvin, "SF and the Novum," *Metamorphoses of Science Fiction: On the Poetics and History of a Literary Genre* (1979), 71.

16. Samuel R. Delany, "Some Reflections on SF Criticism," *Science-Fiction Studies* (1981), 235. The aspect of the sf reading protocol that Delany highlights in this essay is precisely the "alternative workings of the world in which the characters maneuver" ("Some Reflections" 236).

17. On sf/utopian reading practices, see Kenneth M. Roemer, "Perceptual Origins: Preparing Readers to See Utopian Fiction," *Utopian Thought in American Literature* (1988), 7–24; "The Literary Domestication of Utopia," *American Transcendental Quarterly* (1989), 101–122; "Getting 'Nowhere' Beyond Stasis," *Looking Backward, 1988–1888* (1988), 126–146; and his review of Ruppert (below), "Prescriptions for Readers (and Writers) of Utopias," *Science-Fiction Studies* (1988), 88–94. See also Peter Ruppert, *Reader in a Strange Land: The Activity of Reading Literary Utopias* (1986). Working from Wolfgang Iser's studies, Ruppert argues for a "dialectical" method of reading utopias (both traditional and recent) that requires the reader to "engage the terms of the text's dialectic in an inquiry that becomes her own"; for in "actively questioning the formulations provided by the text, the reader participates more fully in a reading that becomes an unfolding of the terms of the dialectic—a dialectic embedded not just in the text but in the social realities with which the text is concerned" (23). For a historical materialist analysis of this dialectical reading process, see Darko Suvin, "Locus, Horizon, and Orientation: The Concept of Possible Worlds as a Key to Utopian Studies," *Not Yet* (1997), 122–137. For more on reading sf, see Marleen Barr, "'The *Females* Do the Fathering!': James Tiptree's Male Matriarchs and Adult Human Gametes," *Science-Fiction Studies* (1986), 42–49; Martha Bartter, "The (Science Fiction) Reader and the Quantum Paradigm: Problems in Delany's *Stars in My Pockets Like Grains of Sand*," *Science-Fiction Studies* (1990), 325–340; Damian Broderick, "Reading SF as a Mega-Text," *New York Review of Science Fiction* (1992), 1, 8–10; Charles A. Ferguson, "Devotional Reading and Science Fiction: The Medieval Saint's Life as a Form of Discourse," *Language in Global Perspective* (1986), 113–122; Lee Cullen Khanna, "The Reader in *Looking Backward*," *Journal of General Education* (1981), 69–79; William Ferdinand Touponce, *Ray Bradbury and the Poetics of Reverie: A Study of Fantasy, Science Fiction, and the Reading Process* (1981). On the related issue of sf fandom and reading, see Chapter 2, n. 12.

18. Joanna Russ, "When It Changed," *Science Fiction: The Science Fiction Research Association Anthology* (1988), 411–418. For a range of criticism on "When It Changed," see Bülent Somay, "Towards an Open-Ended Utopia," *Science-Fiction Studies* (1984); Marleen Barr, "Science Fiction's Invisible Female Man: Feminism, Formula, Word, and World in 'When It Changed' and 'The Women Men Don't See,'" *Just the Other Day: Essays on the Suture of the Future* (1985), 433–437; Donna Perry, "Joanna Russ," *Backtalk: Woman Writers Speak Out* (1993), 287–311; Zoreda M. Lee, "Anglophone Popular Culture in the Mexican University English Curriculum," *Journal of Popular Culture* (1996), 103–114. For the most recent SFRA anthology, see David Hartwell and Milton T. Wolf, eds., *Visions of Wonder: The Science Fiction Research Association Anthology* (1996).

19. In *The Female Man* (1975), the women of the utopian future do not lose, and the loss of the men in the colony is explained in two very different versions. In one the men are said to have died from plague, but in the other they are reported to have been killed by the women in a successful uprising. As well, the struggle of women against the structural power of male privilege (Russ avoids an essentialist position against individual men) does not come down to the punctum of a single invasion and resistance but spreads throughout linear time and alternate universes as female genotypes in parallel realities (like their counterparts in so many liberation movements) carry on the now military, now cultural-political war against the ruling power, whether in the battle zone of Manland or in the U.S. society of the 1960s. As the book ends, a coalition of representative women have joined forces for yet another campaign. On the critical utopia, see Chapter 3.

20. James Tiptree Jr. [Alice Sheldon], "Houston, Houston, Do You Read?" *The Science Fiction Research Association Anthology*, 434–476. For the author's comments, see Alice Sheldon, "A Woman Writing Science Fiction and Fantasy," *Women of Vision* (1988), 43–58. For a range of criticism on "Houston, Houston," see Lowry Pei, "Poor Singletons: Definitions of Humanity in the Stories of James Tiptree, Jr.," *Science-Fiction Studies* (1979), 271–280; Joanna Russ, "Women and SF: Three Letters," *Science-Fiction Studies* (1980), 232–233; Adam Frisch, "Toward New Sexual Identities: James Tiptree, Jr.," *In the Feminine Eye: Science Fiction and the Women Who Write It* (1982), 48–59; Lillian M. Heldreth, "'Love Is the Plan, the Plan Is Death': The Feminism and Fatalism of James Tiptree, Jr.," *Extrapolation* (1982), 22–30; Anne K. Mellor, "On Feminist Utopias," *Women's Studies* (1982), 241–262; Barbara J. Hayler, "The Feminist Fiction of James Tiptree, Jr.: Women and Men as Aliens," *Spectrum of the Fantastic* (1988), 127–132; Veronica Hollinger, "'The Most Grisly Truth': Responses to the Human Condition in the Works of James Tiptree, Jr.," *Extrapolation* (1989), 117–132; Nancy Steffen-Fluhr, "The Case of the Haploid Heart: Psychological Patterns in the Science Fiction of Alice Sheldon ('James Tiptree, Jr.')," *Science-Fiction Studies* (1990), 188–220; Judith Luedtke Seal, "James Tiptree, Jr.: Fostering the Future, Not Condemning It," *Extrapolation* (1990), 73–82; Judith Genova, "Tiptree and Haraway: The Reinvention of Nature," *Cultural Critique* (1994), 5–27.

21. Messner notes that on March 15 the Earth is in a position almost opposite to the orbital location it would occupy on October 19. Therefore, if in October the Earth would be visible as a point of light against the background of the constellation Pisces from *Sunbird's*

position somewhere outside of Mercury's orbit, then from that same position in March the Earth should be visible in Virgo, Pisces' celestial opposite (see 439).

22. As students in my dystopia seminar in spring 1999 pointed out, the "Book of Judy" works like an ideological formation that interpellates each individual "Judy" as she comes along. The new Judys thus add to the growing ideological articulation of their collective reality, living richly *in* a post-revolutionary ideology, not trapped by a narrow "false consciousness." On ideology and false consciousness, see Terry Eagleton, *Ideology: An Introduction* (1991).

23. Messner notes that Lorimer's particular location in space has an astrological significance that recapitulates the competing social paradigms in the story. Caught between Pisces and Virgo, he is positioned between opposite signs in the Zodiac, signs whose characteristics bear resemblance to the subject constructions of the women in the *Gloria* and the men in the *Sunbird:* Pisces are said to be sensitive, nurturing, and idealistic (at times even "starry-eyed") whereas Virgos are practical, analytical, meticulous, even hypercritical and perfectionist.

24. For more on the process of naming, or interpellating, as the means of constructing obedient social subjects, see the key essay by Louis Althusser, "Ideology and Ideological State Apparatuses," *Lenin and Philosophy* (1971), 127–188. See also the discussions in Eagleton, *Ideology,* and Paul Smith, *Discerning the Subject* (1988).

25. On the iconic and discrete registers of the sf/utopian text, see Tom Moylan, *Demand the Impossible: Science Fiction and the Utopian Imagination* (1986), 35–52 (and on the formal affiliation of sf with the literary anatomy and romance rather than the character-centered psychological novel, see 35–38). For more on the negotiation between the worlds of sf and the reader, see Fredric Jameson, "Progress Versus Utopia; or, Can We Imagine the Future?" *Science-Fiction Studies* (1982), 147–158.

26. On the theory and practice of this empowering shift from subjectivity to agency, see Smith, *Discerning the Subject.*

27. See also Phillip E. Wegner, "The Last Bomb: Historicizing History in Terry Bisson's *Fire on the Mountain* and Gibson and Sterling's *The Difference Engine,*" *Comparatist* (1999), 141–151. Wegner brings Jameson's connection of sf and the historical novel to bear on that particular type of sf, the alternative history, that works through the "register of the 'what if' (what if the Confederacy had won the Civil War? what if the United States had lost World War II?)" and "views the present [as] the product of sheer contingency" ("Last Bomb" 141).

28. Jameson offers a major reconsideration of the relationship between realism, sf, and utopian writing in "'If I Find One Good City I Will Spare the Man': Realism and Utopia in Kim Stanley Robinson's *Mars Trilogy,*" *Learning from Other Worlds: Estrangement, Cognition and the Politics of Science Fiction and Utopia* (2000), 303–343; but see also *The Political Unconscious: Narrative as a Socially Symbolic Act* (1981). See Patrick Parrinder's detailed analysis in "*News from Nowhere, The Time Machine* and the Break-up of Classical Realism," *Science-Fiction Studies* (1976), 265–274. He argues that the historically specific complexity of these major utopian and sf novels "is due in part to the generic interactions" with realism in the case of Morris and with the interaction of realism and utopian fiction in Mor-

ris's novel in the case of Wells. As Parrinder puts it: "Morris turns from the degraded world of Dickens to create its negative image in a Nowhere of mutual trust and mutual fulfilment. Wells writes a visionary satire on the utopian idea which reintroduces the romantic hero as explorer and prophet of a menacing future. Both writers were responding to the breakup of the coalition of interests in mid-Victorian fiction, and their use of fantasy conventions asserted the place of visions and expectations in the understanding of contemporary reality. Schematically, we may see Wells's SF novel as a product of the warring poles of realism and utopianism, as represented by Dickens and Morris" (273). See also John Goode, "Gissing, Morris, and English Socialism," *Victorian Studies* (1968), 201–226. Zipes also argues that sf texts, such as Bradbury's *Fahrenheit 451,* tactically appropriate the form of realism, but not its epistemological logic, as a way to further the estrangement effect of the fantastic strategy; see "Mass Degradation of Humanity and Massive Contradictions in Bradbury's Vision of America in *Fahrenheit 451*," *Explorations in Utopian/Dystopian Fiction* (1982), 182–198. See also Eugenio Bolongaro, "From Literariness to Genre: Establishing the Foundations for a Theory of Literary Genres," *Genre* (1994), 277–313. See Chapter 2, n. 35, and Chapter 4, n. 2.

29. James situates this process in terms of the situation and perspective of the *young* sf reader. The young person being inscribed into society (i.e., being interpellated by its institutions, practices, and discourses) who is also reading a set of texts has the added opportunity (if only momentarily or potentially) to interrupt, reconfigure, or perhaps even subvert that "reality": "Children and adolescents spend much of their time trying to decode the weird and alien world in which they live; decoding sf is no different for them, and indeed, working on an understanding of a deliberately coded work such as an sf novel may actually assist them in learning to understand the meaning of the culturally and unconsciously coded world of a mimetic novel, or, indeed, of 'real life'" (*20th Century* 121).

30. Henry Schwarz and Richard Dienst, eds., *Reading the Shape of the World: Toward an International Cultural Studies* (1996). See also Peter Fitting, "To Read the World: Barthes' *Mythologies* Thirty Years Later," *Queen's Quarterly* (1988), 857–871.

Chapter 2

1. See H. Bruce Franklin, *War Stars* (1988), Constance Penley, *NASA/Trek: Popular Science and Sex in America* (1997); and Carol Stabile, *Feminism and the Technological Fix* (1994); and for more on the role of sf in producing and legitimating scientific-military policies and practices, see Andrew Ross and Constance Penley, *Technoculture* (1991); and Andrew Ross, *Strange Weather: Culture, Science, and Technology in the Age of Limits* (1991). Feminist critiques are extensive, but for two early interventions, see Beverly Friend, "Virgin Territory: Women and Sex in Science Fiction," *Extrapolation* (1972), 49–58; and Mary Kenny Badami, "A Feminist Critique of Science Fiction," *Extrapolation* (1976), 6–19. See note 26 below.

2. In *Public Sphere and Experience: Towards an Analysis of the Bourgeois and Proletarian Public Sphere* (1993), Oskar Negt and Alexander Kluge (drawing on Herbert Mar-

cuse) make a strong claim for the subversive power of "fantasy" (the Frankfurt School's term for that psychic impulse that drives all forms of fantastic discourse, as opposed to the literary subgenre of that name). Although fantasy is both escapist and subject to commodification, it nevertheless possesses the potential to overcome alienation by way of estrangement and therefore to bring the critical subject(s) back to an encounter with the existing situation: "Fantasy has a tendency to distance itself from the alienated labor process and to translate itself into timeless and ahistorical forms of production that 'do not and cannot exist.' Thus, fantasy would prevent the worker from advocating for his interests in reality. This danger is not, however, as great as it may appear. . . . As fantasies move farther away from the reality of the production process, the impulse that drives them on becomes less sensitive. Thus, all escapist forms of fantasy production tend, once they have reached a certain distance from reality, to turn around and face up to real situations. They establish themselves at a level definitively separated from the production process *only if* they are deliberately organized and confined there by a valorization interest" (Negt and Kluge 36).

3. Isaac Asimov, introduction to *More Soviet Science Fiction* (1962), 7–13.

4. See Harlan Ellison, ed., *Dangerous Visions* (1967) and *Again, Dangerous Visions* (1972). For the influential British counterpart, see Judith Merril, ed., *England Swings SF* (1968).

5. Young conservative activists in the 1960s, such as Newt Gingrich, also appreciated the delights and didacticism of sf, although, as Suvin suggests in his reader's report, libertarian writers of the quality of Robert Heinlein were usually more astute than the many conservative "Heinleinists" who celebrated the author's work. See, however, Gingrich's cowritten sf novel: Newt Gingrich, William R. Forschen, and Albert S. Hansen, *1945* (1996). For critical analyses of the connection between right-wing tendencies and interest in sf/utopias and popular culture in general, see Peter Fitting, "Utopia Beyond Our Ideals: The Dilemma of the Right-Wing Utopia," *Utopian Studies* (1991), 95–109; and Lawrence Grossberg, *We Gotta Get out of This Place: Popular Conservatism and Postmodern Culture* (1992).

6. For examinations of the U.S. movement that attend to its intellectual and cultural work, see Stanley Aronowitz, *The Death and Rebirth of American Radicalism* (1996), and George Katsiaficas, *The Imagination of the New Left* (1987). For studies of particular moments or movements in the United States, see Marty Jezer, *The Dark Ages: Life in the United States, 1945 to 1960* (1981); Van Gosse, *Where the Boys Are: Cuba, Cold War America and the Making of the New Left* (1993); James Tracy, *Direct Action: Radical Pacifism from the Union Eight to the Chicago Seven* (1996); Frances Fox Piven and Richard A. Cloward, *Poor People's Movements* (1977); Clayborne Carson, *In Struggle: SNCC and the Black Awakening of the 1960s* (1981); Angela Davis, *Angela Davis: An Autobiography* (1974); Philip S. Foner, ed., *The Black Panthers Speak* (1970); Elaine Brown, *A Taste of Power: A Black Woman's Story* (1992); Sara Evans, *Personal Politics: The Roots of Women's Liberation* (1979); Alice Echols, *Daring to Be Bad: Radical Feminism in America, 1967–1975* (1989); Karla Jay and Allen Young, eds., *Out of the Closets: Voices of Gay Liberation* (1972).

7. The success of the challenge can be measured negatively by the increase in state repression of the Left after 1968 (which replayed the repression of the Palmer raids in the 1920s and the McCarthyism of the 1950s). Taking the United States as but one example: the FBI launched its Counter Intelligence Program (COINTELPRO) of surveillance, infiltration, disinformation, provocation, and physical attacks (from beatings to gunfights) against the Black Panther Party, the American Indian movement, the Vietnam Veterans Against the War, the Puerto Rican Young Lords, and others; working illegally within the national borders, the Central Intelligence Agency pursued its parallel program, Operation Chaos; and across the nation police department "red squads" investigated, harassed, and disrupted Left formations in their own locales. See Ward Churchill, *Agents of Repression: The FBI's Secret War Against the Black Panther Party and the American Indian Movement* (1990), and Ward Churchill and Jim Vander Wall, eds., *The COINTELPRO Papers: Documents from the FBI's Secret Wars Against Domestic Dissent* (1990). In his reader's report, Phillip E. Wegner recalls a more positive though sobering expression of the net gains in the following passage (dealing with the suppression of a revolution) from Ursula K. Le Guin's *Dispossessed* (1974): "When they came, marching in their neat black coats up the steps among the dead and dying men and women, they found on the high, grey, polished wall of the great foyer a word written at the height of a man's eyes, in broad smears of blood: DOWN! They shot dead the man who lay nearest the word, and later on when the Directorate was restored to order the word was washed off the wall with water, soap, and rags, but it remained; it had been spoken; it had meaning" (*Dispossessed* 302).

8. See Lefebvre, *The Production of Space* (1991), 46–67; and Negt and Kluge 54–91.

9. The invocation of the "long march" in the New Left imagination had already been expressed by Raymond Williams in *The Long Revolution* (1961). But while Williams was primarily referring to the entire political movement, the leader of the German SDS was making an existential challenge to young activists to think about how they would conduct the coming stages of their lives in terms of their political affiliations and goals.

10. As Aronowitz has observed, an interim move in this process of intellectual radicalization was the simultaneous organization of "post-SDS" formations such as the Movement for a Democratic Society and the New University Conference along with the emergence of radical caucuses in traditional scholarly disciplines and the professions. Although the caucuses met with varying degrees of success, important intellectual and political space was secured in fields such as English, economics, history, political science, and sociology. Along with such academic initiatives, other professionals—scientists, physicians, engineers, teachers, businesspeople—formed organizations against the war and for social responsibility. Of interest to the discussion in this book, Marge Piercy was active in the Movement for a Democratic Society as she moved into writing her first sf work (Aronowitz 85–88).

11. See B. Ruby Rich's *Chick Flicks: Theories and Memories of the Feminist Film Movement* (1998) for a theorized memoir of feminist film culture (including production and criticism, in the context of the political movements) in this same period. On the relation-

ship between feminist politics and feminist sf, see Lisa Hogeland, *Feminism and Its Fictions: The Consciousness-Raising Novel and the Women's Liberation Movement* (1998).

12. The study of the complex and uneven world of sf fandom (and of sf audiences in general) is a project that is still in its early days (and ready to be helped by the methodologies of cultural studies). For historical and critical views (in addition to memoirs of the sf "Golden Age" (1930s–1940s) by authors such as Isaac Asimov, Arthur C. Clarke, and Frederick Pohl), see Sam Moskowitz, *The Immortal Storm: A History of Science Fiction Fandom* (1954); Beverly Friend, *The Science Fiction Fan Cult* (1975); Joe Siclari, "Science Fiction Fandom: A History of an Unusual Hobby," *The Science Fiction Reference Book* (1981), 87–129; Nickianne Moody, "Maeve and Guinevere: Women's Fantasy Writing in the Science Fiction Marketplace," *Where No Man Has Gone Before: Women and Science Fiction* (1991), 186–204; the essays in Constance Penley, ed., *Close Encounters: Film, Feminism, and Science Fiction* (1991); Henry Jenkins, *Textual Poachers: Television Fans and Participatory Culture* (1992); Joe Sanders, *Science Fiction Fandom* (1994); Cheryl Harris and Alison Alexander, *Theorizing Fandom: Fans, Subculture, and Identity* (1998); Camille Bacon-Smith, *Science Fiction Culture* (1999); and Edward James, *Science Fiction in the 20th Century* (1994). On the related issue of sf readership, see Chapter 1, nn. 7, 11, and 17; and on the sf industry and market, see Chapter 6, n. 7.

13. Richard Ohmann, "English and the Cold War," *The Cold War and the University: Toward an Intellectual History of the Postwar Years* (1997), 73–107.

14. See also Terry Eagleton, "The Rise of English," *Literary Theory: An Introduction* (1996); Francis Mulhern, *The Moment of Scrutiny* (1981); Frank Lentricchia, *After the New Criticism* (1980).

15. See Aronowitz, especially chapters 1 and 2. Of particular interest (in light of the position later taken by the critical dystopias) is his analysis of the emergence, in this case in the United States, of what came to be called "cultural studies" as a critique of liberalism and liberal intellectual culture.

16. The formative role played by Marxist thought and analysis in this intellectual and cultural movement in the United States has been surmised and attacked by the Right but has not yet been described and detailed. Influences came from several directions at once. The indigenous U.S. tradition was fed, challenged, and expanded by the theoretical work of Third World national liberation movements and European critical Marxism. This work was furthered in the United States by journals such as *Monthly Review, The Progressive, Studies on the Left, Liberation, Radical America, Root and Branch, Ramparts, Socialist Revolution* (now *Socialist Review*), *Feminist Studies, New Political Science, The Insurgent Sociologist, Catalyst, Radical History Journal, Jump Cut, Sub-Stance, Semiotexte, Telos,* and *New German Critique*. The radical caucuses of the academic organizations also helped, as did independent projects such as the ongoing Socialist Scholars Conference and the Summer Institute in Culture and Society of the Marxist Literary Group (MLG). More recently, the journal of the MLG, *Mediations,* and the journal *Rethinking Marxism,* with its large annual conference, have joined this list of critical Marxist vehicles and venues in the United States. For a discussion of the theoretical and political impact of the Marxist Literary

Group, see Sean Homer, *Fredric Jameson: Marxism, Hermeneutics, Postmodernism* (1998), 28–30.

17. See *Science Fiction Studies* (July 1999). This special issue, "The History of Science Fiction Criticism," includes the following contributions: "Editorial Introduction," 161–163; Arthur B. Evans, "The Origins of Science Fiction Criticism: From Kepler to Wells," 163–187; Gary Westfahl, "The Popular Tradition of Science Fiction Criticism, 1926–1980," 187–213; Donald M. Hassler, "The Academic Pioneers of Science Fiction Criticism, 1940–1980," 213–232; Veronica Hollinger, "Contemporary Trends in Science Fiction Criticism, 1980–1999," 232–263; and "Collective Works Cited and Chronological Bibliography," 263–284. See Hassler's follow-up comments in his own "Editor's Pad" column in *Extrapolation* (1999), 187–189. See also the additions suggested by Neil Barron and David Hartwell and the *Science Fiction Studies* editor Carol McGuirk (going only by her initials, "CM") in "Notes and Correspondence," *Science Fiction Studies* (1999), 514–516. I have included Barron's items in the Bibliography, and Hartwell offers several other items worth noting: The introductions to the Gregg Press editions of significant sf texts that ran from the late 1970s to the early 1980s under Hartwell's general editorship; the uncollected critical essays and reviews by Joanna Russ; the essays in *The Australian SF Review* in the late 1960s and early 1970s; the sf criticism of Leslie Fielder; Robert Heinlein's 1941 Denvention speech; Theodore Sturgeon's 1983 Philcon speech; and the proceedings of the Khatru Symposium on Women in SF. Hartwell notes this about the Khatru work: It was "conducted and published as a special issue of his fanzine in 1975 by Jeff Smith in Baltimore. . . . It is now unobtainable, but a late 1980s reprint was done by SF3, the Madison [Wisconsin] sf society for Wiscon, under the auspices of Jeanne Gomoll" (515). Editor "CM" (Carol McGuirk) adds that the Khatru Symposium involved a "written discussion among Suzy McKee Charnas, Virginia Kidd, Ursula Le Guin, Vonda McIntyre, Raylyn Moore, Joanna Russ, Luise White, Kate Wilhelm, and Chelsea Quinn Yarbro; also contributing were three (as everyone thought) men: Samuel Delany, Jeffrey Smith, and James Tiptree, Jr. The symposium was published as a double issue of the fanzine *Khatru* 3 and 4 (1975). Tiptree was asked to withdraw, as being an annoyingly masculinist voice! (Her persona was revealed in 1976 by the same Jeffrey Smith)" (516). Also on Khatru, see Badami.

18. My own list of influential work in this early period includes the following: Phillip Babcock Gove, *The Imaginary Voyage in Prose Fiction* (1941); J. O. Bailey, *Pilgrims Through Space and Time* (1947); Marjorie Hope Nicolson, *Voyages to the Moon* (1948); Martin Green, "Science and Sensibility. II: Science Fiction," *Kenyon Review* (1963), 699–728; Sam Moskowitz, *The Immortal Storm: A History of Science Fiction Fandom* (1954) and *Explorers of the Infinite: Shapers of Science Fiction* (1963); I. F. Clarke, *Voices Prophesying War, Future Wars, 1763–1984* (1966); Donald A. Wolheim, *The Universe Makers: Science Fiction Today* (1971); and, most significant, Kingsley Amis, *New Maps of Hell: A Survey of Science Fiction* (1960). Hassler describes Amis as the "sometime lecturer at Swansea University in South Wales who came to Princeton in 1959 to lecture on sf. The interesting crux, of course, is that his resulting book . . . not only highlighted what the MLA Seminar [on science fiction], and eventually the SFRA, wanted to do in the academy but also, in its very title, sug-

gested how the work was changing from that of separate pioneers to collective cartographers of a literature" ("Academic Pioneers" 224). See also Eric Jacobs, *Kingsley Amis: A Biography* (1995); Nicholas Ruddick's review, *Science Fiction Studies* (1999), 129–130; and the subsequent exchange between Ruddick and Brian Aldiss in "Notes and Correspondence," *Science Fiction Studies* (1999), 512–513.

19. For more on the necessity of reading and analyzing specific textual traditions (or textual webs, as Delany calls them) on their own terms, see Fredric Jameson, "Progress Versus Utopia," *Science-Fiction Studies* (1982), 147–158; "On Raymond Chandler," *Southern Review* (1970), 624–650; "Third World Literature in the Era of Multinational Capitalism," *Social Text* (1986), 65–88; and (on the difference between aestheticism and populism as responses to mass culture) "Reification and Utopia in Mass Culture," *Signatures of the Visible* (1990), 9–34.

20. In 1997 sf/utopian criticism found a new home in the Modern Language Association with the establishment of the regular discussion group in "science fiction, utopia, and the fantastic." After two years of special sessions that I organized during my tenure on the MLA's Popular Culture Division, in spring 1997, the MLA's Executive Committee approved a proposal for the annual session that was written, submitted, and seen through the channels by Kenneth M. Roemer (with the contributions of scholars, journal editors, and leaders of professional organizations). As an archival document, the proposal includes useful information on the history of sf and utopian studies within and without the MLA; a listing of relevant courses, organizations, journals, scholarship; and a selected listing of papers and sessions on sf and utopia at the MLA between 1949–1965 and 1986–1996. See Roemer, "Petition for an MLA Discussion Group in Science Fiction, Utopian, and Fantastic Literature" (1997).

21. In Britain the SF Foundation, with its archive and its journal, *Foundation: The Review of Science Fiction,* was established in 1971.

22. See Dale Mullen, "Introduction to Science Fiction in Academe," *Science-Fiction Studies* (1996), 371–375.

23. See the essays and lists in the *Science-Fiction Studies* special issue "Science Fiction in Academe" (1996), 371–529. For a comparative look at the teaching of sf in Britain, see Edward James and Farah Mendlesohn, "Science Fiction Courses in Higher Education in Great Britain: A Preliminary Guide," *Foundation* (1993), 59–69. On teaching sf, see Chapter 1, n. 5.

24. See the reports on college courses in the *Science-Fiction Studies* special issue "Science Fiction in Academe," 437–529.

25. Besides the works I discuss in the text, notable books of the 1960s and 1970s include the following: H. Bruce Franklin, *Future Perfect: American Science Fiction of the Nineteenth Century* (1966); Robert Scholes, *The Fabulators* (1967) and *Structural Fabulation* (1975); David N. Samuelson, *Visions of Tomorrow: Six Journeys from Outer to Inner Space* (1969); Robert M. Philmus, *Into the Unknown: The Evolution of Science Fiction from Francis Godwin to H. G. Wells* (1970); Thomas D. Clareson, ed., *SF: The Other Side of Realism* (1971); Patrick Parrinder, *H. G. Wells: The Critical Heritage* (1972), *Science Fiction: A Critical Guide*

(1979), *Science Fiction: Its Criticism and Teaching* (1980); Brian Aldiss, *Billion Year Spree: The History of Science Fiction* (1973); David Ketterer, *New Worlds for Old: The Apocalyptic Tradition, Science Fiction, and American Literature* (1974); Neil Barron, ed., *Anatomy of Wonder* (1976); Lester del Ray, *The World of Science Fiction, 1926–1976* (1979); Eric Rabkin, *The Fantastic in Literature* (1976); Samuel R. Delany, *The Jewel-Hinged Jaw: Notes on the Language of Science Fiction* (1977); Robert Scholes and Eric Rabkin, *Science Fiction: History/Science/Vision* (1977); Gary Wolfe, *The Known and the Unknown: The Iconography of Science Fiction* (1979); Patricia Warrick, *The Cybernetic Imagination in Science Fiction* (1980); Christine Brooke-Rose, *A Rhetoric of the Unreal: Studies in Narrative and Structure, Especially of the Fantastic* (1981); and the first edition of the *Encyclopedia of Science Fiction*, edited by Peter Nichols and John Clute (1979). For a larger list of books and essays, see the "Collective Works Cited and Chronological Bibliography" in the *Science Fiction Studies* issue "A History of Science Fiction Criticism" (1999). My list and the *SFS* list are obviously marked by the paucity of women and therefore symptomatically register the institutional sexism and overt gender bias in the field. For a selected list of the feminist scholarship that emerged in the next decade, see n. 26 below.

26. Russ's essays and book reviews were an early contribution to feminist sf criticism, and they became part of an enduring line of critical thought in the field. Of the many publications that have informed this body of work, I would note the following from the 1980s and 1990s: Ursula K. Le Guin, *The Language of the Night: Essays on Fantasy and Science Fiction* (1992); Nadia Khouri, "The Dialectics of Power: Utopia in the Science Fiction of Le Guin, Jeury and Piercy," *Science-Fiction Studies* (1980), 49–61; Vivian Sobchack, *The Limits of Infinity: The American Science Fiction Film* (1980); Marleen Barr, *Future Females: A Critical Anthology* (1981), *Alien to Femininity: Speculative Fiction and Feminist Theory* (1987), and *Feminist Fabulation: Space/Postmodern Fiction* (1992); Catherine McClenahan, "Textual Politics: The Uses of the Imagination in Joanna Russ's *The Female Man*," *Transactions of the Wisconsin Academy of Sciences, Arts, and Letters* (1982), 114–125; Natalie Rosinsky, *Feminist Futures—Contemporary Women's Speculative Fiction* (1984); Kathryn Hume, *Fantasy and Mimesis: Responses to Reality in Western Literature* (1984); Lee Cullen Khanna, "Frontiers of Imagination: Feminist Worlds," *Women's Studies International Forum* (1984), 97–102; Sarah Lefanu, *Feminism and Science Fiction*. Bloomington: Indiana University Press (1988); Elizabeth Cummins, *Understanding Ursula K. Le Guin* (1990); Anne Cranny-Francis, *Feminist Fiction: Feminist Uses of Generic Fiction* (1990); Veronica Hollinger, "Feminist Science Fiction: Breaking up the Subject," *Extrapolation* (1990), 229–239, and "(Re)reading Queerly: Science Fiction, Feminism, and the Defamiliarization of Gender," *Science Fiction Studies* (1999), 23–40; Annette Kuhn, ed., *Alien Zone: Cultural Theory and Contemporary Science Fiction Cinema* (1990) and *Alien Zone 2* (2000); Lucie Armitt, *Where No Man Has Gone Before: Women and Science Fiction* (1991) and *Theorising the Fantastic* (1996); Robin Roberts, *A New Species: Gender and Science in Science Fiction* (1993); Jenny Wolmark, *Aliens and Others: Science Fiction, Feminism, and Postmodernism* (1994); Anne Balsamo, *Technologies of the Gendered Body: Reading Cyborg Women* (1996); Jane Donawerth, *Frankenstein's Daughters: Women Writing Science Fiction* (1997). See also the special

issue edited by Veronica Hollinger, "Science Fiction by Women," *Science-Fiction Studies* (July 1990).The formation of the feminist critical paradigm in sf/utopian studies was also due to the institutional intervention and leadership of women, as seen, for example, in Judith Merril's editorial work, Janice Bogstad's and Jeanne Gomoll's organizing of Wiscon (the feminist fan convention), Vonda McIntyre's and Susan Janice Anderson's editing of *Aurora: Beyond Equality,* Pamela Sargent's editing of the *Women of Wonder* collections, and Veronica Hollinger's editorial role in *Science Fiction Studies.* On feminist work in utopian studies, see Chapter 3.

27. Joanna Russ, introduction to "What Can a Heroine Do," *To Write Like a Woman* (1995), 79.

28. Joanna Russ, "What Can a Heroine Do," *To Write Like a Woman* 79–94.

29. See also Russ's collection of critical essays in *To Write, Magic Mommas, Trembling Sisters, Puritans and Perverts: Feminist Essays* (1985).

30. Darko Suvin, "On the Poetics of the Science Fiction Genre," *College English* (1972), 372–382. The essay was redone as chapter 1, "Estrangement and Cognition," in *Metamorphoses of Science Fiction: On the Poetics and History of a Literary Genre* (1979), 3–16. References are to the *College English* version.

31. Along with Suvin's essay, the issue includes the following: Herbert Lindenberger, "The Idyllic Moment: On Pastoral and Romanticism"; Paul Alpers, "The Eclogue Tradition and the Nature of Pastoral"; Marcia Lieberman, "'Some Day My Prince Will Come': Female Acculturation Through the Fairy Tale"; and Walter Ong, "Media Transformation: The Talked Book." The book review section includes reviews of Geoffrey Hartman's *Beyond Formalism* and Paul Goodman's *Speaking and Language.*

32. For an overview and appraisal of Suvin's body of work to date, see Patrick Parrinder, ed., *Learning from Other Worlds* (2000).

33. That is, what others term the "professional-managerial class"; see Barbara Ehrenreich and John Ehrenreich, "The Professional-Managerial Class," *Between Labor and Capital* (1979), 5–45; Barbara Ehrenreich, "The Professional-Managerial Class Revisited," *Intellectuals* (1990), 173–185; Fred Pfeil, "Makin' Flippy Floppy: Postmodernism and the Baby Boom PMC," *The Year Left: An American Socialist Yearbook, 1985* (1985), 263–295; and Tom Moylan, "Ideology in the Age of Reagan," *Crane Bag* (1985), 117–123.

34. As Wegner suggests, whereas the estrangement effect of sf works through the primacy of the textual novum, in properly modernist texts it does so by way of varieties of formal innovation. Noting this difference helps to explain the formal reasons for sf's didactic nature.

35. A number of critics were moving in this direction. For one important example, see Thomas D. Clareson, ed., *SF: The Other Side of Realism* (1971). The collection includes several essays exploring the relationship of sf to the tradition and formal strategies of realism; indeed, the lead essay by Jules Kagarlitsky, entitled "Realism and Fantasy," in an argument similar to Suvin's, considers sf within the scope of what he calls "realistic fantasy" (31). See also Chapter 1, n. 28.

36. One of the previous generation of sf scholars who influenced Suvin was Amis, who approached sf in terms of a differentiation of worlds based in cognition and innovation:

"Science fiction is that class of prose narrative treating of a situation that could not arise in the world we know, but which is hypothesized on the basis of some innovation in science or technology, or pseudo-science or pseudo-technology" (Amis 14). Suvin clearly works with this formal definition even as he takes it to the level of the social and political.

37. Darko Suvin, "Novum Is as Novum Does," *Foundation* (1997), 26–43. The entire text of the keynote presentation will appear in a forthcoming essay Suvin has provisionally titled "Arguing with the Deluge."

38. Wegner thinks that a similar political and theoretical dismissal could well be the case in the surprising neglect of the concept of Utopia (or the "utopian problematic") in all of Jameson's work.

39. See Carol McGuirk, "NoWhere Man: Towards a Poetics of Post-Utopian Characterization," *Science-Fiction Studies* (1994), 141–155; Darko Suvin, "A Note for the 'Quirks and Quarks' (Moods and Facts?) Dept.," *Science-Fiction Studies* (1995), 137–138; and Carol McGuirk, "On Darko Suvin's Good-Natured Critique," *Science-Fiction Studies* (1995), 138–140. In *Positions and Presuppositions in Science Fiction* (1988), Suvin's further thoughts on the novum are expressed in the preface (*Positions* ix–xvi) and in the reprint of his 1982 essay "The SF Novel as Epic Narration: For a Fusion of 'Formal' and 'Sociological' Analysis" (*Positions* 74–86). A study of the related epistemological issue of the "science question" in Suvin's work would begin with his 1976 essay "'Utopian' and 'Scientific': Two Attributes for Socialism from Engels," *minnesota review* (1976), 59–76. It would then move to "Novum Is as Novum Does," wherein he reaffirms his "quite conscious founding decision in *Metamorphoses,* dating from a silent debate with Brecht in the 1950s, to use the nomination of 'cognition' instead of 'science'" ("Novum Is as Novum Does" 39). Such a study might then consider the connections and differences between his position and that of Sandra Harding, *The Science Question in Feminism* (1986); Nancy Hartsock, "The Feminist Standpoint: Developing the Ground for a Specifically Feminist Historical Materialism," *Money, Sex, and Power* (1983), 231–251; and Donna Haraway, "Situated Knowledges: The Science Question in Feminism and the Privilege of Partial Perspective," *Simians, Cyborgs, and Women: The Reinvention of Nature* (1991), 183–203. See also Suvin's "Afterword: With Sober, Estranged Eyes," *Learning from Other Worlds* (2000)."

40. Ernst Bloch, *The Principle of Hope* (1986), 199.

41. On Bloch's dialogic struggle between his Leninist-Stalinist orthodoxy and his radical understanding of the relationship between history and utopian desire, see Tom Moylan, "Bloch Against Bloch: The Theological Reception of *Das Prinzip Hoffnung* and the Liberation of the Utopian Function," *Not Yet* (1997), 96–122; see also Vincent Geoghegan, "Ernst Bloch: Postsecular Thoughts," *Marxism's Ethical Dimension* (2001).

42. Marc Angenot, "The Absent Paradigm: An Introduction to the Semiotics of Science Fiction," *Science-Fiction Studies* (1979), 9–20

43. Kathleen Spencer, "'The Red Sun Is High, the Blue Low': Towards a Stylistic Description of Science Fiction," *Science-Fiction Studies* (1983), 35–50.

44. Peter Fitting, "Positioning and Closure: On the 'Reading Effect' of Contemporary Utopian Fiction," *Utopian Studies I* (1987), 23–36. See also Chapter 1, nn. 7 and 17.

45. See the discussion of critical utopias in Chapter 3, especially nn. 16, 20.

46. Fredric Jameson, "Cognitive Mapping," *Marxism and the Interpretation of Culture* (1988), 347–360. For a discussion of the connection between sf and cognitive mapping, see Jim Miller, "Post-Apocalyptic Hoping: Octavia Butler's Dystopian/Utopian Fiction," *Science-Fiction Studies* (1998), 336–361. As Miller puts it, sf's capacity for "breaking through history . . . [by] achieving historical consciousness by way of the future rather than the past . . . also makes it a good vehicle for Jameson's 'cognitive mapping,' a new form of political art" (Miller 347). See also Richard Bjornson, "Cognitive Mapping and the Understanding of Literature," *Sub-Stance* (1981), 51–62; Erika Ferguson and Mary Hegarty, "Properties of Cognitive Maps Constructed from Texts," *Memory and Cognition* (1994), 455–473; Eric Chown, Stephen Kaplan, and David Kortenkamp, "Prototypes, Location, and Associative Networks (PLAN): Towards a Unified Theory of Cognitive Mapping," *Cognitive Science* (1995), 1–49.

47. The cultural and intellectual shift from that conference and book to the 1990 cultural studies conference in Oklahoma and the publication of its papers in the 1992 *Cultural Studies* volume is itself a symptom of the uneven process of appropriation of the left/oppositional theory that the new economic order achieved in the realms of academia, publishing, and what was left of the public sphere. See Cary Nelson and Lawrence Grossberg, eds., *Marxism and the Interpretation of Culture* (1988), and Lawrence Grossberg, Cary Nelson, and Paula Treichler, eds., *Cultural Studies* (1992).

48. Fredric Jameson, introduction to "Cognitive Mapping," *Marxism and the Interpretation of Culture* (1988), 347.

49. In his more extensive discussion of cognitive mapping in *Postmodernism, or, The Cultural Logic of Late Capitalism* (1991), Jameson refers directly to sf by way of the work of J. G. Ballard, Philip K. Dick, and cyberpunk in general. I agree with Wegner that the roots of the concept can be traced back through all of Jameson's writing on sf; see the early works, "Generic Discontinuities in SF: Brian Aldiss' *Starship*," *Science-Fiction Studies* (1973), 57–58; "After Armageddon: Character Systems in P. K. Dick's *Dr. Bloodmoney*," *Science-Fiction Studies* (1975), 31–42; "World-Reduction in Le Guin," *Science-Fiction Studies* (1975), 221–230; but also see the later "Science Fiction as a Spatial Genre: Generic Discontinuities and the Problem of Figuration in Vonda McIntyre's *The Exile Waiting*," *Science-Fiction Studies* (1987), 44–59.

50. For more on the question of a materialist, secular notion of transcendence and historical processes of political engagement and change, see Joel Kovel, "Cryptic Notes on Revolution and the Spirit," *Old Westbury Review* (1986), 23–35; *History and Spirit: An Inquiry into the Philosophy of Liberation* (1991); Tom Moylan, "Anticipatory Fiction: *Bread and Wine* and Liberation Theology," *Modern Fiction Studies* (1989), 103–121; "Denunciation/Annunciation: The Radical Methodology of Liberation Theology," *Cultural Critique* (1992), 33–65; "Mission Impossible: Liberation Theology and Utopian Praxis," *Utopian Studies III* (1991), 20–30; and Geoghegan, "Ernst Bloch: Postsecular Thoughts."

51. Fredric Jameson, *The Seeds of Time* (1994), x.

52. Paul Smith, *Millennial Dreams: Contemporary Culture and Capital in the North* (1997), 2.

53. For another critique in this vein, see Terry Eagleton, *The Illusions of Postmodernism* (1997).

54. Darko Suvin, "Two Cheers for Essentialism and Totality: On Marx's Oscillation and Its Limits (as Well as on the Taboos of Post-modernism)," *Rethinking Marxism* (1998), 66–82.

55. See also Anuradha Dingwany and Lawrence Needham, "The Difference That Difference Makes," *Socialist Review* (1996), 5–47.

56. Phillip E. Wegner, "Horizons, Figures, and Machines: The Dialectic of Utopia in the Work of Fredric Jameson," *Utopian Studies* (1998), 68.

Chapter 3

1. Henri Lefebvre, *The Production of Space* (1991), 382.

2. Kenneth M. Roemer, "Petition for an MLA Discussion Group in Science Fiction, Utopian, and Fantastic Literature" (1997); see also Chapter 2, n. 20.

3. See Dale Mullen, "Introduction to Science Fiction in Academe," *Science-Fiction Studies* (1996), 371–375.

4. See "Utopia," a special issue of *Daedalus* (1965).

5. The Society for Utopian Studies in the United States was founded by Merrit Abrash and Arthur O. Lewis. In Britain the Utopian Studies Society was founded in 1988 by Ruth Levitas and others. In Israel the International Communal Studies Association was founded in 1985, and in Italy the Centro Interdipartimentale di Ricerca Sull'utopia at the University of Bologna was founded in 1989 by Vita Fortunati.

6. As Sargent notes, the special issues or sections of *Utopian Studies* map the theoretical scope of the field. Up through 1998, the topics have been on Ernst Bloch, Ursula Le Guin, utopian film, Marge Piercy, early utopian fiction by women, utopian architecture, and Fredric Jameson. The awards given by the Society for Utopian Studies also help to characterize the scope of the field. The Eugenio Battisti Awards to the author of the best article in a volume of *Utopian Studies* have been the following: Vincent Geoghegan, "Remembering the Future" (1990); Peter Fitting, "Utopia Beyond Our Ideals: The Dilemma of the Right-Wing Utopia," and Lee Cullen Khanna, "Beyond Omelas: Utopia and Gender" (1991); Michael Gardiner, "Bakhtin's Carnival: Utopia as Critique," and Kenneth R. Hoover, Mondragón's Answers to Utopia's Problems" (1992); Phillip E. Wegner, "Zamyatin's *We*: A Critical Map of Utopia's 'Possible Worlds'" (1993); Carl J. Guarneri, "The Americanization of Utopia: Fourierism and the Dilemma of Utopian Dissent in the United States" (1994); Michael Gardiner, "Utopia and Everyday Life in French Social Thought" (1995); Robert Appelbaum, "Utopian Dubrovnik, 1659: An English Fantasy" (1996); Michael Gardiner, "A Postmodern Utopia? Heller and Fehér's Critique of Messianic Marxism" (1997); Phillip E. Wegner, "Horizons, Figures, and Machines: The Dialectic of Utopia in the Work of Fredric Jameson" (1998). Winners of the Arthur O. Lewis Award for best paper by a younger scholar at the annual Society for Utopian Studies conference have been the following (names of winners for 1992 and 1994 were not available): Robert Shelton, "Aesthetic An-

gels and Devolved Demons: Wells in 1895" (1986); Erika Gottlieb, "The Function of Goldstein's Book: Time as Theme and Structure in Dystopian Satire," and Libby Falk Jones, "Breaking Silences in Feminist Dystopias" (1987); Peter Bergmann, "Utopianism and Defeatism in Friedrich Nietzsche," and James J. Kopp, "Edward Bellamy and the New Deal: The Revival of Bellamyism in the 1930s" (1988); Robyn S. Roslak, "Organicism and the Construction of Utopian Geography: The Role of the Landscape in Anarcho-Communism and Neo-Impressionism," and Richard Toby Widdicombe, "Eutopia, Dystopia, Aporia: The Obstruction of Meaning in Fin-de-Siècle Utopian Texts" (1989); Kristine Anderson, "Encyclopedic Dictionary as Utopian Genre: Two Feminist Ventures" (1990); Darby Lewes, "Middle-Class Edens: Women's Nineteenth-Century Utopian Fiction and the Bourgeois Ideal" (1991); June Deery, "Ectopic and Utopic Reproduction," and Scott Kelley, "Photo-Utopia and Poetic Representations of the Impossible: The Utopic Figure in Modern Poetic and Photographic Discourse" (1993); Beatriz de Alba-Koch, "The Dialogics of Utopia, Dystopia and Arcadia: Political Struggle and Utopian Novels in Nineteenth-Century Mexico," and Jeremy Stolow, "Utopia and Geopolitics in Theodor Herzl's *Altneuland*" (1995); Nicole Pohl, "'Sweet Place, Where Virtue Then Did Rest': The Appropriation of the Country-House Ethos in Sarah Scott's *Millennium Hall*" (1996); Rebecca Totaro, "English Plague and New World Promise" (1997); Ashlie Lancaster, "Instantiating Critical Utopias" (1998). For more information, see Lyman Tower Sargent, "National Identity and U.S. Utopian Literature" (1999).

7. Of the many books that shaped this body of work, I would note the following: Northrop Frye, *Anatomy of Criticism: Four Essays* (1957); Kenneth Burke, *A Grammar of Motives and a Rhetoric of Motives* (1962); Robert C. Elliot, *The Shape of Utopia: Studies in a Literary Genre* (1970); Peyton Richter, ed., *Utopia/Dystopia* (1975); Kenneth M. Roemer, *The Obsolete Necessity: America in Utopian Writings, 1888–1900* (1976); Frank E. Manuel and Fritzie P. Manuel, *Utopian Thought in the Western World* (1979); Jeanne Pfaelzer, *The Utopian Novel in America, 1886–1896: The Politics of Form* (1984). Important British publications include A. L. Morton, *The English Utopia* (1952); John Ferguson, *Utopias of the Classical World* (1975); J. C. Davis, *Utopia and the Ideal Society: A Study of English Utopian Writing, 1516–1700* (1981); and Barbara Goodwin and Keith Taylor, *The Politics of Utopia: A Study in Theory and Practice* (1982).

8. See Lyman Tower Sargent, *British and American Utopian Literature, 1516–1985: An Annotated, Chronological Bibliography* (1988); the first edition came out in 1979. See also the other major bibliographical work at this time: Glenn Negley, *Utopian Literature: A Bibliography with a Supplementary Listing of Works Influential in Utopian Thought* (1978); Arthur O. Lewis, *Utopian Literature in the Pennsylvania State University Libraries: A Selected Bibliography* (1984). Most important of the book series was the one Sargent coedited with Gregory Claeys on utopianism and communitarianism at Syracuse Press from 1988 to 1996. In recognition of his extensive work, Sargent was the first recipient, in 1997, of the Society for Utopian Studies Distinguished Scholar Award for a lifetime of scholarly contributions.

9. Lyman Tower Sargent, "The Three Faces of Utopianism," *minnesota review* (1967), 222.

10. Lyman Tower Sargent, "Utopia—the Problem of Definition," *Extrapolation* (1975), 137–148.

11. Sargent elaborates on this argument in "The Three Faces of Utopianism Revisited," *Utopian Studies* (1994), 1–38. As he puts it, literary utopias and intentional communities are "historical artifacts that are brought into being at particular times and places and usually by identifiable people whose reasons for doing so are in principle knowable . . . [and among] our jobs as scholars is to try to understand to the best of our ability both the work the author intended and the work the reader creates" ("Three Faces Revisited" 6).

12. Wegner discusses the matter of "perfection" (linking it with Mannheim's notion of "conservative utopia") in his chapter on Orwell in *Horizons of Future Worlds, Borders of Present States: Utopian Narratives, History, and the Nation* (1993); see also his forthcoming book, *Imaginary Communities: Utopia, the Nation, and the Spatial Histories of Modernity*.

13. Darko Suvin, "Defining the Literary Genre of Utopia: Some Historical Semantics, Some Genology, a Proposal, and a Plea," *Studies in the Literary Imagination* (1973), 121–145. The essay was redone as chapter 3, "Defining the Literary Genre of Utopia: Some Historical Semantics, Some Genology, a Proposal, and a Plea," *Metamorphoses of Science Fiction: On the Poetics and History of a Literary Genre* (1979), 37–63. References are to *Metamorphoses*.

14. Suvin benefited from Barthes's work on the process of writing utopia and on utopia as writing—perhaps best expressed in Barthes's *Sade/Fourier/Loyola* (1971). On Barthes's understanding and practice of Utopia as a creative, political process, see Diana Knight, *Barthes and Utopia: Space, Travel, Writing* (1997).

15. Peter Fitting, "The Modern Anglo-American SF Novel: Utopian Longing and Capitalist Cooptation," *Science-Fiction Studies* (1979), 59–76.

16. The relationship between Fitting's phrase "critical and utopian" and my neologism *critical utopia* may seem to be obvious, but it isn't. Although I was familiar with Fitting's ideas on sf and Utopia (from conversation as well as reading), it is a matter of my lasting regret that I simply missed reading his 1979 essay until *after* the publication of both my 1980 essay ("Beyond Negation: The Critical Utopias of Ursula K. Le Guin and Samuel R. Delany") and my 1986 book, *Demand the Impossible: Science Fiction and the Utopian Imagination*. I have long ago apologized in person to Fitting for my faulty scholarship, but I take this opportunity to make that apology and recognition of his work public. And yet the nearly simultaneous emergence of our similar but separate arguments testifies to the political and intellectual structure of feeling that, I argue, informed Left culture in this period (see also n. 20).

17. To be sure, this listing is a descriptive sample of early essays and books that characterized the emergent feminist work in utopian studies—and not a definitive or exhaustive bibliography or genealogy. For a listing of significant works of feminist criticism within the broader field of sf, see Chapter 2, n. 26.

18. Joanna Russ, "Recent Feminist Utopias," *Future Females: A Critical Anthology* (1981), 71–85. The essay was reprinted in Joanna Russ, *To Write Like a Woman;* references are to *To Write Like a Woman.*

19. This powerfully expansive political quality—in substance and audience—puts paid to those critics who regard the feminist utopias as more limited in scope and indeed as a sign of Utopia's reduction into a discourse of concern only to what later gets tagged as "special interest groups." See, for example, Krishan Kumar, *Utopia and Anti-Utopia in Modern Times* (1987). In his discussion of Le Guin's *Dispossessed* and the other feminist utopias, he writes of how Utopia has gone into decline in quality, relevance, and appeal and thus has "fragmented, both in its form and in its audience" (420).

20. Moylan, *Demand.* See also Tom Moylan, "Beyond Negation: The Critical Utopias of Ursula K. Le Guin and Samuel R. Delany," *Extrapolation* (1980), 236–254. Besides Russ's "Recent Feminist Utopias," other studies that caught the political and formal logic and consequences of this textual movement include Fredric Jameson, "World-Reduction in Le Guin," *Science-Fiction Studies* (1975), 221–230; Fitting, "The Modern Anglo-American SF Novel" (1979); Darko Suvin and Marc Angenot, "Not Only but Also: On Cognition and Ideology in SF and SF Criticism," *Science-Fiction Studies* (1979), 168–179; Darko Suvin, "The SF Novel as Epic Narration: For a Fusion of 'Formal' and 'Sociological' Analysis" (1982), which is reprinted in *Positions and Presuppositions in Science Fiction* (1988); Peter Ruppert, *Reader in a Strange Land: The Activity of Reading Literary Utopias* (1986); Kumar, *Modern Times* (1987); Frances Bartkowski, *Feminist Utopias* (1989); Angelika Bammer, *Partial Visions: Feminism and Utopianism in the 1970s* (1991). A key element in the critical utopian strategy is its emphasis on *process* rather than product or telos; this is captured in Bammer's argument for maintaining "the concept of utopia as process," for in "the face of external and internal challenges to legitimate both its ends and its means, it is all too easy for even the most progressive movement to foreclose process and construct an image of utopia as historical telos" (Bammer 48). In a later work, Lucy Sargisson as well argues, from a feminist standpoint, for a utopianism of process; see *Contemporary Feminist Utopianism* (1996). See also Ruth Levitas's questioning of the emphasis on process in *The Concept of Utopia* (1990).

21. As well, the critical utopias resonate—logically and chronologically—with Lefebvre's sense of critical knowledge conveyed in his concept of *connaissance,* which, as he puts it, "embodies both a self-criticism which relativizes [knowledge], and a critique of what exists, which naturally becomes more acute when political stakes (or politics at stake) and strategies are under scrutiny"; see *Production of Space*, 368.

22. Levitas's critique of the critical utopias focused on their failure to address the issue of political transformation in a substantial way. Although I take her point, I think she underestimates the investigation of activism and political strategies that constitutes the core of the discrete narratives of the works by Le Guin, Delany, Russ, and especially Piercy. Perhaps symptomatic of the changing situation, Kim Stanley Robinson pays even more attention to the process of transition in his 1990s utopias (*Pacific Edge, Antarctica,* and the Martian trilogy).

23. See the special section "The Work of Fredric Jameson," *Utopian Studies* (1998): Peter Fitting, "The Concept of Utopia in the Work of Fredric Jameson," 8–18, and Phillip E. Wegner, "Horizons, Figures, and Machines," 58–74. The section also includes the following: Tom Moylan, "Introduction," 1–8; Ian Buchanan, "Metacommentary on Utopia, or Jameson's Dialectic of Hope," 18–31; Staci von Boeckmann, "Marxism, Morality, and the Politics of Desire: Utopianism in Fredric Jameson's *The Political Unconscious*," 31–51; Bryan N. Alexander, "Jameson's Adorno and the Problem of Utopia," 51–58; and Fredric Jameson, "Comments," 74–78.

24. Fredric Jameson, *Marxism and Form* (1971), 110–111.

25. Fredric Jameson, *The Political Unconscious: Narrative as a Socially Symbolic Act* (1981), 286.

26. Fredric Jameson, "Reification and Utopia in Mass Culture," *Signatures of the Visible*, 29.

27. On sf's political maneuvers in the 1950s, Fitting refers readers to Judith Merril's account in "What Do You Mean: Science? Fiction?" in *SF: The Other Side of Realism* (1971), 53–95.

28. Fredric Jameson, "Progress Versus Utopia; or, Can We Imagine the Future?" *Science-Fiction Studies* (1982), 151.

29. Fredric Jameson, "Of Islands and Trenches: Neutralization and the Production of Utopian Discourse," *Diacritics* (1977), 6.

30. Wegner's formulation echoes the work of Williams and Miguel Abendsour, which argued that a shift from an emphasis on systemic design to that of heuristic provocation occurred in the literary utopia in the 1850s. Although their argument casts useful light on utopian texts since the 1850s, it does not account for the utopian textual work as described by Marin and Jameson, for, as Marin demonstrates, this dual process of neutralization and figuration was in place even in More's ur-text. See Raymond Williams, "Utopia and Science Fiction," *Problems in Materialism and Culture* (1980), 203–214.

31. See, for example, Fredric Jameson, "Architecture and the Critique of Ideology," *The Ideologies of Theory: Essays 1971–1986* (1988), 35–60.

32. Fredric Jameson, *The Seeds of Time* (1994), 57.

33. Val Gough, "'In the Twinkling of an Eye': Gilman's Utopian Imagination," *A Very Different Story: Studies on the Fiction of Charlotte Perkins Gilman* (1998), 130.

34. See also Fredric Jameson, "Pleasure: A Political Issue," *Formations of Pleasure* (1983), 1–14. Herein Jameson recognizes the place of manifest content as he notes that "the thematizing of a particular 'pleasure' as a political issue . . . must always involve a dual focus, in which the local issue is meaningful and desirable in and of itself, but is also *at one and the same time* taken as the *figure* for Utopia in general" (13).

35. Fredric Jameson, "Comments," *Utopian Studies* (1998), 74–78.

36. For essays on the "double-move" implied in my argument, see Tom Moylan, "Bloch Against Bloch: The Theological Reception of *Das Prinzip Hoffnung* and the Liberation of the Utopian Function," *Not Yet* (1997); Darko Suvin, "Transubstantiation of Production and Consumption: Metaphoric Imagery in the *Grundrisse*," *minnesota review* (1982),

102–115; Norman Finkelstein, "The Utopian Function and the Refunctioning of Marxism," *Diacritics* (1989), 54–65.

37. See *A Catechism of Christian Doctrine* (Baltimore Catechism) (1941) and *A New Catechism: Catholic Faith for Adults* (1967).

38. The case of utopianism in the societies of "actually existing socialism" is a related but separate question and does not enter into this present discussion. But see the second chapter of *Seeds,* "Utopia, Modernism, and Death," in which Jameson examines Utopia in "Second World Culture" through his reading of Andrei Platonov's *Chevengur* (composed in 1927 and 1928 but not published until the 1970s). See also Darko Suvin, "Russian SF and Its Utopian Tradition," *Metamorphoses* (1979), 243–270. Less work has been done on utopianism in colonial, decolonizing, neo-colonial, and post-colonial societies, but Sargent makes a strong case for the need for such work in "The Three Faces of Utopianism Revisited," and stimulated by Sargent's own research, the Society for Utopian Studies has encouraged the submission of conference papers and journal articles in these areas.

39. For a larger historical perspective on this cultural offensive, see Michael Denning's extensive study, *The Cultural Front* (1998).

40. Wegner connects this moment of retrenchment (as the danger of compensatory projects is set against radical resistance and transformation) with the appeal of Gramsci's writings and thus with the moment of Gramsci's political work. As he puts it in his reader's report: "While the 'professionalization' of utopian studies . . . is indeed what allows it to 'survive,' this is also a compensation for and sign of the absence of Utopia . . . in the street, in politics and struggles. Of course, the more positive sense of all this is Gramscian again: pedagogy, even institutional pedagogy, is a form of proto-pre-political labor in times where 'politics' (in a revolutionary sense) is unavailable"; see also "Horizons," 70.

41. The other three antinomic "sorting systems" by which Jameson casts his second look at postmodern culture are Identity and Difference, Time and Space, Nature and Human Nature (see *Seeds* 6–8). It is this deep historical opposition that informs Jameson's capitalization of the word *Utopia:* The typographic distinction enables him to differentiate "Utopia" as the underlying historical force from its particular manifestation in a variety of "utopian" forms. See Preface, n. 1.

42. For an analysis of the contradictory social desires, class positions, and oppositional politics of the militia movement, see Fred Pfeil, "Sympathy for the Devils: Notes on Some White Guys in the Ridiculous Class War," *New Left Review* (1995), 115–124.

43. Daniel Singer, *Whose Millennium? Theirs or Ours?* (1999), 277.

Chapter 4

1. E. M. Forster's story was republished in *The Eternal Moment and Other Stories* (London: Sidgwick and Jackson, 1928), 1–61. I cite the version of "The Machine Stops" that appears in *The Science Fiction Research Association Anthology* (1988), 23–41. For a range of criticism on "The Machine Stops," see Victor De Araujo, *The Short Story of Fantasy: Henry James, H. G. Wells, and E. M. Forster* (1965); Charles Elkins, "E. M. Forster's 'The Machine

Stops': Liberal-Humanist Hostility to Technology," *Clockwork Worlds* (1983), 47–62; Perry Nodelman, "Out There in Children's Science Fiction: Forward into the Past," *Science-Fiction Studies* (1985), 285–296; Richard Toby Widdicombe, "Eutopia, Dystopia, Aporia: The Obstruction of Meaning in Fin-de-Siecle Utopian Texts," *Utopian Studies* (1990), 93–102; Silvana Caporaletti, "Science as Nightmare: 'The Machine Stops' by E. M. Forster," *Utopian Studies* (1997), 32–47; Marcia Bundy Seabury, "Images of a Networked Society: E. M. Forster's 'The Machine Stops,'" *Studies in Short Fiction* (1997), 61–71.

2. Contemporary with Forster's story, Jack London's *Iron Heel* (1908) is arguably a more fruitful text within which to locate the emergence of the dystopian form. For me, however, London's work, though politically preferable to Forster's, remains a borderline case. It is *almost* a dystopia, or perhaps a "proto-dystopia," as Gorman Beauchamp might put it. Published just before "The Machine Stops" and clearly influential on the later dystopias (especially, as Krishan Kumar points out, on Orwell, who listed it in his "chain of Utopia books"), it nevertheless comes to the edge of dystopia but, as I see it, is not yet that new genre; see Kumar, *Utopia and Anti-Utopia in Modern Times* (1987), Orwell quoted on 294. Darko Suvin is also ambivalent about the formal status of the text; in *Metamorphoses of Science Fiction: On the Poetics of a Literary Genre* (1979) he lists London's work along with the "dystopian 'new maps of hell'" in one passage, but in another writes of "London's fusion of Wells and utopianism" as different from "the anti-utopia of Zamyatin, the political 'new maps of hell' of American SF in the 1940s and 1950s, and the satirical SF from the Warsaw Pact countries" (*Metamorphoses* 25, 230). The critic who perceptively catches the borderline quality of the text is Beauchamp; see "Jack London's Utopian Dystopia and Dystopian Utopia," *America as Utopia* (1981), 91–107; and for his notion of the "proto-dystopia" see "The Proto-Dystopia of Jerome K. Jerome," *Extrapolation* (1983), 170–181. See also Nadia Khouri, "Utopia and Epic: Ideological Confrontation in Jack London's *The Iron Heel*," *Science-Fiction Studies* (1976), 174–181; Nathaniel Teich, "Marxist Dialectics in Content, Form, Point of View: Structures in Jack London's *The Iron Heel*," *Modern Fiction Studies* (1976), 85–99; Alessandro Portelli, "Jack London's Missing Revolution: Notes on *The Iron Heel*," *Science-Fiction Studies* (1982), 180–195; and Phillip E. Wegner, *Imaginary Communities: Utopia, the Nation, and the Spatial Histories of Modernity* (forthcoming). Indebted to this work, I see the setting in London's near future as pre-dystopian. Indeed, the fascist regime comes to power in the course of the book, or to put it more formally, the dystopian genre (complete with its eutopian surplus of the future Brotherhood of Man, encoded, as in Orwell and Atwood, in the textual apparatus of the text—in this case a footnote) is born within the pages of this text. See Tom Moylan, "On the Borders of Dystopia: Jack London's *The Iron Heel* and Kim Stanley Robinson's *Antarctica*," *The Dystopian Turn: Science Fiction and Utopia at the End of the 20th Century* (forthcoming).The argument could also be made that this formal and epistemological move from realism to dystopian narrative takes place in H. G. Wells's *Time Machine* (1895), as the Time Traveller moves into the future that then refers back in this emergent dystopian mode to the present of author and his character; see Patrick Parrinder, "*News from Nowhere, The Time Machine* and the Break-up of Classical Realism," *Science-Fiction Studies* (1976), 265–274. See Chapter 1, n. 28.

3. This is the generation of writers that came of age in the first decades of the twentieth century. Mark Hillegas lists their birthdates as follows: Forster, 1879; Zamyatin, 1884; Huxley, 1894; Orwell, 1903; see Mark Hillegas, *The Future as Nightmare: H. G. Wells and the Anti-Utopians* (1967), 5.

4. Hillegas also notes the following: R. H. Benson, *Lord of the World* (1907), Rose Macaulay, *What Not* (1918), A. E. [George Russell], *The Interpreters* (1922), Charlotte Haldane, *Man's World* (1926), David Karp, *One* (1953), William Golding, *The Inheritors* (1955), Franz Werfel, *Star of the Unborn* (1946), Albert Guerard, *Night Journey* (1950), L. P. Hartley, *Facial Justice* (1960), Anthony Burgess, *The Wanting Seed* (1963), and, in the atomic shadow, works like Nevil Shute's *On the Beach* (1957) and Eugene Burdick and Harvey Wheeler's *Fail Safe* (1962). For other titles, see Carter Kaplan, "The Advent of Literary Dystopia," *Extrapolation* (1999), 200–213.

5. A list of dystopian sf film could accompany this body of literary sf. I would begin with *Metropolis* (Lang, 1927), work though examples as varied as *The Invasion of the Body Snatchers* (Siegel, 1956; Kaufman, 1978), *Dr. Strangelove* (Kubrick, 1964), *Dawn of the Dead* (Romero, 1978), *THX 1138* (Lucas, 1970), *Red Dawn* (Milius, 1984), *Brazil* (Gilliam, 1985), *Blade Runner* (Scott, 1982), and come up to recent productions such as *Twelve Monkeys* (Gilliam, 1995), *Gattaca* (Nichol, 1997), *Dark City* (Proyas, 1998), *The Truman Show* (Weir, 1998), *The Matrix* (Wachowski and Wachowski, 1999), and *Pleasantville* (Ross, 1998). I would also include the film versions of *Nineteen Eighty-Four* (Anderson, 1956; Radford, 1984), *Fahrenheit 451* (Truffaut, 1966; Gibson, 2000), *Clockwork Orange* (Kubrick, 1971), and *The Handmaid's Tale* (Schlöndorff, 1990). For the most complete filmography of utopian/dystopian films to date, see Gregory Claeys and Lyman Tower Sargent, *Utopia: The Search for the Ideal Society in the Western World* (2000). See also Peter Fitting, "What Is Utopian Film? An Introductory Taxonomy," *Utopian Studies* (1993), 1–17.

6. See C. S. Lewis, *The Abolition of Man* (1943); Friedrich von Hayek, *The Road to Serfdom* (1944); Karl Popper, *The Open Society and Its Enemies* (1945); and the essays by Arthur Koestler, Richard Wright, Louis Fischer, Ignazio Silone, André Gide, and Stephen Spender in Richard Howard Stafford Crossman, ed., *The God That Failed* (1949). The cluster of these anti-utopian expressions in the 1940s, the time of rising anti-communism, the "end of ideology," and the consolidation of the new economic, political, and cultural systems of the postwar era is itself worthy of study (as is the reassertion of utopianism that followed in the late 1950s).

7. Theodor W. Adorno, "Aldous Huxley and Utopia," *Prisms* (1981), 95–119. The essay was first published in *Prismen: Kulturkritik und Gesellschaft* (1955) (originally written for an Institute for Social Research seminar in Los Angeles in 1941). References are to the English version.

8. Phillip Rahv, "The Unfuture of Utopia," *Partisan Review* (1949), 743–749.

9. Gaylord LeRoy, "A.F. 632 to 1984," *College English* (1950), 135–138.

10. For discussions/critiques of the conservative liberalism found in Rahv and his compatriots, see Alan Wald, *The New York Intellectuals: The Rise and Decline of the Anti-Stalinist*

Left from the 1930's to the 1980's (1987), and Thomas Schaub, *American Fiction in the Cold War* (1991).

11. George Woodcock, "Five Who Fear the Future," *New Republic* (1956), 17–20.

12. Irving Howe, "The Fiction of Anti-Utopia," *New Republic* (1962), 13–16.

13. Lyman Tower Sargent, "Utopia—the Problem of Definition," *Extrapolation* (1975), 137–148.

14. Darko Suvin, ch. 3, "Science Fiction and Utopian Fiction: Degrees of Kinship," in *Positions and Presuppositions in Science Fiction* (1988), 36.

15. John Huntington, "Utopian and Anti-utopian Logic: H. G. Wells and His Successors," *Science-Fiction Studies* (1982), 122–147. In addition to Huntington's essay, this special issue, "Utopia and Anti-Utopia," includes the following: H. G. Wells, "Utopias," 117–122; Fredric Jameson, "Progress Versus Utopia; or, Can We Imagine the Future," 147–159; Tom Moylan, "The Locus of Hope: Utopia Versus Ideology," 159–167; Eugene D. Hill, "The Place of the Future: Louis Marin and His *Utopiques*," 167–180; Portelli, "Jack London's Missing Revolution: Notes on *The Iron Heel*," 180–195; David Ketterer, "Covering *A Case of Conscience*," 195–215.

16. Although freestanding "formal anti-utopias" are relatively rare before the nineteenth century, Kumar locates an early instance in Bishop Hall's *Mundus Alter et Idem*. As an "inverted vision of Cokaygne," Hall's text describes the fat, sluggish, thieving, fighting inhabitants of Crapulia as exemplars of the social corruption the good bishop saw about him (see *Modern Times* 105).

17. For a detailed analysis of *Erewhon*, see Patrick Parrinder, "Utopia After Darwin: *Erewhon* Revisited" (1999).

18. For work on dystopian texts from a feminist perspective, see the essays in Jane Donawerth and Carol Kolmerten, eds., *Utopian and Science Fiction by Women: Worlds of Difference* (1994): Donawerth and Kolmerten, introduction, 1–15; Carol Farley Kessler, "Consider Her Ways: The Cultural Work of Charlotte Perkins Gilman's Pragmatopian Series, 1908–1913," 126–137; Sarah Lefanu, "Difference and Sexual Politics in Naomi Mitchison's *Solution Three*," 153–166; Michelle Erica Green, "There Goes the Neighborhood: Octavia Butler's Demand for Diversity in Utopias," 166–190. See also M. Keith Booker, *The Dystopian Impulse in Modern Literature: Fiction as Social Criticism* (1994) and its companion volume, *Dystopian Literature: A Theory and Research Guide* (1994); and Peter Fitting's review: "Impulse or Genre or Neither?" *Science-Fiction Studies* (1995), 272–281. The difficulty with Booker's extensive survey rests in its thematic approach and its continuing confusion between text and temperament and between anti-utopian and critical utopian positions. Fitting observes that although Booker (in the spirit of Kumar, Sargent, and Jameson) differentiates between dystopia as a type of fiction and as an "oppositional and critical energy or spirit" (Booker, quoted in "Impulse or Genre or Neither?" 272), he still conflates dystopias that critique society with those that critique utopianism. See also Thomas H. Clapper, review of *The Dystopian Impulse in Modern Literature: Fiction as Social Criticism* and *Dystopian Literature: A Theory and Research Guide*, by M. Keith Booker, *Utopian Stud-*

ies (1995), 147–150; and Lyman Tower Sargent, review of *Dystopian Literature: A Theory and Research Guide,* by M. Keith Booker, *Utopian Studies* (1995), 134–139.

19. Lyman Tower Sargent, "The Three Faces of Utopianism Revisited," *Utopian Studies* (1994), 1–38.

20. Although my focus here is on texts and theory, I want to note the importance of Sargent's second category, utopian societies, in terms of the overall impact of Utopia in history. The Communal Studies Association (based in Amana, Iowa) and the Center for Communal Studies (based in Evansville, Indiana) provide an important locus for research on communal, international utopian societies. For a good overview, see Donald E. Pitzer, *America's Communal Utopias* (1997). For an informative review essay, see Michael Cummings, "America's Communal Utopias," *Utopian Studies* (1998), 191–206. Cummings notes the larger significance of this widespread and complex movement, one that has been around, in the West and the East, since the Middle Ages. Speaking specifically of the impact of North American groups, and capturing the basic Utopian-Anti-Utopian opposition, Cummings reminds us that "America's communal utopias have challenged the assumptions of market society, and market society has struck back by undermining or transforming most of them" ("America's Communal Utopias" 191). In this category of utopian work, anti-utopianism enters by way of social theory to attack such social experiments, or (more terribly) it acts physically and psychologically in overt attacks on such communal societies.

21. Contrary to the ideological position expressed in liberal anti-utopianism, Goodwin and Taylor specifically, and significantly, identify liberal democratic theory (LDT) as a recent instance of the anti-utopian temperament as they examine the ways in which it refuses any form of totalizing analysis and anticipatory thought that would radically transform modern industrial-capitalist societies. Cleansed of overt anti-communist hysteria, the cool rationality of LDT posits the primacy of empirical thought and the rule of the majority against the dangerous "fantasies" and radical democracy of utopian projects that actually aim to transform social reality into something better than what now exists; see Barbara Goodwin and Keith Taylor, *The Politics of Utopia* (1982), 92–115.

22. Darko Suvin, "Utopianism from Orientation to Agency: What Are We Intellectuals Under Post-Fordism to Do?" *Utopian Studies* (1998), 162–190.

23. Robert M. Philmus, "The Language of Utopia," *Studies in the Literary Imagination* (1973), 61–78. In addition to the essay, Philmus's 1970 book, *Into the Unknown: The Evolution of Science Fiction from Francis Godwin to H. G. Wells,* was among the breakthrough works in sf studies.

24. Robert M. Philmus, "Swift, Zamiatin, and Orwell and the Language of Utopia," *Visions and Re-Visions: Collected Essays* (forthcoming); pages cited are from typescript copy. I am grateful to Philmus for making a draft of his revision available, and more so for the discussions we had before publication of our respective pieces.

25. Fredric Jameson, *The Seeds of Time* (1994).

26. How this conflict works as well in the regions and nations of the "South," or what used to be called the "Third World" or "developing nations," is a very different question and a subject, as is the question of non-Western utopianism, for another project. Neverthe-

less, those very different situations which also increasingly occur *within* the regions of the North (in its cities, at its margins, among its various peoples, in those sectors of contemporary life which have been written off or newly exploited by the most recent capitalist logic) must underline, surround, and frame the discussion in this study and will emerge from time to time within it as gestures to work not yet done.

27. See Ernst Bloch and Theodor W. Adorno, "Something's Missing: A Discussion Between Ernst Bloch and Theodor W. Adorno on the Contradictions of Utopian Longing," *The Utopian Function of Art and Literature: Selected Essays* (1988).

Chapter 5

1. Karl Marx, *The Letters of Karl Marx* (1979), 30.

2. Raffaella Baccolini, "Gender and Genre in the Feminist Critical Dystopias of Katherine Burdekin, Margaret Atwood, and Octavia Butler," *Future Females, the Next Generation: New Voices and Velocities in Feminist Science Fiction* (2000), 13–34.

3. In addition to "Gender and Genre," see Raffaella Baccolini, "Breaking the Boundaries: Gender, Genre, and Dystopia," *Per una definizione dell'utopia: Metodologie e discipline a confronto* (1992), 137–146; "'It's Not in the Womb the Damage Is Done': Memory and the Construction of Gender in K. Burdekin's *Swastika Night*," *Le trasformazioni del narrarae* (1995), 293–309; "Journeying Through the Dystopian Genre," *Viaggi in Utopia* (1996), 343–357.

4. For an extensive discussion of the place of language in utopian expression, see Robert M. Philmus, "Swift, Zamiatin, and Orwell and the Language of Utopia," *Visions and Re-Visions: Collected Essays* (forthcoming); pages cited are from typescript copy.

5. On the difference between the backward-looking, conservative memory implicated in nostalgia and the forward-bearing, progressive memory allied with progressive change, see Vincent Geoghegan, "Remembering the Future," *Not Yet* (1997), 15–33.

6. Darko Suvin, "The SF Novel as Epic Narration: For a Fusion of 'Formal' and 'Sociological' Analysis," *Positions and Presuppositions in Science Fiction* (1988), 74–86. For another discussion of the relationship between sf/utopia and the epic, see Patrick Parrinder, *Science Fiction: Its Criticism and Teaching* (1980).

7. Suvin's notion of "choice" resonates with Raymond Williams's discussion of "willed transformation" in "Utopia and Science Fiction," *Problems in Materialism and Culture* (1980), 203–214.

8. Although I take Suvin's point, care must be taken to heed feminist critiques of the epic tradition's privileging of the male hero. Yet if the sf novum is that which exceeds the social and formal limits of the present, then it has the potential to transcend the ideological limits of the epic tradition even as it makes use of the epical form. See Russ's commentary on the power of sf to shatter existing gender structures and power relations in "What Can a Heroine Do," *To Write Like a Woman* (1995).

9. Søren Baggesen, "Utopian and Dystopian Pessimism: Le Guin's *The Word for World Is Forest* and Tiptree's "We Who Stole the Dream," *Science-Fiction Studies* (1987), 34–43.

10. Marx: "Men make their own history, but they do not make it just as they please; they do not make it under circumstances chosen by themselves, but under circumstances directly encountered, given and transmitted from the past"; see *The Eighteenth Brumaire of Louis Bonaparte,* in *The Marx Reader* (1997), 156.

11. Jenny Wolmark, *Aliens and Others: Science Fiction, Feminism, and Postmodernism* (1994), 90.

12. Hoda M. Zaki has also found Baggesen's analysis to be compelling and useful; see "Utopia, Dystopia, and Ideology in the Science Fiction of Octavia Butler," *Science-Fiction Studies* (1990), 239–251. Zaki conflates *dystopia* and *anti-utopia,* but she takes the basic point that one end of the dystopian spectrum identifies works that are utopian and progressive and the other names those which are "anti-utopian and conservative" (244).

13. Lyman Tower Sargent, "The Three Faces of Utopianism Revisited," *Utopian Studies* (1994), 9.

14. Darko Suvin, "Utopianism from Orientation to Agency: What Are We Intellectuals Under Post-Fordism to Do?" *Utopian Studies* (1998), 170.

15. Lyman Tower Sargent, "Utopia—the Problem of Definition," *Extrapolation* (1975), 142.

16. In "Swift, Zamiatin, and Orwell and the Language of Utopia," Philmus argues that the "difference between utopia and dystopia finally comes down to a matter of point of view (in all senses of the phrase)" (3). I hope that my overall analysis establishes that this is not the *only* differentiating difference, but Philmus, like Sargent and Roemer, makes a point regarding the critical position of the reader.

17. For her thesis, Maria Varsamopolou is working on the concept of a "concrete dystopia," which she attributes to actually existing social systems, such as the institution of slavery; see "Towards a Definition of Dystopia." 1999.

18. Although I appreciate the spirit and consequences of Suvin's formalist argument that utopia, anti-utopia, and dystopia are *logically* subgenres of sf, I think a more *historically* inflected perspective is also needed—so that the differences between the conditions of the emergence of eutopia in the early moments of modernity and sf (and dystopia) in recent modernity (where *that* begins is another matter) are also taken into account in developing an understanding of the nature and effect of these literary forms. Since the roots of all these forms precede modernity, perhaps the term *estranged* or *nonrealist* or (if properly differentiated from literary fantasy) *fantastic* writing can name the overall category in a way that is both logically and historically appropriate. Nevertheless, I agree that (in the twentieth century, or at least in the second half) all three subgenres are usually conceived, written, and certainly marketed within the generic sphere of sf.

19. In addition, Philmus's distinction, taken from Kenneth Burke, between utopian texts that are "dialectical," thus open and satirical, as opposed to "ultimate," therefore closed and visionary, could provide an additional layer of textual analysis to a study of a dystopian text; see "Swift, Zamiatin, and Orwell and the Language of Utopia."

20. Peter Fitting, "Impulse or Genre or Neither?" *Science-Fiction Studies* (1995), 281n.

21. Raymond Williams, "Utopia and Science Fiction," *Problems in Materialism and Culture* (1980), 203–214.

22. Fredric Jameson, *The Seeds of Time* (1994), 54.

23. Hillegas (like Philmus and others) continues to use the term *anti-utopia* rather than *dystopia,* but he nevertheless catches the significance of Forster's contribution, describing it as the "first full-scale emergence of the twentieth-century anti-utopia," with its dual critique of modern society and the utopian imagination; see Mark Hillegas, *The Future as Nightmare: H. G. Wells and the Anti-Utopians* (1967), 82. Fitting also argues that Forster's story is a rejection of an attempted utopian society. To be sure, at the level of content it is indeed a satiric rejection of the "false utopia" of the Machine Society (and hence of the technological temptation to what was sometimes termed a "utopian" but more accurately was a "socially engineered" solution). As an early instance of the new formal strategy of dystopia, however, it does not refuse all utopian possibility and hence is not a pure anti-utopian narrative (see "Impulse or Genre" 281n).

24. Yevgeny Zamyatin, *We,* written in 1920–1921 and first published in English in 1924. Edition cited is *We* (1993).This early fictional critique of the misdirection of the Soviet revolution was never published in Russian in the author's lifetime. After the first English publication, it was translated into many other languages, but a complete edition did not appear in Russian until 1952. For more on the publication history, see Clarence Brown's introduction to the 1993 edition of *We.* See also Gorman Beauchamp, "Of Man's Last Disobedience: Zamiatin's *We* and Orwell's *1984,*" *Comparative Literature Studies* (1973), 285–301; Darko Suvin, "Russian Sf and the Utopian Tradition," *Metamorphoses of Science Fiction: On the Poetics and History of a Literary Genre* (1979), 243–269; and Phillip E. Wegner, "On Zamyatin's *We:* A Critical Map of Utopia's 'Possible Worlds,'" *Utopian Studies* (1993), 94–117, and his chapters on Zamyatin in *Imaginary Communities: Utopia, the Nation, and the Spatial Histories of Modernity* (forthcoming).

25. George Orwell, *Nineteen Eighty-Four,* first published in 1949.

26. See Krishan Kumar's discussion of Orwell in *Utopia and Anti-Utopia in Modern Times* (1987), 344ff.

27. George Orwell, "Letter to Francis A. Henson," *Collected Essays, Journalism and Letters of George Orwell* (1970), 564.

28. Larry W. Caldwell, "Wells, Orwell, and Atwood: Logic and Eutopia," *Extrapolation* (1992), 338–339. I am grateful to Phillip E. Wegner for alerting me to this essay. As a further indication of Orwell's utopian intention, Wegner notes in the chapter on Orwell in his forthcoming book that the author refused to allow the publication of a Book-of-the-Month Club edition with the appendix (as well as the excerpts from Goldstein's book) removed—even though it meant the potential loss of $40,000 in revenue; see *Imaginary Communities: Utopia, the Nation, and the Spatial Histories of Modernity* (forthcoming).

29. See Robert Paul Resch, "Utopia, Dystopia, and the Middle Class in George Orwell's *Nineteen Eighty-Four,*" *Boundary 2* (1997), 137–176. In his reader's report, Wegner recalls Resch's argument that the "world" of the appendix is truly a "'no place' that cannot exist

given the sociological reality of Oceania. . . . No theory or transition can be imagined from within the limits of Orwell's political ideology" (Resch 158–159).

30. Margaret Atwood, *The Handmaid's Tale,* was first published in Toronto in 1985. I cite the U.S. edition (1986).

31. The term *friendly fascism* might appear simultaneously to understate and overstate the cultural terror and physical violence that permeates contemporary market societies, but as Bertram Gross provocatively employs it to describe the United States in 1980, it echoes the way in which Gilead comes to be accepted by people in small doses, small changes, until of course it is too late; see *Friendly Fascism: The New Face of Power in America* (1980).

32. A further critique of Atwood's liberalism was presented by Tina Lehtoranta in her paper "Feminism in *The Handmaid's Tale* by Margaret Atwood," at the Utopian Studies Society conference, University of Nottingham, 20 June 2000.

33. David N. Samuelson, "*Limbo:* The Great American Dystopia," *Extrapolation* (1977), 76.

34. Frederik Pohl and C. M. Kornbluth, *The Space Merchants,* originally published as "Gravy Planet," *Galaxy* 4.3–5 (June-August 1952), 4–61, 108–159, 104–159; subsequently published in 1953. Edition cited is *The Space Merchants* (1985).

35. Kingsley Amis, *New Maps of Hell: A Survey of Science Fiction* (1960), 113.

36. Frederik Pohl published *The Merchants War* in 1984 as a sequel to *Space Merchants.* In this work endowed with the subsequent utopian optimism of the 1960s and 1970s, the Consies return from their Venusian community and defeat the corporate powers.

37. Philip K. Dick, "Faith of Our Fathers," first published in 1967. Edition cited appears in *The Science Fiction Research Association Anthology* (1988), 353–378. For more developed explorations and speculations within the consumerist belly of the U.S. beast, see especially Dick's novels, from the middle-period in his work: *Martian Time-Slip* (1964), *Dr. Bloodmoney; or How We Got Along Without the Bomb* (1965), *The Three Stigmata of Palmer Eldritch* (1965), *Ubik* (1969).

38. Pamela Zoline, "The Heat Death of the Universe," first published in 1967. Edition cited appears in *The Mirror of Infinity: A Critics' Anthology of Science Fiction* (1970), 285–309.

39. Zoline, quoted by Brian Aldiss, "Foreword to 'The Heat Death of the Universe,'" *The Mirror of Infinity: A Critics' Anthology of Science Fiction* (1970), 288.

40. Barbara Goodwin and Keith Taylor, *The Politics of Utopia* (1982), 27.

41. Robert O. Evans, "The *Nouveau Roman,* Russian Dystopias, and Anthony Burgess," *Studies in the Literary Imagination* (1973), 33 (cited in Sargent, "Three Faces Revisited" 6).

42. See Fitting, "Impulse or Genre or Neither?" 273–276.

43. Marshall Berman, *All That Is Solid Melts into Air: The Experience of Modernity* (1988), 243.

Chapter 6

1. For an overview of this shift, see David Harvey, *The Condition of Postmodernity* (1989), especially 121–201.

2. The emergent regime of millennial capitalism has been described by Eric Alliez and Michel Feher as a new "space of subjection and time of enslavement," in which all social space and time is made available to the cybernetic mechanisms of capital; see Eric Alliez and Michel Feher, "The Luster of Capital," *Zone* (1986), 314–359. The result is what the authors term a "social factorization" in which society itself functions like the factory of the industrial era. That is, all space and time is seized by the discipline of production (whether actively or available in a fallow field for future exploitation). As a result, they argue, humanity is enslaved rather than subjected to the new regime. Formerly free time and spaces become merely unused portions of the social whole that must be made profitable or dumped aside, made derelict, until taken up again when cheaper or desirable or both. Where humanity was once released from the land to work in the factory, to be subjected to capital, now it is released from the workplace to be enslaved in the cyberspace of the transnational corporate machine. This machine tends, on the one hand, "to treat people and 'intelligent' machines as functionally interchangeable terminals—relays in the capitalist social machine" and, on the other hand, "leads to the dereliction of the people and spaces that cannot be 'plugged in' to the network either because they are insufficiently 'informed' or because the information they produce is irreducible to merchandise form" (Alliez and Feher 316–317). See also the discussion and debates between and among the following: Michel Aglietta, *A Theory of Capitalist Regulation* (1979); Giovanni Arrighi, *The Long Twentieth Century* (1994); Robert Boyer, *The Regulation School: A Critical Introduction* (1990); Robert Brenner, "The Economics of Global Turbulence," *New Left Review* (1998), 1–264; Nicholas Costello, Jonathan Michie, and Seaumas Milne, *Beyond the Casino Economy: Planning for the 1990s* (1989); Bennett Harrison and Barry Bluestone, *The Great U-Turn: Corporate Restructuring and the Polarization of America* (1990); Doug Henwood, *A New Economy?* (2000); Alain Lipietz, *Towards a New Economic Order* (1992); Paul Smith, *Millennial Dreams: Contemporary Culture and Capital in the North* (1997); Immanuel Wallerstein, *Geopolitics and Geoculture* (1992) and *Historical Capitalism/Capitalist Civilization* (1996); Ellen Meiskins Wood, *Democracy Against Capitalism* (1995) and *The Origins of Capitalism* (1999).

3. To be sure, real though relative differences of social awareness, social responsibility, and contested political terrain exist between the U.S. situation and the still residual social democratic and even socialist political milieu in Europe. In the present study, of course, it is the harsher, more conservative context in the United States that is the immediate ground out of which the new dystopian sf has emerged. See Jorge Casteñada, *Utopia Unarmed: The Latin American Left After the Cold War* (1993).

4. By the end of Clinton's second term of office in 2000, the Democratic president brought military policy full circle from the Reagan years as he traveled to Europe and Russia to sell the military-industrial complex's dream of a new "son of star wars" missile defense system.

5. The official title was the Personal Responsibility and Work Opportunity Reconciliation Act of 1996 (H.R. 3734 of the 104th Congress, now Public Law 104–193). It was signed into law by Clinton in August 1996.

6. For analyses of the ways in which the rhetoric and ideology of globalization is undemocratically mobilized to legitimate the abandonment of hard-won commitments to

social contracts, entitlements, and care, as well as to justify the continued refusal of higher wages, shorter working weeks, and safe working environments, see Smith, *Millennial Dreams,* especially chapters 1 and 4.

7. That any new works of social critique were to be found in the sf of the 1980s was due to the tenacity of editors, writers, and readers who were willing to work against the changes in publication and distribution practices that were imposed by the restructuring of the publishing industry. Increased profitability demands by new corporate parent companies put more value on producing endlessly repeating sf series rather than singular new works; revised tax laws prevented the holding of backlists of classical sf; and the domination of distribution by a shrinking number of large bookstores narrowed the range of books on offer to readers, who themselves became more vulnerable to the processes of an increasingly defined and controlled market. Nevertheless, small presses, adamant editors in major presses, independent distributors, and the long-standing base of serious sf readers (in fandom and beyond) managed to preserve a creative and courageous commitment to meaningful and challenging work. The feminist, cyberpunk, and new dystopian texts under discussion here were the result of that persistence of vision in the sf community. On the effect of the market on sf, see Nickianne Moody, "Maeve and Guinevere: Women's Fantasy Writing in the Science Fiction Marketplace" (1991); Cristina Sedgewick, "The Fork in the Road: Can Science Fiction Survive in Postmodern, Megacorporate America?" *Science-Fiction Studies* (1991), 11–53; Gary Westfahl, George Slusser, and Eric S. Rabkin, eds., *Science Fiction and Market Realities* (1996); and Camille Bacon-Smith, *Science Fiction Culture* (1999).

8. Bryan N. Alexander, "Jameson's Adorno and the Problem of Utopia," *Utopian Studies* (1998), 51–58. Alexander's essay is part of the special section on "The Work of Fredric Jameson." Taking Alexander's argument, it is this postwar privileging of the dystopian imagination (in negative response to both the material conditions and the resurgence of anti-utopian discourse in the 1940s) that provides the ground for the emergence in the 1960s of the sf-based critical utopia as a textual strategy that draws on the underside of Utopia to critique and refunction the endangered eutopian form of politics and aesthetics.

9. Jameson also notes that these three periods are times when "post-Marxisms" have appeared, when the "end" of categories such as history, ideology, and class has been most loudly proclaimed; see "Five Theses on Actually Existing Marxism," *Monthly Review* (1996), 1–10. See also Jacques Derrida, *Spectres of Marx, State of the Debt, the Work of Mourning* (1994).

10. Jenny Wolmark, *Aliens and Others: Science Fiction, Feminism, and Postmodernism* (1994), 91.

11. Lyman Tower Sargent, "The Three Faces of Utopianism Revisited," *Utopian Studies* (1994), 7.

12. Raffaella Baccolini, "Gender and Genre in the Feminist Critical Dystopias of Katherine Burdekin, Margaret Atwood, and Octavia Butler," *Future Females, the Next Generation: New Voices and Velocities in Feminist Science Fiction* (2000), 16.

13. Ildney Cavalcanti, "Articulating the Elsewhere: Utopia in Contemporary Feminist Dystopias" (1999), 3. See also Elizabeth Mahoney, "Writing So to Speak: The Feminist Dystopia" (1994).

14. Although I take Cavalcanti's point about the formal role of satiric exaggeration, I think it is important to factor in a historical as well as formalist analysis of the relationship between satire and dystopia as distinct (even if closely related) literary forms. I agree with Kumar that the dystopian form is a twentieth-century textual development that has deep roots in the "formal anti-utopia" of the nineteenth century, the "eutopia" that derives from More and others, and classical and modern satire. See Krishan Kumar, *Utopia and Anti-Utopia in Modern Times* (1987), 104–109.

15. In "World-Reduction in Le Guin," Jameson explores possibilities and limits of the formal practice of "radical abstraction and simplification" that he calls "world-reduction." He describes the process as one in which the elements of the empirical world are, in sf texts like Le Guin's, "simplified to the extreme" so that in "this experimental variation on our own empirical universe" we can "relax that tyrannical 'reality principle' which functions as a crippling censorship over" our sense of the word and then develop "alternate versions of a world that has elsewhere seemed to resist even *imagined* change"; see Fredric Jameson, "World-Reduction in Le Guin," *Science-Fiction Studies* (1975), 222–223. Such an "ontological attenuation," he argues, thins out the "sheer teeming multiplicity of what exists, of what we call reality" in order to open the world to critique and, more so, in the work of Le Guin and others in the 1970s, to "become an instrument in the conscious elaboration of a utopia" ("World-Reduction" 223–224). Thus, by "the experimental production of an imaginary situation by *excision* of the real," by a "radical suppression" of some features and exposure of others, the creative work of the sf or utopian text can break through or deviate from hegemonic common sense and offer a critical and subversive form of knowledge to receptive and engaged readers ("World-Reduction" 226).

16. Constance Penley, "Time Travel, Primal Scene," *The Future of an Illusion: Film, Feminism, and Psychoanalysis* (1989), 4.

17. A note on the term *beyond*: When I write of the counter-hegemonic political imagination and practice of the 1990s as moving *beyond* the politics of the 1980s (especially the politics of identity), I am—with Penley, Jameson, and others—referring to a political and cultural move into another conjunctural moment, one that is producing its specific form of analysis and action by dialectically taking the political struggles of the 1980s into that new context. I am *not* speaking of the sort of co-optive dismissal (albeit cast as reformist) of the identity movements that has been articulated in those cultural and political circles that are hegemonically white (certainly male and straight, but also, at times and variously, feminist, conservative, liberal, social democratic, and socialist). Indeed, the new moment (of which the critical dystopias are a part) can *only* work *with and critically through* that previous political effort to establish difference as the basis of counter-hegemonic and progressive work. Only then can the work of organizing a new alliance politics refuse and resist the traditional privileges of white, male dominance and opt instead for an oppositional authority based in the empowered diversity of all involved. To move "beyond" the moment of the 1980s, then, is to move *into* the new conjunctural moment, not to dismiss or move *against* the insights and victories of identity politics. An implicit consequence of this position is its critique and transcendence of the once timely work of Ernesto Laclau and Chantal Mouffe; see *Hegemony and Socialist Strategy: Towards a Radical Democratic Politics*

(1985). For a careful discussion of these issues and clarifications, see Anuradha Dingwaney and Lawrence Needham, "The Difference That Difference Makes," *Socialist Review* (1996), 5–47.

18. Peter Fitting, "Unmasking the Real? Critique and Utopia in Four Recent Films," paper, Society for Utopian Studies conference, San Antonio, Texas, November 1999. For an expanded version of this paper, see Raffaella Baccolini and Tom Moylan, eds., *The Dystopian Turn: Science Fiction and Utopia at the End of the 20th Century* (forthcoming).

19. Lyman Tower Sargent, "U.S. Eutopias in the 1980s and 1990s," lecture, COTEPRA Conference, Centro Interdipartimentale di Ricerca Sull'utopia, University of Bologna, Rimini, Italy, 9 July 2000, n. 1.

20. I am grateful to Sargent for suggesting the pairing of "critical dystopia" versus "anti-critical dystopia." Given my focus, I leave any number of other textual examples to others to analyze for critical or noncritical dystopian properties. In addition to those mentioned, my list of critical texts would also include the following: in sf, the work of Ian M. Banks or Charnas's revived "Holdfast" series; in television, *Babylon Five* or *Buffy, the Vampire Slayer*; in films, from the film version of *Buffy, the Vampire Slayer* (Kuzui, 1992) to the experimental *Pi* (Aronofsky, 1998).

21. In his essay on Butler, Jim Miller also uses the term *critical dystopia* to characterize Butler's textual strategy (and overall attitude toward utopian thought and practice); see "Post-Apocalyptic Hoping: Octavia Butler's Dystopian/Utopian Fiction," *Science-Fiction Studies* (1998), 336–361. In the first section of the essay (entitled "Critical Dystopias/Utopian Pessimism"), he places Butler in the framework of the "postmodern and dystopian writing of the 80s and 90s that is the post-utopian continuation of the feminist utopian tradition," and he then argues that her "Xenogenesis" trilogy and *Parable of the Sower* are "critical dystopias motivated out of a utopian pessimism in that they force us to confront the dystopian elements of postmodern culture so that we can work through them and begin again" (Miller 337). Working with Wolmark's commentary and echoing the logic of Baccolini's argument or the practice of "genre blurring," he argues that "contemporary utopian/dystopian postmodern science-fiction narratives are profoundly 'intertextual' in that their striking hybridity defies easy genre categorization and makes them effective tools with which to 'undermine ostensibly clear-cut distinctions between self and other' and 'explore possibilities for alternative and non-hierarchical definitions of gender and identity within which the difference of aliens and others can be accommodated rather than repressed'" (quoted in Miller 337). See Chapter 8, n. 1.

22. In "Reconsiderations of the Separatist Paradigm in Recent Feminist Science Fiction," *Science-Fiction Studies* (1992), 32–48, Fitting advances a critical perspective on the feminist work of the 1980s. Starting his analysis in the light of Atwood's work—and looking especially at the books by Sargent, Slonczewski, and Tepper—he argues that such works had not so much adapted to the demands of the contemporary situation, as Wolmark suggests, but rather had departed from the spirit of the critical utopia and instead opted for a textual refuge in separatist alternatives that (contrary to those found in Russ or Charnas, for example) were no longer in contestatory tension with the present. He especially sees the concern

with "liminality" as a sign of retreat from the project of political change driven by utopian hope: that is, a marker of the move toward accommodation rather than "mobilizing for change" (43). For a rebuttal, see Pamela Sargent, "On Peter Fitting's Reconsiderations in *SFS* #56," *Science-Fiction Studies* (1992), 271–276. In a related argument, Carol Stabile also challenges the 1980s moment of discourse-based feminist utopianism. Aligning herself with socialist feminism, she argues that "the feminist alternative to the dematerialized, idealist theorizing proposed by many postmodernists has often produced its own version of dematerialized theory" (*Feminism and the Technological Fix* [1994]), 4. She names two tendencies that have pulled away from feminist politics even as they still claim to be part of that project. Although the "technophobic" tendency has more often moved into separatist enclaves informed by an ideology and politics of the woman-and-nature linkage that has little interest in confronting the complexities of the current regime, the "technomania" tendency, tied to Haraway's "cyborg manifesto," has not so much led to its hoped-for radical stance against the system but rather to a reformist place within it. In an apparent embrace of a politics of the local that would claim a liminal space within the dominant system, such "cyborg politics" ends up being absorbed by what it opposes. Neither tendency engages the larger situation. Neither connects with other constituencies to challenge the entire system (see 1-26). Wolmark offers a "critically supportive" assessment of these works in which she argues that the "utopian optimism of the separatist communities depicted in [these novels] is, in the end, insufficient to sustain a radical critique of patriarchy" (Wolmark 86). But for a further critique and supersession of Haraway, see Anne Cranny-Francis's essay "The Erotics of the cy(Borg): Authority and Gender in the Sociocultural Imaginary," *Future Females, the Next Generation: New Voices and Velocities in Feminist Science Fiction* (2000), 145–164. Subsequent to this period, Sargent has noted a marked drop in the number of feminist eutopias published in the 1990s. This drop occurs at the point that the critical dystopian sensibility takes hold (Sargent, conversation, July 2000).

23. The term *cyberpunk* was coined by sf writer Bruce Bethke for a story published in 1982. Writer-editor Gardiner Dozois then used it to describe Gibson's work. The term was subsequently adopted by the writers and editors who identified with the "movement" that coalesced around this new form of near-future sf. See also Bruce Sterling, preface to *Mirrorshades: The Cyberpunk Anthology* (1988), ix–xvi. For a useful account of these developments, see Steve Brown, "Before the Lights Came On: Observations of a Synergy," *Storming the Reality Studio* (1991), 173–178.

24. Peter Fitting, "Hacking away at the Postmodern: William Gibson and Cyberpunk," paper, Popular Culture Association annual meeting, St. Louis, Missouri, 6 April 1989, 8; Darko Suvin, "On Gibson and Cyberpunk SF," *Foundation* (1989), 46.

25. See Jeanne Gomoll, "Open Letter to Joanna Russ," *Aurora* (1986–1987), 7–10; Istvan Csicsery-Ronay, "Cyberpunk and Neuromanticism," *Mississippi Review* (1988), 266–279; Takayuki Tatsumi, "Some Real Mothers: An Interview with Samuel R. Delany," *Science Fiction Eye* (1988), 5–11; Andrew Ross, "Cyberpunk in Boystown," *Strange Weather: Culture, Science, and Technology in the Age of Limits* (1991), 137–167; Thomas Foster, "Incurably Informed: The Pleasures and Dangers of Cyberpunk," *Genders* (1993), 1–10; Sharon Stock-

ton, "'The Self Regained': Cyberpunk's Retreat to the Imperium," *Contemporary Literature* (1995), 588–612. Csicsery-Ronay calls cyberpunk "the vanguard white male art of the age" (267). See also Veronica Hollinger, "Cybernetic Deconstructions: Cyberpunk and Postmodernism," *Storming the Reality Studio* (1991), 203–219. Hollinger reports that one of the strongest indictments of cyberpunk can be found in the 1987 self-criticism made by Bruce Sterling (perhaps the most effective and enterprising cyberpunk writer-editor-promoter) when he noted that its "truly dangerous element is incipient Nietzschean philosophical fascism: the belief in the Overman, and the worship of the will-to-power" (quoted in Hollinger 206). On cyberpunk as a new instance of realism, see Jameson's discussion of cyberpunk in *Postmodernism, or, The Cultural Logic of Late Capitalism* (1991).

26. See Tom Moylan, "Global Economy, Local Texts: Utopian/Dystopian Tensions in William Gibson's Cyberpunk 'Trilogy,'" *minnesota review* (1995), 182–198. In that essay I refer to Larry McCaffery's interview wherein Gibson describes his use of the safety-net metaphor: McCaffery observes that the plot and characters of *Neuromancer* are quite familiar ("the down-and-out gangster who's been fucked over and wants to get even by pulling the big heist"), and asks Gibson if he consciously decided to use such an established framework. In a response that uncannily echoes categories of the Reagan era and explains the accommodations of cyberpunk with the dominant culture, Gibson replies that his inexperience as a novelist led him to seek a narrative "safety net" that could contain his multiple and intense cyberimages. See McCaffery, "An Interview with William Gibson," *Mississippi Review* (1988), 217–237.

27. For an insightful study of this novel, see Laura Chernaik, "Pat Cadigan's *Synners:* Reconfiguring Nature, Science and Technology," *Feminist Review* (1997), 61–84; and Tom Moylan, review of *Synners,* by Pat Cadigan, *American Book Review* (1992), 5, 13.

Chapter 7

1. Kim Stanley Robinson, *The Gold Coast,* first published in 1988. For critical work on Robinson, see Carol Franco, "Dialogical Twins, Post-Patriarchal Topography in Two Stories by Kim Stanley Robinson," *Science-Fiction Studies* (1995), 305–322; "The Density of Utopian Destiny in Robinson's *Red Mars,*" *Extrapolation* (1997), 57–65; "Working the 'In-Between': Kim Stanley Robinson's Utopian Fiction," *Science-Fiction Studies* (1994), 191–211. See also Jameson's essay on the Martian trilogy: "'If I Find One Good City I Will Spare the Man,'" *Learning from Other Worlds* (2000).

2. The other volumes in the Orange County trilogy (entitled "Three Californias" in their New England Press edition) are *The Wild Shore* (1984) and *Pacific Edge* (1990). Following these journeyman studies, what can be seen as Robinson's masterwork, the Martian trilogy, includes *Red Mars* (1992), *Green Mars* (1993), and *Blue Mars* (1996). Robinson states that he began work on the trilogy in 1989, just after *The Gold Coast* was published and just before *Pacific Edge* appeared. Another indicator of his ecological utopianism can be seen in the anthology of short stores he edited; see *Future Primitive: The New Ecotopias* (1994). For insight into Robinson's critical perspective, see the dissertation he wrote, with Jameson as

adviser: *The Novels of Philip K. Dick* (1984). See also *Antarctica* (1997). Working with Baccolini's concept of gender blurring, I read *Antarctica* as a work of its moment, moving beyond *both* eutopian and dystopian categories as it explores (perhaps to the point of the creative exhaustion and transformation of dystopia) new political tendencies at the turn of the twentieth century. Drawing on both subgenres (and also working with the detective genre, the adventure travel narrative, poetry, and expository scientific discourse), it stands as another fine example of the political novel at the end of the century. See Tom Moylan, "On the Borders of Dystopia: Jack London's *The Iron Heel* and Kim Stanley Robinson's *Antarctica*," *The Dystopian Turn* (forthcoming).

3. Kim Stanley Robinson, with David Seed, "The Mars Trilogy: An Interview," *Foundation: The Review of Science Fiction* (1996), 77.

4. See Tom Moylan, "'Utopia Is When Our Lives Matter': Reading Kim Stanley Robinson's *Pacific Edge*," *Utopian Studies* (1995), 1–25.

5. In this work Robinson anticipates the scope and method of the Martian trilogy. In the *Foundation* interview, Seed describes Robinson's work in the later trilogy as an *invitation* "into a new kind of holistic thinking to see how all sorts of different areas of knowledge might inter-relate." Robinson agrees and connects Seed's description with his own embrace of the logic of ecological thought (see Robinson, "Interview" 78).

6. In developing this critical position on straight white masculinity, Robinson implicitly challenges the compromised soft macho positions reinforced by a number of first-wave cyberpunk works. For more on the cultural politics of white male struggles against material and discursive patriarchal power, see Fred Pfeil, *White Guys: Studies in Postmodern Domination and Difference* (1985). For complementary studies of black male struggles, see Hazel Carby, *Race Men* (1998), and Michael Dyson, *Between God and Gangsta Rap: Bearing Witness to Black Culture* (1996). On resistance within male literary practice, see Bertolt Schoene-Harwood, *Writing Men: Literary Masculinities from Frankenstein to the New Man* (2000).

7. In her chapter on Bloch, Cavalcanti refers to Sarah Lefanu's observation in *Feminism and Science Fiction* (1988) that there is "a hidden utopian streak" in dystopian novels by women: "They contain an element of hopefulness that rests on a belief in the power and efficacy of women's speech" (quoted in Cavalcanti 64n).

8. For a wider political perspective on the position Hana occupies, see Cavalcanti, who discusses Luce Irigaray's articulation of a critical space for women as it is "defined more in terms of strategic movement than fixed positionality" (Cavalcanti 66), or as Rosi Braidotti puts it, as it works with "one foot in the system the other outside" (quoted in Cavalcanti 66).

Chapter 8

1. Octavia E. Butler, *The Parable of the Sower,* first published by Four Walls Eight Windows in 1993. I cite the Warner edition of the same year. Octavia E. Butler, *The Parable of the Talents,* first published in 1998.For Butler on *Sower,* see her "Memorial Tribute to

Thomas Clareson" (1994). Among the interviews with Butler, see Frances M. Beal, "Black Women and the Science Fiction Genre: Interview with Octavia Butler," *Black Scholar* (1986), 14–18; Larry McCaffery, "An Interview with Octavia E. Butler," *Across the Wounded Galaxies* (1990), 54–70; Lisa See, "Octavia E. Butler," *Publisher's Weekly* (1993), 50–51; S. W. Potts, "We Keep Playing the Same Record—a Conversation with Octavia E. Butler," *Science-Fiction Studies* (1996), 331–338; Joan Fry, "An Interview with Octavia Butler," *Poets and Writers* (1997), 58–69; C. H. Rowell, "An Interview with Octavia E. Butler," *Callaloo* (1997), 47–66; Therese Littleton and Bonnie Bouman, "Octavia E. Butler Plants an Earthseed," Amazon.com (1999); Mike McGonigal, "Octavia Butler," *Indexed* (1999); Steven Piziks, "Interview with Octavia Butler," *Marion Zimmer Bradley's Fantasy Magazine* (1999). The critical work on Butler is extensive, and it has come primarily from the perspectives of African American studies, feminist studies, and sf studies (although Butler herself has noted an interest among New Age readers, and no doubt New Age criticism, if there is such a thing, will follow). To date, less work has been done on the "Parable" series than on the two previous ones ("Patternmaster"—*Patternmaster* [1976], *Survivor* [1978], *Wild Seed* [1980]—and "Xenogensis"—*Dawn* [1987], *Adulthood Rites* [1988], *Imago* [1989]), but studies that link the "Parable" books with her earlier work will certainly be forthcoming. Among the array of work, see Ruth Salvaggio, "Octavia Butler and the Black Science-Fiction Heroine," *Black American Literature Forum* (1984), 78–81; Donna Haraway, "A Manifesto for Cyborgs: Science, Technology, and Socialist Feminism in the 1980s," *Socialist Review* (1985), 65–107; Sandra Y. Govan, "Homage to Tradition: Octavia Butler Renovates the Historical Novel," *MELUS* (1986), 79–96; Dorothy Allison, "The Future of Female: Octavia Butler's Mother Lode," *Reading Black, Reading Feminist* (1990), 471–478; Angelyn L. Mitchell, *Signifyin(g) Women: Visions and Revisions of Slavery in Octavia Butler's* Kindred, *Sherley Anne Williams's* Dessa Rose, *and Toni Morrison's* Beloved (1992); Michelle Erica Green, "There Goes the Neighborhood: Octavia Butler's Demand for Diversity in Utopias," *Utopian and Science Fiction by Women* (1994), 166–190; Rebecca Johnson, "African American Feminist Science Fiction," *Sojourner: The Women's Forum* (1994), 12–14; Cathy Peppers, "Dialogic Origins and Alien Identities in Butler's *Xenogenesis*," *Science-Fiction Studies* (1995), 47–62; Stacy Alaimo, "Displacing Darwin and Descartes: The Bodily Transgressions of Fielding Burke, Octavia Butler, and Linda Hogan," *Isle* (1996), 47–66; Amanda Boulter, *Speculative Feminisms: The Significance of Feminist Theory in the Science Fiction of Joanna Russ, James Tiptree, Jr., and Octavia Butler* (1996); Roger Luckurst, "'Horror and Beauty in Rare Combination': The Miscegenate Fictions of Octavia Butler," *Women: A Cultural Review* (1996), 28–38; Letetia F. Coleman, *Octavia Butler's Patternist Series: A Cultural Analysis* (1997); Teri Ann Doerksen, "Octavia E. Butler: Parables of Race and Difference," *Into Darkness Peering: Race and Color in the Fantastic* (1997), 21–34; M. Dubey, "Folk and Urban Communities in African-American Women's Fiction: Octavia Butler's *Parable of the Sower*," *Studies in American Fiction* (1999), 103–128. For critical work addressing the utopian/dystopian dimension of *The Parable of the Sower*, see especially Jim Miller, "Post-Apocalyptic Hoping: Octavia Butler's Dystopian/Utopian Fiction," *Science-*

Fiction Studies (1998), and Hoda M. Zaki, "Utopia, Dystopia, and Ideology in the Science Fiction of Octavia Butler," *Science-Fiction Studies* (1990).

2. In interviews, however, Butler often distances herself from utopian writing, as she takes a familiar anti-utopian stance in regard to utopian thought and practice. With McCaffery, she puts it this way: "Personally, I find utopias ridiculous. We're not going to have a perfect human society until we get a few perfect humans, and that seems unlikely. Besides, any true utopia would almost certainly be incredibly boring, and it would be so overspecialized that any change we might introduce would probably destroy the whole system. As bad as we humans are sometimes, I have a feeling that we'll never have that problem with the current system" ("An Interview with Octavia E. Butler" 69). Given this refusal of a utopian or, in our time, critical utopian awareness and emphases on *process* rather than blueprint, the utopian impulses that do emerge in *Sower* grow reluctantly out of the anti-utopian side of the dystopian continuum. And yet this sober caution, this pragmatic stubbornness, produces a militant, critical dystopian narrative. As I note in Chapter 7, Miller recognizes *Parable of the Sower* as a "critical dystopia." He describes the book as a "post-apocalyptic hoping informed by the lessons of the past," arguing that "Butler stares into the abyss of the dystopian future and reinvents the desire for a better world" (Miller 336). Working from the concept of the critical utopia, he argues that Butler generally writes within the feminist utopian tradition even as she contests it: "As an African American woman writing within a largely white woman's tradition, her work often questions the assumptions shared by many white feminist utopian writers. Butler is also far more class-conscious than many other utopian writers. Thus, her largely dystopian fictions challenge not only patriarchal myths, but also capitalist myths, racist myths, and feminist-utopian myths" (Miller 337). Although I agree with his assessment, I argue below that is it the paradoxically pragmatic and apocalyptic dimension of Butler's vision in the second volume that displaces her prophetic/dystopian vision in the first. This is not a surprising development given Butler's own caveats about "utopia."

3. As commentators have pointed out, Mike Davis's critical studies of the political economy and culture of Los Angeles resonate with Robinson's and Butler's fictions; see *City of Quartz: Excavating the Future in Los Angeles* (1992) and *The Ecology of Fear: Los Angeles and the Imagination of Disaster* (1998). Indeed, the last two chapters of *The Ecology of Fear* work with a selection of cyberpunk and dystopian sf to analyze the actual situation in southern California in order to see it not only in terms of its local specificity but also as a microcosm of the entire planetary capitalist society. In *The Ecology of Fear,* Davis traces the ways in which southern California has incrementally suffered the synergistic breakdown Butler envisions, and in this study of the economic exploitation of the area by an amalgam of land developers and city officials, he argues that the apparently "natural disasters" (earthquakes, fires, mud slides, floods) are socially produced by an economic logic (infused by race and class privilege) that is intent on profit and not sustainable and ecologically healthy use.

4. On Olivar and the new debt slavery, Miller notes that the familiar scenario of U.S. corporations moving to places like Mexico to further their exploitive work is "reversed," for "it is not American companies exploiting cheap Mexican labor, but a foreign multinational

taking advantage of cheap, desperate American labor. By inverting the situation, Butler puts the American reader in the shoes not of some oppressed 'Third World' person, but of someone with whom they can more directly identify" (Miller 354).

5. Butler insists that Lauren's condition is psychological not physical. In her interview with Steven Potts, she says Lauren "is not empathic. *She feels herself to be.* Usually in science fiction 'empathic' means that you are really suffering, that you are actively interacting telepathically with another person, and she is not. She has this delusion that she cannot shake. It's kind of biologically programmed into her" (Potts 335, my emphasis). The ramifications of Butler's insistent distinction are worth further consideration. Is this a metaphor that describes an author's position? Is it a symptom of a political vision that is perhaps more idealist than materialist, albeit historical? Or is this an anticipatory figure for an emergent subject position wherein a negative condition (however psychological, it is still genetically produced) could be dialectically negated (and so sublated) and thus become the material basis for a new form of subjectivity that has stronger eutopian potential (since it would significantly help to prevent violence and induce understanding and cooperation)? Here her comment to McCaffery that humanity will not "have a perfect human society until we get a few perfect humans" takes on a slightly different valence, as Lauren can be read as an evolved subject who moves humanity one step closer to (that never to be attained) Utopia *by way of* her very imperfection.

6. Lauren's character is another example of the way Butler creatively deploys a disturbing difference to break open the sutured realty of everyday life and make room for another form of liberated difference. In Michelle Green's words, Butler offers a "dream of a world in which difference can be recognized without prejudice and celebrated," even as she presents that difference by way of apparently negative aliens such as the Oankali in the *Xenogenesis* series or Lauren's painful condition in the *Parable* series (Green, "There Goes" 189).

7. For the basic discussion of "structure of feeling" as a sociopolitical process, see Raymond Williams, *Marxism and Literature* (1977), 128–135.

8. As I note in Chapter 2, Miller recognizes the quality of cognitive mapping in Butler's work and especially links it to the emergence of the Earthseed community: "In addition to presenting us with a critical dystopia that gives us a grim 'cognitive map' of these harsh realties, Butler also leaves us with the notion of an 'Earthseed community,' an inspiring utopian political myth that prizes diversity, but avoids a fragmented identity politics and serves as a good model for the kind of 'new political art' called for by Jameson" (Miller 349). Although Miller's use of the term *myth* is troublesome, his point about Butler's text and its political stance and impact is well taken.

9. Butler, in her interview with Fry: "I examined a lot of the problems [of society] in *Parable of the Sower,* and now [in *Parable of the Talents*] I'd like to consider some of the solutions. Not *propose* solutions, you understand—what I want to do is look at some of the solutions that human beings come up with when they're feeling uncertain and frightened, as they are right now" (Fry 68–69). Like Moses looking into the Promised Land, Butler in *Sower* comes to the edge of a critical utopia by way of her critical dystopian narrative, but then in the second volume she pulls back into a more pragmatic approach. In doing so, she

steps away from a utopian trajectory just as it involves exploring, indeed *proposing,* some radical yet historically situated directions rather than reworking ones we already have with us. Given this stance, I argue that her "realism" shifts her series narrative, by way of the science fictional flight to the stars, from an engaged prophetic text to an apocalyptic one.

10. On "pocket utopia," see Kim Stanley Robinson, *Pacific Edge* (1990).

11. See Williams, *Marxism and Literature,* 121–127.

12. The metaphysical, abstract utopian tendency of *Talents* is precisely the sort of development that Zaki identifies in her critique of Butler's earlier novels. For a critique of a similar move in another sf work, see Tom Moylan, "Ideological Contradiction in Clarke's *The City and the Stars,*" *Science-Fiction Studies* (1977), 150–157.

13. Butler seems intent on pursuing a narrative based more in the sort of future history familiar to space exploration plots rather than the further reaches of dystopia. In her Amazon.com interview, she notes that in *Talents* Lauren turns into "the kind of person who might sometime after death be thought of as a god," albeit a very flawed and problematic god; she then explains that she is thinking about four more volumes that will offer "parables" of the "trickster," "teacher," "chaos," and "clay" (meaning each to be another name of "god"). It is clear that Butler plans to take her ongoing series outward into the galaxy, apocalyptically exploring "different experiences of people who go out, experiences with religion, and settling a new world" (Littleton and Bouman 2, 5).

Chapter 9

1. Marge Piercy, *He, She and It,* first published, 1991. Piercy's body of work in sf; realist and historical fiction; poetry; drama; and critical, expository, and popular essays is extensive; see the "Marge Piercy" Web site (http://www.capecod.net/~tmpiercy/index.html) for a biography and a relatively complete bibliography. For relevant nonfiction by Piercy, see "Active in Time and History," *Paths of Resistance: The Art and Craft of the Political Novel* (1989), 91–123; and "Telling Stories About Stories," *Utopian Studies* (1994), 1–3; see also her poem "The Book of Ruth and Naomi," *Reading Ruth: Contemporary Women Reclaim a Sacred Story* (1994), 159–160. In general, see her contributions to the critical journal *Tikkun.* For recent interviews, see Dawn Gifford, "Marge Piercy: A Class Act," *Off Our Backs* (1994), 14–17; K. Rodden, "A Harsh Day's Light: An Interview with Marge Piercy," *Kenyon Review* (1998), 132–143. For critical work, see Tom Moylan, *Demand the Impossible: Science Fiction and the Utopian Imagination* (1986); Nan Nowik, "Mixing Art and Politics: The Writings of Adrienne Rich and Marge Piercy," *Centennial Review* (1986), 208–218; Robert Philmus, "Men in Feminist Science Fiction: Marge Piercy, Thomas Berger, and the End of Masculinity," *Science Fiction Roots and Branches: Contemporary Critical Approaches* (1990), 135–150; Patricia Ruth Marks, *Re-writing the Romance Narrative: Gender and Class in the Novels of Marge Piercy* (1991); Sue Walker and Eugenie Hamner, eds., *Ways of Knowing: Essays on Marge Piercy* (1991); M. Keith Booker, "Woman on the Edge of a Genre: The Feminist Dystopias of Marge Piercy," *Science-Fiction Studies* (1994), 337–350; June Deery, "Ectopic and Utopic Reproduction: *He, She and It,*" *Utopian Studies* (1994), 36–49; Peter

Fitting, "Beyond the Wasteland: A Feminist in Cyberspace," *Utopian Studies* (1994), 4–16; Helen A. Kuryllo, "Cyborgs, Sorcery, and the Struggle for Utopia," *Utopian Studies* (1994), 50–55; Sherry Lee Linkon, "'A Way of Being Jewish That Is Mine': Gender and Ethnicity in the Jewish Novels of Marge Piercy," *Studies in American Jewish Literature* (1994), 93–105; Vara Neverow, "The Politics of Incorporation and Embodiment: *Woman on the Edge of Time* and *He, She and It* as Feminist Epistemologies of Resistance," *Utopian Studies* (1994), 16–36; Kerstin W. Shands, *The Repair of the World: The Novels of Marge Piercy* (1995).

2. Piercy, "Telling Stories," 1.

3. See the "Marge Piercy" Web page for information on her political history. Her biography discusses her involvement with the movements of the 1960s and 1970s: from opposition to the French Algerian War and the U.S. Vietnam War to her work in the civil rights, women's, and ecology movements, Piercy was an early and deeply involved activist. She was affiliated with Students for a Democratic Society and Movement for a Democratic Society (the grouping), and she was one of the founders of the National Action Committee on Latin America. Since the mid-1980s, she has also been involved in progressive Jewish movements and the work for Jewish renewal. Fitting locates Piercy's radical vision in the social and political culture of the 1960s and 1970s, and he sees her work as simultaneously anticipating, working with, and superseding the cyberpunk moment of the 1980s. He argues that if the "cyber-improvement" highlighted in *He, She and It* parallels aspects of cyberpunk, its "primary interlocutors" are "not so much the cyberpunks, but those feminists and utopians who continue to argue for the 'natural' and the organic as a model for social change" ("Wasteland" 6). Neverow also has extensively examined the "epistemology of resistance" that runs though Piercy's work, especially in her sf volumes, *Woman on the Edge of Time* and *He, She and It*. She argues that the way of knowing and engaging with the world that shapes Piercy's creative and political methodology is fundamentally feminist but also connected with her anti-capitalist, anti-racist vision, and most recently with her critically engaged recognition of the radical liberatory elements of Jewish political culture: "Both novels promote a version of cultural feminist epistemology focused on the politics of personal agency and communal responsibility, contrasting the life-affirming, female-identified cultures with destructive male-dominated cultures" (Neverow 17).

4. Neverow connects Piercy's focus on subversive storytelling with her overall political and creative methodology: "The narrative strategies of *Woman on the Edge of Time* make this destabilization of discourse particularly evident through Malkah's storytelling which, like re-memory in Toni Morrison's *Beloved,* makes the traumas of the past bearable, makes a liveable future possible, makes history a validation of community rather than a system of domination. Malkah uses narrative to orient not only herself, but her granddaughter, Shira, . . . Yod, and us as readers" (Neverow 19). Piercy's critical method is also evident in her own commentary on the Golem material: "I was again very self-consciously operating in (that is to say, *with and against*) the golem tradition" ("Telling Stories" 2, my emphasis).

5. Piercy describes Yod as a "cyborg"; however, Fitting has rightly pointed out that Yod is actually an *android* whereas Nili is a *cyborg*: "By calling Yod a cyborg, Piercy has . . . confused matters. For most science fiction readers, Yod would be called an "android," a hu-

manoid robot rather than a cyborg. The distinction is important. . . . A cyborg is the physical bonding of human and machine—a human who has in some way been augmented or enhanced. A robot or android on the other hand, is a new entity, built or grown from organic and/or non-organic materials" ("Wasteland" 5, and nn. 3 and 4). This accurate distinction thus makes both Yod and Joseph androids; Nili is the "true cyborg," as Fitting puts it. Indeed, this distinction actually works better in underscoring Piercy's point about the ultimate difference between Yod and Nili, and it further supports the outcome wherein Yod's existence and future potential end, whereas the "new human" that Nili, the cyborg, represents continues.

6. Booker elaborates on the economic-political position of the Glop and notes that the zone's "relative independence from direct domination by the multis" makes it a "potential source of social and cultural revival," especially in the "locus of utopian energies" occupied by the Coyote gang; he also refers to the slang used in the Glop as "a sort of literalization of Bakhtinian heteroglossia that incorporates diversity and genuine historical change, both of which are anathema to the multis" ("Woman on the Edge" 344, 345). For more on the economic "discipline" of "disposable populations in the current conjuncture, see Evan Watkins, *Throwaways: Work Culture and Consumer Education* (1993).

7. Several critics have noted the overlap and interplay between Mattapoisett and Tikva; see Kuryllo, and Piercy's comments in "Telling Stories."

8. See the "Marge Piercy" Web site for translations of the Yiddish and Hebrew words used in *He, She and It*.

9. Neverow provides the following background on sources for the name *Nili*: It "is an acronym of a Hebrew phrase, 'Netzah Israel Lo Y'shaker,'" meaning "the glory of Israel will not fail" (I Samuel 15:29), but it is also the name of a Jewish underground intelligence group organized during World War I. As she explains, the "organization was actively opposed by the leaders of another mainstream group, Yishuv . . . which regarded Nili as 'adventurous, irresponsible, and dangerous to the security of the Yishuv'" (Neverow 23). Neverow further notes that Piercy's refunctioning of Jewish radicalism in light of her contemporary political position (which includes her critique of the Israeli state and its policies toward the Palestinian people) also leads her to associate Nili's character with the diverse and radical subject position celebrated by Audre Lorde, a poet Piercy herself recognized in one of her poems. As Neverow observes: "Perhaps it is not coincidental that Nili, who comes from the Black Zone, from the stony radioactive desert, can claim many of the same identities as Audre Lorde, defining herself as black, mother, lesbian, feminist, warrior, activist, woman. And Piercy, in 1993, eulogizes Lorde, radical feminist thinker, passionate advocate of woman's ways of knowing, with exquisite images of stones—obsidian, which can 'take an edge, can serve as a knife in ritual or combat,' carnelian, rose marble, garnet, sand—in her poem 'Elegy in rock, for Audre Lorde'" (Neverow 24).

10. See Neverow for an extended discussion of the events of the narrative in light of the history of resistance and self-defense in the Jewish community: "The novel stresses even more fiercely than *Woman on the Edge of Time* the ethical dilemma of resistance, the urgency to rebel before it is too late. . . . However, both *Woman on the Edge of Time* and *He,*

She and It make it very clear that resistance must be entirely voluntary, not coerced. As the records of the Jewish resistance indicates [*sic*], individuals were entitled to choose their own fates—to flee, to hide, to fight, to submit—so long as they did not betray other members of their community. . . . Those who decided to fight did so freely—and had to assume the guilt for retaliations against the non-combatants" (Neverow 31). See also Fitting, who takes the question up to the situation created by the Israeli state: "Piercy recasts the question of the limits to the right of self-defense in terms of her own Jewishness and the utopian experiment that is Israel. . . . *He, She and It* is a serious reconsideration of one of the most critical challenges of the utopian project: the limits to self-defence. It asks us to consider whether the use of violence in the building and preservation of a better society means that violence—the very violence which the new society rejects—will nevertheless become an integral part of that society" ("Wasteland" 11). As Neverow puts in it her concluding paragraph: "The issues of choice, coercion, and control are crucial to the denouement of both novels—only by resistance to the death, only by taking embodiment to the point of dissolution, can the violence of incorporation be averted. Thus, the transcendent gesture of sacrifice [Connie's in *Woman on the Edge of Time* and Yod's in *He, She and It*] and the pragmatic connectedness of immanence are fused in Piercy's feminist epistemology of resistance, offsetting disturbingly abstract and alienated male viewpoints in the novels" (Neverow 32).

11. Booker traces how Yod transgresses multiple boundaries in the course of the narrative: He notes that by construction he is human and machine, by design he is male and female, and that he is also the creative product of "both the high-tech tradition of science fiction and . . . the kabbalistic traditions of Jewish mysticism, to which he is linked through Piercy's inclusion of the parallel story of the 'golem' Joseph" ("Woman on the Edge" 347).

12. The stories of Shira and Yod call forth a range of issues, debates, and personal and political responses from readers and critics. They resonate with specific dimensions and debates in Left, feminist, and radical Jewish communities, and they lead outward to the Left cyborg politics articulated by Donna Haraway in "A Manifesto for Cyborgs: Science, Technology, and Socialist Feminism in the 1980s," *Socialist Review* (1985), 65–107. As Piercy describes her own concerns about the imbrication of the personal and political: "I am . . . very interested in the degree of sophistication of the socializing and inter-personal mechanisms of a society. . . . How does that society deal with loneliness and alienation? How does it deal with getting born, growing up and learning, having sex, making babies, becoming sick and healing, dying and being disposed of?" ("Telling Stories" 2). Many commentators have insightfully focused on these matters from a number of viewpoints; my particular (and therefore necessarily limited) focus in this reading is on the public, political dimension of the discrete narrative and the iconic detail.

13. The political position of Tikva as well as the overall position represented by the entire anti-Y-S alliance resonates with one of the links to the "Marge Piercy" Web page. Radical leftist, pacificist, and rabbi Arthur Waskow offers his own answers in "Ten Questions on Tikkun Olam of the Future" (*tikkun olam* meaning "healing the world"). He argues that

the "common barrier to social justice and spiritual renewal and the earth-web of life is the global corporation and economic globalism. Its search for maximum short-term profit smashes small cultures, wrecks regional economies, destroys habitats and species, eats up all the time that could be used for spiritual renewal and grass-roots volunteer democratic participation, and endangers the earth-web itself." He also identifies the "four networks or clusters of . . . progressive Jewish activists" as "economic/racial justice activists," "feminists especially concerned with gender equality and gay rights," "Middle East peace activists" and "eco-Jewish environmental activists"; he then suggests that these groupings need to overcome their separation from each other (and I would think, by his political logic, from similar and parallel non-Jewish groups) and work toward developing a "common worldview" and "organizational connection"; see "Ten Questions on Tikkun Olam of the Future," available: http://www.shalomctr.org/html/comm08.html.

14. In her acknowledgments Piercy recognizes her debt to Haraway and her "Manifesto for Cyborgs," but I would argue that her own vision and narrative supercedes cyborg politics. For a socialist-feminist critique of Haraway that has many similarities to the tone of Piercy's narrative, see Stabile. Piercy also recognizes the influence of the work of William Gibson and others in the cyberpunk mode, but again—generous as she is to Gibson and other cyberpunkers—her own work (and the critical dystopia in general) both anticipates and goes beyond that particular development. Fitting, for example, argues that Piercy's new dystopia "has causes and meaning which certainly do not correspond to the depoliticized translation of some punk aesthetic" ("Wasteland" 7).

15. Yod, however, does offer at least a rough sketch of the possible subject formation of a post-patriarchal, post-masculinist, post-homophobic male; although like its several siblings, as a model for this new subject Yod is still a work in progress, one that will only be taken forward by actually existing men in their own lives and struggles. For a precursor of Yod, see the figure of Davy in Russ's *Female Man.*

16. On the process of tapping the progressive potential of traditional culture, see Luke Gibbons, *Transformations in Irish Culture* (1996).

17. Despite its concrete utopian elements, *Woman on the Edge of Time* has gaps and silences that are symptomatic of its own conditions of production within the limits of a capitalism that desires global hegemony. The most troubling absence in Piercy's near-future geography is the nation-state itself as a contested terrain for a democratically class-based economic regulation and control of the corporations—an intervention that would subordinate capital's will to profit to the social needs of the entire population. Although she does detail a political vision and agency, she gives only a passing sketch of the regional state-regulatory bodies in Norika and Europa and a weakened United Nations. Otherwise, it appears that her narrative possibilities are limited by the ideology of globalism as it effaces the potential of the state as a source of regulating capital and redistributing wealth. For an important study of the relationship between the nation-state and the utopian imagination, see Phillip E. Wegner, *Imaginary Communities: Utopia, the Nation, and the Spatial Histories of Modernity* (forthcoming). For one account of what could be done in the present historical moment, see Pierre Bordieu, *Acts of Resistance: Against the Theory of the Market* (1998);

see also Robinson's Martian trilogy and *Antarctica* for other ways of exploring the contradictory but potentially progressive potential of state power.

18. For more on storytelling and counter-narrative, see Jack Zipes, *Creative Storytelling: Building Community, Changing Lives* (1995); and Chris Ferns, *Narrating Utopia: Ideology, Gender, Form in Utopian Literature* (1999).

19. In doing so, Yod continues the long tradition of rewriting fairy tales for the cultural and political needs of the historical moment. On the fairy-tale tradition and its history of formal and political contestation, see the body of work that Jack Zipes has published, especially *Breaking the Magic Spell: Radical Theories of Folk and Fairy Tales* (1979); *Fairy Tales and the Art of Subversion* (1983); *Don't Bet on the Prince: Contemporary Feminist Fairy Tales in North America and England* (1986); *The Trials and Tribulations of Little Red Riding Hood: Versions of the Tale in Sociocultural Context* (1993); *Happily Ever After: Fairy Tales, Children, and the Culture Industry* (1997); *When Dreams Come True: Classical Fairy Tales and Their Tradition* (1999).

20. Piercy's discussion of learning, knowledge, and history is developed within the tradition of feminist standpoint theory and feminist epistemology. See Billie Maciunas, "Feminist Epistemologies in Piercy's *Woman on the Edge of Time*," *Woman's Studies* (1992), 249–258; and key works such as Sandra Harding, *The Science Question in Feminism* (1986); Nancy Hartsock, "The Feminist Standpoint," *Money, Sex, and Power* (1983), 231–251; and Donna Haraway, "Situated Knowledges," *Simians, Cyborgs, and Women* (1991), 183–203. For a complementary argument within the critical Marxist tradition, see Ruth Levitas's essay on the difference between abstract and concrete utopian thought: "Educated Hope: Ernst Bloch on Abstract and Concrete Utopia," *Not Yet* (1997), 65–79.

21. See Evan Watkins's *Throwaways* for a developed argument for an oppositional socialist politics of "repair" (rather than the present regime of acquiescence to a race for endless and meaningless innovation).

Chapter 10

1. Hesiod, "Works and Days," *The Utopia Reader* (1999), 7. Whereas the epigraph to this chapter expresses Hesiod's "dystopian" side, the following section, perhaps better known, shifts to the "utopian" side of his account:

> Nothing for toil or pitiful age they cared,
> but in strength of hand and foot still unimpaired
> they feasted gaily, undarkened by sufferings.
> They died as if falling asleep; and all good things
> were theirs, for the fruitful earth unstintingly bore
> unforced her plenty, and they, amid their store
> enjoyed their landed ease which nothing stirred
> loved by the gods and rich in many of herd.

To be sure, the metaphor of darkness in regard to things dystopian is one that is rich in meaning but vexed with history when it comes to fundamental matters of race, racism, whiteness, and white supremacy. This is a major question for a major study, but see Toni Morrison, *Playing in the Dark: Whiteness and the Literary Imagination* (1992); and to the immediate point of the roots of ancient Greek culture, see Martin Bernal, *Black Athena* (1987).

2. See Krishan Kumar, *Utopia and Anti-Utopia in Modern Times* (1987), 100.

3. Terry Eagleton, "Utopia and Its Opposites," *Necessary and Unnecessary Utopias: Socialist Register 2000* (1999), 31.

4. Peter Fitting, "The Concept of Utopia in the Work of Fredric Jameson," *Utopian Studies* (1998), 11.

5. Ruth Levitas, "Utopia as Literature, Utopia as Politics," *Zeitgenössische Utopieentwürfe in Literatur und Gesellschaft* (1997), 123.

6. On the question of the "utopian impulse" and "utopianism" outside and beyond the Western, modern tradition that bears those names, see Lyman Tower Sargent, "The Three Faces of Utopianism Revisited," *Utopian Studies* (1994), 1–38, and "Is There Only One Utopian Tradition?" *Journal of the History of Ideas* (1982), 681–689.

7. On the complementary interplay of analytic and imaginative forms of critical cognition, see Darko Suvin's conclusion to *Positions and Presuppositions in Science Fiction* (1988): "SF as Metaphor, Parable and Chronotope (with the Bad Conscience of Reaganism)," 189.

8. Tracing Morrison's exploration of Utopia through all her work is another extensive project. One contribution has been made by Jewell Parker Rhodes: "Toni Morrison's *Beloved:* Ironies of a 'Sweet Home' Utopia in a Dystopian Slave Society," *Utopian Studies* (1990), 77–93. Rhodes argues that Utopia in Morrison's novel is "not a place or moment in time, rather utopia is a process of reliving memories, recalling pleasures and pains, and succeeding in loving the self and maintaining this sense of self while joining and loving others. . . . Sweet Home, like slavery in general, becomes compatible with the notion of utopia as a process. Sweet Home is a reference point, a significant focal point for a time. It is a memory to be remembered, rendering knowledge and experience to shape a sweeter tomorrow" (90–91).

9. In spring 1999 Kathryn Mitchell, a student in George Mason University's master's program in creative writing wrote an independent study paper that focused on Robinson's poetry in *Antarctica*. In "Poetry in the Extreme," she presents a substantial analysis of the poetics of Robinson's sf text, arguing that it not only helps to "visualize a subtly changing landscape" but also "to provide a meta-narrator, an oracle signaling plot direction and symbolizing prevailing conditions, both environmental and social." The poems, therefore, provide her with the central line from which she reads the entire text. I can only hope that one day this poet who is also an astute critic of poetry and culture will take my advice and publish this paper. For more of Robinson's poetry, see his volume *The Martians* (1999).

10. Fredric Jameson, *The Seeds of Time* (1994), 65.

11. Dave Brower (Sierra Club activist and co-organizer with David Foster, director for district 11 of the United Steelworkers of America, of the Alliance for Sustainable Jobs and the Environment, at the anti-WTO demonstrations in Seattle, 28 November to 2 December 1999), quoted in Jeffrey St. Clair, "Seattle Diary: It's a Gas, Gas, Gas," *New Left Review* (1999), 92.

12. Subcommandante Marcos, "Open Letter to the World," August 1997; quoted in John Berger "Against the Great Defeat of the World," *Race and Class* (1998/1999), 3.

13. For more on the nonsynchronous function of radical culture, see Ernst Bloch, *Heritage of Our Times* (1991), and "Nonsynchronism and the Obligation to Its Dialectics," *New German Critique* (1977), 22–39. See also Angelika Bammer, *Partial Visions: Feminism and Utopianism in the 1970s* (1991).

14. For another argument on the need not to linger any longer in this dystopian moment than necessary, see Phillip E. Wegner, "'A Nightmare on the Brain of the Living': Messianic Historicity, Alienations, and *Independence Day*," *Rethinking Marxism* (2000), 65–86.

15. St. Clair, "Seattle Diary"; see also Katharine Ainger, "The Battle in Seattle," *Red Pepper* (1999), 16–19; William K. Tabb, "The World Trade Organization? Stop World Takeover," *Monthly Review* (2000), 1–13; and the video *N30 WTO Meltdown: Big Rattle in Seattle* (2000).

16. For a critique of the compromised strategy of managing and petitioning, see Paul Smith, *Millennial Dreams: Contemporary Culture and Capital in the North* (1997), 53–57. Smith describes this accommodationist position as one that oscillates between the "dull default position of the efficient management of everything that exists and the heady renewal of futurism (between a left positivism and a left magic?)" (55).

Bibliography

Adorno, Theodor W. "Aldous Huxley and Utopia." *Prisms*. Trans. Samuel Weber and Shierry Weber. Cambridge: MIT Press, 1981. 95–119.

______. "Aldous Huxley und die Utopie." *Prismen: Kulturkritik und Gesellschaft*. Baden-Baden: Suhrkamp Verlag, 1955. 112–143.

______. *Minima Moralia*. 1951. Trans. E. F. N. Jephcott. London: Verso, 1974.

______. *Negative Dialectics*. New York: Continuum, 1994.

"After Seattle: A New Internationalism?" Special issue. *Monthly Review* 52.3 (July/August 2000).

Aglietta, Michel. *A Theory of Capitalist Regulation: The US Experience*. Trans. David Fernbach. London: New Left Books, 1979.

Ainger, Katharine. "The Battle in Seattle." *Red Pepper* 66 (November 1999): 16–19.

Alaimo, Stacy. "Displacing Darwin and Descartes: The Bodily Transgressions of Fielding Burke, Octavia Butler, and Linda Hogan." *Isle* 3.1 (Summer 1996): 47–66.

Albanese, Denise. *New Science, New World*. Durham, N.C.: Duke University Press, 1996.

Albinski, Nan Bowman. *Women's Utopias in British and American Fiction*. New York: Routledge, 1988.

Aldiss, Brian. *Billion Year Spree: The History of Science Fiction*. Garden City, N.Y.: Doubleday, 1973.

______. Introduction to "Zoline." In *The Mirror of Infinity: A Critics' Anthology of Science Fiction*. Ed. Robert Silverberg. San Francisco: Canfield, 1970. 287–292.

Aldiss, Brian, and David Wingrove. *Trillion Year Spree: The History of Science Fiction*. New York: Avon, 1986.

Alexander, Bryan N. "Jameson's Adorno and the Problem of Utopia." *Utopian Studies* 9.2 (1998): 51–58.

Alkon, Paul. "Dystopian Postscript." In *Transformations of Utopia: Changing Views of the Perfect Society*. Eds. George Slusser, Paul Alkon, Roger Gaillard, and Danièle Chatelain. New York: AMS, 1999. 317.

Alliez, Eric, and Michel Feher. "The Luster of Capital." *Zone* 1 and 2 (1986): 314–359.

Allison, Dorothy. "The Future of Female: Octavia Butler's Mother Lode." In *Reading Black, Reading Feminist*. Ed. Henry Louis Gates Jr. New York: Meridian, 1990. 471–478.

Althusser, Louis. "Ideology and Ideological State Apparatuses." In *Lenin and Philosophy and Other Essays*. New York: Monthly Review Press, 1971. 127–188.

Amis, Kingsley. *New Maps of Hell: A Survey of Science Fiction*. New York: Harcourt Brace, 1960.

Anderson, Benedict. *Imagined Communities: Reflections on the Origin and Spread of Nationalism*. London: Verso, 1983.

Angenot, Marc. "The Absent Paradigm: An Introduction to the Semiotics of Science Fiction." *Science-Fiction Studies* 6.1 (March 1979): 9–20.

Angenot, Marc, and Darko Suvin. "A Response to Professor Fekete's 'Five Theses.'" *Science-Fiction Studies* 15.3 (November 1988): 324–333.

Annas, Pamela J. "New Worlds, New Words: Androgyny in Feminist Science Fiction." *Science-Fiction Studies* 5.2 (July 1978): 143–156.

Appadurai, Arun. "Disjuncture and Difference in the Global Cultural Economy." In *The Phantom Public Sphere*. Ed. Bruce Robbins. Minneapolis: University of Minnesota Press, 1993. 269–297.

______. "Patriotism and Its Futures." *Public Culture* 5 (1993): 411–429.

Armitt, Lucie. *Theorising the Fantastic*. London: Arnold, 1996.

______, ed. *Where No Man Has Gone Before: Women and Science Fiction*. New York: Routledge, 1991.

Aronowitz, Stanley. *The Death and Rebirth of American Radicalism*. New York: Routledge, 1996.

Arrighi, Giovanni. *The Long Twentieth Century: Money, Power, and the Origins of Our Times*. London: Verso, 1994.

Asimov, Isaac. Introduction to *More Soviet Science Fiction*. New York: Collier, 1962. 7–13.

Baccolini, Raffaella. "Breaking the Boundaries: Gender, Genre, and Dystopia." In *Per una definizione dell'utopia: Metodologie e discipline a confronto*. Ed. Nadia Minerva. Ravenna: Longo, 1992. 137–146.

______. "Gender and Genre in the Feminist Critical Dystopias of Katherine Burdekin, Margaret Atwood, and Octavia Butler." In *Future Females, the Next Generation: New Voices and Velocities in Feminist Science Fiction*. Ed. Marleen Barr. Boston: Rowman and Littlefield, 2000. 13–34.

______. "'It's Not in the Womb the Damage Is Done': The Construction of Gender, Memory, and Desire in Katherine Burdekin's *Swastika Night*." In *Le trasformazioni del narrare*. Eds. E. Sciliani, A. Cecere, V. Intononti, and A. Sportelli. Fasano: Schena, 1995. 293–309.

______. "Journeying Through the Dystopian Genre: Memory and Imagination in Burdekin, Orwell, Atwood, and Piercy." In *Viaggi in Utopia*. Eds. Raffaella Baccolini, Vita Fortunati, and Nadia Minerva. Ravenna: Longo, 1996. 343–357.

Baccolini, Raffaella, and Tom Moylan, eds. *The Dystopian Turn: Science Fiction and Utopia at the End of the 20th Century*. Forthcoming.

Bacon-Smith, Camille. *Science Fiction Culture*. Philadelphia: University of Pennsylvania Press, 1999.

Badami, Mary Kenny. "A Feminist Critique of Science Fiction." *Extrapolation* 18.1 (Winter 1976): 6–19.

Baggesen, Søren. "Utopian and Dystopian Pessimism: Le Guin's *The Word for World Is Forest* and Tiptree's 'We Who Stole the Dream.'" *Science-Fiction Studies* 14.1 (March 1987): 34–43.

Bailey, J. O. *Pilgrims Through Space and Time: Trends and Patterns in Scientific and Utopian Fiction*. New York: Argus, 1947.

Bakhtin, M. M. *The Dialogic Imagination: Four Essays*. Ed. Michael Holquist. Trans. Caryl Emerson and Michael Holquist. Austin: University of Texas Press, 1981.

Balsamo, Anne. *Technologies of the Gendered Body: Reading Cyborg Women*. Durham, N.C.: Duke University Press, 1996.

Bammer, Angelika. *Partial Visions: Feminism and Utopianism in the 1970s*. New York: Routledge, 1991.

Barr, Marleen. *Alien to Femininity: Speculative Fiction and Feminist Theory*. Westport, Conn.: Greenwood, 1987.

______. "'The *Females* Do the Fathering!': James Tiptree's Male Matriarchs and Adult Human Gametes." *Science-Fiction Studies* 13.1 (March 1986): 42–49.

______. *Feminist Fabulation: Space/Postmodern Fiction*. Iowa City: University of Iowa Press, 1992.

______. *Future Females: A Critical Anthology*. Bowling Green, Ohio: Bowling Green University Press, 1981.

______. *Future Females, the Next Generation: New Voices and Velocities in Feminist Science Fiction*. Boston: Rowman and Littlefield, 2000.

______. "Science Fiction's Invisible Female Man: Feminism, Formula, Word, and World in 'When It Changed' and 'The Women Men Don't See.'" In *Just the Other Day: Essays on the Suture of the Future*. Ed. Luk de Vos. Antwerp: EXA, 1985. 433–437.

Barr, Marleen, and Nicholas D. Smith, eds. *Women and Utopia: Critical Interpretations*. Lanham, Md.: University Press of America, 1983.

Barron, Neil, ed. *Anatomy of Wonder: A Critical Guide to Science Fiction*. New York: Bowker, 1976.

______. *Anatomy of Wonder 4: A Critical Guide to Science Fiction*. New York: Bowker, 1995.

Barron, Neil, David Hartwell, and CM [Carol McGuirk]. "Notes and Correspondence: Bibliography of Sf Criticism in #78." *Science Fiction Studies* 26.2 (November 1999): 514–516.

Barthes, Roland. *Sade/Fourier/Loyola*. Paris: Éditions du Seuil, 1971.

______. *Sade/Fourier/Loyola*. Trans. Richard Miller. New York: Hill and Wang, 1976.

Bartkowski, Frances. *Feminist Utopias*. Lincoln: University of Nebraska Press, 1989.

Bartter, Martha. "The (Science Fiction) Reader and the Quantum Paradigm: Problems in Delany's *Stars in My Pockets Like Grains of Sand*." *Science-Fiction Studies* 17.3 (November 1990): 325–340.

Baruch, Elaine Hoffman. "Dystopia Now." *Alternative Futures* 2.3 (Summer 1979): 55–67.

______. "A Natural and Necessary Monster: Women in Utopia." *Alternative Futures* 2.1 (Winter 1978/1979): 29–49.

Baruch, Elaine, and Ruby Rohrlich, eds. *Women in Search of Utopia*. New York: Schocken, 1984.

Baudrillard, Jean. *America*. London: Verso, 1986.

Beal, Frances M. "Black Women and the Science Fiction Genre: Interview with Octavia Butler." *Black Scholar* 17.2 (March-April 1986): 14–18.

Beauchamp, Gorman. "Cultural Primitivism as Norm in the Dystopian Novel." *Extrapolation* 19.1 (Winter 1977): 88–96.

______. "From Bingo to Big Brother: Orwell on Power and Sadism." In *The Future of Nineteen Eighty-Four*. Ed. Einer J. Jensen. Ann Arbor: University of Michigan Press, 1984. 65–85.

______. "Future Words: Language and the Dystopian Novel." *Style* 8 (1974): 462–476.

______. "Jack London's Utopian Dystopia and Dystopian Utopia." In *America as Utopia*. Ed. Kenneth M. Roemer. New York: Burt Franklin, 1981. 91–107.

______. "Of Man's Last Disobedience: Zamiatin's *We* and Orwell's *1984*." *Comparative Literature Studies* 10 (1973): 285–301.

______. "The Proto-Dystopia of Jerome K. Jerome." *Extrapolation* 24.2 (Summer 1983): 170–181.

______. "Resentment and Revolution in Jack London's Sociofantasy." *Canadian Review of American Studies* 13.2 (Fall 1982): 179–192.

______. "Technology in the Dystopian Novel." *Modern Fiction Studies* 32.1 (Spring 1986): 53–63.

______. "Utopia and Its Discontents." *Midwest Quarterly* 16 (1975): 161–174.

______. "Zamiatin's *We*." In *No Place Else: Explorations in Utopian and Dystopian Fiction*. Eds. Eric S. Rabkin, Martin H. Greenberg, and Joseph Olander. Carbondale: Southern Illinois University Press, 1983. 56–77.

Benedikt, Michael, ed. *Cyberspace: First Steps*. Cambridge: MIT Press, 1991.

Benford, Gregory. "Is Something Going On?" *Mississippi Review* 47/48 (1988): 218–223.

Benjamin, Walter. "Theses on the Philosophy of History." *Illuminations*. Trans. Harry Zohn. New York: Schocken, 1969.

Bennett, Tony. "Texts, Readers, and Reading Formations." *Bulletin of the Midwest Modern Language Association* 16.1 (Spring 1983): 3–17.

Berger, Harold. *Science Fiction and the New Dark Age*. Bowling Green, Ohio: Bowling Green University Press, 1976.

Berger, James. *After the End: Representations of Post-Apocalypse*. Minneapolis: University of Minnesota Press, 2000.

Berger, John. "Against the Great Defeat of the World." *Race and Class* 40.2/3 (1998/1999): 1–4.

Berman, Marshall. *All That Is Solid Melts into Air: The Experience of Modernity*. New York: Viking, 1988.

Bernal, Martin. *Black Athena: The Afroasiatic Roots of Classical Civilization*. New Brunswick, N.J.: Rutgers University Press, 1987.

Bjornson, Richard. "Cognitive Mapping and the Understanding of Literature." *Sub-Stance* 30 (1981): 51–62.

Blish, James [William Atheling Jr., pseud.]. *The Issues at Hand: Studies in Contemporary Magazine Science Fiction*. Chicago: Advent, 1964.

Bloch, Ernst. "Dialectic and Hope." Trans. Mark Ritter. *New German Critique* 9 (Fall 1976): 3–11.

______. *Heritage of Our Times*. Trans. Neville Plaice and Stephen Plaice. Berkeley: University of California Press, 1991.

______. "Nonsynchronism and the Obligation to Its Dialectics." Trans. Mark Ritter. *New German Critique* 11 (Spring 1977): 22–39.

______. *The Principle of Hope*. Trans. Neville Plaice, Stephen Plaice, and Paul Knight. 3 vols. Cambridge: MIT Press, 1986.

Bloch, Ernst, and Theodor W. Adorno. "Something's Missing: A Discussion Between Ernst Bloch and Theodor W. Adorno on the Contradictions of Utopian Longing." In *The Utopian Function of Art and Literature: Selected Essays*. Trans. Jack Zipes and Frank Mecklenburg. Cambridge: MIT Press, 1988. 1–18.

Bolongaro, Eugenio. "From Literariness to Genre: Establishing the Foundations for a Theory of Literary Genres." *Genre* 25 (1994): 277–313.

Booker, M. Keith. *The Dystopian Impulse in Modern Literature: Fiction as Social Criticism*. Westport, Conn.: Greenwood, 1994.

______. *Dystopian Literature: A Theory and Research Guide*. Westport, Conn.: Greenwood, 1994.

______. "Woman on the Edge of a Genre: The Feminist Dystopias of Marge Piercy." *Science-Fiction Studies* 21.3 (November 1994): 337–350.

Bordieu, Pierre. *Acts of Resistance: Against the Theory of the Market*. New York: New Press, 1998.

Bordieu, Pierre, and Loïc J. D. Wacquant. *An Invitation to Reflexive Sociology*. Chicago: University of Chicago Press, 1992.

Boulter, Amanda. *Speculative Feminisms: The Significance of Feminist Theory in the Science Fiction of Joanna Russ, James Tiptree, Jr., Octavia Butler*. Diss. Ann Arbor: UMI, 1996.

Boyer, Robert. *The Regulation School: A Critical Introduction*. Trans. Craig Charney. New York: Columbia University Press, 1990.

Braverman, Harry. *Labor and Monopoly Capital: The Degradation of Work in the Twentieth Century*. New York: Monthly Review Press, 1974.

Brenkman, John. *Culture and Domination*. Ithaca, N.Y.: Cornell University Press, 1987.

Brenner, Robert. "The Economics of Global Turbulence." *New Left Review* 229 (May/June 1998): 1–264.

Brin, David. "Starchilde Harold, Revisited." *Mississippi Review* 47/48 (1988): 23–27.

Broderick, Damian. "Reading SF as a Mega-Text." *New York Review of Science Fiction* (1992): 1, 8–10.

Bronner, Stephen Eric. *Socialism Unbound*. New York: Routledge, 1990.

Brooke-Rose, Christine. *A Rhetoric of the Unreal: Studies in Narrative and Structure, Especially of the Fantastic*. Cambridge: Cambridge University Press, 1981.

Brown, Clarence. Introduction to *We*, by Yevgeny Zamyatin. New York: Penguin, 1993. xi–xxvi.

Brown, Elaine. *A Taste of Power: A Black Woman's Story*. New York: Pantheon, 1992.

Brown, Steve. "Before the Lights Came On: Observations of a Synergy." In *Storming the Reality Studio*. Ed. Larry McCaffery. Durham, N.C.: Duke University Press, 1991. 173–178.

Browning, William Gordon. *Anti-Utopian Fiction: Definition and Standards for Evaluation*. Diss. Ann Arbor: UMI, 1966.

______. "Toward a Set of Standards for Everlasting Anti-Utopian Fiction." *Cithara* 10.7 (December 1970): 18–32.

______. "Zamiatin's *We:* An Anti-Utopian Classic." *Cithara* 7.2 (May 1968): 13–20.

Buchanan, Ian. "Metacommentary on Utopia, or Jameson's Dialectic of Hope." *Utopian Studies* 9.2 (1998): 18–31.

Bukatman, Scott. "Postcards from the Posthuman Solar System." *Science-Fiction Studies* 18.3 (November 1991): 343–358.

______. *Terminal Identity: The Virtual Subject in Postmodern Science Fiction*. Durham, N.C.: Duke University Press, 1993.

Burke, Edmund. *Reflections on the Revolution in France*. Dublin, 1791.

Burke, Kenneth. *A Grammar of Motives and a Rhetoric of Motives*. Cleveland: World, 1962.

Burton, Robert. *The Anatomy of Melancholy*. Oxford: Henry Cripps, 1628.

Burwell, Jennifer. *Notes on Nowhere: Feminism, Utopian Logic, and Social Transformation*. Minneapolis: University of Minnesota Press, 1997.

Butler, Octavia. "Memorial Tribute to Thomas Clareson." Videocassette. Science Fiction Research Association. 1994.

Caldwell, Larry W. "Wells, Orwell, and Atwood: (EPI)Logic and Eu/topia." *Extrapolation* 33.4 (Winter 1992): 333–345.

Caporaletti, Silvana. "Science as Nightmare: 'The Machine Stops' by E. M. Forster." *Utopian Studies* 8.2 (1997): 32–47.

Carby, Hazel. *Race Men*. Cambridge: Harvard University Press, 1998.

Carson, Clayborne. *In Struggle: SNCC and the Black Awakening of the 1960s*. Cambridge: Harvard University Press, 1981.

Casteñada, Jorge. *Utopia Unarmed: The Latin American Left After the Cold War*. New York: Vintage, 1993.

A Catechism of Christian Doctrine [Baltimore Catechism]. Paterson, N.J.: St. Anthony Guild Press, 1941.

Cavalcanti, Ildney. "Articulating the Elsewhere: Utopia in Contemporary Feminist Dystopias." Diss. University of Strathclyde, 1999.

Chernaik, Laura. "Pat Cadigan's *Synners:* Reconfiguring Nature, Science and Technology." *Feminist Review* 56 (1997): 61–84.

Chomsky, Noam. *Profit over People: Neoliberalism and Global Order.* New York: Seven Stories, 1999.

______. *Year 501.* Montreal: Black Rose, 1993.

Chown, Eric, Stephen Kaplan, and David Kortenkamp. "Prototypes, Location, and Associative Networks (PLAN): Towards a Unified Theory of Cognitive Mapping." *Cognitive Science: A Multidisciplinary Journal of Artificial Intelligence, Linguistics, Neuroscience, Philosophy, Psychology* 19.1 (1995): 1–49.

Churchill, Ward. *Agents of Repression: The FBI's Secret War Against the Black Panther Party and the American Indian Movement.* Boston: South End, 1990.

Churchill, Ward, and Jim Vander Wall, eds. *The COINTELPRO Papers: Documents from the FBI's Secret Wars Against Domestic Dissent.* Boston: South End, 1990.

Cixous, Hélène. "Laugh of the Medusa." In *New French Feminisms.* Trans. Keith Cohen and Paula Cohen. Ed. Elaine Marks and Isabel de Courtivon. Brighton, England: Harvester, 1980. 245–254.

Claeys, Gregory, ed. *Modern British Utopias, 1700–1850.* 8 vols. London: Pickering, 1997.

______. *Utopias of the British Enlightenment.* Cambridge: Cambridge University Press, 1994.

Claeys, Gregory, and Lyman Tower Sargent, eds. *The Utopia Reader.* New York: New York University Press, 1999.

______. *Utopia: The Search for the Ideal Society in the Western World.* Catalogue for an exhibition at the New York Public Library and the Bibliothèque Nationale de France. New York: New York Public Library, 2000.

Clapper, Thomas H. Review of *The Dystopian Impulse in Modern Literature: Fiction as Social Criticism,* by M. Keith Booker. *Utopian Studies* 6.2 (1995): 147–149.

______. Review of *Dystopian Literature: A Theory and Research Guide,* by M. Keith Booker. *Utopian Studies* 6.2 (1995): 149–150.

Clareson, Thomas D., ed. *SF: The Other Side of Realism.* Bowling Green, Ohio: Bowling Green University Press, 1971.

______. *Some Kind of Paradise: The Emergence of American Science Fiction.* Westport, Conn.: Greenwood, 1985.

Clarke I. F. *Voices Prophesying War, Future Wars, 1763–1984.* London: Oxford University Press, 1966.

Clute, John. *Strokes: Essays and Reviews, 1966–1986.* Seattle: Serconia, 1988.

Clute, John, and Peter Nichols, eds. *Encyclopedia of Science Fiction.* New York: St. Martin's, 1993.

Coleman, Letetia F. *Octavia Butler's Patternist Series: A Cultural Analysis.* Diss. Ann Arbor: UMI, 1997.

Cortiel, Jennifer. *Demand My Writing: Joanna Russ/Feminism/Science Fiction.* Liverpool: Liverpool University Press, 1999.

Costello, Nicholas, Jonathan Michie, and Seaumas Milne. *Beyond the Casino Economy: Planning for the 1990s.* London: Verso, 1989.

Cranny-Francis, Anne. "The Erotics of the cy(Borg): Authority and Gender in the Sociocultural Imaginary." In *Future Females, the Next Generation: New Voices and Velocities in Feminist Science Fiction*. Ed. Marleen Barr. Boston: Rowman and Littlefield, 2000. 145–164.

______. *Feminist Fiction: Feminist Uses of Generic Fiction*. Cambridge: Polity, 1990.

Crossman, Richard Howard Stafford, ed. *The God That Failed*. New York: Harper, 1949.

Csicsery-Ronay, Istvan. "Cyberpunk and Neuromanticism." *Mississippi Review* 47/48 (1988): 266–279.

______. "The SF of Theory: Baudrillard and Haraway." *Science-Fiction Studies* 18.3 (November 1991): 387–405.

Cummings, Michael S. "America's Communal Utopias." *Utopian Studies* 9.2 (1998): 191–206.

Cummins, Elizabeth. *Understanding Ursula K. Le Guin*. Columbia: University of South Carolina Press, 1990.

Daniel, Jamie Owen, and Tom Moylan, eds. *Not Yet: Reconsidering Ernst Bloch*. London: Verso, 1997.

Davis, Angela. *Angela Davis: An Autobiography*. New York: Random House, 1974.

Davis, J. C. *Utopia and the Ideal Society: A Study of English Utopian Writing, 1516–1700*. Cambridge: Cambridge University Press, 1981.

Davis, Mike. *City of Quartz: Excavating the Future in Los Angeles*. New York: Vintage, 1992.

______. *The Ecology of Fear: Los Angeles and the Imagination of Disaster*. New York: Henry Holt, 1998.

______. *Prisoners of the American Dream*. London: Verso, 1986.

Dayton, Tim. "The Mystery of Pre-history: Ernst Bloch and Crime Fiction." In *Not Yet: Reconsidering Ernst Bloch*. Eds. Jamie Owen Daniel and Tom Moylan. London: Verso, 1997. 186–201.

De Araujo, Victor. *The Short Story of Fantasy: Henry James, H. G. Wells, and E. M. Forster*. Diss. Ann Arbor: UMI, 1965.

de Certeau, Michel. *The Practice of Everyday Life*. Berkeley: University of California Press, 1984.

Deery, June. "Ectopic and Utopic Reproduction: *He, She and It*." *Utopian Studies* 5.2 (1994): 36–49.

Delany, Samuel R. *The American Shore: Meditations on a Tale of Science Fiction by Thomas M. Disch*. Elizabethtown, N.Y.: Dragon, 1978.

______. "Generic Fictions: Science Fiction and Mundane." In *The Technological Imagination: Theories and Fictions*. Eds. Teresa de Lauretis, Andreas Huyssen, and Kathleen Woodward. Madison, Wis.: Coda, 1980. 175–193.

______. "Is Cyberpunk a Good Thing or a Bad Thing?" *Mississippi Review* 47/48 (1988): 28–35.

______. *The Jewel-Hinged Jaw: Notes on the Language of Science Fiction*. Elizabethtown, N.Y.: Dragon, 1977.

______. "Reading Modern American Science Fiction." In *American Writing Today*. Ed. Richard Kostalanetz. Troy, N.Y.: Whitson, 1991. 517–528.

______. "Science Fiction and 'Literature'—or, The Conscience of the King." In *Visions of Wonder: The Science Fiction Research Association Anthology*. Eds. David Hartwell and Milton T. Wolf. New York: Tor, 1996. 442–458.

______. "The Semiology of Silence." *Science-Fiction Studies* 14.2 (July 1987): 134–165.

______. *Shorter Views: Queer Thoughts and the Politics of the Paraliterary*. Hanover, N.H.: University Press of New England, 1999.

______. *Silent Interviews: On Language, Race, Sex, Science Fiction, and Some Comics. A Collection of Written Interviews*. Hanover, N.H.: Wesleyan University Press, 1994.

______. "Some Reflections on SF Criticism." *Science-Fiction Studies* 8.3 (November 1981): 233–240.

______. *Starboard Wine: More Notes on the Language of Science Fiction*. Pleasantville, N.Y.: Dragon, 1984.

______. *Times Square Red, Times Square Blue*. New York: New York University Press, 1999.

de Lauretis, Teresa. "A Sense of Wa/onder." In *The Technological Imagination: Theories and Fictions*. Eds. Teresa de Lauretis, Andreas Huyssen, and Kathleen Woodward. Madison, Wis.: Coda, 1980. 159–174.

Deleuze, Gilles. *Présentation de Sacher-Masoch*. Paris: Editions de Minuit, 1967.

del Ray, Lester. *The World of Science Fiction, 1926–1976*. New York: Ballantine, 1979.

Denning, Michael. *The Cultural Front: The Laboring of American Culture in the Twentieth Century*. London: Verso, 1998.

Derrida, Jacques. *Spectres of Marx, State of the Debt, the Work of Mourning*. Trans. Peggy Kaumf. New York: Routledge, 1994.

Dews, Peter. *Logics of Disintegration: Post-Structuralist Thought and the Claims of Critical Theory*. London: Verso, 1987.

Dingwaney, Anuradha, and Lawrence Needham. "The Difference That Difference Makes." *Socialist Review* 26.3–4 (1996): 5–47.

Doerksen, Teri Ann. "Octavia E. Butler: Parables of Race and Difference." In *Into Darkness Peering: Race and Color in the Fantastic*. Ed. Elisabeth Ann Leonard. Westport, Conn.: Greenwood, 1997. 21–34.

Donawerth, Jane L. *Frankenstein's Daughters: Women Writing Science Fiction*. Syracuse, N.Y.: Syracuse University Press, 1997.

Donawerth, Jane L., and Carol Kolmerten, eds. *Utopian and Science Fiction by Women: Worlds of Difference*. Syracuse, N.Y.: Syracuse University Press, 1994.

Dreze, Jean, and Amartya Sen. *Hunger and Public Action*. Oxford: Clarendon, 1989.

Drucker, Peter. *Post-Capitalist Society*. New York: Harper, 1993.

Dubey, M. "Folk and Urban Communities in African-American Women's Fiction: Octavia Butler's *Parable of the Sower*." *Studies in American Fiction* 27.1 (Spring 1999): 103–128.

Dutschke, Rudi. "On Anti-authoritarianism." Trans. Salvator Attanasio. In *The New Left Reader*. New York: Grove, 1969. 243–254.

Dyson, Michael. *Between God and Gangsta Rap: Bearing Witness to Black Culture*. London: Oxford University Press, 1996.

Eagleton, Terry. *Ideology: An Introduction*. London: Verso, 1991.

______. *The Illusions of Postmodernism*. Oxford: Blackwell, 1997.

______. *Literary Theory: An Introduction*. 2nd ed. Minneapolis: University of Minnesota Press, 1996.

______. "Pretty Much Like Ourselves." Review of *Modern British Utopias, 1700–1858*, ed. Gregory Claeys. *London Review of Books*, 4 September 1997: 6–7.

______. "Utopia and Its Opposites." In *Necessary and Unnecessary Utopias: Socialist Register 2000*. Eds. Leo Panitch and Colin Leys. New York: Monthly Review Press, 1999. 31–41.

Echols, Alice. *Daring to Be Bad: Radical Feminism in America, 1967–1975*. Minneapolis: University of Minnesota Press, 1989.

______. "'We Gotta Get out of This Place': Notes Toward a Remapping of the Sixties." *Socialist Review* 22.2 (April-June 1992): 9–35.

Ehrenreich, Barbara. "The Professional-Managerial Class Revisited." In *Intellectuals*. Minneapolis: University of Minnesota Press, 1990. 173–185.

Ehrenreich, Barbara, and John Ehrenreich. *Long March, Short Spring: The Student Uprising at Home and Abroad*. New York: Monthly Review Press, 1969.

______. "The Professional-Managerial Class." In *Between Labor and Capital*. Ed. P. Walker. Boston: South End, 1979. 5–45.

Eliav-Feldon, Miriam. *Realistic Utopias: The Ideal Imaginary Societies of the Renaissance, 1516–1630*. Oxford: Clarendon, 1982.

Elkins, Charles. "E. M. Forster's 'The Machine Stops': Liberal-Humanist Hostility to Technology." In *Clockwork Worlds*. Ed. R. D. Erlich. Westport, Conn.: Greenwood, 1983. 47–62.

Elkins, Charles, and Darko Suvin. "Preliminary Reflections on Teaching Science Fiction Critically." *Science-Fiction Studies* 6.3 (November 1976): 263–270.

Elliot, Robert C. *The Shape of Utopia: Studies in a Literary Genre*. Chicago: University of Chicago Press, 1970.

Evans, Arthur B. "The Origin of Science Fiction Criticism: From Kepler to Wells." *Science Fiction Studies* 26.2 (July 1999): 163–187.

Evans, Robert O. "The *Nouveau Roman*, Russian Dystopias, and Anthony Burgess." *Studies in the Literary Imagination* 6 (Fall 1973): 27–38.

Evans, Sara. *Personal Politics: The Roots of Women's Liberation in the Civil Rights Movement and the New Left*. New York: Knopf, 1979.

Ewen, Stuart. *Captains of Consciousness: Advertising and the Social Roots of Consumer Culture*. New York: McGraw-Hill, 1976.

Faludi, Susan. *Backlash: The Undeclared War Against American Women*. New York: Crown, 1991.

______. *Stiffed: The Betrayal of the American Man*. New York: Morrow, 1999.

Ferguson, Charles A. "Devotional Reading and Science Fiction: The Medieval Saint's Life as a Form of Discourse." In *Language in Global Perspective: Papers in Honor of the 50th An-*

niversary of the Summer Institute of Linguistics, 1935–1985. Dallas: Summer Institute of Linguistics, 1986. 113–122.

Ferguson, Erika, and Mary Hegarty. "Properties of Cognitive Maps Constructed from Texts." *Memory and Cognition* 22.4 (1994): 455–473.

Ferguson, John. *Utopias of the Classical World.* London: Thames and Hudson, 1975.

Ferns, Chris. *Narrating Utopia: Ideology, Gender, Form in Utopian Literature.* Liverpool: Liverpool University Press, 1999.

Finkelstein, Norman. "The Utopian Function and the Refunctioning of Marxism." *Diacritics* 19.2 (1989): 54–65.

Fischlin, Daniel, Veronica Hollinger, and Andrew Taylor. "'The Charisma Leak': A Conversation with William Gibson and Bruce Sterling." *Science-Fiction Studies* 19.1 (March 1992): 1–17.

Fitting, Peter. "Beyond the Wasteland: A Feminist in Cyberspace." *Utopian Studies* 5.2 (1994): 4–16.

______. "The Concept of Utopia in the Work of Fredric Jameson." *Utopian Studies* 9.2 (1998): 8–18.

______. "Hacking away at the Postmodern: William Gibson and Cyberpunk." Paper presented at the Popular Culture Association annual meeting. St. Louis, Missouri, 6 April 1989.

______. "Ideological Foreclosure and Utopian Discourse." *Sociocriticism* 7 (1988): 11–25.

______. "Impulse or Genre or Neither?" *Science-Fiction Studies* 22.2 (July 1995): 272–281.

______. "The Lessons of Cyberpunk." In *Technoculture*. Eds. Constance Penley and Andrew Ross. Minneapolis: University of Minnesota Press, 1991. 295–315.

______. "The Modern Anglo-American SF Novel: Utopian Longing and Capitalist Cooptation." *Science-Fiction Studies* 6.1 (March 1979): 59–76.

______. "Positioning and Closure: On the 'Reading Effect' of Contemporary Utopian Fiction." In *Utopian Studies I*. Eds. Gorman Beauchamp, Kenneth M. Roemer, and Nicholas D. Smith. Lanham, Md.: University Press of America, 1987. 23–36.

______. "Reality as an Artificial Construct: A Reading of Five Novels by Philip K. Dick." *Science-Fiction Studies* 10.2 (July 1983): 219–236.

______. "Recent Feminist Utopias: World Building and Strategies for Social Change." In *Mindscapes*. Eds. George E. Slusser and Eric Rabkin. Carbondale: Southern Illinois University Press, 1989. 155–163.

______. "Reconsiderations of the Separatist Paradigm in Recent Feminist Science Fiction." *Science-Fiction Studies* 19.1 (March 1992): 32–48.

______. "'So We All Became Mothers': New Roles for Men in Recent Utopian Fiction." *Science-Fiction Studies* 12.2 (July 1985): 156–183.

______. "To Read the World: Barthes' *Mythologies* Thirty Years Later." *Queen's Quarterly* 95 (Spring 1988): 857–871.

______. "*Ubik:* The Deconstruction of Bourgeois SF." *Science-Fiction Studies* 2.1 (March 1975): 47–54.

______. "Unmasking the Real? Critique and Utopia in Four Recent Films." In *The Dystopian Turn: Science Fiction and Utopia at the End of the 20th Century*. Eds. Raffaella Baccolini and Tom Moylan. Forthcoming.

______. "Utopia Beyond Our Ideals: The Dilemma of the Right-Wing Utopia." *Utopian Studies* 2.1&2 (1991): 95–109.

______. "Utopian Effect/Utopian Pleasure." In *Styles of Creation: Aesthetic Technique and the Creation of Fictional Worlds*. Eds. George Slusser and Eric Rabkin. Athens: University of Georgia Press, 1992. 153–167.

______. "What Is Utopian Film? An Introductory Taxonomy." *Utopian Studies* 4.2 (1993): 1–17.

Foner, Philip S., ed. *The Black Panthers Speak*. Philadelphia: Lippincott, 1970.

Foote, Bud. "A Conversation with Kim Stanley Robinson." *Science-Fiction Studies* 21.1 (March 1994): 51–66.

Fortunati, Vita. *La letteratura utopica inglese: morfologia e grammatica di un genere letterio*. Ravenna: Longo, 1979.

Foster, John Bellamy. *Marx's Ecology: Materialism and Nature*. New York: Monthly Review Press, 1999.

Foster, Thomas. "Incurably Informed: The Pleasures and Dangers of Cyberpunk." *Genders* 18 (Winter 1993): 1–10.

______. "Meat Puppets or Robopaths? Cyberpunk and the Question of Embodiment." *Genders* 18 (Winter 1993): 11–31.

Fox, R. W., and T. J. J. Lears, eds. *The Culture of Consumption*. New York: Pantheon, 1983.

Fraenger, Wilhelm. *Hieronymous Bosch*. Trans. Helen Sebba. New York: Dorset, 1989.

Franco, Carol. "The Density of Utopian Destiny in Robinson's *Red Mars*." *Extrapolation* 38.1 (Spring 1997): 57–65.

______. "Dialogical Twins, Post-Patriarchal Topography in Two Stories by Kim Stanley Robinson." *Science-Fiction Studies* 22.3 (November 1995): 305–322.

______. "Working the 'In-Between': Kim Stanley Robinson's Utopian Fiction." *Science-Fiction Studies* 21.2 (July 1994): 191–211.

Franklin, H. Bruce. *Future Perfect: American Science Fiction of the Nineteenth Century*. London: Oxford University Press, 1966.

______. *War Stars*. London: Oxford University Press, 1988.

Freedman, Carl. *Critical Theory and Science Fiction*. Hanover, N.H.: Wesleyan University Press, 2000.

______. "Science Fiction and Critical Theory." *Science-Fiction Studies* 14.2 (July 1987): 180–200.

Friend, Beverly. *The Science Fiction Fan Cult*. Diss. Ann Arbor: UMI, 1975.

______. "Strange Bedfellows: Science Fiction, Linguistics, and Education." *English Journal* 62 (1973): 998–1003.

______. "Virgin Territory: Women and Sex in Science Fiction." *Extrapolation* 14.4 (Winter 1972): 49–58.

Frisch, Adam. "Toward New Sexual Identities: James Tiptree, Jr." In *In the Feminine Eye: Science Fiction and the Women Who Write It.* New York: Ungar, 1982. 48–59.

Frow, John. *Marxism and Literary History.* Cambridge: Harvard University Press, 1986.

Fry, Joan. "An Interview with Octavia Butler." *Poets and Writers* 25.2 (March/April 1997): 58–69.

Frye, Northrop. *Anatomy of Criticism: Four Essays.* Princeton, N.J.: Princeton University Press, 1957.

______. "Varieties of Literary Utopias." In *Utopias and Utopian Thought.* Ed. Frank E. Manuel. Boston: Beacon, 1965. 323–347.

Fukuyama, Francis. *The End of History and the Last Man.* New York: Free Press, 1992.

______. *Trust: The Social Virtues and the Creation of Prosperity.* New York: Free Press, 1996.

Gardiner, Michael. *The Dialogics of Critique: M. M. Bakhtin and the Theory of Ideology.* New York: Routledge, 1992.

Genova, Judith. "Tiptree and Haraway: The Reinvention of Nature." *Cultural Critique* 27 (1994): 5–27.

Geoghegan, Vincent. *Ernst Bloch.* New York: Routledge, 1996.

______. "Ernst Bloch: Postsecular Thoughts." In *Marxism's Ethical Dimension.* London: Macmillan, forthcoming.

______. "Remembering the Future." In *Not Yet: Reconsidering Ernst Bloch.* Eds. Jamie Owen Daniel and Tom Moylan. London: Verso, 1997. 15–33.

______. *Utopianism and Marxism.* London: Methuen, 1987.

Geras, Norman. "Minimum Utopia: Ten Theses." In *Necessary and Unnecessary Utopias: Socialist Register 2000.* Eds. Leo Panitch and Colin Leys. New York: Monthly Review Press, 1999. 41–53.

Gibbons, Luke. *Transformations in Irish Culture.* South Bend, Ind.: University of Notre Dame Press, 1996.

Giddens, Anthony. *The Third Way: The Renewal of Social Democracy.* Cambridge: Polity, 1998.

Gifford, Dawn. "Marge Piercy: A Class Act." *Off Our Backs* 24.6 (1994): 14–17.

Gomoll, Jeanne. "Open Letter to Joanna Russ." *Aurora* 10.1 (Winter 1986–1987): 7–10.

Goode, John. "Gissing, Morris, and English Socialism." *Victorian Studies* 12.2 (1968): 201–226.

Goodwin, Barbara. "Perspectives on Several Utopias: Steven Lukes's Professor Caritat." *Utopian Studies* 9.2 (1998): 210–219.

Goodwin, Barbara, and Keith Taylor. *The Politics of Utopia: A Study in Theory and Practice.* London: Hutchinson, 1982.

Gosse, Van. *Where the Boys Are: Cuba, Cold War America and the Making of the New Left.* London: Verso, 1993.

Gough, Val. "'In the Twinkling of an Eye': Gilman's Utopian Imagination." In *A Very Different Story: Studies on the Fiction of Charlotte Perkins Gilman.* Eds. Val Gough and Jill Rudd. Liverpool: Liverpool University Press, 1998. 129–144.

Govan, Sandra Y. "Homage to Tradition: Octavia Butler Renovates the Historical Novel." *MELUS* 13.1–2 (Spring-Summer 1986): 79–96.

Gove, Phillip Babcock. *The Imaginary Voyage in Prose Fiction*. New York: Columbia University Press, 1941.

Gramsci, Antonio. *Selections from the Prison Notebooks*. Ed. and trans. Quintin Hoare and Geoffrey Nowell Smith. New York: International Publishers, 1971.

Green, Martin. "Science and Sensibility. I: Science for the Layman. II: Science Fiction." *Kenyon Review* 25.4 (Fall 1963): 699–728.

Green, Michelle Erica. "There Goes the Neighborhood: Octavia Butler's Demand for Diversity in Utopias." In *Utopian and Science Fiction by Women: Worlds of Difference*. Eds. Jane L. Donawerth and Carol Kolmerten. Syracuse, N.Y.: Syracuse University Press, 1994. 166–190.

Greenblatt, Stephen. *Marvelous Possession: The Wonder of the New World*. Chicago: University of Chicago Press, 1991.

Gross, Bertram. *Friendly Fascism: The New Face of Power in America*. New York: M. Evans, 1980.

Grossberg, Lawrence. *We Gotta Get out of This Place: Popular Conservatism and Postmodern Culture*. New York: Routledge, 1992.

Grossberg, Lawrence, Cary Nelson, and Paula Treichler, eds. *Cultural Studies*. New York: Routledge, 1992.

Gutiérrez, Gustavo. *A Theology of Liberation: History, Politics, Salvation*. Trans. Caridad Inda and John Eagleson. Maryknoll, N.Y.: Orbis, 1973.

Habermas, Jürgen. *The New Conservatism*. Trans. Shierry Weber Nicholsen. Cambridge: Polity, 1989.

Hall, Stuart. "Brave New World." *Socialist Review* 21.1 (January-March 1991): 53–57.

Haraway, Donna. "A Manifesto for Cyborgs: Science, Technology, and Socialist Feminism in the 1980s." *Socialist Review* 80 (March-April 1985): 65–107.

______. "Situated Knowledges: The Science Question in Feminism and the Privilege of Partial Perspective." In *Simians, Cyborgs, and Women: The Reinvention of Nature*. New York: Routledge, 1991. 183–203.

Harding, Sandra. *The Science Question in Feminism*. Ithaca, N.Y.: Cornell University Press, 1986.

Hardt, Michael, and Antonio Negri. *Empire*. Cambridge: Harvard University Press, 2000.

Harlow, Barbara. *Resistance Literature*. London: Methuen, 1987.

Harris, Cheryl, and Alison Alexander. *Theorizing Fandom: Fans, Subculture, and Identity*. Cresskill, N.J.: Hampton, 1998.

Harrison, Bennett, and Barry Bluestone. *The Great U-Turn: Corporate Restructuring and the Polarization of America*. New York: Basic, 1990.

Hartsock, Nancy. "The Feminist Standpoint: Developing the Ground for a Specifically Feminist Historical Materialism." In *Money, Sex, and Power*. London: Longman, 1983. 231–251.

Hartwell, David, and Milton T. Wolf, eds. *Visions of Wonder: The Science Fiction Research Association Anthology*. New York: Tor, 1996.

Harvey, David. *The Condition of Postmodernity: An Enquiry into the Origins of Cultural Change*. Oxford: Blackwell, 1989.

______. *Justice, Nature and the Geography of Difference*. Oxford: Blackwell, 1996.

Hassler, Donald M. "The Academic Pioneers of Science Fiction Criticism, 1940–1980." *Science Fiction Studies* 26.2 (July 1999): 213–232.

______. "Editor's Pad." *Extrapolation* 40.3 (Fall 1999): 187–189.

Haug, Frigga. "Feminist Writing: Working with Women's Experience." *Feminist Review* 42 (1992): 16–32.

Hayden, Dolores. *The Grand Domestic Revolution: A History of Feminist Design for American Homes, Neighborhoods, and Clinics*. Cambridge: MIT Press, 1981.

______. *Seven American Utopias: The Architecture of Communitarian Socialism, 1790–1975*. Cambridge: MIT Press, 1975.

Hayek, Friedrich A. von. *The Road to Serfdom*. Chicago: University of Chicago Press, 1944.

Hayler, Barbara J. "The Feminist Fiction of James Tiptree, Jr.: Women and Men as Aliens." In *Spectrum of the Fantastic*. Ed. Donald Palumbo. Westport, Conn.: Greenwood, 1988. 127–132.

Heldreth, Lillian M. "'Love Is the Plan, the Plan Is Death': The Feminism and Fatalism of James Tiptree, Jr." *Extrapolation* 23.1 (Spring 1982): 22–30.

Henwood, Doug. *A New Economy?* London: Verso, 2000.

Hertzler, Joyce Oramel. *The History of Utopian Thought*. New York: Macmillan, 1923.

Hill, Eugene D. "The Place of the Future: Louis Marin and His Utopiques." *Science-Fiction Studies* 9.2 (July 1982): 167–180.

Hillegas, Mark R. *The Future as Nightmare: H. G. Wells and the Anti-Utopians*. London: Oxford University Press, 1967.

Hinkelammert, Franz J. *The Ideological Weapons of Death: A Theological Critique of Capitalism*. Trans. Phillip Berryman. Maryknoll, N.Y.: Orbis, 1986.

"A History of Science Fiction Criticism." Special issue. *Science Fiction Studies* 26.2 (July 1999): 161–284.

Hobsbawm, Eric. *The Age of Extremes*. New York: Pantheon, 1994.

Hogeland, Lisa. *Feminism and Its Fictions: The Consciousness-Raising Novel and the Women's Liberation Movement*. Philadelphia: University of Pennsylvania Press, 1998.

Hollinger, Veronica. "Contemporary Trends in Science Fiction Criticism, 1980–1999." *Science Fiction Studies* 26.2 (July 1999): 232–263.

______. "Cybernetic Deconstructions: Cyberpunk and Postmodernism." In *Storming the Reality Studio*. Ed. Larry McCaffrey. Durham, N.C.: Duke University Press, 1991. 203–219.

______. "Feminist Science Fiction: Breaking up the Subject." *Extrapolation* 31 (Fall 1990): 229–239.

______. "'The Most Grisly Truth': Responses to the Human Condition in the Works of James Tiptree, Jr." *Extrapolation* 30.2 (Summer 1989): 117–132.

______. "(Re)reading Queerly: Science Fiction, Feminism, and the Defamiliarization of Gender." *Science Fiction Studies* 26.1 (March 1999): 23–40.

Homer, Sean. *Fredric Jameson: Marxism, Hermeneutics, Postmodernism*. New York: Routledge, 1998.

hooks, bell. *Killing Rage*. New York: Henry Holt, 1995.

Howe, Irving. "The Fiction of Anti-Utopia." *New Republic,* 23 April 1962: 13–16.

Hudson, Wayne. *The Marxist Philosophy of Ernst Bloch*. London: Macmillan, 1982.

Hume, Kathryn. *Fantasy and Mimesis: Responses to Reality in Western Literature*. London: Methuen, 1984.

Huntington, John. "Thinking by Opposition: The 'Two-World' Structure in H. G. Wells's Short Fiction." *Science-Fiction Studies* 8.3 (November 1981): 240–255.

______. "Utopian and Anti-Utopian Logic: H. G. Wells and His Successors." *Science-Fiction Studies* 9.2 (July 1982): 122–147.

Huyssen, Andreas. *Twilight Memories: Marking Time in a Culture of Amnesia*. New York: Routledge, 1995.

Hynes, James. "Robot's Rules of Disorder: Cyberpunk Rocks the Boat." *In These Times,* 23 November-6 December 1988: 18–19.

Jacobs, Eric. *Kingsley Amis: A Biography*. London: Hodder and Stoughton, 1995.

Jacoby, Russell. *The End of Utopia: Politics and Culture at the End of Apathy*. New York: Basic, 1999.

James, Edward. "Building Utopias on Mars, from Crusoe to Robinson." *Foundation: The Review of Science Fiction* 68 (Autumn 1996): 64–75.

______. *Science Fiction in the 20th Century*. London: Oxford University Press, 1994.

James, Edward, and Farah Mendlesohn. "Science Fiction Courses in Higher Education in Great Britain: A Preliminary Guide." *Foundation: The Review of Science Fiction* 59 (Autumn 1993): 59–69.

Jameson, Fredric. "After Armageddon: Character Systems in P. K. Dicks' *Dr. Bloodmoney*." *Science-Fiction Studies* 2.1 (March 1975): 31–42.

______. "Architecture and the Critique of Ideology." In *The Ideologies of Theory: Essays 1971–1986*. Vol. 2: *The Syntax of History*. Minneapolis: University of Minnesota Press, 1988. 35–60.

______. *Brecht and Method*. London: Verso, 1998.

______. "Cognitive Mapping." In *Marxism and the Interpretation of Culture*. Eds. Cary Nelson and Lawrence Grossberg. Urbana: University of Illinois Press, 1988. 347–360.

______. "Comments." *Utopian Studies* 9.2 (1998): 74–78.

______. "Culture and Finance Capital." In *The Cultural Turn: Selected Writings on the Postmodern, 1983–1998*. London: Verso, 1998. 136–162.

______. "'End of Art' or 'End of History'?" In *The Cultural Turn: Selected Writings on the Postmodern, 1983–1998*. London: Verso, 1998. 73–93.

______. "Five Theses on Actually Existing Marxism." *Monthly Review* 47.11 (April 1996): 1–10.

______. "Generic Discontinuities in SF: Brian Aldiss' *Starship*." *Science-Fiction Studies* 1.2 (July 1973): 57–58.

______. "'If I Find One Good City I Will Spare the Man': Realism and Utopia in Kim Stanley Robinson's *Mars Trilogy*." In *Learning from Other Worlds: Estrangement, Cognition and the Politics of Science Fiction and Utopia. Essays in Honour of Darko Suvin*. Ed. Patrick Parrinder. Liverpool: Liverpool University Press, 2000. 303–343.

______. "Introduction/Prospectus: To Reconsider the Relationship of Marxism to Utopian Thought." *minnesota review* 6 (Spring 1976): 53–59.

______. *Late Marxism: Adorno, or the Persistence of the Dialectic*. London: Verso, 1990.

______. *Marxism and Form*. Princeton, N.J.: Princeton University Press, 1971.

______. "Of Islands and Trenches: Neutralization and the Production of Utopian Discourse." *Diacritics* 7.2 (June 1977): 2–21.

______. "On Raymond Chandler." *Southern Review* 6.3 (Summer 1970): 624–650.

______. "Ontology and Utopia." *L'Esprit Créator* 34.4 (1994): 46–64.

______. "Pleasure: A Political Issue." In *Formations of Pleasure*. London: Routledge and Kegan Paul, 1983. 1–14.

______. *The Political Unconscious: Narrative as a Socially Symbolic Act*. Ithaca, N.Y.: Cornell University Press, 1981.

______. *Postmodernism, or, The Cultural Logic of Late Capitalism*. Durham, N.C.: Duke University Press, 1991.

______. "Progress Versus Utopia; or, Can We Imagine the Future?" *Science-Fiction Studies* 9.2 (July 1982): 147–158.

______. "Reification and Utopia in Mass Culture." In *Signatures of the Visible*. New York: Routledge, 1990. 9–34.

______. "Science Fiction as a Spatial Genre: Generic Discontinuities and the Problem of Figuration in Vonda McIntyre's *The Exile Waiting*." *Science-Fiction Studies* 14.1 (March 1987): 44–59.

______. *The Seeds of Time*. New York: Columbia University Press, 1994.

______. "Third World Literature in the Era of Multinational Capitalism." *Social Text* 15 (1986): 65–88.

______. "Thoughts on the Late War." *Social Text* 28 (1991): 142–147.

______. "World-Reduction in Le Guin: The Emergence of Utopian Narrative." *Science-Fiction Studies* 2.3 (November 1975): 221–230.

Jay, Karla, and Allen Young, eds. *Out of the Closets: Voices of Gay Liberation*. New York: Douglas, 1972.

Jay, Martin. *Marxism and Totality: The Adventures of a Concept from Lukács to Habermas*. Berkeley: University of California Press, 1984.

Jenkins, Henry. *Textual Poachers: Television Fans and Participatory Culture*. New York: Routledge, 1992.

Jezer, Marty. *The Dark Ages: Life in the United States, 1945 to 1960*. Boston: South End, 1981.

Jhally, Sut. "The Political Economy of Culture." In *Cultural Politics in Contemporary America*. Eds. Ian Angus and Sut Jhally. New York: Routledge, 1989. 65–81.

Johnson, Rebecca. "African American Feminist Science Fiction." *Sojourner: The Women's Forum* (February 1994): 12–14.

Jones, Gwyneth. *Deconstructing the Starships: Science, Fiction, and Reality*. Liverpool: Liverpool University Press, 1999.

Kagarlitsky, Jules. "Realism and Fantasy." In *SF: The Other Side of Realism, Essays on Modern Fantasy and Science Fiction*. Ed. Thomas D. Clareson. Bowling Green, Ohio: Bowling Green University Press, 1971. 29–53.

Kaplan, Carter. "The Advent of Literary Dystopia." *Extrapolation* 40.3 (Fall 1999): 200–213.

Kateb, George. *Utopia and Its Enemies*. New York: Free Press, 1963.

Katsiaficas, George. *The Imagination of the New Left*. Boston: South End, 1987.

Kellner, Douglas, and Harry O'Hara. "Utopia and Marxism in Ernst Bloch." *New German Critique* 9 (Fall 1976): 11–35.

Kessler, Carol Farley. "Bibliography of Utopian Fiction by United States Women, 1836–1988." *Utopian Studies* 1.1 (1990): 1–58.

______. "Consider Her Ways: The Cultural Work of Charlotte Perkins Gilman's Pragmatopian Series, 1908–1913." In *Utopian and Science Fiction by Women: Worlds of Difference*. Eds. Jane L. Donawerth and Carol Kolmerten. Syracuse, N.Y.: Syracuse University Press, 1994. 126–137.

______. *Daring to Dream: Utopian Stories by United States Women*. Boston: Pandora, 1984.

Ketterer, David. "Covering *A Case of Conscience*." *Science-Fiction Studies* 9.2 (July 1982): 195–215.

______. *New Worlds for Old: The Apocalyptic Tradition, Science Fiction, and American Literature*. New York: Doubleday-Anchor, 1974.

Khanna, Lee Cullen. "Frontiers of Imagination: Feminist Worlds." *Women's Studies International Forum* 7.2 (1984): 97–102.

______. "The Reader in *Looking Backward*." *Journal of General Education* 33 (1981): 69–79.

______. "The Subject of Utopia: Margaret Cavendish and Her Blazing-World." In *Utopian and Science Fiction by Women: Worlds of Difference*. Eds. Jane Donawerth and Carol Kolmerten. Syracuse, N.Y.: Syracuse University Press, 1994. 15–35.

Khouri, Nadia. "The Dialectics of Power: Utopia in the Science Fiction of Le Guin, Jeury, and Piercy." *Science-Fiction Studies* 7.1 (March 1980): 49–61.

______. "Utopia and Epic: Ideological Confrontation in Jack London's *The Iron Heel*." *Science-Fiction Studies* 3.2 (July 1976): 174–181.

"Kim Stanley Robinson." Available: http://www.fantasticfiction.co.uk/authors/Kim_Stanley Robinson.htm.

Klein, Naomi. *No Space, No Jobs, No Logo: Taking Aim at the Brand Bullies*. New York: Picador, 2000.

Knight, Damon. *In Search of Wonder*. Chicago: Advent, 1956.

Knight, Diana. *Barthes and Utopia: Space, Travel, Writing*. Oxford: Clarendon, 1997.

Kolmerten, Carol. *Women in Utopia: The Ideology of Gender in the American Owenite Communities*. Bloomington: Indiana University Press, 1990.

Kovel, Joel. "Cryptic Notes on Revolution and the Spirit." *Old Westbury Review* 2 (Fall 1986): 23–35.

______. *History and Spirit: An Inquiry into the Philosophy of Liberation.* Boston: Beacon, 1991.

Kuhn, Annette, ed. *Alien Zone: Cultural Theory and Contemporary Science Fiction Cinema.* London: Verso, 1990.

______, ed. *Alien Zone 2: The Spaces of Science Fiction Cinema.* London: Verso, 2000.

Kumar, Krishan. *From Post-Industrial to Post-Modern Society.* Oxford: Blackwell, 1996.

______. *Utopia and Anti-Utopia in Modern Times.* Oxford: Blackwell, 1987.

______. *Utopianism.* Minneapolis: University of Minnesota Press, 1991.

Kumar, Krishan, and Stephen Bann, eds. *Utopias and the Millennium.* London: Reaktion, 1993.

Kuryllo, Helen A. "Cyborgs, Sorcery, and the Struggle for Utopia." *Utopian Studies* 5.2 (1994): 50–55.

______. "A Woman's Text in the Wild Zone: The Subversiveness of Elizabeth Gaskell's *Cranford.*" *Utopian Studies II.* Eds. Michael Cummings and Nicholas Smith. Lanham, Md.: University Press of America, 1989. 102–108.

Laclau, Ernesto, and Chantal Mouffe. *Hegemony and Socialist Strategy: Towards a Radical Democratic Politics.* Trans. Winston Moore and Paul Cammack. London: Verso, 1985.

Landmann, Michael. "Talking with Ernst Bloch: Korcula, 1968." *Telos* 25 (Fall 1975): 165–185.

Lane, Ann J. Introduction to *The Charlotte Perkins Gilman Reader: "The Yellow Wallpaper" and Other Fiction.* New York: Pantheon, 1980.

Latour, Bruno, and Steve Woolgar. *Laboratory Life: The Social Construction of Scientific Facts.* Princeton, N.J.: Princeton University Press, 1986.

Layoun, Mary. "A Small Reflection on a Dream Thrice Removed of Hope from a Refugee Camp." In *Not Yet: Reconsidering Ernst Bloch.* Eds. Jamie Owen Daniel and Tom Moylan. London: Verso, 1997. 224–231.

Lee, Zoreda M. "Anglophone Popular Culture in the Mexican University English Curriculum." *Journal of Popular Culture* 30.1 (Summer 1996): 103–114.

Lefanu, Sarah. "Difference and Sexual Politics in Naomi Mitchison's *Solution Three.*" In *Utopian and Science Fiction by Women: Worlds of Difference.* Eds. Jane L. Donawerth and Carol Kolmerten. Syracuse, N.Y.: Syracuse University Press, 1994. 153–166.

______. *Feminism and Science Fiction.* Bloomington: Indiana University Press, 1988. (British edition: *In the Chinks of the World Machine: Feminism and Science Fiction.* London: Woman's Press, 1988.)

Lefebvre, Henri. *Everyday Life in the Modern World.* Trans. Sacha Rabinovitch. New Brunswick, N.J.: Transaction, 1984.

______. *The Production of Space.* Trans. Donald Nicholson Smith. Oxford: Blackwell, 1991.

Le Guin, Ursula K. *The Language of the Night: Essays on Fantasy and Science Fiction.* Rev. ed. New York: HarperCollins, 1992.

Lehtoranta, Tina. "Feminism in *The Handmaid's Tale* by Margaret Atwood." Paper presented at the Utopian Studies Society conference. University of Nottingham, 20 June 2000.

Lentricchia, Frank. *After the New Criticism*. Chicago: University of Chicago Press, 1980.

LeRoy, Gaylord. "A.F. 632 to 1984." *College English* 12.3 (1950): 135–138.

Levitas, Ruth. *The Concept of Utopia*. Syracuse, N.Y.: Syracuse University Press, 1990.

______. "Educated Hope: Ernst Bloch on Abstract and Concrete Utopia." In *Not Yet: Reconsidering Ernst Bloch*. Eds. Jamie Owen Daniel and Tom Moylan. London: Verso, 1997. 65–79.

______. "For Utopia: The (Limits of) the Utopian Function in Late Capitalist Society." Bristol University, 1999. Typescript.

______. "Utopia as Literature, Utopia as Politics." In *Zeitgenössische Utopieentwürfe in Literatur und Gesellschaft*. Ed. Rolf Jucker. Amsterdam: Rodopi, 1997. 121–137.

Lewis, Arthur O. *Utopian Literature in the Pennsylvania State University Libraries: A Selected Bibliography*. University Park: Pennsylvania State University Libraries, 1984.

Lewis, C. S. *The Abolition of Man*. London: Oxford University Press, 1943.

Linkon, Sherry Lee. "'A Way of Being Jewish That Is Mine': Gender and Ethnicity in the Jewish Novels of Marge Piercy." *Studies in American Jewish Literature* 13 (1994): 93–105.

Lipietz, Alain. *Mirages and Miracles: The Crises of Global Fordism*. Trans. David Macey. London: Verso, 1987.

______. *Towards a New Economic Order*. Trans. M. Slater. London: Oxford University Press, 1992.

Littleton, Therese, and Bonnie Bouman. "Octavia E. Butler Plants an Earthseed." 1999. Available: http://www.cyberhaven.com/books/sciencefiction/butler.html.

Luckurst, Roger. "'Horror and Beauty in Rare Combination': The Miscegenate Fictions of Octavia Butler." *Women: A Cultural Review* 7.1 (1996): 28–38.

Lukács, Georg. *The Historical Novel*. Trans. Hannah Mitchell and Stanley Mitchell. Lincoln: University of Nebraska Press, 1983.

Luke, Tim. "Culture and Politics in the Age of Artificial Negativity." *Telos* 35 (Spring 1978): 55–73.

Maciunas, Billie. "Feminist Epistemologies in Piercy's *Woman on the Edge of Time*." *Woman's Studies* 20 (1992): 249–258.

Mahoney, Elizabeth. "Writing So to Speak: The Feminist Dystopia." Diss. University of Glasgow, 1994.

Mandel, Ernest. *Late Capitalism*. Rev. ed. London: New Left Books, 1972.

Mannheim, Karl. *Ideology and Utopia: An Introduction to the Sociology of Knowledge*. Trans. Louis Wirth and Edward Shils. New York: Harcourt, 1936.

Manuel, Frank E., and Fritzie P. Manuel, eds. *French Utopias*. New York: Free Press, 1966.

______. *Utopian Thought in the Western World*. Cambridge: Harvard University Press, 1979.

"Marge Piercy." Available: http://www.capecod.net/~tmpiercy/index.html.

Marin, Louis. "Disneyland: A Degenerate Utopia." *Glyph* 1 (1977): 397–420.

______. "Theses on Ideology and Utopia." *minnesota review* 6 (Spring 1976): 71–76.

______. *Utopics: The Semiological Play of Textual Spaces*. Trans. Robert A. Volrath. Atlantic Highlands, N.J.: Humanities Press, 1984.

______. *Utopiques: Jeux d'espaces*. Paris: Editions de Minuit, 1973.

Marks, Patricia Ruth. *Re-writing the Romance Narrative: Gender and Class in the Novels of Marge Piercy*. Diss. Ann Arbor: UMI, 1991.

Marx, Karl. *The Eighteenth Brumaire of Louis Bonaparte. The Marx Reader*. Ed. Christopher Pierson. London: Polity, 1997.

______. *The Grundrisse*. Harmondsworth, England: Penguin, 1973.

______. *The Letters of Karl Marx*. Ed. Saul Padover. Englewood Cliffs, N.J.: Prentice-Hall, 1979.

Marx, Karl, and Frederick Engels. *The Communist Manifesto*. London: Verso, 1998.

"Marxism and Utopia." Special supplement. *minnesota review* 6 (Spring 1976).

Massey, Doreen. "Politics and Space/Time." In *Place and the Politics of Identity*. Eds. M. Keith and S. Pile. New York: Routledge, 1993. 141–162.

McCaffery, Larry. "An Interview with Octavia E. Butler." In *Across the Wounded Galaxies*. Urbana: University of Illinois Press, 1990. 54–70.

______. "An Interview with William Gibson." *Mississippi Review* 47/48 (1988): 217–237.

______, ed. *Storming the Reality Studio*. Durham, N.C.: Duke University Press, 1991.

McClenahan, Catherine. "Textual Politics: The Uses of the Imagination in Joanna Russ's *The Female Man*." *Transactions of the Wisconsin Academy of Sciences, Arts, and Letters* 70 (1982): 114–125.

McGonigal, Mike. "Octavia Butler." *Index*, 23 December 1999. Available: http://www.index-magazine.com/indexm/indexed/butler.html.

McGuigan, Jim. *Culture and the Public Sphere*. New York: Routledge, 1996.

McGuirk, Carol. "NoWhere Man: Towards a Poetics of Post-Utopian Characterization." *Science-Fiction Studies* 21.2 (July 1994): 141–155.

______. "On Darko Suvin's Good-Natured Critique." *Science-Fiction Studies* 22.1 (March 1995): 138–140.

McHenry, Susan. "Otherworldly Vision: Octavia Butler." *Essence* 29.10 (February 1999): 80.

McKay, George. "Metapropaganda: Self-Reading Dystopian Fiction: Burdekin's *Swastika Night* and Orwell's *Nineteen Eighty-Four*." *Science-Fiction Studies* 21.3 (November 1994): 302–315.

Mellor, Anne K. "On Feminist Utopias." *Women's Studies* 9.2 (1982): 241–262.

Merril, Judith. *England Swings SF*. Garden City, N.Y.: Doubleday, 1968.

______. "What Do You Mean: Science? Fiction?" In *SF: The Other Side of Realism*. Ed. Thomas D. Clareson. Bowling Green, Ohio: Bowling Green University Press, 1971. 53–95.

Miller, Jim. "Post-Apocalyptic Hoping: Octavia Butler's Dystopian/Utopian Fiction." *Science-Fiction Studies* 25.2 (July 1998): 336–361.

Mitchell, Angelyn L. *Signifyin(g) Women: Visions and Revisions of Slavery in Octavia Butler's* Kindred, *Sherley Anne Williams's* Dessa Rose, *and Toni Morrison's* Beloved. Diss. Ann Arbor: UMI, 1992.

Mitchell, Kathryn. "Poetry in the Extreme." George Mason University, 1999. Typescript.

Moody, Nickianne. "Maeve and Guinevere: Women's Fantasy Writing in the Science Fiction Marketplace." In *Where No Man Has Gone Before: Women and Science Fiction*. Ed. Lucie Armitt. New York: Routledge, 1991. 186–204.

Moore, John. "An Archaeology of the Future: Ursula Le Guin and Anarcho-Primitivism." *Foundation: The Review of Science Fiction* 63 (Spring 1995): 32–40.

Morrison, Toni. *Playing in the Dark: Whiteness and the Literary Imagination*. Cambridge: Harvard University Press, 1992.

Morton, A. L. *The English Utopia*. London: Lawrence and Wishart, 1952.

Moskowitz, Sam. *Explorers of the Infinite: Shapers of Science Fiction*. New York: World Publishing, 1963.

______. "The First College-Level Course in Science Fiction." *Science-Fiction Studies* 23.3 (November 1996): 411–423.

______. *The Immortal Storm: A History of Science Fiction Fandom*. Westport, Conn.: Hyperion, 1954.

Moylan, Tom. "Anticipatory Fiction: *Bread and Wine* and Liberation Theology." *Modern Fiction Studies* 35.1 (Spring 1989): 103–121.

______. "Beyond Negation: The Critical Utopias of Ursula K. Le Guin and Samuel R. Delany." *Extrapolation* 21.3 (Fall 1980): 236–254.

______. "Bloch Against Bloch: The Theological Reception of *Das Prinzip Hoffnung* and the Liberation of the Utopian Function." In *Not Yet: Reconsidering Ernst Bloch*. Eds. Jamie Owen Daniel and Tom Moylan. London: Verso, 1997. 96–122.

______. "'Dare to Struggle, Dare to Win': On Science Fiction, Totality, and Agency in the 1990s." In *Science Fiction, Critical Frontiers*. Eds. Karen Sayers and John Moore. London: Macmillan, 2000. 48–61.

______. *Demand the Impossible: Science Fiction and the Utopian Imagination*. London: Methuen, 1986.

______. "Denunciation/Annunciation: The Radical Methodology of Liberation Theology." *Cultural Critique* 19 (1992): 33–65.

______. "Global Economy, Local Texts: Utopian/Dystopian Tensions in William Gibson's Cyberpunk 'Trilogy.'" *minnesota review* 43/44 (Fall/Spring 1995): 182–198.

______. "Ideological Contradiction in Clarke's *The City and the Stars*." *Science-Fiction Studies* 4.2 (July 1977): 150–157.

______. "Ideology in the Age of Reagan." *Crane Bag* (Dublin) 8.2 (Fall 1985): 117–123.

______. Introduction to the special section "The Work of Fredric Jameson." *Utopian Studies* 9.2 (1998): 1–8.

______. "The Locus of Hope: Utopia Versus Ideology." *Science-Fiction Studies* 9.2 (July 1982): 159–167.

______. "'Look into the Dark': On Dystopia and the Novum." In *Learning from Other Worlds: Estrangement, Cognition and the Politics of Science Fiction and Utopia. Essays in Honour of Darko Suvin*. Ed. Patrick Parrinder. Liverpool: Liverpool University Press, 2000. 51–71.

______. "Mission Impossible: Liberation Theology and Utopian Praxis." *Utopian Studies III*. Eds. Michael Cummings and Nicholas D. Smith. Lanham, Md.: University Press of America, 1991. 20–30.

______. "On the Borders of Dystopia: Jack London's *The Iron Heel* and Kim Stanley Robinson's *Antarctica*." In *The Dystopian Turn: Science Fiction and Utopia at the End of the 20th Century*. Eds. Raffaella Baccolini and Tom Moylan. Forthcoming.

______. "People or Markets: Some Thoughts on Cultural Studies and Corporate Studies." *Social Text* 44 (Fall/Winter 1995): 45–61.

______. Review of *Synners* by Pat Cadigan. *American Book Review* 14.2 (June-July 1992): 5, 13.

______. "Utopia and Postmodernity: Six Theses." In *The City Within: Rhetoric, Utopia, and Technology*. Ed. Jean Randolph. Banff, Canada: Banff Centre for the Arts, 1992. 3–14.

______. "'Utopia Is When Our Lives Matter': Reading Kim Stanley Robinson's *Pacific Edge*." *Utopian Studies* 6.2 (1995): 1–25.

Mulhern, Francis. *The Moment of Scrutiny*. London: Verso, 1981.

Mullen, Dale. "Introduction to Science Fiction in Academe." *Science-Fiction Studies* 23.3 (November 1996): 371–375.

Murphy, Patrick. "Reducing the Dystopian Distance: Pseudo-Documentary Framing in Near-Future Fiction." *Science-Fiction Studies* 17.1 (March 1990): 25–40.

Negley, Glenn. *Utopian Literature: A Bibliography with a Supplementary Listing of Works Influential in Utopian Thought*. Lawrence: Regents Press of Kansas, 1978.

Negley, Glenn, and J. Max Patrick. *The Quest for Utopia: An Anthology of Imaginary Societies*. New York: H. Schuman, 1952.

Negt, Oskar. "Ernst Bloch—the German Philosopher of the October Revolution." Trans. Jack Zipes. *New German Critique* 4 (Winter 1975): 3–17.

______. "The Non-synchronous Heritage and the Problem Propaganda." Trans. Jack Zipes. *New German Critique* 9 (Fall 1976): 46–71.

Negt, Oskar, and Alexander Kluge. *Public Sphere and Experience: Towards an Analysis of the Bourgeois and Proletarian Public Sphere*. Trans. Peter Labanyi, Jamie Owen Daniel, and Assenka Oksiloff. Minneapolis: University of Minnesota Press, 1993.

Nelson, Cary, and Lawrence Grossberg. *Marxism and the Interpretation of Culture*. Urbana: University of Illinois Press, 1988.

Neverow, Vara. "The Politics of Incorporation and Embodiment: *Woman on the Edge of Time* and *He, She and It* as Feminist Epistemologies of Resistance." *Utopian Studies* 5.2 (1994): 16–36.

A New Catechism: Catholic Faith for Adults. Trans. Kevin Smyth. New York: Herder and Herder, 1967.

Nichols, Peter, and John Clute, eds. *Encyclopedia of Science Fiction*. Garden City, N.Y.: Doubleday, 1979.

Nicolson, Marjorie Hope. *Voyages to the Moon*. New York: Macmillan, 1948.

Noble, David. *America by Design: Science, Technology, and the Rise of Corporate Capitalism*. London: Oxford University Press, 1977.

Nodelman, Perry. "Out There in Children's Science Fiction: Forward into the Past." *Science-Fiction Studies* 12.3 (November 1985): 285–296.

Nowik, Nan. "Mixing Art and Politics: The Writings of Adrienne Rich and Marge Piercy." *Centennial Review* 30.2 (1986): 208–218.

Nunan, E. E., and David Homer. "Science Fiction and Teaching: Science, Science Fiction, and a Radical Science Education." *Science-Fiction Studies* 8.3 (November 1981): 311–330.

Ohmann, Richard. "English and the Cold War." In *The Cold War and the University: Toward an Intellectual History of the Postwar Years*. New York: New Press, 1997. 73–107.

______. *English in America: A Radical View of the Profession*. London: Oxford University Press, 1976.

Orwell, George. "Letter to Francis A. Henson." In *Collected Essays, Journalism and Letters of George Orwell*. Eds. Sonia Orwell and Ian Angus. 4 vols. Harmondsworth, England: Penguin, 1970. 564.

Panitch, Leo, and Colin Leys, eds. *Necessary and Unnecessary Utopias: Socialist Register 2000*. New York: Monthly Review Press, 1999.

Parrinder, Patrick. *H. G. Wells: The Critical Heritage*. London: Routledge and Kegan Paul, 1972.

______. "Imagining the Future: Zamyatin and Wells." *Science-Fiction Studies* 1 (Spring 1973): 37–41.

______, ed. *Learning from Other Worlds: Estrangement, Cognition and the Politics of Science Fiction and Utopia. Essays in Honour of Darko Suvin*. Liverpool: Liverpool University Press, 2000.

______. "*News from Nowhere, The Time Machine* and the Break-up of Classical Realism." *Science-Fiction Studies* 3.3 (November 1976): 265–274.

______. *Science Fiction: A Critical Guide*. London: Longman, 1979.

______. *Science Fiction: Its Criticism and Teaching*. London: Methuen, 1980.

______. "Utopia After Darwin: *Erewhon* Revisited." Paper presented at "A Millennium of Utopias" conference. University of East Anglia, 23–26 June 1999.

Patai, Daphne. "Beyond Defensiveness: Feminist Research Strategies." In *Women and Utopia: Critical Interpretations*. Eds. Marleen Barr and Nicholas D. Smith. Lanham, Md.: University Press of America, 1983. 148–169.

______, ed. *Looking Backward, 1988–1888*. Amherst: University of Massachusetts Press, 1988.

______. "Utopia for Whom?" *Aphra* (Summer 1974): 2–16.

Pei, Lowry. "Poor Singletons: Definitions of Humanity in the Stories of James Tiptree, Jr." *Science-Fiction Studies* 6.3 (November 1979): 271–280.

Penley, Constance, ed. *Close Encounters: Film, Feminism, and Science Fiction*. Minneapolis: University of Minnesota Press, 1991.

______. *NASA/Trek: Popular Science and Sex in America*. London: Verso, 1997.

______. "Time Travel, Primal Scene, and the Critical Dystopia." In *The Future of an Illusion: Film, Feminism, and Psychoanalysis*. Minneapolis: University of Minnesota Press, 1989. 63–83.

Peppers, Cathy. "Dialogic Origins and Alien Identities in Butler's *Xenogenesis*." *Science-Fiction Studies* 22.1 (March 1995): 47–62.

Perry, Donna. "Joanna Russ." In *Backtalk: Woman Writers Speak Out*. New Brunswick, N.J.: Rutgers University Press, 1993. 287–311.

Pfaelzer, Jeanne. "The Changing of the Avant-Garde: The Feminist Utopia." *Science-Fiction Studies* 15.3 (November 1988): 282–294.

______. "The Sentimental Promise and the Utopian Myth: Rebecca Harding Davis's 'The Harmonists' and Louisa May Alcott's 'Transcendental Oats.'" *American Transcendental Quarterly* 3.1 (March 1989): 85–100.

______. *The Utopian Novel in America, 1886–1896: The Politics of Form.* Pittsburgh: University of Pittsburgh Press, 1984.

Pfeil, Fred. "Makin' Flippy Floppy: Postmodernism and the Baby Boom PMC." In *The Year Left: An American Socialist Yearbook, 1985.* London: Verso, 1985. 263–295.

______. "Sympathy for the Devils: Notes on Some White Guys in the Ridiculous Class War." *New Left Review* 213 (September/October 1995): 115–124.

______. *White Guys: Studies in Postmodern Domination and Difference.* London: Verso, 1985.

Phillips, Kevin. *The Politics of Rich and Poor: Wealth and the American Electorate in the Reagan Aftermath.* New York: Harper, 1990.

Philmus, Robert M. *Into the Unknown: The Evolution of Science Fiction from Francis Godwin to H. G. Wells.* Berkeley: University of California Press, 1970.

______. "The Language of Utopia." *Studies in the Literary Imagination* 6.2 (Fall 1973): 61–78.

______. "Men in Feminist Science Fiction: Marge Piercy, Thomas Berger, and the End of Masculinity." In *Science Fiction Roots and Branches: Contemporary Critical Approaches.* Eds. Garnett Rhys and R. J. Ellis. New York: St. Martin's, 1990. 135–150.

______. "Swift, Zamiatin, and Orwell and the Language of Utopia." In *Visions and Re-Visions: Collected Essays.* Forthcoming.

Piccone, Paul. "The Crisis of One-Dimensionality." *Telos* 35 (Spring 1978): 43–55.

Piercy, Marge. "Active in Time and History." In *Paths of Resistance: The Art and Craft of the Political Novel.* Ed. William Zinsser. Boston: Houghton Mifflin, 1989. 91–123.

______. "Telling Stories About Stories." *Utopian Studies* 5.2 (1994): 1–3.

Pitzer, Donald E. *America's Communal Utopias.* Chapel Hill: University of North Carolina Press, 1997.

Piven, Frances Fox. "Is It Global Economics or Neo-Laissez Faire?" *New Left Review* 213 (September-October 1995): 107–114.

Piven, Frances Fox, and Richard A. Cloward. *Poor People's Movements.* New York: Pantheon, 1977.

Piziks, Steven. "Interview with Octavia Butler." *Marion Zimmer Bradley's Fantasy Magazine* 37 (1999). Available: http://www.mzbfm.com/butler.htm.

Polak, Fred L. *The Image of the Future: Enlightening the Past, Orientating the Present, Forecasting the Future.* 2 vols. Trans. Elise Boulding. New York: Harper and Row, 1962.

Popper, Karl. *The Open Society and Its Enemies.* London: Routledge and Kegan Paul, 1945.

Portelli, Alessandro. "Jack London's Missing Revolution: Notes on *The Iron Heel.*" *Science-Fiction Studies* 9.2 (July 1982): 180–195.

Porush, David. "Frothing the Synaptic Bath." In *Storming the Reality Studio.* Ed. Larry McCaffrey. Durham, N.C.: Duke University Press, 1991. 1–17.

______. "Prigogine, Chaos, and Contemporary SF." *Science-Fiction Studies* 18.3 (November 1991): 367–387.

Potts, S. W. "We Keep Playing the Same Record—a Conversation with Octavia E. Butler." *Science-Fiction Studies* 23.3 (November 1996): 331–338.

Pringle, David. *The Ultimate Guide to Science Fiction: An A-Z of Science Fiction Books by Title*. 2nd ed. New York: Scolar, 1995.

Rabkin, Eric. *The Fantastic in Literature*. Princeton, N.J.: Princeton University Press, 1976.

Rahv, Phillip. "The Unfuture of Utopia." *Partisan Review* 16.7 (1949): 743–749.

Reich, Robert. *The Work of Nations: Preparing Ourselves for 21st Century Capitalism*. New York: Knopf, 1991.

Renault, Gregory. "Science Fiction as Cognitive Estrangement: Darko Suvin and the Marxist Critique of Mass Culture." *Discourse* 2 (1980): 113–141.

Resch, Robert Paul. "Utopia, Dystopia, and the Middle Class in George Orwell's *Nineteen Eighty-Four*." *Boundary 2* 24.1 (Spring 1997): 137–176.

Rhodes, Jewell Parker. "Toni Morrison's *Beloved:* Ironies of a 'Sweet Home' Utopia in a Dystopian Slave Society." *Utopian Studies* 1.1 (1990): 77–93.

Rich, B. Ruby. *Chick Flicks: Theories and Memories of the Feminist Film Movement*. Durham, N.C.: Duke University Press, 1998.

Richter, Peyton, ed. *Utopia/Dystopia*. Cambridge, Mass.: Schenkman, 1975.

Roberts, Robin. *A New Species: Gender and Science in Science Fiction*. Urbana: University of Illinois Press, 1993.

Robinson, Kim Stanley. *The Novels of Philip K. Dick*. Diss. Ann Arbor: UMI, 1984.

Robinson, Kim Stanley, with David Seed. "The Mars Trilogy: An Interview." *Foundation: The Review of Science Fiction* 68 (Autumn 1996): 75–81.

Rodden, K. "A Harsh Day's Light: An Interview with Marge Piercy." *Kenyon Review* 20.2 (1998): 132–143.

Roemer, Kenneth M., ed. *America as Utopia*. New York: Burt Franklin, 1981.

______. "Getting 'Nowhere' Beyond Stasis." In *Looking Backward, 1988–1888*. Ed. Daphne Patai. Amherst: University of Massachusetts Press, 1988. 126–146.

______. "The Literary Domestication of Utopia, There's No 'Looking Backward' Without Uncle Tom and Uncle True." *American Transcendental Quarterly* 3.1 (March 1989): 101–122.

______. "1984 in 1894: Harben's *Land of the Changing Sun*." *Mississippi Quarterly* 26.1 (Winter 1972–1973): 29–42.

______. *The Obsolete Necessity: America in Utopian Writings, 1888–1900*. Kent, Ohio: Kent State University Press, 1976.

______. "Perceptual Origins: Preparing Readers to See Utopian Fiction." In *Utopian Thought in American Literature*. Eds. Arno Heller et al. Tübingen, Germany: Gunter Narr Verlag, 1988. 7–24.

______. "Petition for an MLA Discussion Group in Science Fiction, Utopian, and Fantastic Literature." Internal document. Modern Language Association, 20 February 1997.

______. "Prescriptions for Readers (and Writers) of Utopias." *Science-Fiction Studies* 15.1 (March 1988): 88–94.

Rose, Mark. *Alien Encounters: Anatomy of Science Fiction*. Cambridge: Harvard University Press, 1981.

Rosenthal, Pam. "Jacked In: Fordism, Cyberpunk, Marxism." *Socialist Review* 21.1 (January-March 1991): 79–105.

Rosinsky, Natalie M. *Feminist Futures—Contemporary Women's Speculative Fiction*. Diss. Ann Arbor: UMI, 1984.

Ross, Andrew. *Strange Weather: Culture, Science, and Technology in the Age of Limits*. London: Verso, 1991.

Ross, Andrew, and Constance Penley. *Technoculture*. Minneapolis: University of Minnesota Press, 1991.

Rowbotham, Sheila, Lynne Segal, and Hilary Wainwright. *Beyond the Fragments: Feminism and the Making of Socialism*. Boston: Alyson, 1979.

Rowell, C. H. "An Interview with Octavia E. Butler." *Callaloo* 20.1 (Winter 1997): 47–66.

Ruddick, Nicholas. "*Kingsley Amis: A Biography* by Eric Jacobs." *Science Fiction Studies* 26.1 (March 1999): 129–130.

Ruddick, Nicholas, and Brian Aldiss. "Notes and Correspondence: In Defense of Kingsley Amis. A Response." *Science Fiction Studies* 26.3 (November 1999): 512–513.

Ruppert, Peter. *Reader in a Strange Land: The Activity of Reading Literary Utopias*. Athens: University of Georgia Press, 1986.

Russ, Joanna. *How to Suppress Women's Writing*. Austin: University of Texas Press, 1983.

______. *Magic Mommas, Trembling Sisters, Puritans and Perverts: Feminist Essays*. Trumansburg, N.Y.: Crossing Press, 1985.

______. "Recent Feminist Utopias." In *Future Females: A Critical Anthology*. Ed. Marleen Barr. Bowling Green, Ohio: Bowling Green University Press, 1981. 71–85.

______. *To Write Like a Woman: Essays in Feminism and Science Fiction*. Bloomington: Indiana University Press, 1995.

______. "Towards an Aesthetic of Science Fiction." *Science-Fiction Studies* 2.2 (July 1975): 112–119.

______. "Women and SF: Three Letters." *Science-Fiction Studies* 7.2 (July 1980): 232–233.

Salvaggio, Ruth. "Octavia Butler and the Black Science-Fiction Heroine." *Black American Literature Forum* 18.2 (Summer 1984): 78–81.

Samuelson, David N. "*Limbo:* The Great American Dystopia." *Extrapolation* 19.1 (Winter 1977): 76–87.

______. *Visions of Tomorrow: Six Journeys from Outer to Inner Space*. New York: Arno, 1969.

Sanders, Joe. *Science Fiction Fandom*. Westport, Conn.: Greenwood, 1994.

Sanderson, Richard. "The Two Narrators and the 'Happy Ending' of *Nineteen Eighty-Four*." *Modern Fiction Studies* 34.4 (Winter 1988): 587–595.

Sargent, Lyman Tower. *British and American Utopian Literature, 1516–1985: An Annotated, Chronological Bibliography*. New York: Garland, 1988.

______. "Is There Only One Utopian Tradition?" *Journal of the History of Ideas* 43.4 (October 1982): 681–689.

______. "National Identity and U.S. Utopian Literature." Plenary lecture at the Comparative Thematic Network Project (COTEPRA) conference, Centro Interdipartimentale di Ricerca Sull'utopia, University of Bologna, Bertinoro, Italy, 27 November 1999.
______. *New Left Thought: An Introduction*. Homewood, Ill.: Dorsey, 1972.
______. "Political Dimensions of Utopianism." In *Per una definizione dell'utopia: Metodologie e discipline a confronto*. Ed. Nadia Minerva. Ravenna: Longo, 1992. 185–210.
______. *Political Thought in the United States: A Documentary History*. New York: New York University Press, 1997.
______. Review of *Dystopian Literature: A Theory and Research Guide,* by M. Keith Booker. *Utopian Studies* 6.2 (1995): 134–139.
______. "The Three Faces of Utopianism." *minnesota review* 7.4 (1967): 222–231.
______. "The Three Faces of Utopianism Revisited." *Utopian Studies* 5.1 (1994): 1–38.
______. "U.S. Eutopias in the 1980s and 1990s." Lecture at the Comparative Thematic Network Project (COTEPRA) conference, Centro Interdipartimentale di Ricerca Sull' utopia, University of Bologna, Rimini, Italy, 9 July 2000.
______. "Utopia—the Problem of Definition." *Extrapolation* 16.2 (Spring 1975): 137–148.
______. "Women in Utopia." *Comparative Literature Studies* 10 (December 1973): 302–316.
Sargent, Pamela. "On Peter Fitting's Reconsiderations in *SFS #56*." *Science-Fiction Studies* 19.2 (July 1992): 271–276.
Sargisson, Lucy. *Contemporary Feminist Utopianism*. New York: Routledge, 1996.
______. *Transforming Bodies*. New York: Routledge, 2000.
Sassen, Saskia. *The Global City: New York, London, Tokyo*. Princeton, N.J.: Princeton University Press, 1991.
Sayers, Karen, and John Moore, eds. *Science Fiction, Critical Frontiers*. London: Macmillan, 2000.
Sayre, Robert, and Michael Löwy. "Figures of Romantic Anti-Capitalism." *New German Critique* 32 (Spring-Summer 1984): 42–93.
Schaub, Thomas Hill. *American Fiction in the Cold War*. Madison: University of Wisconsin Press, 1991.
Schiller, Herbert I. *Culture Inc.: The Corporate Takeover of Public Expression*. London: Oxford University Press, 1989.
Schoene-Harwood, Bertolt. *Writing Men: Literary Masculinities from Frankenstein to the New Man*. Edinburgh: Edinburgh University Press, 2000.
Scholes, Robert. *The Fabulators*. London: Oxford University Press, 1967.
______. *Structural Fabulation: An Essay on the Fiction of the Future*. South Bend, Ind.: University of Notre Dame Press, 1975.
Scholes, Robert, and Eric Rabkin. *Science Fiction: History/Science/Vision*. London: Oxford University Press, 1977.
Schulz, H. J. "Science Fiction and Ideology: Some Problems of Approach." *Science-Fiction Studies* 14 (1987): 165–179.
______. "Waiting for the Barbarians." *Journal Wired* 1 (Winter 1989): 107–118.

Schwarz, Henry, and Richard Dienst, eds. *Reading the Shape of the World.* Boulder, Colo.: Westview, 1996.

"Science Fiction by Women." Special issue. *Science-Fiction Studies* 17.2 (July 1990).

Seabury, Marcia Bundy. "Images of a Networked Society: E. M. Forster's 'The Machine Stops.'" *Studies in Short Fiction* 34.1 (Winter 1997): 61–71.

Seal, Judith Luedtke. "James Tiptree, Jr.: Fostering the Future, Not Condemning It." *Extrapolation* 31.1 (Spring 1990): 73–82.

Sedgewick, Cristina. "The Fork in the Road: Can Science Fiction Survive in Postmodern, Megacorporate America?" *Science-Fiction Studies* 18.1 (March 1991): 11–53.

See, Lisa. "Octavia E. Butler." *Publisher's Weekly,* 13 December 1993: 50–51.

Seed, David, ed. *Anticipations: Essays on Early Science Fiction and Its Precursors.* Syracuse, N.Y.: Syracuse University Press, 1995.

Shalom Centre. "Action Guide to Support Israeli-Palestinian Peacemaking." 1999. Available: http://www.shalomctr.org/html/peace03.html.

Shands, Kerstin W. *The Repair of the World: The Novels of Marge Piercy.* Westport, Conn.: Greenwood, 1995.

Sheldon, Alice. "A Woman Writing Science Fiction and Fantasy." In *Women of Vision.* Ed. Denise DuPont. New York: St. Martin's, 1988. 43–58.

Shiner, Lewis. "Confessions of an Ex-Cyberpunk." *New York Times,* 7 January 1991: A19.

Shippey, Tom, ed. *Fictional Space: Essays on Contemporary Science Fiction.* London: Oxford University Press, 1991.

Shohat, Ella, and Robert Stam. *Unthinking Eurocentrism: Multiculturalism and the Media.* New York: Routledge, 1994.

Shor, Ira. *Culture Wars: School and Society in the Conservative Restoration, 1969–1984.* London: Routledge and Kegan Paul, 1986.

Siclari, Joe. "Science Fiction Fandom: A History of an Unusual Hobby." In *The Science Fiction Reference Book.* Ed. Marshall B. Tymn. Mercer Island, Wash.: Starmont, 1981. 87–129.

Siebers, T., ed. *Heterotopia: Postmodern Utopia and the Body Politic.* Ann Arbor: University of Michigan Press, 1994.

Singer, Daniel. *Whose Millennium? Theirs or Ours?* New York: Monthly Review Press, 1999.

Sivanandan, A. "Globalism and the Left." *Race and Class* 40.2/3 (1998/1999): 5-21.

Slusser, George. "Literary MTV." *Mississippi Review* 47/48 (1988): 279–288.

Slusser, George, Paul Alkon, Roger Gaillard, and Danièle Chatelain, eds. *Transformations of Utopia: Changing Views of the Perfect Society.* New York: AMS, 1999.

Smith, Jeffrey, ed. "Khatru Symposium on Women in SF." In *Women in Science Fiction: A Symposium.* Ed. Jeffrey Smith. Baltimore: J. D. Smith, 1975.

Smith, Paul. *Discerning the Subject.* Minneapolis: University of Minnesota Press, 1988.

______. *Millennial Dreams: Contemporary Culture and Capital in the North.* London: Verso, 1997.

Sobchack, Vivian. *The Limits of Infinity: The American Science Fiction Film.* South Brunswick, N.J.: A. S. Barnes, 1980.

Soja, Edward W. *Postmodern Geographies: The Reassertion of Space in Critical Social Theory.* London: Verso, 1989.

Somay, Bülent. "Towards an Open-Ended Utopia." *Science-Fiction Studies* 11.1 (March 1984): 25–38.

Spencer, Kathleen. "'The Red Sun Is High, the Blue Low': Towards a Stylistic Description of Science Fiction." *Science-Fiction Studies* 10.1 (March 1983): 35–50.

Spinrad, Norman. "On Books: The Neuromantics." *Isaac Asimov's Science Fiction Magazine* 104 (May 1986): 180–190.

Spivak, Gayatri Chakravorty, with Ellen Rooney. "In a Word: Interview." *Differences* 1.2 (1989): 124–156.

St. Clair, Jeffrey. "Seattle Diary: It's a Gas, Gas, Gas." *New Left Review* 238 (November/December 1999): 81–97.

Stabile, Carol A. *Feminism and the Technological Fix.* Manchester, England: University of Manchester Press, 1994.

Stableford, Brian M. *Scientific Romance in Britain, 1890–1950.* London: Fourth Estate, 1985.

Steffen-Fluhr, Nancy. "The Case of the Haploid Heart: Psychological Patterns in the Science Fiction of Alice Sheldon ('James Tiptree, Jr.')." *Science-Fiction Studies* 17.2 (July 1990): 188–220.

Sterling, Bruce. "Letter from Bruce Sterling." *REM* 7 (April 1987): 4–7.

______, ed. *Mirrorshades: The Cyberpunk Anthology*. New York: Ace, 1988.

Stillman, Peter. "The Limits to Behaviorism: A Critique of B. F. Skinner's Social and Political Thought." *American Political Science Review* 69.1 (March 1975): 202–13.

______. "The Past Decade of the History of Utopian Thought." *Utopian Studies* 1.1 (1990): 103–110.

______. "Public and Private in Margaret Atwood's *The Handmaid's Tale* and *Bodily Harm*." *Q/W/E/R/T/Y* 8 (1998). Available: http://www.univ-pau.fr/~parsons/qwerty.html#qwerty8.

Stillman, Peter, and S. Anne Johnson. "Identity, Complicity, and Resistance in *The Handmaid's Tale*." *Utopian Studies* 5.2 (1994): 70–86.

Stockton, Sharon. "'The Self Regained': Cyberpunk's Retreat to the Imperium." *Contemporary Literature* 36.4 (1995): 588–612.

Suvin, Darko. "Afterword: With Sober, Estranged Eyes." In *Learning from Other Worlds: Estrangement, Cognition and the Politics of Science Fiction and Utopia. Essays in Honour of Darko Suvin*. Ed. Patrick Parrinder. Liverpool: Liverpool University, 2000.

______. "Defining the Literary Genre of Utopia: Some Historical Semantics, Some Genology, a Proposal, and a Plea." *Studies in the Literary Imagination* 2 (Fall 1973): 121–145.

______. "Locus, Horizon, and Orientation: The Concept of Possible Worlds as a Key to Utopian Studies." In *Not Yet: Reconsidering Ernst Bloch*. Eds. Jamie Owen Daniel and Tom Moylan. London: Verso, 1997. 122–137.

______. *Metamorphoses of Science Fiction: On the Poetics and History of a Literary Genre.* New Haven, Conn.: Yale University Press, 1979.
______. "A Note for the 'Quirks and Quarks' (Moods and Facts?) Dept." *Science-Fiction Studies* 22.1 (March 1995): 137–138.
______. "Novum Is as Novum Does." *Foundation: The Review of Science Fiction* 69 (Spring 1997): 26–43.
______. "On Gibson and Cyberpunk SF." *Foundation: The Review of Science Fiction* 46 (Autumn 1989): 40–51.
______. "On the Poetics of the Science Fiction Genre." *College English* 34.3 (December 1972): 372–383.
______. *Positions and Presuppositions in Science Fiction.* Kent, Ohio: Kent State University Press, 1988.
______. "Revelation vs. Conflict: A Lesson from No Plays for a Comparative Dramaturgy." *Theatre Journal* 46.4 (December 1994): 523–538.
______. "Science Fiction and the Novum." In *The Technological Imagination: Theories and Fictions.* Eds. Teresa de Lauretis, Andreas Huyssen, and Kathleen Woodward. Madison: Coda, 1980. 141–159.
______. "Transubstantiation of Production and Consumption: Metaphoric Imagery in the *Grundrisse.*" *minnesota review* 18 (Spring 1982): 102–115.
______. "Two Cheers for Essentialism and Totality: On Marx's Oscillation and Its Limits (as Well as on the Taboos of Post-modernism)." *Rethinking Marxism* 10.1 (Spring 1998): 66–82.
______. "'Utopian' and 'Scientific': Two Attributes for Socialism from Engels." *minnesota review* 6 (Spring 1976): 59–76.
______. "Utopianism from Orientation to Agency: What Are We Intellectuals Under Post-Fordism to Do?" *Utopian Studies* 9.2 (1998): 162–190.
______. "Where Are We? Or How Did We Get Here? Is There Any Way Out? or, News from the Novum." *Science Fiction, Critical Frontiers.* Eds. Karen Sayers and John Moore. London: Macmillan, 2000. 3–22.
Suvin, Darko, and Marc Angenot. "Not Only but Also: On Cognition and Ideology in SF and SF Criticism." *Science-Fiction Studies* 6.2 (July 1979): 168–179.
Suvin, Darko, and David Douglas. "Jack London and His Science Fiction: A Select Bibliography." *Science-Fiction Studies* 6.2 (July 1976): 181–187.
Tabb, William K. "The World Trade Organization? Stop World Takeover." *Monthly Review* 51.8 (January 2000): 1–12.
Tatsumi, Takayuki. "Some Real Mothers: An Interview with Samuel R. Delany." *Science Fiction Eye* 1.3 (March 1988): 5–11.
Taussig, Michael. *Shamanism, Colonialism, and the Wild Man: A Study in Terror and Healing.* Chicago: University of Chicago Press, 1987.
Teich, Nathaniel. "Marxist Dialectics in Content, Form, Point of View: Structures in Jack London's *The Iron Heel.*" *Modern Fiction Studies* 22 (Spring 1976): 85–99.

Touponce, William Ferdinand. *Ray Bradbury and the Poetics of Reverie: A Study of Fantasy, Science Fiction, and the Reading Process.* Diss. Ann Arbor: UMI, 1981.

Tracy, James. *Direct Action: Radical Pacifism from the Union Eight to the Chicago Seven.* Chicago: University of Chicago Press, 1996.

United Nations Development Program, ed. *Human Development Report, 1996.* London: Oxford University Press, 1996.

"U.S. Students Leave Shopping Malls to Sign up for Grassroots Protest." *Guardian,* 20 November 1999: 21.

"Utopia." Special issue. *Daedalus* 94.2 (Spring 1965).

"Utopia and Anti-Utopia." Special issue. *Science-Fiction Studies* 9.2 (July 1982).

Vaihinger, Hans. *The Philosophy of "As If": A System of the Theoretical, Practical and Religious Fictions of Mankind.* New York: Harcourt, 1924.

Varsamopolou, Maria. "Towards a Definition of Dystopia." University of Nottingham, 1999. Typescript.

Vauchez, André. *The Spirituality of the Medieval West: The Eighth to the Twelfth Century.* Trans. Colette Friedlander. Kalamazoo, Mich.: Cistercian Publications, 1993.

Voight, Andreas. *Die Socialen Utopien.* Leipzig: G. J. Goschen'sche Verlagshandlung, 1906.

Von Boeckmann, Staci. "Marxism, Morality, and the Politics of Desire: Utopianism in Fredric Jameson's *The Political Unconscious.*" *Utopian Studies* 9.2 (1998): 31–51.

Wald, Alan. *The New York Intellectuals: The Rise and Decline of the Anti-Stalinist Left from the 1930's to the 1980's.* Chapel Hill: University of North Carolina Press, 1987.

Walker, Sue, and Eugenie Hamner, eds. *Ways of Knowing: Essays on Marge Piercy.* Mobile, Ala.: Negative Capability, 1991.

Wallerstein, Immanuel. *After Liberalism.* New York: New Press, 1995.

______. *Geopolitics and Geoculture.* Cambridge: Cambridge University Press, 1992.

______. *Historical Capitalism/Capitalist Civilization.* London: Verso, 1996.

______. *Utopistics.* New York: New Press, 1999.

Walsh, Chad. *From Utopia to Nightmare.* London: Geoffrey Blas, 1962.

Warrick, Patricia. *The Cybernetic Imagination in Science Fiction.* Cambridge: MIT Press, 1980.

Waskow, Arthur. "Ten Questions on Tikkun Olam of the Future." Available: http://www.shalomctr.org/html/comm08.html.

Watkins, Evan. *Throwaways: Work Culture and Consumer Education.* Stanford: Stanford University Press, 1993.

Webster, Sarah, and Libby Falk Jones, eds. *Feminism, Utopia, and Narrative.* Knoxville: University of Tennessee Press, 1990.

Wegner, Phillip E. "Horizons, Figures, and Machines: The Dialectic of Utopia in the Work of Frederic Jameson." *Utopian Studies* 9.2 (1998): 58–74.

______. *Horizons of Future Worlds, Borders of Present States: Utopian Narratives, History, and the Nation.* Diss. Ann Arbor: UMI, 1993.

______. *Imaginary Communities: Utopia, the Nation, and the Spatial Histories of Modernity.* Berkeley: University of California Press, forthcoming.

______. "The Last Bomb: Historicizing History in Terry Bisson's *Fire on the Mountain* and Gibson and Sterling's *The Difference Engine*." *Comparatist* 23 (1999): 141–151.

______. "'A Nightmare on the Brain of the Living': Messianic Historicity, Alienations, and *Independence Day*." *Rethinking Marxism* 12.1 (2000): 65–86.

______. "On Zamyatin's *We*: A Critical Map of Utopia's 'Possible Worlds.'" *Utopian Studies* 4.2 (1993): 94–117.

Wells, H. G. "Utopias." *Science-Fiction Studies* 9.2 (July 1982): 117–122.

Westfahl, Gary. *The Mechanics of Wonder: The Creation of the Idea of Science Fiction*. Liverpool: Liverpool University Press, 1998.

______. "The Popular Tradition of Science Fiction Criticism, 1926–1980." *Science Fiction Studies* 26.2 (July 1999): 187–213.

Westfahl, Gary, George Slusser, and Eric S. Rabkin, eds. *Science Fiction and Market Realities*. Athens: University of Georgia Press, 1996.

Whalen, Terrence. "The Future of a Commodity: Notes Toward a Critique of Cyberpunk and the Information Age." *Science-Fiction Studies* 19.1 (March 1992): 75–89.

Whyte, William Hollingsworth. *The Organization Man*. New York: Simon and Schuster, 1956.

Widdicombe, Richard Toby. "Eutopia, Dystopia, Aporia: The Obstruction of Meaning in Fin-de-Siecle Utopian Texts." *Utopian Studies* 1.1 (1990): 93–102.

Williams, Raymond. *George Orwell*. New York: Columbia University Press, 1971.

______. *The Long Revolution*. London: Chatto & Windus, 1961.

______. *Marxism and Literature*. London: Oxford University Press, 1977.

______. *Problems in Materialism and Culture*. London: Verso, 1980.

______. *The Year 2000*. New York: Pantheon, 1983.

Wolfe, Gary K. *The Known and the Unknown: The Iconography of Science Fiction*. Kent, Ohio: Kent State University Press, 1979.

Wolheim, Donald A. *The Universe Makers: Science Fiction Today*. New York: Harper and Row, 1971.

Wolmark, Jenny. *Aliens and Others: Science Fiction, Feminism, and Postmodernism*. Iowa City: University of Iowa Press, 1994.

Wood, Ellen Meiskins. *Democracy Against Capitalism: Renewing Historical Materialism*. Cambridge: Cambridge University Press, 1995.

______. *The Origins of Capitalism*. New York: Monthly Review Press, 1999.

Wood, Susan. "James Tiptree, Jr., 1915–." In *Science Fiction Writers: Critical Studies of the Major Authors from the Early Nineteenth Century to the Present Day*. Ed. Everett Bleiler. New York: Scribners, 1982. 531–541.

______. "Space, Time and Gender: The Impact of Cybernetics on the Feminist Utopia." *Foundation: The Review of Science Fiction* 62 (Winter 1994/1995): 22–31.

Woodcock, George. "Five Who Fear the Future." *New Republic*, 16 April 1956: 17–20.

"The Work of Fredric Jameson." Special section. *Utopian Studies* 9.2 (1998).

World Bank. *Poverty and Hunger*. Washington, D.C.: World Bank, 1986.

Zaki, Hoda M. *Phoenix Renewed: The Survival and Mutation of Utopian Thought in North American Science Fiction, 1965–1982*. New York: Stormont, 1988.

———. "Utopia, Dystopia, and Ideology in the Science Fiction of Octavia Butler." *Science-Fiction Studies* 17.2 (July 1990): 239–251.

Zipes, Jack. *Breaking the Magic Spell: Radical Theories of Folk and Fairy Tales*. London: Heinemann, 1979.

———. *Creative Storytelling: Building Community, Changing Lives*. New York: Routledge, 1995.

———. *Don't Bet on the Prince: Contemporary Feminist Fairy Tales in North America and England*. London: Methuen, 1986.

———. *Fairy Tales and the Art of Subversion: The Classical Genre for Children and the Process of Civilization*. London: Heinemann, 1983.

———. *Fairy Tale as Myth, Myth as Fairy Tale*. Lexington: University of Kentucky Press, 1994.

———. *Happily Ever After: Fairy Tales, Children, and the Culture Industry*. New York: Routledge, 1997.

———. "Introduction: Ernst Bloch and the Obscenity of Hope." *New German Critique* 45 (Fall 1988): 3–9.

———. "Introduction: Toward a Realization of Anticipatory Illumination." In *The Utopian Function of Art and Literature: Selected Essays of Ernst Bloch*. Trans. Jack Zipes and Frank Mecklenburg. Cambridge: MIT Press, 1988.

———. "Mass Degradation of Humanity and Massive Contradictions in Bradbury's Vision of America in *Fahrenheit 451*." In *Explorations in Utopian/Dystopian Fiction*. Eds. Martin Greenberg, Joseph Olander, and Eric Rabkin. Carbondale: Southern Illinois University Press, 1982. 182–198.

———. *The Trials and Tribulations of Little Red Riding Hood: Versions of the Tale in Sociocultural Context*. 2nd ed. New York: Routledge, 1993.

———. *When Dreams Come True: Classical Fairy Tales and Their Tradition*. New York: Routledge, 1999.

Žižek, Slavoj. *The Ticklish Subject: The Absent Centre of Political Ontology*. London: Verso, 1999.

———. "When the Party Commits Suicide." *New Left Review* 238 (November/December 1999): 26–48.

Literary Bibliography and Filmography

Fiction and Poetry

Abbott, Edwin. *Flatland: A Romance of Many Dimensions*. London: Seely and Co., 1884.
Acker, Kathy. *Empire of the Senseless*. New York: Grove, 1988.
A. E. [George Russell]. *The Interpreters*. London: Macmillan, 1922.
Aldiss, Brian. *Starship*. New York: Criterion, 1959.
Andreae, Johann. *Christianopolis: An Ideal State of the Seventeenth Century*. 1619. Reprint, trans. F. E. Held. New York: Oxford University Press, 1916.
Atwood, Margaret. *The Handmaid's Tale*. 1985. Reprint, Boston: Houghton Mifflin, 1986.
Auden, W. H. "The Unknown Citizen." *Listener* 22.551 (August 1939): 215.
Auster, P. *The New York Trilogy*. London: Faber and Faber, 1987.
Banks, Ian M. *Consider Phlebas*. New York: Bantam, 1991.
Bellamy, *Looking Backward: A. D. 2000–1887*. Boston: Ticknor, 1888.
Benson, R. H. *Lord of the World*. London: Pittman, 1907.
Bisson, Terry. *Fire on the Mountain*. New York: Arbor House, 1988.
Bradbury. Ray. *Fahrenheit 451*. New York: Ballantine, 1953.
Bradley, Marion Zimmer. *The Shattered Chain*. New York: Daw, 1976.
Brust, Steven, and Emma Bull. *Freedom and Necessity*. New York: Tor, 1997.
Bull, Emma. *Bone Dance*. New York: Ace, 1991.
Bulwer-Lytton, Edward. *The Coming Race*. London: Blackwood, 1871.
Burdekin, Katherine [Murray Constantine, pseud.]. *Swastika Night*. New York: Feminist Press, 1985.
Burdick, Eugene, and Harvey Wheeler. *Fail Safe*. New York: McGraw Hill, 1962.
Burgess, Anthony. *Clockwork Orange*. London: Heinemann, 1962.
______. *The Wanting Seed*. London: Heinemann, 1963.
Butler, Octavia E. *Adulthood Rites*. New York: Warner, 1988.
______. *Dawn*. New York: Warner, 1987.
______. *Imago*. New York: Warner, 1989.
______. *Kindred*. New York: Doubleday, 1979.
______. *Mind of My Mind*. New York: Doubleday, 1977.

______. *The Parable of the Sower.* New York: Four Walls Eight Windows, and New York: Warner, 1993.

______. *The Parable of the Talents.* New York: Seven Stories Press, 1998.

______. *Patternmaster.* New York: Doubleday, 1976.

______. *Survivor.* New York: Doubleday, 1978.

______. *Wild Seed.* New York: Doubleday, 1980.

Butler, Samuel. *Erewhon.* London: Trubner and Co., 1872.

Cabet, Etienne. *Travels in Icaria.* Trans. Robert P. Sutton. Macomb, Ill.: R. P. Sutton, 1985.

______. *Voyage et aventures de lord Villiam Carisdall en Icarie.* 1840.

Cadigan, Pat. "Rock On." In *Mirrorshades: The Cyberpunk Anthology.* Ed. Bruce Sterling. New York: Ace, 1988. 35–43.

______. *Synners.* New York: Bantam, 1991.

Callenbach, Ernest. *Ecotopia: A Novel About Ecology, People, and Politics in 1999.* Berkeley: Banyan Tree Books, 1975.

Capek, Karel. *The War with the Newts.* Trans. M. and R. Weatherall. London: Allen and Unwin, 1937.

Charnas, Suzy McKee. *The Conqueror's Child.* New York: Tor, 1999.

______. *The Furies.* New York: Tor, 1994.

______. *Motherlines.* New York: Berkley, 1978.

______. *Walk to the End of the World.* New York: Ballantine, 1974.

Chesterton, G. K. *The Napoleon of Notting Hill.* London: John Lane, 1904.

Clarke, Arthur C. *The City and the Stars.* New York: Harcourt, 1956.

Connolley, Flynn. *The Rising of the Moon.* New York: Ballantine, 1993.

Delany, Samuel R. *Dhalgren.* New York: Bantam, 1975.

______. *The Einstein Intersection.* New York: Ace, 1967.

______. *Triton.* New York: Bantam, 1976.

DeLillo, Don. *Underworld.* New York: Simon and Schuster, 1997.

Dick, Philip K. *Dr. Bloodmoney; or How We Got Along Without the Bomb.* New York: Ace, 1965.

______. "Faith of Our Fathers." *Dangerous Visions.* Ed. Harlan Ellison. Garden City, N.Y.: Doubleday, 1967. 175–204. In *Science Fiction: The Science Fiction Research Association Anthology.* Eds. Patricia S. Warrick, Charles G. Waugh, and Martin H. Greenberg. New York: HarperCollins, 1988. 353–378.

______. *Martian Time-Slip.* New York: Ballantine, 1964.

______. *The Three Stigmata of Palmer Eldritch.* Garden City, N.Y.: Doubleday, 1965.

______. *Ubik.* Garden City, N.Y.: Doubleday, 1969.

Dostoyevsky, Fyodor. *The Brothers Karamazov.* 1879. Reprint, trans. Ignat Avsey. Oxford: Oxford University Press, 1994.

Elgin, Suzette Hayden. *The Judas Rose.* New York: Daw, 1986.

______. *Native Tongue.* New York: Daw, 1984.

Ellison, Harlan, ed. *Again, Dangerous Visions.* Garden City, N.Y.: Doubleday, 1972.

______, ed. *Dangerous Visions.* Garden City, N.Y.: Doubleday, 1967.

Elphinstone, Margaret. *The Incomer.* London: Women's Press, 1987.

______. *A Sparrow's Flight*. Edinburgh: Polygon, 1989.
Forster, E. M. "The Machine Stops." *Oxford and Cambridge Review* 8 (Michaelmas Term 1909): 83-122. In *Science Fiction: The Science Fiction Research Association Anthology*. Eds. Patricia S. Warrick, Charles G. Waugh, and Martin H. Greenberg. New York: Harper-Collins, 1988. 23–41.
Gearhart, Sally. *The Wanderground: Stories of the Hill Women*. Watertown, Mass.: Persephone, 1979.
Gibson, William. *Count Zero*. New York: Ace, 1987.
______. "The Gernsback Continuum." In *Mirrorshades: The Cyberpunk Anthology*. Ed. Bruce Sterling. New York: Ace, 1988. 1–11.
______. *Mona Lisa Overdrive*. New York: Bantam, 1988.
______. *Neuromancer*. New York: Ace, 1984.
Gibson, William, and Bruce Sterling. *The Difference Engine*. London: Gollancz, 1990.
Gilman, Charlotte Perkins. *Herland*. 1915. Reprint, ed. Ann Lane. New York: Pantheon, 1980.
Gingrich, Newt, William R. Forschen, and Albert S. Hansen. *1945*. Riverdale, N.Y.: Baen, 1996.
Golding, William. *The Inheritors*. London: Faber and Faber, 1955.
______. *The Lord of the Flies*. London: Faber and Faber, 1954.
Guerard, Albert. *Night Journey*. New York: Knopf, 1950.
Haldane, Charlotte. *Man's World*. London: Chatto and Windus, 1926.
Haldeman, Joe. *Forever War*. New York: St. Martin's, 1974.
Harris, Robert. *Fatherland*. New York: Random House, 1992.
Hartley, L. P. *Facial Justice*. London: Harnish Hamilton, 1960.
Hartwell, David, and Milton T. Wolf. *Visions of Wonder: The Science Fiction Research Association Anthology*. New York: Tor, 1996.
Heinlein, Robert A. *Stranger in a Strange Land*. New York: Putnam, 1961.
Hesiod. "Works and Days." Trans. Jack Lindsay. In *The Utopia Reader*. Eds. Gregory Claeys and Lyman Tower Sargent. New York: New York University Press, 1999. 7.
Hoban, Russell. *Ridley Walker*. New York: Washington Square, 1982.
Horace. *Ars Poetica: The Art of Poetry*. Trans. James Hynd. Albany: State University of New York Press, 1974.
Huxley, Aldous. *Brave New World*. Garden City, N.Y.: Doubleday, 1932.
______. *Brave New World Revisited*. New York: Harper, 1958.
______. *Island*. New York: Harper, 1962.
Kadrey, Richard. *Metrophage*. New York: Ace, 1988.
Kafka, Franz. *The Penal Colony*. 1919. In *The Penal Colony: Stories and Short Pieces*. Trans. Willa Muir. New York: Schocken, 1948.
Karp, David. *One*. New York: Vanguard, 1953.
Keiller, Patrick. *Robinson in Space*. London: Reaktion, 1999.
Koestler, Arthur. *Darkness at Noon*. New York: Macmillan, 1941.
Le Guin, Ursula K. *Always Coming Home*. New York: Harper, 1985.
______. *The Dispossessed*. New York: Harper, 1974.

———. *Four Ways to Forgiveness*. New York: Harper, 1995.
———. *The Left Hand of Darkness*. New York: Ace, 1969.
———. *The Word for World Is Forest*. New York: Berkley, 1976.
Lem, Stanislaus. *Solaris*. 1961. Reprint, trans. Joanna Kilmartin and Steve Cox. New York: Walker, 1970.
Lewis, C. S. *That Hideous Strength*. London: John Lane, 1945.
Lewitt, S. N. *Cybernetic Jungle*. New York: Ace, 1992.
London, Jack. *The Iron Heel*. 1908. Reprint, Edinburgh: Rebel, 1999.
Luceno, Richard. *The Big Empty*. New York: Ballantine, 1993.
———. *A Fearful Symmetry*. New York: Ballantine, 1989.
———. *Illegal Alien*. New York: Ballantine, 1990.
Macaulay, Rose. *What Not*. London: Constable, 1918.
Madsden, Catherine. "Commodore Bork and the Compost." *The Witch and the Chameleon* 5/6 (1976): 16–19.
Marlowe, Christopher. *Doctor Faustus*. 1604. Reprint, ed. Michael Keefer. Peterborough, Ontario: Broadview, 1991.
McIntyre, Vonda N., and Susan Janice Anderson. *Aurora: Beyond Equality, Amazing Tales of the Ultimate Sexual Revolution*. New York: Fawcett, 1976.
Merril, Judith, ed. *England Swings SF*. Garden City, N.Y.: Doubleday, 1968.
Mixon, Laura J. *Glass Houses*. New York: Tor, 1992.
More, Thomas. *Utopia*. 1516. Reprint, trans. Ralph Robynson. Boston: Bedford, 1999.
Morris, William. *News from Nowhere*. 1890. Reprint, London: Reeves and Turner, 1891.
Morrison, Toni. *Beloved*. New York: Knopf, 1997.
———. *Paradise*. New York: Knopf, 1998.
Nabokov, Vladimir. *Bend Sinister*. New York: Holt, 1947.
———. *Invitation to a Beheading*. 1938. Reprint, trans. Dimitri Nabokov. New York: Putnam, 1959.
Orwell, George. *Nineteen Eighty-Four*. New York: Harcourt, 1949.
Pfeil, Fred. *Goodman 20/20*. Bloomington: Indiana University Press, 1986.
Piercy, Marge. "The Book of Ruth and Naomi." In *Reading Ruth: Contemporary Women Reclaim a Sacred Story*. Eds. Judith A. Kates and Gail Twersky Reimer. New York: Ballantine, 1994. 159–160.
———. *Breaking Camp*. Hanover, N.H.: Wesleyan University Press, 1968.
———. *City of Darkness, City of Light*. New York: Fawcett, 1996.
———. *Dance the Eagle to Sleep*. New York: Fawcett, 1970.
———. *He, She and It*. New York: Knopf, 1991. (British edition: *Body of Glass*. London: Michael Joseph, 1992.)
———. *The High Cost of Living*. New York: Harper, 1978.
———. *Small Changes*. Garden City, N.Y.: Doubleday, 1973.
———. *Vida*. New York: Summit, 1980.
———. *Woman on the Edge of Time*. New York: Knopf, 1976.
Plato. *The Republic*. Trans. Richard Sterling. New York: Norton, 1985.

Platonov, Andrei. *Chevengur.* 1927. Reprint, trans. Anthony Olcott. Ann Arbor: Ardis, 1978.

Pohl, Frederik. *The Merchants War*. New York: St. Martin's, 1984.

Pohl, Frederik, and C. M. Kornbluth. *The Space Merchants*. 1953. Reprint, New York: St. Martin's, 1985.

Pynchon, Thomas. *Vineland*. Boston: Little, Brown, 1990.

Rand, Ayn. *Anthem*. London: Cassell, 1938.

Reynolds, Mack. *Commune 2000*. New York: Bantam, 1974.

Rich, Adrienne. "Dreamwood." In *Time's Power*. New York: Norton, 1989.

Robinson, Kim Stanley. *Antarctica*. New York: HarperCollins, 1997.

______. *Blue Mars*. New York: HarperCollins, 1996.

______. *The Gold Coast*. New York: Tor, 1988.

______. *Green Mars*. New York: HarperCollins, 1993.

______. *The Martians*. London: HarperCollins, 1999.

______. *Pacific Edge*. New York: Unwin Hyman, 1990.

______. *Red Mars*. New York: HarperCollins, 1992.

______. *The Wild Shore*. New York: Ace, 1984.

Robinson, Kim Stanley, ed. *Future Primitive: The New Ecotopias*. New York: Tor, 1994.

Russ, Joanna. *The Female Man*. New York: Bantam, 1975.

______. "When It Changed." *Again, Dangerous Visions*. Ed. Harlan Ellison. Garden City, N.Y.: Doubleday, 1972. 233-241. In *Science Fiction: The Science Fiction Research Association Anthology*. Eds. Patricia S. Warrick, Charles G. Waugh, and Martin H. Greenberg. New York: HarperCollins, 1988. 411–418.

Russo, Richard Paul. *Carlucci's Edge*. New York: Ace, 1995.

______. *Carlucci's Heart*. New York: Ace, 1997.

______. *Destroying Angel*. New York: Ace, 1992.

______. *Subterranean Gallery*. New York: Tor, 1989.

Sargent, Pamela. *The Shore of Women*. New York: Crown, 1986.

Sargent, Pamela, ed. *More Women of Wonder: Science Fiction Novelettes by Women About Women*. New York: Vintage, 1976.

______, ed. *The New Women of Wonder: Recent Science Fiction Stories by Women About Women*. New York: Vintage, 1978.

______, ed. *Women of Wonder: The Classic Years*. New York: Harcourt, 1995.

______, ed. *Women of Wonder: The Contemporary Years*. New York: Harcourt, 1995.

______, ed. *Women of Wonder: Science Fiction Stories by Women About Women*. New York: Vintage, 1974.

Shakespeare, William. *The Tempest*. 1611. Reprint, New York: Norton, 1997.

Shelley, Mary. *Frankenstein: or The Modern Prometheus*. London: Lackington, Hughes, Harding, Mayor & Jones, 1818.

Shepard, Lucius. *Life During Wartime*. New York: Bantam, 1987.

Shiner, Lewis. *Deserted Cities of the Heart*. New York: Bantam, 1989.

Shirley, John. *Eclipse*. New York: Blue Jay, 1985.

———. *Eclipse Corona*. New York: Warner, 1990.

———. *Eclipse Penumbra*. New York: Warner, 1988.

Shute, Nevil. *On the Beach*. London: Heinemann, 1957.

Sinclair, Upton. *The Jungle*. Garden City, N.Y.: Doubleday, 1906.

Skinner, B. F. *Walden II*. New York: Macmillan, 1948.

Slonczewski, Joan. *A Door into Ocean*. New York: Arbor House, 1986.

Stapledon, Olaf. *Last and First Men: A Story of the Near and Far Future*. London: Methuen, 1930.

———. *Odd John: A Story Between Jest and Earnest*. London: Methuen, 1935.

———. *Star Maker*. London: Methuen, 1937.

Steinbeck, John. *Grapes of Wrath*. New York: Viking, 1939.

Sterling, Bruce. *Islands in the Net*. New York: Ace, 1989.

———. *Schizmatrix*. New York: Ace, 1986.

Suvin, Darko. "Growing Old Without Yugoslavia." *Science-Fiction Studies* 21.1 (March 1994): 124.

Tepper, Sherri. *The Gate to Women's Country*. New York: Doubleday, 1988.

Tiptree, James, Jr. [Alice Sheldon]. "Houston, Houston, Do You Read?" *Aurora: Beyond Equality*. Eds. Vonda McIntyre and Susan Anderson. New York: Fawcett, 1976). 36-98. In *Science Fiction: The Science Fiction Research Association Anthology*. Eds. Patricia S. Warrick, Charles G. Waugh, and Martin H. Greenberg. New York: HarperCollins, 1988. 434–476.

———. "We Who Stole the Dream." *Out of the Everywhere and Other Extraordinary Visions*. New York: Ballantine, 1981. 89–115.

——— [as Racoona Sheldon]. "Your Faces, O My Sisters! Your Faces Filled of Light." In *Aurora: Beyond Equality*. Eds. Vonda McIntyre and Susan Janice Anderson. New York: Fawcett, 1976.

Tuttle, Lisa. "The Cure." In *Light Years and Dark*. Ed. Michael Bishop. New York: Berkley, 1984. 372–382.

Updike, John. *Toward the End of Time*. New York: Fawcett, 1997.

Vidal, Gore. *Messiah*. New York: Dutton, 1954.

Vonnegut, Kurt, Jr. *Player Piano*. New York: Scribners, 1952.

Waugh, Evelyn. *Love Among the Ruins*. London: Chapman and Hall, 1953.

Wells, H. G. *A Modern Utopia: A Sociological Holiday*. London: Chapman and Hall, 1905.

———. *The Time Machine*. London: Heinemann, 1895.

Werfel, Franz. *Star of the Unborn*. Trans. Gustave O. Arlt. New York: Viking, 1946.

Williams, Walter Jon. *Hardwired*. New York: Tor, 1986.

Wittig, Monique. *Les Guérillères*. Paris: Editions de Minuit, 1969.

———. *Les Guérillères*. Trans. David LeVay. New York: Viking, 1969.

Wolfe, Bernard. *Limbo*. New York: Random House, 1952.

Zamyatin, Yevgeny. *We*. 1924. Trans. Clarence Brown. New York: Penguin, 1993.

Zoline, Pamela. "The Heat Death of the Universe." *New Worlds Magazine* (July 1967). In *The Mirror of Infinity: A Critics' Anthology of Science Fiction*. Ed. Robert Silverberg. New York: Harper and Row, 1970. 293–307.

Film and Video

Alien. Dir. Ridley Scott. 1979.

Alien: Resurrection. Dir. Jean-Pierre Jeunet. 1997.

Alien 3. Dir. David Fincher. 1992.

Aliens. Dir. James Cameron. 1986.

Blade Runner. Dir. Ridley Scott. 1982.

Brave New World. Dir. Leslie Libman and Larry Williams. 1998.

Brazil. Dir. Terry Gilliam. 1985.

Buffy, the Vampire Slayer. Dir. Fran Rubel Kuzui. 1992.

A Clockwork Orange. Dir. Stanley Kubrick. 1971.

Contact. Dir. Robert Zemeckis. 1997.

Dark City. Dir. Alex Proyas. 1998.

Dawn of the Dead. Dir. George Romero. 1978.

Dr. Strangelove or: How I Learned to Stop Worrying and Love the Bomb. Dir. Stanley Kubrick. 1964.

E.T.: The Extraterrestrial. Dir. Steven Spielberg. 1982.

Fahrenheit 451. Dir. François Truffaut. 1966.

Fail Safe. Dir. Sidney Lumet. 1964.

The Fifth Element. Dir. Luc Besson. 1997

Gattaca. Dir. Andrew Nichol. 1997.

The Handmaid's Tale. Dir. Volker Schlöndorff. 1990.

Hardware. Dir. Richard Stanley. 1990.

Independence Day. Dir. Roland Emmerich. 1996.

The Invasion of the Body Snatchers. Dir. Don Siegel. 1956.

The Invasion of the Body Snatchers. Dir. Philip Kaufman. 1978.

Johnny Mnemonic. Dir. Robert Longo. 1995.

Liquid Sky. Dir. Slava Tsukerman. 1982.

The Man in the Grey Flannel Suit. Dir. Nunnally Johnson. 1956.

The Man Who Fell to Earth. Dir. Nicholas Roeg. 1976.

The Matrix. Dir. Andy Wachowski and Larry Wachowski. 1999.

Max Headroom. Dir. Rocky Morton and Annabel Jankel. 1985.

Men with Guns. Dir. John Sayles. 1997.

Metropolis. Dir. Fritz Lang. 1927.

Mission to Mars. Dir. Brian De Palma. 2000.
Nineteen Eighty-Four. Dir. Michael Anderson. 1956.
Nineteen Eighty-Four. Dir. Michael Radford. 1984.
N30 WTO Meltdown: Big Rattle in Seattle [video]. Dir. Leon and Guerillavision. 2000.
On the Beach. Dir. Stanley Kramer. 1959.
Pi. Dir. Darren Aronofsky. 1998.
Pleasantville. Dir. Gary Ross. 1998.
The Postman. Dir. Kevin Costner. 1997.
Red Dawn. Dir. John Milius. 1984.
Robocop. Dir. Paul Verhoeven. 1987.
Solyaris. Dir. Andrei Tarkovsky. 1972.
The Terminator. Dir. James Cameron. 1984.
THX 1138. Dir. George Lucas. 1970.
The Time Machine. Dir. George Pal. 1960.
The Truman Show. Dir. Peter Weir. 1998.
Twelve Monkeys. Dir. Terry Gilliam. 1995.
2001: A Space Odyssey. Dir. Stanley Kubrick. 1968.

Index

Printed in the United Kingdom
by Lightning Source UK Ltd.
114267UKS00002B/15

9 780813 397689